DIASPORA

ALSO BY HOWARD M. SACHAR

DIASPORA

An Inquiry into the Contemporary Jewish World

HOWARD M. SACHAR

PERENNIAL LIBRARY
Harper & Row, Publishers
New York, Cambridge, Philadelphia, San Francisco
London, Mexico City, São Paulo, Singapore, Sydney

A hardcover edition of this book is published by Harper & Row, Publishers, Inc.

Grateful acknowledgment is made for permission to reprint:

On pp. 438–439: Lines from "The 'Mountain Jews' of Soviet Russia" by Joshua Rothenberg from the November 1967 issue of *Jewish Frontier*, Volume 34, Number 10.

Designer: Sidney Feinberg

Map on pages 484–485 by George Colbert

First PERENNIAL LIBRARY edition published 1986.

Library of Congress Cataloging-in-Publication Data
Sachar, Howard Morley, 1928–
    Diaspora.

    "Perennial Library."
    Bibliography: p.
    Includes index.
    1. Jews—Diaspora. 2. Jews—History—1945–
I. Title.
DS134.S22   1986   909'.04924   84-48190
ISBN 0-06-091347-9 (pbk.)

86 87 88 89 90 MPC 10 9 8 7 6 5 4 3 2 1

In memory of Samuel Sachar,
the grandfather who pioneered the family emigration to America,
and thereafter quietly rescued two generations of kinsmen

Gratitude is herewith expressed to the American Jewish Congress, whose Beverly and Harvey Karp Foundation helped to underwrite the research for this book. The volume will be used in the Congress's "National Agenda Series."

Contents

Acknowledgments

As the personal tone of its chapters suggests, this volume is based on first-hand investigation as well as on reading. During the course of my travels, I have been favored with the help of scores of knowledgeable individuals. Most of them are described or quoted in the text. Those who are not can only be listed here, with heartfelt thanks.

Germany and Austria

Dr. Sybil Milton, chief archivist of the Leo Baeck Institute; Mrs. Johanna König, first secretary of the Embassy of the Federal Republic of Germany in Washington; Dr. Niels Hansen, ambassador of the Federal Republic of Germany in Tel Aviv; Saul Kagan, executive director of the Conference on Jewish Material Claims Against Germany; Dr. Ernst Löwenthal, journalist; Miss Inge Schilzer, assistant to the general director, Jewish Community Council of Berlin; Albert Klein, film critic, and Rayah Klein, artist; Andreas Nahama, student; Dr. Monika Richarz, historian; Dr. Herbert Steiner, director of the Archives of the Austrian Resistance; Dr. Jonny Moser, former executive director of the Jewish Community Council of Vienna; Dr. Ivan Hacker, president of the Union of Jewish Community Councils of Austria

Italy

Dr. Sergio della Pergola, Institute of Contemporary Jewry, Hebrew University; Dr. Bice Migliau, director of the Jewish Community Center, Rome; Fritz Becker, director emeritus of the World Jewish Congress, Rome; Luciano Tas and Lea Tas, editors of *Shalom;* Professor Giorgio Sacerdote, attorney

Scandinavia

Dr. Michael Suess, scientist; Jan-Erik Levy, executive director, and Stefan Meisels, associate executive director, Jewish Federation, Stockholm; Daniel Koverman, director of the Jewish Community Center, Stockholm; Mrs. Janina Waril, director of the Judaica Foundation, Stockholm

France

Edward Roditi, author and journalist; Henri Wormser, banker; Michel Gourfunkle, foreign editor of *Valeurs Actuelles;* Dr. Doris Bensimon-Donath, sociologist; Adam Loss, director, and Mrs. Gaby Cohen, associate director, United Jewish Welfare Fund of France; Mrs. Jacqueline Kellerman, director of the Jewish Community Council of France; Georges Levitte, field director emeritus of the American Jewish Joint Distribution Committee, Paris; André Amar, former president of the United Jewish Appeal of France and of the World Jewish Congress, French Section; Dr. Bernhard Blumenkranz, director of the Jewish Archives; Bezalel Fedida, former director of the Sephardic Section, Jewish Agency, Paris; Serge Cwajgenbaum, director of the World Jewish Congress, Paris; Shimon Samuels, director of the Anti-Defamation League, Paris; Mrs. Nivès Fox, director of the American Jewish Committee, Paris; Michael Shaked, former emissary of the Jewish Agency, Paris

Great Britain

Dr. S. I. Roth, director, and Dr. Elizabeth Eppler, associate director, Institute of Jewish Affairs; Barnet Litvinoff, journalist, author of *A Peculiar People;* Dr. Martin Gilbert, Merton College, Oxford; Geoffrey Paul, editor of the *Jewish Chronicle;* Henry Shaw, former director, Hillel House, University of London; Hilda Margulies, social worker; Richard Hellman, attorney; Ronald Green, businessman; the late Albert Cooperman, businessman

Australia and South Africa

Dr. Peter Medding, Institute of Contemporary Jewry, Hebrew University; Aleck Goldberg, executive director, and Messrs. Gustav Saron and Denis Diamond, former executive directors, South African Jewish

Board of Deputies; Dr. Marcus Arkin, executive director of the Zionist Federation of South Africa; Dr. Frank Bradlow, historian

Moslem Nations

Shlomo Cohen-Sidon, president of the Association of Egyptian Immigrants in Israel; Asher Hissin, former president of the Association of North African Immigrants in Israel; Michael Lewan, former executive assistant to Congressman Stephen Solarz, Washington, D.C.; the late Ezra Hadad, former director of the Department of Oriental Affairs, Histadrut, Tel Aviv

Spanish-Speaking World

Sevio Levinsky, chairman of the Association of Latin American Immigrants in Israel; Professor Chaim Avni, Institute of Contemporary Jewry, Hebrew University; Dr. David Schers, research director of the Jewish Agency, Buenos Aires; Elias Zviklich, attorney; José Pascar, former professor of law, University of La Plata; Dr. Adolfo Huberman, Jewish Teachers Institute, Buenos Aires; Zalman Wassertzug, journalist; Alfredo Berlfein, director of the American Jewish Joint Distribution Committee, Buenos Aires; Dr. Abraham Rosenvasser, professor emeritus of history, University of Buenos Aires; Jacobo Kovadloff, director of the Department of Latin American Affairs, American Jewish Committee

Brazil

Dr. Bernardo Akerman and Dr. Lucia Akerman, physicians; José Mindlin, industrialist; Asher Rosenvit, educator; Francisco Gothilf, director of *Mosaico TV;* Professor Eva Alterman Bly, Department of Sociology, University of São Paulo; Dr. Walter Rehfeld, Institute of Jewish Studies, University of São Paulo; Stefan Hamburger, businessman; Wolf Wolf, businessman

Communist Eastern Europe

Imre Heber, president of the Central Board of Hungarian Jews; Ferenc Katona, journalist; Charles Fenyvesi, journalist; Dan Regen-

streiff, counselor of the Federation of Jewish Communities of Romania;
Dr. Theodor Lavie, historian; Saul Cratianu, writer; Shlomo Leibovitz,
director of the East European Department, Foreign Ministry of Israel;
David Giladi, former ambassador of Israel to Hungary; Dr. Andrei
Strichan, former professor of aesthetics, University of Bucharest; Miss
Eva Gruber, former lecturer in economics, University of Bucharest

Soviet Union

Leonard Schroeter, attorney, author of *The New Exodus;* Jerry
Goodman, executive director of the National Conference on Soviet
Jewry; Professor Muriel Atkin, Department of History, George Washington University; Professor Mordechai Altshuler, Department of History, Hebrew University; Zalman Abramov, attorney, chairman of the
Israel Council on Soviet Jewry; Vladimir Lazaris, attorney; Dr. Mikhail
Agursky, cyberneticist; Dr. Aleksandr Luntz, mathematician; Evgeni
Deborin, engineer; Viktor Dubin, engineer; Shmuel Azarik, theatrical
designer; Aleksandr Ovchinkov, statistician; Aleksandr Shipovage, engineer; Shlomo Ben-Oren, chairman of the Association of Georgian Immigrants in Israel

I must express appreciation, as well, to Abraham Karlikow, director
of the Department of Foreign Affairs, American Jewish Committee; Dr.
Daniel Thursz, executive vice-president of B'nai B'rith; Mark Friedman,
director of cultural activities, World Jewish Congress; Heinz Wegener,
director of the Deutscher Akademischer Austauschdienst, Berlin; Bruce
Martin, director of the Research Facilities Office, Library of Congress.

Professor Henry Solomon, dean of the Graduate School and chairman of the Faculty Research Committee, George Washington University, ensured that I was spared the heaviest expenses of transcribing my
manuscript. His support throughout the past decade and a half has
made him a collaborator in my publications. There are other collaborators. Among them are my father, Dr. Abram L. Sachar, who for
thirty years has read and offered commentary on my work; and my wife,
Eliana, who for two-thirds of that period has subjected herself to the
identical regimen. My family has altogether been obliged to shift for
itself during my travels of the last three years. That ordeal, at least,
ends here.

Kensington, Maryland
March 30, 1984

DIASPORA

Prologue

Monsieur Mondial

In January 1982, I sat with Gerhart Riegner in his comfortable, tastefully furnished apartment on Geneva's Avenue Wendt. Approaching seventy, Riegner was short and overweight. The spectacles on his rotund, owlish face, together with his formal bearing, lent him a distinctly pedantic appearance. Riegner was a *Yecke*, a German Jew. The son of a prosperous Berlin lawyer, he had himself been trained in the law, and was embarked upon graduate work at Heidelberg when the Nazi rise to power altered his plans. Leaving Germany in 1933, he continued his studies at the Institut des Hautes Études Internationales in Geneva, where he received his doctorate in jurisprudence in 1935. His parents and sisters had fled that year to the United States. As he made ready to join them, Riegner was presented suddenly with an unexpected career challenge. Nahum Goldmann, executive director of the World Jewish Congress, was seeking an international lawyer as his assistant in Europe. When Goldmann tendered the offer to Riegner, the young man accepted enthusiastically. Here at last was an organization willing to defend Jewish rights in a period of increasingly malevolent racism.

His task was to fight on all fronts, but specifically before the League of Nations. Despite his youth and his lack of official status at the League, Riegner's early efforts were not unimpressive. In 1935, when the citizens of the Saar voted to rejoin Germany, Riegner persuaded the League to elicit Berlin's assurance of unhindered Jewish departure from the Saar. Three years later, he won the case against Romania, providing the documented brief with which the League condemned the Bucharest government for persecuting non-Romanian minorities. Otherwise, the young man's exertions were all but futile. The antisemitic campaign of Hitler and of the East European Fascist regimes mounted in savagery. Nothing seemed capable of inhibiting it.

With the outbreak of World War II, the petitions and briefs of international lawyers became entirely irrelevant. The German conquest of Poland, then of Western Europe, and finally Hitler's invasion of the Soviet Union, placed the very survival of European Jewry in the balance. Through his League of Nations acquaintances, Riegner was able to secure copies of Nazi antisemitic legislation in the various occupied territories. Each afternoon, too, a French train arrived at the Swiss frontier. There its engineer delivered to Riegner's awaiting secretary envelopes addressed to "Monsieur Mondial," the pseudonym by which Riegner already was widely known among his Jewish contacts. Their enclosed material was essentially newspaper clippings and private (coded) letters sent by Riegner's correspondents in Europe, and from them a pattern gradually emerged of large-scale Jewish deportations in France, in the Lowlands, in the Greater Reich. Riegner dispatched this information to New York. By 1942, he and his associates in the World Jewish Congress were well informed of the deteriorating circumstances of the hostage Jewish populations, even of mass atrocities in the Polish ghettos. Yet as late as the spring of that year they were unaware of the Nazi blueprint for exterminating the Jewish people. The fate of the transported Jews remained a mystery.

Then, in July 1942, a bombshell was suddenly dropped in Riegner's lap by a German Gentile, Eduard Schulte. Schulte was chairman of a huge mining corporation, and his position evidently gave him access to important Nazi officials. From them he had learned that a plan was under discussion in Hitler's inner councils for deporting the entire Jewish population of occupied Europe to the east, where it would be liquidated. A staunch anti-Nazi, Schulte confided his shocking information to a Swiss friend, who immediately informed Dr. Benjamin Sagalowitz, press officer of the Swiss Confederation of Jewish Communities. Sagalowitz in turn telephoned Riegner in Geneva.* The two men met the following afternoon in Lausanne. Stunned by Sagalowitz's account, Riegner thereupon journeyed to Zurich to interview Schulte's Swiss friend personally. The latter repeated the story. For the next two days

---

*Honoring a promise to Schulte, Riegner himself never divulged the German industrialist's role in this episode. Rather, in 1982, Schulte's identity was discovered by two Jewish scholars.

Riegner contemplated its implications. Reports had been coming in lately, describing mass Jewish arrests in France and Belgium, in Germany and Austria. They seemed to corroborate Schulte's account. The emerging pattern suggested that a carefully formulated plan for the Jews' destruction was indeed already in operation.

Riegner moved quickly. Exploiting his access to the United States diplomatic pouch, he first dispatched a cable to the World Jewish Congress's New York office. He followed it with an identical message to London, this time using the British pouch. The British recipient was Sidney Silverman, a respected member of Parliament and a proud Jew. Riegner's decision to send a backup cable proved to be shrewd. As he feared, the State Department refused to deliver the message to the Congress's office; but through his connections in the British War Office, Silverman managed to convey the information to New York. Upon receiving it, Goldmann and Rabbi Stephen Wise, founder of the Congress and a renowned Jewish spokesman, departed immediately for Washington. There they handed the report personally to Under Secretary of State Sumner Welles. Welles was incredulous. He asked the two Jewish leaders not to publicize the report until the State Department could confirm it with the Vatican (which had an extensive information network in Europe). Wise and Goldmann agreed. The weeks passed. No information was forthcoming from Rome. Finally, in October, Goldmann instructed Riegner to prepare another dossier and give it to Leland Harrison, the United States minister in Bern.

By now, Riegner had a wealth of confirming data, including accounts smuggled in from Poland to the representative of the Agudat Israel (Orthodox) movement in Switzerland, and the personal testimony of two East European Jews who had escaped and recently made their way into Swiss territory. One of these survivors was Gabriel Zivian, a Latvian who had witnessed the massacre of Riga's Jews eight months earlier. The other was a man known only as Itten, a Polish Jew who had been "selected out" as a slave laborer for the Wehrmacht near Stalingrad. As a driver for a German officer, Itten had learned the full story of the liquidation of Jews on the Eastern front. The officer, who was an anti-Nazi, personally helped Itten escape. Once he reached Paris, Itten contacted several Jewish friends, who managed to smuggle him across the Swiss border. More dead than alive when he reached Geneva, Itten was hospitalized. An attending physician, hearing his half-delirious account, immediately telephoned Riegner. Riegner then questioned Itten for hours. The latter's description of systematic murder tallied with Riegner's other intelligence. All this material went into the report given to Leland Harrison, who sent it forthwith to Washington.

By then, eleven weeks had passed since Riegner had dispatched his original cable. In the meanwhile, independent evidence on the destruction of vast numbers of Jews had been reaching London and Washington from the Polish government in exile, the Red Cross, and Swedish and Spanish diplomats. Until then, the Allied governments had remained silent, concerned that these atrocity stories would divert attention and energy from the war itself, or, in the words of one Foreign Office official, "waste a disproportionate amount of . . . time in dealing with the wailing Jews." Breckinridge Long, the State Department's immigration officer, had asked that Riegner's information, transmitted through the diplomatic pouch, no longer be made available to "private persons," that is, to Wise and Goldmann. But the account dispatched by Leland Harrison was simply too overwhelming to be ignored. When Sumner Welles read it, he called in the two Jewish leaders to apologize for his earlier hesitation. The question at this point was the appropriate Allied response. By then, the Nazis had been defeated at Stalingrad, and the tide had turned in the war. Wise and Goldmann suggested that this was the moment for the Allied governments to issue a decisive warning to the Nazi leaders. When the proposal reached him, President Roosevelt agreed. At his request, London joined Washington in releasing the stark facts of mass Jewish extermination and in warning the Axis officials and their collaborators that they would be held collectively and personally responsible for this unprecedented crime.

Soon afterward, in the spring of 1943, Wise was able to persuade Roosevelt to establish a War Refugee Board. The idea was Riegner's. In a long cable, he had outlined practicable steps to help and possibly extricate a number of still accessible Jewish communities—in Transdniestria, Hungary, Bulgaria, and Unoccupied (Vichy) France. Riegner's suggestion produced a certain limited action. Through the intercession of Secretary of the Treasury Henry Morgenthau, Jr., Roosevelt granted the World Jewish Congress the right (later extended to other Jewish organizations) to disburse funds—Jewish funds only— throughout Europe in an effort to save Jews. The War Refugee Board would monitor this disbursement. Accordingly, through the World Jewish Congress and the American Jewish Joint Distribution Committee, thousands, then hundreds of thousands, and ultimately millions of dollars were spent on the care and feeding of Jews in southern France and in parts of Romania and Bulgaria. With these funds, some ten thousand Polish Jewish children were transported to Iran, and from Iran to Palestine.

Riegner's achievements were less than far-reaching, however, within the context of the Nazi "Final Solution." In 1939, the world Jewish population was estimated at slightly over 16.5 million. During the Holocaust, more than a third of this number—5,934,000—were destroyed. Before the war, Europe encompassed a Jewish population of 9.5 million. After the war, the number was closer to 3.5 million. Before the war, 57 percent of the world's Jews were to be found in Europe. After the war, the figure was 32 percent. What the losses entailed not merely in flesh, blood, and indescribable suffering, but in talents, skills, and often genius, as well as in religious institutions and in cultural and economic influence, is beyond calculation, even two generations after the fact.

A Transfusion from America

Among the populations liberated by the Anglo-American forces, approximately 2.5 million uprooted civilians were dispersed throughout Western and Central Europe, and at least 2 million others remained scattered in the east. At the outset, the Allied military governments in the various western zones of occupied Germany and Austria moved swiftly to repatriate these displaced persons. By late 1945, most of them were returned to their homes. Yet a core of some 100,000 "DPs" remained; and these were almost entirely East European Jews. Packed into the barracks of their former concentration camps, living on army rations or—later—United Nations relief funds, the DPs stubbornly refused to be shipped back to Poland, Hungary, or Romania, to the charnel houses of their families, to populations whose antisemitism had played an important collaborative role in the Nazi extermination program. If housing and food already were inadequate for them, their circumstances deteriorated even further in 1946–47 under an influx of another 150,000 East European Jews, most of these from Poland. The newcomers were in flight from the revived Jew-hatred of their former homelands. Congestion in the American zones of Germany and Austria soon increased almost intolerably. The authorities no longer classified the "infiltrees" as displaced persons; only the war was recognized as a cause of displacement, and the newcomers were declared ineligible for United Nations care.

It was the Joint Distribution Committee, the principal arm of overseas American Jewish philanthropy, that accepted the task of supplying provisions for some 250,000 displaced persons. Indeed, the number of refugees dependent on the "Joint" continued to grow. In the spring of 1947, an additional 20,000 Romanian Jews migrated through Hungary to the American zone of Austria. Some 10,000 more Jews arrived in the British zone of Germany, 1,500 in the French zone, and fully 18,000 in Italy. There were also approximately 10,000 Jewish refugees maintained in France and elsewhere in liberated Western Europe, and 32,000 in the Allied zones of Germany, Austria, and Italy who barely subsisted outside the camps. In Eastern Europe too, as in North Africa, the Joint operated canteens, hospitals, clinics, schools, and orphanages to sustain hundreds of demoralized Jewish communities. So it was, by the summer of 1947, that the Joint was providing succor to a vast commonwealth of 750,000 desperately impoverished Jews.

Although the administrative burden of the refugee camps began to ease with the growing pace of "underground" migration to Palestine in 1947 and 1948, the financial burden on the Joint remained overwhelming. In conjunction with the Jewish Agency, the Joint found itself subsidizing the journey of tens of thousands of Jews across the Alps to Mediterranean ports—and then, after May 15, 1948, sharing responsibility with the Jewish Agency for sending most of the DP population to Israel. Meanwhile, it continued its relief and rehabilitation programs in Eastern Europe. From the end of the war, then, until 1952, the Joint disbursed $353 million in supplies and services to reconstruct the shattered lives of Jews overseas. It was a Jewish Marshall Plan. And like its counterpart, the aid supplied by American Jews was responsible for nothing less than the revival of Europe's most cruelly mutilated people.

The circumstances of those Jewish survivors who remained in Europe, as well as the fate and fortune of Diaspora Jews in many other lands and continents, are the subject of this book. It is a volume that deals with the "third world" of contemporary Jewry, with approximately 4.5 million individuals who live, or who have lived until recent years, beyond the frontiers both of Israel and of North America. Their collective destinies are perhaps less well known to readers in the United States, Canada, and Israel, those to whom this book is largely directed, and whose own Jewish communities have already been extensively chronicled.

I

The Vortex of Guilt:
Germany and Austria

Wiedergutmachung *in Germany*

"The infusion of philanthropy from America and the West unquestionably revived the Jewish survivors," Gerhart Riegner observed. "But it was only a physical revival, you see. The task of rebuilding their lives in Europe and overseas was much too far-reaching to be borne exclusively by the Joint." Was it not more appropriate, Riegner continued, for those who had thrust European Jewry into this devastation to bear at least part of the cost?

Obviously, at war's end, Germany too was a ruined land, its own population hungry and freezing. But within the ensuing few years a combination of Marshall Plan aid and free market economics, as well as the diligence of the German people, began to produce important results. By 1951, the nation was sufficiently recovered to join the European Coal and Steel Community. It was at work again, its *Wirtschaftswunder* was under way. Indeed, there was a certain obscenity in the contrast between Germany's reviving affluence and the near-bankruptcy of little Israel. Fully 100,000 of the Jewish state's new immigrants were living in tents. The Israeli treasury had all but exhausted its foreign exchange reserves. The issue of German compensation plainly had assumed a new urgency.

In fact, it was an issue that had been discussed for at least a decade. First raised in 1941 by Nahum Goldmann, it was subsequently developed by a committee of German Jewish refugees, led by Dr. Siegfried Moses (who later would serve as comptroller-general of Israel). By war's end, Moses's committee had outlined the basic components of a plan for German reparations. These were to be based on individual Jewish claims, on the claims of Jewish institutions, and on the collective claims of the Jewish people in their effort to build the Jewish National Home in Palestine.

The concept of reparations was not foreign to the Allies. At the Yalta and Potsdam conferences they had agreed to impose a reparations obligation of $20 billion on defeated Germany. But the formula devised by the World Jewish Congress was a very different proposition. It envisaged the payment of German reparations not to a sovereign state with which the Third Reich had been at war, but to the Jewish people as a whole. The notion was too revolutionary for the Allied delegations who attended the Paris Reparations Conference in 1945. In its place, two years later, General Lucius Clay, military governor of the American zone of occupied Germany, authorized a modest compromise gesture to the Jews. Jewish property confiscated by the Nazis would be disposed of and its proceeds used to rehabilitate Jewish victims. Britain and France later approved similar laws for their occupation zones. The concept was equitable in theory, but in practice it required individual Jews to file claims, each of which first had to be approved by one or another of the states of the Bundesrepublik, the Federal Republic of (West) Germany. The bureaucratic ordeal was endless, and all but heartbreaking. Few Jews were prepared to go through with it. By 1953, only 11,000 applications had been filed, and a mere $83 million paid out by the various German *Länder*.

In 1949 and 1950, however, Dr. Noah Barou, a vice-president of the World Jewish Congress, and Gerhart Riegner, by then the Congress's general director, began discussing with West German officials alternative means of compensation. In March 1950, they finally won confirmation from the Adenauer government that the principle of collective reparations could serve as a basis for negotiations. The German chancellor was entirely serious about *Wiedergutmachung*, making amends to the Jews. Only by doing so, he was convinced, could his nation win acceptance by the West as a trustworthy partner. Accordingly, in January 1951, Israel's Prime Minister David Ben-Gurion made the first move. After extensive consultations with Nahum Goldmann, who had recently moved up to the presidency of the World Jewish Congress, Ben-Gurion sent notes to the four Allies, announcing a Jewish claim for $1.5 billion in reparations against the new Germany. The sum was calculated on the basis of Israel's role in absorbing half a million Jewish victims of the Nazis at a per capita expense of $3,000. Reactions to the claim were varied. Moscow did not bother to answer it ($500 million of the claim was against East Germany). The Western Allies acknowledged Israel's case, but observed that there was no way to force the Bundesrepublik to pay this sum. They advised Israel to negotiate directly with Bonn.

No diplomatic issue could have raised profounder complications for the Jewish state. Among its citizens, emotions ran high against contact of any sort with Germany. Survivors of the death camps launched demonstrations of protest, went on hunger strikes, even threatened suicide. Menachem Begin, leader of the right-wing opposition, warned direly of violence if Ben-Gurion went ahead with his plan. Ben-Gurion did. In January 1952, the prime minister requested the Knesset's permission to enter into formal talks with Bonn, reminding the members that if the request was not granted, Israel would forfeit more than a billion dollars in heirless Jewish property. "Let not the murderers of our people also be their heirs!" he cried. And despite the violence outside—the surging crowds, the wail of sirens, the explosion of tear gas canisters—and the fury of Menachem Begin and his partisans within, the measure passed.

The next initiative on the Jewish side was taken by Nahum Goldmann. Lithuanian-born and educated in Germany, the World Jewish Congress president was a man of unusual linguistic and diplomatic virtuosity. With Riegner's assistance now, he patiently and adroitly co-opted twenty-two national and international organizations into a Conference on Jewish Material Claims against Germany—in effect, a central address for the Jewish people—and won the endorsement of this body for negotiations with Bonn. Thereupon, the Israeli government and the Jewish Claims Conference designed a common strategy. Talks with the Germans subsequently began on the "neutral" territory of Wassenaar, near The Hague, Netherlands, in March 1952.

Sitting at the conference table in Wassenaar's ancient ducal castle were the German delegation, the Israeli delegation, and the delegation of the Jewish Claims Conference. Talks began in a chilly atmosphere, with no handshakes, and care taken to avoid using the German language. English was spoken. The Israelis related their claim for a billion dollars to the expense of absorbing half a million refugees. The Claims Conference asked $500 million for the rehabilitation of Jewish victims outside Israel. The German negotiators accepted in principle the obligation to pay, but rejected the Israeli and Jewish demands as too high, and offered approximately half the sum. An impasse soon developed, and on March 31 the Israeli and Jewish delegates returned home.

Hereupon, Adenauer intervened personally. At a private meeting in his home, he assured Nahum Goldmann that Germany would be flexible, that the issue of reparations was a matter not of financial horse trading but of moral obligation.

Several weeks later, the delegations resumed their negotiations, and eventually they reached a compromise agreement. It was signed in a quiet ceremony on September 10, 1952, in the Luxembourg City Hall. The "Treaty of Luxembourg" consisted of three related, but separate, agreements. The first, between Israel and the Bundesrepublik, was the *Shilumim,* or reparations, agreement. Under its terms, Bonn would provide Israel with goods and services equivalent to 3 billion German marks (some $700 million), to be transmitted in annual allotments over fourteen years. The second protocol was an agreement with the Jewish Claims Conference for Bonn to initiate new legislation to provide indemnification and property restitution to individual victims of Nazi persecution. The last protocol, also with the Claims Conference, obliged Bonn to make a flat cash payment of DM 450 million to the Conference—through Israel—for the rehabilitation of Nazi victims living outside Israel. In all, the sum of DM 3.45 billion ($820 million) in goods, services, and cash would be paid to Israel and to the Claims Conference in New York.

The Engine of Jewish Recovery

The Germans paid punctiliously. By the time the *Shilumim* deliveries to the Jewish state were completed in 1965, the Bundesrepublik had dispatched some 1,450,000 tons of goods. There was virtually no area of Israel's economy that was not transformed by the shipments—of industrial equipment, telecommunications, housing materials, vessels and harbor facilities, power-generating plants. Rescued from the threat of insolvency, the Zionist republic subsequently entered its period of major economic growth. Yet, although initially less dramatic, the two protocols signed between Germany and the Claims Conference exerted an equally far-reaching influence on Jewish life. Under the second of the two agreements, Bonn provided over $100 million for the rehabilitation of Jewish victims outside Israel's frontiers. Between 1954 and 1964, these Claims Conference allocations helped underwrite Jewish communal revival in some forty countries, particularly in Western and Central Europe, whose surviving members were beggared, their possessions looted, their religious and educational institutions ruined.

Thus, of the German "rehabilitative" funds allocated by the Claims Conference in the first decade, some three-quarters were applied exclusively to social welfare, including cash relief, medical care of the aged, child care, resettlement assistance, and vocational training. The remaining Conference expenditures, approximately $20 million, were devoted to cultural and educational reconstruction. Dozens of synagogues and community centers were built or enlarged with this money. Some 165 Jewish schools were constructed or refurbished. Each year, scholarship funds enabled 15,000 to 18,000 students to attend Jewish day schools or teachers' training colleges. Local communities were provided with subventions for cultural and educational programs. Money still went far in the early postwar decades, and the Claims Conference staff administered it imaginatively.

Even more significant in promoting Jewish revival, however, was the direct payment of German funds to individual survivors of the Nazi era. Under the Treaty of Luxembourg, West Germany had agreed to enact laws providing both for personal indemnification and for the restitution of property. In meeting these obligations, Bonn subsequently enacted two legislative landmarks. The first was the Federal Indemnification Law (BEG), passed in 1953, and the second was the Federal Restitution Law (BRUEG), passed in 1957. BEG superseded all the old laws of the former military governments and individual German states. Under its terms, victims of the Nazis or victims' dependents would be compensated from a central fund and under a central authority. They would be indemnified for loss of life or limb; for damage to health, business opportunities, or professional careers; for deprivation of liberty, interruption of vocational training; and for loss of pensions and insurance rights.

Thus, for *Freiheitsschaden*—loss of freedom—the Bundesrepublik paid four marks (approximately one dollar at the post-1948 exchange rate) for each day a person had been imprisoned in a Nazi concentration camp or confined to a ghetto or forced to wear the yellow star. Payments similarly were made to individuals whose education had been interrupted under the Nazis. Thus, if a Jewish medical student had been prevented from continuing his studies, he could receive up to ten thousand marks in *Wiedergutmachung*. Payments also were made to artists, writers, scholars, and other intellectuals whose education had been completed, but whose careers had been destroyed. Claimants who already had been well established in their professions until Hitler wrecked their livelihoods were remunerated for life in the form of monthly pensions—and very generous ones. No matter how many years earlier a civil servant had fled Germany, or what other vocation he had since embraced, Bonn assumed that he had actually persevered in his old profession, as though the Third Reich had never existed. Such civil servants even received "promotions" during their phantom careers, which entitled them to larger pensions than they would have received otherwise. Those who had lost family breadwinners in concentration camps similarly were given lifetime pensions as dependents or heirs. Pensions also were mailed to those who had suffered "reduction in earning power" as a result of imprisonment, beatings, or physical and psychological distress in concentration camps.

Under the provisions of the BEG, beneficiaries were not limited to former citizens of Germany, but included all victims of Nazism who had been "stateless persons" as of January 1, 1947. This signified in practice all Jews who had not returned to their former countries. For example, a Polish Jew who had returned to Poland was not eligible; the payments obviously would fall into the hands of the Communist regime. But if, as was usually the case, he had gone to Israel, the United States, or other non-Communist nations, he was eligible. A French Jew returning to his former homeland could not claim; but a French Jew settling in non-Communist lands beyond France could. Moreover, Jews who resumed their citizenship in their former West European homelands—that is, French Jews, Belgian Jews, Dutch Jews—were covered by bilateral treaties subsequently negotiated and signed between Bonn and some twelve Western governments. Under these agreements, the Bundesrepublik agreed to pay a total of one billion marks. Accordingly, Jews who resumed their lives in these various nations applied directly to their own governments for compensation. All things considered, the indemnification law (BEG) not only was administered fairly but was repeatedly amended in ensuing years, each time adding new categories of beneficiaries and making adjustments for inflation.

Under the terms of the Federal Restitution Law (BRUEG), moreover, victims of Nazism were compensated for the loss of their individual property. Clearly, this applied only to former citizens of Germany; but even in Germany, it was impossible to restore actual physical property. Personal possessions had long since disappeared, or had changed hands too many times to be traced. Instead, an equivalent financial reimbursement was provided for household or business furnishings, for bank accounts, securities, precious metals, and other movable properties the Nazis had confiscated. Compensation under the restitutions provision became as open-ended as did the indemnifications payments.

It was evident, then, that Bonn had assumed a tremendous financial obligation under these various collective commitments. By 1961, the indemnification and restitution authorities alone employed some four thousand persons, and kept several hundred special judges and clerks busy at the immense task of *Wiedergutmachung*. If there were delays in the first years, these were rarely due to obstructionism, but more commonly to the shortage of well-trained personnel; and in the course of time the machinery began to work smoothly. Thus, under the original indemnification law (BEG) and its two revisions, some 4,276,000 claims had been submitted by 1973 (twenty years after passage of the legislation), and 95 percent of these had been processed. Payments to Nazi victims reached DM 32 billion, or over $10 billion, and 75 percent of these went to Jews residing outside Germany. Within the same twenty-year period, fully 278,000 annuities were in force, requiring monthly payments of DM 11,680,000 ($36,236,000).

In those two decades, payments to Israel and the Jewish Claims Conference, payments of indemnifications and restitutions, amounted each year to over 5 percent of Germany's national budget—and continued through the ensuing decade. By 1984, the totality of West German payments (including those dispensed under bilateral agreements with other West European states) had exceeded DM 60 billion. It is estimated that by the end of the century, Bonn will have paid out some DM 86 billion under these various obligations. Money obviously would never compensate for the trauma of the Nazi epoch. Nonetheless, the prodigious outpouring of German funds, far more than the Adenauer government had ever envisaged, played a major role in the economic growth of Israel, in the rehabilitation of hundreds of thousands of Jewish survivors worldwide, and in the revival of Jewish communal life in Western Europe.

The Remnant Jewry of Postwar Germany

Of the various Western European Jewish communities, the most important in the pre-Hitler era had been that of Germany itself. At its apogee in 1925, it comprised 564,000 individuals, and 503,000 even as late as 1935. Then, during the first six years of Nazi rule, 350,000 Jews fled the country, leaving some 214,000 by 1939. Of these latter,

180,000 perished in Hitler's concentration camps. Possibly 20,000 others survived in Europe, including those who had been confined to the "privileged" concentration camp of Theresienstadt, or had gone underground. But the figure was uncertain. Since the majority of survivors were *Mischlingen*, children of mixed marriages, they appeared to be linked to the Jewish community by only nominal ties; the reconstruction of Jewish life in Germany presumably would have been the least of their concerns. Anyway, Germany was in ruins, and there appeared to be little inducement for them to remain. Almost every German Jew of intellectual, scientific, or academic stature had left Germany during the 1930s or had perished in the Holocaust. It was unlikely that any of the 350,000 German Jews who had departed for other lands would be persuaded now to return.

Indeed, leaders of Jewish organizations abroad were unanimously opposed to the very notion of Jews resuming their lives in Germany. A few German Jewish leaders in the United States and Israel proposed imposing a rabbinical ban of excommunication even on those who remained in Germany. The Jewish Agency formally deprived Jews in Germany of the right to send delegates to the World Zionist Congress. To the Zionists, the spectacle of Jewish refugees settling anywhere but in Palestine constituted a betrayal, and a return of Jews to Germany a particularly unforgivable one. Not every German Jewish émigré shared this view. One who did not was a man with the unlikely name of Karl Marx, who returned from exile to become editor of a German Jewish weekly, the *Allgemeine Wochenzeitung der Juden in Deutschland*. By 1961, Marx's newspaper had grown to a circulation of 48,000 subscribers, three-quarters of them non-Jewish German politicians, libraries and associations, and German Jews abroad. Like a chamber of commerce booster, Marx fervently championed a bigger and better Jewry in Germany, and denied most of the charges of antisemitism in a nation where he himself had achieved some prominence.

Among those staying on or returning, however, few evinced much interest in Jewish cultural or religious activity. They tended to be more concerned with the future of German democracy. These were Jews who had been active in Weimar politics and who felt a duty to reconstruct the old democratic parties or their former trade unions. Among them were Ludwig Rosenberg, who rose eventually to the chairmanship of Germany's trade union federation; Otto Wollenberg, who became political editor of the federation's weekly newspaper; Siegmund Weltlinger, a former Berlin banker who served as alderman in the Berlin municipal council, Jeanette Wolff, a beloved grandmotherly figure who had lost her husband and two of her children in a concentration camp, and who became a Social Democratic deputy from Berlin in the Bundestag. Otherwise, the only significant group of German Jews eager to return were approximately 7,000 who had escaped to Shanghai in 1938–39; after the war, some 2,500 of these managed to get back. Yet, despite the brief revival of "native" Jews, by 1952 the Jewish population of Germany appeared to be waning. Of the survivors, at least 3,000 had died from the belated effects of their wartime ordeal. Emigration further reduced their numbers. Between 1945 and 1952, approximately 7,000 left for Israel and the United States. Of the 16,000 or 17,000 who remained, at least half had married non-Jews, and the children of these couples rarely were brought up in the Jewish faith. Entire pages of Marx's *Wochenzeitung* were filled with advertisements requesting marriage partners, and announcing deaths.

Then, from 1952 to 1961, West Germany experienced a totally unexpected influx of over 20,000 Jews. Approximately a fourth of them came from East Germany, where some 8,000 Jews had remained following the establishment of two separate states in 1949. From its inception, the Communist regime of the Deutsche Demokratische Republik had not found it necessary to provide these survivors either with restitutions or indemnifications. Walter Ulbricht and his colleagues in the Pankow government insisted that such "largess" would have represented discrimination against other victims of Nazism. To be sure, Jewish communal institutions were protected. Synagogues and Jewish old age homes were reestablished in East Berlin, Dresden, and Leipzig, and there were Jewish *Gemeinden*—communal councils in those cities. Individual Jews at first rose to prominence. Thus, Paul Meker, Lea Grundig, and Erich Jungmann were active members of the Communist Party central committee. Albert Norden was the East German propaganda minister. Gerhard Eisler was director of the state television and radio service. Heinrich Abusch served as Ulbricht's executive assistant, and Friedrich-Karl Kaul was chief legal prosecutor for the Communist regime. The prewar writers Arnold Zweig and Anna Seghers were received back with honor and became public monuments. In the early 1950s, however, when Stalin adopted antisemitism as a political weapon, Ulbricht swiftly fell into line and many Jewish public figures lost their positions. The majority of East German Jews hurriedly fled to

West Germany. Despite the relaxation of the antisemitic campaign in later years, none returned. By 1984, perhaps 1,500 Jews remained in the Deutsche Demokratische Republik, 400 of them in East Berlin.

Many of those who arrived in West Germany joined the ranks of Jewish pensioners. But others developed useful, even important careers. Dr. Fritz Grunsfeld of Düsseldorf was one of them. "We were Germans to the core," Grunsfeld reminisced during our interview in 1981. (A bachelor in his mid-seventies, he shared an apartment in a good neighborhood with his spinster sister, a retired dentist.) Indeed, the Grunsfelds were originally Prussians. Their father, a prosperous merchant of Halle, was a decorated officer-veteran of World War I. Fritz Grunsfeld was a successful international lawyer until the Nazis deprived him of his practice. In 1943, he, his sister, his mother, and his father were deported to Theresienstadt, where both parents died. Grunsfeld and his sister held on until they were liberated by the Red Army. For a while they resumed their professions in Leipzig, in East Germany. Then, in 1952, the Slansky trial in Czechoslovakia, and the ensuing "anti-Zionist" purges in the German Democratic Republic, launched a new era of Jewish oppression. (In our interview, Grunsfeld dropped his voice as he described those terror-ridden days.) In late autumn, he and his sister loaded their possessions into their tiny Czech automobile and crossed the frontier from East to West Berlin.

With the intercession of family friends, Grunsfeld was offered a judgeship in Düsseldorf. He was fully aware that the North Rhine–Westphalia state administration had selected him for "image" purposes. Even so, he accepted the job on the spot, and held it for the next twenty years, until he was promoted to an appeals court that specialized in restitution cases. Another Jew served on the panel of judges, a lawyer who had returned from Israel. Was it appropriate, I wondered, for a Jew to decide cases in which nearly all the claimants were fellow Jews? "I suspect that it was precisely for that reason that I was chosen," Grunsfeld replied equably. "Those who experienced the Nazi horrors firsthand were better equipped to pass judgment on them." In any case, his own reputation was one of consistent fairness, and he was eventually appointed president of the court. Although not personally religious, moreover, Grunsfeld made a point of observing all the Jewish holidays, attending every meeting of the local B'nai B'rith lodge, and serving as a board member of the Jewish Gemeinde.

What, then, was Grunsfeld's attitude toward the new Germany?

"There are millions of good Germans," he observed calmly, "and for that matter, there are plenty of bad Jews." His rationale was one I had heard from nearly every other Jew I had met in Germany. "One cannot live in the past, worrying about who was a Nazi and who was not. I have received much help from many good Germans, and I admire and love this people." That much was evident. When he spoke of his hero, the archconservative politician Franz-Josef Strauss, he emphasized that only such a man was "capable of standing up to the Russians." Grunsfeld may have been proud of Israel, eagerly corresponding with relatives there, but the notion of joining them was out of the question. Gazing at his composed features, his stolid, thoroughly Germanic manner, I was reminded of Theodor Herzl's comment on Arthur Schnitzler, the Austrian Jewish writer. "Schnitzler? No, he belongs here as much as Schubert or Mozart." This man was at home.

If it was not mere expediency that kept Grunsfeld in Germany, possibly this was less true of the thousands of other German Jews in Israel, England, or Latin America who returned following the passage of the Indemnification Law of 1953 (BEG). In contrast to straitened little Israel, the opportunity for economic security in Germany was compelling to the returnees. A law passed by Bonn in 1961 offered former German Jewish citizens an immediate grant of DM 6,000 (approximately $2,000), and every assistance from the housing authorities, upon their repatriation to West Germany or West Berlin. Those who accepted were generally the old, sick, or destitute. By the early 1960s, they were making their way back at the rate of nearly one hundred a month. Once settled in, they tended to retire from active life and to live on their pensions, comfortable again in familiar German-speaking surroundings. Several thousand kept their Israeli passports as insurance policies; but virtually none ever left Germany again.

Nor were all of them pensioners. A significant minority of German Jewish lawyers returned from abroad to earn solid livelihoods from the vast machinery of restitutions and indemnifications. By 1984, these numbered close to a thousand. Others among them went into public life. Thus, Herbert Weichmann became mayor of Hamburg and rose to the presidency of the Federal Bundesrat. Eric Kaufmann became Adenauer's legal adviser, and played a decisive role in negotiating the Bundesrepublik's emergence to sovereignty in 1955. Kurt Glaser became senator of public health for Hamburg. Joseph (Asher) Neuberger, a returnee from Israel, served as minister of justice for North

Rhine—Westphalia, and later as a judge on the federal supreme court; while another former émigré, Dr. Rudolf Katz, served as deputy president of the same court. Paul Herz, who lived out the war years in the United States, became a Social Democratic senator and city planner for West Berlin. Hans Hirschfeld served as Berlin's director of public information.

Interestingly enough, there were few businessmen among the repatriates. Although their firms were restored to them almost without exception, they preferred to remain abroad as silent partners in these companies. Among the rare Jewish businesses that flourished again under their former owners was the mighty M. M. Warburg Bank in Hamburg. Located on the Ferdinandstrasse, a street of banks commanding a dramatic view of the bay, the firm's premises, stone and steel, blended naturally into the financial district's staid German topography. So did the Warburg dynasty. Its roots went back to the medieval town of Warburg. In the seventeenth century, one member established a bank in Hamburg. Other family members later settled in Denmark, Sweden, and (eventually) the United States. Hamburg remained their base, however. By the beginning of the twentieth century, M. M. Warburg had become the second-largest merchant bank in Germany and played a major role in the growth of the imperial economy.

The chapter closed with the Nazi accession, of course. In 1938, M. M. Warburg & Co. was expelled from the Reichsbank consortium and its assets were transferred to "Aryan" receivers. Yet by then, Eric Warburg, son of the bank's director, had established a new firm in his own name in New York. A veteran of the kaiser's army, he enlisted in the United States Army Air Corps in 1942. Commissioned a captain, then trained for combat intelligence, Warburg participated in the Allied landings in North Africa, in the invasion of Sicily, of Normandy, in the liberation of Paris, in the Battle of the Bulge. By war's end he held the rank of colonel, and had been awarded decorations by the American, British, and French governments. It was probable that Warburg's determination to share actively in the war against Nazism was influenced, at least in part, by Jewish pride. His family had always been staunchly identified Jews. Its sense of responsibility for Jewish welfare extended to both sides of the Atlantic. In New York, Felix Warburg, Eric's uncle, had been the founding chairman of the Joint Distribution Committee during World War I. Thirty years later, after World War II, Edward Warburg (who had participated in the Normandy invasion with his cousin Eric) served as the Joint's chairman in a period when that philanthropy's vastly expanded program made Jewish history. In the immediate postwar period, Eric Warburg returned to Hamburg. There he turned over one of the homes of the family's Kösterburg estate to Youth Aliyah, for the care of Jewish refugee children who were trained for life in Palestine.

The process of regaining control of the bank was more complicated. Warburg found it necessary to return from New York many times in the late 1940s and early 1950s to handle the negotiations. During those years, he resisted the appeal of the United States high commissioner, John McCloy, to settle permanently and help restore the economy of Hamburg. But in 1954, the transfer of the bank was accomplished, and Warburg was faced with a painful decision: whether to return to Germany with his wife and children and resume direct control of the bank's operations, or to remain in New York as the firm's "silent partner"—as virtually all former German Jewish businessmen preferred to do. He returned. A wealthy man, Warburg could not have been motivated by financial considerations alone. As a Jew, scion of a people, of a family, with a unique international background, conceivably he experienced a sense of mission in sharing the process of European integration. By the 1950s, it was hardly to Germany alone that he was returning, but rather to a Western Europe moving rapidly toward mutual interdependence.

Since the end of the war, when every "normal" consideration would have dictated a punitive approach, Warburg had retained his faith in Germany's capacity to democratize itself and to energize the rest of Europe. He counseled his friend John McCloy against carrying out the Morgenthau Plan, a draconian blueprint for reducing the country essentially to a pastoral state. One did not democratize a nation by turning its people from Nazism to communism, he warned. As his bank steadily regained its former leadership, participating in Germany's vast economic boom, Warburg acquired a reputation as a wise counselor to leading figures in both of Germany's major parties. *Schnitzler? No, he belongs here as much as Schubert or Mozart.* Still dynamic in his eighties, Warburg is widely admired by his countrymen as the very model of the "good European."

Ostjuden *and Jewish Revival*

By the mid-1950s, prominent old-line German Jews such as Grunsfeld and Warburg, or Feuchtwanger (an eminent Munich banker) and Rosenthal (a millionaire Selb porcelain manufacturer), had become a diminishing minority within the Jewish minority. It was not simply that the old, the ill, and the pensioners were the norm. Rather, German Jews were being inundated by newcomers from Eastern Europe. Although most of the quarter-million Jewish displaced persons who were located on German soil after the war had gone to Israel by the early 1950s, some fifteen thousand Polish, Hungarian, or Romanian Jews remained as permanent residents. Most had earned a small stake as petty traders, and had acquired enough German to take up livelihoods in the reviving German economy. Within the ensuing years, perhaps eleven thousand of them became citizens (and about two thousand of them married non-Jewish Germans). They were not an easy group. Many had been twisted by their wartime ordeal and now were further warped by the anomaly of their presence in Germany. Much of their notorious irascibility doubtless was a form of projected self-contempt, and they swore that their children at least would be sent to Israel. Ultimately, they comprised 95 percent of the Jewish community of Munich, and nearly that large a proportion in Frankfurt. Some opened restaurants and bars in the less savory areas around the railroad stations. But most invested their initial earnings in small or middle-sized retail and wholesale shops, often specializing in jewelry, textiles, furs, leather goods, and produce.

Others branched out further yet, and a few even achieved impressive economic success. Arthur Brauner, son of a Lodz lumber dealer, bought a partnership in a small motion picture company. By the early 1960s, his two firms, Central Cinema Corporation (CCC) and Alfa, had produced 150 films and Brauner himself was Germany's most successful independent film mogul. Of the eighteen smaller German film companies in 1984, three were owned by Jews. There were other recent Jewish tycoons, in fur, in chocolate, in jewelry. But for the most part, the *Wirtschaftswunder* passed by German Jews and *Ostjuden* together. The largest numbers in both communities remained pensioners, with a small mixture of lawyers and an occasional professor, publisher, or journalist. It was a minority that bore little resemblance to the Jewish economic and cultural aristocracy of pre-Nazi Germany.

The most enduring impact of the East European influx was upon Jewish communal life. The founders of the early postwar Gemeinden were German Jews. Middle-aged or older, they were often partners of mixed marriages and were rarely religiously observant. Their haste in reviving the Jewish Gemeinden within days after the German surrender was entirely pragmatic. By identifying themselves as Jews, they ensured their right to additional rations from the Allied authorities. But whatever their motives, these self-styled Gemeinde leaders succeeded in organizing a powerful *Zentralrat,* a Central Council, of the Jews in Germany. The role of this body was narrowly functional. It was to promote Jewish legal and economic interests, particularly in restitution matters; to act as the Jewish spokesman in Germany; to monitor German progress toward democracy; and to encourage legislative measures against antisemitism. The Zentralrat's secretary-general, Dr. Henryk van Dam, was German-born, as were the early secretaries-general of many of the individual Gemeinden. A lawyer during the Weimar period, and married, typically, to a Gentile, van Dam gave only secondary attention to Jewish cultural and religious activities. Civil rights were his major concern.

By the late 1940s and early 1950s, East European survivors began joining the Gemeinde boards in larger numbers, and eventually infiltrated the leadership positions. Managing restituted Jewish communal property, they succeeded often in lining their own pockets. So frequent and embarrassing were the episodes of malfeasance that no "decent" Jew would participate in the Gemeinde committees. It was fifteen or twenty years before most of the early officials were purged and leadership in the Gemeinden became honorable again. With the exception of Berlin and Munich, however, that leadership has remained essentially in the hands of the East Europeans.

There are seventy-three Gemeinden currently in Germany. I visited three of them. In Hamburg, the Jewish communal offices are located on the ground floor of an IBM office building. High glass doors lead into the reception room, for there is nothing clandestine about being a Jew in Hamburg, a city with a strong anti-Nazi record. Its first two postwar mayors were Jews, and the most recent, Herbert Weichmann, also served as a member of the federal Bundesrat. Weichmann, in fact, had been offered the presidency of the Bundesrepublik, but had declined. ("I was not prepared to be used quite that obviously for the sake of postwar Germany's new image," he admitted to me.) Not far from the Gemeinde office, facing a broad square, is a magnificent new synagogue. Its banquet halls and auditorium can accommodate up to 4,000 people, but they are rarely used by the city's Jewish population of 1,400. I was received by the Gemeinde's executive secretary, Günther Singer. German-born of Polish parents and a survivor of Auschwitz,

Singer, a heavyset man in his late fifties, explained that the Jews of
Hamburg, like those of other German cities, were predominantly East
European, with a substantial minority of Iranian rug dealers. The younger Jews were mainly in business. Most were registered in the Gemeinde, where their dues, as elsewhere in Germany, were calculated at
the rate of 10 percent of their income taxes.

Was Herr Singer optimistic about the future of Jewish life in Hamburg? He was unsure. It was an aging community, essentially weighted
toward pensioners. And what of relations with the non-Jewish population? Here the executive secretary had no complaints. The isolated
cases of antisemitism that had come to his attention were not serious.
Even so, he would not count himself an optimist, and was totally unim-
pressed by Herbert Weichmann's faith in the German future. "They
weren't here during the war, these high and mighty Kaiserjuden," he
scoffed. "They don't know what the average German is capable of.
Weichmann meets only with rich, important people." Why, then, did
Singer not emigrate to Israel after 1948? "I could not bring myself to
abandon my old mother," he replied. His children? They, too, were
working in Hamburg.

In Munich, whose Jewish community is second in size only to
Berlin's, the Gemeinde functions in a rather anonymous, older building, its halls narrow and dark, its doors triple-locked (unlike Hamburg,
Munich had been a bastion of Nazism). Within, the corridors resonate
with whispers and murmurs in Yiddish or Yiddish-German. A wide variety of boldface notices on bulletin boards announce forthcoming concerts, lectures, Hebrew courses. From the outset, the Gemeinde's
German-born chairman, Hans Lamm, a soft-spoken, congenial man, has
been in the unique position of administering the affairs of Jews who are
largely aliens both to Munich and to Germany. Although these
Ostjuden have abandoned much of their prewar religiosity, their public
institutions at least function within the structure of traditionalism. Their
four synagogues are Orthodox. Their canteens, nursery school, elementary school, old age home, and community center are strictly kosher.
There is little evidence of "assimilation" among either the young or the
old. Here, too, there are far more Jewish young people than in any
other German city. Only 12 percent of Munich's approximately four
thousand Jews are over sixty, and their average age is the lowest of any
German Jewish community. Some five hundred children attend religious school, and nearly that many participate in various Jewish youth

clubs. Quite insular, few of the youngsters here maintain contacts out of school with non-Jews. No other Jewish community is as ethnocentric, as Zionist, or as generous in its contributions to Israeli causes. From the early 1960s on, several hundred of Munich's Jewish youth have gone to Israel for their military service, rather than fulfill it in Germany (a choice permitted under German law); and dozens of young Jews volunteered for service in Israel during the 1967 and 1973 Middle East wars. Is it possible, then, to verify the conclusion of Leo Katcher, a shrewd commentator on the German Jewish scene, that Munich Jews are living "under the twin shadows of fear and memory of Munich's Nazi past"?

The observation presumably would not be endorsed by many hundreds of Munich *Ostjuden*, who remain intensely Jewish in their loyalties but who have done well in this typically postwar boom city. Joseph Domberger, for one, does not appear to be sitting on his suitcase. Stocky, middle-aged, with jet-black hair and mustache adorning a cherubic face, Domberger was born in Drogobych, in Polish Silesia. Fleeing in the wake of the German invasion, his family traveled to Romania, and from there ultimately to Palestine. It was in Palestine that Joseph Domberger attended school, joined the Haganah—the Jewish underground—rose to officer's rank in the Israeli army, even was appointed military adjutant to Prime Minister Moshe Sharett. His father meanwhile returned to Europe, eventually settling in Munich to become a successful property developer. For the while, the son continued to serve Israel. Dispatched to Argentina early in the 1950s, however, on a mission for Israel Bonds, Joseph Domberger decided to go into business for himself; over the next ten years he developed a successful plastics company in Buenos Aires.

With his ties to Israel long since cut, Domberger found it easier in 1964 to join his father's thriving company in Munich. ("How could I leave my father?") His misgivings about the Germans were not borne out—then or later. His wife, a Swiss Jew whom he had met in Argentina, reported that their son was a favorite of his Christian teachers and classmates. "We have never encountered a single episode of antisemitism during our entire life in Germany," the Dombergers assured me. Through his Munich-based firm, Domberger has branched out as a developer of apartment buildings, hotels, department stores, industrial buildings, in Germany and elsewhere in Europe. Lately his partners have included prominent local entrepreneurs, among them Edmond de Rothschild in Geneva.

When Domberger arrived in Munich, his fellow *Ostjuden* were altogether parochial, "self-ghettoized." Closing their shops at 6 P.M., they also closed off all their relationships with the Gentile world. It was Jewish identity of a sort, but hardly a creative one. Thus, borrowing from the model he had encountered in Buenos Aires, Domberger organized a club, Hebraica, that sponsored lectures on Jewish cultural themes. At the request of the B'nai B'rith regional office in Basel, in 1966 he transformed the club into the revived B'nai B'rith lodge of Munich, the third postwar lodge in Germany. Its first hundred members were the most respected Jews in town; for the European tradition of B'nai B'rith was elitist. Under Domberger's aegis, a second lodge was established later in Munich, then five others elsewhere in Germany. These lodges subsequently became centers of Jewish cultural life in Germany, far more than did the local Gemeinden. Their interfaith meetings were addressed by the nation's leading politicians. ("They regard it as a privilege to be invited.") Eclectic in his Jewish activities, Domberger served also as president of the United Jewish Appeal, of Israel Bonds, as a board member of the local Gemeinde, and of the Gesellschaft für Christliche-jüdische Zusammenarbeit—the Christian-Jewish Cooperation Association. Yet B'nai B'rith remained his first love. By 1977, he was elected president of the order's European Council, and was subsequently reelected twice. As a major European Jewish leader, he was taken seriously by the leading statesmen of Germany.

"No," he insisted, "we are not living on our suitcases any longer. Years ago, Jews here were regarded as pariahs by the Jewish world. If they visited Israel they were ashamed to admit that they were living in Germany. They would dissemble, intimating that they lived in Zurich, or Vienna, or else that they were on the verge of leaving. No longer. We must end this hypocrisy for the sake of our children. They ought not to be ashamed of living in Germany. If we are here, obviously we must live a rich and vital Jewish life. In the long run, that can only benefit Israel. But we are here to stay." I pressed him on the point. With his ties to Israel, would he not prefer to make Tel Aviv or Haifa his base? Sitting in his luxurious home on the fashionable Kaskadenweg, surrounded by the plaques and scrolls of his accumulated Jewish and German testimonials, I could have anticipated Domberger's answer. It was identical to Herbert Weichmann's: "We must reject Hitler's plan to make Europe Judenrein."

Philosemitism and the Upsurge of Jewish Settlement

The West German government and important sectors of the German public cooperated in this Jewish revival. In the immediate aftermath of the war, a formidable residue of antisemitism lingered on. A survey in 1947 disclosed that four out of ten Germans in the American zone of occupation continued to distrust Jews. Later attempts at denazification and democratization under American auspices were largely ineffectual; the very notion of reeducation was suspect as an occupation measure. Then, with the establishment of the Bundesrepublik in 1949, the task of organizing a functioning democracy was placed entirely in German hands. Dominating public life for the next ten years, the Adenauer government observed all the correct democratic forms, even outlawed the neo-Nazi Socialist Reich Party.

Yet Adenauer and the other Christian Democratic leaders seemed content to denounce antisemitism rather than actively to promote interfaith understanding. The result of this somewhat flaccid policy could be seen in an upsurge of vandalism against Jewish cemeteries. Between 1955 and 1959, fully 175 such desecrations occurred. On Christmas Eve 1959, the new synagogue in Cologne was defaced with swastikas, and within the next fortnight, synagogues and Jewish community centers in Wiesbaden, Koblenz, Ingelheim, Memmingen, and Bamberg were similarly desecrated. The vandals were found to be little more than juvenile delinquents, but the episodes deeply shocked German public opinion. In January 1960, representatives of twenty student and other youth organizations demonstrated by torchlight against antisemitism and neo-fascism. The Jewish Zentralrat and individual Gemeinden were deluged with telegrams and letters of shocked sympathy. Many Germans sent donations to Youth Aliyah.

Several other factors contributed to this new attitude of remorse. One was a far-reaching change in the postwar German social climate. For the first time in decades, the nation was experiencing uninterrupted material prosperity; and, simultaneously, Western democratic values were acquiring a solid foothold among large segments of the German people. In the 1960s, moreover, Germany was all but inundated by millions of East European refugees and foreign workers from throughout the Common Market. In this increasingly heterogeneous nation, Jews would not have stood out even if they had returned by the hundreds of thousands. Not least of all, the abduction of Adolf

Eichmann in 1960, and his trial in Israel the following year, seemed to shock the Germans out of their complacency. For German youth, the trial supplied answers their parents had never given them. As they followed the Jerusalem court sessions in the German press or on television, they grasped the truth at last of the horrors their nation had committed. Fully twenty thousand of these young people visited Israel between 1961 and 1967. Some traveled in youth groups, some on their own, and many arrived to work in kibbutz settlements or in development towns.

But if the Eichmann trial fostered a new understanding between Germans and Israelis, it even more dramatically influenced Germany's approach to Nazi war crimes and to local Jews. In 1964, Bonn adopted a statute of limitations for the trial of Nazis accused of murder, to go into effect on May 8, 1965, the twentieth anniversary of Germany's surrender. Outraged, the Israeli government, American Jewish organizations, and numerous influential German intellectuals protested vigorously. Taken aback, Bonn promptly reversed itself and removed all limitations on the prosecution of Nazi murderers. By 1983, some eighty thousand Germans had been sentenced by the courts of individual *Länder*, and more than sixty thousand other investigations still were being undertaken by state prosecutors. The Central Agency for the Prosecution of Nazi Criminals, functioning in Ludwigsburg, a small town near Stuttgart, employed a staff of over one hundred attorneys, judges, and researchers, who worked tenaciously to bring the crimes of Germany's past to light and judgment.

At the same time, state and municipal governments appeared to vie with each other in providing financial aid to Jews. Beyond restitutions and indemnifications, their help throughout the 1950s and 1960s included an unending subsidy of Jewish communal institutions. Some forty-five synagogues were built or restored. In Bonn, the handsome new synagogue was constructed across the street from the foreign ministry, a tangible reminder to visiting diplomats of Germany's concern for its Jews. In Frankfurt, the magnificent rebuilt Spanish Byzantine synagogue on Freiherr von Steinstrasse cost the state of Hesse 800,000 marks. As in many other communities, the building remains empty except on the Jewish High Holidays (not more than 4,200 Jews live in Frankfurt). Additional synagogues were constructed or refurbished in Berlin, Hamburg, Hagen, Duisburg, Münster, Mülheim, Saarbrücken, Heidelberg, Mainz, Paderborn, Hannover, and Wiesbaden. Nothing is lacking except worshipers to fill them. But for the German authorities, it has been a matter of honor, obligation—and image. Thirty-nine libraries and three institutes of Jewish studies have been established, and communal Gemeinden have been subsidized in whole or in part.

West Berlin, with its six thousand Jews, offers the most vivid example of this *Wiedergutmachung*. The city has always had a special meaning for Jews. At its peak in 1925, Berlin Jewry numbered 173,000 and was the cultural cynosure of West European Jewish life. By war's end, barely two thousand survivors remained here. Although nearly all were either *Mischlingen* or intermarried Jews, most took part in organizing the postwar Gemeinde. Heinz Galinski, who became the Gemeinde's professional director, would have been rejected with contempt by the cultivated German Jewish community of the prewar era. A Silesian, a concentration camp survivor whose wife and parents perished in a Nazi gas chamber, Galinski was a shrewd politician of limited education, somewhat akin to an American political boss. He soon perfected the art of browbeating the local Berlin municipality into funding Jewish communal activities, and eventually into underwriting construction of the handsome Gemeinde building itself on the Fasanenstrasse. Chatting with me in his office in January 1982, Galinski assured me that he could pick up the telephone and get what he wanted from "the most important people in the government," that he was invited to every municipal function as "the official representative of the Jewish community." As I contemplated this indelicate man, it occurred to me that he may have been precisely the right individual to deal with Germans, with their vulnerable consciences, their respect for authority, their lingering susceptibility to intimidation.

Unlike the early 1950s, then, when the Adenauer government found it necessary to chivy public opinion toward material restitution, in the 1960s and 1970s it was public opinion that prodded the government to launch new programs for German reeducation, to make clear to the younger generation the depths of German responsibility for the Nazi epoch. To that end, teachers were reoriented and textbooks and other teaching materials revised to unveil the Nazi past, and to explain the horrors of unchecked antisemitism. This reeducation extended to military officers' training schools. Enlisted in the campaign, too, were the government-controlled radio and television, and a Federal Center for Political Education to provide schools and other public educational facilities with material on Jews and antisemitism. Employing legions of social psychologists, film artists, writers, and editors, the Center disseminated over a million pamphlets about Israel, about concentration camps and Jewish refugees.

A movement of vigorous philosemitism, *Aktion Sühnezeichen*—Operation Penance—strengthened the effort of consciousness-raising. Its original founders were a group of influential German pastors, who demanded that Nazi guilt be accepted by all German youth. The earliest spokesmen asked the Jews "to allow us—with our hands and other means—to do something good as a token of reconciliation." Led by writers, scholars, and other intellectuals, together with the original nucleus of clergymen, Aktion Sühnezeichen encouraged acts of contrition ranging from individual gestures of personal "atonement and penance" to an organized interest in Judaism. Between 1959 and 1967, several thousand young men and women performed menial, unpaid work for Jewish institutions throughout Western Europe and in Israel. In Germany itself they participated in volunteer repair work in synagogues and Jewish cemeteries, initiated memorial exhibits, even published several books on the Holocaust. Groups of schoolchildren cleaned and decorated Jewish cemeteries and also fashioned musical instruments as gifts for Israeli schools, among other activities of contact and goodwill. A new order of German Protestant nuns, the Ecumenical Sisterhood of Mary, worked quietly in Jewish old age homes and private homes both in Germany and in Israel. Germans also collected scholarship funds for Israeli youths willing to study in Germany, and invited Jews to spend vacations in Germany.

As early as 1951, after Martin Buber accepted the prestigious Goethe Prize, books by Jewish writers rapidly became an intellectual vogue. Reprint lists carried the works of Else Lasker-Schüler, Nelly Sachs, Gertrude Kollmar, Kurt Tucholsky, and Ernst Toller. By the late 1960s and early 1970s, a German publisher seemed almost duty-bound to publish at least one Jewish title a year. In every German city I visited, it was rare to pass a bookstore without encountering works by prominent Jewish writers in the window display (in 1981–82, the principal figure appeared to be Gershom Scholem). Biographies of other influential Jewish figures, such as Sigmund Freud, Hermann Cohen, Moses Hess, Chaim Weizmann, Max Bodenheimer, David Ben-Gurion, and Moshe Dayan, continue to sell well. Books have appeared on the Talmud, the Cabalah, on historic Jewish communities in Berlin, Nuremberg, Frankfurt. At the same time, numerous lectures on Judaism and Jewish history have been well attended in hundreds of independent adult education programs throughout the country. Circles for the study of Jews and their history operate in many German cities. In 1979, a Hochschule für Jüdische Studien was established in Heidelberg and jointly funded by the Jewish Zentralrat and the federal government. Currently, three-quarters of its 160 students are German Jews. Almost every major university offers courses on Jewish religion and history.

Professor Richard Rürup teaches one of these at Berlin's Technical University. A slim, bearded, mild-mannered gentleman in his mid-forties, Rürup was trained as a general historian at Göttingen. Eventually he was drawn to the study of the Jews, and particularly of German antisemitism. Aware of the deep-rooted interest in the subject, and the growing professionalization of German Jewish studies, he won important funding from the Deutsche Forschungsgemeinschaft to build the Technical University's Judaica collection and to provide graduate fellowships. In 1982, the program was enlarged into a Zentrum für Antisemitismusforschung. Rürup's own course, "Jewish Emancipation and Antisemitism in Central Europe," has become one of the star offerings in the university's program of social studies. Was it philosemitism? I asked. Rürup thought not. "Actually, I believe the philosemitism of the 1960s and early 1970s is waning. A new generation is growing up, no longer personally conscience-stricken about the role of their parents—who were themselves youngsters during the Nazi epoch. As an example, in the 1950s the disproportionately important role of Jews in German economic and cultural history was played down, for fear of touching upon a sensitive subject. No longer. Jewish history can now be studied with complete objectivity. If the Jews played a larger-than-life role in German history, we can cope with that fact, for we have been sensitized to pluralism, to the right of minorities to be different, to have 'personalities' of their own." I found the explanation reassuring. It augured better for German-Jewish relations than did a sentimental philosemitism.

The number of Jews in Germany meanwhile has been steadily rising since the early 1970s. In addition to the 32,000 Jews officially registered in the Gemeinden of seventy-three organized communities, there are approximately 10,000 Jewish "floaters" who have not yet appeared on the Gemeinden's rolls, but whose children someday may. Among the newcomers there has been an unanticipated recent influx of perhaps

4,000 Soviet Jews who emigrated to Israel but grew disenchanted there. Like their East European predecessors after World War II, many of them are barely eking out an existence as dealers in trinkets and secondhand clothes in the back streets of Frankfurt, Hamburg, and Munich. But other "floaters" are veteran residents of Tel Aviv and Haifa. They are often a less than desirable element. Again, like their East European counterparts of the 1940s, not a few of them operate shady bars in the larger cities. Their precise numbers are unknown, but the figure commonly cited is between 2,500 and 3,000.

Some two hundred Israeli students, finally, are studying in German universities. I spotted one of them lunching in the canteen of Berlin's Jewish Gemeinde on the Fasanenstrasse. A *sabra*, a native of Jerusalem, he was something of a beatnik, unshaven, wild-haired. Seated beside him was his German—Gentile—girlfriend. Five years earlier, he explained, he had come to study aeronautical engineering at the Technical University. By now he had his M.A., as well as his assistantship, and was "considering" the possibility of remaining on another five years until he received his doctorate. Would he return then to Israel? He grinned slyly. "As of now, I plan to. But how do I know how I'll feel five years from now?" Meanwhile, he remained active in the Gemeinde. Across the table sat another student, chatting with a neighbor in fluent German. He turned out to be the son of Soviet Jews who had emigrated to Israel, then settled in Berlin. I queried the young man on his plans. "As of now, I expect to return to Israel," he replied, "but it will depend on the job I'm offered. I'm making no commitments." Each year, fewer of them do.

Austria: Affronted Innocence

On November 9, 1966, a district court in Vienna sentenced Wilhelm and Johann Mauer, forty-eight and fifty-two years old, to prison sentences of twelve and eight years respectively for their participation in the wartime mass murder of the Jews of Stanislav, in eastern Poland. What was startling about the trial was not the mildness of the sentences, but the fact that the defendants had been found guilty at all. In an earlier trial the previous spring, the Mauer brothers had been acquitted by a jury of their neighbors in Salzburg, many of whom were subsequently revealed to be ex-Nazis themselves. The presiding judges refused to accept the verdict. Remanding the Mauers to prison, they asked the Austrian high court to authorize a new trial. The court concurred and also ordered a change of venue. Accordingly, in October and November, the Mauers were retried in Vienna and found guilty. Had it not been for the pressure of world opinion, the brothers probably would have been acquitted in the second trial, as well. Even so, the sentences, for the murder of thousands of Jews, were an insult to intelligence and justice.

Only two months earlier, SS Hauptsturmführer Franz Novak had similarly been acquitted of mass murder. It was the Novak acquittal that had galvanized the American press and international Jewish organizations into unprecedented criticism. From the United States, Canada, Britain, and Israel, protests flooded into Austrian legations. In Vienna, some two thousand young people denounced the acquittal, marched into the center of the city and sat down, paralyzing traffic. The Jews of Austria added their own protests. It happened that the Austrian government was planning a huge "freedom celebration" on October 25, 1966, to commemorate the tenth anniversary of the Allied military departure. Speeches were scheduled by the chancellor, the cardinal, and leaders of the three religions. Hereupon Chief Rabbi Akiba Eisenberg shocked the Austrians by wiring the chancellor: "You may celebrate. We shall mourn." While the festivities went on in Vienna as scheduled, Eisenberg conducted a memorial service in the capital's main synagogue. Not less than ten thousand Jews attended, nearly the entire Jewish population of the city, clogging the streets for blocks around the synagogue. Over the loudspeakers, the rabbi told the assembled listeners: "The youth of Vienna is growing up in an atmosphere where they see how mass murderers are acquitted and their government makes no protest."

Rabbi Eisenberg hardly exaggerated. Before and after the war the Austrian record on the Jews was a reeking scandal. In some ways the nation's tradition of antisemitism was even more deeply ingrained than Germany's. As an intellectual and political movement, it could be traced back to August Rohling, the professor of theology who in 1870 published one of the first antisemitic classics, *The Talmud Jew,* and encompassed such pioneers of late-nineteenth-century Jew-hatred as Georg von Schönerer and Vienna's Mayor Karl Lueger. Under the latter's incumbency, Jews were excluded from all municipal offices and non-Viennese Jews were briefly denied the right to live in the capital. By the turn of the century, several flagrantly antisemitic political parties had emerged. In the universities, Jews were openly ridiculed and provoked. In 1907, a parliamentary motion to exclude Jews from gymnasia and universities was barely defeated. And in the poisonous racism of the post-Habsburg period, a convention of university deans passed a resolution in 1925 to bar Jews from any academic post. By 1936, two years before the Anschluss, 537,000 Austrians were registered Nazis in a population of seven million.

Following the Anschluss and the outbreak of the war, when Austria comprised 8 percent of the Greater Reich, about a third of the functionaries working for the SS extermination program were Austrians, and almost half the six million Jewish victims of the Final Solution ultimately were killed by Austrians. Austrians commanded the four Polish death camps of Treblinka, Sobibor, Maidanek, and Belzec, where some two million Jews perished. Along with Hitler himself, Ernst Kaltenbrunner, the Gestapo chief, was Austrian. So was Adolf Eichmann, and so were many members of his staff. In the Netherlands, two Austrians, Arthur Seyss-Inquart and Hans Rauter, directed the annihilation of 110,000 Dutch Jews. Of the 5,090 names on the list of war criminals active in Yugoslavia, where two million people were killed, 2,499 were Austrian. Over a thousand Austrians participated in the Einsatzkommandos, SS hunter-killer teams on the Soviet front.

But even as this noteworthy record was being compiled, the Allies issued the Moscow Declaration in November 1943, outlining the sympathetic postwar position they would adopt toward Austria as "the first free nation to fall victim to Hitlerite aggression." Thus, at the Potsdam Conference in 1945, the Vienna government was exempted from reparations payments, thereby confirming the Austrians' sense of detachment from their country's Nazi past. Under the scrutiny of the Allied occupation powers, the Austrian parliament enacted a war criminals law in 1945. Yet it was not until 1963 that a prosecuting agency was established to put the measure into effect, and only as a result of continuous pressure by foreign Jewish organizations. Once Austria regained its sovereignty in 1955, most of its Nazi war criminals had been granted amnesty by various presidential decrees. The occasional trials that did take place usually ended with acquittals. Austrian Nazis who were tried and convicted in other lands enjoyed full civil rights upon returning home.

Only the briefest mention of the Nazi past—the period between 1918 and 1945—appeared in Austrian school texts. Professors with flagrant Nazi backgrounds were permitted to continue teaching. Not less than thirty-five organizations in Austria were known to be antisemitic, and twenty of them were actively engaged in promoting their ideals. While none occupied a major position in public life, they functioned in a climate of official indifference—unlike Germany, where such groups, if not actually outlawed, were watched closely. Indeed, it was precisely this moral vacuum that induced Simon Wiesenthal to establish his Documentation Center of Nazi War Crimes not in Germany but in Vienna. He knew his Austrians.

The nation's attitude of self-forgiveness was particularly evident in its treatment of Jewish financial claims. As late as 1935, the Viennese Jewish community was Europe's third largest, numbering 200,000, nearly 3 percent of Austria's population. At the time of the Anschluss in March 1938, at least 185,000 Jews were still living in the Austrian capital, and at the outbreak of the war, perhaps 66,000. By then, 48,000 Jews already had been deported and some 4,000 managed to emigrate; but of the rest, only 9,000, or one out of seven, survived. Together with those who had perished, or had fled earlier by the tens of thousands, the survivors had been cruelly despoiled by the Nazi regime. In 1946, the Austrian government committed itself to the full restitution of property to Nazi victims. Yet it soon became evident that Jewish claims fell into a different category. When Jews pressed their appeals, they were officially informed that they were entitled only to properties currently "identifiable" in Austria; otherwise, they would have to look to Germany for restitution. Under this guideline, a Jew who had left a store filled with goods would receive back nothing but an empty storeroom. Before the war, most Viennese Jews had rented their flats. Accordingly, they were not entitled to restituted housing in the postwar years. Subsequent Austrian restitution laws made no provision to compensate Jews for the exorbitant and confiscatory taxes imposed on them after the Anschluss. Nor was recognition given to heirless Jewish property; this reverted to the state. To the tens of thousands of Jewish survivors abroad claiming restitution, the Austrian government emphasized that transfers to foreign countries "would constitute a burden on the Austrian economy."

This coldly uncompromising stance was based upon a premise accepted by the nation's two major political parties from the beginning, namely, that Austria itself had been a victim of aggression. "It is not Austria that should make restitution," insisted the spokesman of the Socialist Party in 1946, "but rather Austria to which restitution should be made." As a result, the government flatly rejected the notion of

German-style indemnifications. The single concession extracted from Vienna by the Jewish Claims Conference was a "relief fund" for Austrian Jews who could prove they had lost their liberty—that is, who had actually been confined in concentration camps. At that, Vienna established the fund only after the Claims Conference persuaded West Germany to contribute half its capital; and payments to Jewish victims never exceeded half the amount paid out in German indemnifications for the identical damage. In this fashion, then, survivors of one of Europe's oldest, largest, and most distinguished Jewish communities were essentially disenfranchised from *Wiedergutmachung*, whether financial or moral.

A Community in Limbo

Central Friedhof, Vienna's largest cemetery, maintains its Jewish memorial chapel at 11 Simmerlager Hauptstrasse. Restored ten years after its destruction on Kristallnacht in November 1938—the night when the Nazis launched a mass destruction of synagogues in the Greater Reich—the site evokes poignant memories. Along its tree-lined main avenue stand the tombs and mausoleums of the Austrian Rothschilds; of Arthur Schnitzler; of Adolf Lieben, dean of the philosophy faculty at the University of Vienna; of Ignaz Brüll, teacher of Gustav Mahler; and of scores of other greats. Here, too, is the monument to Dr. Hirsch Chajes, last chief rabbi of Vienna, whose remains have been transferred to Israel. Scattered through the Jewish section of the cemetery are many small memorial tablets, honoring victims of the Nazi terror not actually buried at Central Friedhof. The contrast between cemetery and city reveals a profound discontinuity. Few Jews now live in the old Jewish quarter near the Karmeliter market. Rather, the precarious history of Jewish fortunes in Vienna is kept alive almost exclusively in street markers, plaques, and old buildings. Judengasse and Judenplatz are simply names from another era. The Chasidic and other Orthodox houses of prayer are tucked away where only their congregations can find them. Today, there is but one authentic and recognizable synagogue, the Seitenstettengasse. It may well symbolize the trepidation with which Jews still live on in the Austrian capital. Erected in 1826, the Seitenstettengasse is an impressive, even beautiful structure, with twelve gilt pillars and a starry blue dome. It is also concealed behind an apartment house on a narrow, cobblestoned street—the imperial stipulation under which it was originally constructed. Ironically, the synagogue's obscure location alone saved it from destruction on Kristallnacht.

Vienna's importance in postwar Jewish life has been essentially as a transit point for Jews from the East. After 1945, Austria was second only to Germany in its concentration of displaced persons. Numbering 44,000 in Austria by 1947, nearly all of them came from Poland, Romania, and Hungary, and they were scattered among the various Allied zones of occupation. As in Germany, a small minority—3,000 or 4,000—decided to remain on. At first they lived a marrano life as hidden Jews, dispersed throughout the city, often dealing on the black market, struggling to subsist. The 1,500 or 1,800 Viennese Jewish survivors would have nothing to do with them, and least of all with the Chasidim, who arrived from Hungary in greater numbers after 1946, and who opened small textile, jewelry, and fur businesses. But the newcomers were younger than the Austrian Jews, and their uninterrupted trickle of immigration outbalanced the rising death toll of the "veterans." Twenty years later, the influx of *Ostjuden* comprised 80 percent of Vienna's 12,000 Jews.

Over the decades, they have evolved into a reasonably middle-class community. Although there are perhaps two hundred doctors and lawyers among them, most Austrian Jews are small businessmen, still disproportionately represented in textiles, furs, and jewels, but also scattered in other wholesale and retail activities. A few have done very well. A former DP, Simon Moscovitch, has become an important banker and adviser to the ministry of finance. Arthur Liksa, also a former DP, is a millionaire furrier. Inevitably, too, an important minority has prospered through shadier activities. As in Germany, there are barkeepers and brothel owners among them, former black marketeers whose role in currency and diamond dealing remains suspect at best. The sordid Jewish underground is yet another legacy of the Holocaust, of a horror that gave the unscrupulous a head start in survival.

Dr. Avraham Hodik is associate director of the Vienna Jewish Kultusgemeinde. His office, on the second floor of the Gemeinde's glass-and-steel building, looks out on a collage of homes and gardens. In his thirties, fair-skinned and heavyset, Hodik wears a skullcap. Born a Gentile, he converted to Judaism in his twenties, then spent a number of years in Israel before returning to Vienna. Some 6,500 Jews belong to the Gemeinde, he reported, and an additional 4,500 or so are unregistered. Of the latter, approximately two thousand are Soviet Jews, and three or four hundred are Israelis. The Gemeinde has long since passed from the hands of native Viennese into those of Polish and Hungarian refugees, who are the heirs to well-established traditions of Jewish political action in their former countries. The most recent Gemeinde election reflects the Jewish community's growing economic security; the centrists have taken over from the Socialists. The Gemeinde seems to be a vital organization, in any case, operating a Jewish community center, an old age home, a clinic, a Jewish primary day school attended by a minority of Vienna's Jewish children, and an afternoon school attended by a majority. In the early postwar years, the Joint contributed the largest part of the Gemeinde's budget. Since then, funding has come from assessments that are calibrated to the members' income tax payments—the traditional Central European pattern. The municipality covers the small remaining deficit, perhaps 10 percent of the budget.

Despite the infusion of East Europeans, Austrian Jewry remains an aging community. Two-thirds of its members are over sixty. If the largest numbers of them have achieved security, a small residue of perhaps a thousand continues to receive social welfare help from the Gemeinde. Traditional in their religious loyalties, most Jews still prefer to remain inconspicuous. They are uncomfortable when Israeli personalities appear on the television screen, and in the late 1970s and early 1980s they positively squirmed at the charmless Menachem Begin. It is significant that Simon Wiesenthal receives no contributions from Jews in Vienna. A former Gemeinde official, Dr. Jonny Moser, apparently spoke for many when he suggested to me that Wiesenthal is "obsessed, with no sense of perspective. He keeps old wounds alive." Nor have Viennese Jews been entirely happy with the fact that until recently, Bruno Kreisky, a Jew, served as Austria's chancellor.

Kreisky is an authentic paradox for modern Austria. Friends and enemies alike have long regarded him as one of the nation's ablest politicians. After a brief stint in prison following the Anschluss, he left the country in 1938. Afterward, he found refuge in Stockholm, and in 1945 became Austria's first postwar diplomatic representative in Sweden. Yet politics, not diplomacy, was his métier. A veteran Social Democrat, he began his parliamentary career in his native country in 1951. Later, as secretary of state from 1953 to 1959, and then as foreign minister until 1966, Kreisky was largely responsible for charting Austria's neutralist role in world affairs. Throughout those years of eminence, nevertheless, he often admitted to journalists that "there are two things I can never achieve in [Catholic] Austria because of my Jewish origin: to become head of my party or to become the nation's chancellor." Suddenly, in the election of 1970, by his party's and country's choice, he became both. In fact, Kreisky no longer meaningfully identified himself with the Jewish people, even as his militant Socialist background permitted him no accommodation with the Austrian Zionist movement. Once in office, his attitude toward Israel was coolly "objective."

Kreisky made his position on the Jewish state unmistakably clear in one of the most spectacular, and least understood, acts of his incumbency. On September 28, 1973, two Palestinian terrorists kidnapped three Soviet Jewish emigrants and an Austrian customs official at a railroad station outside Vienna and rushed them off to the international airport. The abductors then demanded that the government fly them to an unspecified Arab country, where the Jewish hostages could be exchanged for Arab prisoners held in Israel. They also demanded that the transit of Soviet Jewish emigrants through Austria to Israel be stopped. An emergency meeting of the Austrian cabinet took place. During the ensuing four hours of deliberation, Kreisky and his associates worked out the "compromise" of closing the Jewish Agency hostel at Schönau Castle. Soon afterward, the hostages were released by the terrorists, who were flown out of Vienna to Libya. Kreisky announced later that the decision had been taken with a "heavy heart," that his "foremost consideration" had been the need to save the lives of the hostages. Schönau had been in danger before, he explained, and Austria could not allow itself to become a secondary theater of operations in the Arab-Israeli conflict.

The chancellor had a point. Even earlier, the Austrian government had received several threats against Schönau. The previous January, six Arabs had been arrested with incriminating evidence of a plan to attack the castle. Earlier yet, in a precautionary move, the government had ordered security at Schönau increased, with some 100 police assigned to round-the-clock duty. This was an unprecedented measure by Austrian standards, for 523 police were responsible for the entire province of Vorarlberg (in which Schönau was located), with its 271,000 inhabitants. Moreover, Schönau had become a kind of extraterritorial Israeli enclave, doubly protected by armed Israeli guards; Austrian police had not been allowed inside. Few sovereign governments would have tolerated such an arrangement. Yet Kreisky stressed in his broadcast after the cabinet meeting that Austria had made it possible for thousands of Soviet Jewish emigrants (by then, slightly over 100,000) to enter the country, and that the government would continue to allow transit facilities to Soviet Jews with valid exit permits. The reassurance did not assuage the Israeli government or public. Rather, on October 2, Prime Minister Golda Meir paid an urgent visit to Vienna, but failed to change Kreisky's decision on Schönau. By then, the government of Israel had become so distracted by the Schönau episode that it lost sight of vital security problems closer to home. Three days later, the Arabs launched their Yom Kippur offensive against an Israeli nation taken entirely by surprise.

Notwithstanding the Schönau decision, Kreisky was still distrusted by many Austrians. They remained acutely conscious of his background and aware that he had a brother living in Israel, until the latter's death in 1973. Political writers tended to describe Kreisky as "too clever," "tricky," "shrewd," "a useful outsider in difficult times." His party was defeated in the spring 1983 elections, for reasons that probably had little to do with his Jewishness; but the distrust was a characteristic Austrian reaction. A public opinion poll in November 1974 revealed that 70 percent of adult Austrians nurtured antisemitic feelings, and of these, 21 percent felt that it would be best if there were no Jews at all in Austria. Latent antisemitism unquestionably remained stronger among Austrian politicians than among their counterparts in Germany. Right-wing deputies in parliament actually boasted of their "subconscious antisemitism." On Palm Sunday 1974, the first of a series of articles on "The Jews in Austria" appeared in the Vienna mass circulation daily *Neue Kronen-Zeitung*. Purporting to be a documented history, the introductory article quoted from a large number of antisemitic publications, and used controversial statistics to imply a "judaization" of the arts, literature, politics, and other areas. Moreover, the intended serialization was preceded by an aggressive advertising campaign, including posters displaying the Austrian flag with the Star of David in the middle and a caption reading: "The Jews in Austria—for decades a taboo in this country," and featuring a rabbi who was hardly less than an antisemitic caricature. In response to vigorous Jewish protests, the Austrian press council finally was bestirred to condemn the series as potentially inflammatory. After running several installments, the *Neue Kronen-Zeitung* decided to cancel the rest.

Meanwhile, by the mid-1970s, prosecution of Nazi criminals had come to a standstill. A new criminal code of 1974 all but foreclosed the possibility of future trials, and the department in the ministry of the interior that dealt exclusively with these crimes was terminated. Nor have there been significant changes in restitution laws during the last two decades. A final codicil was passed in 1975, entitling victims of Nazi persecution who had received no restitution under any law to payments of 15,000 Austrian shillings—about $1,000. The effect of this feeble gesture in any case was dissipated in 1982 and 1983 by a spate of anti-semitic violence. First, a homemade bomb exploded outside the apartment of Rabbi Eisenberg. This episode was followed by a series of bombings and machine gun attacks against the Seitenstettengasse Synagogue. Although the perpetrators were caught and revealed to be youthful PLO sympathizers, many Viennese suspected that rightist and neo-Nazi groups were becoming even more active and violent (however politically insignificant).

These are the people among whom Austrian Jews live, and they react accordingly, with discretion. Possibly a combination of fear and Central European formality makes it difficult now for a visitor to reach Viennese Jews. The latters' conventional good manners alternate with gratuitous displays of rudeness, as if to protect their cherished privacy. It was only with some difficulty that I managed to persuade the functionaries of the Gemeinde to agree to an appointment. "I can give you one hour," Avraham Hodik informed me—although he was entirely courteous once I arrived. Well, each country gets the Jews it deserves, the old adage has it. In Austria, many seem to resemble the national self-parody, "Herr Karl," the perennial accommodator, endlessly on the qui vive. If their numbers are not declining, neither is their vitality growing. They remain a colorless vestige of a once powerful and brilliant Jewry. Rabbi Eisenberg still insists that the community is viable and has a future. These Jews have a future as Austria has a future. It is of more than passing interest that the little nation survives in large measure on tourists, who are attracted almost exclusively to the cultural relics and architectural monuments of a former imperial glory.

II

A Prolonged Convalescence in Western Europe

Two Peoples of the Book: The Netherlands

In March 1958, while living in Israel, I entered into correspondence with the Netherlands Cultural Foundation on behalf of a scholarship program then being established at Brandeis University for overseas students. Later, visiting with the foundation's committee in Amsterdam, I was received with exceptional warmth. "It will be a privilege for our students to study at Brandeis," the director assured me. "We Dutch are reared on the Bible, you know. For us, the Jews are God's holy people." In response, I discerned a certain symbolism in the fact that I had written the director from my apartment on Tel Aviv's Rembrandt Street, and that she had responded from her office on Amsterdam's Jozef Israels Lane.

It was more than an exchange of amenities. My visit to Amsterdam took me past a heroic statue of a dockworker on Jonas Dam Mayerplein, between the massive Great Ashkenazic Synagogue and the Portuguese Synagogue. Erected in 1952, the sculpture is a monument to the stevedores who defied the Nazis eleven years earlier by walking off their jobs to protest the roundup of 435 young Jews in Amsterdam's old Jewish quarter; later, transport workers and others joined the strike. To commemorate this act of defiance, Queen Wilhelmina added the words "Heroic–Resolute–Merciful" to the Amsterdam coat of arms. Elsewhere in the city, three bridges on the Weeperstraat memorialize Dutch rabbis who perished in Auschwitz. The Anne Frank House is a national museum, its two adjoining houses converted into the International Youth Center of the Anne Frank Foundation (young Germans are by far the most numerous foreign visitors). A statue of Anne Frank stands in the Jankersjof. There is an Anne Frank School in Amsterdam and an

Anne Frank Square in Utrecht. Memorials to murdered Jews, most of them bearing Hebrew and Dutch inscriptions, are to be found in all the nation's larger cities. Innumerable streets, public places, and gardens are named for Jews. Spinoza House in The Hague is a national shrine.

Jewish freedom in this land extends back to the struggle of the Dutch against Spanish rule in the seventeenth century, and the asylum given Jewish fugitives from the Inquisition. The identical hospitality was extended to Central and East European Jews during the nineteenth and twentieth centuries. At the time of the Nazi invasion in May 1940, 140,000 Jews were living in the Netherlands, 30,000 of them refugees from the Third Reich. Approximately two-thirds of this population were engaged in trade and commerce, with a substantial minority in the professions. The role of Jewish scholars, writers, musicians, and scientists in the nation's cultural life was as distinguished here as elsewhere in the West. It was their Jewish communal life that was much less vital. A more thoroughly acculturated Jewry was not to be found in Europe. By the 1930s, the typical Netherlands Jew was as "solid" a citizen as his Dutch counterpart. The thoroughness of Jewish integration counted for little after 1940, of course. Within the next two and a half years, 110,000 Jews were deported to Auschwitz, to Sobibor, and to a few smaller camps. About 6,000 survived. Together with approximately 21,000 others, who had fled the country before the German occupation, and some 3,000 who were hidden by Dutch friends and neighbors, the survivors comprised less than a fourth of their prewar population. The 27,000 Jews who returned tended to concentrate in Amsterdam rather more than before 1940; but otherwise they quickly reestablished their former eminence in commerce and the professions.

There were wounds that lingered, however. In the immediate aftermath of the war, the Netherlands government turned over several thousand Jewish war orphans to Christian homes. The children were well cared for. In later years, the Jewish community sought the return of these youngsters to Jewish institutions. The effort proved to be complicated, and often harrowing. Among the 1,750 Jewish children left without parents or near relatives, 400 still were living with Christian foster parents as late as 1954. An especially traumatic episode, more prolonged than most, but by no means atypical, involved two Dutch Jewish orphans, Anneke Beekman and Rebecca (Betty) Milhado. During the war, both girls were reared in the Catholic faith by foster mothers, in Hilversum and Heerlen. In February 1949, when Anneke Beekman was awarded to Jewish guardians by the supreme court, she disappeared from the home of her foster mothers, the Misses van Moorst. Betty Milhado was kidnapped twice by her foster mother. In both cases the women were arrested, but none disclosed the girls' whereabouts.

After several years, the case of the missing children became a cause célèbre. The matter was raised in press and parliament, with all the leading newspapers supporting Jewish communal appeals for the return of the girls. In 1954, it was learned that Anneke Beekman had been smuggled into Belgium by her latest guardian, Mrs. Geertruida Langendijk. Two additional years of private legal maneuverings ensued before the Dutch government finally asked Brussels for the extradition of Mrs. Langendijk's sister, who had been involved in the abduction. The Belgian government refused the request on technical grounds. Finally, in November 1957, the woman surrendered to the Dutch authorities to serve a three-month jail sentence. Four years later, then, Anneke Beekman and Betty Milhado were located in Belgium. On their own, they returned to the Netherlands. In their teens by then, both girls made it plain they were practicing Catholics and intended to remain within the Church of Rome. They were lost to the Jewish people. These episodes kept the memory of the Holocaust vivid well over a decade after the war. In the Netherlands more than elsewhere in Western Europe—more even than in France, where such cases were not uncommon—perhaps by reason of the nation's otherwise exemplary democracy, they became something of an obsession among the remnant Jewish community.

The goodwill of the Dutch government meanwhile remained exemplary both in the vigorous postwar prosecution of Nazi war criminals and collaborators, and in the restitution of Jewish property. Special restitution courts were established within months after the war. Homes and shops were returned to their Jewish owners almost immediately. In 1953, a parliamentary law allocated the equivalent of $7 million to recompense Jews for their untraceable chattels and securities. These funds were provided by a nation that, far more than Austria, had been the victim of Nazi aggression, and that did not have assurances of future compensation by West Germany. In the end, Bonn did in fact work out a bilateral agreement with the Netherlands and eleven other nations for a lump sum reparations payment of DM 1 billion ($250 million). With their share of this money, the Dutch were able to deal even more generously with Jewish survivors and their organizations. By 1973, the

Dutch government had paid to the Association of Dutch Jews in Israel approximately $5 million to help their former compatriots there. Infirm or destitute victims of the Holocaust who remained in the Netherlands continued to receive pensions.

This record of solicitude bespoke the unique status of "the People of the Book" in the eyes of the Dutch, and particularly of Dutch Protestants. Nowhere else in Europe were representatives of the government, often of the royal family, as likely to attend Jewish communal affairs, and especially Jewish memorial commemorations. Jewish religious and historical matters were given ample coverage by the nation's press. The last three mayors of Amsterdam have been Jews. Friendship for Israel was deep, and at times passionate. During the Six-Day War of 1967, thousands of Dutch young people conducted a sympathy march for Israel in Amsterdam, and hundreds joined Jewish friends in offering their services to the Israeli embassy in The Hague. The outbreak of the Yom Kippur War in 1973 produced an identical outpouring of solidarity, with pro-Israel demonstrations throughout the country, and church appeals for funds on behalf of Israel.

Yet this exceptional political and economic security has not led to meaningful Jewish demographic growth. As late as 1984, the Jewish population remains at the early postwar figure of about 28,000 (in a Dutch population of 14 million). Dutch Jewry is an aging community, moreover, with a lower birth rate and a higher death rate than the population at large. Intermarriage has also markedly influenced these developments. Mixed marriages between all groups have increased in the Netherlands since the war, but among Jews the rate of increase, 185 percent, is by far the largest. The Holocaust sharply reduced the number of prospective Jewish mates, while the nation's famed postwar atmosphere of social freedom has reinforced the Jews' assimilationist tendencies.

On the one hand, Dutch Jewry still appears to be well structured for communal purposes. The leaders of the three religious "trends" (Orthodox, Liberal, and Sephardic) cooperate on issues affecting Jewish well-being. With the aid of a Claims Conference grant of $1,146,000, the community operates a superb old age home, a day school, and several competent afternoon schools. There are many lectures and a good deal of journalism on Jewish cultural matters. Jewish art exhibitions are well attended. Annual fund-raising drives contribute to communal and Israeli needs, and there is much coming and going between the Netherlands and Israel. On the other hand, over 40 percent of Dutch Jews remain unregistered with any of the three community organizations. Possibly less than a thousand Jews regularly attend Sabbath services. Only about four hundred youths receive Jewish education of any kind following their Bar or Bat Mitzvahs. During the war, most of the country's rabbis and lay leaders were killed, and for years afterward there were no rabbis or Jewish teachers at all outside Amsterdam. The shortage of Jewish communal personnel remains, despite occasional infusions from Israel. Notwithstanding the eminence of Dutch Jewish authors and critics, few of these today are writing on Jewish themes, and fewer yet belong to synagogues or to other Jewish organizations. There has been an almost total absence of Dutch Jewish historiography, whether scholarly monographs or profiles of eminent Dutch Jewish figures who disappeared in the war.

In the absence of historical works, Dutch Jewry is likely to remain known to posterity, to the Dutch population, and to Jews abroad mainly from fiction or memoirs, most notably, of course, *The Diary of Anne Frank*. In the mind of the typical Dutch Christian, the image of the Jew as a composite of the Old Testament figure, the perennial martyr, and the dynamic Israeli continued to linger well into the 1970s. During the same period, the Israelis were similarly guilty of idealizing the Dutch, until the latter, out of a mixture of sympathy for Palestinian refugees and concern for stable sources of oil, began in recent years to encourage the Common Market nations to support the PLO. By the 1980s, it is evident that neither people is quite as willing to romanticize the other any longer, whether as the nation quintessentially of Rembrandt, on the one hand, or as the race archtypically of Jozef Israels, on the other.

Belgium: Continental Jerusalem

In November 1965, the Belgian people mourned the death at the age of eighty-nine of Queen Mother Elizabeth, widow of the revered King Albert. She had been a symbol of tolerance and stability in a nation rent by a traditional hostility between Dutch-speaking Flemings and French-speaking Walloons. The queen mother also had a special place in the hearts of Belgium's Jews. Her courage and solicitude on their behalf were legendary. She maintained a cordial friendship with Chaim Weizmann, the Zionist leader. After Hitler's rise to power in Germany, Elizabeth offered Albert Einstein hospitality in her palace;

and during the Nazi occupation, she interceded personally to save many Jewish children and aged persons. After the war, she was the first member of a royal family to visit the new Jewish state.

The queen mother's concern for the Jews was typical of the Belgian people's. On the eve of the German invasion, about 90,000 Jews lived in this tiny land, where they comprised 1 percent of the population. Most were immigrants, predominantly from Eastern Europe, together with 14,000 more recent fugitives from Germany. Divided between Antwerp and Brussels, they were largely self-employed, and played a notable role in the diamond trade, which indeed was largely in their hands. Diamonds and other precious stones were a historic Jewish vocation; they were safe, portable assets for an insecure people. Then, as now, Antwerp was the center of the diamond industry. Its dealers were quick to exploit the newly discovered stones of the Belgian Congo and the city accordingly attracted Jewish dealers who maintained close links with their clients throughout the world, a majority of whom was also Jewish. For its part, the Belgian government was appreciative of this unique Jewish contribution to the nation's economy. Jews enjoyed no less security here than in Holland.

The German Wehrmacht invaded on May 10, 1940, and completed its occupation of the little country within a fortnight. For the ensuing year and a half the Jewish community was systematically reduced to pariah status. In March 1942, the first deportations began. As in the Dutch Netherlands, hundreds of Gentiles risked their lives by hiding Jews, supplying them with forged documents, temporarily adopting their children. The Belgian underground published instructions for helping Jews. Queen Elizabeth and Cardinal van Rooey appealed to the German military governor to exempt from deportation the few thousand Jews who were Belgian citizens. In fact, the governor agreed, but was unable to keep his promise. Of the 65,000 Jews who remained in Belgium during the autumn of 1940, not less than 40,000 perished. At the time of liberation, some 20,000 Jews were found alive in Belgium. Approximately 12,000 of them were from other countries; the rest were Belgian nationals.

In February 1945, the liberated Belgian government embarked upon the immediate repatriation of all Belgian refugees. These included 26,000 Jews living in England and the United States, the surviving remnant of Belgium's prewar diamond community. Despite the government's efforts, five years would pass before Antwerp's Jewish population reached 15,000, less than a third its number in 1940. By then, there were 42,000 Jews in the country altogether. Most of these were still of foreign origin, and still unnaturalized. Yet they enjoyed the identical civil rights possessed by other Belgians (except for the right to vote and hold office). Their economic integration in the early postwar years went reasonably smoothly. Although the problems of tracing and making restitution for Jewish property were as complicated here as in other European countries, the government resolved them swiftly and equitably. With money provided by Belgium's own reparations treaty with West Germany, a block payment of $30 million was applied to a special pension fund for Belgian Jewish survivors. Between 1953 and 1973, a series of Claims Conference appropriations provided $4,766,000 for Jewish communal needs. Currently, the number of Belgian Jews remains stable at 41,000 in a Belgian population of 9.6 million. Some 24,000 are settled in Brussels, 13,500 in Antwerp, and 1,500 each in Liège and Charleroi.

The nation maintains its tradition of warm hospitality. In the postwar era, right-wing Flemish groups such as the Volksunie, the Boerderband, and the Saint Maartensfonds favored amnesty for Nazi criminals, and antisemitic strictures appeared in their publications and activities. But by the 1950s, Jew-hatred no longer existed in any organized form or in any Belgian political program. Social snobbery and clannishness still remain, of course. In Antwerp, buildings and neighborhoods inhabited by large numbers of Jews have largely been vacated by non-Jews. But in the public sphere, relations have remained impeccable, with the government sensitive to Jewish needs. Judaism is recognized as one of the four national faiths entitled to state subsidies, a tradition that extends back to the nineteenth century, when the Consistoire Centrale Israélite was officially designated the representative body of Belgian Jewry. Like its French counterpart, the Consistoire supervises the administration of synagogues and ratifies the nomination of rabbis and cantors—part of whose salaries are underwritten by the government. The nation's four private Jewish day schools (two in Brussels, two in Antwerp) also receive state subsidies.

An affluent community, the 24,000 Jews of Brussels have developed their own version of a United Jewish Appeal. Contributions are generous and the lion's share goes to Israel. If Brussels Jewry evinces a distinguishing feature, it is its Zionist and secular character. Only a small proportion of the capital's Jews attends its two official synagogues. An even smaller minority of their children, perhaps 20 percent, attends Jewish day schools. Dispersed in many trades and scattered throughout the city, the Jews of Brussels are far more eclectic in their interests than are their kinsmen in Antwerp. They tend to participate in general rather than Jewish communal activities, and possibly 30 percent of them have intermarried.

In sharp contrast, the Flemish city of Antwerp encompasses one of the last *shtetls* in the world. Even more than before the war, diamonds and Orthodoxy are the forces that unite the city's Jews. Four-fifths of their breadwinners work in the diamond industry, mainly in the "upper" commercial strata, where they function essentially as dealers and brokers. Most of their transactions are conducted in the buildings of the four principal diamond exchanges, which in turn are concentrated within a small perimeter, the Pelikanstraat district, in the heart of Antwerp. In these exchanges, Jewish membership is overwhelming—perhaps 80 percent. On the Jewish High Holidays, the exchanges are completely empty, and banks transacting business with the diamond industry are closed. The exchanges themselves are not simply trading centers, for that matter, but forums of Jewish life in which members discuss Jewish communal matters and reach decisions that later are formally approved by the various Jewish organizations. Bulletin boards on all four exchanges contain notices of Jewish funerals, Jewish memorial services, Jewish meetings, and two of the restaurants in the diamond exchange are kosher.

The element of trust is vital in the diamond trade, and religious Orthodoxy, curiously enough, is often regarded as the ultimate guarantee of a Jew's honesty. By the 1980s, their numbers swollen by two or three thousand émigrés from Israel, at least half of Antwerp's Jews are Orthodox, an extraordinary proportion for a Western city. Indeed, one component of the Orthodox group, numbering perhaps a thousand families, is Chasidic, and encompasses in turn six smaller communities, half of them Romanian or Hungarian, each living in a ghetto within a ghetto. Walking through the area in the winter of 1981, I had the impression of a transplanted Mea Sh'arim, the ultra-Orthodox quarter of Jerusalem. Men were not only bearded here, but scores of them wore the traditional Chasidic beaver hats and black frock coats. Women wore shawls and long sleeves. There are two large private Jewish day schools in Antwerp, one belonging to the Chasidim, the other to the somewhat more Westernized "traditional" community. They are attended by fully

85 percent of Antwerp's Jewish children. On its own, Antwerp Jewry also supports an extensive network of communal offices and facilities, including a B'nai B'rith home, a youth center, an old age home, an institute for Jewish learning, a teachers' seminary, a cultural center, a Jewish museum, as well as a lavishly equipped Maccabi sports stadium.

If the city's Jews maintain little contact with Antwerp's Gentile majority, their segregation is self-imposed, particularly by the Orthodox establishment. What contact would they wish, anyway, with the non-Jewish world? Their business activities are confined almost exclusively to an industry they themselves monopolize. It is an ethnocentrism that is regarded with perfect equanimity by their neighbors. The diamond trade has given employment to over twelve thousand workers (in 1984), after all, and has contributed significantly to the city's wealth. The Jewish enclave is simply a pluralistic fact of life that has long since been institutionalized as an integral, if exotic, feature of the landscape.

Greece: A Sephardic Flame Guttering Out?

Greek Jewry was a somnolent community at the beginning of the twentieth century, numbering approximately 13,000 souls and scattered almost evenly between the mainland and the Dodecanese. A temporary demographic growth dated from the Balkan Wars of 1912–13, when large areas of former Ottoman Macedonia, including the port of Salonica, passed into Greek hands. Salonica's 80,000 Jews comprised the single largest Sephardic—Spanish-descended—community in the Balkans, and their Ladino dialect became a kind of lingua franca for the port city's entire population. Most of Salonica's trade, industry, artisanry, and dockworking were controlled by Jews, and on the Sabbath and other Jewish holidays the harbor was virtually shut down. The dominance was short-lived. As a consequence of the Greco-Turkish War of 1920–22 and the ensuing population exchange between the two countries, the vast influx of Smyrniot (Greek) refugees into Salonica reduced the proportion and influence of the town's Jewry. Jewish security was also threatened by Greek political and economic pressure. The government's policy of hellenization undermined the Ladino school system. A series of antisemitic riots were tolerated. As a result, several thousand Jews departed, to France, Latin America, and Palestine. By 1939, the Jewish population of Salonica had dropped to 60,000. Perhaps 70,000 Jews remained in Greece at large.

The German invasion of April 1941 doomed this community altogether. Almost immediately Jews were evicted from their homes, arrested, taken as hostages. Those who managed to flee to the Italian zones of occupation were protected; but at the end of September 1943, all of Greece came under German military rule. Thousands of Jews already had died of starvation and ill-treatment in forced labor battalions. Now, under the direction of SS General Jurgen Stroop (the officer who liquidated the Warsaw ghetto), systematic roundups of Jews were carried out in Salonica, in Athens, on the islands of Corfu, Crete, and Rhodes. In the end, approximately 58,000 Greek Jews were annihilated, most of them in Auschwitz. By the time of the Allied liberation in late 1944, no more than 12,000 Jews were found alive in the country, the majority of them in Athens.

Their condition was even more desperate than that of the Greek population at large, which was suffering from a famine crueler than anywhere else in Europe. The Jews were starving, half-naked, roofless. Each day after the liberation, scores of them died of disease and exposure. There was little government assistance available, and after 1944 the developing Greek civil war prevented the Joint Distribution Committee from helping Jewish survivors. The authorities meanwhile were sluggish in restoring confiscated Jewish property, for they were unwilling to dispossess thousands of Greeks. It was known, too, that most of the Jewish survivors belonged to the leftist EAM-ELAS camp in the civil war, the underground forces that earlier had helped save many Jews during the Nazi occupation. Accordingly, as the fighting reached its climax in 1948–49, the royalist press chose to label Marxism a "world Jewish intrigue." Jews were accused of fostering heresy, of seeking to weaken the Orthodox Church as a barrier to communism. In Salonica and Athens, taxes on Jewish shopkeepers were assessed at a much higher level than on Greek businessmen, and impoverished Jewish families often were denied help from government welfare centers on the grounds that "Jewish charities" were available. It was in these years of postwar discrimination that the majority of Jewish survivors emigrated to Israel.

Today, barely 5,000 Jews remain in Greece (3,000 of them in Athens, 1,500 in Salonica) among a population of nine million. Their economic circumstances unquestionably have improved. Most Jews are small merchants, interspersed with a few dozen doctors, lawyers, accountants, and pharmacists. They are highly acculturated. "You cannot distinguish the Jews from the rest of the Greeks," insists Marcel Yoel, editor of the Greek Jewish newspaper, *Israelitiki Epitheorissia*. "There are not two communities. We are [simply] Greeks who belong to a different religious group." And it is true that Jews and Christians generally coexist without serious friction. Yet there were several recurrences of antisemitism in the late 1970s. A book by a journalist, John Foiurakis, *Zionist Conspiracies*, imputed to the Jews "historical designs" on Greece. The charge was repeated by another journalist, Petros Diacoyiannis, in his volume *The Flesh Eaters*. During the same period, Shlomo Nahmia, a young Jewish engineer and the son of a leading member of Greece's Central Jewish Committee, died under mysterious circumstances while serving in the army. Suspicion lingered that he had been driven to suicide by antisemitic bullying.

Whatever the depth of latent antisemitism, it has not induced Greek Jews to maintain a low profile. They have taken an active part in Greek life, even in the political arena, and a few have played a role in several governments. During the 1974 national election campaign, Jews were courted as a voting bloc. The New Democracy (Center) Party of Prime Minister Constantine Karamanlis made a special point of naming Miltiadis Evert, the minister of industry, as its liaison with the Jewish community. Evert's father, the police chief of Athens during the wartime Nazi occupation, had saved the lives of many Jews by providing them with false identity papers. Most Greek Jews did in fact vote for the New Democracy Party, although for reasons that probably related to their middle-class status. On the other hand, when the Socialists came to power in the 1981 election, one of their first acts was to grant diplomatic status to the PLO, and in the summer of 1982 Prime Minister Andreas Papandreou greeted Yasser Arafat when the latter arrived in Greece following the Israeli expulsion of PLO forces from Lebanon. With a large and vulnerable diaspora of its own kinsmen scattered throughout the Arab world, Greek regimes tend to adopt a pro-Arab stance in international affairs, even to display a rather shocking permissiveness toward Arab violence against El Al airplanes and passengers on Greek territory. Although there does not appear to be a conscious spillover of this pro-Arab policy into domestic antisemitism, the Greek Jewish community remains concerned, and in recent years its institutions have been kept under police guard.

Greek Jews still maintain the old Ottoman tradition of working collectively through a central organization, in this case the Central Jewish

Committee. With the help of a $1 million Claims Conference grant, the committee since 1955 has operated a Jewish day school in a wealthy Athens suburb. It is a less than impressive institution. Three of its five staff members are Israelis, and its classes extend only to sixth grade. Afterward, students attend schools affiliated with the Orthodox Church. Mixed marriages are common. In Greece, as in Israel and most of the Arab countries that similarly belonged to the Ottoman Empire, civil marriage does not exist. Until a few years ago, any Jew seeking to marry "out" was forced by the Jewish community to go abroad or to be married by a priest. In an effort to "face realities," however, the Athens Jewish community decided in 1977 to permit mixed marriages for a two-year trial period "in order to prevent the rejection of Judaism by those Jews who want to marry Greeks." The rabbi of Athens grudgingly agreed to officiate at these ceremonies. The trial period has since been extended. Yet there is a very real danger that this vestigial minority may not endure, whatever adjustments and compromises it makes. Once a community whose principal enclave, Salonica, was the economic center of the modern Sephardic world, Greek Jewry in the late twentieth century is approaching the threshold of exotica.

Italy: The Duce as Patron

In the Roman darkness, half a dozen leather-jacketed youths were spray-painting a hammer and sickle on the wall of a public building, affixing placards that exhorted the citizens of Italy to vote for *Il Partito Communista*. Loping toward them in my American greatcoat, I asked in pidgin Italian for the direction of Via Nomentana. In the mist, the teen-agers gaped at me. Then, after only a few moments' hesitation, they set about putting me on a correct course. One of the youths insisted on drawing a simple diagram for me on a notepad. Not to be outdone, another accompanied me down the street to ensure that I had my bearings. I did. In less than fifteen minutes I reached Via Nomentana.

It was a street of affluent villas. Formidably constructed in stone, the homes were more than imposing. In January 1982, they were heavily barricaded. Bruno Zevi's residence was among them. A thick, high wall and a steel door barred the way. I rang the buzzer and identified myself into the speaker box. After ten minutes or so, the gateway opened and Zevi himself admitted me. There was no mistaking his handsome Roman features, his stocky, muscular body; I had seen photographs of him in his published biography. He apologized for the delay. "We must be careful these days. This is a bad time for Rome." It was an understatement. Italy was convulsed by disorder, the Red Brigades running amok. "Haven't you seen any of those gangsters yet?" he asked.

Later, in his home, I understood Zevi's particular vulnerability. As a renowned architectural critic and teacher, he was a man of influence. His political views were centrist. His forthright Jewishness and Zionism, too, could hardly have endeared him to leftist or third world partisans. As he elaborated upon those ideas, it was apparent that he had developed a sophisticated rationale for a "new Judaism" based upon a combination of "relativity" (extensive quotes from Einstein), the "unconscious" (Freud and Buber were invoked here), and a creative Jewish "dissonance" (inspired by Arnold Schönberg). Zevi had written on the subject at length, even had managed to interweave his notions of Jewish uniqueness and "spatial" architecture. Could this richly cultured man be a Roman Jew, I wondered, a member of perhaps the most notoriously inbred Jewish community in Western Europe?

Roman he was. His family was one of the thirty who belonged to the Scuola Tempio—the "Temple School" of Jews whose ancestors had been carried in chains from Palestine to Rome as prisoners of Titus, 1,900 years before. Like the Jews who arrived in Rome during the later centuries of the empire, his family lived in the squalor of the Trastevere ghetto, along the Porto d'Ottavio, the oldest, most malarial section of the capital. It was not until 1880, a decade after the Risorgimento and Jewish emancipation, that large numbers of Roman Jews began to move out of the old ghetto area. Even today, some 4,000 of Rome's 12,000 Jews remain on in Trastevere, concentrated mainly in an area of a few square blocks. They maintain their identity in a network of institutions, operate their own synagogues, clinic, hospital, orphanage, and welfare agencies. Educated in the same Jewish school, they rarely marry outside their own group. Until very recently, they were as poor as any Jewish subcommunity in Western Europe, and even today a few hundred of them continue to subsist as ragpickers or pushcart peddlers.

The Zevis escaped this fate when Bruno's grandfather, Benedetto, was chosen as one of the two Jews permitted to study medicine in each generation. Later, during a malaria epidemic, he distinguished himself sufficiently to be allowed to treat Gentile patients, and was given the right to settle elsewhere in Rome. (He did not avail himself of the opportunity, but his son did later.) In other Italian cities, Jews were beginning to share fully in the blessings of emancipation, and to make their mark on Italian life. During the latter nineteenth century, Graziado Isaiah Ascoli became the nation's most influential philologist and Alessandro d'Ancona its most eminent literary critic. Samuel Romain was a distinguished historian of Venice. Senator I. B. Supino was Italy's most respected art historian. Many other Jews became important authors, critics, literary historians. Tullio Levi-Civita was regarded as the greatest of Italy's mathematicians. Cesare Lombroso was the founder of the science of criminology. In the early twentieth century, Senator Pia Foa established the science of modern pathological anatomy. Jewish intellectual prowess continued into the interwar years. Comprising 0.1 percent of the Italian population in 1930, Jews provided 8 percent of the nation's university professors.

They were Italian through and through. Their Jewish faith was regarded by their neighbors (in the words of the historian Cecil Roth) "as an amiable eccentricity rather than as a social mistake." No obstacles blocked a Jew from entering politics. By 1894, eleven Jewish deputies were sitting in parliament. Three years earlier, Luigi Luzzatti had become minister of finance, and in 1909 he was elected prime minister. Leone Wollenberg served as finance minister from 1900 to 1903. General Giuseppe Ottolenghi was appointed minister of war in 1902. Sidney Sonnino, a half-Jew, was prime minister for brief periods in 1906 and 1909–10, and served as foreign minister from 1914 to 1919. Gabriele Pincherl was honorary president of the council of state. Ernesto Nathan was elected mayor of Rome in 1907.

Bruno Zevi's father, Guido, was the first member of the family to leave the ghetto, residing on the fashionable Via Napoli, and later on the even more fashionable Via Nomentana. He could afford it. Serving first as chief engineer of the municipality of Rome, he later developed a lucrative private practice. Like most Italian Jews, he sent his children to state schools. The decision was not taken lightly. The Concordat of 1929 provided for a daily hour of Catholic education in the public schools. While Jewish children were allowed to receive their own religious education during the free hour, the compromise at best was embarrassing to them. Nevertheless, after so many centuries of restriction and seclusion, Italian Jews could hardly ignore or resist the opportunity for acculturation. As a result, the old religious academies, the talmud torahs and yeshivas, began to decay. The Jewish Sabbath was rarely

observed. Between 1930 and 1940, some 30 percent of Jewish marriages were with Gentiles. Zevi's own home may have been somewhat
more traditional than the norm—a Roman legacy. He was Bar
Mitzvahed and the High Holidays and Passover were observed.

The advent of fascism initially was no more significant to Jews than
to other Italians. Indeed, of the fifteen jurists who drew up the Fascist
constitution in 1924, three were Jews. "The Jewish problem does not
exist in Italy," Mussolini insisted in 1929. A year later, he publicly denounced antisemitism as "unworthy of a European nation . . . stupid
and barbarous," and for the next half-decade he continued to describe
Hitler's racial theories as "vulgar nonsense." The Duce also opened his
country's gates to a large number of German Jewish refugees. The Fascist position on Jews abroad was similarly one of active benevolence;
they were envisaged as useful agents in Mussolini's determined campaign of imperialism in the East Mediterranean. Within the Duce's
overseas empire, the 24,000 Jews in Libya, the 4,000 in Rhodes, enjoyed full economic and educational opportunities. In Salonica and the
Levant, Jews were encouraged to apply for Italian nationality. The appointment of an Italian rabbi in Alexandria became a question of national prestige to Mussolini. At the Hebrew University of Jerusalem, a
readership in Italian was maintained by the Italian government. Denied
access to higher education, thousands of young Jews from Eastern Europe were welcomed as students in Italy, and provided with generous
grants.

Even so, growing numbers of Jewish intellectuals joined the anti-
Fascist opposition during the early 1930s. The Zevi family was among
these. Bruno's father was a cousin-in-law and admirer of Chief Rabbi
Angelo Sacerdote, who had misgivings about fascism from the beginning. In 1934, Bruno joined a small anti-Fascist youth group that clan-
destinely circulated seditious literature. Two years later, as a matricu-
lating student at the University of Rome's school of architecture, he
secretly collected funds for the Spanish Loyalists. Neither he nor his
friends were surprised in 1937 and 1938 when Mussolini and Hitler
exchanged visits, and Italy began gravitating into the German orbit.
With the formation of the Rome-Berlin Axis in 1938, the Duce officially
aligned himself with Hitler on the "Jewish problem"—a problem most
Italians had not known existed. The government soon established a special Bureau for Demography and Race Protection. Thereafter, works by
Jews were no longer published or performed in the theater. In August

1938, foreign Jews and their children were excluded from schools and universities and many of the 14,000 refugee Jews who lived in Italy, nearly a third of the total Jewish population, were ordered to leave.

Then, in September 1938, all Jews, citizens and foreigners alike, were dismissed from the state's educational and cultural institutions. Jews were denied the right to enter military service, to own more than 50 hectares of land, to manage enterprises employing more than 100 persons, to occupy positions in banks, the stock exchange, and insurance companies, or to open new businesses. As in the days of Zevi's grandfather, Jewish doctors and lawyers were forbidden to serve Christians. Notices soon excluded Jews from restaurants, cafés, cinemas, and other public places. Within eighteen months, some 5,500 Jews fled Italy—over a tenth of the Italian Jewish population.

It is a revealing insight into the many loopholes and inconsistencies of the antisemitic program that Zevi at first remained both in the university and in the army, and even became an officer in the autumn of 1938. Numerous exceptions were made for "compassionate" reasons, and a vigorous traffic in bribes developed. Nevertheless, Zevi's father was unable to practice his profession, and decided to send his family to Palestine. Here was yet another irony. The Jews of Italy, weak in their religious loyalties and heavily intermarried, had somehow become staunch Zionists. The redemptive effort taking place in the Holy Land appealed to their pride and imagination. The Zevis shared in this sentiment. Thus, an older sister, Auriana, whose lawyer husband was denied the right to practice, departed for Palestine in 1939. A second sister, Marcella, who had married into the Sonnino family, followed soon afterward. Bruno, the youngest of the children, similarly left the country—in his case for England. He had been accepted at the University of London's school of architecture. By the time war broke out, he had also been in correspondence with Harvard, and made plans to study there under Walter Gropius. Early in 1940, he returned to Italy for a last visit with his parents, who themselves subsequently departed for Palestine. The son traveled then to the United States. In 1941, he received his Master of Architecture degree from Harvard.

It was in this period, too, that Zevi married Tullia Bassani. Hers was a distinguished Sephardic family from Ferrara (Giorgio Bassani, a relative, described it in his celebrated 1964 novel, *The Garden of the Finzi-Continis*). In contrast to her husband's angular Roman face, Tullia's features are narrow and delicate, her eyes limpid, heavy-lidded. When we met, she observed that Bruno was something of a prodigy, having emerged from a former Roman ghetto family. It had been a tradition among her forebears that talent was a monopoly of the "northern" people—that is, of the Sephardim. This was also the theory of her cousin Gigliola Columba, who married Guido Lopez-Nunes, grandson of a Sephardi of Ferrara. A short, balding man of sixty at the time of our meeting in January 1982, Lopez-Nunes acknowledged that he was a Sephardi on one side only, that his paternal grandmother, a Tedesci, may have descended from a German Ashkenazic family. Even in Milan, the center of Jewish settlement in the north, Ashkenazic Jews predominated until after World War II. Distinction there lay in wealth, not in pedigree. Milan's community was one of the first to be emancipated in the nineteenth century and, without a ghetto tradition, it shared in the burgeoning prosperity of the north. Lopez-Nunes's own father, Sabatino, was a highly successful playwright who, at the turn of the century, became director of the Society of Authors. The son's childhood, on Milan's Viale Romagna, was spent in a "mixed" neighborhood, in a state school. After his Bar Mitzvah, he rarely stepped into a synagogue. His milieu was thoroughly Italian. Indeed, his father was an early admirer of Mussolini. The disenchantment came only in the latter 1930s, when the market for Sabatino Lopez-Nunes's plays suddenly was closed off, and he himself was dismissed from his position in the Society of Authors. The family survived on his pension and savings. Guido and his brother had to leave school to seek employment.

The Black Years

In June 1940, some 45,000 Jews lived in Italy. Of these, 8,000 were German refugees. Of the rest, 13,000 lived in Rome, 8,000 in Milan, 4,000 in Trieste, 2,700 in Turin, 2,700 in Florence, 2,000 in Genoa, 2,000 in Venice, 1,750 in Livorno, 1,000 in Ancona. With Italy's entrance into the war that month, they found their bank accounts blocked, and by the end of the year half of Italy's Jews had been deprived of their livelihoods. Still, they were not confined to ghettos or forced to wear yellow badges. Conditions even for foreign Jews were hardly barbaric. After the panic-stricken departures in autumn and early winter of 1938, many of these noncitizens returned and were joined by other Jewish fugitives through the initial years of the war, often with the passive acquiescence of the Fascist authorities. In the first seven months of hostilities, some 2,000 Jews succeeded in obtaining passage to Palestine or other sanctuaries. Despite much coming and going, therefore, the Jewish population in Italy remained notably stable. Elsewhere, in France, Greece, and Yugoslavia, local Jews invariably found safety in the Italian zones of occupation; and thus tens of thousands of Jewish lives were saved by Mussolini's unwillingness to have anything to do with the Final Solution. For all his strident verbal antisemitism, the Duce in practice looked the other way as his subordinates extended their protection to Jews.

In May 1943, under intense German pressure, Mussolini called up Italian Jews for service in special "labor brigades." Even these orders were put into effect rather casually, with numerous exemptions. Then, only two months later, on July 25, as Allied forces pushed north from Sicily, Mussolini was overthrown in a coup led by Marshal Pietro Badoglio. It appeared that the gravest threat to Italian Jewry was over. The respite was brief. On September 8, 1943, the Germans sent Badoglio packing, and assumed military control of northern Italy. On November 30, determined to "wipe the slate clean," SS General Karl Wolff issued the order for all Jews to be arrested and interned. Where-upon, in Milan, the Lopez-Nuneses and their kin sought refuge with Gentile friends. That help was given willingly. Indeed, most of the Jews who came through the war owed their survival to friends and neighbors, or even to utter strangers, who gave them shelter.

Guido, eighteen years old, was unwilling to accept a hunted existence. He fled to Lake Maggiore, thirty miles north of Milan, and hired an outboard motorboat. A half-hour trip brought him to the Swiss shore, where he found sanctuary in an internment camp maintained by the Swiss government. Other escaping Jews were less fortunate. Most were sent back. Some committed suicide. Approximately a thousand Milanese Jews who were turned back by the Swiss authorities were caught and liquidated. The Lopez-Nuneses were not among these. Two weeks after Guido reached Switzerland, his parents and brother followed, and were admitted. Sabatino Lopez-Nunes was an admired figure among the Italian-speaking Swiss. The family was given decent treatment in an old age home.

Bruno Zevi was one of the first to discover the fate of Roman Jewry. In March 1943, he volunteered for action as a partisan in Italy. Three weeks after the Allies entered Rome, in May 1944, he was flown there as a radio operator. He set out immediately in quest of relatives. His maternal grandmother, Olympia Bondi, had lived in a comfortable villa on Via Apirle. Fearing the worst, Zevi knocked on the door. It opened. "I nearly went faint," he recalled. The old woman stood there.

The story Olympia Bondi related to her grandson was elaborated upon later by others. On September 24, 1943, SS General Herbert Kappler issued the order for the roundup and deportation of Rome's Jews. In desperation, Ugo Foa, president of the Rome Jewish Community, sent word to Kappler, proposing a deal. Kappler was receptive. As an "interim" measure, the SS commander agreed to accept fifty kilograms of gold, to be paid within thirty-six hours. Foa and his colleagues then frantically began soliciting the rest of the Jewish community. On the afternoon of September 26, Foa also approached Pope Pius XII, through an intermediary, requesting an emergency loan. The pontiff complied on the spot, agreeing to lend the Jews any amount of gold they might need. But by then the collection campaign had reached its goal. Rome Jewry apparently was spared.

Again, their hope was premature. Learning of Kappler's deal, and enraged by it, Adolf Eichmann sent his personal aide, SS Captain Theodor Dannecker, to carry out the Final Solution in Rome under any circumstances. Thereupon the German ambassador to the Vatican, Baron Ernst von Weizsäcker, informed the pope of the impending "betrayal." Pius XII's role at this point was ambiguous. On the one hand, he refused to speak out publicly against the deportation of Jews. His single expression of concern was a declaration by the Vatican newspaper that the pontiff's "universal and paternal succor . . . knows no bounds of nationality, religion, or race." On the other hand, Pius XII directed his clergy to offer the Jews sanctuary. Accordingly, 4,238 Jews found refuge in the monasteries and convents of Rome, and another 477 were sheltered in the Vatican itself. Meanwhile, on Saturday, October 16, Captain Dannecker launched his *Judenrazzia*. Fully 2,091 Jews were caught, including Bruno Zevi's cousin Savino Coen. Many of these Jews had left the convents to return home briefly to bathe for the Sabbath, and it was then that they were seized.

Grandmother Olympia had remained at the convent until the final German departure. So had other relatives, Zevi's aunts, uncles, most of his cousins. So had the majority of Jews. In all, some 10,000 of Rome's 12,500 Jews managed to survive. Despite Mussolini's equivocation and the pope's covert effort to save lives, the Nazi terror had raged unchecked for eighteen months, from the autumn of 1943 to the spring of

1945. Throughout Italy during that period, 7,683 Jews perished, all but about 1,000 of them in extermination camps outside the country. Although the majority of the prewar population survived, they were famished and debilitated. They were also wounded in their Jewish collectivity. Synagogues and libraries had been looted of their richest artifacts and manuscripts. If Jewish communal life had been quite feeble even before the war, it was largely paralyzed after 1943. Its revival now appeared less than assured.

The Republican Era

The legal basis of renewed Jewish security had been established well before the Allied liberation. From December 1943 on, the post-Mussolini governments issued a series of decrees abolishing the racial laws and restoring full equality of citizenship to Jews. In October 1944, the government even offered citizenship to all foreign Jewish refugees in Italy. Although most of the fugitives were waiting to go to Palestine, the liberation drew back a significant number of Italian Jews who had fled elsewhere in Europe. By 1946, some 34,000 of them had resumed their lives in Italy. By then, too, their prewar tendency to concentrate in the bigger cities gained momentum. Rome and Milan encompassed nearly two-thirds of the survivors—13,000 and 9,000, respectively. The once flourishing Jewish communities of Ancona, Pisa, Mantua, Ferrara, and Modena eventually would all but disappear as a result of internal migration and a low birth rate. Even the larger communities of Turin, Florence, Trieste, Venice, and Livorno declined rapidly.

Wherever the survivors lived, they enjoyed the goodwill of the Italian government, which moved swiftly to assure the restitution of their homes and other property. The watchdog of Jewish rights was Rafaele Cantoni, the first postwar president of the Union of Italian Jewish Communities. A lawyer by profession, Cantoni had been active in the underground, and many of the leading postwar members of the government had been his comrades. By testifying to the Italian people's humane treatment of the Jews, he helped assure a tolerable peace treaty for his country, and a place for himself on the drafting committee of the new republican constitution. A dynamic, barrel-chested man, excitable and warmhearted, Cantoni assiduously worked through his friend Enrico de Nicola, president of the Italian republic, to ensure that Jewish rights and needs would be met. For the next decade and a half, Cantoni labored fifteen hours a day on behalf of his people, until he died—literally of overwork, his friends insisted.

In the late 1940s and early 1950s, Italian Jews shared in the general improvement of the nation's economy. They remained in small and medium-sized businesses, for the most part, wholesale and retail. Their most impressive gains occurred in Milan. The great postwar boom city even produced a number of Jewish tycoons, including Astore Mayer, one of the nation's largest paper manufacturers, and Andres Shapiro, a plastic manufacturer. Other Milanese and Roman Jews moved increasingly into the professions. The Jewish middle class was further augmented in the 1950s by refugees from Egypt, Syria, and Lebanon, and ultimately by some three thousand Libyan Jews. By the opening of the next decade, then, Milanese Jewry had acquired a new demographic configuration. Of nine thousand Jews in the city, a third were Ashkenazim, a third were indigenous Sephardic Jews, and a third were Jews from the Moslem world. Whatever their background, they thrived.

Their political role may have been limited in a nation whose first postwar years were dominated by the Christian Democratic Party (associated closely with the papacy). Yet no significant antisemitism existed either officially or among the population at large. It was a source of pride to the Italian people that, so long as Mussolini remained in power, not a single Jew had been mistreated during the war, that the basic humanity of Italian civilization had remained unsullied. Compassion for survivors of the Holocaust was deeply felt. Numerous streets and squares were named for Jews, or for those who had helped Jews, and Jewish organizations and leaders received public awards. Thus, in 1966, the Unione—Union of Italian Jewish Communities—was awarded the government's Gold Medal of Civil Merit. The Jewish community of Milan received the municipality's gold medal in recognition of its welfare and educational work, and its "great dignity in sacrifice" during the years of racial persecution. On the occasion of the republic's twentieth anniversary, President Giuseppe Sarragat named Astore Mayer, president of the Milan Jewish community, a Knight of Labor, the nation's highest public service award.

Bruno Zevi shared in this revival and approbation. When the war ended, he returned to architecture, then became professor of the history of architecture at the University of Venice, and subsequently at the University of Rome. A decade later, he founded and edited the journal

L'Architettura, which soon became the authoritative voice in the profession. He wrote twenty four books. Several of them received international acclaim, and one of them, *Architecture as Space,* was eventually translated into thirteen languages. Zevi's design ideas were incorporated into some of Italy's most renowned architectural projects, including the railroad station in Naples, a vast housing complex in Salerno, the Luigi Einaudi Library in Dogliano, the Italian Pavilion at the Montreal World Fair. Books were published on his work. Universities in Italy and abroad awarded him honorary doctorates.

Meanwhile, Zevi's cousin-in-law Guido Lopez-Nunes in Milan rose to the public relations directorship of the distinguished publishing firm Mondadori. In 1953, he became the advertising director for Motta, the nation's largest candy company, and later was appointed director of the Italian branch of J. Walter Thompson. For Lopez-Nunes, as for Zevi, Jewishness represented no career impediment. Possibly it was an asset in a country that recoiled from any doctrine smacking of its Fascist era.

The Jewish problem in Italy was ultimately one not of security but of cultural revival. Many of the smaller Jewish communities had been laid waste by the war, by desertions, by loss of confidence. Even earlier, many of their wealthiest families had joined the Catholic Church. Between 1931 and 1939, perhaps 10 percent of the Jewish population deserted the faith. The 34,000 or so Italian Jews who remained after 1945 were demoralized, and not a few were anxious to pass unnoticed. Their Jewish communal institutions remained impoverished and heavily dependent on Joint funds and on a Claims Conference subvention of $7,250,000.

Meanwhile, in the hope of energizing the community's spiritual life, the Union of Jewish Communities summoned David Prato from Palestine to resume his prewar position as chief rabbi of Rome. Rabbi Dante Lattes, a distinguished scholar, returned from Tel Aviv to revive the Unione's cultural department and to direct Rome's feeble little rabbinical seminary. These efforts produced no dramatic religious awakening, then or later. Nominally, Italian Jewry was, and remains, Orthodox. With the exception of the more recent Libyan Jewish immigrants, however, few Italian Jews are devout. As in other Western lands, people attend synagogue mainly for reasons of social propriety and gregariousness. Thus, in Rome's Great Synagogue on Lungotevere Cenci, a baroque extravaganza near the gates of the old ghetto, services remain noisy, convivial, with no emphasis whatever on solemnity, dignity, or spiritual inspiration. Nor has there been any meaningful Jewish intellectual revival since the end of the war. While Jews are important in the nation's academic and artistic life, few of them have turned their attention specifically to Jewish culture. In the last decade before the war, it is recalled, approximately 30 percent of Italian Jews married out of the faith. Since then, in Milan, the percentage has approached 40 percent, and in provincial communities the ratio is higher yet. When the monthly journal *Shalom* announces "Jewish" marriages, these are increasingly between Libyan Jews. The reproduction rate of Jews has dropped. Like Jewish communities elsewhere in Western Europe, Italy's is aging.

These bleak trends do not present the full story. A certain cohesiveness is assured by the Jews' very communal structure. In return for the religious and educational services they provide, including marriage performed by a rabbi and burial in a Jewish cemetery, the official communities are authorized to impose taxes on their members at a rate calculated according to personal incomes. As in Germany, Austria, and the Scandinavian countries, most Jews have chosen to register and to pay their "taxes," which have notably improved the funding of communal life in recent years. Jewish youth centers in Rome and Milan (both subsidized by Claims Conference grants) have developed reasonably solid programs of lectures, concerts, exhibitions, and Hebrew and Jewish history classes. In Rome, the Jewish Center is attached to the Great Synagogue, and appears to be well attended. Its staff has successfully organized a major Jewish festival each year in the Trastevere ghetto, with pavilions devoted to Jewish history, Jewish cuisine, Jewish rites, Zionism and Israel. Attended by thousands of Jews and non-Jews, the festival is a typically Roman explosion of excitement and celebration. In 1981, Prime Minister Mario Andreotti was an honored guest. In Milan, with its more sedate northern tradition, a Jewish documentation center has been established, including archives and a quite decent library on contemporary Jewish life.

Important steps also have been taken in the field of education. In belated response to the Concordat of 1929, with its provision for a daily hour of Catholic education in state schools, various Jewish communities in the postwar era launched a major effort of day-school construction— again aided by substantial infusions from the Claims Conference. By the mid-1960s, the program was taking hold, and in ensuing years it became firmly established. As of 1983, not less than 60 percent of all

Italian Jewish children attended Jewish day schools, the highest propor-
ton of any Jewish community in Europe, except for Belgium. Then, late
that same year, the Italian parliament rescinded the Concordat's provision for religious education. The effect of the measure on Jewish day-
school registration has yet to be gauged.

Throughout the 1960s, meanwhile, a series of books appeared on
the nearly extinct regional and ethnic communities of Italy. The Jewish
minority was discovered in this way, when the publishing firm of Mondadori began reprinting Italo Svevo's long-neglected fictional classics,
La Coscienza di Zeno, Senilità, and *Una Vita.* A half-Jew, often called
"the Italian Proust," Svevo concentrated almost exclusively on the assimilated Italian Jewish bourgeoisie of Trieste, and evoked their mentality and ambience in imagery that often was hauntingly authentic.
Conceivably more poignant yet were the writings of Giorgio Bassani,
whose novels and stories dealt with the Jewish middle class of Ferrara
during the years of Fascist persecution. While Svevo and the Jewish
writers Alberto Moravia (a baptized Catholic) and Natalia Ginzburg
rarely portrayed their fictional characters specifically as Jews, Bassani
did, and his books revealed the gradual alienation of Italian Jewry from
the social order under Mussolini. One of his works, *Il Giardino dei
Finzi-Contini,* an exquisitely wrought autobiographical novel of his Italian Jewish provincial childhood, sold 300,000 copies in the 1960s and
won the Viareggio Prize, Italy's most coveted literary award. The
nostalgic interest in vanished Jewish communities suggested that the
Italian people were beginning to sense the irreplaceability of their Jewish leaven. That preoccupation was of course fully shared by the surviving Jews themselves.

It was the State of Israel, however, that proved to be the decisive
influence in fortifying Italian Jewish identity. Zionism affected Milanese
and Roman Jewry alike. Even a Jew as highly acculturated as Guido
Lopez-Nunes, whose father's plays had been received by Italian audiences as enthusiastically as Pirandello's, was swept passionately into
Jewish nationalism. In 1948, he became president of the Zionist Organization of Milan, and served in ensuing years on the executive committee of the Italian Zionist Association. It was the inspiration of Israel that
persuaded Lopez-Nunes to observe the Jewish holidays. For Italian
Jews, the sense of Zionist pride was rekindled initially in the liberation
period, when they first encountered the Palestine Jewish Brigade
among the rescuing British army. The flame blazed even more vividly

during Israel's war of independence in 1948, and supremely during the Six-Day War crisis of 1967.

The reaction of Genoa's tiny Jewish population in 1967 was characteristic. The day war broke out, June 5, hundreds of Genoese Jews poured into makeshift recruiting offices. During the ensuing two weeks, the pro-Israel headquarters became the center of Genoese Jewish life. The various committees worked around the clock, fund-raising, taking blood donations, processing applicants for Israel. Sixty percent of all eligible men and women between the ages of seventeen and thirty-five volunteered to serve in Israel. The outpouring in Rome and Milan, obviously, was much larger. During the October 1973 war, the Italian Jewish population committed itself to provide Israel with the equivalent of one hundred kilos of gold—$1.5 million. The gesture was symbolic as well as generous. It was the thirtieth anniversary of "Black Sabbath," when the Nazis had taken fifty kilos of gold as ransom for the Jews of Rome.

In common with his cousin-in-law and with other Italian Jews, Bruno Zevi fully shared this Zionist dedication. At the time of the Yom Kippur War, he served as chairman of Rome's pro-Israel rally. Yet his renewed sense of identity with his people preceded the birth of Israel and was typically "Latin" in its consciousness of personal dignity. For him, as for thousands of other Jews, that pride was frontally challenged on February 15, 1945, when the Vatican proudly revealed that Rome's chief rabbi, Israel Zolli, had converted to Catholicism. It was uncertain then or later if the rabbi's apostasy was to be regarded as symptomatic of the malaise affecting thousands of other Italian Jews. Without doubt, many had endured a psychic trauma under Nazi rule, and were broken by their ordeal. On the other hand, it was subsequently revealed that Zolli had remained chief rabbi just long enough (four years) to assure himself a sizable pension. He had resigned only two weeks before his baptism and must have been taking Catholic instruction while in office. There were also charges that Zolli was pro-Fascist. He had thought kindly of Mussolini. Several weeks earlier, he had openly defended a local racist. In any case, none of this information was available when the bombshell of Zolli's conversion was dropped. Hearing the news, Bruno Zevi rushed "almost blindly" to the Great Synagogue. There he found the sanctuary and the courtyard packed. Thousands of Jews had gathered spontaneously to voice their horror and outrage.

On the dais stood Alfredo Panzieri, oldest of the city's rabbis. A frail little man, almost deaf, Panzieri had been trapped in the capital during the German occupation. Although all synagogues had been closed, each Sabbath the aged rabbi imperturbably conducted services in the tiny chapel of the Jewish old age home. In October 1943, a contingent of SS troops entered the building, rounding up elderly worshipers for deportation. Panzieri continued with his prayers, unaware of the Germans' presence. Unaware of Panzieri's deafness, in turn, the Germans were dumbfounded by his apparent courage, and left him alone. Now it was this old man who addressed the crowd in the Great Synagogue, speaking gently, even artlessly, of the "joy and honor" of being Jewish. The Jewish chaplain of the American occupying army spoke briefly afterward, expressing the solidarity of American Jews with the Jews of Rome. Umberto Nahon, the Italian-born rabbi of the occupying British Army, added his own comment: "In our tradition, when a man leaves our community, his name must be canceled out." It was the only allusion to Zolli in the service.

The ceremony of reaffirmation lasted three hours, and for Bruno Zevi it was one of the decisive experiences of his life. Nahon's words had voiced his own thoughts. As he left the synagogue, Zolli's mortified daughter approached Zevi, seeking to explain that, as a professor of philosophy earlier at the University of Padua, her father had written many books on the affinity between Judaism and Christianity, and evidently had been carried away. (Later, Zolli became professor of Jewish history at the Lateran College.) Zevi brushed her aside. "Your father does not exist for me," he muttered. "He has never existed." Nor, from that point on, could he bring himself even to mention Zolli's name. Thirty-eight years later, the memory of the episode still caused him pain. His face was hard as he described it. "A third of the Jewish people were liquidated by the Nazis, and then our official 'leader' in Rome chose to betray us. The Vatican would take no satisfaction for encouraging that betrayal, though. They did not know us. We would not be erased that easily."

The Vatican Forgives the Jews

From his vantage point in Switzerland, Gerhart Riegner's dealings with the Vatican extended back to the war years. His effort then was devoted to rescue, and was tragically frustrated. Although Pius XII was willing to offer sanctuary and to lend funds to the Jews of Rome, he was unprepared to confirm the Nazi genocide, much less publicly to condemn it. After the war, Riegner concentrated initially on the return of Jewish children who had found refuge among Catholic families. To that end, he met in Rome with Monsignor Giovanni Montini, the Vatican's acting secretary of state for international affairs (who many years later became Pope Paul VI). Montini procrastinated. "I cannot give orders for the return of those children unless I have their exact addresses," he insisted. Nearly three years passed before the Vatican softened its position, and even afterward individual prelates in the Netherlands, Belgium, France, and Poland were hesitant to cooperate. At the same time, Pius XII fended off repeated appeals by the World Jewish Congress for an encyclical that would decisively repudiate the theological basis of antisemitism. "We shall study the question" was his invariable response.

Then, in 1958, Pius XII died, and was succeeded by Angelo Roncalli, who assumed the papal throne as John XXIII. Renowned for his broad humanity, the new pontiff set out immediately to demonstrate his friendship for the Jews. In 1959, he invested the Israeli ambassador to Italy with the Grand Cross of Sylvester, a gesture of significance inasmuch as the Curia previously had ignored the very existence of Israel. It was during the same year that the Vatican announced plans to convene a Second Lateran Council—Vatican II. The historic gathering was scheduled to meet in 1962 and to continue for three years. Hereupon, Professor Jules Isaac, an eminent French Jewish authority on antisemitism and a man whose own wife and children had been killed by the Gestapo, secured an interview with John XXIII, and asked that the question of antisemitism be placed on the agenda of the forthcoming Council. Responding sympathetically, the pope turned the matter over to Cardinal Augustin Bea, president of the Secretariat for the Promotion of Christian Unity.

Seventy-eight years old, a German-born Jesuit and former confessor of Pius XII, Bea was a leader of the progressive element in the Vatican. He had witnessed the SS roundup of Jews in Rome in 1943, and the memory of that horror had never left him. In later years, he supported Jewish pleas for an encyclical on the Jewish question, but without result. Now at last, in the enveloping compassion of John XXIII, he thought he had found his man. In preparation for Vatican II, therefore, Bea consulted first with Nahum Goldmann and Gerhart Riegner of the World Jewish Congress, who promised to draft a proposed statement in cooperation with other Jewish organizations.

These latter ultimately included B'nai B'rith, the American Jewish Committee, the Board of Deputies of British Jews, the Union of Italian Jewish Communities, the Conseil Représentatif des Israélites de France, and several other broadly based Jewish constituencies. Their negotiations were not easy. Once their compromise draft was submitted in 1960, moreover, it encountered delays by conservative elements within the Vatican. Eventually, a renewed emphasis was provided by Israel's capture of Adolf Eichmann. The 1961 trial sessions in Jerusalem raised painful questions of Christian complicity in the Holocaust. Meanwhile, in December 1961, the (Protestant) World Council of Churches issued a forceful condemnation of antisemitism. Cardinal Bea exploited these embarrassments as he pressed his colleagues for action. Still, the opposition remained. Several members of the Curia were plain and simple reactionaries. Others were susceptible to Arab pressures. In 1963, John XXIII died and his successor was Cardinal Montini, who was enthroned as Paul VI. The new pontiff's traditional suspicions of the Jews were compounded by his support of Roman Catholic claims on Jerusalem, and by the vulnerability of Latin Christians in the Arab world. During his visit to Christian holy places in Israel a year later, Paul's single allusion to Israel was to "the authorities in Tel Aviv."

In the end, it was not only Bea's persistence but strong political pressure from liberal Catholic elements in the United States (among them, President John Kennedy in the White House) that forced a draft declaration through the Lateran Council. While Paul VI and the conservatives persisted in their delaying tactics, in 1965 Bea and his supporters prevailed at last in the fourth and final session of Vatican II. The bishops voted a *Schema* on the Jews. The document was something less than a dithyramb of friendship. Suggesting that all mankind, and not simply part of it, was guilty of the Crucifixion, the *Schema* went on to declare: "Although the Jewish authorities and those who followed their lead pressed for the death of Christ, nevertheless, what happened to Christ in his passion cannot be attributed to all Jews without distinction then alive, or to the Jews today. Although the Church is the new People of God, the Jews should not be represented as rejected by God or accused as if this followed from Holy Scriptures." Finally, the declaration observed that the church "deplore[d] on religious grounds any display of anti-Jewish hatred or persecution."

Many Jewish leaders were disappointed, even cynical. Nor were their reservations allayed by the insensitivity of Paul VI himself, whose first post-*Schema* Easter sermon once again endorsed the notion of the collective guilt of the Jews in the death of Jesus. But Riegner was less pessimistic. He sensed that the declaration would outlive the current papal incumbent. As he saw it, the task was to build from Vatican II, to develop an ongoing relationship with Bea and the latter's associates. The old cardinal promised Riegner to organize a special committee—a "Jewish committee"—to deal with Catholic-Jewish relations under the rubric of his Secretariat for the Promotion of Christian Unity. Then, in late 1967, even as these preparations were being made, Bea died, and the "Jewish committee" expired with him. Riegner was shaken. Unwilling to mark time, however, he turned his efforts to the Protestants, and by 1969 succeeded in establishing a similar committee with the World Council of Churches. He suspected that this development would be heeded by the Vatican, and he was right. Later that same year, Riegner and Goldmann were invited to a papal audience. Visibly affected by Jewish and liberal criticism, Paul VI affirmed his willingness to cooperate with the Jewish people "in the service of common human causes." Several months later, as a token of his goodwill, he authorized the establishment of an International Catholic-Jewish Liaison Committee to discuss Catholic-Jewish relations. He himself would appoint the Catholic members, while the World Jewish Congress and other Jewish organizations would select a delegation from among themselves.

The negotiations bore fruit. In the spring of 1974, the Vatican published a series of "Guidelines and Suggestions for Relations with Judaism." While professing to implement the *Schema* of Vatican II, the "guidelines" in fact went beyond that document. For one thing, the new statement rejected the widespread notion that Judaism was a religion of fear and inflexible law, evincing neither love of God nor love of mankind. The history of Judaism was now declared to be an ongoing one, "creating new and rich religious values." The publication concluded with instructions to Catholics to embark on serious dialogue with Jews at all levels and actively to fight antisemitism. It was an impressive volte-face in Catholic doctrine. Conceivably, the statement would exert a positive impact in nations such as Argentina and Brazil, with their large Jewish communities and their powerful Catholic hierarchies. Moreover, the Vatican gave practical effect to the "guidelines" by dropping its insistence on a Catholic upbringing for the children of mixed Jewish-Catholic marriages. The implications for thousands of such youngsters and their parents were far-reaching.

"There has been a significant change in the church's attitude to Jews since John XXIII and Vatican II," Riegner observed eight years later, "although unquestionably generations will have to pass before the full implications of the *Schema* work their way down to grass roots." Generations, one might ask, before the largest part of the Catholic world would agree to forgive a people that had survived Crusaders' massacres, Inquisitional tribunals, autos-da-fé, ghettos, Easter pogroms, civic disenfranchisement, economic strangulation, and a climactic genocide? But the Jews, of all peoples, could not permit themselves the luxury of cynicism, no more than of naive credulity. If the *Schema* offered even a faint hope of a change in the Vatican's mind and heart, it would be accepted—both gratefully and cautiously.

III

Oases of Uncertain Tranquillity:
Switzerland and Scandinavia

The Bureaucratization of Conscience

Following my two lengthy meetings with Gerhart Riegner at his Avenue Wendt apartment, I permitted myself a brief interval of sightseeing in Geneva. As I passed the old League of Nations buildings, the headquarters buildings of the World Health Organization, the Red Cross, the World Council of Churches, I hardly needed reminder of the unique vantage point this city—this country—had offered "Monsieur Mondial" as he pieced together the first hard evidence of the Holocaust. Here, too, in Switzerland at the turn of the century, the early Zionist congresses had assembled. Since then, other international Jewish organizations, from rabbinical associations to the World Jewish Congress itself, have continued intermittently to choose Switzerland as the venue for their periodic gatherings.

Yet this tidy mountain enclave is also the home of the largest Jewish community in continental Europe that was not directly affected by the Final Solution. Numbering 21,000 in a Swiss population of 7,800,000, the nation's Jews live in three principal regions: 58 percent in the German cantons, mainly in Zurich, Basel, and Bern; 38 percent in the French cantons, principally in Geneva and Lausanne; and 4 percent in the Italian cantons, essentially in Lugano, which encompasses a small, aging, and highly Orthodox community. They are a mélange of cultures. In 1866, shortly after the revised Swiss federal constitution extended civil rights to non-Christians, the first Jewish settlers arrived from Alsace. These were followed by small numbers of immigrants from Eastern Europe in the early twentieth century, and finally by a modest influx of refugees from Hitler's Greater Reich. The nation's stringent naturalization laws restricted Jewish immigration to a much lower quota than in other Western countries. The few Jews who were admitted tended to acculturate swiftly. Swiss immigration policy was even more tightly regulated before and during World War II. Many more Jewish refugees than were accepted were turned back—usually to meet death at the hands of the Nazis. Inhibited by fear of provoking Germany, and by their own undercurrent of racism, the Swiss rationalized their policy by invoking the slogan "The boat is full." Although some 30,000 Jews ultimately found sanctuary in Switzerland during the war years, few were admitted after 1943, when the Nazi extermination program was in full progress. As soon as the war ended, the government moved to repatriate the refugees, and by 1947 only 1,800 remained.

Even now, Switzerland ensures that immigrants can become citizens only with the greatest difficulty. At least 40 percent of the Jews who arrived before or since the war remain unnaturalized. The same obduracy is evident in the government's attitude toward Jewish assets transferred to Switzerland before the war and unclaimed afterward because their owners perished in the Holocaust. For years the World Jewish Congress insisted that these funds should properly be transferred to Jewish relief organizations; and for years the Swiss government insisted on documented "proof" of Jewish ownership. The funds eventually were released to the Schweitzer Israelitische Gemeinde—the Swiss Jewish Federation—and to the Swiss Refugee Committee, but only after a decade and a half of painful and complicated negotiations. "They wore me out," murmured Riegner in exasperated recollection. Was this antisemitism? Riegner preferred to ascribe it to a characteristic Swiss inflexibility on rules and regulations.

In recent decades, however, the Swiss have appeared faintly abashed by their wartime record of callousness to refugees, and perhaps a guilty conscience explains the sanctuary they offered Hungarian refugees in 1956 and Czech refugees in 1968, among them a relatively large number of Jews. In the 1960s, French Switzerland also absorbed hundreds of Jews from North Africa and the Near East. Most of the newcomers went into business, and over the years several of them emerged among Switzerland's wealthiest residents (if not citizens). On the whole, Jews have shared in the postwar Swiss affluence. As in other countries, they are found largely in wholesale and retail commerce, with a substantial minority of professionals. If they encounter little serious antisemitism, they are aware of tacit vocational and social quotas. Less than a dozen Jews are prominent in the federal government or even in the cantonal or municipal administrations. Jews are barred from membership in a few clubs and societies in Zurich. Switzerland continues to maintain a scrupulously neutralist position on Middle Eastern—and other international—issues, an attitude that further encourages Swiss Jews to keep a low profile.

In some degree, Jewish communal life mirrors the provincialism of the host society. There are several national Jewish organizations. The most important of them, the Schweitzer Israelitische Gemeinde, maintains its headquarters in Zurich, and its four thousand dues-paying members help underwrite a large and efficient network of old age homes, summer camps, women's clubs, and Jewish centers. Yet, in federalist Switzerland, the bulk of Jewish activities remains in the hands of local organizations, congregational and other. Linguistic barriers between cantons are mainly responsible for this provincialism; German-speaking Jews maintain little contact with French-speaking Jews. It is all the more remarkable, then, that Swiss Jewry has long been among the world's most generous contributors to Israeli causes. No doubt prosperity is a factor. So, too, is Swiss efficiency, which ensures that nearly every household is covered. Additionally, the Jewish press is more influential here than in any community of equal size. Its *Wochezeitung*, published by the federation, is found in almost every Jewish home, rather like the *Chronicle* in England. And there are several journals and newspapers of good quality sponsored by various individual Jewish organizations.

Despite its structural integrity, Swiss Jewry is not without its problems. Liberal Judaism is all but ostracized by the Jewish establishment. Reigning supreme, the Orthodox rabbinate is quite inflexible, taking a hard line against conversions at a time when the rate of intermarriage is over 40 percent. The Jewish population is aging, and declining as a result. It is an adage that "a wedding of two Jews in Switzerland is rare enough, but a marriage between Swiss Jew and Swiss Jew is a minor miracle." As isolated and cosseted as Switzerland itself, the little Jewish community shares in both the pleasures and the perils of its comfortable seclusion.

Denmark: Tranquillity Revisited

"My mother passed away last month," Chief Rabbi Bent Melchior wrote me in the late autumn of 1982. "You were the last person to share her reminiscences. Would you by chance have a transcript of your conversation?" Regrettably, I did not. My "transcript" consisted of little more than impressionistic notes of my visit to an inconspicuous, rather lower-middle-class neighborhood in Copenhagen, the Nørre Farimagsgade quarter. It was a climb of four stories to the modestly furnished apartment. Meta Melchior, eighty years old, had greeted me warmly. Her features were delicately chiseled, her eyes still luminous. It was a very Central European face.

Those were her origins. Born Meta Schonstein in Leitmeritz, Bohemia, she was the daughter of the local rabbi. In 1906, her father became the assistant to the chief rabbi of Copenhagen. Meta's earliest languages were German at home and Danish at school. Her friends were as likely to be Gentile as Jewish, but the closest of them was a Jewish boy, Marcus Melchior, whose family had lived in Denmark for at least three centuries. In Copenhagen, Melchiors Plads is a street named for Moritz Gerson Melchior, whose summer home was the second home of Hans Christian Andersen. Melchiorsvej is a street named for Moses Melchior, one of Denmark's leading bankers. Marcus Melchior's own parents descended from a less affluent branch of the family, but their roots were a source of pride to them. Others of their Jewish neighbors traced their ancestry back even further, to seventeenth-century immigrants from Germany. Well before the Napoleonic-emancipation era, they enjoyed freedom to travel, to practice their religion in private homes. The constitution of 1849 eliminated the final barrier to equality, Jewish participation in government. By then, the nation's Jewish population had grown to three thousand, most of them settled in Copenhagen.

Thereafter, increasingly acculturated, Danish Jewry began to produce its share of distinguished public figures. Among them were Georg Brandes, the literary critic, and his brother Edvard, leader of Denmark's Liberal Party and twice minister of finance; Herman Trier, president of Parliament; General C. J. de Meza, commander of the Danish army during the war with Prussia in 1864; and, in the twentieth century, Neils Bohr (a half-Jew), the Nobel laureate and "father of atomic energy." If the trend toward acculturation brought with it a certain waning of Jewish identity by the turn of the century, Jewish solidarity was revived by an infusion of four thousand East European Jews in the last decade before World War I. Poor, Yiddish-speaking, somewhat radical in their politics, they had little in common with the indigenous Danish Jews, who ensured that communal leadership remained firmly in their own hands.

Marcus Melchior and Meta worked together in a Jewish youth group, and became engaged during the years he was studying at the Hildesheimer Rabbinical Seminary in Berlin. When he was ordained, in 1921, they were married. Opportunities for young rabbis were limited during the postwar depression. The next years brought Melchior a succession of marginal posts: a pulpit in Tarnowicz, a small German town in the Polish Corridor; then a congregation in Beuthen, Silesia. With the rise of the Nazis, the family returned to Copenhagen, where Melchior scraped by as director of a tiny Jewish afternoon school and by giving private Bar Mitzvah lessons. In time, however, Melchior proved to be a popular guest lecturer in high-school and adult-education programs. His interpretations of Judaism were welcomed by Danish educational authorities, who were intent upon combating the inroads of Nazi antisemitism. During this period, too, with four children to care for, Meta was actively involved in community efforts to provide for hundreds of Jewish refugees who were arriving from Germany.

By World War II, the Jews of Denmark numbered approximately 7,000 in a Danish population of 4.2 million. Of these, 1,300 were off-spring of mixed marriages, and another 1,500 were fugitives from the Greater Reich. This was the minority that was trapped on April 8, 1940, when the German army occupied Denmark. Remarkably, during the first two and a half years of Nazi rule, Jews and non-Jews were treated alike. Denmark was declared a *Musterprotektorat*—a model protectorate—that ostensibly shared a common "Aryan" heritage with Germany. The Nazis sensed, too, that the Danish people would not collaborate in anti-Jewish discrimination. Thus, like many other Danes, the Melchiors' Gentile friends drew closer to them. The change in the family's circumstances was economic. Melchior's lectures at Danish high schools were terminated and he was obliged to struggle again.

The Mobilization of Conscience

The interlude of toleration ended in the summer of 1943. By then, the emergence of a Danish resistance movement had forfeited the country's privileged status. Accordingly, the German administration decided to move against the Jews. In September 1943, Dr. Werner Best, the Nazi gauleiter in Copenhagen, instructed his director of shipping, Georg Duckwitz, to make a number of vessels available for the deportation of Jews. A "good German," Duckwitz was horrified by the request and alerted Danish political leaders. The latter normally would have alerted Chief Rabbi Max Friediger. But several days earlier the Germans had taken Friediger into custody as a hostage. Instead, the information was conveyed to Melchior.

Melchior began informing Jews the next morning, at synagogue prayer services, while Meta and her older children set about telephoning others. Many Danish Gentiles were embarked on the same mission. By the afternoon of September 30, word had reached several thousand Danish Jews. Later that same night, when contingents of SS troops, address lists in hand, began raiding Jewish homes, most of the Jews were gone. With the exception of 202 ill or older people, no one was present. The initial roundup was a failure. It continued for several days, but only 472 Jews in all were captured.

By then, Melchior, his wife, and their children had reached a small inland community, Orlev, fifty-five miles west of Copenhagen. After a ten-day stopover there with a Christian friend, the family traveled north to the coastal town of Falster. In Falster, other Christian friends chartered a boat for their departure to Sweden. The arrangements were typical of the massive effort the Danes conducted to rescue their Jewish population. The success of that effort, and the contrast it offered to the behavior of many other European peoples, has become a subject of historical fascination. Among the explanations for the rescue, one was the proximity of Sweden, a neutral country, which granted the refugees asylum. The laxity of Nazi rule in Denmark also helped. So did the high rate of Jewish-Christian intermarriage, which had reached 40 percent by 1939; in many instances, the Danes were helping their relatives. The fact that the Danes had been forewarned by Duckwitz was also an atypical piece of luck. Finally, many other Germans in Denmark disapproved of the deportations. The Wehrmacht occupation troops were typically older men, often in their forties and fifties, and most preferred to turn a blind eye to Jewish escape. Melchior regarded this last factor as decisive. Years later, he wrote in his autobiography:

> The assumption that the success was due to the colossal stupidity of the Germans, and that they never noticed anything [is untenable]. . . . Of course, the Germans knew perfectly well what was going on and, of course, they could have put a stop to it, had they decided to do so. So, the fortunate thing was that [the occupying army] did not want to. . . . Certainly the Gestapo was eager enough. But it was not strongly represented in Denmark.

On the night of October 8, then, Melchior, his family, and nineteen other Jews were loaded on a small fishing smack in Falster, and in a harrowing, storm-racked journey, transported to the Swedish village of Lilla Beddinge. The local inhabitants, fishermen's families, welcomed the refugees with great kindness. Three days later, the Melchiors and their companions were taken by bus to Malmö, a four-hour journey. There, in an empty high school, they joined hundreds of Jews who had preceded them. During the ensuing two weeks, the Swedish government organized more permanent arrangements. In the end, fully 6,500 rescued Jews were dispersed throughout Sweden, often in makeshift camps, in unused summer pensions, and in rest homes.

Melchior and his family were lodged in the town of Kristianstad. A tiny room was found for them in a third-rate hotel. Meals were provided in various Jewish homes. The children's clothing were odds and ends collected from the neighboring Malmö Jewish community. Arrangements eventually were made for Melchior to serve as the rabbi of the Danish Jewish refugees, with the Stockholm Jewish community providing a tiny stipend. The work obliged Melchior to travel almost continually, visiting the numerous camps, offering spiritual comfort to the refugees, conducting services, lecturing, giving Hebrew lessons, relaying greetings and news from family to family. He became a beloved figure. In March 1944, the Danish government sent word to Melchior that it had appointed him "rabbi of the refugees."

The solicitude of the Danish king and cabinet similarly extended to the 472 Jewish captives who had been sent on to the concentration camp at Theresienstadt. By their frequent inquiries, supplemented by their regular dispatch of Red Cross food parcels, the Danish authorities may well have saved the prisoners' lives. Finally, in April 1945, the Theresienstadt Jews were liberated. The day they were brought home to Denmark, thousands of Danes lined the main route to Copenhagen, waving flags and joyously welcoming them. A month later, the former prisoners were joined by the repatriated refugees from Sweden. The Melchiors' experience was typical. When they unlocked the door of their apartment in Copenhagen, they found that it had been freshly cleaned and painted. Two weeks earlier, the government had warned that no delay would be countenanced in the restitution of Jewish property. There was none. Homes and businesses usually were turned over within days. Subsequent laws reimbursed Jews for confiscated movable goods and securities.

In the first two years after liberation, Melchior was obliged once again to subsist on temporary jobs—tutoring, editing the local Jewish weekly, lecturing. Then, in April 1947, Chief Rabbi Friediger died, and his congregation unanimously elected Melchior to succeed him. Assured of a decent income at last, the family took its place in a Jewish community that was itself regaining its former status and dignity. By then, the children of the East European immigrants had moved out of their vocational ghetto in the needle trades and were becoming businessmen or joining the indigenous Jews in the liberal professions. One of them, Henryk Gruenbaum, became minister for economic affairs. Another, Dr. Stephen Hurwitz, was appointed the national ombudsman, and throughout the 1950s and 1960s remained perhaps the single most respected figure in the government. Only one group of Jews continued on the periphery of both Danish and Jewish life. In 1968, Denmark became the sanctuary for some 2,500 Jews fleeing the upsurge of antisemitism in Communist Poland. Although the newcomers augmented Denmark's Jewish population of 7,500 by nearly 30 percent, most of them were veteran Communists and had long since ceased regarding themselves as Jews. Even more heavily intermarried than the "native" Danish Jews, they were unwilling to join the official Jewish community.

For the ensuing twenty-two years after his election as chief rabbi, meanwhile, Marcus Melchior continued his practice of extensive lecturing before Christian and Jewish groups. He was repeatedly honored—with orders, citations, royal receptions. Meta became the first president of Denmark's Women's International Zionist Organization (WIZO). The Melchiors' six children all participated in B'nai Akiva, the Orthodox Zionist youth organization. It was the family's most creative and rewarding period. In 1969, it ended with Melchior's death. Almost immediately, Bent Melchior, his third son, was elected as the new chief rabbi. The choice was by no means a mere gesture of respect for the late Marcus. By then, Bent Melchior had fulfilled an extensive apprenticeship in Jewish life. At the age of twenty, he had served as a volunteer soldier in Israel's war of independence. Afterward, he studied for five years at Jews College in England, and was ordained a rabbi. A man of broad culture, fluent in four languages, he had earned the respect of the congregation well before his father died.

I sat with Bent Melchior in his ample, somewhat old-fashioned apartment, only two blocks from his mother's flat. Sallow and overweight, a heavy cigar smoker like his late father, he was all business as he evaluated his role in the community. He remained as committed as had Marcus to the Orthodox trend within Judaism. Danish Jewry might not be observant, he remarked, but it expected traditionalism from its leaders. "Here we are so few, we must remain under the same roof." Yet the man was no fanatic. He accepted the importance of "aesthetics," of organ, choir, and a modified Hebrew ritual. There was also room for flexibility elsewhere. By 1982, the intermarriage rate of Jews had climbed to 45 percent. It was a fact of life in this open society, with no sense of guilt. But neither was it synonymous now with assimilation. Bent Melchior saw to that. He was prepared to accept spouses for conversion, to train children of mixed marriages for Bar Mitzvah and for subsequent Jewish involvement. Meanwhile, the structure of the Jewish community remained intact. This was the "Mosaic Community of Faith," the officially recognized Jewish community. Empowered by the state to tax its members, the community raised sufficient funds to underwrite an impressive program of cultural activities. A Jewish day school, funded by a Claims Conference grant, was attended by nearly half the Jewish children of Copenhagen. "Synagogue attendance is our Achilles' heel," admitted Bent Melchior. "Among our young people, Israel, not organized religion, is the focus of identity."

That focus has become somewhat diffused lately. "It was Zionism that made me Jewish," remarked Bent Blüdnikow. The son of Russian Jewish immigrants, a university graduate student in his late twenties, Blüdnikow had no memory of the Holocaust, nor even of traditionalism in the family home. For him and his peer group, Israel had long served as the major source of Jewish creativity. Disoriented, however, by Israel's policies under Menachem Begin, that creativity was beginning to turn inward, toward Danish Jewish history. With considerable effort, Blüdnikow had succeeded in organizing the first Danish Jewish historical society. The local Jewish community was not celebrated for its munificence, and thus far, funding came almost equally from Christians and Jews. Of the eight board members, five were non-Jews, including the chairman. Yet this shared commitment to Jewish cultural survival may have offered insight into the curiously benign and cooperative nature of Jewish-Gentile relations in Denmark. It was the Danish people themselves who erected the imposing monument in the ferry station of Elsinore, a sculptured representation of a Danish fishing boat with Jewish refugees. The symbiosis was, perhaps still is, responsible for the very physical salvation of Danish Jewry.

*

Before 1940, Norway's Jewish population numbered a minuscule 1,450 souls. Nearly half of these perished during the German occupation, and the rest were smuggled into Sweden by the Norwegian underground. After the war, approximately 800 of the fugitives returned home. Their welcome was as heartfelt here as in Denmark. Restitution was immediate. Heirless Jewish property reverted to the Jewish community. Today, perhaps 1,100 Jews, in a Norwegian population of 3.5 million, are concentrated mainly in Oslo, with a tiny satellite community in Trondheim. They maintain synagogues in both cities. Although proud of Israel, they are also proud of their equal status in Norwegian society, and they intermarry at a rate exceeding 50 percent.

Most of Finland's 2,000 Jews remained at home during the war. Inasmuch as their country was allied with Germany, a number of Finnish Jewish soldiers actually fought at the side of German units against the Soviet Union. It was a bizarre juxtaposition, for both Finns and Jews. The Finnish army was never under direct German command, however, and the Helsinki government was able to deny all German requests for jurisdiction over Jewish refugees from Central Europe. Finland's staunch loyalty to its Jews was the more noteworthy in a nation that had given them civil rights much more reluctantly than had Denmark, Sweden, or Norway. Jewish political emancipation had not come in Finland until January 1918, in the aftermath of the Russian Revolution and Finland's declaration of independence. The new republic then adopted a constitution granting equality to all residents of the country.

In the ensuing years, Jews flourished, and quickly achieved their characteristic business profile, with a fair intermingling of professionals. No area of society was closed to them, no more than in Denmark and Norway. The nation's most respected diplomat, Per Jakobson, ambassador to the United Nations, was a Jew, and there were distinguished Jewish figures in the arts and sciences, in journalism and the state television network. Since the 1950s, nevertheless, a slow numerical decline has become evident, the typical consequence of a low birth rate and an intermarriage rate of over 50 percent. The shrinkage is accompanied by a perceptible ebbing of cultural vitality. It is preeminently the magnetism of Israel that sustains Jewish identification.

Sweden: "Aryan" Neutrality

I first met Herman Abrahamsson at a Haifa bus stop in the autumn of 1957. He was a tall chap in his late twenties, with rugged angular features under an unkempt shock of black hair.

"Where from?" I asked.

"Stockholm."

"What brings you here?" I persisted, with the oblique delicacy I had learned from the Israelis. "Zionism?"

"Narishkeit," he sighed. "Utter foolishness. I don't know why I'm here."

The answer appealed to me. We became friends. Yet Herman remained evasive about the circumstances that had brought him to Israel. I was supposed to be the student of history. It would have been more logical to begin with the circumstances that had brought him to Sweden. Twenty-five years would pass before the thought occurred to me.

In the year of Herman's birth, 1929, approximately seven thousand Jews were to be found in Sweden, half of them in Stockholm. Their presence extended back to eighteenth-century emigrations from Central Europe. No Jew was eligible to own property until 1860, to vote until 1866, to stand for public office until 1870. But afterward, their equality was virtually complete. In subsequent years, a number of Jewish families became wealthy, even influential, particularly in journalism and publishing. The population of this quasi-assimilated community was soon equaled and then exceeded by Jewish refugees from tsarist Russia. Herman's parents were among the latter. His father worked as a house painter. Herman, his two brothers and three sisters were raised in Fjurholmsplan, the poorest quarter of south Stockholm. Theirs was a traditional Orthodox upbringing. Only Jewish day schools were lacking; there was no money, no support for them from the acculturated Swedish Jews who dominated the communal institutions. In the public schools, meanwhile, Jewish students were frequently taunted by their classmates. One of Herman's teachers was an avowed antisemite, who outspokenly praised the government's closed-door policy to German Jewish refugees. Yet Herman's bitterest memories were of the snobbery displayed by the native Jews.

The ensuing war years brought little respite to the Abrahamssons' struggle for subsistence. The sons left school to find work. At the age of fourteen, Herman took a job in a factory, attending night classes at a technical high school. With the Nazis riding high in Europe then, Aryan ideology made sharp, if brief, inroads among his classmates and fellow workers. A tall, muscular youth, Herman no longer endured it passively. Once the war shifted against Germany, moreover, neo-Nazi groups began disappearing into the woodwork. Indeed, soon afterward the Swedish government itself found it expedient to adopt a more forth-right pro-Allied stance, even to revise its former exclusionist immigration policy. In late 1943, it admitted 200,000 refugees from neighboring Scandinavian countries. Among these were the 6,500 Jews from Denmark, and an additional thousand from Norway and Finland. In the spring of 1945, the Swedish Red Cross under the presidency of Count Folke Bernadotte interceded with the Nazis to save Jewish concentration camp inmates (the precedent had been established earlier, in Hungary, by the Swedish diplomat Raoul Wallenberg). Hoping still to save his skin, Heinrich Himmler, the SS chief, agreed to release 9,000 of these Jews, who were brought to Sweden more dead than alive in the celebrated "Bernadotte wagons." Although 2,000 of them eventually left the country after the war, most remained. Together with a few hundred Danish and Finnish Jews who similarly chose not to return, the new-comers doubled Sweden's prewar Jewish population. Relatively unskilled, they were dependent in the early postwar years on social welfare care. Some of it was provided by the government, more by the Stockholm Jewish community, most by the Joint.

Herman visited these refugees often, pedaling his bicycle to their encampments at Vikinghill and Lovö, outside Stockholm. It was only then that he became aware of the magnitude of the Holocaust and developed his own raison d'être as a Jew. During his early youth he had belonged to B'nai Akiva, but his interest in Zionism had lain fallow during the war. It revived now with a vengeance. In 1946, emissaries were arriving from Palestine, seeking volunteers for the Haganah, the Jewish underground. There was strong local direction behind the movement. Fritz Hollander, a German-born Jew and owner of one of Stockholm's largest import-export firms, had earlier hurled himself into the Jewish rescue effort; now he was prepared to subsidize anyone who would serve in Palestine. Herman's course was set. It was influenced not only by Jewish pride but by a need to escape the uncompromising Orthodoxy of his father. His older brother, Lennart, had fled the house at the age of sixteen to begin living with a non-Jewish girl. His younger brother, Bernhard, had joined the merchant marine at the age of fourteen. It was time for departure and action.

In mid-1947, the first military instructor arrived from Palestine and opened a camp in Skevik, on the outskirts of Stockholm. Nearly one hundred young Scandinavian Jews turned up for the initial twelve days of training. The sessions were primarily motivational, and they succeeded. Herman was charged now with purpose and enthusiasm. In their own way, so were other Swedish Jews. Far more than before the war, they were participating in activities of the World Jewish Congress and the World Zionist Organization. In 1947, a special appeal on behalf of the Haganah netted 800,000 kronor, an unprecedented sum for Swedish Jews.

The series of training programs ended in April 1948, on the eve of full-scale war in Palestine. Among the youths who had committed themselves to service were 34 Finns, 50 Danes, and 7 Swedes, Herman among them. With "hiking" uniforms provided by Fritz Hollander, the group departed by ferry and train to Paris, then by truck to a staging area outside Marseilles, then to a secret château, "Tirat Zvi," in the French Alps. About 120 young men and women gathered there, most of them from Anglo-Saxon countries, but many from Latin America and Europe. For the next month, the volunteers underwent a training so rigorous that only 80 of them managed to complete the course. Finally, in late May, they embarked from Marseilles on a 120-ton fishing schooner. Following a zigzag course across the Mediterranean to avoid British destroyers, the tiny vessel dropped anchor off Tel Aviv on June 12—a nightmare journey of two weeks.

Once disembarked, the newcomers were moved out by bus to a camp near Netania, where the nucleus of the Machal, the "foreign legion" of Jewish volunteers, was being assembled. Herman was assigned to the Seventy-second Battalion of the Seventh Brigade, an elite fighting force of shock troops. With a potpourri of Italian, British, and Czech equipment, he and his comrades were trained for three more weeks. The first assignment would be a tough one. Their destination was Malkieh, near the Lebanese border, held by Syrian and Iraqi guerrillas. Herman and the twelve companions in his truck immediately came under fire. They remained dug in for the next eight days, in searing heat, on meager rations, under intermittent artillery and small arms fire, taking turns manning a single Bren gun. By the time the youths were relieved, they had suffered four wounded and one killed. It was an acute attack of malaria that struck Herman down, putting him in a hospital for ten days. A week after his release, he was back in action. His assignment this time was an armored car patrol along the Lebanese-Syrian border. Twelve days later, the four-car unit was sent to the Jordan Valley for an attack on the Iraqi army.

It was a major operation, with fully 1,200 troops committed to a night assault. The offensive lasted nearly ten hours. By daylight, the worst was over. The Iraqis had been slaughtered. Among the surviving prisoners, a half-dozen SS veterans were discovered. They were shot on the spot. Herman participated in other actions, other ugly episodes, during the next six months, before suffering a recurrence of malaria. Of his fellow Scandinavians, he learned afterward, ten had been killed. All but one of the casualties were Finns. Tough World War II veterans, they had invariably volunteered for the most dangerous operations.

A Refocused Identity

Herman was discharged from the army in June 1949. At first, he and a group of other Scandinavian volunteers contemplated establishing their own kibbutz, but the Israelis were bankrupt and no money was available for the project. Eventually, Herman and his friends were given their passports and air tickets home. The reunion in Stockholm was joyous, with relatives and friends pouring into the family apartment to welcome him. The reaction of the Swedish Jewish community was more restrained. It had accepted Israel by then, had contributed to it generously; but the notion of giving the demobilized volunteers a helping hand evoked a cool response. In Stockholm, as in Copenhagen, the Jewish community was dominated by the older families, and they were still unwilling to extend themselves on behalf of the local East Europeans.

For a while, Herman was employed by a brother-in-law as a textile salesman. Later, he tried his hand as a carpet salesman. It was a deadening vocation, particularly after his Israeli experience. If there was an interlude of satisfaction, it was provided by Lenke Rothman. Hungarian-born, she was one of the nine thousand Jews who had arrived in the "Bernadotte wagons" near the end of the war. Her parents and seven of her brothers and sisters had been murdered in Auschwitz. Lenke herself was critically ill with tuberculosis, and emotionally traumatized. In the following years, many people cared for her, including the famous poet of the Holocaust, Nelly Sachs, who underwrote her education at the Academy of Art. By the time Herman met and married her in 1954, Lenke had begun a promising career as an artist.

In later years, other East European Jewish refugees arrived, among them 2,500 from Hungary after the abortive 1956 revolution; and twelve years after that, some 1,500 Polish Jews, who were members of the exodus that also streamed into Denmark. In that decade and a half, the Jewish population of Sweden climbed to 15,000, three-quarters of them living in Stockholm, the rest divided between Malmö and Gothenburg. The postwar immigrants provided Swedish Jewish life with a diverse and stimulating character. In the 1980s, the 2,000 Jews in Gothenburg, Sweden's second city, are identified principally with Liberal Judaism. The 3,000 in Malmö remain predominantly Orthodox. Stockholm's 10,000 Jews manage to support Liberal, Conservative, Orthodox, even small Chasidic congregations.

As elsewhere in Scandinavia and Central Europe, the local Jewish communities sustain their activities by imposing "taxes" on registered members. These funds, together with Claims Conference subventions, underwrite a reasonably broad program of lectures, concerts, and adult education classes. The *Judisk Kronika,* published eighteen times a year, is received in the majority of Jewish homes. In Stockholm, the single Jewish day school attracts relatively few students, but a much larger number attends afternoon courses at the Jewish Center. Most of them, too, belong to a variety of Zionist-oriented youth movements. The largest, B'nai Akiva, each year sends between fifty and seventy youngsters on work-study tours of Israel. Few remain in Israel—many more Israelis are "floating" in Sweden—but exposure to Israeli life unquestionably enhances their Jewish commitment.

In 1955, Herman Abrahamsson's Zionist loyalties were mobilized again. He was contacted in May by a middle-aged Israeli who went by the name of Hirsch. The man asked Herman to serve as a "postal box" for information dispatched by Israeli spies in Syria, which would then be sent on to Israel. Herman agreed on the spot. In April 1957, a letter arrived from the Israeli agent in Syria, and Herman dropped it in his coat pocket, intending as usual to turn it over to Hirsch. The doorbell rang. Two detectives stood at the entrance. They inspected the apartment, then ordered Herman to accompany them. At police headquarters, Herman nonchalantly hung up his coat in the anteroom. A panel of detectives then questioned him about his Israeli contacts. Herman denied everything. After an hour or so, he was released, "for the time being." Upon returning to his flat, he raced off in his automobile and disposed of the incriminating letter.

Two days afterward, he was summoned for another interrogation. This time the charges were more specific. Had Mr. Abrahamsson and other Swedish Jews not "fraudulently" lent their passports to Israeli agents for the purpose of smuggling Jews out of Eastern Europe? Herman had—almost a year earlier. He had all but forgotten. As he was informed later, the Romanian government had caught a number of Jews using these illegal passports and notified the Swedish government, which then traced the documents to their true owners. At this point, Herman drew a sigh of relief. Fraudulent use of his passport was a charge he could live with. Subsequently, before a panel of judges, he pleaded guilty. At the same time, he indignantly defended his activity, which, after all, was indistinguishable from the legendary Raoul Wallenberg's use of questionable documents to rescue Jews in wartime Hungary. "If we Jews don't do this for our fellow Jews," he demanded, "then who will do it?" The judges were moved. Herman was fined a nominal two hundred kronor.

Nevertheless, he sensed that it would be appropriate to take a vacation from Sweden, and quickly, lest he be picked up on the much graver charge of complicity in Israeli espionage. Moreover, departure would enable him to break free from his collapsing marriage. Both he and Lenke recognized by then that they were hopelessly mismatched. With restitutions coming from Germany, she would be safe without him. Herman left her the apartment and the car, then made his way via Italy to Israel. In Haifa he registered at a Hebrew-language institute and contemplated settling in Israel permanently. He abandoned the idea within a few months. The heat wilted him. The nation's aggressive politics repelled him. His love for Israel evidently could survive only from afar. In the summer of 1958, too, he learned from his family that the Swedish police were closing their file on him. He could return. By then, his other problem also had been resolved. With Lenke's concurrence, he had secured a divorce from the Haifa rabbinical court.

Yet, when he was back in Sweden, Herman's restlessness continued. In ensuing years he moved from one position to another: a computer firm, an import-export house, a timber company, an advertising agency. Once he briefly opened a little art shop of his own. He rarely failed to land on his feet. Nor did the largest number of other Jews in Sweden, most of whom were active in business, industry, and the professions. If few were as wealthy as Fritz Hollander, nearly all of them earned decent livelihoods. For Herman, economic uncertainty was less of a problem than emotional ambivalence. He maintained some Israeli contacts, and his best friends still tended to be Jews. But otherwise he took little active interest in the Jewish community. The backbiting and status-seeking of communal Jewish politics were not for him. He returned periodically to the Jewish Center to renew his roots, but then drifted away. There were less complicated attractions elsewhere.

An Affinity of Strangers

I reacquainted myself with them during my third visit to Stockholm, in the summer of 1982. The city remained an almost ideal amalgam of the aesthetic and the functional: a blend of traditional and modern architecture, ornate stone-facaded public buildings and gleaming skyscrapers, dignified boulevards, a superb metro system, majestic onion-towered churches, exquisite gardens and restaurants. Prices were shockingly high, but the Swedes could afford them. Their basic health and unemployment needs were met by a government that traditionally had refused to weigh itself down with heavy defense expenditures. It was the self-sacrifice of other nations that allowed this people to flourish under their sparkling northern skies.

Between interviews, I was a weekend guest of Rolf Moser, one of Stockholm's Jewish community leaders. A successful and cultured businessman in his late forties, Moser drove me out for a drink to his country cottage, then to a friend's cottage nearby. The hosts were Jews. So were the four invited couples. All upper-middle-class, all university-trained, all at ease in German or English (for my benefit), they were particularly comfortable with each other. They had Gentile friends, of course, but in recent weeks the Israeli invasion of Lebanon had created a certain awkwardness. It was now Midsummer Fest, a time for relaxation. Better to spend the holiday with those one could be sure of. This cautiousness applied to their plans for their children. Most of the youngsters attended state schools, were encouraged to have Gentile friends. Even so, when they were shipped off for their traditional junior year at an American high school, arrangements invariably were made through the Scandinavian Jewish Youth Federation, and the children were placed with Jewish families. I had to assume, from the distinctly unkosher food in that summer cottage, that the reasons had little to do with religious traditionalism.

This would have been a fair appraisal of the religiosity of Stockholm Jewry altogether. The Great Synagogue at Währendorfsgade was Liberal in the Central European tradition (that is, Conservative by American standards). A charming old building of early-nineteenth-century vintage, designed by a German architect and constructed with a surfeit of dark oak, it was classically Central European in its elaborate fretwork and mullions, its tasteful gold-and-blue enameling. Services were decorous and brief the Sabbath morning when I attended. Typically, less than one hundred people were present. On the High Holidays, attendance was said to be somewhat more respectable. An American rabbi, Morton Narrowe, had presided over the congregation for twenty years, and had become something of a force among Stockholm Jewry in his willingness to accommodate to practical realities. One of those realities, surely, was the permissiveness of Swedish society. Like other Swedes, Jewish couples tended to live together before marriage. Narrowe refrained from moralizing; for, if dealt with heavy-handedly, these young people would not have had the slightest difficulty in acquiring Gentile spouses. As it was, the intermarriage rate for Swedish Jewry hovered at the 50 percent level.

Thus, in 1960, two years after his second sojourn in Israel, Herman Abrahamsson had met Inge-Britt Lundquist. A red-haired Nordic, she had been married earlier to an Israeli, had lived with him in a kibbutz for two years before returning with him to Sweden. They were divorced soon afterward. Herman and Inge-Britt met the following year. For him, she offered the contrast of Nordic straightforwardness and simplicity. For her, he offered the warmth and dark wit Scandinavian women apparently enjoy in Jewish men. They were married several months later. By then, Herman's parents were reconciled to the mores of this strange land; their older son, Lennart, had already gone through two Swedish wives. Inge-Britt's parents could not have cared less. Both sets of parents attended the civil marriage ceremony. A year later, Inge-Britt gave birth to her first child, Michael. It was understood that he would be raised as a Jew. Although the boy attended public school, Herman sent him to afternoon Hebrew classes at the Jewish Center. Thereafter, Michael was Bar Mitzvahed. In 1965, the Abrahamssons had a daughter, Naomi. She, too, received a Jewish upbringing.

In 1969, Herman and Inge-Britt were divorced, and Inge-Britt remarried—a Swedish Gentile this time, a much older man, who died several years later. She and Herman remained close friends. For her part, she took pains that the children continued entirely faithful to their father's tradition. During Michael's high-school year in the United States, he was routinely lodged with a Jewish family. Active in the Maccabi sports club and in B'nai Akiva, he spent a year at the Hebrew

University in 1981 (like his father, celebrating his twenty-first birthday in Israel). That same year, the daughter, Naomi, visited Israel for six weeks with a Habonim Zionist youth group. Inge-Britt joined her there, delighted at the opportunity of renewing contacts with Israeli friends. Both children went through a traditional phase, attending Sabbath synagogue services and observing Jewish dietary laws. Herman was bemused.

The day before departing Stockholm, I attend a welcome-back party for Michael at Inge-Britt's home. The youth is as tall as his father— slim, brown-eyed, good-looking. Eager to use his newly acquired Hebrew, he converses with me in that language quite easily, assures me that he is determined to continue his studies in Jewish and Israeli history. Naomi—also slim, soft-featured, blue-eyed—is attractive and gentle. Their mother beams as we chat, proud of her children. It is twenty years since I have last seen Inge-Britt. She has filled out, but remains a handsome woman, her hair still red, her blue eyes still clear. I notice, too, that she continues to wear the necklace with the Hebrew word *chai* as its pendant. She had worn it when we first met. Herman's current girlfriend (also non-Jewish) chats animatedly with his two older sisters and their husbands. Inge-Britt's mother is there, a thin, white-haired woman, as blue-eyed as her daughter. She and Herman shake hands cordially. The mother's sister, widow of a Jew, wears a large golden Star of David around her neck. "My husband is dead over ten years," she informs me, "but I've never missed attending synagogue on Shabbat." Michael's high-school French teacher arrives with her husband. She hugs Michael, and afterward listens intently as he relates his experiences in Israel. "We Swedes are very interested in Israel, you know," the teacher's husband assures me.

The tolerant, intermarried ménage buzzes away contentedly through the afternoon, eating, drinking, chatting in obvious amiability and mutual goodwill. I believe that I am witnessing a microcosm of Swedish Jewry.

IV

After the Deluge: France

Prewar: Centralism and Gallicization

The largest synagogue in France is the Temple Victoire, named for its site on Paris's rue de la Victoire. More often it is described as the Cathedral Synagogue of Paris, or the Great Synagogue, or even as the Rothschild Synagogue, after the family whose members traditionally have worshiped there. Designed late in the nineteenth century in a neo-Romanesque style by the chief architect of the municipality of Paris, the formidable old building is the property of the City of Paris, for it was underwritten by the municipality and by the Consistoire Israélite. Its sanctuary encompasses three thousand seats, and is dominated by a huge silver menorah positioned before the Ark of the Law and by vast candelabras hanging from its lofty arches. "My father worshiped here," remarked Jacques Trèves. "Quite frequently he was honored with a call to the Torah. It was his due as a member of the Consistoire board."

For Trèves, the observation was a matter not of pride but of simple fact. In his early seventies when we met in the winter of 1981, a fair-skinned man of middle height, shaking slightly with Parkinson's disease, he belonged to a family that had lived in France since the fourteenth century. His grandfather fought in the Franco-Prussian War and was decorated for heroism in the siege of Paris. His father, a renowned orthopedic surgeon, similarly received the Medaille Militaire for distinguished service in World War I. The family apartment on rue de Prony, in Paris's fashionable seventeenth arrondissement, resonated with quiet civility, refined culture, personal distinction. In 1939 Jacques Trèves enrolled in the Haute École Polytechnique, studied there for two years, then remained on for two additional years of graduate work in telecommunications. Afterward, he entered the civil service as a telecommunications engineer in the ministry of posts.

The Trèveses were representative of the veteran French Jewish population. Based in Paris, its roots were largely in Alsace-Lorraine, and to a lesser extent in Provence. By the turn of the century, French Jews had achieved an upward mobility unsurpassed by Jews in any other land. Their ranks included such eminent financiers as Rothschild, Camondo, Cahen d'Anvers, Pereira, Königswarter, Menasche, de Hirsch, d'Almeida. Often titled as counts or barons, they tended to marry among themselves or with more recently established banking dynasties. By 1914, the majority of the country's 120,000 Jews were small-scale manufacturers or wholesale or import-export businessmen; but most of these, too, had become quite comfortable. In the upsurge of liberalism following the Dreyfus Affair, their children moved freely into the professions and the civil service. There were Jewish deputies and senators in parliament, Jewish officers up to the rank of general in the army, Jews in the *hautes écoles* and the Sorbonne, in theater, literature, and the press, including such luminaries as Henri Bernstein, Sarah Bernhardt, Bernard Lazare, Émile Durkheim, André Spire, Léon Blum. The "Belle Époque" before World War I was their golden age in France.

Profoundly gallicized, they envisaged their religious affiliation as a matter purely of "cultism," subordinate to their broader cultural interests. The Trèveses intermittently attended the Temple Victoire, and Jacques Trèves was Bar Mitzvahed; but otherwise the family avoided clannishness. Many of their friends were Jewish, but tended to be gallicized Alsace-Lorrainers like themselves. Acculturation was after all the mandate of emancipation. "To the Jews as individuals, everything. To the Jews as a nation, nothing!" declared Clermont-Tonnère, one of the early champions of Jewish equality. And the bargain, struck by the General Assembly in 1791 and confirmed afterward by Napoleon's Sanhedrin in 1807, remained the guide to Jewish behavior ever after. Jews would pray together, more than occasionally socialize together, but they no longer segregated themselves by neighborhood, and assuredly did not engage in public affairs as a separate bloc.

To foster the Jews' "integration," Napoleon had established the Consistoire Israélite, an elite assembly of Jewish laymen and rabbis who governed French Jewish religious institutions. During the ensuing century and a half, even following the separation of church and state in

1905, the Consistoire determined the regimen of the nation's synagogues and the rationale for Jewish "cultism" within the framework of Gallic civilization. Its chief rabbis interpreted the Consistoire's nominal Orthodoxy in an increasingly "ameliorist" fashion, somewhat to the left of American Conservatism. The lay members of the Consistoire were models of the integrated French Jew. Its president traditionally was a member of the venerated and munificent Rothschild family, and its other members were drawn from the elite of commerce and the professions. Living in Paris's most exclusive faubourgs and socializing freely with Gentiles, they expressed their residual Jewishness by "civilizing," "gallicizing" their coreligionists, and by demonstrating in their own careers that Jews made exemplary citizens.

This was the mission, too, of the best-known of French Jewish philanthropic organizations, the Alliance Israélite Universelle. Devoted to the education of underprivileged Jewish children outside France, particularly Sephardic Jews in North Africa and the Near East (a traditional arena of French imperialism), the Alliance, under the leadership of Baron de Hirsch and Count Camondo, established a vast network of 188 schools in fifteen countries. These institutions provided superior education and fostered admiration for all that was most "noble, most equitable, most liberal, most human in the genius of our country." Fidelity to the obligations of French citizenship, then, to the French *mission civilisatrice*, was a central motif of the veteran Jewish community.

Little contact existed between that community and some 170,000 East European Jews who arrived in France between 1906 and 1939. Gravitating mainly to Paris, the newcomers by World War II comprised two-fifths of the Jewish population of the capital and approximately half the number of Jews in France altogether. As in other Western countries of refuge, they tended to settle in the poorer metropolitan neighborhoods. Thus, Belleville, comprising essentially the nineteenth and twentieth arrondissements, became Paris's most densely congested Jewish quarter after World War I, followed closely by the *ploetzl* (a Yiddish term for "area of settlement") in the fourth arrondissement. Heavily concentrated in the textile and apparel trades, the East Europeans were the authentic pioneers of France's modern textile industry, as their kinsmen had been earlier in New York's Lower East Side. Much to the dismay of the established Jewish community, the immigrants were Yiddish-speaking and ethnocentric. They shunned the Consistoire in favor of their own makeshift synagogues, their own kashrut commissions and religious schools, and—increasingly—their own ardently left-wing Bundist (Socialist) societies. "We were great snobs toward the East European Jews in those days," admitted Trèves. "They did not seem to fit into our tradition, and for us they were a plain and simple embarrassment."

Ironically, the danger that confronted French Jewry in the 1930s made no distinction between native and East European Jews. Antisemitism was hardly a new phenomenon for either group. Jacques Trèves's father had fought in the streets during the Dreyfus Affair, and remained deeply scarred by the experience. Thirty years later, he still tended to judge friends or politicians by their behavior during that crisis. But it was a closed chapter, he believed. Neither he nor his friends discerned a threat to themselves as Jews in the postwar period, despite the growing class hatreds bred by the depression and by the emergent German-Italian Axis. When antisemitism resurfaced with unexpected virulence during the 1936 Popular Front government of Léon Blum, the leaders of the French Jewish establishment insisted that the hostility was directed at the "boorish" and "noisome" East European newcomers. "The immigrants who arrive among us with their memories and habits of Poland, Romania, and elsewhere," argued Baron Robert de Rothschild, president of the Consistoire of Paris, in a speech of 1934, "retard the assimilation process and help create xenophobic feelings among Frenchmen."

The baron did not entirely misjudge the danger. Although French right-wing antisemitism of the 1930s made few distinctions, the newcomers unquestionably were the more vulnerable to xenophobia. A majority of them had not yet acquired French citizenship, and successive French governments, even the Popular Front, attempted to cope with the depression by imposing employment quotas for foreigners. In the winter of 1938–39, the Daladier cabinet went so far as to authorize the deportation of thousands of East European aliens—among whom Jews were heavily, if not preponderantly, represented. As it launched roundups and arrests of foreigners who participated in strikes, the government also invoked a new law to strip French nationality from naturalized Frenchmen whom it judged "unworthy of the title of French citizen." The warning was clear to those immigrant Jews who presumed to criticize the policy of appeasing Nazi Germany. More ominously, a plan was under discussion to make use of the French territory of Madagascar as a "reservation" for refugee Jews. In 1938, the Daladier cabinet several times alluded to this African island as a possible solution to the "Jewish question." The groundwork for the collaborationist Vichy regime was already well laid.

1940–44: A Shattering of Illusions

In the spring of 1940, the 340,000 Jews in France represented less than 1 percent of the nation's population of 45 million. Of this minority, barely 150,000 were native-born. The aliens included 50,000 refugees from Nazi-dominated Central Europe, and 35,000 who had lately arrived as fugitives from Belgium and Holland. The rest were East Europeans. Whatever the vindictiveness of recent government policy, none of the immigrants dreamed that their lives were hanging in the balance. And this surely was furthest from the minds of native-born Jews like Jacques Trèves and his family.

When the war began, Trèves's father was recalled to the army and placed in command of a military hospital in Brittany. Jacques Trèves was mobilized as a first lieutenant, assigned to a signal corps unit in Alsace. The German blitzkrieg struck in the spring of 1940. In late June, Trèves was wounded in a strafing attack and captured by a German patrol. Afterward, he was placed in a French military hospital under German command. Inspecting Trèves's identity papers, the German chief surgeon noted the religious designation—*Israélite*—and ignored it. The Battle of France was over. Almost immediately, large numbers of Jews fled south to the Vichy-unoccupied-zone, until by the end of 1940 some 195,000 of them were concentrated there. Approximately 120,000 Jews remained in Occupied France. Jacques Trèves was among the latter. A decorated veteran, he was sure he would be safe if he returned home. And, indeed, at the outset he was allowed to resume his civilian career as a telephone engineer for the postal ministry. His brother, Jean-Louis, remained a prisoner of war, but was not singled out for discriminatory treatment. Eventually, Dr. Trèves also journeyed back to Paris and embarked again on his medical practice.

Yet the "legal" basis of their return was soon destroyed as the SS took control of Jewish affairs. In the autumn of 1940, the German administration ordered a census of all Jews, the registration of all Jewish enterprises for purposes of "aryanization" (that is, expropriation). In April 1941, Jews were forbidden to engage in a wide variety of professional and clerical occupations, and soon afterward were obliged to wear the yellow star. Subsequently, they were denied use of public transportation and access to public facilities. Then in May and August 1941, the first roundups of foreign Jews began. Finally, in May 1942, Adolf Eichmann arrived in Paris with a mandate to deport all Jews, regardless of French citizenship. Their initial destination was an internment camp in Drancy, a suburb of Paris. From there they would be packed in cattle cars and shipped directly to Auschwitz.

The Trèveses were not among the victims. Jacques Trèves secretly crossed the demarcation line to the Vichy zone at the end of 1940. Soon afterward, his family joined him. They found lodgings at Auvergne, in a hotel filled with other Jewish fugitives. For a while, the father was allowed a limited practice, exclusively among Jews. The respite was brief. It was the intention of the Pétain-Laval government to restore the country to its original Gallic, authoritarian, "homogeneous" ideals. Jews were the earliest victims of this policy. On July 12, 1940, twelve days after Pétain assumed his role as head of state in Vichy, the government established a commission to strip French citizenship from all recently naturalized inhabitants who were found to be "undesirable." In this fashion, six thousand Jews were immediately deprived of their passports. Other regulations followed quickly, disqualifying Jews and other "undesirable" foreigners from practicing medicine or law. Then, in October, a Statut des Juifs was enacted, defining Jews on racial lines, then excluding them—foreign-born and native alike—from responsible positions in the public services. Jews might hold menial jobs only if they had served in the armed services in World War I or had distinguished themselves in the 1939–40 campaign. It was this provision that initially saved the Trèves family.

The antisemitic legislation gained momentum. An edict of October 7 swept away the Crémieux Decree of 1870, a law that had granted citizenship to the sizable Jewish population of Algeria. Soon afterward, a Commisariat des Affaires Juives was established under a notorious antisemite, Xavier Vallat, to supervise the administration of the Statut des Juifs. A tighter Jewish quota was immediately authorized for businesses and professions. Large numbers of Jewish enterprises and property holdings were "aryanized." It was the "internment" camps, however, established for foreign Jews, that represented one of the darkest chapters of the Vichy period. Some ten thousand individuals were packed into these wretched barracks-communities under appalling conditions. Despite the best efforts of Jewish charities, three thousand persons died there.

In November 1942, following the Allied invasion of North Africa, German troops swept across the demarcation line and extended their occupation to all of France. The SS had already embarked on the Final Solution in the occupied areas. Now, under Hitler's personal order of December 10, the deportation campaign was to be extended to the entire country. As in the occupied zone, roundups and deportations no longer discriminated between native and foreign-born Jews. Moreover, the Vichy authorities cooperated as fully in these measures as had the local police in Occupied France. They had already prepared a detailed census of Jews for their dragnet. In 1942, some 43,500 Jews were deported to the occupied zone. During 1943–44, another 33,500 Jews were shipped on to Drancy—and Auschwitz.

As it happened, February 1943 proved to be a turning point in German-Vichy relations. In that month Pierre Laval, the Vichy vice-president, had agreed to conscript several hundred thousand young Frenchmen for labor in Germany. This act of collaboration was universally detested, and soon undermined public cooperation in other pro-Nazi measures—even in the roundup of Jews. The Germans henceforth were obliged to move on their own. The shipments to Drancy picked up again in the summer of 1943. There were no exemptions: neither citizens, nor former POWs, nor military veterans. The only hope for Jews was to hide or escape. But it had become a more realistic hope, due to public disaffection. A key factor in saving Jews unquestionably was the effort of Jewish organizations themselves. One of these was the Joint, which until the German occupation of the Vichy zone continued to pour in millions of dollars to local Jewish agencies and rescue groups. Among the latter were the Éclaireurs Israélites (the Jewish branch of the French Scout movement), the Young Zionists, the Organisation Juive de Combat (the Jewish branch of the French underground). These and other groups fabricated identity papers, hid children, smuggled Jews into Switzerland, Spain, or areas of Italian military occupation.

Yet while some Jews continued to escape with the help of these organizations, there were numerous instances of local compassion, particularly among the French clergy. The Trèveses were among those who managed to evade the dragnet in the Vichy zone with the help of non-Jewish friends, who secured them false identity papers. Jacques Trèves was not oblivious of the debt he owed these Gentiles. Even so, bitterly recalling the collaborationist record of Vichy, he could not refrain from observing later that "what was extraordinary was not that so many Jews perished, but that the majority survived." It was an apt evaluation. By the summer of 1944, some 74,000 Jews had been deported from France to the killing centers of Poland. A third of this number were French citizens, the rest were foreign refugees. Another 14,000 Jews died in Occupied and Vichy France as a consequence of detention camp conditions or of spot executions. Of the prewar Jewish population of 340,000, a total of 90,000 perished.

A Welcome Renewed

Following the liberation in the summer of 1944, Trèves and his family returned to their apartment in Paris. Unlike most Jewish dwellings, it had not been confiscated and sold. A devoted maid had remained there, claiming it as her own. Trèves's father instantly resumed his practice, with a senior appointment to a government hospital. Trèves himself was asked to rejoin the army, and was given command of communications for an infantry division. At the time of his discharge in 1947, he had achieved the rank of lieutenant colonel. In October of the same year, he married Francine Shreiber. Sharing his Alsatian Jewish origins, she was the daughter of a physician, a friend of Trèves's father (and a second cousin of the renowned journalist Jean-Jacques Servan-Shreiber). Grand Rabbi Jacob Kaplan presided at the nuptials in the Temple Victoire. Afterward, Trèves advanced rapidly in the postal ministry. Within three years, he was placed in charge of the entire telephone system of France and Algeria. Following the birth of their son and daughter, the family moved to a handsome apartment on Boulevard Émile Lanzière. For Trèves, faith in his native land had been revindicated.

So, too, apparently, was it for other survivors. With sublime disregard of the recent Vichy epoch, the eminent French Jewish writer Edmond Fleg expressed his renewed optimism in 1945: "Antisemitism as a doctrine and as a social attitude has never taken root in France. Had the Germans not occupied France during those tragic years, we should never have seen a Jewish Statute. Now, after their sinister presence, France is in the process of again becoming what she always has been since the French Revolution, the least antisemitic country in Europe."

If Fleg's account of the past was blindered, his prognosis for the future was prescient. The provisional government was determined to purge the nation of its wartime shame. With a relentlessness that Vichy itself could not have surpassed, it launched into a long series of war crimes trials, prosecuting and convicting thousands of collaborators. One feature of this exorcism was the annulment by decree of all the antisemitic laws of the Vichy regime. Jews who had been dismissed from government service by Vichy were immediately reinstated. Confiscated Jewish property was expeditiously returned. Within two years after the liberation, nearly all French Jewish citizens were back in their homes and business premises. Nonetheless, tens of thousands of displaced persons and former non-citizens remained almost totally without means; for a second component of the national exorcism was the virtual carte blanche extended to Jewish immigrants. Fully 55,000 Jewish DPs were to avail themselves of the opportunity, raising the postwar Jewish population to approximately 300,000 by 1951.

The care, lodging, and rehabilitation of many of these refugees soon became a vast burden. The government could hardly bear it alone; France was all but bankrupt in the first years after the war. Moreover, the former refugees were not yet French citizens, and thus were ineligible in any case for government assistance. The task of caring for them was taken on largely by the Jewish welfare services, most of these receiving their principal support from American Jewry—from the Joint. Over a decade passed before French Jews were able to assume a major share of their welfare expenditures. Even so, by the early 1950s the nation's circumstances began to improve. In 1954, France received its proportion of German reparations, a treaty payoff of DM 1 billion, much of which the government subsequently disbursed to victims of Nazi oppression. More important, the national economy itself was reviving, and the Jewish population substantially shared in the recovery.

France's residue of antisemitism had not been entirely expunged. One issue that kept it alive among rightist, clerical groups was the disposition of Jewish children who had been left in the care of Christian families during the Nazi occupation. This painful question surfaced in various countries, but nowhere in Western Europe did it flare up more controversially. A widely publicized case was that of the Finaly children. Immediately after the Anschluss in 1938, Dr. Fritz Finaly and his wife fled Austria for France and settled in Grenoble. Their sons, Robert and Gerald, were born in 1941 and 1942. With the German conquest of France, the Finalys placed their children in a Catholic school. In February 1944, both parents were deported, never to return. Friends arranged for the children to be moved to another Catholic institution, and eventually they were entrusted to Antoinette Brun, director of the municipal nursery of Grenoble. Mlle Brun also cared for eight other Jewish children, whom she later returned to their parents. But the Finaly youngsters she attempted to keep, despite the efforts of Dr. Finaly's three surviving sisters to obtain custody over them. By 1948, the aunts resorted to legal proceedings. The case dragged on until 1952, when the appeals court of Grenoble confirmed the decision for the children to be turned over to one of the aunts, Mrs. Hedwigge Rossner, a citizen of Israel. Still Mlle Brun refused to give up the boys, and in February 1953 she spirited them across the Pyrenees to Spain, where all trace of them was lost.

At this point, the arrest of Mlle Brun, of an abbess of the Order of Notre-Dame de Sion, and of several Basque priests who had been accomplices to the kidnapping, transformed the Finaly affair into a cause célèbre. Public opinion was sharply divided. Mlle Brun's supporters alluded to her heroism in saving Robert and Gerald Finaly, and denounced "Jewish ingratitude." She had become the children's "true mother," the argument went, more so than a strange aunt who had never seen them and who now sought to take them away from France. Arguments—sentimental, nationalist, legalistic—filled thousands of columns in newspapers and magazines. Then a much more critical issue developed. Many Frenchmen supported the argument of *La Croix,* the official organ of the Catholic Church in France, that "the church is a perfect society that has authority over those who have become its members by baptism." Guy de Rothschild, president of the Consistoire Israélite Centrale, commented sharply on "ideological kidnappings," and intimated that the church itself must have been involved. Was this not another Mortara Affair (the notorious abduction of a Roman Jewish child a century earlier)? Hereupon, alarmed by the upsurge of anticlerical passions, Cardinal Gerlier, primate of Gaul, entered into negotiations with Grand Rabbi Kaplan and with representatives of the Finaly family. In March 1953, an agreement was reached. The children would be brought back without police intervention, and all proceedings against the abductors would be dropped by the Finaly family.

Even then, additional months passed before Basque priests returned the boys to France, where they were conveyed to the temporary custody of a French Jewish leader, André Weil. The church-state controversy raged on. In late summer of 1953, however, the children's aunt, Mrs. Rossner, decided their future by summarily taking them off to Israel. All charges and countercharges eventually were dropped, and the Finaly affair guttered out. Yet its impact on French Jews was lasting. Whatever their individual backgrounds, they had been united on the Finaly issue as on no other since the liberation. It had reminded many of them that their security, ostensibly assured after the Dreyfus Affair, then horrifyingly betrayed during the Occupation and Vichy, was still not guaranteed, even by the strenuous liberalism of the postwar government.

Indeed, antisemitism remained quite vocal among France's traditionally xenophobic petite bourgeoisie. Pierre Poujade spoke for this group. A small-town shopkeeper, Poujade first captured public attention in 1953 when he mobilized a group of colleagues to resist the government's tax collectors. Afterward, he organized a national Association for the Defense of Shopkeepers and Artisans, and several months before the 1956 elections he converted his movement into a party and entered candidates in every district. Attacking the "Jewish magnates" and "Israelite potentates of the great stores who wish to ruin small commerce," the Poujadists exploited the combination of lower-middle-class frustration and insularity, winning more than fifty seats in the National Assembly. Yet, once Poujadism reached the legislature, it was almost immediately exposed as politically mindless and racked by defection and dissension. Poujade's speeches and press releases continued to hammer away at Jewish "economic parasitism," but within a year failed any longer to evoke national resonance. Even more decisive in blunting the threat of racism was the nation's flourishing economy. Linked with the painful memory of the Occupation-Vichy epoch, the resurgence of postwar France offered little nourishment to a serious antisemitic movement.

By the mid-1950s, the Jews of France were satisfied that they had achieved optimal political security and a new plateau of economic opportunity. There was hardly an area of public life in which they were not winning distinction. Among widely respected figures of the 1950s and 1960s were the political commentator Raymond Aron and his brother Robert, a historian and essayist; the sociologist Georges Friedmann; the economist Robert Mosse; the novelists Joseph Kessel (member of the French Academy) and four postwar winners of the Prix Goncourt—Anna Langfus, Roger Ikor, Romain Gary, and André Schwartz-Bart. As in other Western nations, Jews were prominent in theater and cinema. Active in all phases of the economy, from the textile industry to heavy steel and machinery (the automobile manufacturer André-Gustave Citroën was a Jew, as was Marcel Dassault, chairman of France's leading military aircraft combine), Jews similarly played their traditional role in high finance. The Rothschilds continued to rank as the largest of the nation's private bankers. Their investments extended from the Peugeot automobile company to Club Méditerranée.

The combination of acceptance and eminence was particularly striking in politics. Jews were everywhere represented, except in the far right. René Mayer served briefly as premier of a Socialist coalition government in 1953, even as Daniel Mayer (no relation) succeeded Guy Mollet as secretary-general of the Socialist Party. Jules Moch served as minister of the interior in a number of Socialist governments. Charles Lussy was president of the Socialist bloc in the Chamber of Deputies. Michel Debré, the converted son of Jewish parents, served as premier in the de Gaulle government of 1958. Rarely did the Jewishness of these figures evoke special comment in the French press, not even during the last years of the Fourth Republic, when a Jewish premier, Pierre Mendès-France, became the nation's most conspicuous figure.

The descendant of a Sephardic family that had lived in France since the seventeenth century, the son and grandson of decorated war heroes, Mendès-France had been trained in the law. He was elected to parliament in 1932 and served until the outbreak of the war. Enlisting then as an air force officer, he escaped Nazi capture in 1940 by making his way to North Africa. Although he was arrested and imprisoned by the Vichy regime in Morocco for desertion, he escaped again, this time reaching England, where he joined the Free French air force. For the next two years, he flew as a bombardier in raids over Europe. In September 1944, following liberation, he served briefly as minister of national economy in the provisional government, then took his former seat in the Chamber. In those years, Mendès-France rose swiftly to the leadership of the "progressive" wing of the Socialist Party, and in that capacity he was chosen premier in 1954.

Forty-seven years old, trim, dark, and square-jawed, Mendès-France was a vigorously independent man who touted milk in a land of wine-drinkers. With a wide public following, and at the height of his powers, the new premier introduced a disciplined program of Keynesian reforms that succeeded in reactivating his nation's sluggish economy. Yet his most impressive success was in negotiating an end to the Indochina War, a conflict that had raged for eight years and taken a heavy toll of France's manpower and wealth. Operating under a tight deadline at the Geneva Peace Conference, Mendès-France managed against all odds to formulate the compromise of a de facto division of Vietnam into Communist and non-Communist sectors, thus permitting a face-saving French withdrawal from the Indochinese quagmire. Earlier, he had negotiated acceptable terms for withdrawal from Morocco and Tunisia. By these accomplishments, Mendès-France won the respect of every major political group in the nation. A virtual Mendèsist cult soon developed in France. As it happened, this popularity failed to ensure the survival of his parliamentary majority in the tumultuous world of French politics. After seven months, the Socialist Party split into factions, and he left the premiership. Yet Mendès-France remained a beloved national figure, a symbol of all that was honorable in the French Socialist tradition.

If the nation's acceptance of Jews approached philosemitism, part of the reason could be ascribed to widespread admiration of Israel, whose growing prowess conceivably assuaged France's sense of guilt for the Vichy deportations. By the mid-1950s, too, Frenchmen and Israelis faced a common enemy in Gamal Abd al-Nasser. The Egyptian president was launched upon a campaign of subversion equally against the French presence in Algeria and the Israeli presence as an independent state in the Middle East. The alliance eventually was cemented in October 1956, during the Franco-Israeli military collaboration in the Sinai-Suez War. For nearly a decade after that successful venture, both nations remained linked in a tight, mutually supportive friendship. Serving as Israel's diplomatic mentor and principal source of weapons, the French expressed their friendship to the Jewish state by other gestures at home. An influential pro-Israel bloc developed in the Chamber of Deputies. The Alliance France-Israël included in its membership the nation's most respected political and cultural leaders. There could be little doubt that much of this friendship for "our gallant little ally" subliminally influenced the popular attitude toward Jews altogether. Even French rightists (among the strongest advocates of the Israeli partnership) found it difficult to make distinctions between *Israéliens* and *Israélites*, between the Jews of Israel and the Jews of France.

If the era between the Dreyfus Affair and World War I was known as the "golden age" of French Jewry, so the decade and a half following World War II might have been regarded as a "second golden age," a period when the Jewish question once again became a weathervane of France's reconfirmed liberalism. Perhaps an insight into this renewal of equality and security was provided by the nearly forty Parisian streets, avenues, and squares named for Jews, many of them figures—like Heine, Spinoza, or Mendelssohn—who had not themselves been French citizens, but who had lived or died in Paris. Engraved in stone and brass, the Jewish presence this time manifestly was intended to be permanent.

The Survival of Noblesse Oblige

Until the nationalization measures inaugurated by the Mitterrand government in the early 1980s, the Rothschild Bank remained the largest private financial institution of its kind in France. Its headquarters on rue Laffitte was an austerely modern eight-story building of steel and glass. Alain de Rothschild greeted me cordially in his penthouse office on the top floor. He was a striking figure, gray hair framing a narrow, cleanly sculpted face. Tall, slim, casually dressed in sport jacket and slacks, he appeared much younger than his seventy-two years. To my pleased surprise, he addressed me in perfect English. "I had an English nanny," he explained. "My brother and I were raised like little British lords. My father [Robert de Rothschild, nephew of the famed Edmond] really didn't have much time for the children. Too busy with his public responsibilities—the Consistoire and all that."

It was the family tradition. The Paris branch had been established in 1812 by James, youngest of the five sons whom Meyer Amschel Rothschild dispatched from the Frankfurt ghetto to the principal capitals of Europe. Granted the patent of baron in 1822, James became an important figure in the world of international finance. His bank by then had become the most powerful of the *hautes banques,* the small group of private institutions whose capital was generated by a single family or by intimate associates, hidden from public scrutiny, dealing mainly with governments. The Rothschild Bank's capital in fact was many times that of the Bank of France. James died in 1868 and was succeeded as chairman of the Paris branch by his eldest son, Alphonse. With his brothers Gustave and Edmond, Alphonse de Rothschild built railroads, served as a director of the Bank of France, and helped guarantee the staggering indemnity imposed on the nation by Germany in 1871. The three brothers also fitted easily into French high society, for they were thoroughly Parisian and polished.

At the same time, the Rothschilds maintained a deep commitment to French Jewry. Raised in a home faithful to Jewish practices, they accepted the leadership of the Jewish community in the tradition of noblesse oblige, and were generous with their time and money. The barons themselves were chairmen of at least four Jewish organizations, their wives of three out of six women's Jewish charitable committees. Rothschild patronage was instrumental in building the Temple Victoire, in founding the Société des Études Juives in 1879, in establishing the Jewish hospital, old age home, orphanage, primary school, and in providing innumerable scholarships. But the family's most important leadership role was played in the Consistoire Israélite, the "government" of the Jewish religious establishment. Alphonse served as president of the Consistoire Centrale, his brother Gustave as president of the Consistoire de Paris. In this capacity, the Rothschilds traditionally made good the organization's deficits. Indeed, their munificence on behalf of Jewish causes was so far-reaching that French Jews became accustomed to sparing themselves effort or expense of their own. The tradition continued through the 1920s and 1930s, a process known as the "Rothschildization" of French Judaism. Alain learned it from his father, Robert, a Jew so proudly identified that he had challenged a man to a duel in the period of the Dreyfus Affair. "We were no longer strictly observant," Alain recalled, "but we were Bar Mitzvahed, recited Hebrew prayers each night. Above all, we knew what our duty was."

They understood their duty no less as Frenchmen. Alain and his brother Elie were raised on stories of French military prowess. Both brothers were called up in September 1939, and assigned to the Maginot Line. It was there that they were captured during the German breakthrough in the late spring of 1940. Their cousin Guy de Rothschild escaped at Dunkirk, and eventually rejoined the Free French. Another family member, Philippe de Rothschild, fled to Morocco, was imprisoned with Mendès-France, then escaped and reached England, to fight again. Alain de Rothschild meanwhile was taken off to a POW camp in Germany. His identity was swiftly determined by his captors, but he was treated correctly. Rather, it was his French fellow officers who made it plain that a Jew was unwanted in their quarters. The memory of the experience caused him pain for decades afterward. At war's end, repatriated to France, Alain de Rothschild was determined— "militantly determined"—to serve the cause of the Jews. Upon his father's death, he accepted the presidency of the Consistoire Centrale as a matter of family obligation. In ensuing years, he worked hard to justify his incumbency.

There was little choice. The Holocaust had ravaged any alternative Jewish leadership. Vichy's willingness to sacrifice noncitizens first doomed the community of East European immigrants and their offspring. Not more than 35,000 of the nearly 120,000 immigrant Jews who had inhabited Paris in 1939 returned from the death camps or from other countries. The ideologies—Zionist, Yiddishist, pluralist—that had been fostered by the immigrant community failed to revive initially in the postwar period. Those who survived in greatest numbers were the veteran Jewish citizens. Ironically, their leaders remained much less dejudaized than native middle-class Jews, for their Judaism was aristocratic and patriarchal. "As a Rothschild," Alain explained, "I owed it to the family." Accordingly, the "establishment" organizations were the first to revive—the Consistoire and the Alliance Israélite Universelle. These two pillars of prewar Jewish communal life were joined in turn by the Conseil Représentatif des Israélites de France. Founded in the Vichy zone in 1943 by refugee members of the Jewish old guard, the CRIF was envisaged as spokesman for all the principal surviving organs of French Jewry. During the liberation period, it was the CRIF, in liaison with the Alliance and the French section of the World Jewish Congress, that defended Jewish rights, and that later became the watchdog of Jewish restitution. Typically, Alain de Rothschild was offered, and accepted, its presidency.

Under his leadership, the CRIF quite fair-mindedly attempted to co-opt both the immigrant and the nativized groups to formulate a common Jewish position in dealing with the government. This goal was not always manageable. By the 1950s the influx of displaced persons and later European refugees had swollen the immigrant population to approximately 60 percent of French Jewry. Impoverished, still disoriented to French life, many of these survivors had been nurtured on militant leftist, even Communist, ideologies. Their aggressive tactics in the struggle to win control of the CRIF nearly destroyed this roof organization. It was not until the period of the Stalinist Doctors' Plot in 1953 that the Communists were publicly discredited, and grudgingly abandoned their efforts to dominate the affairs of the CRIF.

It was not ideological dissent alone that limited the efforts of the Consistoire and the CRIF to resuscitate the Jewish community. Despite France's gradual economic revival, French Jewish institutions continued for many years to suffer from an acute shortage of funds. This time, the Rothschilds could not make up the deficits; their own fortunes were still too depleted or disorganized. Moreover, French citizens were notoriously reluctant to pay their taxes, and French Jews tended to adopt this tradition in their own communal affairs. As elsewhere in Europe, then, the burden of rehabilitation fell mainly on American Jews—that is, upon the Joint. But in this case, the Joint's director in Europe, Dr. Joseph Schwartz, was determined that French Jewry make use of American largess with maximum efficiency, and then begin to raise additional funds on its own. The precedent had been set by the United States government itself, after all, which had tendered Marshall Plan aid on condition that the various European nations first rationalize their economics.

Schwartz's challenge was met. In 1949, the French Jewish leadership established a central organization for the solicitation and distribution of funds. Known as Fonds Social Juif Unifié, it was akin to the federations that had long been central to American Jewish life. Typically, the Fonds Social's first president was Elie de Rothschild, Alain's brother. Its board of directors was drawn from the prewar paladins of industry, commerce, banking, and academia. In fact, these were capable individuals. They ensured that Joint money henceforth was spent rationally and equitably, with appropriate shares going to a wide variety of Jewish schools, hospitals, orphan homes—as well as to the Alliance and Consistoire themselves. A year later, the Fonds Social launched its own fund-raising drive. The proceeds initially were less than impressive, and as late as 1952 the Joint was still underwriting more than half of Jewish communal expenditures. Even so, French Jewry at least had developed a structure for collection and distribution, and in the next few years the gap between the amounts raised and spent would narrow dramatically.

By 1955, the most debilitating economic problems created by the war apparently had been surmounted. Yet religious and cultural revival came far more slowly. Despite the Joint's transfusions, as late as the mid-1950s barely twenty-five synagogues were functioning throughout France. The Consistoire at first displayed little initiative or imagination in attracting the more recent European immigrants, or in providing for their specialized religious needs. Rather, the typical consistorial rabbi envisaged himself as an official rather than as a spiritual leader of his synagogue. Outside the domain of ritual and ceremony, his influence was extremely limited. And in any case, there were not many rabbis left—only twenty-one of the sixty who had belonged to the Consistoire in 1939.

Similarly, in the first decade after the liberation, French Jewry failed to develop an extensive network of Jewish day schools or even afternoon schools. In Paris and its suburbs, the total number of students attending the thrice-weekly afternoon synagogue classes in 1955 was not more than 2,400, in a local Jewish population of 145,000. One Jewish primary school, and two secondary schools operated in the capital. In the provinces, the ratio was even lower. The single exception was Alsace, where state funding continued to be provided for synagogues and day schools (church and state had not been separated here), and where a lively Jewish cultural tradition survived. Otherwise, religious and cultural fervor had died out among the main body of French Jewry. The Rabbinical School of France, established in the previous century, was attended by fewer than a dozen students, and was all but moribund.

Indeed, no central agency of any kind for Jewish cultural activity existed in the country. The Alliance maintained a Jewish library close by Paris's clamorous Montmartre. The handful of rather second-rate Yiddish dailies enjoyed a combined circulation of barely fifteen thousand. Following the liberation, a number of Jewish periodicals appeared, disappeared, and reappeared. In the mid-1950s, one of these was *Évidences*—a French version of the American *Commentary*—which was published by the Paris office of the American Jewish Committee; and a Zionist bimonthly, *La Terre Retrouvée*. Both were of good quality. The Consistoire put out a little semimonthly magazine, *Le Journal de la Communauté*, chiefly filled with notices of religious holidays, Bar Mitzvahs, and marriages. A similar gazette was published in Strasbourg. There existed no French Jewish publishing house.

A small group of French Jewish writers continued to produce. They spanned three generations. Eminent among them in the early-1950s were the "patriarchs," Edmond Fleg, André Spire, and Henri Herz, all poets. In the second generation were Armand Lunel, a novelist from Provence; Elian Finberg, born in Palestine but writing in French; and Albert Cohen, novelist and poet. Finally, a handful of newcomers included Emmanuel Seydoux, a poet; David Scheinbart, André Schwartz-Bart, and Elie Wiesel, the latter two foreign-born Holocaust survivors; and Arnold Mandel, an old-line French Jew and the group's most respected novelist. It was a tiny constellation, and within a few years the "patriarchs" would be gone. Even Zionism failed as a rejuvenating intellectual force. By the mid-1950s, the various Zionist groups were concentrating almost exclusively on fund-raising for Israel. These efforts were by no means negligible. The Fédération Sioniste experienced a significant revival after the birth of Israel. Following the Sinai-Suez campaign in 1956, it raised the impressive sum (for France) of $1,125,000. Nevertheless, during the first postwar decade, Zionism as a cultural influence remained weaker in France than in any other Western European country.

Edmond Fleg's optimism notwithstanding, it was apparent by then that the Occupation-Vichy experience had inflicted a deep psychic wound that only slowly, even belatedly, was working its way through French Jewry—natives and immigrants alike. Evidence of this trauma could be seen in an upsurge of conversions and name changes during the late 1940s and early 1950s. The former was a new phenomenon. Until the war, acculturation had been a natural, spontaneous process rather than a deliberate attempt to "pass." In the framework of prewar French secularism, there had been little need for Jews to make any concessions to Christianity. Following the liberation, however, an acute Jewish anxiety emerged. Once the enduring seriousness of their Jewish identity was plain to French Jews, a substantial minority reacted by seeking escape. The wave of conversions to Catholicism was particularly evident in the smaller cities and towns of the provinces, where no Jew could hide his Jewishness. In all, as many as fifteen thousand French Jews converted after 1945. The more common alternative was that of "administrative disidentification," the use of a long-standing French law that permitted citizens of foreign origin to gallicize their names. Before the war, thousands of Jews had availed themselves of this right. Afterward, the numbers increased tenfold.

Arnold Mandel, the distinguished novelist-essayist, pungently summarized the condition of French Jewry. Most of the Jewish intellectuals of France who strained their wits trying to rediscover Judaism were "explorers without maps or compasses," he argued. Before Hitler, there had been an authentic German Jewish culture, at once genuinely German and genuinely Jewish. As Mandel observed, there had never been a comparable Franco-Jewish culture. "France, the motherland of emancipation, accepted the Jew only by making an abstraction of his Jewishness." Currently, Zionism was much more important than Judaism as a movement or an ideology—"to the extent that it is important at all."

In Mandel's view, unless some vital new development appeared, there existed a serious possibility of "the disappearance of organic Judaism in France, and its survival [mainly] in the form of an 'examination of conscience' by individuals." It was an incisive appraisal. If French Jewry in large measure had been a self-deluded population before the war, afterward it had become a minority so palpably lacking in communal élan that it hovered at the threshold of cultural exhaustion.

V

A Demographic Revolution: France

The Maghreb Hinterland

In the first decade after liberation, an infusion of immigrants from North Africa and the Middle East launched a far-reaching change in the ethnic composition of French Jewry. Some 35,000 of the newcomers arrived from Syria, Egypt, and Turkey, and from the Maghreb, France's vast North African empire. As late as 1948, approximately 500,000 Jews were living in French North Africa. Fully 285,000 of them were concentrated in Morocco. Algeria accounted for another 135,000, and Tunisia for an estimated 105,000. Most traced their ancestry to Berber tribesmen who had been converted to Judaism nearly a millennium before, and whose vernacular, Judéo-Berber, afterward remained distinct from that of their Moslem neighbors. A smaller number were Sephardim, descendants of Spanish Jews; and some of these maintained their own Ladino dialect.

Among the North African Jews, the Moroccans were by far the most deprived, economically and culturally. Reduced to near-pariah degradation, they lived in wretched ghettos that frequently were swept by epidemics and by native mobs. They enjoyed virtually no political rights. To be sure, functioning by tradition within a *millet*—quasi-autonomous—regime of their own, they were permitted to adjudicate their personal and communal affairs before their own rabbinical courts. The establishment of the French protectorate in 1912 assured them of more extensive physical security and even a degree of economic improvement. But as late as 1948, perhaps half the Moroccan Jewish working population survived as peddlers and artisans, the rest as small shopkeepers, clerks, or manual laborers. Except for a handful of affluent families, urban Jews by and large continued to live in their own dis-

...ll vulnerable to disease and to occasional outbursts of local ...violence.

...n the other hand, their concentration in Marrakech, Casablanca, and Fez provided them with certain educational advantages. Their children had access to Alliance Israélite Universelle schools, which successive French governments discreetly supported as effective disseminators of French culture. By 1939, forty-five Alliance schools in Morocco educated fully a third of all Jewish children. Although the majority still received a more parochial Hebrew and talmudic schooling, the beacon of French culture shone before their eyes too; for they understood well that it was the protection and tolerance of the French that enabled them to maintain their religious and cultural traditions in relative peace. The Vichy interregnum clearly represented a painful setback to Moroccan Jewry, but at least it was a brief one. The economic hardships of the postwar period endured somewhat longer. During the latter 1940s and early 1950s, the Joint was obliged to provide relief for tens of thousands of Moroccan Jews.

Yet the principal threat to Moroccan Jewry emerged from two major political changes. The first was the establishment of Israel and the Palestine war of 1948, which unleashed Moslem pogroms. The worst of the violence was felt in neighboring Libya, where a chain reaction of attacks eventually caused the flight of 32,000 Jews to Israel and Italy during the ensuing years. In Morocco itself, however, crowds of Berber hooligans invaded the Jewish sector of Oujda in June 1948, massacring scores of inhabitants, wounding more than a hundred others, and pillaging shops and homes. This assault, too, touched off a wave of emigration to Israel, mainly by the poorest and most devout; by 1952, approximately 70,000 Jews had departed. The second political development was the emergence of a fiery Moroccan nationalism. In the early 1950s, a mounting series of riots and demonstrations against the French protectorate brought the country to the verge of revolution; and in 1954 France's Prime Minister Mendès-France committed his government to Moroccan independence within two years. The prospect of Berber rule deeply unsettled Morocco's remaining Jewish population. It was at this point that Gerhart Riegner and several of his colleagues in the World Jewish Congress succeeded in establishing contact with the Moroccan Istiqlal—nationalist—leadership. A series of clandestine discussions followed in Europe. Eager for Jewish support abroad, the Berber spokesmen guaranteed their Jewish "brothers" full constitutional rights

and political security in a free Morocco, as well as the right to emigrate
to Israel or France.

Indeed, upon achieving independence in 1956, the new Moroccan
regime honored its promise. Proclaiming complete equality for all inhabitants, the government included a Jew in its first cabinet, and continued to protect Jewish interests. It was economic, not political, failure
that determined the Jews' course. With the loss of French capital and
industry, the nation was reduced to near-bankruptcy. The likelihood of
economic collapse was particularly frightening to those Jews who remained, most of them now middle-level or small businessmen. Even
before the end of the French protectorate, some 104,000 Jews had left
the country, a majority of them settling in Israel. Now, during the first
ten months of Moroccan independence, another 33,000 Jews left the
country. This time, their goal was almost exclusively France. The
newer émigrés were not only petite bourgeoisie. Many came from the
remaining pockets of ghetto peddlers and artisans. In recent years, they
had received discouraging accounts of economic hardships and second-
class status from their kin in Israel.

The Moroccan government meanwhile continued to assure its remaining Jewish citizens of their security, and to recruit additional Jews
into the government. In 1967, during the Six-Day War, King Hassan
ordered the arrest and prosecution of anyone engaged in anti-Jewish
violence or propaganda. Yet emigration quietly continued throughout
the 1960s and early 1970s, and the government made no serious effort
to restrict it. By 1984, the Moroccan Jewish population had declined
from 285,000 to 17,000. Although 190,000 of these emigrants had departed for Israel, a substantial minority, approximately 65,000, settled
in France, where they joined some 10,000 kinsmen who had preceded
them before World War II, or who had re-emigrated there from Israel.

Tunisia: The Jews of Enterprise

The growing Moroccan enclave in France was augmented by other
Jews from the Maghreb. One of them was Ya'akov (Richard) Uzan.
When interviewed by the author in 1981, Uzan operated a small kosher
restaurant on Paris's rue Ambroise-Thomas. He was a chunky man in
his late thirties, his goatee nicely embellishing a delicate face. His
French was crystalline, each syllable bitten off with impeccable clarity.
Surely, most of his life was spent in France? "Just the opposite," he

replied, beaming. In fact, he had been born and reared in Tunis. His grandfather, Yosef Uzan, had been a ritual slaughterer, had dressed in the native djellaba and spoken Judéo-Berber. Uzan's father, Isak, wore European clothing, but remained punctiliously Orthodox. Ya'akov himself grew up in Bellical, a mixed Berber-Jewish residential quarter. Relations between the two peoples were amicable enough, although no Jew ever was a guest in a Moslem home, nor a Moslem in a Jewish home. (Social contacts with the French were unthinkable.) It was a tolerable existence. Tunisia, with its long Mediterranean coastline and temperate climate, was a kind of North African Switzerland. Of its 3,500,000 inhabitants at the end of the war, some 105,000 were Jews; and like Uzan, fully 70 percent of these lived in Tunis. Nearly half earned their—adequate—livelihoods as workers, the rest as small shopkeepers and clerks.

Under the French protectorate, the Jews of Tunisia enjoyed physical security and civil equality. Except for some 17,000 Jews who had served in the French army, Paris did not grant the Tunisians French citizenship en bloc, as it did the Jews of Algeria. Otherwise, as in Morocco, the sultan's government respected the autonomy of the Jewish community and even contributed financially to Jewish communal institutions. Jewish needs also were covered by various local and international organizations, including the Joint, ORT (the Organization for Rehabilitation and Training), the Jewish Agency, and of course the Alliance. Ya'akov Uzan attended an Alliance school until the age of fourteen. Although he and his brothers studied at a parochial afternoon school, observed a kosher diet and the major Jewish holidays, their ties to Judaism were becoming increasingly superficial. Completing his secondary education in a French lycée, and working in his uncle's sporting goods shop, young Uzan shared his friends' admiration for French civilization. He accepted Zionism, of course, but essentially as an abstraction. Some 18,000 Tunisian Jews had departed for Israel between 1948 and 1953; yet these were essentially poor and backward Jews from the *bled*, the Moslem interior. Few urban Jews were interested in joining them. By 1952, letters from kinsmen in Israel reinforced the familiar litany of border dangers, of enforced relocation to agricultural settlements, of inferior economic and social status.

In the following years, tensions mounted between the Tunisian Neo-Destour nationalists and the French administration. The sequence of bombings and retaliations increased in scope and ferocity. The Jews were deeply unsettled. They maintained friendly enough relations with both sides (far more than in Morocco); yet their businesses were hard hit by the months of strikes, violence, and mass arrests. Privately, the nationalist leaders assured their Jewish contacts that an independent Tunisia would guarantee equality for all citizens. Habib Bourguiba, leader of the Neo-Destour Party, endorsed this commitment personally. Many Jews were prepared to accept it. As late as 1954, there existed no particular antipathy toward them among the population at large. Indeed, numbers of Jews like the Uzan family supported the Neo-Destour in its struggle for self-rule. In 1956, when Tunisia finally was granted its independence, Ya'akov Uzan and several of his Jewish friends joined in the street celebrations, locking arms with Moslem acquaintances. Jewish security was unaffected at first. Most of the civil service remained French, and French troops stayed on in the crucial ports and bases of the country. Public order was maintained. Several Jews held prominent positions in the cabinet and public administration, and others were influential journalists. Jews were among Prime Minister (later President) Bourguiba's closest friends and associates. In every respect, they enjoyed identical civil and political rights with Moslems, and the government continued partially to subsidize Jewish communal activities.

Even so, Jews were concerned about their economic stability under a Moslem regime. In 1955, on the eve of independence, the nation's Jewish population totaled approximately 90,000. By 1963, it had fallen to 60,000. As in Morocco, poorer and more devout Jews had left earlier for Israel. The largest numbers of those departing now settled in France. Although a majority still remained in Tunisia, their ambivalence was abruptly resolved by a shattering military confrontation between the Tunisians and the French. Early in 1962, responding to nationalist pressures, President Bourguiba decided to reclaim the port and arsenal of Bizerte, facilities that had been reserved to France by earlier treaty agreement. When he ordered his troops into the protected area, however, they were annihilated. An orgy of strikes and rioting then followed, and soon the nation's economy was all but paralyzed.

For the Jews, caught in this chauvinist upheaval, it was not the time to risk further delay. Within the following year, their remaining population was halved. Afterward, a steady, if slower, exodus continued. It was influenced both by the government's increasingly militant pro-Arab stance on the Israel issue and by its shift toward domestic socialism.

The cabinet had already declared a state monopoly in sugar, coffee, tea, fruits, grain, hides, and cattle. Thousands of Jewish businessmen accordingly witnessed the elimination of their occupations. It was only a question of time, most believed, before they were liquidated altogether as a commercial element. Departure now would mean the abandonment of homes and businesses—the transfer of capital abroad had recently been disallowed—but younger Jews were unwilling to procrastinate. With or without resources, they made for the harbors and embarked for France. Later, their parents followed. By 1965, some 80,000 Tunisian Jews were living in France. Less than 8,000 remained behind.

It was in 1965 that the Uzans departed as a family. Sensing that their little sporting goods shop was a closed chapter, they simply left the key in the door of their flat and walked out. With them they took their suitcases, their steamship tickets, and a total of three thousand French francs. Nothing more was permitted. As father, mother, four brothers and sisters, one daughter-in-law, and four children prepared to climb into the caravan of awaiting taxis, several of their Moslem neighbors begged them to stay. "Don't go, Isak," they pleaded with the father. "There's no reason for you to leave."

"It's not because of you," he replied, tears in his eyes. "You are my brothers."

"You belong here with us," insisted Émile Benzaqin, the family's oldest Moslem friend. His father had delivered animal carcasses to Grandfather Yosef Uzan's abattoir. "What awaits you in France? Have you a job there? Family there?"

Benzaqin's words haunted the father throughout the voyage to Marseilles. The Jewish Agency representative at least had promised him housing and employment in Israel. What awaited him in France? Except for a distant cousin, there were no relatives, no assurance of a job, not even certainty that the French government would renew his family's three-month visitors' visas. It was Ya'akov who stiffened his resolve. "It's a rich land, Papa," he reminded his father. "Our best hope. It always was."

Algeria: The Jews of Status

For the Jews of Algeria, France was not simply the protector. It was the *patrie*. They numbered 135,000 at war's end, a community less than half the size of Moroccan Jewry. Yet if they represented a mere 1.4

percent of Algeria's ten million inhabitants, they comprised nearly 14
percent of the country's 950,000 European settlers. Unlike their fellow
Jews in the Maghreb, Algerian Jews were largely of Sephardic origin,
tracing their roots back to Spain. Reduced to *dhimmi*—second-class—
status under Moslem rule in the ensuing centuries, they were also the
first of the Maghreb Jews to enjoy the blessings of French rule, in 1830.
Indeed, forty years later, Paris extended French citizenship to Algerian
Jewry, as it had at the outset to the country's other European inhabitants. Henceforth, unlike their kinsmen in Tunisia and Morocco, Algerian Jews shared all the rights and privileges of Frenchmen. Living
mainly in Algiers, Oran, and Constantine, they were a commercial element, by and large, although of a somewhat more advanced status than
in Tunisia and Morocco. Several thousand of them also held positions in
the civil service.

"It was a not uncomfortable life," recalled André Bensimon, taking
his ease in a not uncomfortable apartment on Paris's Avenue Gambetta.
He was a compact, rather hard-featured man, his brown hair and ruddy
(possibly vinous) complexion belying his seventy years. A flawless
French-speaker, Bensimon was married to the eminent French sociologist Doris Bensimon-Donath, and a visitor would have been hard-
pressed to imagine his grandfather dressed in the Berber djellaba,
speaking Arabic. The grandfather had been a jeweler who eventually
progressed from the Jewish quarter in the malodorous Casbah to a
somewhat more Europeanized working-class neighborhood in the port
area. By then he had adopted Western clothing and was speaking a
tolerable French. It was a matter of survival. He and his fellow Jews
had suffered even more acutely from the Dreyfus Affair than had the
Jews of France; for the colons of Algeria were as xenophobic as any
irredentist minority in Europe. Well into the twentieth century, even
the best-educated Algerian Jews were never quite accepted by these
Europeans. If Jews attended French schools, moved freely in commercial and professional life, became successful lawyers and doctors, they
still found themselves in a social ghetto.

Bensimon's father, a small textile merchant, had served in a French
regiment during World War I. Returning from the Macedonian front
chronically ill with malaria, he died in 1927. That same year, André
Bensimon was admitted to the École Normale. Upon completing his
studies in 1933, he was appointed an instructor in a primary school in
Lira al-Mezen, a small Berber town near the Atlas Mountains. In earlier years, André Bensimon's background had been typically Jewish. He

had been Bar Mitzvahed, attended a talmud torah twice weekly, observed the dietary laws and all the Jewish holidays. Nevertheless, by the time he embarked on his teaching career, he had become as thoroughly enamored of French secular values as had other young Algerian Jews. It was a love affair that went unreciprocated by the colons. Their right-wing antisemitism became particularly virulent during the 1930s, when hatred of Léon Blum's Popular Front government erupted into riots, the vandalization of synagogues and Jewish shops in Algiers, the murder of a score of Jews in Constantine. Ironically, the Algerian Berbers did not participate in this violence. Their relations with the Jews were civil.

After the outbreak of World War II, Bensimon became a machine gunner in a Zouave regiment and was shipped to France. In May 1940, he and his entire unit were taken prisoner by the onrushing German Wehrmacht. Several days later, as they were force-marched to Paris, Bensimon and eighteen or twenty of his Algerian Jewish comrades escaped, then made their way to Marseilles, and from Marseilles to Constantine. Reaching their homes in Algeria, however, they were immediately drummed out of the army, together with all other Jewish soldiers. It was the beginning of a Vichy antisemitism that, typically, was as vindictive in the Maghreb as in France itself. Algerian Jews were stripped of their French citizenship. Jewish functionaries were purged from the administration, their children expelled from French schools. Unable to resume his teaching career, Bensimon worked in his brother-in-law's textile shop. The ordeal lasted two and a half years, until November 1942, when American troops liberated French North Africa. It was indicative of the colons' pro-Vichy sympathies that virtually the only local inhabitants to cooperate in the liberation were Jews. Even after the Allied landings, a year passed before Jewish political rights were restored, and then mainly as a result of intense pressure from international Jewish organizations.

Bensimon returned to teaching, to a "quality" school in Algiers's Bab al-Wad quarter. The period of normalcy and security endured barely a decade. By the mid-1950s, Moslem resentment of French rule had burgeoned into a full-scale insurrection. The Jewish reaction to the ensuing slaughter and counterslaughter was confused. Bensimon and his friends, most of them Socialists, sympathized with the FLN—Berber nationalist—demands for self-determination. Not a single major act of Berber terrorism had been committed against Jews, after all. Indeed, the nationalist leadership repeatedly assured the Jewish community of its safety and equality in a future Algerian state. Yet it was known that much of the FLN's equipment was coming from Egypt's President Nasser, and the prospect of being governed by a regime beholden to one of Israel's most implacable enemies was unsettling. As a result, the majority of Algeria's Jews remained in the background, publicly neutral, privately still hoping for a last-minute reprieve from a French departure.

The hope was not to be realized. Once de Gaulle consolidated his power in France, in 1959, he made clear his intention to phase out the colons' privileged status in Algeria. Worse yet, during the ensuing transitional period of French withdrawal, Berber xenophobia unexpectedly burst out against the Jews. In the last week of 1960, widespread anti-Jewish riots culminated in the pillaging of the Great Synagogue of Algiers. Although the violence was immediately repudiated by the FLN leadership, the Jewish community was deeply unnerved. Nor was it reassured by the French government's decision in July 1962 to withdraw its army and to accord full sovereignty to Algeria by the end of the year. It was then that the totality of the European settlement, 950,000 colons, embarked on a vast collective exodus to France. Their homes, estates, businesses, their public institutions—the legacy of a century and a quarter of French rule—all were left behind. The 135,000 Jews of Algeria shared in the departure.

Until this moment, the Israeli government had been confident that Algerian Jewry would follow the example of tens of thousands of other Maghreb Jews, particularly those of Morocco, and settle in Israel. The expectation was naive. The long process of gallicization had done its work. Of French nationality and culture, the Jews of Algeria were intent upon claiming all the rights extended to other colons. Paris had guaranteed them loans, housing, employment, and social welfare services once they reached France. Straitened little Israel could hardly match these benefits. Ultimately, less than 5,000 Jews chose to go to Israel. Of the rest, over 120,000 returned "home." Closing the doors to their apartments, they drove their automobiles to the ports, abandoned them there, and boarded the vessels waiting to carry them off to Marseilles and Toulon. André Bensimon's sister, Azula, and her family went that route late in 1962.

Bensimon did not join them at first. His aged mother was unwilling to abandon her little flat. Moreover, friends in the French ministry of education had asked him to remain in Algeria as director of Algiers's College Condorcet, a haute école for talented native youngsters, and he had accepted. The offer was linked to a vast aid program by which Paris still hoped to maintain a "special relationship" with the successor Algerian regime. Most of the college's two thousand students were Moslem, as was the faculty. Bensimon's relations with them were cordial. His eventual decision to leave in 1965 was dictated by his health; he suffered from a recurrent stomach ulcer. By then, less than four thousand Jews remained in Algeria, essentially the inhabitants of the backward Atlas Mountain communities. On the eve of Bensimon's departure, his colleagues tendered him an emotional farewell party. The moment was bittersweet. No need to be maudlin, Bensimon reassured himself. Paris was waiting.

The Avalanche of Maghreb Jewry

France was still open terrain for the Maghreb newcomers. The nation's wartime manpower losses and chronically low birth rate endangered its prospects for economic and military revival. The government regarded massive immigration as the solution. In the aftermath of both world wars, newcomers had arrived essentially from other European lands. Now, in the 1950s and 1960s, the largest numbers of them were coming from North Africa and the Middle East. The tidal wave included 25,000 refugees from Egypt, perhaps 65,000 from Morocco, 80,000 from Tunisia, and fully 120,000 from Algeria. Their presence more than doubled France's Jewish population within two decades. Thus, by 1970, French Jewry totaled 670,000, and suddenly had become the fourth-largest Jewish community in the world. Of this hugely augmented enclave, 350,000 Jews were of North African origin.

Their process of adjustment was by no means painless. The majority of the Tunisians and Moroccans were not citizens. To be sure, as Jews rather than Berbers, they were regarded as aspirants to French civilization, and few were ever denied the right to remain. But neither were most of them eligible for government welfare benefits. They were obliged to turn instead to the Jewish social service agencies. In the early 1950s, however, French Jewry itself barely had recovered from the trauma of the war, and the community's resources were strained to the limit. Welfare measures remained erratic and disorganized. "We took several Moroccan Jewish children into our home for about six weeks, until lodgings could be found for them," Jacques Trèves recalled. "We knew what it meant to be refugees." Chastened by their wartime experience, other native Jewish families displayed a similar compassion. Voluntarism was the key in these first years.

Then, later in the decade, with German reparations payments forthcoming, the Fonds Social Juif Unifié opened absorption centers in Paris and Marseilles to guide the newcomers into available housing and employment. "We stayed with distant relatives in Marseilles when we first arrived [in 1965]," Ya'akov Uzan explained, "but afterward a representative of the Fonds Social directed us on to Paris. There, another representative helped us find an apartment in Belleville, even stocked it with food and secondhand furniture. The Fonds Social also located a doorman's job for my father in a bank. I was luckier. They found a spot for me in a small textile factory." Uzan smiled proudly then. "Between us, we managed." They managed better than had the East European immigrants in the interwar period. They spoke French. This time the economy was booming. Virtually all the Moroccan and Tunisian newcomers were literate (unlike many of those who went to Israel), and 30 percent of them had even received a secondary education.

Their most urgent problem was housing. Arriving in family groups, large numbers of Maghreb Jews were crowded into Paris's marginal Belleville quarter. During the 1920s and 1930s, it is recalled, this poor workingman's area had become a major focus of settlement for the East Europeans. Afterward, Nazi deportations all but liquidated Belleville's Jews. The Jewish welfare organizations now reversed the process. Filling the vacuum left by the East Europeans, the Maghreb immigrants worked in leatherware ateliers, in small-scale clothing manufactories. Others found jobs as plumbers, mechanics, electricians. If few of the Moroccans or Tunisians achieved integration into the nation's social structure, by the end of the 1950s they had at least won their economic foothold.

Between 1962 and 1965, the influx from Algeria had to be absorbed. Among its 940,000 transplanted colons were 120,000 Jews. Although the newcomers added significantly to the widening beachhead of North African immigrants, they preferred to regard themselves as "veteran" French. They had arrived in the country with French passports, after all, and with the attendant rights of French citizenship. The status entitled them to the government's repatriation assistance, which included travel expenses, a cash grant equivalent to about $200 a person, social insurance, provisional housing until the newcomer found suitable accommodation wherever he wished to settle. If he had been a civil servant in Algeria, the government was committed to finding him a similar position in France. If he had been a merchant, he was given a loan on easy terms to reestablish himself in business. Additionally, he was eligible for the usual supplementary benefits extended to all Frenchmen: unemployment payments for large families, free secondary, vocational, and university education for his children.

"I myself didn't take a franc from the Jewish social services," recalled André Bensimon proudly. "It wasn't necessary. Employment was provided for me almost immediately right here in Paris, at the École Pigier." His experience was typical. Algerian Jews needed and received very little Jewish help. Fully 72 percent of their men had received a secondary education. The ethnic barriers that had handicapped their advancement under colonial rule in Algeria scarcely existed in France. A middle- and lower-middle-class group in the Maghreb, they earned their livelihoods in France now as modest shopkeepers in the textile, clothing, and costume jewelry trades, as proprietors of small workshops, as government clerks, teachers, pharmacists, and lawyers. Their integration into the French economy was all but painless.

It was the Algerian immigration, too, that effected a significant shift in French Jewry's geographical distribution. Before and immediately after the war, Jews had settled overwhelmingly in the Paris region, with a much smaller enclave in Alsace-Lorraine. Large numbers of Algerians similarly gravitated to the capital. The more affluent among them tended to gather along the rue du Faubourg Montmartre and the Faubourg Poissonnière, establishing boutiques, restaurants, and bars, creating the street atmosphere of Algiers or Oran. Others congregated extensively in thirty-five or forty Paris suburbs, including Asnières, Blanc-Mesnil, Meaux, Nanterre, Orly, Créteil, and particularly in the commune of Sarcelles, eleven miles from the heart of Paris, where by 1984 some eleven thousand of them were housed in a dense complex of middle-class apartment units. Yet barely 30 percent of the Algerian Jewish immigrants migrated to the Paris area. The government saw to it that the majority did not. Faced with a tidal wave of nearly a million Europeans (and Jews) from Algeria, the ministry of absorption was determined not to permit the continued overconcentration in the capital. Rather, by offering swift employment and priority housing elsewhere in the country, it induced the repatriates to disperse more widely throughout the provinces.

In the case of the Jews, about a third settled along the southern, Mediterranean coast. Others were distributed almost evenly in other regions. As late as 1984, to be sure, Paris and its satellite communities encompassed over 340,000 Jews. Alsace-Lorraine contained some 36,000. But newer Jewish communities unexpectedly burgeoned out. Before the war, approximately 10,000 Jews had lived in Marseilles; by 1984, the port city's Jewish population had grown to 85,000—of whom the majority were Algerians. Before the war, 7,000 Jews had resided in Lyons; in 1984, there were 34,000. The Jews of Toulouse, less than 1,000 in 1939, numbered 28,000 by 1984. The Jews of Nice totaled barely 600 before the war; by 1984, the figure was 30,000. Additionally, over 100,000 Jews were scattered throughout smaller cities and towns elsewhere in France.

A Reverse Acculturation

The Maghreb newcomers transformed the very character of French Jewry. During the 1960s, Judéo-Arabic replaced Yiddish as the community's second language. The North Africans may not have been uniformly traditional Jews. But whatever the differences between the Europeanized Algerians and the ethnocentric Moroccans and Tunisians, the residue of Maghreb self-identity tended to be more authentically Jewish than the pale "cultism" of the native Jews. To their credit, the paladins of the Consistoire and the Fonds Social were prepared to support the newcomers in rebuilding their communal lives. Thus, for the first time in sixty years, a major program of synagogue construction was launched throughout France. Care was taken to re-create the Sephardic architectural pattern, to publish and distribute prayerbooks following the Sephardic-North African rite, to develop an Eshel Sephardic seminary for the training of teachers, youth leaders, rabbis, and cantors.

On the whole, education became a basic priority for this metamorphosed community. The facilities of the three Jewish day schools in Paris were substantially improved. New talmud torah schools were opened in Paris and the provinces. In Strasbourg, a quality Akiva day school provided for 450 students, at least 300 of them North African. In 1951, only 8 percent of Marseilles Jewish children were receiving any form of religious education. By 1966, the ratio tripled. By 1981, it quadrupled. The proliferation of facilities was largely underwritten by Claims Conference grants to the Fonds Social; and through the Fonds Social, to the Consistoire. It was Claims Conference funding, too, that permitted the construction of a network of Jewish community centers, an innovation heretofore unknown in Europe. Devised along the American model, these buildings went up throughout France in the 1960s and 1970s. With their attractive premises and broad-ranging social and cultural programs, they became important magnets for younger North African Jews, who traditionally regarded themselves as a separate community rather than as members of a "cult."

For that matter, formal religiosity was beginning to wane even among the younger Moroccans and Tunisians, and well before their departure from the Maghreb. In France, the process gained momentum—and continues to do so. It has gone hand in hand with upward mobility. The newcomers are integrated far more solidly now within the French economy. The measure of their success is visible in Belleville, once the very heart of the Paris ghetto. Few Jews still live in this decrepit area, but the businesses they operate there apparently are thriving. In addition to hundreds of retail shops, workshops, and warehouses, there have also sprung up many scores of little restaurants, bakeries, and butcher shops, all flashing neon Stars of David. The names are classically Maghreb Jewish—Zeitoun, Zeinati, Benhaim, Romani—and the proprietors are largely Tunisians. Parisians of all backgrounds come for the *couscous, arissa, addas,* and other spicy Maghreb dishes.

In France at large, the Moroccans still tend to lag behind, but most of the Tunisians and Algerians share the bourgeois standards and values of the Europeans. Their children attend the universities in growing numbers and are increasingly represented among France's professionals. In adapting to the secular influences of contemporary France, more than half the North Africans have admitted in recent years that they are far less religiously observant than in their countries of origin. On the other hand, if their Judaism has faded, their commitment to ethnic identity remains unshaken. It is still all but unthinkable for them to marry among non-Jews. Their emotional loyalty to Israel is intense, and so, increasingly, is their determination to make their mark in Jewish communal life. Thus, while the lay positions in the Consistoire remain in the hands of the Rothschilds and of other well-born native Jews, the North Africans have achieved a near-monopoly of the rabbinate itself. The latest chief rabbi, André Sirac, is an Algerian. Nearly all the students at the rabbinical seminary are Maghreb or Egyptian Jews. From the late 1960s on, the North Africans have served effectively on the various Jewish public committees, occupying half the seats on the board of the Fonds Social, a third on the CRIF, nearly half on the Appel Juif Unifié.

Perhaps the conclusive evidence of their integration is the extent of their intermarriage with Jews of European background. By 1984, more than half of all North African marriages have been with Ashkenazi Jews. The phenomenon can be attributed partly to France's historic indifference to racial or ethnic origins, but even more to the economic and educational progress of the North Africans themselves. Ya'akov Uzan married a native French girl, born in Paris of Algerian Jews who had settled in France fifty years earlier. "Snobbery between communities?" he scoffed. "There is no racial snobbery between the Ashkenazim and the North Africans altogether. Not in this open society." His evaluation was endorsed by Jacques Trèves. "I would not have the faintest objection to my daughter marrying a Sephardic Jew," he stated flatly. His daughter, an attractive, thirty-year-old doctoral student (of Japanese literature) at the Sorbonne, offered a qualification. "Well, we are snobs, possibly," she admitted, "but we are not racists." Behind these observations one sensed a tacit awareness that French Jewry had been slowly atrophying for at least a century, and that the influx of tens of thousands of "integral" Jews may have provided a decisive transfusion.

. . . A Tentative Cultural Renaissance

This is the conviction of André Neher. We first met at his apartment in Jerusalem. He was a very charming man in his early seventies. A member of the Alsatian Jewish elite, Neher until 1940 had been a professor of German literature at the University of Strasbourg. It was the war and his life under Vichy that redirected his career. He turned his mind almost exclusively to Judaism, and after the liberation he became his university's first professor of Jewish studies. It was appropriate that he should do so in Alsace. The laws on separation of church and state did not apply here, and Neher accordingly enjoyed both government financial support and the moral backing of a Jewish community that, with Antwerp's, was the last citadel of Orthodoxy in Western Europe. Strasbourg also boasted the finest Jewish high school on the continent. Many pious North African families, who feared raising their children in Paris, were drawn to the Jewish communities of Alsace. Not a few of these young people became Neher's students—then went on from the

University of Strasbourg to assume positions of leadership in Jewish life. In Paris, meanwhile, Jewish students at the Sorbonne and other universities had access to Leon Ashkenazi's Centre Universitaire d'Études Juives. Now in his sixties, Ashkenazi was born in Oran, the son of Algeria's chief rabbi, and attended the University of Algeria. In the late 1940s, he moved to Paris to assist Robert Gamzon, founder of the Jewish Scouts and an underground war hero, in establishing a college of Jewish studies. Upon Gamzon's death, Ashkenazi became the school's director. With the financial help of the Fonds Social, he enriched its curriculum to attract university students, and won a limited accreditation from the Sorbonne. Currently, several hundred students are attending branches of the Centre Universitaire.

Are these developments harbingers of a Jewish cultural renaissance? It is faintly possible. On the one hand, not more than 5 percent of Jewish children are enrolled in day schools and barely that many attend Sabbath services. If France is a committedly secular society, this is hardly less true of French Jews. Few of the North African rabbis possess intellectual depth, and fewer yet seem to generate an appeal to younger people, whether of European or North African background. The Lubavitcher Chasidim have attracted several hundred young Jews. At the other end of the religious spectrum, Liberal Judaism maintains a thriving synagogue on Paris's rue Copernic. Its normal Sabbath turnout of perhaps four or five hundred individuals is considerably higher than that of a typical Orthodox synagogue. Some of its popularity can be attributed to the intellect and charm of its young British-born rabbi, Michael Williams. But two smaller Liberal congregations, in Nice and Marseilles, also appear to be growing impressively. Liberal Judaism may yet become a force in French Jewry, although, as of now, it remains a far weaker movement than in England, whose Jewish community is half the size of France's.

The most significant development in French Jewry is not to be found in its suspect religiosity, but in its increasingly forthright ethnic pride and confidence. The integral Jewishness of the newcomers has proved to be infectious, and the younger generation, whether of Maghreb or Ashkenazic origin, has repudiated its forebears' more characteristic Diaspora timorousness. If young Jews had been asked before World War II, "Are you Jewish?" conceivably more than two-thirds would have failed to answer or would have dissembled. In 1969, about 90 percent of the Jewish university students queried in Paris answered this question affirmatively. Indeed, many of them displayed an interest in enlarging their knowledge of Jewish culture. From the mid-1950s on, there has been a palpable revival of Jewish identity among Jewish intellectuals. When intermarried, they appear increasingly likely to ask their spouses to convert and their children to be Bar Mitzvahed. One of France's most distinguished publishing houses, Calmann-Lévy, has issued a series of books of Jewish interest, including translations of Robert Paxton's account of the Vichy epoch, Hannah Arendt's work on totalitarianism, Isaiah Berlin's reflections on Jewish history, an anthology on Soviet Jewry edited by Lionel Kochan. Meanwhile, the French section of the World Jewish Congress has conducted biennial symposia among Jewish intellectuals, as have the Alliance and several youth groups, and participation in these events has been surprisingly large. From the latter 1960s, the roster of Jewish scholars who have turned their attention to Jewish subjects is even more impressive. In truth, nothing has quite matched it in any other European Jewish community.

Of wider general interest, perhaps, are the growing numbers of French Jewish novelists, poets, and essayists writing on Jewish themes. Through the 1950s and 1960s, the Holocaust remained their obsession. Thus, André Schwartz-Bart's *The Last of the Just* won the Prix Goncourt in 1959; and Jean-François Steiner's controversial piece of fictional journalism, *Treblinka*, elicited comparable interest. So, too, did Piotr Rawicz's *Blood from the Sky* and Anna Langfus's *The Last Shore*. Several of these authors, as well as many others, appeared to have been profoundly influenced by Sartre's *Réflexions sur la question juive*, an essay that dominated the theoretical approach to racial questions after 1947. Sartre's passion for provocative definition left its impact on Robert Misrahi, in the latter's densely abstract volume, *La condition réflexive de l'homme juif*. Albert Memmi produced a fascinating account of his Tunisian ghetto childhood in his widely acclaimed *Statue de sel* (Pillar of Salt). While often acute in its observations, Memmi's *Portrait d'un juif*, dedicated to "Sartre, homme libre," and its sequel, bearing the Sartrean title *La libération du juif*, were clearly written under the spell of existential dialect and fervor. Steiner's *Treblinka* also sought to fit the facts of the tragedy into the French pursuit of paradox—that it was "the Jewish will to live" which led both to the Jews' "complicity" in their own destruction and to their heroic revolt against their oppressors at Treblinka.

In contrast, much of French Jewish writing in the 1960s and 1970s read like an anguished quest for identity. Thus, Jacques Kanzmann's *Qui Vivae* revealed the shoddier aspects of the resistance movement in its story of a young Jewish outcast during the Occupation. Another example of Jewish marginality was Georges Friedmann's *Fin du peuple juif*. An eminent Marxist sociologist, Friedmann had given little thought to his Jewishness until the Occupation. Later, in the 1960s, while visiting Israel, he reached the strikingly unoriginal conclusion that the cultic nature of the Jewish people was outmoded and that the Israeli nation had become its vital center. Along with Friedmann, other postwar writers have displayed a similar animus toward "fossilized Orthodoxy," and have found in Israel the solution to the Jewish dilemma. This discovery apparently liberates them from the need to understand Judaism in order to write about Jews. The passion for elegant oversimplification, as well as the tendency to draw sweeping generalizations on a meager reservoir of basic Jewish information, remains one of the great temptations of French—and French Jewish—intellectualism.

This characteristic struck me with particular force during a visit to Manès Sperber, one of French Jewry's most acclaimed essayists. Born in Prague in 1909 of Galician parents, Sperber had been active in the Socialist and Communist movements during the 1930s. Early in the war he detached himself from the army, fled to Switzerland, and there turned to writing on Jewish issues. With only the vaguest knowledge of Jewish history or of the Hebrew language, he managed afterward to contribute regularly to *Évidences,* the French version of *Commentary*. A small man with a wizened face, Sperber received me in his spacious apartment off the rue de Montparnasse. His principal interest, he reminded me, was in the "special relationship" between Judaism and psychology. As a student of the unconscious, he was a great admirer of Buber, of the "genius of mysticism." I had read two of Manès Sperber's books. They displayed an interesting, if rather portentous, effort to understand biblical figures—and his own belated reaffirmation of Judaism—in psychological terms. This psychologizing (narcissistic?) approach is shared by André Chouraqui, an Algerian Jew, originally a lawyer, then a sociologist of Maghreb Jewry, who in a series of autobiographical works has made much of his near "assimilation" and of the "spiritual crisis" that brought him back to Judaism and the Jewish people. Such greathearted acts of return have always puzzled me. Even if they were not factitious, what exclamations of gratitude are they supposed to evoke from the reading audience?

A Belated Zionization

Many of these writers have been seeking to come to terms not only with their Jewishness (an old theme) but with the new dimension that has been provided by the State of Israel. Until well into the 1950s, Zionism exerted little impact upon French Jewry. The East Europeans who had been its most vigorous partisans were largely annihilated. While thousands of displaced persons supported the movement after the liberation, they were preoccupied with their own concerns. So were the North Africans, however much they transferred their characteristic Maghreb ethnocentrism to emotional support for Israel. It was not until after the Sinai-Suez campaign of 1956, and the subsequent intensification of Jewish Agency activity in France, that admiration for Israel became a vogue among Jews and non-Jews alike. In the following years, some ten universities added Hebrew to their curricula, and the Sorbonne and Strasbourg developed broader programs of Jewish studies.

Commitment to Israel took on a new urgency during the Middle East crisis of 1967. As elsewhere in Western Europe, large demonstrations were mounted. Outside the Israeli embassy in Paris, nearly 100,000 people stopped traffic for hours. In Marseilles, 7,000 people demonstrated; 20,000 in Strasbourg; 4,000 in Nice. A special coordinating committee of Jewish organizations under the chairmanship of Baron Guy de Rothschild was hastily formed to launch an emergency fundraising campaign. The result was a vast outpouring of contributions, a phenomenon altogether new in the experience of French Jews, a majority of whom still were immigrants themselves. Following the Six-Day War there was even a modest emigration to Israel, principally of North African Jews, although several members of the elite also departed, including André Neher.

From 1967 on, others of France's leading Jewish intellectuals and prominent families began to redefine their attitude to the Jewish state. The most celebrated among them was the political writer Raymond Aron. A highly assimilated Jew and a critic of Zionism, Aron had frequently warned the Israelis not to make claims upon the patriotism of their kinsmen in France. Then came the Six-Day War, followed by President de Gaulle's irascible observation that the Jews were an "elite" and "domineering" people. Outraged, Aron responded in a series of essays published under the title *De Gaulle, Israël, et les Juifs*. He drew a scathing analogy between de Gaulle's comment and the observation made in 1942 by Xavier Vallat, the notorious commissioner for Jewish affairs under Vichy, that "the Jew is a foreigner [whose] natural rights as a member of a superior race, born to dominate the world, made him want to rule it." In the course of attacking de Gaulle and French anti-semitism, Aron now admitted to a certain tortured identification of interest with Israel:

> But I also know, more clearly than in the past, that in the event of the State of Israel being destroyed . . . I should be wounded in the very depths of my being. In this sense, I have confessed that a Jew can never achieve a perfect objectivity where Israel is concerned.

A similar change of attitude could be discerned in the remarks of Guy de Rothschild in 1970: "Our personality has been altered during centuries of hate and insult," the baron declared in April that year, commemorating the centenary of the Israeli agricultural settlement of Mikveh Israel, founded by the Alliance Israélite Universelle, "and we have projected upon Israel our very essence."

Jacques Trèves's response was equally revealing of the native Jewish community's embrace of Israel. During the 1967 crisis, he and his family joined the pro-Israel demonstration. The following year they visited Israel, and were moved by the sights and sounds of Jewish pride and self-confidence. In 1972, Trèves's brother, Jean-Louis, emigrated to Israel. Characteristically, Trèves himself has sought to preserve an "equable" balance. "We also want to preserve a French Jewish civilization," he insisted. For the North African majority, however, there was no qualification or ambivalence. Their Jewishness afterward was largely identified with the destiny of Israel. Interrogated in 1968, the inhabitants of the largely Maghreb Jewish *banlieu* of Sarcelles emphasized by a majority of 63 percent that Israel had become the principal focus of their Jewishness.

The experience of the June 1967 crisis also led to the formation of a centralized fund-raising organization on behalf of Israel and local Jewish charities. Until then, 80 percent of all charitable funds raised among French Jews had gone to the Fonds Social. Barely 20 percent had gone to Israel, under a separate drive conducted by the Keren HaYesod. Following Guy de Rothschild's emergency appeal during the Six-Day War, however, the French Jewish leadership decided that the Fonds Social and the Keren HaYesod henceforth should organize a joint appeal, the Appel Juif Unifié, on the American model, and guarantee Israel its "fair share." That fair share has turned out to be slightly more than half, a distribution that would have been unthinkable in the 1950s. It is the proof of French Jewry's unanimous support now of Israel. So is the leadership on the board of the Appel Juif Unifié, for since 1968 it has included (together with many North Africans) some of the distinguished names of French Jewry, among them the Rothschilds, Grand Rabbi Jacob Kaplan, Georges Wormser, Marcel Bleustein-Blanchet. In France, as elsewhere in the Diaspora, commitment to Israel has become an integral component of Jewishness itself.

A *Putative Anti-Zionism*

De Gaulle's widely publicized remark of November 27, 1967, that the Jews "remain what they have always been, that is, an elite people, self-assured and domineering," could be seen as a reappraisal of sorts after the philosemitism of the postwar era. Having extracted France from Algeria, de Gaulle and his right-centrist successors, Georges Pompidou and Valéry Giscard d'Estaing, adopted an undisguised pro-Arab stance in foreign affairs. The decisive shift away from Israel, in turn, allowed a certain leeway for the emergence of antisemitism. In effect, and surely unintentionally, the government blurred the already tenuous distinction in French minds between *Israélite* (Jew) and *Israélien* (Israeli). This was, after all, still the nation that had produced the Vichy regime, and there were subterranean influences, quite independent of Israel, that lent themselves to racist exploitation. One was the growing fear of the nation's large foreign population. By the 1970s, France had become the habitat for five million foreigners, two million of them North African Moslems. With the mounting economic difficulties of the ensuing decade, the prewar policy of bureaucratic xenophobia was apparently revived. Tens of thousands of unemployed or otherwise "undesirable" Berbers and Middle Eastern Arabs suddenly were deported to their countries of origin. No Jews were affected, but the threat implicit in these palpably racist administrative measures was ominous. So was the revival of right-wing anti-intellectualism, as it was exposed by the Algerian conflict and its aftermath, and particularly as it was exacerbated by the student uprisings of the late 1960s.

Antisemitism still remained unacceptable as a political policy; throughout the 1960s and 1970s, no political party openly invoked it. Following the *Schema* issued by Vatican II, moreover, the French episcopate in 1969 established a Committee for Relations with Judaism and vigorously condemned Jew-hatred. Nevertheless, an event of serious Jewish concern was the publication in 1965 of *Les Juifs*, by Roger Peyrefitte, a former diplomat. Under the guise of an investigation of Jewish life, the author made Judaism appear odious and ridiculous, and disingenuously ascribed Jewish ancestry to a large number of well-known persons. For example, de Gaulle was really "Kolb" and was, of course, Jewish. The Rothschild family, whom Peyrefitte had libeled, sued the author and publisher, forcing the removal of a number of objectionable passages. Yet by then the book had been widely publicized and read. Four years later, in the southern provincial town of Orléans, ugly rumors began to circulate of young women mysteriously disappearing in Jewish-owned boutiques, then being smuggled by white slavers to the Middle East. Although the Jews of Orléans numbered only 500 in a population of 88,000, many of the city's inhabitants appeared to have worked themselves into a delirium against the handful of Jewish proprietors. The national Jewish organizations eventually were able to mobilize the French press in a campaign against "medievalism." But it was evident that a dangerous substratum of judeophobia lingered on in the provinces.

A subtle but more wide-ranging threat was the emergence of the Nouvelle Droite, a loose constellation of technocrats and journalists that moved onto the intellectual scene during the early and mid-1970s. Conducting an increasingly well-coordinated campaign against "Judeo-Christian" ethical values, against "Jewish monotheism," political egalitarianism, and other expressions of humanitarian tolerance, the New Rightists proposed a clearly racist elitism based on pseudoscientific premises. Its avant-garde was called GRECE—Groupement de Recherche et d'Études pour la Civilisation Européenne—which professed to be a cultural rather than a political movement. Among its estimated membership of ten thousand, GRECE included a number of well-connected young intellectuals, some even of ministerial rank. One of its subsidiaries, the Club de l'Horloge, consisted of 120 selected *hautes écoles* graduates. Apparently, GRECE's intention was to infiltrate the power structure. In this effort, it had an important ally in the press magnate Robert Hersant, owner of a chain of provincial dailies, of *Le Figaro*, and of the even more widely read newspaper *France-Soir*. A veteran antisemite, Hersant in the 1930s was active in several pro-Nazi groups, and was a close friend of Darquiet de Pellepoix, who succeeded Xavier Vallat as commissioner for Jewish affairs under Vichy.

The ideology of the Nouvelle Droite was also apparent in gangs of adolescent hoodlums. In the late 1970s and early 1980s, small bands of Paris high school students took to distributing extreme rightist Front de la Jeunesse tracts and attacking their Jewish schoolmates with brass knuckles and iron bars. The years after 1978 generally witnessed a sharp rise in antisemitic scrawling on subway walls and storefronts, desecrations of tombstones, distribution of antisemitic leaflets, and the bombing of the headquarters of human rights organizations such as the International League Against Antisemitism (LICA). Near the end of 1978, a suspicious fire broke out in the synagogue of the Paris suburb of Drancy, the town in which the Nazis had operated their central deportation camp. Several months later, another fire broke out in the temporary hall made available to the Drancy Jews. In March 1979, a bomb was detonated in Paris's kosher student restaurant on rue Médicis, at noon, when it was filled with diners. Scores of young people were injured, some permanently maimed.

This rising temper of anti-Jewish violence was taking place in the nation that, through the late 1960s and the 1970s, had adopted the most critical anti-Israel attitude in Western Europe. It was not unlikely that some, even most, of the outrages, such as the bombing of the Jewish student canteen, were tactics in a Palestinian terror campaign, in which local Arab extremists also were participating (although it was doubtful that the perpetrators included any significant number of North African Berbers; as in the Maghreb itself, relations between these Moslems and North African Jews were generally tolerable). But it was a matter of concern to the Jewish community that the government seemed unwilling to take vigorous antiterrorist measures. For several years, Gerhart Riegner and other officials of the World Jewish Congress had been entreating French authorities to sign an international agreement against terrorism. Sensitive to Arab pressures, however, both the Pompidou and the Giscard cabinets were unwilling to equate political violence, which they described as a "spillover" of the Middle East war, with simple criminality. Under this interpretation, insurance companies were not obliged to reimburse Jewish victims of terrorism. Bombings and other atrocities were classified simply as acts of war.

Thereafter, the violence steadily mounted. During late September 1980, five Parisian synagogues and other communal institutions, including a school and a nursery, were machine-gunned. Although the attacks occurred at night and did not inflict casualties, the Jewish leadership was sufficiently alarmed to end the listing of their offices in telephone directories or even by their full names on door plaques. Acronyms were their only identification. Thus, even now, the Paris office of the World Jewish Congress is identified as the CJM (Congrès Juif Mondial). Other listings are, variously, CRIF, FJUS, AJU, AJC—nothing more. It is a question not of shame but of self-protection.

This technique availed little for the Liberal synagogue on Paris's rue Copernic, in the middle-class sixteenth arrondissement. It is a rather nondescript building, with its title, Union Libéral Israélite, modestly etched on a wall, and its distinguishing features as a house of worship revealed only on the inside of the courtyard. At 7:30 P.M. of October 3, 1980, a bomb exploded at the entrance to the synagogue. The Sabbath evening service was by chance running late; otherwise, hundreds of congregants might have been killed or wounded on the steps outside. As it was, several worshipers inside were wounded, and four passersby were killed, one of them an Israeli tourist who happened to be walking down the street; the others, non-Jews who lived in the neighborhood. Later, an anonymous telephone call to the police claimed responsibility for the explosion on behalf of the "Front d'Action pour une Nouvelle Europe," a small, illegal, neo-Nazi group. The claim was discounted. It was not unlikely that Arabs were responsible. Some weeks earlier, in Antwerp, Arabs had fired on a busload of Jewish students, killing one child.

This time, public indignation was overwhelming. Whatever the recent unpopularity of Israel under the Begin government, the atrocity on rue Copernic had been committed against a house of worship, and with enough savagery to have killed dozens, possibly hundreds, of men, women, and children. François Mitterrand and other Socialist Party leaders visited the synagogue to express their solidarity with the Jewish community. Other dignitaries from the municipality, from other parties, representatives of other faiths, arrived to pay their condolences. Their palpable goodwill soon afterward was mobilized into one of the truly extraordinary mass demonstrations in recent French history. A movement known as Le Renouveau Juif—Jewish Renewal—was at least partly responsible. Here we must go back.

The Challenge of Pluralism

Since 1967, the government's frigid attitude toward Israel, and the hostility of leftist "anti-imperialists," had persuaded a number of younger Jews that a more dynamic advocacy was required on behalf equally of Israel and of French Jewry. The first effort to provide an alternative to the Rothschild-dominated establishment was launched by one Henri Hajdenberg, a lawyer still in his twenties. The son of Polish immigrants who had settled in Belleville between the wars, Hajdenberg had maintained only perfunctory Jewish interests since his Bar Mitzvah. Like most of the Jews of his generation, however, he still regarded Israel as the bedrock of his Jewish identity. The Six-Day War then became the decisive experience in his life. Together with thousands of other Jews, he volunteered for service in Israel, and briefly worked there in a kibbutz.

Returning to Paris, Hajdenberg was appalled by the anti-Israel, and at times the seemingly antisemitic, posture taken by the New Left—a number of whose leaders were themselves Jews. To confront this danger, he organized a militant "defense association," a group of young Jews who did not hesitate to use iron bars and brickbats in clashes with radical elements. But neither did Hajdenberg and his friends overlook the "timidité" (Hajdenberg's word) of the Rothschilds and their colleagues among the Jewish leadership. Meeting with Guy de Rothschild, Hajdenberg failed to persuade the eminent banker to criticize de Gaulle and to endorse the strategy—understandably "horrifying" to the acculturated Jewish elite—of a Jewish voting bloc. Someday these mandarins would pay, Hajdenberg vowed to his friends, and it would not be in money.

From then on the young lawyer's mission was to organize direct political action on behalf of Israel. His closest ally in this endeavor was his cousin Daniel Buk. An engineer, Buk was married to a Tunisian Jewish girl, the daughter of recent immigrants. His connections with his wife's family and circle of friends had given him an insight into a rich vein of Jewish ethnocentrism waiting to be tapped. In the mid-1970s, then, the two cousins and their friends organized a "Comité Juif d'Action," and made their first order of business the creation of media happenings. The most dramatic of these was staged in May 1974, following the United Nations condemnation of Zionism as racism. Entitled "Twelve Hours for Israel," the event took the form of a day of celebration, entertainment, and political propaganda in the capital's Port de Versailles exhibition area. Months of preparation were required, and help was provided enthusiastically by hundreds of young Jews, North Africans and Europeans alike. The Appel Juif Unifié and several other key Jewish organizations were prevailed upon to finance the undertaking. The larger political parties deemed it expedient to send representatives. In all, some eighty thousand people attended. For the French government and public, the event was an astonishing revelation of Jewish solidarity.

Afterward, the committee sought to maintain its contacts with the Appel Juif Unifié, then under the chairmanship of Elie de Rothschild. But these became increasingly tense. Rothschild and his colleagues warned Hajdenberg not to politicize their activities, not to create the impression of a Jewish voting bloc. Hajdenberg and Buk in turn made no commitment, observing only that their course of action was dictated by the behavior of the government. In the spring of 1977, the Giscard cabinet, under Arab pressure, decided to release the imprisoned PLO terrorist Abu Daoud, one of the planners of the Munich Olympics massacre. The decision was taken only months before the scheduled Paris municipal election. Hajdenberg's and Buk's action committee thereupon launched a vigorous campaign against the government candidate for the third arrondissement, supporting instead a member of Mitterrand's Socialist Party. The latter won handily. Shaken, the Giscard cabinet immediately sponsored a bill prohibiting racial or religious discrimination in commercial transactions—by then a common practice of French companies in search of Arab business—in effect, declaring acquiescence in the Arab boycott to be a crime. The government retained an escape clause, however, which it used soon afterward to avoid any prosecution that might affect relations with oil-producing countries. At that point, Hajdenberg and Buk knew what had to be done. Yet their plans to organize a national Jewish voting bloc were thwarted by lack of funds. Although sharing in the outrage at the government's duplicity, the Rothschilds and other board members of the Appel Juif Unifié and of CRIF vetoed any financial support for direct political action. Hereupon the young action committee members decided to go outside the Jewish establishment to fulfill their strategy.

As it developed, they were provided with effective guidance by an Israeli emissary, Avi Primor. In his mid-forties, a slim, handsome man, Primor was a veteran in his country's diplomatic service, which included an earlier stint as counselor of the Israeli embassy in Paris. He had recently been sent back from Jerusalem as a representative of the Jewish Agency. Primor's insight into young French Jews was shrewd. The Israeli connection, he knew, was the one sure technique for mobilizing their latent ethnic pride. Accordingly, he advised Hajdenberg and Buk to direct their efforts to the North African neighborhoods, and to recruit extensively from among young Maghreb Jews. The committee in this fashion could be transformed into a mass action organization, the Renouveau Juif. Once the inhabitants of Sarcelles and the other North African communities were given status as members of a broadened directorate, they would generate a far wider support from their own relatives and friends.

The approach almost immediately proved effective. In April 1980, the Port de Versailles became the site for another pro-Israel celebration, this time a gathering of 150,000 Jews, more even than the pope had attracted on his recent visit to the French capital. It was an electrifying event. In large degree it was made so by Hajdenberg's direct attack on the Giscard d'Estaing government. To ensure that there was no misunderstanding of his purpose, or of the discipline now expected of French Jews as a voting bloc, Hajdenberg had invited the Socialist candidate, François Mitterrand, to share the platform with him. Mitterrand had accepted. Further, a straw vote was taken on the spot, a "referendum" on Giscard's Middle East policy. Not surprisingly, the vote registered 99 percent against the president.

Alain and Guy de Rothschild had felt it politic to appear at the exhibition. Silently, they witnessed this astonishing political demonstration. And silently, with tightly controlled emotions, they listened as Hajdenberg then launched into a harsh condemnation of the French Jewish establishment. That leadership had been unconscionably evasive, Hajdenberg declared. It had not spoken out forthrightly on Middle Eastern issues, and the consequences in French policy toward Israel had been disastrous. "The establishment countenances assimilation," Hajdenberg proclaimed finally. "We cannot go on this way." It was a possibly well-meaning effort to arouse Jewish self-respect. Yet the attack on the Rothschilds was cruelly unfair. Each of the dynasty's brothers and cousins had devoted his talents, efforts, and money unstintingly to the welfare of his people. They had been the principal fund-raisers and contributors to Israeli causes. Hajdenberg's broadside, which presumably had been influenced by Avi Primor, was an intolerable affront. Several hours later, Guy de Rothschild telephoned the Jewish Agency leadership in Jerusalem, demanding that Primor be recalled. The demand was met. In some measure, this sharp riposte by French Jewry's most influential family had its effect. Ostracized by the major institutions, Hajdenberg and the Renouveau Juif were blocked afterward in their efforts to share in the "official" Jewish leadership. For over a year, the movement conducted meetings, but failed to maneuver the establishment into adopting a public stance on the forthcoming elections.

It was on October 3, 1980, following several earlier anti-Jewish outrages, that the bomb exploded at the Liberal Synagogue on rue Copernic. At the funeral for the Israeli woman who had been killed in the blast, Alain de Rothschild murmured to Rabbi Williams: "I would never have believed a Frenchman capable of doing such a thing." Tears streamed down the baron's cheeks. After his ordeal at the hands of his fellow officers in the war, after his people's ordeal under Vichy, Rothschild's faith in his country was, at best, high-minded. But several days later, attending the funeral service for a Portuguese boy who had also been killed in the explosion while passing the synagogue on a bicycle, Rothschild had hardened sufficiently to take note of Giscard d'Estaing's continued absence and silence. "It's a scandal," he whispered bitterly to a companion. "We haven't heard a word from the president." In fact, the Jewish community had already heard enough from Giscard's prime minister, Raymond Barre, on the night of the explosion. Speaking at a televised press conference, Barre remarked: "The terrorists' target was a Jewish synagogue, but they only succeeded in killing innocent Frenchmen." At the time, the premier did not yet know that one of the victims was a presumably non-"innocent" Israeli woman. By then, neither the Rothschilds nor the other leaders of the principal Jewish organizations objected when Hajdenberg and his colleagues of the Renouveau Juif took it upon themselves to mount a protest demonstration against the bombing.

The event began the following afternoon. Embarking from the steps of the rue Copernic Synagogue itself and continuing for four hours along the Champs Élysées to the gates of the presidential palace, the march was joined by approximately 100,000 persons. By no means were all of them Jews. While Jewish communal officials walked in the vanguard of the throng, they were flanked by a delegation of mayors wearing tricolored sashes. Behind them, delegations of bemedaled Jewish war veterans were accompanied by representative groups from all the major political parties, from labor unions, feminist organizations, Freemasons. Elsewhere, in a dozen cities throughout the country, similar marches were held: in Marseilles, Grenoble, Montpellier, Nîmes, Lyons, Strasbourg, Nancy, and others. That same evening, the National

Assembly held a special session, with one speaker after another rising to denounce the evils of antisemitism. Finally, after a moment of silence, the assembly adjourned to permit some of its members to march.

Until the autumn of 1980, most political commentators had predicted the reelection of Giscard. Hajdenberg, Buk, and their colleagues in the Renouveau Juif were unwilling to accept that prognosis. They purchased large advertisements in the newspapers and circulated posters, warning against the government's role in constructing the Iraqi nuclear reactor. In the last weeks before the election in April 1981, Hajdenberg's committee held "information sessions" on the Middle East with parliamentary delegates and mayors (data were supplied by the Israeli embassy), then ran a final series of advertisements, offering a detailed, factual account of Giscard's Middle East record, including his petulant criticism of the Camp David accords. The elections then produced a decisive victory for Mitterrand.

Plainly, the opposition to Giscard's leadership was nationwide, and not the result of only one issue. Yet it was significant that the predominantly Jewish arrondissements in Paris had voted unanimously against Giscard, and would again in the final runoff election. Additionally, the French Jewish vote may have been responsible for the election of some forty deputies. The public had been made keenly aware of a powerful Jewish voting bloc, the first ethnic bloc of its kind in contemporary French history. The Jews had adopted the Renouveau Juif's slogan: "A dignity vote is a sanction vote." For his part, Mitterrand, the new president, honored his campaign pledge to become the first French head of state to pay an official visit to Israel.

What of the Renouveau's threatened campaign against the Jewish establishment itself? That remains latent. As I questioned them, the lay and professional leaders of French institutional life all but vied with each other in the warmth of their admiration for the Rothschild family. Henri Wormser, a native Alsatian Jew (whose father had been Clemenceau's chef de cabinet), a banker himself and chairman of CRIF's political committee, noted that the Rothschilds had always represented the most liberal element in the capitalist camp. The French Left invariably had maintained excellent relations with them. "If the Rothschilds have been accepted as our leaders, it is because they are unique among the capitalist breed. They are entirely apolitical, with no ax to grind." Wormser's sentiments were echoed by the leadership of CRIF, of the Fonds Social, of the Appel Juif Unifié, of the Consistoire; and not a few of these vice-chairmen or committee chairmen were of North African ancestry. Indeed, since the early 1950s, the Rothschilds themselves had been among the most forthright advocates of communal democratization—"so long as the process is orderly and responsible."

The process actually had been initiated in the latter 1960s, under the impact of a series of student uprisings. Students and other traditionally underrepresented elements of the French Jewish population now began to insist upon wider participation in communal leadership (even as French students at large were demanding wider influence in French public affairs). The board of the Fonds Social was the first to agree. Under a new constitution adopted in 1972, the federation's membership was opened to anyone over eighteen who paid a very small membership fee, and to any Jewish association, regardless of its character. Since then, board elections have been conducted by a single ballot, on the basis of geographic division. It is an unexceptionably democratic system, and it has done away with closed doors and with oligarchical decision-making. From the outset, no one applauded it more heartily than did Guy de Rothschild, chairman of the Appel Juif Unifié. Alain de Rothschild, meanwhile, encouraged similar changes in CRIF, the representative spokesman of French Jewry. "The sooner our younger elements are exposed to the responsibility of communal leadership, the better my family and I will like it," he insisted, in the course of our conversation. "I've been trying to resign my chairmanship for three years now, but they won't let me." His smile was wistful.

"It's not likely that our family tradition can go on," he continued. "In my father's time, in my uncle Edmond's time, wealthy people didn't have to be clock-watchers. They could come and go as they pleased. No longer. We don't have the time anymore." He hesitated. "Yet who does? A younger man trying to make a fortune can't do it, either. I don't know what the answer is. Certainly we don't want to turn our communal affairs over to professional executives, as you've done in the United States, with all that careerist empire-building. Possibly the answer lies with the younger technocrats, who will know how to make up for limited time with expert management. I don't know." Later, as our discussion ended, he returned to the point again. "In one respect, that young Hajdenberg is right, though. We can't sustain the burden ourselves much longer."

It seemed an accurate assessment. By then, one of Alain's cousins, Edmond de Rothschild, president of France's Bonds for Israel campaign and a major investor in Israel, had moved his business headquarters from Paris to Geneva. Several months later, Guy de Rothschild announced that the Mitterrand government's decision to nationalize the family banks had left him no alternative but to transfer the family's base of operations to New York. Elie de Rothschild, president of the Appel Juif Unifié, had given no indication yet of his intention of pulling up stakes; but, by common recognition, Elie was the least influential of the Rothschild dynasty, and his responsibilities did not seem likely to be sustained by his children (who, like the children of Guy and Alain, are the products of mixed marriages). In the summer of 1982, Alain de Rothschild departed for New York to prepare the transfer of his offices and key personnel from Paris. He was in his New York apartment two months later when he was fatally stricken by a massive coronary, at the age of seventy-two. No deluge would follow. Among the earliest of the "mandarins" to grasp the changing personality of French Jewry, he had presided gracefully and modestly over his people's decisive era of transition.

VI

The Jews of Complacence: Great Britain

The Jetsam and the Grand Dukes

It was a seedy, lower-middle-class neighborhood in Edgware. My walk from the underground station took me past Cypriot greengrocers, Jamaican bakeries and butcheries, Pakistani restaurants. Arnold Wesker's home, a narrow and aged three-story structure, appeared comfortable enough. There was no central heating, of course, but space enough to raise three children. "Not Mayfair, but not the East End, either," Wesker remarked with a chuckle. "It wouldn't do to move too far from my roots." One of Britain's most acclaimed playwrights, he had won success largely by drawing on his Jewish background. Audiences and critics admired the "pungency," the "authenticity," of his work. We sat in his book-strewn study, warmed by an electric heater. He was short. A mod hairdo provided the setting for his delicate Jewish features. "It was hell," he declared straight out. "This wasn't a case of at least not knowing we were poor. We knew it, all right."

For Wesker and his Russian immigrant parents, life in Whitechapel, the main thoroughfare of London's East End, was a cold-water flat on the upper floor of a tenement, toilet facilities on the landing shared with the family below. His parents worked in a sweatshop, sewing clothes on subcontract from a factory. They were leftist. Arnold Wesker himself identified with that tradition as a youth. So did tens of thousands of other impoverished immigrant Jews and their children. My own great-uncle, a newcomer from Lithuania after World War I, had also spent his formative years in the East End, struggling to gain a foothold. "No, sir, the Grenadier Guards Band wasn't waiting to greet *me* at Waterloo Street Station," he recalled in mordant amusement. His family tradition had been Orthodox, and somehow it had remained unshaken by socialism. There had been tens of thousands like him, too.

Orthodox or Bundist or more leftist yet, the immigrant Jews poured through that common East End funnel, nearly 100,000 of them between 1880 and 1914. It was centered on the two westernmost parishes of the borough of Stepney—essentially Whitechapel and St. George's in the East—and spilled over into the adjacent area of Mile End and Bethnal Green. At its peak in 1914, the East End contained 90 percent of London's Jews, and reproduced the mores and flavor of East European Jewish life. During the 1920s and 1930s, Jews still constituted a third of the inhabitants of Stepney, still were largely employed in the "Jewish trades"—tailoring, cabinetmaking, taxi driving, occasionally small retail shops. As in New York's Lower East Side, or in Paris's Belleville, Yiddish culture prevailed. The newspapers tended to be quite leftist, their journalism the articulation of poverty.

Yet the culture of Bundist socialism and *Yiddishkeit* was rapidly dissipated. By World War I, a majority of Jewish children attended the local schools. After the war, virtually all Jewish youngsters did. Their generation displayed a characteristic passion for education, for mastering the idiom and ambience of the widely admired Anglo-Saxon civilization. The pace of their social acceptance never matched the speed of their acculturation, and surely not at the pace of their fellow Jews in the United States. "This country," remarked Wesker, with a mock grimace, "moves with the speed of a stomach turning." The newcomers knew they were unpopular. There were isolated riots against Jewish workers early in the century. Later, the postwar depression produced an organized antisemitic movement, Sir Oswald Mosley's Union of Fascists. Nationalist xenophobia unquestionably was weaker in Britain than on the Continent. Democracy was solidly rooted here. Even so, the forays of Mosley's Blackshirts into Whitechapel convinced Wesker and his friends that the one enduring solution to unemployment and antisemitism was a root-and-branch "Socialist" transformation of society. For thousands of young Jews subsisting in the congested flats of the East End, the god of Marxism had not yet failed.

Neither, ironically, had the patronage of the Anglo-Jewish "aristocracy." In a parallelism of the Jewish experience in France and the United States, the high-water epoch of East European Jewish immigration was also the apogee of Jewish *arrivisme* among the British elite. Jews like Sir George Jessel, Sir Rufus Isaacs, Herbert Samuel, and Edwin Montagu were members of British cabinets or governments. These were the paladins of an earlier, far more acculturated Jewish population that by 1880 numbered approximately sixty thousand—half of them

Sephardim, half Central European Ashkenazim. No conditions had been laid down for *their* settlement, after all, as there had been for French Jewry by the Paris Sanhedrin or for German Jewry by the Prussian Diet. They had been more fully accepted in Britain than in any other European nation, except possibly Italy. In their golden age, between the 1870s and 1920s, they produced nearly a quarter of Britain's (nonlanded) millionaires. Their wealth was concentrated in the City, the financial center of Greater London, among bankers, stockbrokers, and investors such as the Rothschilds, the Montefiores, the Montagus, the Goldsmids.

In public estate as in private wealth, these were the "Grand Dukes" of Anglo-Jewry, members of that tight, much intermarried group of families that at the turn of the century comprised the Anglo-Jewish establishment. At the very top of the pyramid sat a comminuted oligarchy of less than a dozen clans, equally divided between old Sephardim and Central Europeans. One of their most eminent figures was Sir Robert Waley-Cohen, who served as managing director of the Shell Petroleum Corporation until the 1930s. Sir Robert, through his ancestor Levi Barent Cohen, who came to London in the 1780s, was related to nearly every other leading family in Anglo-Jewry: to the Rothschilds, the Montefiores, the Goldsmids, the Samuels. Indeed, collateral alliances linked most of the important dynasties, from the Franklins to the Montagus to the Sassoons. Only the august Rothschilds remained apart, marrying largely among their own cousins. As in France during the same period, moreover, these older families all but monopolized the leadership of Anglo-Jewry in the same paternalistic spirit of their own businesses, handing down responsibility from father to son. Animated by a consuming sense of noblesse oblige, they worked through institutions they themselves had founded and directed, emulating the British aristocracy in relying on volunteerism and the co-option of wealth and talent.

The oldest of these Jewish public bodies, tracing back to the eighteenth century, was the Board of Deputies of British Jews, whose representatives were elected by the nation's synagogue congregations and (in subsequent years) by other Jewish organizations and associations. At no time was the Board endowed with an official standing. Yet, as a purely voluntary body, meeting once a month, it exerted a certain leadership at a time when legally recognized Gemeinden, kahals, and consistoires were the norm on the Continent. The Board achieved its widest prestige in the mid-nineteenth century, under the presidency of the renowned Sir Moses Montefiore, when it played a leading role in the achievement of Anglo-Jewish political emancipation. For many decades afterward, however, the Board essentially marked time, bestirring itself occasionally in the early 1900s and after World War I against the imposition of immigration restrictions. Its revived sense of purpose and urgency awaited the 1930s, the period of Mosley and the British Union of Fascists. Then, from 1933 on, the Board operated as the central coordinating body in the Jewish struggle against nativist reaction. It was the Grand Dukes who also founded the Jewish Board of Guardians to care for the Jewish poor, developing under its patronage a broad network of welfare agencies and activities that played a central role in the life of the East European immigrant population.

By the same token, it was the intertwined network of Jewish millionaires that determined the structure of Anglo-Jewish religion. Their model, not surprisingly, was the Church of England. In 1868, the wealthy elders (Rothschilds, Montagus, and Samuels among them) of a group of London synagogues agreed to merge their separate congregations, their separate endowments, and their nonprofessional staffs into a "United Synagogue" under the spiritual leadership of the "Chief Rabbi of the Great Synagogue." In 1870, an Act of Parliament allowed other synagogues in and out of London to become constituent members. Thereafter, the bulk of the East European immigrants tended almost automatically to join the United Synagogue, to acquiesce tacitly in the leadership of the aristocrats, even in the latter's version of Judaism, which was nominally Orthodox but increasingly anglicized and modernized. Almost imperceptibly over the years, changes in ritual had been authorized by successive chief rabbis. Sermons were delivered in English, services were shortened, and synagogue worship came to possess an air of decorum, which the immigrants regarded as cold, but which their children accepted insofar as they accepted religion at all.

This was the structure of Anglo-Jewish communal life as late as the 1930s. Over its institutions the Grand Dukes continued to reign supreme. The majority of them were still bankers and brokers, and many were titled. The Waley-Cohens were the most ubiquitous and the most involved in Jewish affairs, while the Rothschilds were the most influential and munificent. Between them and their relatives and friends, they were the chairmen or vice-chairmen of the Board of Deputies, the Board of Guardians, the United Synagogue, and of virtually every other Jewish body of consequence—most of which they themselves created and maintained. The social stratification of Britain was altogether emulated within the Anglo-Jewish community.

War and Communal Transformation

This traditionalist state of affairs was abruptly stirred by the emergence of Nazism. Between 1933 and 1941, fully 60,000 German-speaking refugees were added to Britain's Jewish population of 200,000. While the new influx was only a third the size of the earlier East European immigration, it was concentrated in a much shorter period. The nation's response to these beleaguered Jews was not ungenerous. To be sure, the government's attitude was influenced in 1933 by the oldest of Jewish pledges, the commitment of the Anglo-Jewish leadership that "all expense [of accommodating the refugees] will be borne by the Jewish community without ultimate charge to the state." Even so, a voluntary Academic Assistance Council helped to find positions in British universities for refugee scholars, and many private citizens offered the hospitality of their homes to the newcomers. Harold Macmillan, MP, sheltered forty Czech Jews in his house in Sussex. Former Prime Minister Stanley Baldwin launched an appeal fund for aid to the refugees. In December 1938, a society for the "Care of Children from Germany" arranged for the immigration of nearly ten thousand Jewish children, most of whom were then lodged with foster parents, Jewish and non-Jewish. The quiet, unassuming kindness of these families represented the nobler side of British character.

There was another side. The British Medical Association opposed the admission of more than a small number of refugee doctors, and no refugee doctor or dentist was allowed to practice until the war created a shortage. Some newspapers warned against "misguided sentimentalism," the dangers of unemployment, or "outbursts of antisemitism." After the war began, the refugees were designated as "enemy aliens." During the fifth-column panic of 1940, some thirty thousand foreign nationals—most of them Jewish refugees—were confined in grim internment centers and nearly eight thousand were deported to Canada and Australia. In the first two years of the war, the government took the lead in barring Jewish escape routes to England from the Continent and prevented the shipment of food and medicines to the ghettos and concentration camps of Europe.

This coldhearted reaction to human tragedy may have been animated by a fear of Jews flooding into Palestine, even if indirectly, via England. Yet a more decisive factor in the government's implacable bureaucratism was simply the low priority given to Jewish rescue. Jews were exposed as defenseless by then, and thus of little international consequence. They were no longer the "great world force" whom Lloyd George had courted in World War I. More than occasionally, officials responded to Jewish entreaties and demands with undisguised irritation. "The Jews have done nothing but add to our difficulties by propaganda and deeds since the war began," complained J. S. Bennett of the Colonial Office. The view was echoed in September 1944 by A. R. Dew of the Foreign Office, who argued that "a disproportionate amount of the time of this office is wasted in dealing with these wailing Jews."

The rise of Nazism affected British Jewry in many ways. The most obvious impact was financial, for the local community bore the immense burden of assisting German Jewish refugees, and eventually all other European Jews, who managed to reach England. The Board of Deputies, formerly the genial patron of Anglo-Jewish advancement, was now obliged to reorient itself as a major defense organization against revived domestic antisemitism. Most important of all, the rise of the Third Reich accelerated the growth and triumph of Zionism among Anglo-Jewry, and with it a transformation among its ranks. As in France, the old guard—including members of the Rothschild family—scorned the very notion of political Zionism. The East Europeans had embraced it early on, but somewhat ineffectually during their years of settlement and impoverishment.

It was only when Chaim Weizmann and Harry Sacher, both of Russian Jewish background, had succeeded in extracting the Balfour Declaration from the War Cabinet in November 1917 that the older families began to be outflanked. Until then, whenever a Jew wished to approach authority he did so through the Jewish establishment. Weizmann now had opened out a direct contact with the government; the East European community at last had its foot in the door of Whitehall. Soon afterward, with the establishment of the Jewish National Home in Palestine under British mandate, London became the fulcrum of international Zionism; and the Zionist Federation offices in Great Russell Street became the nerve center of the Zionist world. The movement accordingly gained in prestige among Anglo-Jewry itself.

During the next twenty-five years, the Grand Dukes still managed to preserve their leadership of the Board of Deputies, and ensured that the Board maintained a discreetly "non-Zionist" position. Yet their traditional role as advocates for Anglo-Jewry no longer remained uncontested. Increasingly, the rank-and-file membership of the Board reflected the preponderance of East Europeans. Besides Weizmann himself, the challenge to the old guard was issued by another East European Jew. Born in the tsarist Pale of Settlement and reared in London's East End, Selig Brodetsky had achieved a brilliant record as a scholarship student at Cambridge. By 1924, at the age of thirty-one, he was professor of mathematics at Leeds University, and eleven years later was elected national president of the Association of University Teachers. An ardent Zionist, Brodetsky emerged as the spokesman of the growing East European majority in the Board of Deputies. He was elected as the Board's president in 1939, and overwhelmingly reelected in 1943. By then, Zionists had taken over the Board's executive and all its key committees. Henceforth, this body's ethnocentric and Zionist orientation in Jewish affairs was decisively fixed.

The Immigrant Community Comes of Age

The influence of the East Europeans was exerted not only through force of numbers. By the eve of World War II, they had also begun to pull their weight economically. As in the United States, the children of the immigrants were intent on going into business for themselves, on becoming "respectable" members of the middle class. They succeeded within the space of little more than one generation. By 1942, a survey conducted by the *Jewish Chronicle* discovered that 60 percent of Jewish men were self-employed (the national figure was 6 percent). Retailing was the typical route, particularly in the electrical supply business, the radio industry, scrap metal, textiles, clothes, jewelry, and foodstuffs. Even as it required only a few pounds to equip a tailor's workshop, so the establishment of a small radio shop, a clothing store, or a scrap metal enterprise was equally inexpensive. English-speaking by then, thousands of second-generation Jews soon achieved entrepreneurial status.

A few did even better. Arnold Weinstock, son of an immigrant tailor, joined his father-in-law's electrical and radio business, then went on after a series of dazzling takeovers to become chairman of a mammoth company with annual sales in the 1960s approaching the billion-pound mark, and embracing three of the proudest names in British engineering—General Electric, English Electric, and Associated Engineering Industries. In various areas, other Jewish businessmen imaginatively developed the concept of bulk purchase to supply decent-quality merchandise at reasonable prices. The trend toward mass-market retailing had begun even before World War I, but it was not until the interwar period that the enormous purchasing power of the British working classes, whose real wages actually rose through the depression, were fully tapped. Thus, Montague Burton climbed out of the East End to build a network of six hundred shops retailing tailor-made suits, and by the eve of World War II he dominated the mass tailoring business. After serving in the Royal Flying Corps in World War I, John Cohen, son of a Whitechapel tailor, traded in surplus military foodstuffs, then began setting up grocery stores with the help of his large family. Sensing the imminent shift to the suburbs in England, Cohen exploited long-term leases and the leverage of bulk purchasing to sell at cut-rate prices. After some forty years of aggressive buying, advertising, and expansion, his company, Tesco, forged ahead to become one of the largest chains of food stores in England.

Other Jews displayed the same shrewd instinct for the mass market. Barnett Salmon and the four Glueckstein brothers, sons of nineteenth-century German Jewish immigrants, were the first to discern that the respectable Victorian family longed for a respectable place to drink a nice cup of tea. To meet that need, Salmon and the Gluecksteins provided cheap, clean establishments where nonalcoholic beverages and refreshments were sold. Under the name Lyons, they extended their collection of tearooms from London to other British cities. By the mid-1920s, the Lyons white-and-gold decal had become part of the national landscape. By 1969, at the height of its fortunes, the chain had a turnover of £129 million, sold 39 percent of all the ice cream eaten in Britain, owned a quarter of the frozen food market, and also operated a string of restaurants and hotels.

The paragon of entrepreneurial drive may well have been Isaac Wolfson. Sitting in his vacation home in Rehovot, Israel, in the summer of 1981, Wolfson was a stocky man, his mane of white hair set off by thick black eyebrows. Well into his eighties, he spoke in the rich accents of his native Scotland, and with the intensity and enthusiasm of a much younger man. "I was the poorest of the poor," he recalled, with a kind of perverse glee, "so many of us that we didn't know where one began and the other left off." In fact, Wolfson was one of eleven chil-

dren of an immigrant furniture-maker who lived in the slums of
Glasgow. After a brief stint working for his father, he moved to London
in 1920 and began selling clocks, mirrors, and upholstery covers. His
main chance came in 1930, when he was hired as chief buyer for the
Great Universal Stores, a Jewish-owned mail order company, and two
years later he bought a 40 percent stake in the company with the help
of his father and a stockbroker friend.

Streamlining and rationalizing the company in the midst of the depression, Wolfson counted on the purchasing power of the British working classes. Beginning in 1934, too, he embarked on a campaign to buy
up small retail businesses for GUS (and for his own personal holdings).
He continued these purchases during World War II. Although a great
deal of money was circulating then, entrepreneurs often lost patience,
disheartened by wartime price controls and shortages of material. Wolfson had the postwar in mind, and his gamble paid off. Since the early
1970s, Great Universal Stores has become Western Europe's largest
mail order chain. Additionally, through private loans, Wolfson has acquired partnerships for himself in a wide string of diverse companies in
Britain, Canada, South Africa, Hong Kong, the Netherlands, France,
and Israel. In his old age, he divulges no information on his private
fortune. "I live modestly," he insists. "I own no yachts, country houses,
strings of racehorses. This villa in Israel is my one indulgence." But the
fact that he has given some £50 million to charity, including two entire
colleges in Oxford and Cambridge, named after him, and innumerable
benefactions to Jewish and Israeli causes, provides some estimation of
his immense wealth.

Possibly even better known than the vast Wolfson conglomerate,
because it is more visibly identified under its own imprimatur, is the
chain of Marks and Spencer stores. Arriving as a youth from Bialystok
in 1882, Michael Marks began as a stall operator in Leeds, then eventually graduated to a covered market hall, a "penny bazaar." Marks
worked on a low profit margin, but his volume soon enabled him to
branch out to additional penny bazaars in different northern English
towns. By the time he died in 1908, he left behind a prosperous and
rapidly expanding company. In ensuing years, under the direction of
Marks's son, Simon, and son-in-law, Israel Sieff, the firm began market-
ing a wider range of better-quality goods; then, during the 1930s, concentrated on building "superstores," and on larger-scale bulk buying.
By the eve of World War II, Marks and Spencer was operating 234

stores. By 1984, it was operating twice that many—nearly half of them in Canada. Bigger, handsomer, more appealing than their predecessors, these emporiums offer an almost limitless range of merchandise, and provide attractive embellishments to the main streets of every British town and city of consequence. In 1972, when Marcus Sieff, younger son of Israel Sieff, became chairman, Marks and Spencer was already selling 10 percent of all the clothes marketed in Britain. Its annual profits by then exceeded £239 million.

Other vocations besides mass merchandising were pioneered and largely preempted by East European Jews and their children. Thus, two out of three major cinema theater chains, Odeon and Granada, were built by Jewish entrepreneurs. Currently, a sizable proportion of the entertainment business, stretching from Associated Television to London's Palladium, is in the hands of the three Grade brothers, who started life as tap dancers in the music halls of the East End. During the postwar real estate boom, at least one hundred people made a personal fortune of over £1 million in land. It is estimated that fully three-quarters of them were Jews, usually the sons of immigrants. Names like Max Rayne, Jack Cotton, Charles Clore, and Harry Hyams became synonymous with entrepreneurial dash. Through the talents of these men, old Georgian and Victorian buildings were demolished in almost every town center, to be replaced by gleaming steel office blocks. Harold Samuel, who in 1969 acquired the huge (but ailing) City of London Real Property Company, became in one fell swoop the single largest property owner in the world. A clue to Jewish success in property development may well have been a certain hardheaded objectivity. For the children of East European immigrants, property had never been enveloped in mystique, as it had for more traditional Englishmen. It was simply another commodity whose profit potential lay substantially unrecognized. And Jewish investors were prepared to take the risks involved.

By 1970, of the five hundred leading companies listed in the *Times* (London) index, twenty-three were Jewish, and their number has since nearly doubled. They include Marks and Spencer, Great Universal Stores, Montague Burton, Lyons, Granada, Sears Holdings, City Centre Properties, General Electric, Associated Engineering Industries, Shell, ICI—altogether a major cross-section of the British economy. By the same token, Jews have virtually preempted the manufacture and distribution of clothing, footwear, and all consumer goods sold through chain stores, and of course a large share of property development.

In recompense for their efforts, some of them have achieved the official recognition that counts most in Britain—induction into the knighthood, even occasionally into the peerage. Isaac Wolfson is Sir Isaac Wolfson. Both Simon Marks and Israel Sieff moved from baronetcy to barony, as did Sieff's son, Marcus. The registry of knighthood has included the widest spectrum of Jewish entrepreneurs, from Sir Arnold Weinstock to Sir John Cohen to Sir Lew Grade. The Salmons and Gluecksteins of Lyons Tearooms have boasted among them two privy councillors, seven knights, six commanders of the British Empire, three members of Parliament, the chairman of the Greater London Council, a high court judge, and a cabinet minister. These and other titled Jews have tended to bear their eminence with varying degrees of diffidence, from the genial unpretentiousness of Sir Isaac Wolfson and Sir John Cohen to the rather overpowering self-esteem of Lord Marcus Sieff, the current chairman of Marks and Spencer (whose office in Baker Street, with its retinue of flunkies, has been compared to Mussolini's). Whatever their self-image, the image they projected to others as early as the 1950s was of an immigrant community that within the space of two generations had propelled itself to security and a reasonable degree of social acceptance—even by the standards of the older nativized Jewish establishment.

Moving Out

As late as 1914, it is recalled, fully nine-tenths of London Jewry, some 200,000 people, were concentrated in the East End. After World War I, the pattern began to shift, and by 1930 less than a third of London's Jews still made their homes in Stepney and Bethnal Green. This migration was accelerated by World War II. Large areas of Stepney were flattened by Luftwaffe bombing, and many families were evacuated elsewhere. At the same time, rent controls placed housing in the more desirable northern and northwestern parts of London within the means of numerous East End dwellers. Because the main underground lines connected East London with the suburbs north of the Thames, the cynosure for London Jewry became the northern boroughs of Edgware, Willesden Green, and to a lesser degree the boroughs of Hendon, Finchley, and Wembley. Edgware was and has remained a somewhat charmless place, comfortable without being expensive, greatly favored by families that have reached a modest level of affluence. The row houses are heavily Jewish, one *mezuzah* after another affixed to the doorposts, the main streets well supplied with synagogues and delicatessens. As late as the 1980s, London Jews have remained considerably less suburbanized than Londoners in general; they tend to prefer the metropolis to the countryside. Among their third and fourth generations, there seems to be a distinct inclination for the inner London boroughs of Hackney and Westminster.

The residential pattern has long since shifted in other communities, as well, with older Jewish areas such as Cheetham in Manchester and Cheepeltown in Leeds declining in favor of new suburban enclaves. Nevertheless, the centrality of London in Anglo-Jewish life has increased (the opposite of the patterns in the United States and France). By 1984, of an Anglo-Jewish population estimated at between 360,000 and 390,000 (no official figures are available), Manchester still contains 30,000; Leeds, 18,000; Glasgow, 13,400; Liverpool and Brighton, 7,500 each; Birmingham, 6,300; Cardiff, 5,000; Southend and Westcliff, 4,000; Bournemouth, 3,500; Newcastle and Southampton, 3,000; while Belfast, Edinburgh, Leicester, Nottingham, and Sheffield sustain Jewish communities of approximately 1,000 each. These figures represent a growth of provincial Jewry from 90,000 at the turn of the century to the current number of some 120,000. Yet the rise of London Jewry to perhaps 240,000, fully two-thirds of British Jewry, indicates a doubling of the capital's population since 1900.

Does the improvement in their status affect Jewish political behavior? Well ensconced today in the middle and upper-middle income brackets, British Jews might have been expected to vote Conservative. There is even precedent for this affiliation. A century ago, wealthy Jews exerted a certain influence within the Tory Party, and as late as 1900, of the twelve Jewish MPs, eight were Tories. Yet throughout the first third of the twentieth century, most Jews, even affluent Jews, gravitated increasingly to the Liberals. The party was conservative enough not to put off Jewish millionaires, yet was trusted by Jews of all income levels for its traditional championship of religious liberty. As a result, when the Liberals declined as a major force after World War I, Jewish representation in politics similarly declined for many years. The Conservative Party had become identified with a certain genteel antisemitism. On the other hand, socialism had lost its initial appeal for the

East European immigrants; during the interwar period, the Labor Party tended to pick its MPs from among the Gentile working classes. It was only after World War II that Jews began turning in increasing numbers to Labor. The change was largely a reaction to the Conservatives' post-war record of anti-Zionism and thinly disguised antisemitism (Churchill notwithstanding). By the 1950s, almost all Jewish MPs were Laborites.

The best-known of them was Sidney Silverman. Liverpool-born, the son of an impoverished Russian immigrant, Silverman had become a confirmed Socialist in his teens. As a conscientious objector in World War I, he served two years' imprisonment, and half starved by refusing to eat nonkosher food (it was not a matter of piety but of principle). In 1927, Silverman opened a modest solicitor's office in Liverpool and devoted his major efforts to the dockworkers. Police and bigoted magistrates soon learned to respect this pocket battleship who steamed out with all guns blazing in the cause of his working-class clients. Elected MP in 1935 for Nelson and Colne, a constituency he represented until his death, Silverman attacked the Tories with scorn and passion. At the same time, he threw himself into the struggle on behalf of Hitler's victims. As chairman of the British section of the World Jewish Congress, he used all his legal knowledge and parliamentary skill to call his nation's attention to the Nazi atrocities. It was Silverman, we recall, whom Riegner used to inform the Allies of the Final Solution. After the war, horrified by the spectacle that met his eyes in Bergen-Belsen, Silverman helped draft the White Paper on Nazi crimes against the Jews and also became an impassioned Zionist. His attacks in the House of Commons on Foreign Secretary Ernest Bevin, the archenemy of Jewish independence in Palestine, were merciless, and on one occasion actually drove Bevin out of the House. But eventually Silverman's whiplash sarcasm and refusal to compromise, as well as his hatred of his party's line on Vietnam, got him expelled from Labor's parliamentary faction and induced Prime Minister Harold Wilson to threaten to "muzzle" him and the other "dogs" if they persisted.

Although forty-two Jewish MPs in the House of Commons in 1970 were Laborites, their influence within the party was never substantial. Like Silverman, most of them were left-wingers, and during the postwar years Labor was dominated by centrists such as Attlee, Gaitskell, and Wilson. Harold Laski, once Labor's major theorist, saw his influence swiftly erode following the victory over Churchill in 1945. From the 1960s on, Jewish progressives have tended increasingly to vote their pocketbooks and social status, much as do other Englishmen. Currently, with the issue of antisemitism or even anti-Zionism no longer urgent, most Jews have divided their votes almost evenly, and in recent years there has been a resurgence of Conservative Jewish MPs. Indeed, in 1982 Jews served at all echelons of Margaret Thatcher's government. Sir Issac Wolfson's nephew David was the prime minister's administrative chief of staff. Sir Keith Joseph, one of three Jewish cabinet ministers, was her closest domestic adviser. With Jewish voters influenced by the identical economic and security questions that preoccupy other Englishmen, it is almost unthinkable for them to regard themselves as a separate ethnic community. Even occasional surveys of Jewish voting patterns have embarrassed the leadership of the Board of Deputies, who quickly reject any notion of a "Jewish vote" in the pattern of the United States or, increasingly, of France. For British Jews, political "objectivity" is the proof of their acculturation.

N. M. Rothschild & Sons is located in New Court, on St. Swithins Lane, in the heart of the City. It is the headquarters of the House of Rothschild in England. Functional in its steel and marble, the building was erected in 1965 to replace the palazzo-like structure built in 1867, which itself was the successor to the Rothschilds' first London office in 1804. The vice-chairman, Sir Claus Moser, awaited me. He was a tall, lean, balding man of sixty, his brown eyes lending warmth to finely drawn features. Although his manner at first was typically reserved, he was direct and, in time, engaging. "I've never felt anything other than a German Jew," he confessed, a remark he had made publicly in a television interview several days earlier.

Moser was born into a distinguished Berlin banking family. His grandfather and father held the controlling interest in the Fromberg Bank, one of the German capital's largest private financial institutions. If the life was one of affluence, it was also one of high culture, particularly of musical culture. Both parents, Moser himself, his brother and sister, were talented pianists. The family fled in 1936, settling in England. The father had been transferring funds to London as early as the 1920s, and their financial circumstances as a result were better than those of most of their fellow refugees. Numbering sixty thousand by World War II, these new immigrants represented one of every seven Jews in Great Britain. They were also a far more bourgeois and cultured element than their East European predecessors, adapting much more rapidly to British life. The German and British ambiences were not that far apart. Dignity was the key.

The Mosers settled into a comfortable suburban home in Putney. The two sons attended a boarding school in Surrey, and were well treated. "It was British decency and sportsmanship at its best," Claus Moser recalled. He also saw the British at their worst. In May 1940, his family was among those interned as "enemy aliens," and was obliged to live behind barbed wire in a Liverpool detention camp. Six months passed before the Mosers were allowed to return to their home in Putney. Claus (he had dropped the German *K* by then) was enrolled in the London School of Economics. In 1943, he was graduated with first-class honors in statistics. Following a three-year stint with the RAF, he accepted a lectureship in statistics at the School of Economics. He published prolifically. Two of his books, *Survey Methods in Social Investigation* and *British Towns*, became classics, and he was appointed a full professor while still in his thirties.

Moser's success was characteristic of the German Jewish immigrant group, which provided hundreds of faculty members at Britain's universities, and several thousand physicians, scientists, musicians, publishers, and businessmen of high standing and recognition. Two German Jews, Sir Hans Kreb and Sir Ernst Chain, became Nobel laureates. Moser himself in 1961 was appointed a statistical adviser to the prime minister's committee on higher education. In that capacity, he supervised the formulation of a report proposing that Britain's universities be opened to thousands of qualified students through an extensive government scholarship program. The recommendation was put into effect and its impact on British education was far-reaching. For his role, Moser was made Commander of the British Empire, and in 1967 appointed director of the office of central statistics, a permanent undersecretaryship that represented the highest rank in the civil service.

By then, other Jews, of East European and Central European backgrounds alike, had moved into the top echelons of the civil service. Among them were Sir Ben Barnett, chairman of the Commonwealth Telecommunications Board; Sir Andrew Cohen, permanent undersecretary of the ministry of overseas development and a former governor of Uganda; Sir Edgar Cohen, permanent representative to the Organization for European Economic Cooperation; Sir Ben Lockspeiser, secretary of the department of scientific and industrial research; Sir Solly Zuckerman, chief scientific adviser to the ministry of defense. The question of their Jewishness was never raised. Moser himself was always a proud, if nonobservant, Jew. His relations with his colleagues were excellent. Indeed, he was a close friend of Prime Minister Edward Heath; their mutual love of music created a bond.

In 1977, Lord Evelyn de Rothschild asked Moser to join his bank as vice-chairman with special responsibility for the intelligence unit of *The Economist*, a Rothschild-owned journal. Thereafter, Moser served as the bank's principal financial adviser to clients ranging from the government of Singapore to Britain's largest universities. Widely respected for his erudition, both economic and musical, he was elected chairman of the board of governors of Covent Garden in 1974, and in that position immediately assumed a major responsibility for London's cultural scene. The commingling of his three careers—academic, financial, musical—in effect represented a paradigm of the German Jewish role in British life.

Yet an affinity for the liberal professions is increasingly characteristic of Jews of all backgrounds in Britain, as elsewhere. Comprising less than 1 percent of the British population, Jews represent 3 percent of all university students, 5 percent of the nation's doctors, 9 percent of its lawyers. Their role as academicians is beginning to approach that of American Jews, and at every level. In the past two decades, the president of one Oxford college was not only a Jew but an American, Arthur Goodhart, a member of the Lehman banking clan. David Daiches, son of a Scottish rabbi, was dean of the School of English and American Studies at Sussex University. Max Beloff, Gladstone Professor of Government, resigned his chair at Oxford in 1972 to become president of University College of Buckingham. Both Beloff and Martin Gilbert, a fellow of Merton College, Oxford, a distinguished biographer of Churchill and the author of a number of semipopular works on the Holocaust, have emphasized that their Jewishness has created no obstacle whatever to their academic careers or to those of their Jewish colleagues. Sir Isaiah Berlin, professor of social and political theory at Oxford, has emerged as the most legendary figure in Britain's entire academic constellation. In 1966, Berlin was appointed first president of Wolfson College, and since then has been showered with honors, including a baronetcy, the Order of Merit, membership in the British Academy, and later the Academy's presidency.

A useful index to Jewish prominence in the learned professions is the rising number of Jews elected as fellows of the Royal Society (from twelve in 1948 to forty-nine in 1983) and as fellows of the British Academy (from four to twenty-two in the same period). The reservoir of Jewish professionals also includes many hundreds of Jewish musicians, composers, directors, producers, writers, playwrights. Today it is no longer possible to find any significant area of British life from which Jews are excluded.

The Quality of Faith

The instinct for respectability is also evident in Anglo-Jewry's "ecclesiastical" affiliations. Presently, no less than 470 synagogues are functioning in the United Kingdom, half of these in Greater London. The United Synagogue represents some 200 of them and lists 40,000 families on its rolls. With an income of £1.5 million a year, this largest of Jewish religious organizations still wields enough influence to nominate the chief rabbi, whose authority extends to Ashkenazic congregations not only in Britain but throughout the entire Commonwealth except for Canada. The United Synagogue also supports Jews College, which trains Orthodox rabbis, supplies Jewish chaplains, underwrites much of the budget for religious education, and provides religious instruction for Jewish students in state schools. Until the 1960s, this record of institutional service was all that the United Synagogue's members asked of it. Orthodox in their affiliation out of respect for their parents or grandparents, most second- or third-generation Jews were content that their religious establishment, like that of the wider British community, remain bland, tolerant, gentle, accepting rabbinical students and proselytes with minimal qualifications, and by and large avoiding the strictures of "legalism." Currently, the typical British rabbi embodies a certain pallid blending of English and Jewish cultures— rather like a Jewish version of an English parson, down to the canonical collar.

Meanwhile, the Federation of Synagogues, established in 1887 by a committedly traditional group of East European immigrants, has continued to hold its own, with 176 constituent congregations (in 1984), most of these considerably smaller and less affluent than their counterparts in the United Synagogue, but with a respectable membership of 17,000 families. Efforts to unite the two groups have invariably failed. In addition, there is an ultra-Orthodox group that developed in the interwar period, the Union of Orthodox Hebrew Congregations, better known as Adat. Founded by Hungarian immigrants, it has tended in recent decades toward the self-segregating practices of Chasidism, and its congregations are found largely in the Stamford Hill section of London. It was also the militant new group of Orthodox refugees from Central and Eastern Europe that challenged the historically tolerant consensus within the United Synagogue itself. The strident fundamentalism of this element ultimately exhausted the patience of the president of the United Synagogue, Ewen Montagu. In 1962, Montagu surrendered his post to Isaac Wolfson, the famed millionaire, in the hope that Wolfson's wealth and standing among the immigrant community would enable him to control the unruly new faction. Soon after, the so-called Jacobs Affair unfolded.

Louis Jacobs, son of a Manchester working-class family, had received his ordination at Jews College, then had gone on to Oxford to study philosophy and comparative religion. In 1954, at the age of thirty-four, he was called to the pulpit of the New West End Synagogue in London's fashionable Bayswater district, where his keen intellect made an immediate impact. In his preaching, as in two of his books, Jacobs restated traditional Judaism in terms congenial to the twentieth-century mind. He raised objections to only a few Orthodox precepts, essentially the Mosaic authorship of the Torah, the textual accuracy of other parts of the Bible, and the doctrines of physical resurrection and punishment in the world to come. But it was these reservations that the fundamentalists regarded as "apostasy." In 1959, Jacobs became a faculty member at Jews College, with the understanding that he would replace the principal, who was to retire shortly. The school's reputation had declined in recent decades, and Jacobs seemed to be the man capable of revitalizing its curriculum and faculty. From the college, it was also assumed that he would eventually succeed Chief Rabbi Israel Brodie. Meanwhile, it was Brodie who controlled the appointment of the principal of Jews College.

The first chief rabbi to be British-born and Oxford-educated, Brodie was a less forceful personality and surely less of a scholar than his predecessors, and during the 1950s he tended to defer to the sternly Orthodox members of his religious court. Under their pressure, he announced in 1961 that he would not approve Jacobs's eventual appointment as principal. Whereupon Jacobs relinquished his tutorship. At this point, all but one of the honorary officers of Jews College resigned in protest, the events created a tempest in Jewish organizational circles, and even the national press gave them a certain attention. After a few months, however, the Jacobs Affair seemed to have run its course. Two years went by. Finally, in 1963, Bayswater's New West End Synagogue acted to bring Jacobs back to his old post. Under the constitution of the United Synagogue, however, it was the chief rabbi who was authorized to certify this appointment, and Brodie refused to do so. The Jacobs Affair immediately revived and burgeoned into a cause célèbre in the Jewish community. Despite the avalanche of criticism from the membership of the United Synagogue itself, Brodie insisted that rabbis were obliged to accept the literal interpretation of the Torah in all its details. In fact, this was the first time that acceptance of fundamentalist tenets had been made a condition of appointment in the United Synagogue, which historically was known for its latitudinarianism. Accepting the challenge, the New West End Synagogue voted overwhelmingly to disregard the chief rabbi's ban.

The next step was up to Sir Isaac Wolfson, as president of the United Synagogue. Far from being a moderate, Wolfson made much of the fact that he was a man of simple piety, a *frum* (observant) sort of chap, who accepted the Torah without reservation, and who detected in his vast business success the hand of God. Hurriedly summoning the United Synagogue council, Wolfson authorized a resolution expelling the New West End Synagogue management committee from office. The resolution was seen as a triumph not only of "traditionalism" over "heresy," but also—in view of the opposition to the measure led by Baron Edmund de Rothschild and some of the famous names in Anglo-Jewry—of new money over old money. The garish publicity that followed in the British press and television was far more extensive than in the initial phase of the affair. For British Jews, a notoriously self-effacing community, the embarrassment was acute. Yet for Jacobs and the synagogue, the decision was without practical effect. After having been removed from office, the management committee simply founded its own, independent, New London Synagogue—headed, of course, by Jacobs. From this pulpit, Jacobs afterward launched no radical innovations within Anglo-Jewry. An amiable man, he limited himself subsequently to expressions of mild concern about the future of Anglo-Judaism and the danger of the United Synagogue's becoming ultra-Orthodox ("something entirely alien to our British tradition," he assured me).

Other alternatives to the Orthodox establishment have not been lacking. Reform Judaism currently supports twenty-six congregations, with a membership of ten thousand families. Emerging from the moderate and cautious nineteenth-century tradition of German Liberal Judaism, Reform in England was not modernist enough for the taste of Claude Goldsmid Montefiore. The scion of two distinguished Anglo-Jewish houses, Montefiore joined with Lily Montagu in the early 1900s to pioneer Liberal Judaism, a far more revisionist version of its German namesake. Over the ensuing decades, British Liberal Judaism came to match Reform in size and influence. Currently, the movement lists some twelve thousand families on its rolls. In theory, the Liberal movement is somewhat closer to early American Reform, while British Reform continues to adhere to the more traditionalist approach of German Liberalism. Both movements long remained immune to Zionism, an attitude that for years inhibited their popularity. That stance eventually changed with the Holocaust and the birth of Israel. Liberal and Reform Jews alike made their peace with Zionism. Additionally, in a period of growing intermarriage, both movements were more hospitable to converts. Their major era of growth accordingly was in the 1940s and 1950s. In 1956, the Reform movement opened its own theological seminary, later called Leo Baeck College. Eventually the seminary was underwritten by both groups, even as both established a joint Council of Liberal and Reform Rabbis. Yet the two movements together have attracted barely 10 percent of the United Synagogue's membership.

The latter, meanwhile, under its most recent chief rabbi, Immanuel Jakobovits—German-born and rigid in his theology—continues to maintain its domination over British Jewry. It has sustained this primacy despite the loss of intellectual vitality, the erosion of public reputation that attended the Jacobs controversy, and a remorseless legalism that severely discourages conversions. Evidently British Jews, like British Gentiles, are unable or unwilling to shake themselves loose from tradition. "It's very British to be Orthodox establishment," sighed Jacobs. "It's very British to be conservative."

But if Anglo-Jewry as a whole, through habit and sheer inertia, tolerates the United Synagogue's authority, it has been unwilling to allow its children to vegetate in quite the same torpor. Until well after World War II, a majority of Jewish pupils received their religious education in late afternoon synagogue classes that were conducted by ill-equipped instructors. After undergoing Bar Mitzvah, few youngsters continued to study. During the 1950s, visiting Jewish educators from the United

States repeatedly advised that a broad spectrum of day schools, offering a solid program of Jewish studies, was urgently needed. In fact, for over two decades British Jews had been tentatively moving in that direction, and with the help of the British government itself. In an effort to improve the nation's antiquated school facilities, Parliament in 1944 enacted the Butler Education Act, authorizing government funding to religious denominations that constructed new schools on their own. British Jewry's response was typically languid, however, for half the costs were to be borne by the community itself. Even so, a network of Jewish day schools began to emerge. The momentum for this development was further accelerated by the growing influx of West Indian and African immigrants into middle-class neighborhoods, and of their children into neighborhood schools. Confronting this development, British Jews responded, as did many of their American kin, with a belated discovery of the values of private Jewish education.

Currently, the day schools range from ultra-Orthodox, Chasidic institutions (distinctly submarginal), to the Yavneh Association's first-rate King David schools, to Carmel College, a secondary school of the highest quality. Their classes are attended by sixteen thousand children, or 14 percent of the Jewish school population. By contrast, 60 percent of Catholic children attend Catholic schools. Nevertheless, the ratio of one out of seven Jewish youngsters in parochial schools is a meaningful increase since the prewar period, and the ratio is steadily climbing.

Whatever the future impact of the day school movement, the quality of religious-educational life among British Jews remains exceptionally shallow. A survey conducted by the *Jewish Chronicle* in 1978 suggested that less than half the families even of children who belonged to Jewish youth movements or who attended day schools observed the Sabbath, and a quarter did not observe Yom Kippur. The central feature of Anglo-Jewish religious life continues to be the Bar Mitzvah, and after that, fund-raising, which of course is not religious at all but associated rather with Israel and the fear of antisemitism. As in many other Western Jewish communities, the integuments binding Anglo-Jewry appear to be neither faith nor a shared cultural heritage, but a kind of unfocused Zionism and the instinct for conviviality with one's own kind.

A Diffusion of Communal Vitality

Woburn House is the organizational center of British Jewry. Some six or seven stories high, on Upper Woburn Place, in central London, the aging structure is the headquarters of the Board of Deputies as well as many others of the Jewish community's principal institutions and agencies. A spacious auditorium shares the ground level with the Jewish Museum, containing an impressive display of artifacts, photographs, and documents extending back through five centuries of Anglo-Jewish history. On the morning of my visit, the auditorium was filled with perhaps three hundred of the Board's deputies—slightly more than half the required quorum—in their monthly convocation.

From my vantage point in the balcony, the participants seemed fairly evenly divided between men and women, and most of them were on the down side of fifty. Large numbers of the men wore skullcaps for the occasion, a display of piety that characteristically evaporated later at the main exit. The atmosphere was informal, with a great deal of *shul*-like chatter, interspersed with occasional admonitions for silence, and more than occasional dozing. No surprises there; I had not been led to expect the paladins of Anglo-Jewish social or cultural life. Synagogue committee chairmen, Zionist women's chairpersons, members of Hebrew school and adult education boards, these middle-class patrons and matrons bore no resemblance to the elegant Sir Claus Moser or to the formidable Lord Marcus Sieff. They were nothing more or less than representative of their constituents—and possibly of Anglo-Jewry at large.

As I took my seat, the subject under discussion was Margaret Thatcher's recent address on the occasion of the Board's annual banquet. The prime minister had criticized Israel's recent annexation of the Golan Heights, and the delegates now were vigorously debating an appropriate collective reply. The arguments pro and con were interrupted from time to time with cries of "Hear, Hear" or "Shame." All very reminiscent of the House of Commons. So were the endless committee reports that followed. It was the report of the committee on Jewish defense and group relations that elicited the delegates' complete attention. Antisemitism was at issue. Monitoring occasional Fascist and other anti-democratic groups, the committee also had the task of encouraging government legislation against incitement; of supplying hundreds of speakers each year to lecture on Jews and Judaism at schools, colleges, adult classes, clubs, societies.

Was the vigilance still warranted in the 1980s? Surely not as much as in earlier decades. Between 1945 and 1948, underground Zionist violence against British personnel in Palestine had touched off serious anti-Jewish outbreaks in England for the first time in nearly thirty years.

Exploiting the angry mood, Sir Oswald Mosley had formed a new "Union" party, essentially a collection of young toughs who set out to provoke clashes with Jews. By 1953, Mosley's effort had guttered out. The booming postwar economy had largely eradicated the remaining pockets of ethnic tensions. In later years, other fringe groups occasionally surfaced, dredging up the old libels. One of these, Colin Jordan's National Front, gained a certain publicity during the economic crisis following the 1973 Middle East war. Membership in the National Front reached perhaps twenty thousand, then swiftly declined with the end of the Arab oil blockade. Fluctuating primarily with the employment situation, these movements received no substantial backing from any important group. In the past two decades, moreover, hundreds of thousands of "coloreds" have poured in from throughout the Commonwealth, establishing new ghettos, and public attention has focused on them.

If there is a residual danger for Britain's Jewish minority, it lies in a possible "spillover" of anti-Israel sentiment. Outspoken in its criticism of Israel in recent years, the British press, especially the *Times*, is not always careful to distinguish between Israelis and Diaspora Jews. Thus, during my own visit to London, an episode of Arab unrest in the West Bank elicited a *Times* headline reading: "Jews Break Arab Legs." Other press accounts dealt with the "collapse of Jewish morality"—in Israel, as it turned out. The Board's concern was not unwarranted, then, as press and television commentators appeared to be obsessed with Israel's wrongdoings, alleged or real. The potential existed for a diffusion of identification between Israelis and Jews.

As I sat in the balcony of the auditorium in Woburn House, the committee reports—on foreign affairs, adult education, disarmament, Holocaust commemorations—droned on amid the low counterpoint of chitchat and housewifely gossip. They provided little insight into this community's values and priorities. A better source of information would have been the *Jewish Chronicle*. Published weekly, the *Chronicle* is incomparably the most professional, and most respected, Jewish newspaper in the Diaspora. Its latest circulation of 70,000, including 4,000 subscribers in the United States, assures it of a minimum of 300,000 readers. It is also one of the oldest newspapers in Britain, having been founded early in the nineteenth century, and is certainly the oldest Jewish newspaper in any language in the world. Yet the *Chronicle* did not transcend the limitations of a communal bulletin until William

Frankel became its editor in 1958. A lawyer by training, Frankel immediately broadened the *Chronicle*'s coverage from local Jewish events to developments of Jewish consequence throughout the world. He was also determined to prod the Anglo-Jewish community into serious thought. Thus, during the Jacobs controversy, the *Chronicle* forthrightly attacked the "medievalism" of the chief rabbinate. Additionally, Frankel was intent upon exposing his readers to the brilliant young group of postwar Jewish writers. He suspected that the latter's views were both fresh and acerbic.

He was not wrong. The new crop of authors included Bernard Kops, Brian Glanville, Wolf Mankowitz, Peter Shaffer, Harold Pinter, and Arnold Wesker, among others. In addition to their fiction, they were arguably the nation's best playwrights. As matters turned out, they also had very definite ideas about the quality of Jewishness in England. In 1948, Brian Glanville was the first to come to terms with his background, in a cool, somewhat acidulous, study of London Jewish suburban life. His confrontation took the form of a novel. Entitled *The Bankrupts*, and set in Golders Green, the sprawling Jewish middle-class suburb in northwest London, the book provided a rather cheerless picture of domineering parents, weak children, and an altogether shallow subculture. Indeed, as a mirror to their world, the novel was a sobering jolt for Anglo-Jewry. Then, in 1960, Frederick Raphael and Gerda Charles published their own mercilessly critical pictures of Anglo-Jewish life. Subsequently, Glanville, Raphael, and Charles were bracketed together as the "Golders Green School." It was this "school," too, that heralded the onrush of a new wave of books and plays by Jews about Jews. Few quite matched the caliber of Bellow's or Malamud's works in the United States, but some were interesting, even enduring. These included Wolf Mankowitz's *Make Me an Offer*, William Goldman's *The East End My Cradle*, Alexander Baron's *With Hope Farewell*, Dannie Abse's *Ash on a Young Man's Sleeve*, and Bernard Kops's *The Hamlet of Stepney Green*. A new younger writer, Bernice Rubens, won the Booker Prize, Britain's premier literary award, with her third novel, *The Elected Member*, a grim account of an Orthodox Jewish family coping with a heroin addict in its midst.

It was a measure of William Frankel's imagination, then, even his courage, that he persuaded Glanville, Pinter, Kops, Wesker, Mankowitz, Shaffer, Abse, and Baron to write articles for the *Chronicle,* describing what they envisaged to be the impact of their Jewish backgrounds on their creative work. With hardly an exception, the authors insisted that Jewishness had exerted virtually no influence on their writing, that they regarded the Jewish tradition altogether with a distinct lack of enthusiasm. It was an unanticipated commentary. Indeed, the series immediately provoked howls of outrage from the *Chronicle*'s rather staid, middle-class constituency. Nonetheless, Frankel had performed an important service (the *Chronicle*'s soaring circulation testified to the fact) by laying bare a harsh and important truth. In England, Jewish intellectuals were not attracted to Jewish life. Surveys in later years merely confirmed this discovery. Out of the scores of Anglo-Jewish artists, three or at most four were "active" in the Jewish community. At the outbreak of the Six-Day War in 1967, to be sure, a hurriedly formed Writers' Committee for Israel obtained the support of nearly every Jewish writer in Britain—but also of many non-Jewish writers. And soon afterward the committee lapsed. Even where their work was unmistakably Jewish in tone, as in the case of Wesker, Abse, Mankowitz, Kops, or Raphael, Jewish artists clearly preferred to remain outsiders.

Perhaps there was a certain fey justice to this repudiation. The Anglo-Jewish middle class is itself largely uninterested in higher culture. As notoriously philistine as its British counterpart, the Jewish community shares the British sense of pragmatism, neither respecting nor particularly trusting intellectuals. The contrast with France, and its profound admiration for intellectualism, could hardly be more vivid. In the early 1960s, Anthony Blond, an enterprising young publisher, convinced himself that there was a rich Jewish market waiting to be tapped, and brought out a number of titles with specifically Jewish themes. He lost money on all of them. Another publisher, Valentine Mitchell, a subsidiary of the *Jewish Chronicle,* sputtered along for twenty-four years, publishing about half a dozen titles annually, including *The Diary of Anne Frank* and Leonard Stein's magisterial *The Balfour Declaration,* without making money. The firm eventually was sold in 1975. In the early 1970s, the *Chronicle*'s own literary supplement was reduced to a quarterly, and now appears only twice a year. The novelist and MP Maurice Edelman tried to establish a Jewish periodical that "could look *Commentary* in the face" (at a time when *Commentary* was a Jewish magazine), but found no backers. The *Jewish Quarterly,* once a superior scholarly and literary review, eventually went defunct. Little wonder that the two thousand or so Jewish intellectuals have tended to remain as indifferent to the Jewish community as the latter has to them. Britain's intellectual ambience in any event can hardly be equated with that of the United States, which in recent decades has been charged with acute awareness of its regional heritage as well as of the impact of ethnicity. Unlike the Americans, the British have never countenanced a forthright tradition of cultural pluralism.

The somnolence of Anglo-Jewish religious and cultural life is paralleled by demographic decline. Investigations conducted by the Board of Deputies suggest that the Anglo-Jewish population in 1983 probably is closer to 360,000 than to the 390,000 figure more commonly cited, and even that number is uncertain. Jewish families in Britain average less than two children per family unit. The rate of intermarriage is climbing; in 1976, the Board of Deputies estimated the figure at 20 percent. If these statistics are less than foreboding by the standards of the Continent, there appears little chance that the children of mixed marriages will remain Jewish in any meaningful numbers, particularly when the rabbinate makes conversions all but impossible. Uncertainty about the Jewish demographic future has led Chaim Bermant, the most prolific commentator on the Anglo-Jewish scene and a man who does not share the rabbinate's vested interest in dire prognostications, to prophesy that "as a community [the Jews of England] seem on the way to extinction." A well-worn lament, of course, heard in every Jewish community in modern times.

The Voice of Jerusalem

There has been at least one dependable talisman for Anglo-Jewish identity. Discussions at Woburn House on the Israeli annexation of the Golan Heights awakened the delegates from their lethargy. Heads were raised. Eyes shone with passion. The Board of Deputies had to take a position, after all. Admittedly, its resolutions would exert no *serious* impact on the London stock exchange, but could the members simply accept Prime Minister Thatcher's recent criticism without a word of protest? The focus of Anglo-Jewry's emotional loyalties could not be left in doubt. Those loyalties had been dramatically fortified by the Middle Eastern crisis of 1967. The response then was as overwhelming in Britain as in other Diaspora communities. Ten thousand people attended a mass rally for Israel at the Royal Albert Hall. Community leaders and other prominent Jewish businessmen lobbied members of Parliament.

Eight thousand young people registered for service in Israel by the end of June, and over a thousand of them actually departed.

The financial response was massive. The machinery of fund-raising, the Joint Palestine Appeal, remained essentially in the hands of the Marks, Sieff, and Sacher families—whose forebears in their turn had been Chaim Weizmann's earliest patrons. During the 1960s and 1970s, Lord Marcus Sieff and Michael Sacher ran the Zionist Federation almost as if it were a branch of Marks and Spencer. In large measure, the Joint Palestine Appeal functioned as a branch of the Zionist Federation, and the JPA's fund-raising dinners over the years had become as much a part of the Jewish calendar as the High Holidays. Yet contributions tripled and quadrupled during the June 1967 crisis. As always, the blue-chip group of millionaires gathered to make their gifts on the top floor of Marks and Spencer's headquarters in Baker Street. At the same time, telegrams were pouring out of JPA headquarters at Rex House, calling other supporters to meetings in synagogues throughout the country. And people gave as they never had in their lives. Within a period of some two months, British Jews raised a total of £6 million, a higher amount proportionately than the sum contributed by American Jewry.

In the years since, the Joint Israel Appeal (the name was updated) has functioned as one of numerous fund-raising causes for Israel. Almost every ancillary Israeli enterprise or institution—religious, educational, cultural, medical—has organized its own constituency, and they have raised over £2.5 million a year throughout the 1970s and early 1980s. With the Zionist Federation and its sister groups, they publish various periodicals, foster Hebrew studies, and sustain intensive public relations programs. As an ideology, however, Anglo-Zionism for some years has appeared to be losing its élan. At most, 10,000 British Jews have emigrated to Israel since 1948, and only a minority of these have become Israeli citizens. Few of the Zionist Youth Movement's 6,500 members have been persuaded to settle in Israel. As far back as the 1960s, the Zionist Federation decided to branch into the field of Jewish education, and within the ensuing decade and a half it established its own impressive network of day schools with a student population of 12,000. Otherwise, Zionism in Britain, as in other Western Jewish communities, has been disoriented by Israel's rightist government, and its growing uncertainty of purpose has tended to blur Israel's role in the Anglo-Jewish community.

In truth, Anglo-Jewish organizational life altogether remains notably pedestrian. There are seemingly unlimited societies and programs— actually, some three hundred different ones—revolving around synagogues, Zionism, or welfare. The numbers of Jewish aid societies that predated the welfare state now impressively supplement it with an agglomeration of Jewish hospitals, old age homes, flats and almshouses for the elderly, as well as perhaps sixty Jewish clubs and organizations. Except for the waning mystique of Zionism, however, there is little of solid Jewish cultural content in their programs. Large numbers of Jewish charity committees function as hardly more than disguised matrimonial clubs. In that respect, they compete with Bournemouth, with its large array of Jewish hotels crowning the East Cliff, Britain's equivalent of the Catskills. The absence of leadership may be a key to this somnolence. The religious establishment is a bore. The mandarins of Zionism remain in their vast local enterprises and majestic residences, and few make even a token gesture of settling in Israel. The writers and academicians offer Anglo-Jewry meager intellectual fare compared to the feast that presently enriches American Jewish life and education. There are capable professionals in the Jewish organizations, but they enjoy little of the status and influence of their counterparts in the United States or even in France.

Painfully absent are men like Sir Barnett Janner. Whitechapel-born and -bred, a lawyer by profession, Sir Barnett had been the Liberal MP for Whitechapel from 1931 to 1935, and subsequently the Labor MP for Northwest Leicester. During his career in the House of Commons, many Jews regarded him as "their" MP. Whenever any Jewish issue arose at home or abroad, Sir Barnett could be depended upon to raise the matter publicly in the House or privately with the minister or government department concerned. A broad-shouldered, thickset man, with a large head and a boxer's profile, Janner at one time or another held almost every office of consequence in the Jewish community. Presidency of the Board of Deputies was for him the natural platform to continue his championship of the Jewish cause. The selflessness of his devotion to his people was beyond question.

There is no reason to doubt that an equivalent devotion is shared by Greville Janner, Sir Barnett's son and the most recent president of the Board of Deputies. Like his late father, Greville Janner holds a seat in the House of Commons; but in appearance and style he bears little resemblance to Sir Barnett. Rather slight and bespectacled, he has been described as the ferret where his father was the bulldog. My impression of him as he presided over the monthly meeting at Woburn House was of a witty, urbane, even effervescent man, a skilled parliamentarian and a facile speaker. Several evenings later, I was a guest at a dinner party he hosted for the visiting president of the Hungarian Jewish Community. The affair took place at the Royal Horse Guards Hotel. Some eighteen or twenty Jewish communal leaders and their wives were present. Janner hurried about the dining room, shaking hands and bussing the wives. He wore a skullcap, as did all the men present. It was the last night of Chanukkah and a menorah waited on the table. Lighting the candles, Janner led the guests in a full-throated rendition of the Chanukkah chants. Throughout the dinner—British kosher at its worst, a soppy unfilleted fish with boiled potatoes and peas—Janner was endlessly on the alert, roaming the table, chatting animatedly, backslapping, shaking hands.

As the "leader of Anglo-Jewry," he explained to me, he had access to the prime minister "anytime I like." The Board of Deputies was not simply the "guardian of Anglo-Jewry" but the "buffer" between the British government and Israel. "In fact, I had a visit with [Foreign Secretary] Lord Carrington just this afternoon," he confided. To my left, a woman, a social welfare executive who was listening in on our discussion, caught my eye. With a faint shrug, she smiled cryptically. Was she sharing my thought: that between the Board's leadership and the chief rabbinate's, one's reaction could only be wry demurral or silence? The spectacle was by no means sad, only tepid and colorless, possibly as irrelevant as the aura of movement projected by a Jewish community that remains far more adept at exploiting its common denominator of ethnic gregariousness than at responding imaginatively to new religious and intellectual challenges.

VII

The Progeny of Empire:
Australia and South Africa

Respite in Oceania

In January 1788, the first flotilla of convict transport ships dropped anchor in Sydney harbor, and among its nearly eight hundred prisoners were eight Jews. These included sixteen-year-old Esther Abrahams of London, sentenced to an Australian penal farm for stealing a piece of lace. Shortly after her release some years later, she married the colonial governor of New South Wales. Possibly as many as a thousand Jewish convicts, most of them sentenced for petty thievery or fencing, reached the Australian colonies by 1844, before the practice of shipping felons was terminated.

Australia's first voluntary Jewish settler was the colorful and enterprising Barnett Levey, who arrived in 1821 to join his brother, a well-to-do former convict. Levey soon established himself as a merchant, and later founded and directed Australia's first theater. In common with the majority of his fellow Jews, he intermarried and had his children baptized. From the mid-1840s on, Jewish newcomers were free and middle-class, intent upon exploiting the virgin continent's seemingly limitless commercial potential. The nineteenth century was a boom era for Australia. The thriving wool market, later the discovery of gold, drew substantially larger numbers of British immigrants. By 1881, the Jewish population had reached nine thousand, slightly more than half of them in Sydney, the capital of New South Wales, and in Melbourne, the capital of Victoria. They maintained a respectable nucleus of synagogues, part-time Jewish schools, welfare and philanthropic societies. At no time did they encounter serious prejudice. Their fellow colonists were aliens, too; and Australia lacked those classes that elsewhere tended to be antisemitic, a hard-pressed petite bourgeoisie and an aristocratic ruling elite. Except for the convicts among them, Jews from the beginning enjoyed full civil and political rights.

Between the 1880s and World War I, an influx of East European immigrants more than doubled the Jewish population. Again, settling mainly in Sydney and Melbourne, the newcomers began as small retailers, then forged upward on the crest of the thriving frontier economy. Several of them achieved a distinction unimaginable to their kin in Britain. Thus, John Monash, whose parents were Viennese immigrants of Polish descent, was trained as a civil engineer at the University of Melbourne and later qualified as a patent attorney. Fluent in German and French, Monash became familiar with the use of reinforced concrete in Europe, and was one of its pioneers in Australia. By 1914, he was elected president of the Victoria branch of the Institute of Engineers.

Monash's enduring fame ultimately was achieved as a military leader. While a student, he joined the university company of the Victoria Rifles, and later moved steadily up the ranks of active reservists. In 1908 he was promoted to lieutenant colonel and given command of the Australian Intelligence Corps, the precursor of the general staff. Then, in 1918, he was appointed commander of the Australian Expeditionary Force in France. Monash's ensuing success as a general was due in large measure to his "big business" mentality, which the vast complexity of a modern army required. His breakthrough tactics against the German line at Le Hamel in the summer of 1918, involving the combined use of tanks, airplanes, and motor transport, were far in advance of contemporary practice and foreshadowed the "joint operations" of World War II. Lloyd George called Monash "the most resourceful general in the whole of the British Army," and Liddell Hart wrote in his *Times* obituary that Monash "had the greatest capacity for command in modern war among all those who held command." Decorated many times over, knighted, granted almost every honor the governments of Australia and Great Britain could bestow, Monash at the time of his death in 1931 was the most respected Australian of his generation.

His achievements preceded by a good twenty years those of the most successful East European immigrants. Zalman Komesarov came from the Ukrainian village of Berdiansk in 1913. With his wife and two children, he arrived in Melbourne with five British pounds, and soon turned to the greenhorn's typical occupation, peddling. His route took him by train from Melbourne to Yarram, the terminus of the one-hundred-mile railroad line. From there he carried his merchandise from farm to farm, returning home each weekend. Typical also was his decision to anglicize his name, to Kaye. Within three years, he had saved enough to open his own haberdashery in a Melbourne suburb. When the business flourished during the boom of World War I, and in the years that followed, he brought over family members from the Ukraine.

They arrived with little time to spare, as it happened. The world depression struck Australia hard, and Kaye nearly went bankrupt. With a quarter of the nation's work force unemployed, legislation was passed in the early 1930s to shut off immigration from Southern and Eastern Europe. Jews who had arrived earlier somehow maintained their economic foothold, even provided their children with a decent education. Borrowing tuition money from the bank, Kaye registered his own sons in good private schools. At the age of eight, William, the youngest, and the first to be born in Australia, began attending Scotch College, a combined primary-secondary school operated by the Presbyterian Church. John Monash had gone there. Although young Kaye's school friends were as likely to be Gentile as Jewish, he experienced occasional social discomfort, particularly when he was excused from religious classes. He and other Jews, after all, represented the most visible minority in Australian society. Concentrated in the principal metropolitan areas, their names were on a wide variety of retail shops, on law and medical offices. Some even then had achieved eminence as bankers, financiers, brewers, and clothing manufacturers.

A thousand miles to the east, across the Tasmanian Sea, a smaller but otherwise nearly identical Jewish community had been established in New Zealand. There 2,350 Jews were living in 1921. Tight immigration restrictions limited their growth to barely 3,470 by 1945. The majority were East Europeans, and they were distributed equally in the two major cities of Auckland and Wellington, with a tiny enclave in Christchurch. Enjoying full civil rights, they prospered. Although most of them were wholesale and retail merchants, several Jews (of German extraction) won public distinction. As far back as the nineteenth century, Sir Julius Vogel was twice elected prime minister (in 1873 and 1876), while Sir Arthur Myers served as minister of munitions in World War I. There were five Jewish mayors of Auckland, and almost every city had a Jewish chief magistrate at one time or another. Sir Wolf Fisher and several Jewish colleagues pioneered the nation's steel mills, its brewing and hotel industries. As elsewhere, however, an unspoken gulf separated even the most prominent Jews from extensive social contact with Gentiles.

In Australia, the curious mixture of frontier egalitarianism and residual conservative snobbery was evident in the career of Sir Isaac Isaacs. Born in Melbourne, the son of Polish immigrants, Isaacs became a successful lawyer, then entered political life. After occupying a number of ministerial positions in Victoria province, he was appointed a high court judge and later, in 1930, chief justice of Australia. The following year, James Scullin, the Conservative prime minister, asked Isaacs to become the first native-born Australian governor-general. The nomination was sharply criticized. King George V was said to have been reluctant to confirm it. In Australia, anti-Jewish prejudice was not confined to the tight little Anglo-Australian oligarchy. Before World War I, *Bulletin,* a nationalist weekly, invented the character of John Bull-Cohen, a British imperialist functioning as the instrument of Jewish financiers. Now, fifteen years later, Isaacs's prospective appointment encountered a similar nationalist opposition. But eventually it went through. Once Isaacs assumed office, moreover, he became as beloved and respected a figure as Monash had been.

Young William Kaye was largely oblivious of these crosscurrents within the nation's political and social life. In the opportunities that mattered, Australia was still the freest of nations, and Jews rarely encountered obstacles in the day-to-day conduct of their affairs. Their little Orthodox synagogues went up in any neighborhood of their settlement and choice. Reared in a traditional home, William Kaye attended an afternoon *cheder,* a parochial Hebrew school, down the street. Yet the unique openness of Australian life ultimately drew him, his brothers, and most of his generation away from Orthodoxy and into the recently established Liberal temple. The goal of nativization also encouraged higher education. In 1937 Kaye began to study law at Melbourne University, where his brothers Myer and Peter were medical students.

World War II intervened. In 1941 Kaye volunteered for the navy, his older brother Peter for the army. In a Jewish community of thirty thousand, four thousand young men and women enlisted in the armed services. As a sublieutenant, Kaye was assigned to convoy duty on the New Guinea run. His fiancée worked at naval headquarters. Mustered out in 1946, Kaye completed his law studies and passed the bar examinations in record time, then secured a clerkship with a respected Anglican firm. A handsome, red-haired, blue-eyed young man with a good war record, he encountered no difficulties whatever as a Jew. In time, he was invited to join a firm of prominent non-Jewish barristers. The economy was flourishing. The nation's political processes were operating smoothly. Kaye and his generation of native-born Jews faced the future with every confidence.

Immigration and Inculturation

By then, leadership in the Jewish community had passed to second-generation Jews of East European background. They were no longer an isolated community. Their younger members had ranged the battlefronts of the world and had strengthened their bonds with Jewish kinspeople abroad. After the Holocaust, Zionism became as urgent a cause here as it was among East European Jews in other countries. Indeed, the full passion of that sentiment was soon turned upon the Australian Liberal government. A cordial relationship developed between the Zionist leaders Max Frelich and Horace Newman, and Dr. Herbert Evatt, Australia's minister for external affairs. As chairman, later, of the UN General Assembly's ad hoc Committee on Palestine, Evatt vigorously steered his colleagues to their vote in favor of Partition on November 25, 1947, and thus all but ensured the General Assembly resolution four days later. The Zionism of a tiny Australian minority group thereby played a certain limited role in the birth of Israel.

This forthright expression of pluralism would not have been widely acceptable to Australians in the prewar era. Before 1940, they still tended to regard themselves as an outpost of Anglo-Saxon civilization, and they fully supported the priority given British immigrants. Yet their elitism did not survive the war. The danger of Japanese invasion between 1941 and 1943 convinced both major political parties that future security depended upon a much larger population. Immigration would have to be enlarged dramatically; and, if necessary, half of it might even be non-British. Between 1945 and 1965, then, over 2,000,000 immigrants poured into Australia, raising the nation's population from 7,400,000 to 11,500,000 (it is 14 million today). At least 58 percent of the newcomers were non-British, and by 1965 they comprised 20 percent of Australia's total population and 30 percent of its urban population. Many of the newcomers were of distinctly non-Nordic stock. Thus, Melbourne came to have the largest Greek community in the world outside of Athens.

The Jews participated in this growth. Between 1940 and 1961, their population doubled, to 60,000. Currently, it approaches 70,000. Immigration accounted for the largest part of the growth. Of the 40,000 newcomers, virtually all were former East European refugees. As late as 1984, two of three Australian Jewish adults had spent their lives in Nazi-held Europe. The influx represented more than a transformation of Australian Jewry. It was a rebirth. Nothing like it had occurred in any other major Diaspora community except France's. By and large, the postwar immigrants avoided the older Jewish enclave in Sydney and gravitated to Melbourne, a more polyglot city. Today, Melbourne's Jewish population has reached 36,000; Sydney's is 30,000.

As elsewhere, the new arrivals rapidly became self-supporting. Although they were given generous assistance by the Australian Jewish Welfare and Relief Society, they were helped even more by the postwar Australian economic boom. As of 1984, not less than 70 percent of Jewish breadwinners are either employers or self-employed (in contrast to 10 percent of the Australian working population). Most are businessmen, of course, while their children typically have been drawn to the professions. Virtually all of them have moved, or plan to move, to the suburbs of Prahran and Moorabbin in Melbourne; of Randwick, Woollahra, Waverley, and North Shore in Sydney. Like other Australians, the Jews tend increasingly to vote their pocketbooks, and from the early 1970s on, they have been abandoning their traditional fidelity to the Labor Party in favor of the more moderate Liberals. The latter, once regarded as the citadel of "Anglo" snobbery, have long since become as pro-Israel and pro-immigration as the Laborites.

With a quarter of the national adult population foreign-born, "multiculturalism," the Australian version of cultural pluralism, has increasingly been accepted as the norm. The new context is as congenial to the Jews as to the other ethnic groups. One among many immigrant communities, they no longer feel social pressures to conform. Rather, they have been inclined to develop their own institutions and organizations even more vigorously. Young people's associations, Zionist societies, Jewish cultural movements of all trends have developed, even a Yiddish theater in Melbourne with a semiprofessional repertory company. Welfare and philanthropic organizations have expanded and become more professionalized. In direct emulation of Britain's Board of Deputies, provincial boards of deputies were founded in the post-

World War II period, then coordinated under an Executive Council of Australian Jewry. The latter is now the community's voice to the "outside" world. Jewish identification with Israel, profoundly intensified during the 1967 Middle East crisis, has continued to hold firm. Far more than in Britain, day-school education has become a major fact of Australian Jewish life. In the mid-1980s, Sydney's Jewish community supports three day schools with 1,200 students, maintains eight kindergartens, and educates a third of the city's Jewish children. In Melbourne, eight schools are educating fully 90 percent of the city's Jewish children of primary-school age and 50 percent of secondary-school age. One of these schools, Mount Scopus College, is the largest Jewish private school in the world.

In New Zealand, the trend has been in the opposite direction. Orthodox synagogues remain the hub of Jewish religious life in Wellington, Auckland, and Christchurch, and continue to function under the "authority" of the chief rabbi in London. B'nai B'rith lodges similarly have developed in the principal cities since the 1960s, and Zionist societies have been active since the end of World War I. Even so, assimilation tends to be far more extensive in New Zealand, and the high rate of intermarriage, estimated at 35 percent, together with an insignificant immigration, accounts for the minuscule growth of the Jewish population to about 4,500 (out of New Zealand's population of 3.1 million) in 1984. The process works both ways, of course. The tiny demographic base has inhibited the development of any significant communal vitality. Yet in Australia, and notably in Melbourne, it is not only pluralism but plain and simple insularity that has affected every aspect of a community two-thirds of whose members still are European-born, and who are consciously resistant to the wider opportunities of acculturation. A survey in 1967 revealed that only 22 percent of the nation's Jews belonged to non-Jewish organizations, and barely a third admitted to having non-Jewish friends. There is little evidence that, since then, the ratio has changed substantially.

This parochialism has tended to repel the children of the immigrants. University-educated and thoroughly australianized, they have not hesitated to criticize their parents' "ghettoization." A collection of essays entitled *Jews in Australian Society* (Melbourne, 1973) stresses this theme. One contributor writes:

> Perhaps our trouble is that in seeking to retain social cohesion we have taken on too many of the less attractive features of Australian society. There

is a crudeness and coarseness about Melbourne Jews that grates, albeit it is a part of the whole nouveau riche pattern of the society. . . . [It is revealed] in the narrowness of the Jewish community . . . precisely because there is so little to preserve. . . . Melbourne ultimately will remain an important Jewish centre, but because of schools built and trees planted, not because of cultural, intellectual or spiritual values. . . . I find the Jewish community in Melbourne can offer me very little, and I regret that it seems to be offering so little to Australia.

This denigration is not the only augury of incipient weakness. As in other Western countries, following the wave of immigration, Australian Jewry is failing to reproduce itself. From the late 1950s on, few Jewish families have reared more than two children.

It is evident, too, that the younger generation is adopting Australia's relaxed ambience. The nation's genial and open-spirited society, its qualities of fairness, camaraderie, and good sportsmanship, are useful correctives for a traditionally insecure minority group. Few obstacles of any kind have barred the Jews' way in life. Since the 1960s, there have been Jewish lord mayors of Sydney and Melbourne, members of the federal and state parliaments in both major parties, department heads and commission chairmen, key advisers to prime ministers. In 1978, Sir Zalman Cowen, a distinguished legal scholar and vice-chancellor of the University of Queensland, was appointed governor-general of Australia, thereby becoming the second Jew to hold this office. William Kaye also flourished in his profession. Appointed a Queen's Counsel in 1962, he represented some of the nation's largest corporations. In 1966, he was elected chairman of the Victoria Bar Association (whose first chairman, earlier, also was a Jew), then in 1971 was elected president of the Australian Bar Association. One year later, he was appointed judge of the Supreme Court of the State of Victoria.

The first Jew to hold this position, Kaye was the object of much pride within the Jewish community, which in ensuing years took even greater satisfaction in his forthright identification with every important Jewish and Zionist cause. His judicial colleagues, meanwhile, regarded him as the "quintessential Australian" in his quiet integrity and low-keyed fairness, his love of sports and genial public-spiritedness. "But that's the danger facing Australian Jewry," he confesses. "Life is simply too easy for us. It's an outdoor, pleasant, comfortable existence—and a shallow and materialistic one. It's precisely the kind of thing that's eroding the Jewish interests of our young people. In this country, it's a far greater danger than antisemitism." The example of American Jewry is cited to reassure him. "The Jews of America are a tiny minority, too," he agrees. "Yet their response to a pluralistic society has been to exert a certain impact not only upon American society but upon Jewish culture altogether. We have nothing like it in Australia. I can't envisage a single important Jewish achievement ever coming out of this country."

Kaye may be right in his prognosis for Australian Jewry. A California-like hedonism and self-satisfaction rarely generate the intellectual tensions that have been unique to Jewish creativity. It is a prospect of security and emotional relaxation, on the other hand, for which nine-tenths of the Jews of the world would settle unhesitatingly and gratefully.

South Africa: Calvinist Promised Land

The Voortrekker Monument in Pretoria memorializes the nineteenth-century Afrikaner farmers who uprooted their families in the Cape Province and moved deep into the veld to escape British rule. Their ordeal is inscribed in friezes here, wall to wall: their long trek by ox wagon into a remote and forbidding interior; the tenacity of their defense against waves of attacking Zulu tribesmen along the Blood River; the vitality of their autonomous republics and indigenous Afrikaans language and culture. Drawing inspiration from the Bible, these flinty Dutch and Huguenot pioneers regarded themselves as modern Israelites, fleeing alien bondage, establishing a white Calvinist Jerusalem in a promised land of their own. The parallel is vivid between the Afrikaners and the Zionist pioneers in Palestine. Even as the Zionists struggled to maintain their foothold against a hostile Arab majority and an increasingly antagonistic British mandatory regime, so the Afrikaners nurtured the memory of their own Great Trek, their own short-lived republics, their own struggle against British imperialism, their own fear of being swept away by hordes of surrounding "natives." That linked heritage would explain much of their intermingled destinies in ensuing years, no less than the militance of their respective national consciousnesses.

Even on the shores of South Africa itself, for that matter, the two peoples—Afrikaners and Jews this time—were not strangers to each other from the beginning. In 1652, when the Dutch East India Company dispatched Jan van Riebeeck to establish a refueling station at the Cape of Good Hope, a tiny nucleus of Dutch Sephardic Jews acted as managers in the enterprise and engaged in barter trade with the local Hottentot tribes. A century later, when the British planted their flag at the Cape, Sephardic Jews again helped the newcomers to develop industry there. In the first half of the nineteenth century, small numbers of British and German Jews arrived in Cape Town, Grahamstown, and Port Elizabeth. Beginning as itinerant merchants (*smousers*, as the Afrikaners called them), the newcomers traveled from the Cape in ox or mule wagons, dragging themselves up mountain passes toward the veld in search of isolated farm villages. Ultimately, a number of these smousers built stores, and a few became prominent merchants.

Newer opportunities beckoned in the 1850s, when veins of diamonds were unearthed in the northeastern corner of the Cape Colony. Only two decades later, gold fields were discovered in the Witwatersrand reef of the Transvaal. Some two or three thousand Jews were among the cascade of fortune seekers that poured into the country afterward. Most of them still were of British or German origin, and most still came as smousers or as storekeepers. Yet a smaller group was found among the important diamond buyers in those early days of prospecting, and adventurers such as Alfred Beit, Barney Barnato, Lionel Phillips, David Harris, and Harry Mosenthal made fortunes in this trade. With the funds they accumulated in the diamond industry, moreover, Barnato and Phillips also became investors and later company directors in several Transvaal gold mines.

Ranging even farther afield, Samuel Marks, a Lithuanian immigrant, applied his profits from the diamond and gold fields to exploit the coal deposits of the Transvaal, then to develop an iron and steel industry nearby, then a series of ancillary industries including brick-and-tile works, a glass factory, a brewery and a distillery, fruit- and meat-preserving plants, a jam factory, a tannery and boot factory. With rare intuition, Marks foresaw the economic potential of the Vaal River basin and acquired extensive land and mineral interests there, linking them in turn with his industrial enterprises. Some of these undertakings failed, but many succeeded, and all of them helped prime the pump of the Transvaal's industrial development. Although few other Jews were to be found yet in the upper reaches of commerce and industry, increasing numbers of them won security as small middlemen, filling the niche between the large moneyed interests of the gold fields and the agricultural economy of the Afrikaners.

After 1881, a far larger wave of Jews poured in from Eastern Europe, over 90 percent of them from Lithuania. Close enough to the Baltic for access to a window on the world, these *Litvaks* were inspired by the success of their compatriot Samuel Marks. With their traditionally hardheaded business acumen, they too sensed the economic possibilities of South Africa. In family groups, the Litvaks embarked then by the hundreds and thousands, at first establishing themselves in the Cape Colony, later moving extensively into the interior. They followed the initial pattern of the early Central European Jews, beginning as smousers with their packs in their wagons, then opening small shops. Most settled in Johannesburg, the rough-and-ready new capital of the mineral-rich Transvaal. In 1893, the numbers of Jews in Johannesburg rose to 6,000, then to 12,000 in 1899—and to 15,000 in the Transvaal at large. Their relations with the Afrikaners were amicable. The Lithuanian newcomers unquestionably valued the British connection, with its link to the great and liberal democracy of the motherland. Indeed, a majority of the Jews in the Afrikaner republics joined in the general exodus of *Uitlanders*—non-Afrikaners—during the Boer War. But following the end of hostilities, virtually all of them returned.

In ensuing years, the Jews broadened their base in South Africa. A number of them began playing a role in Transvaal public life, as municipal councillors in Johannesburg and other cities and towns. In 1909, Harry Grauman became the first Jewish mayor of Johannesburg. Other Jews were elected to the Transvaal and Cape legislative councils. When the new Union of South Africa came into being in 1910, the initial membership of the federal parliament included seven Jews. The continued influx of Jewish immigrants, most of them still Lithuanians, reflected their awareness of the unlimited future apparently opening in this South African cornucopia. In 1933, numbering 70,000, Jews comprised 4.5 percent of the country's white population.

The Afrikaners' Vindication

Since the end of the Boer War, British dominion was a reconfirmed fact of life in South Africa. So was British preeminence in South African trade, finance, and industry. Yet the Afrikaners, who represented over half the nation's Europeans on the eve of World War I, were hardly standing still. Although essentially an agricultural and a small-town population, concentrated in the two inland provinces of Transvaal and the Orange Free State, they were keenly aware of their emergent demo-

graphic strength and of their latent economic power. Steeped in Calvinism, they nurtured a deep-seated resentment of British rule. The
moderates among their leaders, men such as Louis Botha and Jan
Christiaan Smuts, were prepared to achieve a working accommodation
with the British, and during World War I even allied themselves with
the empire. But in 1924, the right-wing National Party swept into office. Committed to a chauvinist policy of "South Africa for the South
Africans" (that is, for the Afrikaners), Prime Minister James Hertzog
was intent upon enlarging the Afrikaner presence in the public affairs of
the Union. For six years, his government packed the civil and military
services with Afrikaners.

In the 1930s, when the depression brought Smuts back to power in
a moderate "United" coalition government, the right-wingers set about
organizing a new "purified" Nationalist Party, even more implacably
xenophobic than its predecessor. Further embittered by widespread
unemployment, the Afrikaner extremists were convinced that the solution to their problems lay in evicting the "foreigners," that is, the British and the Jews, who dominated the industrial and commercial sectors
of the economy. The new militancy emerged during a period of growing
European crisis. In the event of war, would South Africa again ally itself
with Britain? Smuts felt a moral obligation to do so. The Nationalists
stridently opposed the very notion. When war broke out in September
1939, the cabinet in fact supported Smuts's decision to join the Allies;
but the majority was very narrow. As events developed, it would be the
last gasp of moderation. In opposition for the ensuing nine years, the
Nationalists continued to fan the flames of Afrikaner rancor. And finally,
in the election of May 1948, their moment of vindication arrived.

It was the moment of truth for the Jews, too. From the beginning of
their settlement in South Africa, they had linked their destiny to the
liberal, urban civilization of the British population. Even in the predominantly Afrikaner Transvaal, where the largest number of Jews
lived, they preferred to have their children educated in English-speaking schools and universities. The mounting chauvinism and racism of
the Afrikaner right wing deeply concerned them, and the unexpected
antisemitism of the National Party was even more of a shock. This
stance was first adopted in 1930, when the incumbent Nationalist government proposed a bill to limit drastically European, and specifically
East European, immigration. Dr. Daniel Malan, serving then as minister of the interior, stated his government's rationale explicitly when he

warned that the "alarming rise of alien non-Nordic stock immigrants will threaten the homogeneity of the white population." To the Jews' consternation, the bill found wide support in English as well as Afrikaner circles, and was passed.

Until then, the Jews had not been aware that feelings against them were running so high. Perhaps they had grown complacent. Heavily engaged in commerce, they were a highly visible element in the cities. By 1937, too, Jews comprised a third of the total annual immigration. The public reaction should not have been a revelation to them. Nor did that reaction abate with the immigration act. Throughout the 1930s, public pressure mounted to stop the influx of Jews from Nazi Germany, and was translated into the Aliens Act of 1937. Much of the anti-British and antisemitic chauvinism of the pre-World War II era was heavily influenced by Nazi propaganda. Without specifically endorsing Nazism, the National Party nevertheless adopted a brutally plainspoken antisemitic position, advocating a ban on the further immigration of Jews as one of the "elements which cannot be assimilated by the South African nation or which are a hindrance or dangerous to society." From then on, in parliament, in the press, on the political hustings, the Nationalist spokesmen—Dr. Malan, Eric Louw, H. F. Verwoerd—repeatedly demanded a "quota system" to reduce Jewish participation in the nation's economic life. In 1943, the party's branch in the Transvaal formally banned Jews from membership.

One consequence of this growing menace was the enhanced role of the Jewish Board of Deputies. Modeled on the British prototype, the Board was founded early in the twentieth century, and consisted of affiliated organizations—synagogues, welfare bodies, social, cultural, or Zionist societies. Its leadership of South African Jewry in matters of immigration and naturalization had been established by the 1930s, and thereafter its principal activity was to monitor and refute anti-Jewish propaganda, and to foster better relations with other sectors of the European population. Failing to block the Aliens Act in 1937, or to achieve the passage of anti-defamation legislation, the Board discreetly turned its energies to the campaign against the National Party. In the 1930s and 1940s, its executive council encouraged Jews to give financial assistance to the candidates of Smuts's United Party. In fact, that encouragement was hardly needed. Jews were spontaneously mobilizing behind Smuts, and with every resource at their disposal. In the elections of 1938 and 1943, the effort was successful. But in 1948 it failed;

the Nationalists won by a slender margin. Dr. Daniel Malan, the arch-rightist, was inaugurated now as the new prime minister. It was a thunderbolt for the Jews of South Africa. They walked the streets in a daze, haunted by fears of an impending Nazi regime on South African soil. The Board of Deputies was at a loss. Should it seek to approach the new government? Should Jews emigrate to Britain? To Israel? Or should they stand fast and attempt to resist the imminent program of militant Afrikanerdom? It was a terrifying moment.

Apartheid and Accommodation

As it happened, the Nationalist leadership had been rethinking its own relationship with South African Jewry. A year before the election, Malan released a statement intimating that his party had shifted its position on the Jews. He did not make the remark capriciously. A seasoned politician, he had learned from his 1943 defeat that a party tainted by Nazism was vulnerable to national and international pressures. It appeared wiser now to break with "foreign ideologies" and to concentrate on purely South African issues. For Malan, the most important of those issues was no longer antisemitism, or even British imperialism. It was the need to confront the "black peril." The new emphasis henceforth would be upon *apartheid,* enforced segregation, and "regulation" of the nonwhite races. In launching this program, the Nationalists would have limited their freedom of action in alienating the Jews, a powerful middle-class element that comprised 15 percent of white Johannesburg. Only six weeks after the election, then, Malan met with leaders of the Jewish Board of Deputies and assured them that his government favored "nondiscrimination" toward any sector of the white population; and that he, personally, was uninterested in any further talk about the "so-called Jewish question."

The Board leaders were immensely relieved by Malan's olive branch. For their part, they were prepared to meet him more than halfway. Indeed, from then on they gradually settled into the position that the Board of Deputies was a "nonpolitical body." In 1951 its chairman declared: "The Board emphatically disapproves of attempts to persuade Jews as a group to vote for any one political party." It was a complete reversal of policy, but the government welcomed the statement at its face value. Thereafter, while the National Party remained in power, specifically anti-Jewish legislation was never again proposed, and over the years antisemitism was all but eradicated as a factor in public life. The Jewish leaders in turn learned to close their eyes to the emerging program of discrimination against other races and peoples.

Obviously, de facto apartheid long antedated the Nationalist victory of 1948. White supremacy and the uncompromising social separation of the races were deeply rooted in the experience of the British no less than of the Afrikaners, of Smuts and the United Party no less than of Malan and the Nationalists. Convinced that they were interpreters of the Divine Will, however, Malan and his colleagues went much further now in institutionalizing apartheid. Their new legislation of racial separatism not only was grim and uncompromising, but was enforced under uniquely harsh judicial constraints. In 1951, the government laid down its own definition of "communism," under which almost anyone of liberal opinions on the race issue could be subjected to prosecution. When a groundswell of outraged black and colored opposition developed against the apartheid program, the government launched a series of "treason trials" in the mid-1950s against suspected black and white agitators. In the aftermath of the "Sharpeville Massacre" of protesting blacks in March 1960, savage new repressive measures were enacted, precipitating the flight of scores of white liberals and distinguished public figures, who feared arrest and detention. When the Macmillan cabinet in Britain severely condemned the South African regime, the Nationalists in their turn decided to sever the last of their country's relationships with the British Crown. By referendum in 1961, South Africa proclaimed itself an independent republic.

Jews were prominent among those who opposed the apartheid program. Throughout the 1950s and early 1960s, Jewish names kept appearing in every echelon of the struggle—among reformist liberals and Communists, in the courts (whether as defendants or as counsels for the defense), in the lists of "bannings" (political quarantine), and among those who fled the country to evade arrest. During the treason trial that began in December 1956, when 156 people were prosecuted on charges of "conspiring to overthrow the state by violence and replace it with a Communist state," twenty of the twenty-three white defendants were Jews. At one stage, the prisoners' chief defense counsel was a renowned Jewish lawyer, Israel Meisels. The trial dragged on over five years, until the government finally gave in and released the accused on lack of evidence. In July 1963, the police captured the leadership cadre of the African Umkonto we Sizwe underground. Of the seventeen people ar-

rested, five were whites, and all of these were Jews (four of the arrested
made a spectacular escape while awaiting trial). When the secret African Resistance Movement was crushed in 1964, it became evident
again that many Jews were involved. The following year, the South
African security police managed to penetrate the Communist underground, and four of the thirteen people arrested and tried were Jews.
Jews represented less than 3 percent of South Africa's 4.2 million
whites by 1960, but they may have comprised 60 percent of the nation's
white political defendants. Eventually all "radicals," Jews or otherwise,
were purged from the country between 1960 and 1965. Yet it was plain
that the old Jewish tradition of social activism died hard.

The overwhelming majority of Jews did not participate in radical or
illegal activities of any kind. Nevertheless, Jewish voters all but unanimously withheld their support from the National Party. Of the nine
Jews in Parliament during the first decade after the Nationalist victory,
all represented the United Party—the party of Smuts—except for one
or two belonging to the tiny Labor Party. The single most respected
spokesperson for the liberal tradition in Parliament altogether was
Helen Suzman. The daughter of Lithuanian Jewish immigrants and the
wife of a Johannesburg physician, Mrs. Suzman launched her parliamentary career in 1943 from the affluent Houghton district of Johannesburg, and she remained in the legislature continually afterward. In
1959, disenchanted with her United Party's lingering conservatism on
the racial issue, Mrs. Suzman broke away to found the Progressive
Party. It was a daring move, and in the 1961 election all the Progressives lost their seats, except for her. In subsequent elections, nevertheless, she was faithfully supported by her Houghton constituents—
more than half of whom were affluent Jewish business and professional
families. Within the next few years, eleven other Progressives finally
were elected to Parliament to fortify Mrs. Suzman's eloquent and lonely
campaign for racial justice. All of them were returned from districts
with large Jewish constituencies.

One of Mrs. Suzman's most devoted allies was Ellen Hellman, similarly the daughter of a Houghton Jewish family. The first woman to
earn a doctorate at the University of Witwatersrand, doing her research
on the problems of urban blacks, Mrs. Hellman played an active role in
the South African Institute of Race Relations, which had been established in 1929 with the financial support of white liberals, many of them
Jews. In ensuing years, during the war and the postwar period, she

edited a number of books for the institute, dealing with the problems of racial inequalities. In the latter 1950s, she served as a trustee of the Treason Trial Defense Fund, then as a founding member of the Progressive Party. Well into the 1960s, she worked with Helen Suzman, Israel Meisels, Sidney Kentridge, Hannah Jaffe, and other Jewish liberals in fighting the government's program of apartheid in all its aspects. Occasionally, her home was raided by the police, but she was not deterred. In 1979, in Mrs. Hellman's eightieth year, Witwatersrand awarded her an honorary doctorate for her "pioneering work" in the cause of urban blacks, and—by implication—for a lifetime devoted to the cause of racial justice.

Jewish involvement in liberal causes did not go unremarked in Nationalist and other Afrikaner circles. A letter to *Die Transvaler* in 1961 expressed a typical Afrikaner reaction:

> We as Afrikaners would very much like to learn why the Jews work so conspicuously in every sphere against the government's *apartheid* policy, because their names appear most prominently as advocates for all agitation movements. . . . What do they aim at with their liberalistic policy of mingling between White and non-White? . . . Our Jewish friends work against *apartheid* in every field by indecent commiseration with the natives, encouragement of intermingling, support of integration and advocacy of social levelling in city councils and Parliament. . . . We wish to bring to our Jewish friends' attention that these actions will not be observed without consequences by South Africans as a whole.

But in fact, Afrikaner criticism against the Jewish community was misplaced. It is recalled that, following Prime Minister Malan's 1948 discussion with leaders of the Board of Deputies, Jewish communal policy underwent a marked change, and thereafter the Board refused to take a stand on issues not directly related to the Jewish community. After all, the Board was not a church or even a synagogue, its executive council insisted, but mainly a defense agency. It had not been founded to serve as the "conscience of the community." Henceforth, not even the 1960 Sharpeville Massacre provoked the Board of Deputies or the Jewish press to break its silence.

Indeed, when Prime Minister Malan retired to private life in 1953, to be succeeded by Johannes Strydom, the Jewish National Fund inscribed Malan's name in its Golden Book "as recognition of his contribution to better racial understanding in South Africa." Upon the election of Hendrik Verwoerd as prime minister in 1958, the Board of

Deputies sent a group of emissaries to extend formal congratulations. On the fiftieth anniversary of the Union of South Africa, an editorial in the Board journal, *Jewish Affairs,* contained no mention of apartheid. This politic behavior was also characteristic of the rabbinate, although moral condemnations of apartheid were not lacking from Anglican and, to a lesser degree, from Catholic clergymen. In September 1966, when Prime Minister Verwoerd, an ardent racist with a pro-Nazi record during the prewar and war years, was stabbed to death in Parliament, mourning services were conducted in synagogues throughout the country. In their sermons, the Orthodox chief rabbi of Transvaal and his colleagues in other synagogues paid homage to Verwoerd's "statesmanship and integrity."

On a personal basis, in recent decades, Jews have tended to display greater kindness to their black and colored employees than have the Afrikaners or even the British. Jewish businessmen have played leading roles in improving wages, and extending unemployment and social welfare compensation to nonwhite employees. Public opinion research polls repeatedly indicate that Jews are far more tolerant of nonwhites than are any other white group. At the same time, Jewish political preferences increasingly reflect those of English-speaking Gentiles of comparable social and economic status. Thus, most Jews were inclined to vote for the middle-of-the-road United Party rather than for the tiny Progressive Party—long after the United Party's virtual demise as a political force. Today a common witticism has it that Jews speak like Progressives, vote for the United Party, and privately hope that the National Party will remain in power to guard the status quo. Middle class and prosperous in the 1970s and 1980s, they have taken apartheid for granted and try to think about it as little as possible.

The Other Homeland

Cecil Margo stands well over six feet tall. Balding, his complexion still ruddy, he belies his seventy-one years, as his easy geniality belies his prestige as one of his nation's most decorated war veterans and as justice of the South African Supreme Court. The son of Lithuanian immigrants, one of six children, Margo was born and reared in Johannesburg. His home was traditionally Jewish, with all holidays and folk customs observed. Zionism was central to the family's life. Every visiting Zionist of importance—Shmaryahu Levin, Nachum Sokolow,

Vladimir Jabotinsky—was a dinner guest in the Margo household. Cecil and his brothers and sisters afterward listened raptly as these prophets of Jewish nationalism lectured before packed auditoriums of Johannesburg Jews.

Nowhere else in the Jewish world, conceivably, was Zionism so integral a feature of Jewishness as in South Africa. It was an ideology the Litvaks brought with them in their spiritual baggage. A mosaic of ethnic and racial traditions, South African society itself encouraged this kind of nationalist identity. Here, alone in the Diaspora, the Zionist Federation was the first national Jewish organization, founded in 1898 and antedating by more than a decade the Board of Deputies. Nearly all the country's rabbis embraced Zionism at the outset, including the Reform rabbis. It was out of this fused British and Jewish-Zionist tradition that Cecil Margo emerged, graduating secondary school and enrolling in the University of Witwatersrand in 1932. With many other Jewish students at "Wits," he was a member of the Student Zionist Association. It was the Jewish scheme of things.

So was Margo's decision to study law. The professions exerted the identical attraction for second-generation Jews here as in other Diaspora communities (one of Margo's brothers became a doctor, another an architect). Receiving his degree in 1937, Margo was called to the bar the same year. Trial work was his special interest. His first-rate mind, engaging personality and infinite willingness to put in long hours ensured the success of his barrister's practice. His other passion was flying. At Witwatersrand, he had joined the University Cadet Squadron, and in 1937 he won his wings and a commission in the Royal South African Special Reserve. He polished his skills afterward, flying about the country in light Gypsy Moths and Tiger Moths.

Upon the outbreak of World War II, Margo joined his brothers and most of his friends in the armed services. In late 1940, he became a bomber pilot in East Africa, flying nineteen missions against Italian supply depots before being transferred to Egypt in June 1941. Subsequently his missions were against Germans, first in Crete, then in North Africa. It was murderous work, flying through heavy antiaircraft fire and swarms of Messerschmitt 109s. His squadron took many losses. Margo's luck held, as it did in his ensuing battle action in the Sicilian and Italian campaigns. Late in 1944, he was given command of the RSAF's famed Twenty-fourth Squadron. By the time the war in Europe ended, he had flown 150 missions, achieved the rank of lieutenant colonel, been awarded additional decorations. He returned home a national hero.

The war record of South African Jewry was altogether a solid one. Yet it had no effect in liberalizing the government's immigration policy. The Afrikaner majority in parliament refused to add to the "Anglo" voting lists, particularly if the immigrants were European Jewish survivors. Even Prime Minister Smuts, traditionally friendly to the Jews and a warm supporter of Zionism—as a member of the British War Cabinet in 1917, he had been one of the authors of the Balfour Declaration—felt constrained to bow to nationalist pressures. "First and foremost," he insisted, "the solution to the Jewish question is free immigration to the Jewish National Home in Palestine." What South African Jew could disagree with so forthright a Zionist position? In the postwar period, then, Zionist political meetings overshadowed all other Jewish communal interests. The Board of Deputies and the Zionist Federation, their leadership often interchangeable, worked unremittingly on behalf of Jewish statehood in Palestine.

In 1947, moreover, the Zionist leadership was discreetly recruiting Jewish war veterans for service in Palestine, and providing refresher courses for them on farms outside Johannesburg and Cape Town. By May 1948, the intensity of this effort no longer was animated by ideological Zionism alone. Malan and the Nationalists had triumphed in the election, and for many South African Jews, the establishment of a Jewish state had become indispensable as a reserve homeland. During the ensuing Palestine war, fully 646 volunteers from South Africa participated in Israel's armed forces, the largest proportionate contribution of any Diaspora community, and fifty times larger than American Jewry's.

The role of South African air force veterans was particularly crucial. In 1948, Margo's legal practice was flourishing, not unaided by his distinguished war record. In June of that year, a cable arrived from David Ben-Gurion, asking him to organize Israel's air force. Although Margo was married and the father of a small son by then, his response was all but reflexive. He flew out of South Africa within the week. The night of his arrival in Israel, he was rushed to military headquarters on Tel Aviv's HaYarkon Street. There the nation's military commanders— Ya'akov Dori, Yigael Yadin, Chaim Laskov—described for him the parlous circumstances of their little air force. The few available Dakotas and Czech ME-109s were being used exclusively in support of army ground action. There was no planning section, no maintenance section, no intelligence branch. Margo was appalled.

Conferring intensely with the headquarters staff, and on a near-round-the-clock basis, Margo succeeded in hammering out a list of priorities. It took him nearly a week. Procurement was the first order of business, with emphasis less on the hodgepodge of transports and fighters than on all-purpose fighter-bombers that would be suited to Israel's climate and small scale of operations. He took the plan to Ben-Gurion, who approved it on the spot. Others of Margo's recommendations were put into action. Among them was the organization of a methodical training program. Maintenance was upgraded for quick makeshift operations, and a spare-parts system was worked out. The air force was taken out of army hands. Non-Jewish mercenaries were rapidly phased out of command positions, and Jewish veterans of the various Allied air forces took their places. There were some 820 volunteers from Western countries, including 300 from the United States, 110 from Britain, 70 from Canada, 100 from other countries, and 150 from South Africa. English became the operative language for the air force. An integrated command structure was established. Appropriate intelligence, briefing, and debriefing procedures were worked out. A schedule of tactical and strategic objectives was formulated.

By the time most of these changes were in place, the war itself was winding down. Israel's survival had been assured. Margo had given the little nation a year of service. He returned now to Johannesburg and resumed his law practice. Early in 1948 he had applied for "silk," the senior position of Queen's Counsel, and the title was conferred in 1949. In ensuing years, a wealthy man, living with his wife and three sons in a large home in the choice Oakland section of Johannesburg, Margo gave generously of his funds and time to the Israel United Appeal. So did South African Jews at all levels. Few had recovered from the trauma of the Nationalist victory in 1948. For most of them, subliminally, Israel remained a potential beachhead for their own families.

By a curious twist of history, the South African government became a protector of that beachhead. Empathy between Afrikaner Calvinism and Zionism had long been a fact of life. During Israel's struggle for independence, Afrikaner newspapers vigorously championed the Israeli cause. Their support was fortified by hatred of the British, and also by a thinly disguised hope that a sovereign Jewish homeland might end once and for all the danger of mass Jewish immigration to South Africa. Disregarding British pressure, Smuts had extended de facto recognition to the newborn State of Israel only two days before the elections that brought his defeat. Upon assuming office, Prime Minister Malan in turn found an easy way to inspire Jewish confidence. In May 1948, he trumped Smuts's gesture by recognizing Israel de jure. In later weeks, the Nationalist government closed its eyes to the dispatch of Jewish military volunteers and large quantities of Jewish funds to Israel. In 1953, Malan became the first head of government to visit Israel.

In ensuing years, Malan and his successors continued to allow the Jewish community exemption from South Africa's stringent regulations against currency transfers abroad, permitting the dispatch of up to 10 million rand a year to Israel. As much as any factor, it was fear of losing this exemption that weighed heavily ever after on South African Jews, that inhibited their criticism of the government's racial policies. It also helped resolve a moral dilemma plaguing the consciences of thousands of their young people. The latter recognized that Judaism imposed a moral imperative to oppose racial discrimination. But there was a national Jewish imperative, too, and this was to foster the one and ultimate solution for the Jewish condition, namely, strengthening the Jewish state; and the Nationalist government was helping in that process.

South African Jewry has not rested in its exertions on Israel's behalf. The Zionist Federation remains by far the most important organization in Jewish life. Under its aegis, the Israel United Appeal conducts biennial campaigns that are unmatched in the Diaspora for their generosity—and this in a nation that does not grant tax exemption for such contributions. Additional fund-raising campaigns over the years have been conducted on behalf of numerous individual Israeli causes. Most of these organizations function within the premises of the Zionist Federation Building, a formidable six-story complex in downtown Johannesburg, rather like an American corporation headquarters. Within its labyrinth are to be found scores of offices, batteries of computers and photocopiers, a staff of two hundred people, a huge canteen, a fleet of six automobiles. Coverage given to Israel in the South African Jewish press invariably exceeds reporting of local Jewish events and activities. Currently, some 5,500 South African Jews are living in Israel.

The accommodation between South African Jewry and the Nationalist government has not been without its crises. In 1961, the Israeli government engaged in a diplomatic effort to win the friendship of the black African states, and in July of that year it cast its vote with the Afro-Asian bloc in the United Nations, condemning South Africa's program of apartheid. Outraged, South African Foreign Minister Eric

Louw thereupon publicly requested that "South African citizens who have racial and religious ties with Israel" express their disapproval of the "hostile and ungrateful" action of Israel. The demand made headlines in South Africa, with the Afrikaans press unanimously expressing its resentment of Israel. Under tremendous Jewish pressure, then, both the Zionist Federation and the Board of Deputies felt obliged to issue statements repudiating Israel's action. Although many liberal Jews and Gentiles were shocked by this expediency, Afrikaner resentment at least seemed mollified. Several months later, however, the UN General Assembly voted on a proposal to impose economic and diplomatic sanctions on South Africa. While most of the Western nations voted against the resolution, ensuring its defeat, Israel again supported it. This was the last straw for the Pretoria government. It disallowed all further Jewish money transfers to Israel, thereby crippling Zionist fund-raising in South Africa.

Again, under heavy pressure equally from the government and the badly shaken Jewish community, the Board of Deputies felt impelled to criticize Israel's stand publicly. The government was not assuaged. The ban on fund transfers remained. Worse yet, there occurred a certain revival of popular antisemitism. Harsh statements against Jews were made in Parliament, swastika daubings appeared periodically on synagogues, and a few cemeteries were desecrated. In June 1963, a bomb blast damaged the Jewish War Monument in the Johannesburg Jewish cemetery. Letters to both the Afrikaans and the English press leveled charges of Jewish disloyalty. And the obsequious response of the Board of Deputies and the Zionist Federation leadership, intent upon dissociating South African Jewry from Israel's diplomatic stance, alienated thousands of young Jews.

It was the Six-Day War of 1967 that resolved the crisis. A wave of public sympathy for Israel swept over South Africa, then admiration for Israel's spectacular victory. Stirred to its depths, the Jewish community plunged into a mass fund-raising effort, and some eight hundred young South African Jews departed again as volunteers. The leaders of the Board of Deputies and the Zionist Federation renewed their urgent appeal for the government to waive its ban on money transfers. At this point, the new prime minister, Balthazar Vorster, decided to grant the request on "purely humanitarian grounds." Whereupon 20 million rand ($30 million) was dispatched to Israel. During the 1973 Yom Kippur War, too, the sympathy of the South African government and people remained with Israel. "What is happening to [Israel] today may happen to us tomorrow," stated Defense Minister Pier Willem Botha. "We will find practical ways of showing our goodwill towards Israel." That goodwill, as it happened, was influenced by the black African nations' sudden termination of diplomatic ties with Israel. In 1974 and 1975, Israel and South Africa raised their own diplomatic representation to ambassadorial level, and in April 1974, Prime Minister Vorster visited Israel. The Jews of South Africa breathed more easily.

Affluence and Inner-Directedness

If Johannesburg, its skyscrapers thrusting out of the Transvaal veld, is South Africa's Houston, Cape Town is the nation's San Francisco. Older, more sedate, still redolent of British colonialism in its charming villas and Victorian-style restaurants and hotels, its blazered schoolchildren and parasoled nannies, Cape Town looks out benignly at the surrounding checkerboard of farms and vineyards, on the waters of the Atlantic mingling with those of the Indian Ocean. In 1982, Constantia, an affluent Cape Town suburb, became the headquarters of my visit. There I ensconced myself in the mansion of my third cousin Manuel Sachar and recorded the odyssey of his success.

A heavyset man in his late sixties, his blue eyes and snub nose framed in a gentle moon face, Manuel reminisced easily and modestly. What false pride could there be, anyway, for a white man living in a nation producing more diamonds and platinum than the rest of the world altogether? In a country turning out 74 percent of the gold of the non-Communist world, 90 percent of Africa's coal? Could the soil of any other nation possibly be more fecund? What other white society had access to so endless a source of cheap black labor? It was a matter of simple gravity, then. The wealth trickled down inevitably. Manuel took no self-satisfaction in the phenomenon.

Born in an impoverished Lithuanian village, one of four children, he shared with his family the enforced tsarist transplantation of Jews inland during World War I. An older brother disappeared in 1917 to join the Red Army, and was never seen again. The rest of the family survived, and returned to Lithuania. In 1930, Manuel was sent off to South Africa to establish a foothold there. His younger brother, Israel, followed two years later, and by 1935 the family was reunited in Cape Town. At the outset, the brothers were the providers, operating two small drapery

shops in Cape Town. Four years later, Manuel and a cousin purchased
a failing general store called Grand Bazaar. The cost was high, two
thousand pounds, but the site offered potential. Keeping his profit margin low and counting on volume, Manuel benefited from the war boom,
and the Grand Bazaar moved steadily into the black.

In 1947 he opened two new stores, again selling quality goods at
reasonable prices. In effect, Grand Bazaar was South Africa's first discount merchandiser. By 1950 the stores were thriving. The family
moved out of Woodstock, a Jewish ghetto area, to the Gardens, then
several years later to the upper-middle-class Sea Point district—following the traditional Jewish migration pattern in Cape Town. In the
mid-1960s, Manuel opened three more stores. In 1968 he incorporated
his company, and the number of Grand Bazaar stores grew even more
rapidly. By then, Manuel was following the Marks and Spencer technique of buying likely sites, quickly selling them to banks or insurance
companies, then leasing them back for ninety-nine years. In 1983 he
opened five new stores, raising the total to twenty-three, and propelling
Grand Bazaar to the top ranks among South Africa's discount chains.

Like others of the nation's large discount firms, Grand Bazaar has
been a typically Jewish innovation. It is also typical in its willingness to
open its stores in colored and black areas, to hire nonwhite employees,
to offer them the salary and promotion opportunities enjoyed by white
employees. In this respect, Manuel Sachar's business career is a paradigm of the essentially mercantile role played by Jews in the South
African economy. But increasing numbers of Jews have also moved into
the lighter industries, particularly clothing, leather goods, furniture, tobacco processing, and candy-making. More recently they have turned
to the service industries. Today, half the nation's hotels are Jewish
owned, including the Sun Group, South Africa's largest chain. The
theater and cinema chains similarly have been built by Jews. Some two-
thirds of South Africa's Jews have remained in commerce, however.
Supermarket chains like Manuel Sachar's Grand Bazaar network have
been their pioneering contribution.

As in other Diaspora communities, Jews are also found in disproportionate numbers in the liberal professions. Currently, 22 percent of the
Jewish working population earn their livelihoods in these fields. Jews
comprise 12 percent of South Africa's doctors and dentists, 11 percent
of its accountants, nearly 10 percent of its lawyers. Cecil Margo's career
exemplifies this pattern. In 1971 he was appointed a justice of the

Transvaal Province Division of the Supreme Court. It was no longer an eyebrow-raiser for a Jew to achieve that distinction. As of 1984, six Jews are among the twenty-five members of Margo's court, and at various times Jews have been members of the appellate division of the Supreme Court—equivalent to the United States Supreme Court. Jews have also been active participants in the cultural life of South Africa, although exclusively in the English-speaking milieu. Jewish academicians, writers, musicians, theatrical directors and producers are among the most eminent in the nation.

Yet their after-hours life still tends to be almost exclusively Jewish. Although the benefits (for traditionalists) of an inner-directed community include one of the Diaspora's lowest intermarriage rates—perhaps less than 10 percent—there has been little escape for the Jew wearied by his parish affairs. Even a great lawyer like Israel Meisels, the defense counsel of the treason trials, spent his leisure among his own people, as national chairman of the Board of Deputies, then of the Zionist Federation. Synagogue attendance remains an accepted expression of Jewish living. Most of the congregations still describe themselves as Orthodox. They remain linked organizationally in provincial federations, each with a chief rabbi. During the 1950s, the chief rabbi of the Transvaal and the Orange Free State, Dr. Louis Rabinowitz, the possessor of a rich command of Jewish lore and of a dynamic personality, exerted a substantial influence on Jewish life. Rabinowitz's successor, Bernard Casper, a pleasant man of vaguely spiritual appearance, has failed to evoke the same respect. In the Cape, the Orthodox rabbinate cast an even feebler shadow during the 1960s and 1970s. The Reform movement established itself rather late, in 1933, and currently embraces only 10 percent of South African Jewry. Resented by the Orthodox leadership, Reform rabbis were obliged for years to fight an uphill battle to win recognition. Even now, in Johannesburg, the Orthodox chief rabbi scurries off the dais when his Reform counterpart approaches the lectern to deliver an address. The unseemly internecine feuding, combined with the temperate climate and secular attractions of Sabbath weekends, has tended in recent years to undermine religious influences altogether among younger Jews.

It is secular Jewish life that has increasingly consumed the energies of South African Jewry. Here the results have been impressive. They are to be found in a superb amalgamation of family service, old age homes, sick funds, and burial, helping hand, and other benevolent societies. One of the most significant advances of the post–World War II period has been in Jewish education, especially in day schools. From the outset, these were fostered largely by the Zionist movement, operating within the nation's historic tradition of multiculturalism. For the last two decades, over half the Jewish children in South Africa have been enrolled in these institutions. The Board of Deputies remains the spokesman for South African Jewry to the government and to communities abroad. It operates an employment bureau, a library, a museum, a prestigious lecture service. Its monthly journal, *Jewish Affairs*, is of excellent quality and is found in every Jewish home. But as a leadership force, the Board has lost ground steadily to the Zionist Federation, which engages by far the largest quantity of Jewish funds and energies.

Portents

Returning to South Africa in June 1982, I encountered striking changes in a land I had visited eight years earlier. A number of the more humiliating features of apartheid had been modified. The separate entrances and separate hours at railroad stations, post offices, theaters, and parks were gone. In government buildings, in large stores and small shops, even in the best restaurants and hotels of every city on my itinerary, the races were mingling as freely as in the streets. The pass laws, requiring blacks to leave Johannesburg by nightfall and return to their authorized urban compound at Soweto, remained on the books, but were not enforced. Whites no longer enjoyed a monopoly of well-paying jobs. The new moderation in fact reflected pressures on the Nationalist government that could not safely be ignored. Until 1974, South Africa had been protected to the north by Rhodesia and by the Portuguese colonies of Angola and Mozambique. The sea was its protection in the northeast. Then, unexpectedly, Portugal stepped out of Angola and Mozambique. Several years later, Rhodesia acquired its own majority black government and was transformed into Zimbabwe. In 1976, a serious eruption occurred in the Soweto ghetto, inflicting numerous casualties on white functionaries working there. At that point, it became a matter of urgency for the South African regime to inaugurate a selective, if largely cosmetic, relaxation in its racial policies.

The government's cautious accommodation to the "winds of change" similarly permitted Jewish communal leaders to speak out more forthrightly on apartheid. After lengthy and anguished deliberation, the

Board of Deputies in 1978 issued a new statement of its position in *Jewish Affairs,* urging "every member of our community to strive for peaceful change—in particular for the elimination of unjust discrimination—so that all, regardless of race, be permitted and encouraged to achieve the full potential of their capabilities and live in dignity and harmony." This time, lightning did not strike from Pretoria. Meanwhile, there were other, private, more characteristic Jewish reactions to the new political developments in southern Africa. At the highest level, Harry Oppenheimer, the chairman of De Beers, Ltd., was quietly "diversifying" $2 billion of his company's assets in overseas investments. So were other (professing) Jews, although in different ways.

Manuel Sachar prided himself on his strong Zionist affiliations and his tireless efforts to provide money and other assistance to Israel. In 1947, he made his initial investment in the Holy Land, a modest £250 share in the Palestine-South Africa Investment Company. After 1967, when the South African government eased its restrictions on currency transfers to Israel, he embarked on a major reinvestment program. It was all strictly within the letter and spirit of the law, for Pretoria insisted that the income from these investments be returned to South Africa, and Manuel complied. In 1970, he and a group of other South African Jews bought control of Peltours, an eminently successful Israeli touring company. In 1977, he purchased a site in Tel Aviv and financed the construction of a sizable office building there. "I've never lost a cent in Israel," Manuel observed proudly. But did he regard these investments strictly as commercial ventures? "Of course not," he replied in full candor. "I'm deeply fond of South Africa. But if anything happens, we'll have a place in Israel." What did he fear might happen? He shrugged. It was an ancestral, atavistic Jewish shrug. Thousands of South African Jews share his skepticism that this El Dorado can be preserved indefinitely against the threat—of what? Afrikaner anti-semitism again? Not likely. It is the black ocean this time.

The Jewish population already has declined, from 118,000 in 1948 to approximately 105,000 by 1984. The figure cannot be exact. Some 20,000 Israelis are floating around the country in search of a quick fortune. But the "nativized" community unquestionably is shrinking. The Anglo-Jewish writer Chaim Bermant recalled his visit to a Jewish day school in South Africa. "My wife and I spoke to the sixth form . . . and asked how many of the students proposed to go to Israel when they left school. About a quarter of the hands went up. When we asked how many proposed to make their home in South Africa, not a *single* hand went up." There it was. In the aftermath of the Soweto riots in 1976, fully 6,000 Jews, most of them younger people, departed within the space of two years. Since then, many hundreds of others have left annually, some for Israel, the majority for other English-speaking countries. Those with exportable professional skills are particularly well represented in this exodus. Since my visit, I have thought of the people I had come to know best: Ellen Hellman, whose daughter is married to an Englishman in Oxford; Frank Bradlow, a distinguished Cape Town historian, whose three children live in England and Europe; Cecil Margo, whose three sons are all professionals, one a psychiatrist in London, the other two lawyers in the United States.

Manuel Sachar is fortunate. His oldest son, at least, remains with him in the business. The middle son is practicing as a clinical psychologist in London. His daughter, the youngest, is firmly settled in Jerusalem as an apprentice film director. "Rochelle stands in for us in Israel," remarked Manuel, neither with resignation nor with false pride. "She's guarding the beachhead."

VIII

Stepchildren of the East:
The Moslem World and India

Turkey: Sephardic Elegy

In 1492, some 200,000 Jews were evicted from Spain by royal decree and cast adrift on the sea-lanes of the world. Carrying with them a proud Sephardic (Iberian) heritage of intellectual acuity and personal dignity, they settled extensively throughout the Mediterranean basin and the Near East. Smaller numbers traveled on to the Western Hemisphere. Yet, in the late twentieth century, it is only in Turkey that the Sephardic community can be found in its original ethnic purity; for here over 95 percent of the Turkish Jewish population is Sephardic. Earlier, the families of these Jews had been scattered throughout the Ottoman Empire, particularly in the Balkans, and even in Asia Minor. But from the 1920s on, the focal point of Turkish Jewish settlement tended to be Istanbul, notably in the old Galeta section on the northern shore of the Golden Horn, and Balat, on the southern shore. Traces of this semi-ghetto can be found today in streets and alleys where scores of tiny synagogues lie abandoned.

Under the Ottoman Empire, Jewish security was well protected. Jews served as prime ministers, as finance and foreign ministers, as eminent members of the commercial and professional community. As late as 1914, individual Turkish Jews figured among the intellectual aristocrats of the Jewish world, and their seminary in Constantinople traditionally provided the chief rabbis of Iraq, Egypt, Libya, Yemen, and of the Sephardic community in Palestine. But of Turkey's approximately eighty thousand Jews on the eve of World War I, most belonged to the lower middle class, earning their livelihoods as craftsmen or small merchants, the latter operating their shops in the Grand Bazaar cheek by jowl with Greek and Armenian tradesmen. In the early 1920s, they were joined by kinsmen from Bulgaria and Greece, who had been ruined in the upheavals of the two Balkan wars, the First World War, then the ensuing Greco-Turkish War.

After World War I, the Ottoman Empire was dismantled and Turkey became a republic under an aggressively modernizing leader, Mustafa Kemal. The initial decades of postwar republican rule were uneasy ones for the Jews. As an integral feature of the national transformation, the Kemal regime forcibly secularized or eliminated the religious institutions of Turks and non-Turks alike. Thus, the Alliance Israélite Universelle schools, in which the largest numbers of Jewish children received their education, were closed; and so, gradually, were other Jewish private schools. Even in the few surviving afternoon synagogue classes, Hebrew was not taught at all. Ladino, the traditional dialect of Sephardic Jews, gradually was abandoned even as a spoken tongue. Possibly half the country's seventy-five synagogues (in 1920) were confiscated and, like Turkey's mosques and churches, often were transformed into museums. In the prevailing climate of Turanian chauvinism, the Jews were now regarded as a "non-Turkish" element. For the first time since their settlement in this land, they were barred from the civil service, deprived of import and export licenses, and subjected to discriminatory property taxes. Indeed, in 1942, a mounting wave of pro-Nazi xenophobia produced the notorious Varlik Vergisi, a property tax that ruined thousands of jewish—and Greek and Armenian—businessmen, before it was dropped finally under Allied pressure in 1944.

It was principally those Jews whose estates had been devoured by the Varlik Vergisi, as well as other, poorer Jews, who departed for Western countries and Israel in the post–World War II years. The Turkish government made no effort to block their departure or the transfer of their meager savings. By 1967, as a result, not more than 42,000 Jews continued on in Turkey, and since then the figures have been reduced to 21,000, less than a tenth of 1 percent of the nation's total population of 31 million. Three-quarters of these Jews live in Istanbul. The famed Jewish merchant population of Izmir (Smyrna) was reduced from 15,000 to 4,000. Edirne (Adrianople), which as late as World War II encompassed 14,000 Jews and boasted possibly the most tightly knit Jewish community in the East—the home of Joseph Caro, author of the *Shulchan Aruch,* a city in which some thirteen synagogues and a renowned talmudical academy thrived in the years before World War I—lost its entire Jewish population to Israel.

Turkey's remaining Jews are largely businessmen or professionals. Although few are wealthy, some do well, particularly the dealers in automotive supplies, rubber, textiles, and farm tools, or the stylish retail merchants whose shops can be found in the better streets. They live comfortably, by and large, in apartments and villas in Istanbul's northern suburbs. Whatever the vicissitudes of democratic government in postwar Turkey, Jews no longer are singled out for discrimination— although most are still inclined to exercise their Jewishness discreetly. The rise of Israel has had no adverse affect on them. The Turks are Sunni Moslems, but they dislike the Arabs, even as they have developed a certain unspoken admiration for Israel as a progressive warrior nation. While adhering to a pro-Arab line in the United Nations, the Ankara government maintained until recently a consulate in Jerusalem, and has allowed Turkish Jews to visit Israel as often as they like.

The most enduring Jewish disability in republican Turkey has been religious and cultural. In the nineteenth and early twentieth centuries, as we recall, Turkish Jews still enjoyed a world reputation for scholarship. Even in recent years, a chief rabbi and his council have presided authoritatively from their headquarters building in the Beyogulu district over the religious affairs of Istanbul Jewry, applying strict Orthodox law to such traditionally "personal status" questions as marriage, burial, and inheritance. In recent decades, however, religious observance has become as nominal among Turkish Jews as among most of their counterparts in Europe. Although four Jewish day schools still function in Istanbul, 90 percent of Jewish children attend state schools or, whenever possible, the small number of elite foreign schools (French, British, German) that are allowed to teach in their national languages. Among the younger generation, Jewishness is a matter of ethnicity, and is sustained by a score of Jewish sports, cultural, and "friendship" clubs. Jews socialize largely with Jews, marry almost exclusively among themselves. Few of them aspire to "pass" into a society that they regard as intellectually inferior in every respect. Their rate of reproduction is a solid three per family. But if they are in no sense a moribund Jewry, they are a pale shadow of the renowned minority enclave that, as recently as World War I, was the most creative and distinguished Sephardic community in the Diaspora.

Egypt: The Hubris of Europeanization

If Turkish Jews boasted a lineage of four centuries, the majority of Egypt's 66,000 Jews (in 1945) traced their native settlement back less than four decades. Most were born in the Near East, but not in Egypt. Some were émigrés from the former Ottoman provinces of Syria, Lebanon, and Palestine, from North Africa and Corfu. During the 1920s and 1930s, they came precisely to shed their Asian inheritance, for Egypt under British rule offered refugees the opportunity of special "status" under European consular protection. As a result, the newcomers regarded themselves increasingly as "Europeans," members of that privileged economic and social class that included hundreds of thousands of British, French, Italians, and Greeks. Later, to be sure, this favored extraterritoriality was withdrawn as a result of the Anglo-Egyptian Treaty of 1936; and by the eve of World War II, nearly four-fifths of the Jews in Egypt were stateless. Yet, as "local subjects," they still enjoyed full legal protection in their personal lives and business affairs, without the corresponding responsibilities of citizenship.

They were almost exclusively a middle-class community. Beginning as petty merchants in Cairo and Alexandria, they flourished rapidly in both cities. Together with the Greeks and the Armenians, they owned or managed the finest shops on Suleiman Basha and Ali Basha streets, and operated the most important textile firms in Cairo's Musky commercial quarter. Hundreds of Jewish financiers served as executives in Egypt's banking and insurance systems. Jewish brokers played leading roles in the currency and cotton exchanges and in the stock market. Other Jews prospered as doctors and lawyers. The economic boom of World War II consolidated their already formidable position. Living for the most part in their own neighborhoods, the Harat al-Yahud, in Cairo and Alexandria, the Jews spoke mainly French—the language of haute culture—among themselves. Numbers of Jewish families began purchasing homes in Cairo's attractive residential quarters of Heliopolis, Daher, and Zamalek, together with the nouveaux riches of the other minority communities. They rarely encountered prejudice. Indeed, the larger Egyptian firms vied with each other in engaging Jewish executives. If nationalist hatred festered beneath the surface of Egyptian public life, it was directed toward the British, rarely toward the other minorities, and least of all toward the Jews.

Egyptian Jews maintained a strong cohesiveness and community discipline. They established their own elaborate network of—principally Alliance—schools, of Maccabi and HaKoach sports clubs, B'nai B'rith lodges, hospitals, mutual aid societies, youth, literary, and drama circles, and private associations of Sephardic, Ionian, and Italian Jews. As in other Near Eastern lands, their extensive cluster of synagogues functioned under the legally recognized authority of rabbinical courts. The government in fact obliged them to pay "taxes" to support their semiautonomous community, and they did so willingly. Affluent and Europeanized, they were less observant than were the Jews of North Africa, possibly even of Turkey. Yet they guarded their ethnic and cultural, if not their religious, traditions fiercely.

Central among those traditions in the 1920s and 1930s was Zionism. Modern Hebrew was taught in all the Alliance schools. Zionist journals, libraries, and drama groups were active. Jews collected money for the Jewish National Fund, went to Palestine on visits, even invested money there. Then, in the late 1930s, Egypt began to identify increasingly with the Arab cause, and Jews found it useful to become circumspect in their Zionist loyalties. In 1938 and 1939, the militant right-wing fringe groups, Ikhwan al-Muslemin (Moslem Brotherhood) and Misr al-Fatat (Young Egypt), were setting a new and ominous tone, calling for a boycott of Egyptian Jewish businesses, issuing lists of prominent Jewish merchants and communal organizations. That same year, a number of Jewish institutional offices were bombed. Although anti-Jewish violence came to an abrupt end with the martial law of World War II, it was plain that xenophobia was mounting among a people that until the 1930s had maintained a wide distance between themselves and so-called integral Arabs.

By the end of the war, King Farouk's militant new pan-Arab stance encouraged an authentically anti-Jewish fanaticism in Egypt. For the first time, newspaper editorials advised Egyptian Jews to refrain from Zionist activities. In November 1946, anti-Jewish demonstrations in Cairo and Alexandria were spurred on by the pro-royalist press. Hooligans smashed and ransacked Jewish shops, looted a synagogue in Cairo. Ultimately, it was the Palestine partition debate in the United Nations, the creation of the State of Israel, and the Arab-Israeli War in 1948–49 that threatened the very survival of Egyptian Jewry. In 1947, a Companies Law was enacted, requiring at least 75 percent of all employees in private businesses to hold Egyptian citizenship. The blow was a crippling one for Jewish enterprises. On May 15, 1948, the day

Egypt launched its invasion of Palestine, hundreds of Egyptian Jews were arrested, ostensibly for Zionist plotting. Two weeks later, the government was empowered to confiscate the property of individuals whose activities were "detrimental to the state"; and shortly afterward the holdings of some hundred Jewish merchants and companies were sequestered. In August and September 1948, Egyptian nationals alone were permitted to serve as brokers on the stock exchange, then to practice medicine. Jewish businesses were looted, and bombs planted in Jewish neighborhoods killed and wounded 252 individuals. Additionally, Jews were persuaded to "contribute" hundreds of thousands of pounds to the Egyptian army.

The assassination of Prime Minister Mahmud al-Nuqrashi by an Ikhwan gunman in December 1948 finally brought the terrorism to a halt. The new premier, Ibrahim al-Hadi, immediately and courageously emptied the prisons of "Zionist suspects"—Jews—and filled them with members of the Ikhwan itself. The nation slowly returned to normal, to its characteristic easygoing indolence. The circumstances of Egyptian Jewry soon improved. In July 1949, the government released substantial portions of confiscated Jewish assets. Jewish schools were authorized to reopen, a Jewish communal newspaper to resume publication. Most significantly of all, "non-Moslems" were allowed to leave the country again. Thus, taking advantage of the opportunity, some thirty thousand Jews disposed of their homes and businesses between 1949 and 1951, transferred their holdings to European banks, and summarily departed for France and Italy—and a third of these in turn went on to Israel. Fully three-fifths of Egyptian Jewry remained, however, cautiously optimistic that stability would continue.

That expectation lasted barely three years. In 1952, a "Colonels' Revolution" overthrew King Farouk and established a republic under military rule. Within the next eighteen months, Gamal Abd al-Nasser emerged as undisputed leader of the officers' junta. Deliberately fanning the flames of anti-British and anti-Israel hostility, Nasser focused public rancor on the European "monopoly" of Egyptian economic life. British, French, Greek, and Italian entrepreneurs were closed out of the national market. The Jews, in turn, were singled out as an Israeli fifth column. In December of 1954, Nasser exploited a treason trial of eleven Egyptian Jews, who were convicted of spying for Israel, to brand the entire Egyptian-Jewish population as a "nest of traitors." During the ensuing winter months, Jewish shops were boycotted, Jewish importers deprived of their licenses, Jewish stockbrokers and cotton brokers denied access to their former underwriting houses. It was no less difficult for Jews to leave the country, even when exit visas were available. The market for Jewish properties had collapsed and the government prohibited money transfers abroad. Each month, the few hundred Jews who were allowed departure for Europe took with them the smallest fraction of their savings. Few of the thirty-seven thousand or so who remained managed to salvage their estates or careers.

For this hostage Jewry, Egypt's humiliation in the Sinai-Suez War of 1956 was a disaster even more far-reaching than the original Palestine War. Once again, the European minorities provided a convenient target. Tens of thousands of British, French, Italian, and Greek inhabitants were expelled from Egypt, their businesses confiscated. Yet retribution against the Jews was harshest of all. Within the space of a year, 21,000 of them were shipped out of the country. None was allowed to take with him more than thirty Egyptian pounds. Other Jews were permitted to leave on their own initiative, although under the same financial constraints. By the end of 1959, approximately 36,000 Jews had departed for Israel, France, Italy, or Brazil, and other, smaller groups followed in ensuing years. By June 1967, not more than 3,000 remained.

Their climactic ordeal took place in the aftermath of the Six-Day War. Shocked to near-hysteria by the scope of its military debacle, the Nasser government arrested hundreds of Jews, including the aged rabbis of Cairo and Alexandria, and interned them in concentration camps. Three years passed before the prisoners were released. Most of them eventually succeeded in departing Egypt by paying out all they owned in bribes. The three or four hundred sick or aged Jews who remained lived essentially on funds transmitted by the Joint or by other overseas Jewish philanthropies. Of these, barely two hundred survived to extend tearful greetings to Menachem Begin in Cairo's Sharei Shamayim Synagogue, during the Israeli prime minister's visit of April 1979, a month after the signing of the Egyptian-Israeli peace treaty.

Syria: The Malevolence of Political Insecurity

Victor Basrawi* was forty-three years old. The muscle tone gone in his face and body, he appeared to be at least fifteen years older. Sitting in his living room in a shabby working-class apartment in southeast

---

*The subject's family name has been changed to protect relatives currently living in Syria.

Brooklyn, his dark eyes peered anxiously through heavy spectacles. "We go back thousands of years in the Middle East," he insisted. "We are *'Musta'arabin* [Arabized Jews]." It was possible. Although the Basrawis were Aleppines, and numerous Aleppo Jews were descendants of sixteenth-century Sephardic immigrants, others unquestionably shared a more ancient and indigenous lineage. All of them in any case mastered the art of adaptation. The father, Musa, had changed his name to Michel under the French mandate. The mother, Latife, became Liliane. Middle class, the Jews of Aleppo and Damascus alike tended to enroll their children in French—Alliance and Mission Laïque—schools. The family had lived for generations in Bah'sita, the old Jewish commercial quarter downtown, but the success of the Basrawis' leather goods store in the 1930s allowed them to join the Jewish emigration to a better, upper-middle-class neighborhood in the Jamalyal district. There Victor Basrawi was reared with his nine brothers and sisters, attended a parochial talmud torah, then a Mission Laïque secondary school.

As late as 1947, some 26,000 Jews were living in Syria, a population divided almost equally between Damascus and Aleppo. Each community zealously maintained its own institutions and folk mores. Despite their parochialism, their circumstances were not uncomfortable. Earlier, under the listless Ottoman administration, they had endured no serious political disabilities, and had even achieved a certain eminence in commerce. Under French rule, they shared in the dramatic upsurge of the Levant's economy. To be sure, none of the Jewish communities profited quite as impressively as did the 5,000 Jews of Beirut, Lebanon. The Beirutis were favored in their affluence, living at the gateway to Mediterranean trade. Moreover, they continued to enjoy political security in this sophisticated mercantile nation well after the French departure and the establishment of Lebanese independence in 1946—and even following the birth of Israel two years after that. Jews remained in the Lebanese civil service. As late as 1962, several Jews participated in the Lebanese delegation to the United Nations. Offering refuge to the Jews of Syria after the Palestine War of 1948, Lebanon was the one Arab state in which Jewish numbers actually increased following Israeli independence, from 5,700 (in the 1944 census) to 9,000 in 1949. Afterward, emigration to Israel and to other nations swiftly depleted this population, to 4,000 in 1967, to 1,000 in 1972, and to less than 200 by 1984.

Syria was a different story for the Jews. During the last years of the

French mandate, there were occasional violent demonstrations against the "supporters of Zionism." In 1945, the director of the Alliance school in Damascus was murdered. Following the United Nations partition resolution in November 1947, a series of anti-Jewish outbursts in Aleppo were climaxed by the sacking of the Bah'sita quarter. Seven years old then, Victor Basrawi was beaten by a crowd of Moslem teenagers. The family shop was looted. Hundreds of Jewish businessmen experienced the same fate. The poorer Jews made no effort to remain. Selling or abandoning their homes, they bribed their way across the Lebanese frontier. Those who sought to rebuild their lives were either the wealthy or others who simply feared risking imprisonment by illegal departure.

The Basrawis were among these. In the aftermath of the Palestine War, their lives and those of their Jewish neighbors were beset with new and far graver difficulties. Their identification papers were stamped with the word *Musawi* (Mosaic—i.e., Jewish). Most of their schools were closed. To inhibit illegal Jewish departure, and the possible augmentation of Israel's military manpower, the government in 1948 prohibited the sale of Jewish property, and five years later froze Jewish bank accounts. Most chilling of all, Jews were subject to arrest and prosecution or were obliged to visit the police station daily as an earnest of their good behavior, whenever their children and other close relatives succeeded in escaping.

The Basrawis' modest leather goods shop barely scraped along, struggling to obtain materials through uncertain import licenses. For them, as for the remaining four or five thousand Jews in Aleppo, the consuming obsession by then was to clear out. The father, Michel, was exploring the possibility of escape as early as 1950. As he began negotiations with Arab contacts, however, a friend, Murad Ahan, was seized by the Deuxième Bureau on suspicion of organizing an emigration ring. The man's fingernails were torn out, his body burned with cigarettes. By the time he was released after a week of "interrogation," he had lost the sight in one eye and his sense of equilibrium. Michel Basrawi instantly dropped his plans and devoted his full attention to his shop. From time to time, his apartment was scoured by police in search of incriminating evidence.

In 1957, the vise tightened. "Encouraged" to remain within their home cities, Jews no longer were issued driving licenses. The pressure soon became intolerable. That winter, Victor's younger brother

Édouard "disappeared." Later, the family was discreetly informed that
he had been smuggled over the mountains to Lebanon. In the immediate aftermath of his departure, the parents were called to police headquarters and asked to explain their son's absence. When they could not,
they were ordered to report daily to give an accounting on their other
children. Yet for Victor, there was never a doubt that he would make
the attempt on his own. He said nothing to his parents or to his remaining brothers. It was an unspoken rule among Jews to avoid implicating
their families.

In March 1958, then, the week of his eighteenth birthday, Victor
Basrawi traveled by bus to Damascus. There he located his contact, a
taxi driver named Samir. A veteran smuggler of Jews, Samir set his
price at three hundred pounds—in advance. Victor paid. That night the
taxi carried him through a mountain pass to a village on the Syrian side
of the border. "You're on your own," whispered Samir. "Half a kilo-
meter on foot will bring you into Lebanon." It did. Reaching the Lebanese village of Haloué, Basrawi flagged down a truckdriver and
requested a lift to Beirut. Instead, the Arab took him to the village
mukhtar, who promptly locked him in a room, then several hours later
had him driven back to the frontier under armed guard.

A contingent of Syrian police waited. Stripping and searching the
youth on the spot, the Syrians threw him into a van and drove him
straightaway to Damascus. Finally, after a week and a half, he was
driven to Aleppo. At the local police station, his parents were waiting.
Smiling, the guards instructed the Basrawis to wait. They escorted the
young prisoner into another room. There, calmly and systematically,
they set about beating him with rubber truncheons. Hearing his
screams, his mother fainted. Days went by, then weeks. There were
repeated beatings and kickings and moments when the terrified youth
lost track of time altogether. After three months, he was released into
the custody of his parents.

Victor Basrawi was determined to try again. Each week, news came
of others who somehow had escaped. In June 1959, he and two friends
were put in touch with a "reliable" Arab guide. The sum of one thousand pounds was agreed upon. They traveled by bus to Homs. The
Arab guide was there, and he drove them to the border, then personally led them by foot through a series of passes and across a river.
Lebanon awaited them. So, once again, did a contingent of Syrian military police—on the Lebanese side of the frontier. With their guns, the

MPs prodded the young Jews into a truck. Basrawi and his companions were transported back to Homs, then locked in a precinct station. The commandant, Abu Hakim, was a huge, burly man, a specialist in dealing with "Communists." Flanked by a dozen guards, he launched into an "instruction session" with his Jewish captives. Whips and electrodes were used. The ordeal continued for two days. Afterward, Basrawi and the others were carried off to yet another police station. This time they were locked in the "tank," a vast chamber containing nearly one hundred other Jewish prisoners. The latter, too, had been captured while attempting to cross the border, and had undergone torture.

The following day, Basrawi, his companions, and some thirty other prisoners were transported by van to Mazzah Military Prison in Damascus. The three friends were given their own cell. Although they were spared further beatings, they now faced slow starvation. In the ensuing forty days of detention in Mazzah, Basrawi lost nearly a pound a day. He was failing when, suddenly, he was transferred back to the precinct station. There he was fed adequately. He learned afterward that his parents had saved him by paying baksheesh to the commandant. Subsequently, the three young Jews were carried off to Homs, to another investigation at the local police headquarters, and from there at last to court. The ordeal seemingly had come to an end. An honest man, the judge was astonished that any Syrian citizen should have been arrested for traveling across the Lebanese border, a journey that was strictly within the law. Some 400,000 Syrians were working in Lebanon on a semipermanent basis, after all. He ordered the prisoners released forthwith.

Basrawi and the others walked out of the courtroom. Their families were waiting. Quickly embracing, they hurried to waiting taxis. Before they could drive off, four jeeps careened to the curb. The women screamed. The senior police officer smiled. "What one softhearted judge does is his business," he explained, "but we have to investigate these boys for other crimes." The "other crimes" were not specified. Basrawi was confined to the local jail with his friends for the next sixty-six days. Near the end, convinced that he had nothing further to lose, he embarked on a hunger strike. It was an unprecedented protest. Confused by it, the warden arranged Basrawi's immediate transfer to a prison in Damascus. There he remained another twenty days, continuing his hunger strike. Eventually, he and his two companions were interrogated by a group of senior military officers, who presented each of them with a typed sheet of paper. "It's a confession that you were fleeing to Israel," explained a colonel, "that you were planning to join the Israeli army to fight Syria. Sign it and you'll be released." They signed.

They were carried back again to Mazzah Prison. For the next two weeks, they were interrogated twice daily by another team of military officers. One of these was an Egyptian colonel (this was the period of the United Arab Republic) assigned to the Mudhakkarat, the Syrian military intelligence branch. The Egyptian was shocked by the brutality of the local police. Possibly it was this man who intervened. On December 13, 1959, fully six months after his initial capture in Lebanon, Basrawi was allowed legal counsel. The lawyer was one of the most famous in Damascus; Basrawi's parents had retained him at a staggering fee. The very fact that the case was going to court gave hope that the young prisoners soon would be released. They were. "I'm a busy man," snapped the attorney to the Basrawis as their son was discharged from prison. "Try to keep him out of trouble. Next time you may never know if he's captured."

Victor Basrawi had learned his lesson. Returning to Aleppo, to his work at the family shop, he dutifully visited the local police headquarters each day. The official sentence for attempting to escape had been raised by then to twelve years; yet, as the lawyer had warned, many Jews did not survive to serve it. Evidently one had to learn to live in this prison-nation. There were still ways to accommodate. In 1964, all Jews were denied import licenses. Normally, this would have been a death blow to their businesses. But soon almost every Jewish merchant engaged his Arab proxy, serving, for a handsome commission, as the owner of record. The fiction probably fooled no one, but government officials cynically tolerated it in return for discreet payoffs. Remarkably, during the 1960s, the Basrawis even managed to open two additional shops.

It was a grim decade, nevertheless. The inauguration of a radical Ba'athist regime in 1962 launched a new era of political tension, and this in a country already notorious for its lawlessness and political instability. The government's essential purpose thenceforth was to militarize Syrian public life and to intensify public hostility toward the "imperialist" West and Israel. Worse yet, a power struggle ensued between rival Ba'athist factions, and in February 1966 a military coup brought Colonel Salah Jadid to power. The Jadid regime in turn was comprised mainly of Alawites, adherents of a small Moslem minority sect. Enjoying little public support, it barely survived two armed revolts in 1966 and 1967. Under the circumstances, it was not the strength of the Alawite cabinet that frightened the Jews, but its vulnerability. To compensate for political weakness, Jadid and his colleagues now openly championed the one cause that was universally popular, a war of liberation against Israel.

Accordingly, it was the Six-Day War that ended any lingering Jewish hopes for security. The fanaticism of the mob, the harrowing press and television accounts of the mass extermination awaiting the Israelis, convinced the Basrawis and their friends that their days in this land were numbered, whether or not they fled. And indeed, in the aftermath of Syria's defeat, under the regime of President Nureddin al-Atassi—Jadid's even more bloodthirsty successor—the Jewish community suffered an upsurge of arbitrary arrests, kidnappings, and permanent disappearances. No Jew thenceforth was allowed to travel more than three miles from his home. The director of the Jewish section of the Mudhakkarat, a diminutive officer named Muhammad Machele, was a sadist who delighted in terrorizing Jews, even halting them in the street and striking them across the face. By 1971 and 1972, out of sheer despair, the remaining few thousand Jewish men—and some women—began to run the grave risks of flight once again. With the endless distribution of baksheesh, some of these people managed to develop new contacts and exit routes through Turkey, occasionally even through Lebanon.

Two of Basrawi's younger brothers, Albert and Robert, were among those prepared to take the gamble. In March 1973, Albert's brother-in-law was shot in cold blood at the door of his home by an Arab hooligan. The police went through the motions of an investigation, then let the matter drop. Any danger was preferable now to existence in this land. For a payment of three thousand pounds each, Albert, Robert, and Albert's wife, Colette, engaged a taxi driver who was known to have a shrewd knowledge of the terrain. The Arab spirited them over the border to Lebanon, and from there to safety. A day later, the Mudhakkarat called in Albert's and Robert's parents for questioning. The old couple was not physically maltreated, but the interrogation was aggressive. It continued for three days, until the intelligence officers were satisfied that the parents had known nothing of their sons' plans. In any case, the Jewish exodus no longer could be stemmed. In the earlier

years, between 1948 and 1961, approximately 15,000 Jews had succeeded in fleeing the country. Afterward, the rate had slowed. But in
the nightmare period between 1963 and 1973, another 6,000 found
ways to cross the frontier. By the end of the 1970s, not more than 5,000
Jews altogether remained in Syria. Of these, some 4,000 were in
Damascus. The Aleppine community had dropped to 600.

In early 1975, Jewish circumstances suddenly registered an unexpected, if slight, improvement. By then President Hafez al-Assad, who
had succeeded the psychotic Nureddin al-Atassi, had undergone the
trauma of the Yom Kippur War. His economy had been savagely bat-
tered. In the course of the diplomatic negotiations of 1974–75, it became as clear to him as to Anwar al-Sadat in Egypt that only the
diplomatic support of the United States would lever Israeli troops off
Arab soil. To cultivate American goodwill, Assad, like Sadat, was prepared to adopt a certain flexibility in his relations with Washington. In
February 1974, a young Jewish congressman from Brooklyn, Stephen
Solarz, whose constituency included several thousand Jews of Syrian
extraction, visited Damascus as a member of a congressional delegation.
During an interview with Assad, Solarz managed to persuade the Syrian
president that Washington would regard the fate of the Syrian Jewish
minority as an earnest of the Ba'athist government's promised new
moderation. During the next two years, then, Assad lifted restrictions
on the transfer of Jewish property. Two Jewish schools were reopened.
Several Jewish students were admitted to the university. Jews were
issued drivers' licenses and Jewish businessmen were allowed to apply
for import licenses again.

More significantly yet, a number of Jews managed to obtain passports and exit visas for business trips abroad. The opportunity was
hardly open-ended. Jewish applicants were required to post large bonds
(the equivalent of $6,000) and to leave family members behind. Victor
Basrawi was one of a small minority of Jews who could afford the payment. Early in 1975, he was given a six-week travel permit to visit the
United States. Ostensibly, his purpose was to arrange supplies for his
family's leather shops. Once reaching New York, however, Basrawi
made straight for Congressman Solarz's Brooklyn office. There he was
taken in hand by Sylvia Wurf, Solarz's executive assistant for Syrian
Jewish affairs. In her latter sixties, a gentle-featured widow, Mrs. Wurf
already had become a legendary figure to the Syrian Jewish community
in Brooklyn. Over the years, she had developed a network of connec-

tions in the State Department, recruiting help on behalf of Syrian refugees, exploiting every loophole in United States immigration laws. Nearly always, she secured permanent-resident papers—green cards— in record time, helping the Syrians find employment and housing. She allowed no bureaucratic obstacle to stand in her way, or any physical impairment. Mrs. Wurf was blind.

With her help, then, Basrawi secured his green card only three weeks after his arrival. He returned immediately to Syria. In 1980, he made a return trip to New York. Within days, he arranged the admission of three of his six children to a religious school in Brooklyn. Afterward, flying home with the school documents in hand, he persuaded the Syrian authorities to allow him yet a third visit to the United States. The three sons who had been accepted for schooling were permitted to accompany him (after all, they were not going to Israel). But his wife, Ariela, and the other children remained as hostages in Aleppo. So did his shops, his apartment, his automobile. Now Basrawi confronted the gravest challenge of his life. If he and the three children were not back before the exit visas expired, in six months, retribution would be meted out to his family at home. It was vital to move quickly to extricate Ariela, their two daughters and one young son. Describing his odyssey, Basrawi became intentionally vague at this point in his account, offering few details on his subsequent arrangements. By devious and circuitous means, evidently, contacts were made with relatives of Syrian officials. With the help of wealthy Syrian Jews in New York, funds were discreetly passed to numbered bank accounts in Switzerland. Travel documents were altered, and the exit permits of the three sons in New York were mailed back to Aleppo for use by the remaining children.

In the end, everything depended upon the reliability of the exit zone that had been found, the willingness of border police to look the other way at the right moment. It was a terrifying gamble. "I would never have taken it, if even the faintest alternative had existed," Basrawi admitted afterward. In December 1982, Ariela and the children embarked on their assigned route through the Lebanese mountain chain. It was a trek of nine hours—for a woman of forty, two daughters of seventeen and fifteen, and a boy of eleven. When Basrawi described this episode afterward, his ruined body shook visibly. "Nine hours in that darkness, over those rocks and thistles," he whispered. "A whole family's lives hanging in the balance. You understand, monsieur? And I, sitting by this telephone, knew the night, the very hour of their departure. Those nine hours I was living or dying by this telephone with them, waiting, waiting. . . ." At four-thirty the following morning, the telephone rang. "It was Beirut. Ariela on the line. She and the children were safe." As he relived the moment, Basrawi's eyes behind their thick spectacles visibly misted over. "Afterward, Sylvia, here"—he gestured to Sylvia Wurf, sitting across the room—"made the necessary arrangements to bring the family to New York. All they had to do was reach the United States. Sylvia could be depended on to take care of the rest."

Ariela Basrawi was seated beside her husband. Three weeks had passed since she had fled Syria, hardly enough time to put her new surroundings in focus. Had she yet recovered from the experience? Smiling tightly, she said nothing. Instead, she rolled down her thick knee stockings, displaying shins crisscrossed with livid welts. Basrawi moaned softly. "Would you like to see the children's legs?" he asked then. "It was all those thistles and thorn bushes they had to cross through, you see. It left them some souvenirs."

Two days after Ariela and the children vanished from Aleppo, the Mudhakkarat swept down on Basrawi's old parents. Once again they were grilled for days, but in the end they were spared imprisonment. So were Basrawi's two sisters and their husbands and children—the remainder of the family in Syria. Rather, the government simply confiscated Victor Basrawi's shops, his automobile, closed off all the rooms of his apartment except one, where his parents were living. "There they will remain," murmured Basrawi, "and there, sooner or later, they will die. They will never leave Aleppo." Was there ever a possibility, he was asked, that he or others of his family who had escaped would go to Israel? Basrawi hesitated "Thousands of our people went to Israel in the first years after 1948," he explained then. "They were the poorer elements. But for us, who were accustomed to a somewhat higher standard of living . . ."

His prognosis for the once venerable and distinguished Syrian Jewish community was also an old story. The tiny remnant staying behind appeared to have won a certain precarious physical security. Assad was no friend, but Atassi before him had been worse. And after Assad, one wondered, in the event the Sunni Moslem majority erupted and overthrew the hated Alawite regime? Yet another old story. It was a faint, tentative preference for a known and predictable tyrant over the explosive fury of the mob that lay in wait.

Yemen: The Impulsion of Messianism

In February 1880, a bedraggled procession of some five hundred men, women, and children appeared on the outskirts of Jerusalem. Dark-skinned, they were slight of stature and quite emaciated. Their leader sought an audience with the Chacham Bashi, the Jewish community's chief rabbi. Escorted to the rabbi's court, the elder of the band explained, in Arabic, that they were Jews, and that they had arrived from Yemen. It seemed unlikely at first. An obscure little kingdom tucked into the southwestern corner of the Arabian peninsula, Yemen lay well beyond the frontier of any known Jewish settlement. Nevertheless, growing acquaintance with the newcomers erased any doubts that their ritual, at least, was authentically Jewish. The family genealogies they carried with them suggested, too, that a Jewish presence in Yemen extended back conceivably eighteen hundred years, to the historic Exile from Palestine. Indeed, within six centuries after their arrival, they had succeeded in judaizing Yemen's royal household; and the monarch Yusuf Dhu-Nuwas afterward secured the conversion to Judaism of thousands of his subjects. Here was the clue to the newcomers' physical resemblance to Arabs. Many, if not most, of them were lineal descendants of these converts.

The era of large-scale proselytization was fleeting. By the end of the ninth century, the disciples of Islam swept into their fold the entire (pagan) population of the Middle East. Ultimately, the Jews of Yemen were transformed into a *dhimmi*—non-Moslem, but God-respecting, minority. Denied the right to engage in agriculture, they were obliged to behave circumspectly in the presence of their Moslem neighbors, to pay special taxes, to live in an isolated quarter of the capital, Tsan'a, and of other towns. Their status improved slightly after 1872, when the Ottoman army conquered Yemen. Jews were permitted to build new quarters and synagogues, and were exempted from the obligation of collecting animal carcasses. Yet, living in a society governed by Shi'ism, the least tolerant version of Islam, they remained untouchables, subjected to heavier taxes and to more humiliating restrictions than Jews elsewhere in the Moslem world, with the possible exception of Iran. Confined to the towns and cities, the Jews became Yemen's artisans. Their exquisite leatherwork and jewelry were highly prized by the Arabs, who paid well for them. The Jews may have enjoyed a higher standard of living than did the Arabs. Even so, they were far poorer than Jews anywhere else, and they remained small, underfed, and susceptible to a high mortality rate.

They remained intensely observant, as well, punctiliously following the minutest of biblical rules and regulations. Moreover, as devotees of the Cabalah, they sustained the messianic vision of a return to the Holy Land. It was in 1880 that the dream of Return was suddenly transformed into reality. By sailing ship and caravan, tales reached the imamate of Yemen of Jews from far-off nations who had arrived in the Land of Israel to reclaim the ancient hope of Zion. Whereupon, in near-delirium, some one hundred Jewish families from Tsan'a promptly sold their homes and set out for Palestine. Sailing up the Red Sea to Suez in tiny dhows, they continued afterward by land to Alexandria, then by steamer to Jaffa, and again by foot to Jerusalem. These were the five hundred trembling and awestruck Yemenites who first entered the Holy City and opened the window on a world passed by. Each year afterward, they were joined by hundreds of their kin, until by 1948 the Yemenite population in Palestine, swollen by immigration and natural increase, had already reached forty thousand.

The birth of Israel was the ultimate augury of redemption for the imamate's remaining Jews. By then, life in Yemen had become insupportable. Enraged by the defeat of Arab forces in the Palestine War, mobs began pouring through the Jewish quarters of Tsan'a, Te'ez, Dama, Rada'ah—pillaging and burning. Hereupon, the imam decided to place no obstacles in the way of the Jews' departure, so long as they left all their property to the government. For a fixed sum, the Jewish Agency in turn persuaded the sheikhs whose territories lay between the imamate and the British Crown Colony of Aden to let the Jews pass through. Across this bleak terrain, then, Yemen's remaining Jews made their way by foot down the coast. By the time they arrived at the hastily organized Joint transit camp in Hashed, adjoining Aden, most of them were walking skeletons. Nursed back to health, they were ultimately loaded onto transport planes at the RAF airport at Khornasar and flown to Israel. Between January 1949 and June 1951, 48,000 of these Jews were borne to safety by the Jewish Agency's "Operation Magic Carpet." The Yemenites thus became the one Jewish community in the world that was transplanted virtually in its entirety to the Holy Land.

Iraq: Farewell to Babylon

Tracing their ancestry to the first of Jewish diasporas, that of ancient Babylon, the Jews of Iraq comprised the oldest Jewish population on earth. No Jewry in the Middle East was ever more thoroughly arabized.

Dark of skin, they were physically almost indistinguishable from their Arab neighbors. Arabic was their language at home and in the street. Unlike Jews elsewhere in Arab lands, moreover, few of them possessed biblical names. They blended almost completely into the ethnographic landscape. By 1914, they numbered some 115,000, and were dispersed mainly between Baghdad, Basra, and Mosul. After the Young Turk Revolution of 1908, the Jews of Iraq became Ottoman citizens in the fullest sense of the word, spared the need any longer to pay poll taxes as *dhimmis* or to live in ghetto neighborhoods. They were allowed to send delegates to the Ottoman parliament in Constantinople, to serve in the law courts and municipal councils.

If they experienced lingering insecurities, these were dissipated almost completely upon the establishment of the British mandate. In ensuing years, four Jews sat in the Iraqi parliament. Sassoon Effendi ben Ezekiel, scion of Iraqi Jewry's most distinguished family, served as minister of finance. Throughout the 1920s and 1930s, Jewish children attended government schools and universities. Among Middle Eastern Jews, the Iraqis achieved unsurpassed prosperity. As far back as the nineteenth century, the opening of the Suez Canal vastly augmented the importance of Baghdad and Basra in the developing British trade with the Orient. Sharing in that commerce, Iraqi Jewish businessmen gradually won a decisive share in their nation's foreign trade, exceeding that of Moslem, Christian, even European merchants. Under the British mandate, Jews were major contractors for the occupying army, owners of the principal import-export houses, leading executives in local branches of British companies and in the British administration itself. Numbering approximately 140,000 in 1939, Iraqi Jews had achieved an economic and educational distinction unequaled in the Moslem world, except for Egypt. Although they had become somewhat lax in their religious observance, they maintained a firm ethnocentrism, and scrupulously married only among themselves.

Their favored circumstances changed drastically after the outbreak of World War II. With Britain on the defensive in the Middle East, a pro-Nazi military cabal briefly assumed control of the Iraqi government in May 1941. For several weeks, Jews were subjected to arrests and beatings. Eventually, the British launched a counteroffensive that sent the dissident Arab officers into flight. But when Iraq's Jews celebrated their anticipated rescue, the Arab population erupted suddenly in riots, killing over two hundred Jews and injuring hundreds of others. Only the arrival of the British army restored order. Then, in the early post-war years, demonstrations against Zionism mounted in intensity, and with them anti-Jewish propaganda. In the spring of 1948, the withdrawal of British garrisons from Iraq posed an acute danger to the Jewish minority. All the more so when the Palestine War began in May 1948. Anti-Jewish chauvinism in Iraq reached fever pitch. Zionism was made a capital offense, and hundreds of Jews were arrested and tried on this charge. A number of Jewish detainees were subjected to heavy fines, others to imprisonment. One Jew, convicted of selling arms to Israel, was sentenced to death and hanged in Basra.

By September 1949, the worst of the hysteria finally abated. Martial law was abolished. Yet the economic ordeal was only beginning for the Jews. Most of their import-export and banking licenses were revoked. Despairing of their future in Iraq, several thousand Jews arranged to be smuggled across the border to Iran, and from there to Israel. Even the wealthiest and most respected Jewish businessmen now recognized their vulnerability, and were merely awaiting a safer opportunity to clear out. That chance materialized on March 9, 1950. The government announced that Jews wishing to emigrate to "occupied Palestine" would be permitted to do so, on condition that they renounce their Iraqi citizenship. Immediately, thousands of Jewish householders lined up at the makeshift registration offices. Some 14,000 backward Jews from the mountainous Kurdish territories poured into the larger cities, camping in synagogue courtyards. In fact, this "Ezra and Nehemiah Operation" was organized in its entirety by the Jewish Agency, which had won permission to use the Baghdad airport for charter flights to Israel. The Iraqi regime's purpose in allowing the emigration was not difficult to fathom. The flight of Jewish businessmen and bureaucrats would open their positions to local Arabs. More important, the government could make instant use of Jewish assets in coping with its endemic financial crisis. The situation was not unlike the later eviction of Egyptian Jewry, in 1956–57.

By the end of 1950, fully 65,000 Jews had left the country for Israel. Selling off their homes and businesses at distress prices, they departed with only the smallest residue of their savings. Some 55,000 or 60,000 Jews decided to wait, in the hope that market conditions would improve. But early in 1951, with obvious government concurrence, acts of violence against Jews broke out again, including synagogue bombings and mob attacks on Jewish quarters. When the remaining Jewish inhabitants hurried to sell out for whatever they could get, they soon discovered that they had waited too long. In March of that year, all Jewish assets were frozen; emigrating Jews afterward were permitted to take with them only forty pounds each. By June 1951, the deadline for legal emigration, some 110,000 Jews had relinquished their citizenship and departed. Another 13,000 Jews had earlier fled illegally, via Iran. As a consequence, Jewish assets valued at the equivalent of $200 million were transferred to the government, which then proceeded to auction them off for hard cash.

By 1952, only 6,000 Jews remained in the country. Their circumstances remained uncertain at best. Having risked everything by staying on beyond the grace period of departure, they were forbidden now to leave the country altogether. Although permitted to engage in business, they were denied employment in the civil service. Intermittent changes of government eased restrictions on Jewish travel and the disposal of property—in 1955 and 1958, for example. Yet those who "failed to return" were deprived of their citizenship, and their property was confiscated. By June 1967, a mere 3,000 Jews continued on in Iraq. The Six-Day War was their coup de grâce. In the aftermath of the Arab defeat, the Iraqi government summarily imprisoned scores of Jewish merchants on the pretext of smuggling money out of the state. In March 1968, Jews again were forbidden to sell their property, and a major portion of their future salaries or profits subsequently were to be "deposited" in a government account.

In January 1969, nine prominent Jewish businessmen were sentenced to death on charges of spying for Israel, and several days later they were hanged in a Baghdad square, to the cheers of thousands of onlookers. In August, two more Jews were hanged and scores of others were tortured to death secretly in Iraqi jails. In this fashion, the grim Abd al-Salaam Aref regime sought to divert public attention from its domestic failures. The overt persecution of Iraqi Jews ended only in 1971, as a consequence of intense pressure by Western governments. Thereafter, the final remnant was allowed to leave Iraq, although without money or property of any kind. If there was consolation to be discerned in this tragedy, it was that the largest numbers of the vast Babylonian reservoir of 140,000 Jews at least had emerged with their lives, and subsequently managed to resume useful and productive careers in Israel.

Iran: Aborted Awakening

Farajollah Rahimzadeh,* a slim, bespectacled man of fifty-two, articulate and ingratiating, reminisced in the living room of his comfortable Beverly Hills home. Born into a family of small merchants, he was reared in Hamadan, a middle-sized town some 250 miles from Tehran. It was the site of an ancient Persian Jewish community and, legend has it, birthplace of the folkloristic ancestors Mordechai and Esther. Until the twelfth century, this vast nation encompassed a Jewish population of conceivably 600,000. Scattered to other parts of the Middle East afterward, they left a residual community of between 110,000 and 120,000 by the eve of World War I. One factor in their dispersion was the brutality of Moslem rule. Like Yemen, Iran followed the militant trend of Shi'ite Islam. In harsh contrast to the Ottoman Empire, government policy in Tehran remained uncompromising in its theocratic fundamentalism. Iranian Jews were subjected to painful humiliations and extortions. Heavily ghettoized, branded by the Shi'ite mullahs as ritual "polluters," they were forbidden to walk in the rain lest water touching them come in contact with Moslems. Until the coup that established the Pahlavi dynasty in 1925, and even for several years afterward, Jewish men faced harassment and beatings, occasional murders; their women, kidnapping and rape. Traditionally denied the right to practice agriculture, driven from the guilds of crafts and commerce, Jews over the centuries had been confined to roles as itinerant peddlers, moneylenders, musicians, amulet-makers, tinkers, cesspool cleaners, sellers of liquor—in short, to vocations that were shunned by Moslems as forbidden or socially unacceptable.

A certain improvement in their status took place under Pahlavi rule. Determined to crush the power of his nation's ecclesiastical hierarchy, the new shah launched into a Kemal-style program of modernization. The juridical authority of the mullahs was limited to the narrowest features of Moslem personal status. Jews were allowed increasingly to ply their crafts, to carry on "normal" commercial activities under the protection of secular courts. With the advent of the new shah, Mohammad Reza Pahlavi, in 1941, a few Jews even were accepted into the civil service, and Jewish children began to attend state schools. It was not until the latter 1940s, however, that public education was acknowl-

---

*The subject's name has been changed to protect family members in Iran.

edged as the right of Jewish as well as of Moslem youngsters. Farajollah
Rahimzadeh was among the more fortunate ones. As early as the 1930s,
he had managed to attend an Alliance Israélite Universelle primary
school, a state high school, and then at the age of eighteen to secure a
clerical position in a Tehran bank. In time, he was engaged in a sub-
managerial position in the government's department of social insurance. Keeping his Jewish identity to himself, he studied at the
University of Tehran in the evenings, concentrating on statistics and the
German language. Rahimzadeh was in the vanguard of a growing migration of Jews from the smaller towns to the larger cities—to Isfahan,
Shiraz, and particularly Tehran. During the oil boom of the 1950s and
1960s, the population shift was accompanied by a parallel Jewish trend
toward middle-class vocations and status. Although large numbers of
Jews continued as bazaar merchants, a significant minority became importers, automobile dealers, spare-parts distributors, even factory
owners.

In professional life and state service, too, Jews were beginning to
win recognition under the benign rule of the younger shah. During
Rahimzadeh's youth, in the 1940s, many Jewish parents were careful to
give their children Iranian names—like his own. Even so, few Jews
were admitted to the universities, and still fewer to law and medical
schools, or to state service. But policies and mores were changing with
economic progress. In 1965, the department of social insurance sent
Rahimzadeh to Frankfurt, to study actuarial statistics. Although his Jewish identity was known by then, he continued to win promotions, and
eventually was appointed manager of the department's central research
bureau. In that capacity, he was one of the three highest-ranking Jews
in the government. Other Jews were achieving eminence as scientists,
university professors, and directors of research institutes, as doctors,
lawyers, journalists. Like Rahimzadeh, they made their homes in fashionable suburbs and sent their children to state schools. In no other
Middle Eastern country, surely, did Jewish circumstances improve as
dramatically within as short a period. It was the opposite of the Jewish
fate in Arab countries after the rise of Israel.

By the same token, Mohammad Reza Pahlavi reacted equably to
Jewish statehood. In 1950, his government extended de facto recognition to Israel; then, in 1960, de jure recognition—although without establishing diplomatic relations. Following Israel's spectacular victory in
the Six-Day War, the shah admitted publicly that the two countries had

long maintained important economic and commercial ties. Israel's airline, El Al, was operating by then on a regular schedule between Tel Aviv and Tehran. Many Israeli technical experts were working in Iran as advisers. Since 1957, Israel had been receiving most of its oil from Iran. From the outset, moreover, Iranian Jews were free to emigrate to Israel. Those who first availed themselves of the opportunity tended to be poorer, more devout Jews. Between 1948 and 1955, approximately 28,000 departed, and another 22,000 followed between 1956 and 1966. The 74,000 or so who remained generally belonged to the wealthier business and professional classes.

Even these last regarded themselves as traditionalists. They respected the dietary laws, the principal Jewish holidays, and married exclusively among themselves. Nevertheless, acculturation and affluence were beginning to exert their influence. As a boy, Rahimzadeh was quite observant. The pattern changed during his adulthood. Following his parents' example, he gave his own two sons typically Persian names. Unlike his parents, he provided them with no Hebrew training at all. The venerable Persian Jewish dialect was gradually abandoned as Jews in Tehran moved from the older ghetto areas to the city's mixed quarters. Throughout the 1960s, at least half of Rahimzadeh's friends were non-Jews. In every respect, the Jews' altered sociology matched the tempo of Iran's economic progress. As late as 1976, the political situation in the country appeared quite stable, and with it Jewish security. Jews were fully aware of the nation's widespread corruption, of course. Bribery affected every echelon of the economy, from state contracts, in which the shah's relatives took their cut, to middle-level private enterprise. Yet, together with other businessmen, Jews adjusted, learning to pay baksheesh for every major deal that was thrown their way.

By the latter 1970s, it was impossible even for the most acculturated and sanguine Iranian Jews to ignore the nation's growing social ferment. In the midst of the burgeoning oil wealth, the gap was widening ominously between the classes. Inflation raged, as vast quantities of hard currency were squandered on useless armaments. The mullahs and ayatollahs, who had never reconciled themselves to the shah's 1963 land reform act, with its appropriation of religious foundation lands for public sale, were alarmed by the growing secularization of society in later years. Under the accumulation of these resentments and concerns, strikes and demonstrations against the shah's regime gained in intensity throughout 1977 and 1978. The nation's 75,000 Jews watched these developments with increasing anxiety. Most of them still went about their business, although keeping a low profile. Jews who lived in the outlying towns began moving in larger numbers to the cities. Others, more affluent, established bank accounts overseas.

Rahimzadeh also now began transferring substantial quantities of funds to the United States. His older son, Nami, had just departed for Ohio State University, intending to become a premedical student. It was Nami who opened the family account in Columbus. The move came none too soon. Before Rahimzadeh's eyes, thugs attacked shops, theaters, government agencies, including the department of social insurance itself. In the autumn of 1978 he sent his younger son, Aziz, to live with Nami in Columbus. Again, his timing was astute. In December of that year, a letter arrived from the "Purge Committee of the Islamic Revolution," warning Rahimzadeh and his family to leave within two weeks or face death "for continuing to help the shah." During the next few days Rahimzadeh said nothing. Finally, after careful deliberation, he asked the director of his department for a ten-day leave "to register my son in university in the United States." The request was granted. Rahimzadeh moved cautiously. Purchasing round-trip tickets for his wife and himself, he withdrew only a few thousand dollars from his bank account. He left his freezer stocked with food, his automobile in his garage, and he and his wife packed only two suitcases. In the first week of December 1978, Rahimzadeh and his wife flew out of Tehran airport for their "ten-day visit." They did not return. Others were following the same course. In February 1979, the last month before the fall of the shah, some thirty thousand Jews packed their bags and cleared out. Like Rahimzadeh, they had upholstered their foreign bank accounts in advance.

By then, abusive placards and threats were directed specifically against Jews. Several Jewish-owned hotels and homes were burned, and two fire-and-bomb attacks were launched against the El Al office in Tehran. Leading ayatollahs publicly warned Jews to cease acting as defenders of "Zionist aggression." No one was spared. Two years earlier, in February 1977, Dr. Mirza Tzedek,* dean of science and chairman of the physics department at the University of Isfahan, a man of international reputation, was conducting his weekly seminar when eight or

---

*This name, too, has been altered to protect the subject's family.

nine masked men broke into the classroom, rushed toward him, and clubbed him to the ground. The students did not move or speak; they summoned an ambulance only after the assailants departed. Unconscious, Tzedek was carried off to the hospital, where he underwent surgery for a fractured skull. Three months passed before he could return to teaching. In the summer of 1978, after facing a half-year of student rioting, Tzedek decided to resign as dean of science. It was too visible a position for a Jew.

In Paris during this same period, Ayatollah Khomeini and his supporters assured Western journalists that, under their anticipated Islamic government, Jews would be allowed to remain in Iran and prosper. Those who opposed the shah were anti-Israel, they argued, not anti-Jewish. The distinction was fake. "The exalted Prophet [Mohammed] has already observed that the Jews are a race of ruin and destruction," wrote Khomeini in a 1970 article, "that they lie in wait against the nearby Moslems, and that they want to make the Moslems suffer great calamities. . . ." In Iran itself, the revolutionists echoed this harsher line, warning that Jews had always exploited Moslems and continued to do so both in Israel and in Iran. Weeks after the revolution triumphed, however, Khomeini and his spokesmen insisted that Iran's Jews had nothing to fear from an Islamic republic, that they would be allowed to sell their property and go wherever they wished, including Israel. Meanwhile, the Israeli embassy was ordered closed, and its premises were turned over to Yasser Arafat and the PLO. Even then, the ayatollah cordially greeted successive delegations of Iranian Jewish leaders, and repeated his commitment to full security for the Jews. He reminded them that the constitution of the new Islamic republic defined Zoroastrians, Jews, and Christians as "recognized minorities" who were "free to perform their religious rites and ceremonies," and asserted that Moslems were bound to treat non-Moslems with "good moral conduct" and to "observe their fundamental rights."

At the outset, the Jews suffered from the economic chaos in Iran, from severe shortages, rationing, and soaring inflation, in common— and seemingly indiscriminately—with other citizens. But soon a number of specifically anti-Jewish refinements were added. Professor Mirza Tzedek was among the first to sense the cutting edge of revived Shi'ite fanaticism. Five months after the revolution, he traveled back to Isfahan to resume his teaching. Within days, student groups visited his office and politely "suggested" that he not continue on as a member of the faculty. Even as he considered this suggestion, his salary was halted by the university administration. Other Jewish faculty members were also persuaded to resign. Throughout the country by then, Jews were fearful of appearing in public, of eating in restaurants. Storekeepers would not allow them to touch food on the shelves, and surrogate buyers had to be found.

Then, in May 1979, Habib Elghanian, a millionaire businessman and president of the Anojan Kalimian, the federation council of Iranian Jewish communities, was seized, tried on charges of "Zionist spying," and summarily executed. In April 1980, Albert Danielpour, a prominent Jewish industrialist, was tried by a local court in Hamadan for "Zionist conspiracy," found guilty, and executed. His two brothers, who had managed to flee abroad, were tried in absentia and sentenced to death. In ensuing months, nine Jewish businessmen were arrested, tried on the identical charge of "aiding Zionism," and shot by firing squad. A wave of terror passed through the Jewish population. Which of them had not maintained contact with friends and relatives in Israel over the years? In the months following the revolution, an additional 10,000 Jews managed to clear out before the restrictions against emigration could be put into force. The government was fearful of a hemorrhage of capital and talent, and soon all exits for both were closed. With the outbreak of war between Iran and Iraq in September 1980, no Iranian, whether Moslem or Jew, was allowed an exit visa. The rule was absolute. Nearly 40,000 Jews had fled during the months immediately preceding and following the revolution, but the remaining 35,000 were now locked inside the country.

Ingenuity still found ways. It happened that Iranians working in the Persian Gulf emirates were paid in blue-chip Kuwaiti currency. Contacts accordingly were established with relatives of these workers in Europe and the United States. At a heavy discount, arrangements were made to bank Iranian rials in their local Iranian accounts. The Kuwaiti money in turn was sent abroad, where it was converted and deposited in special accounts for Jews. Mirza Tzedek negotiated this transaction through his brother-in-law in London. Paying a heavy price in baksheesh, he arranged afterward for his wife, his two children, and himself to be smuggled across the Pakistani frontier, and from there to fly to Madrid. In Madrid, Tzedek was able to secure United States visas for the family on the strength of a teaching invitation from California State University. Several hundred other Jews used variations on the same technique to make their way across the Pakistani or Turkish borders. Yet the majority did not. Most did not possess the necessary funds or contacts. Most, too, were fearful of exposing their families to the risk of arrest and almost certain execution.

Of the 40,000 Jews who had managed to depart earlier, at least 80 percent settled in the United States, and the largest numbers of these took up residence in southern California, where the climate and economic potential were especially appealing. Another 10 percent went to Europe. Only 10 percent chose to settle in Israel. Whatever their destination, virtually all these émigrés were middle class, and some of them were quite affluent. Those who stayed were not. The pattern was in striking contrast to the Israel-bound emigration of the 1950s and 1960s, when poor Jews had departed and wealthy Jews had remained behind. Moreover, the last-minute exodus of middle-class Jews was a serious blow to their communal institutions, which had depended on the elite to cover their deficits.

Jewish communal life as a result was left in serious disarray. The chief rabbi of Tehran, Yedidyah Shoft, departed the country in September 1980 after receiving threatening telephone calls. The Anojan Kalimian continued to function, but only under "reliable"—that is, government-appointed—leadership. Synagogues remained open in Tehran, Shiraz, Mashhad, and other large Jewish centers, but Jewish schools were nationalized, their curricula tightly regulated and dejudaized, their facilities opened to substantial numbers of Moslem students. Other Jewish institutions, among them clinics and old age homes, continued to operate, but these, too, were required to open their premises to Moslems. The balance was a delicate one. Jewish leaders felt obliged to call a series of meetings to proclaim their loyalty to the Islamic republic, to commemorate the anniversary of the revolution and the "martyrs" who fell defending it.

In Beverly Hills, meanwhile, Farajollah Rahimzadeh took little comfort in the spacious home he was able to purchase for his family, in the funds he was able to spirit out. His parents, his brothers and sister and their families, remained in Iran. He still corresponded with them, was even able to speak to them by telephone. "So far, they are all right, I believe. I'm even hopeful that the oppression of Jews hasn't reached mass proportions." At his side, his younger son, Aziz, nodded reassuringly. "Khomeini seems to be exercising a certain restraining influence on the ultra-fanatics in his regime," Rahimzadeh continued. "But after Khomeini goes . . ." His eyes clouded over, and he shook his head.

India: The Children of Placidity

Elsewhere in the Orient, even beyond the Moslem world, pockets of Jewish life similarly extended back for centuries, even millennia. India was preeminent among them. At its height in 1947, the Jewish population here numbered approximately 26,000, and was divided among three distinct subcultures. The largest consisted of the Bene Israel—Children of Israel—a Marathi-speaking group that claimed as ancestors Jews who had journeyed from Palestine in antiquity, traveling along trade routes to the Orient that had been opened by King Solomon. Settling on the Konkan coast of western India, a flourishing trade center in that era, and residing mainly in towns and larger villages, the Bene Israel in ensuing centuries were known among their Indian neighbors as the Shanwar Tellis—Saturday Oilmen—referring both to their traditional vocation until the eighteenth century as seed-oil pressers, and to their abstention from work on Saturdays.

In time, these early Israelites apparently adapted to India's prevalent caste system, segregating between light- and dark-skinned Jews, and observing other Hindu practices, among them the ban on eating meat. Otherwise, they kept their Jewish patronymics, such as Abraham, Jacob, David, Joseph, Elijah, or Solomon, although their last names usually were Indian. The Bene Israel also observed the basic Jewish holidays, recited the traditional Hebrew prayers, and maintained the strict separation of the sexes. Over the centuries, their version of Judaism may have become diluted and corrupted, at least until visiting Western missionaries in the early nineteenth century revived their knowledge of Hebrew and the Bible. In the mid-1700s, meanwhile, some two thousand of the Bene Israel, approximately one-third their total number, left their towns and settled in Bombay to work as clerks in the East India Company, then later in the British administration. Opening their first synagogues in Bombay in 1796, they were joined in ensuing decades by approximately six thousand Jews from Arab lands, mostly from Baghdad. Well educated in Jewish lore, comparatively wealthy, the "Baghdadis" disdained any social contact with the Bene Israel, whom they regarded as not "pure Jews."

"Pure" or not, during the nineteenth century the Bene Israel became more prosperous and better educated under British rule. Thanks to Bombay's role as an international trade center, they also became increasingly aware of Jewish communities elsewhere. Their desire to rejoin the wider Jewish world was given a new urgency in 1947 with the establishment of India's independence. The civil service, in which they had occupied a favored position under British rule, conceivably would offer their jobs to Hindus now. On the other hand, the birth of Israel a year later seemed to provide the answer to their prayers. Their decision to move to the Holy Land admittedly was not reached without a certain trepidation. The Bene Israel had been isolated from the Jewish mainstream for many centuries, had absorbed numerous Hindu traditions, were vague about their origins, conceivably had proselytized and intermarried. They sensed that others might doubt the authenticity of their Jewishness. Even so, they felt that they had no choice.

As they began settling in Israel, their fears initially seemed justified. The Israeli rabbinate was hesitant to accept them as genuine Jews. Once in a Jewish land, however, the Bene Israel were not prepared to be consigned to limbo. They launched an anguished collective protest, including demonstrations before the Knesset and other appeals for public support. They won that support. Shocked by the national uproar, the rabbinate relented and legitimized the Bene Israel as "authentic" Jews. Afterward, thousands of other Bene Israel moved to Israel. Less than five thousand of them now remain in India, essentially in Bombay, where they continue to live near the central railroad station, in tenement neighborhoods of narrow alleys and unprepossessing little shops. Still devout in their religious loyalties, they maintain four synagogues and three prayer halls. Following India's independence and the abolition of the caste system, distinctions between the aristocratic Baghdadis and the Bene Israel finally evaporated. But the rapprochement was largely academic. Within a few years, the majority of the Baghdadis also emigrated. In their case, the destination was not Israel, but England or other Commonwealth nations.

Interestingly enough, the "purest" Jewish community in India, if not the oldest, is a tiny enclave in Cochin, a city of some 45,000 in the state of Kerala on the western, Malabar coast, about 650 miles south of Bombay. The Cochin Jews trace their ancestry back at least 1,500 years, possibly further. Brilliant traders in international commerce during the late Middle Ages, they were granted autonomy by the local raj, and in 1565 even were permitted to build their homes and synagogues close to the royal compound. This favored status was interrupted by the Portuguese occupation of Malabar several years afterward. A lengthy and bitter period of Catholic persecution followed. But in the eighteenth century the Malabar territory was conquered by an expedition dispatched from the Netherlands. Thereafter, under the patronage of the tolerant Dutch, Cochin Jews resumed their former commercial eminence and maintained it as well throughout the succeeding era of British rule.

Numbering about 2,500 by the early 1940s, the Cochinis were a palimpsest of cultures. Dutch influence lingered in the architecture of the Jewish quarter—"Jew Town"—with its quaint housetops and Old World appearance. Apart from their use of English as the language of education and social refinement, Jews spoke the native Malayalam as their daily vernacular, and Hindu influences remained as evident in their customs as among the Bene Israel. One of those influences was a debilitating caste system that fractured the tiny community into "white Jews" and "black Jews." The former lived in a somewhat more affluent quarter of "Jew Town." Within two decades after the independence of India, however, most of the Cochin Jews departed for Israel. Some two hundred remain.

Currently, not more than seven thousand Jews of all backgrounds live in India. The majority are Bene Israel, most of these still in Bombay. Despite their fragile demographic base, their Judaism survives in extraordinarily vital form. Thus, in December 1968, the three remnant groups joined in gala festivities to commemorate the four hundredth anniversary of Cochin's first, Paradesi, synagogue. Government authorities cooperated generously in the fete—in part to ensure that India's pro-Arab position on the international scene should not be misunderstood as anti-Jewish. On the last day of celebration, many public notables attended, among them Prime Minister Indira Gandhi, who made a speech from the rostrum of the Paradesi synagogue. In remarks broadcast throughout India, Mrs. Gandhi reminded her listeners that the "ancient, harmonious, and honorable" story of Indian Jews demonstrated again how vital it was for modern India to be a secular nation in which religious passions should have no place. She assured her audience that the "Jewish community of India has rendered . . . notable service in many fields. It has contributed men of distinction to business and industry, to the civil service and the armed forces, and to the world of scholarship." Then, smiling, the prime minister concluded her address with the Hebrew expression of congratulations: "Mazal Tov."

IX

The Legacy of Iberia:
Spain and Central America

Exile and Afterglow

Several years before World War I, Max Luria, an American philologist, was studying the dialects of Monastir, a Serbian town with a considerable Jewish minority. Chatting with two old Jewish women, he observed that the language of Spain resembled that of Monastir's Jews. At this point, Luria recalled, one of the women gathered "the last dying embers of pride and remarked with fire . . . 'Ma somuz ispañolis [But we are Spanish]!'" Both the woman's Ladino accent and her pride of ancestry were quintessentially Sephardic (from *Sepharad*, the Hebrew word for Spain). One of the most renowned of contemporary Sephardim, the writer and Nobel laureate Elias Canetti, described an episode of his youth, when he and an Ashkenazi friend were taunted as "Yids." "Pay no attention to it," Canetti's mother reassured her son (again in Ladino). "That was meant for Kornfeld [the Ashkenazi], not for you." "You"—the Sephardic Jews—were descendants, after all, of perhaps the most brilliant and fecund community in the history of the Diaspora, the Jews of medieval Spain and Portugal. It was unthinkable that they should be confused with Ashkenazim, Jews whose ancestry traced back to the sterile feudal society of Central Europe or to the squalid Pale of Settlement of tsarist Russia.

This hubris had been cruelly challenged in the late fifteenth century, when the largest numbers of Spanish Jewry, some 200,000 individuals, were expelled from their Iberian homeland as Jews traditionally had been cast adrift elsewhere, ruined and penniless, uncertain of future sanctuary. Most of the émigrés eventually settled in various provinces of the Ottoman Empire, particularly in the Balkans and in Turkey itself, as well as in the coastal cities of North Africa and the Arab Near East. But several thousand others found refuge in Italy, in the Netherlands, in England. Numbering between 200,000 and 300,000 in the latter seventeenth century, the descendants of these fugitives still comprised the majority of the world Jewish population.

Throughout the Mediterranean world, Sephardic Jews assiduously preserved the cultural legacy of medieval Iberia. In North Africa and Syria, to be sure, they integrated in some degree into the local oriental Jewish communities; and in Italy they adapted easily to the sophisticated ambience of the Renaissance. But elsewhere, and notably in Turkey and the Balkans, they guarded their Sephardic religious and social traditions, their familial and social exclusivity, their native Ladino dialect. A medieval Castilian, transliterated into Hebrew script, Ladino in the end became the lingua franca of virtually all Jews in Turkey and Ottoman Europe. As late as 1940, of some 300,000 Balkan Jews (outside Romania and western Serbia), nearly 250,000 were Sephardim. Even as the original Spanish Jewish poets had lamented their exile from the soil of Israel, so now, in a latter-day exile, Sephardic Jews continued to idealize the fields, mountains, gardens, and rivers of Moslem Spain. That unrequited love was expressed by a sixteenth-century marrano, Luis de Carvajal:

> Adiós España, tierra bonita,
> tierra de la consolación. . . .

For nearly two centuries after the expulsion from Spain and Portugal, the tradition of Sephardic intellectual acuity was maintained by such renowned figures as Joseph Caro, the talmudic codifier of Safed; Baruch Spinoza, the Amsterdam philosopher; Menasseh ben Israel, the rabbi-diplomat who negotiated the resettlement of Jews in England. The financial acumen of the Sephardim produced the famed bankers, importers, and exporters of Holland and the West Indies. Yet by the eighteenth century, economic conditions had deteriorated in the Balkans and the Near East, where a majority of the Sephardim lived, and where they shared in this atrophy. Their loss of vigor was evident in their demography, as well. By the eve of World War I, the Sephardic birth rate had declined to zero population growth; and by 1939, of approximately 16.5 million Jews in the world, "pure" Sephardim did not exceed 700,000. Faced with this loss of critical mass, and fearful of inundation by the Ashkenazic tide, the Sephardim took refuge in their pride of ancestry. As late as the eighteenth century, they disdained social relations with non-Sephardic Jews, and as late as the twentieth century they refused to intermarry with them. Under no circumstances would they worship with them in the same synagogue. In marked contrast to the Ashkenazim, whom they regarded as uncouth, they cultivated a reserved manner and a fastidious attention to dress. Even the Sephardic stevedores of Salonica, or the vendors of the *pan de España* in the streets of Smyrna, poignantly sought to maintain their Spanish *grandesa*.

In the end, their exclusivity could not save their lives. During World War II, the Sephardic communities of southeastern Europe were liquidated as brutally as were their Ashkenazic counterparts in Poland and Central Europe. Throughout the Balkans, the only major Sephardic populations to escape destruction were those of Bulgaria, a Nazi ally and hence able to protect its Jews, and of neutral Turkey. Today, as has been seen, a bare 15,000 Jews remain in Istanbul, and barely 4,000 in Izmir (Smyrna) and Edirne (Adrianople). The renowned Hispanic Jewish traditions of the Balkans and Asia Minor, still vigorous only two generations ago, currently are all but moribund. Ladino, too, has faded as a common language; its few remaining journals are published in Roman characters. In Turkey, Ladino newspapers and journals are banned altogether. Among the Sephardic communities of North Africa and the Levant, Ladino was initially undermined by French, the language of the Alliance schools. As a consequence of their near-extinction in the Old World, then, it is the more remarkable that there are still Sephardim to be found who defiantly add the traditional abbreviation "S. T." to their signatures: *Sephardi Tahor*—"pure Sephardic."

Strategic Outposts in the New World

It is an irony of history, as well, that the governments of fifteenth-century Spain and Portugal, the monarchies that expelled their Jews, unwittingly laid the groundwork for a Jewish presence in their overseas empires—and thus for the survival of the Jewish component in Hispano-Portuguese civilization. They accomplished this unintended feat by permitting converts to buy their way into expeditions to the New World, including Columbus's, and to trade in the overseas colonies. In this fashion, Mexican Jewish history virtually began with the Spanish conquest, and as many as half the Spanish inhabitants of Mexico City in the sixteenth century may have been of Jewish origin. For several decades in that period, their merchants actually dominated much of the international trade of Central America. The evidence is compelling, too, that most of these New Christians were marranos, secretly professing Jews.

Even larger numbers of marranos were to be found among Portuguese New Christians than among their Spanish counterparts. Taking fullest advantage of royal land grants and exemptions from taxation, several thousand of these clandestine Jews played a decisive role in fostering the growth of early sixteenth-century Brazil. The first to cultivate sugar plantations along Brazil's northern coast, they owned as many as half the 120 sugar mills operating there by the early seventeenth century. An island 300 miles from Belém to this day bears the name of its marrano founder, Fernando Noronha. For a while, too, Dutch Sephardim were a major factor in the distribution of refined Brazilian sugar throughout Europe; and when the Dutch West Indies Company launched its Brazilian campaign in 1624, the northern "sugar" provinces were captured with significant local Jewish assistance. By the mid-seventeenth century, Jews enjoyed a wider degree of religious freedom in Dutch Brazil than anywhere else in the Western world, except for the Netherlands themselves. Numbering some three thousand, they comprised perhaps half the country's civilian European population.

The golden interlude ended in 1654, after Portugal reconquered northern Brazil. Terrified of another Inquisition, many Jews fled to the interior. There, over the generations, they merged into the native population. Yet some managed to reach other lands, including one small contingent of twenty-four Jews who found refuge in the Dutch West India Company's outpost of Nieuw Amsterdam in North America. Jews also settled in Dutch Curaçao, a 370-square-mile island off the coast of Venezuela, where they were recognized as Dutch citizens and granted religious freedom. By 1715, numbering approximately two thousand, Jews accounted for a third of Curaçao's white population, and represented the single largest (identified) Jewish settlement in the Western Hemisphere altogether. In later years, the majority of these sugar magnates intermarried and dropped their Jewish affiliations; but in the interval, Curaçao Jewry remained the hub of an Antilles Jewish population that extended throughout the British West Indies and even into several of the French West Indian islands.

*

Revival in Central America

It was the haunting fear of a Spanish or Portuguese reconquest of Latin America that continued to inhibit Jews from resettling there until quite late in the nineteenth century, long after most of the native populations had won their independence. When the connection finally was revived, Mexico was the initial port of call. Ladino-speaking Sephardim characteristically were the first to venture to return. Arriving from Turkey and the Balkans in 1863, and numbering less than two hundred, these *turcos* began as peddlers of household and farm goods. Indifferent to the contempt of Mexico's white aristocracy, the newcomers remained proudly conscious Jews. Upon winning a foothold in the country, they made it their first order of business to arrange religious services in private dwellings. Their first synagogue, Mount Sinai, erected in Mexico City in 1912, remains in use by Syrian Jews. There are today in Mexico perhaps 3,500 Sephardim, many of whom are engaged in smaller-scale manufacture of clothing.

In the late nineteenth century, their presence was augmented by several hundred Jews from Central Europe. One of these, José Yves Limantour, became the financial genius of the Porfirio Díaz regime and was largely responsible for putting Mexico on the gold standard and consolidating the railroads into a single national system. Other Central European Jews participated in Mexican mining and railroads, and several became editors and teachers. But it was only in the 1920s, when the United States imposed restrictions on East European immigration, that large numbers of Polish and Romanian Jews altered their route southward. Some 25,000 immigrated to Mexico before World War II. Like their Sephardic predecessors, most of these *Ostjuden* began as door-to-door peddlers or operated tiny market stalls. The war boom of the 1940s ultimately guaranteed their economic security. In the postwar years, the East Europeans branched out into textiles, furniture manufacturing, chemicals, film production, and imports and exports in general. Today, their children and grandchildren are also among Mexico's most prominent engineers and doctors. Numbering approximately forty thousand in a population of sixty million—the fourth-largest Jewish community in Latin America—virtually all of them are living in Mexico City. They make their homes in the capital's exclusive Hipódromo, Chapultepec, and Polanco quarters.

Notwithstanding this economic success, Mexican Jews remain di-

vorced from their country's political life. In the nineteenth century, the
government had barred the foreign-born and their offspring from elec-
tive political office and other key posts. Aimed at the Spaniards and
their descendants, who continued to dominate the Mexican economy as
wealthy landlords, the legislation affected Jews and other immigrant
groups, as well. It became the tradition in ensuing years for Mexican
Jews to devote their "extracurricular" energies mainly to their own communities. As elsewhere, each Jewish immigrant group established its
own *kehilla*—its communal organization. The East Europeans' was the
largest. By the 1950s, its splendid headquarters building on Acapulco
Street had become the focus of a broad and generous cultural and philanthropic life embracing a network of day schools, a Yiddish theater, a
choir, a first-rate old age home, and a cultural center. Today, this dense
nucleus of social and cultural facilities is paralleled by nearly two dozen
Conservative, Orthodox, and Reform synagogues. Meanwhile, smaller
groups of Central European Jews, approximately six thousand in all,
who arrived as refugees from Hitler, founded their own German- and
Hungarian-language kehillas. The Unión Sefaradi, finally, remains Mexican Jewry's smallest communal organization.

Although maintaining their autonomy, these various Jewish subcultures have established a Comité Central Israelita de México to deal
with the government and others of the nation's public institutions. It
reveals much of the basically secular ethos of Mexican Jewry that the
single meeting place in which these communities freely mingle is the
Centro Deportivo Israelita, the Jewish sports center. With its magnificent building, its huge auditorium, gymnasiums, tennis courts, its
Olympic-sized swimming pool and sculptured gardens, the center may
well be the most dazzling social-sports complex of its kind in Mexico
City. Like its counterpart Hebraica complexes in Buenos Aires and São
Paulo, it is a characteristically lavish testament to Jewish ethnocentrism
and gregariousness.

A school network, however, represents Mexican Jewry's proudest
communal and cultural accomplishment. Before 1914 and even between
the wars, the government itself encouraged the nation's various ethnic
minorities—Spaniards, French, Americans, Germans—to provide their
own educational facilities. The tiny Jewish community wasted no time
in responding to this challenge. Today, the Jewish school system ranges
from Yiddish and Hebrew secular institutions to an Orthodox Yavne
school. Not less than 85 percent of Mexican Jewish children attend

their classes, in buildings that are the last word in modernity, possessing the finest equipment and the nation's best (and best-paid) teachers. No other Diaspora community can boast anything superior in accommodations or staff, not even South African or Australian Jewry.

The rather frenetic quality of Mexican Jewish communal life, its skein of synagogues, schools, centers, journals, and newspapers, has emerged perhaps less from the classic Jewish sense of insecurity than in other, larger Latin American nations. Since its early-twentieth-century revolutionary period, Mexican politics have been liberal and anticlerical. Jews have not been confronted here with overt, church-generated antisemitism. Nor has the government ever indulged in anti-Jewish attitudes or activities. Unlike Argentinians or populations of essentially European lineage, the Mexicans do not replenish historic prejudices from Old World reservoirs. At worst, Jews occasionally have been identified with the disliked *gringos* to the north. In 1982, during the Lebanon war, press attacks on Israel were sharp, and several Jewish institutions were attacked—probably by PLO groups or sympathizers. The violence quickly subsided. At no time have Mexican Jews faced a threat to their safety or freedom of action. Nevertheless, over the years, they have remained an inner-directed and rather self-satisfied minority, a materialistic group both in their private lives and in their communal activities. In the tradition of their wealthy non-Jewish neighbors, their homes, perhaps even their consciences, are barred and locked to the Indian and mestizo majority population.

A Renewed Sephardic Foothold in the Caribbean

The underappreciated Sephardic legacy, both in Mexico and in other Central American countries, consists not only of precedent but of progeny. The lineal descendants of the nineteenth-century *turcos*, and of the earlier Sephardic settlers, currently number at least 100,000 throughout all Latin America, and some 44,000 in the Caribbean basin alone. Wherever they settled, they were invariably the first to establish Jewish communal organizations, to enter into discourse with the native population in a mutually negotiable language. As in the seventeenth and eighteenth centuries, it was the privileged little Sephardic enclave in the Netherlands Antilles that remained the mother settlement for them all. Secure and prosperous under Dutch rule, Curaçao Jewry managed to nourish other Jewish congregations in the New World well into the latter 1800s. Its own spark may have been nearly extinguished by then, and the descendants of this privileged gentry today are more frequently encountered among the island's Gentile majority. Yet there remains a nucleus of identified Jews, almost evenly divided between Sephardim and a mixture of Central and East European merchant families. Their intermittent religious life is conducted in a single Reform synagogue.

It should not be surprising that the oldest pockets of uninterrupted Jewish life in the Caribbean basin are to be found in island archipelagos of Dutch, British, even French possession. Here the Inquisition had never functioned. In Surinam, just north of Brazil and west of French Guiana, some 500 Jews remain in the capital city of Paramaribo. They, too, are but a remnant of a once-flourishing Sephardic population, a community that dispersed after a series of bloody slave uprisings in 1825. Paramaribo still abounds with traces of a rich Jewish past. Houses are to be found with *mezuzahs* attached to the doorposts. Sephardic names occasionally appear in shop windows. Otherwise, more than in Curaçao and Aruba, Surinam Jewry has become largely Ashkenazic, although mainly of Central European refugee origin. Under the Union Jack, meanwhile, Jamaica became an early haven for Brazilian Jewish fugitives. Even now, most of the island's 250 Jews are of Sephardic ancestry. Comfortable merchants and hoteliers in a popular vacation retreat, they have little difficulty supporting Jamaica's one synagogue. British Trinidad and Barbados offer a dispiriting contrast. Both islands are on the fringes of the tourist itinerary. Their 200 or 250 Jews are aged former refugees, subsisting on shabby retail shops.

Elsewhere, Jewish circumstances have been uneven among the smaller, independent republics of Central America. In the little coffee-producing nation of El Salvador, with its four million inhabitants, the three hundred Central European Jews who thrived as coffee exporters as recently as a decade ago have almost all left, despairing of their future in a land racked by a sapping, Marxist-led guerrilla insurrection. Guatemalan Jewry continues to hang on, a respectable seven or eight hundred. Its roots extend back more than a century, to Sephardic immigrants from the Caribbean islands. Yet the Sephardim are outnumbered twice over now by Ashkenazic Jews, several hundred of them descendants of turn-of-the-century arrivals from German Posen, the others Polish refugee families dating from the 1930s. Although Guatemala suffers from chronic political unrest, and once, in the 1960s, from a noisy—if ineffective—antisemitic vice-president, Clemente Rojas, this political instability has not seemed to unnerve the Jewish minority. A middle-class, reasonably prosperous enclave of shopkeepers, they sustain an active communal life, replete with a Jewish day school and a handsome sports center.

Tiny Costa Rica, with its modest population of 2,300,000, has long enjoyed a reputation as the most literate and stable republic in the Caribbean. Its tradition of religious permissiveness in modern times has been unsurpassed even in the Dutch- and British-ruled islands. Almost all the country's 2,400 Jews are of Polish origin—most of them from the same Polish town, Zelechow. Their emergence as Costa Rica's preeminent bourgeois element has been steady and largely unresented. Their communal life is warm and vigorous. Maintaining two large synagogues and an active Zionist society, they send most of their children to an excellent day school. The government has been enthusiastic in its admiration for Israel, which in turn has organized several technical projects for Costa Rica. It is a subject of mild and friendly popular interest that Luis Monge Alvarez, president of Costa Rica (in 1983), is married to a Jewish woman.

Except for their origins, the Jews of Panama share the demographic profile of Costa Rican Jewry. Numbering approximately four thousand in a population of two million, they comprise the third-oldest Jewish community in the Caribbean basin, after Curaçao and Mexico. Sephardic Jews from the West Indies began arriving in this isthmus nation as early as 1875, a quarter-century before Panama won its independence from Colombia. The first synagogue on the Central American mainland was erected in Colón. Later, other Jews arrived from Syria, to found a separate religious community. After the construction of the canal, and the establishment of a United States protectorate over Panama, numbers of Russian Jews began to arrive. In the 1930s, they were joined by fugitives from Nazi Germany. As elsewhere, each community developed its own kehilla. Comprising the largest group, the East Europeans have built a handsome community center that includes among its ample facilities a day school that currently is attended by 80 percent of Panama's Jewish children. Profiting from the nation's status as a free-trade zone and from its international trade connections, Panamanian Jewry has flourished in importing, retailing, distributing. Jews have served in high public office. Dr. Max Del Valle was vice-president of Panama and once a presidential candidate. The imminent return of the canal to the

Panamanian government has evoked some concern but little anxiety among the country's Jews. Few of them are leaving.

No Latin American nation displayed a more consistent hospitality toward Jews, or elicited a more equivocal response, than the Dominican Republic. As early as 1881, a former Dominican president, General Gregorio Luperón, approached officials of the Alliance Israélite Universelle in Paris with a proposal that Jewish victims of tsarist pogroms be resettled in Dominica. Luperón's invitation plainly was motivated by a desire to import Jewish brains and enterprise. His economy needed both. It received neither. In those days, Russian Jewry's destination was the bountiful United States. Then, over a half-century later, the notion was revived during the international conference on refugees at Évian-les-Bains, France, in July 1938. Again, a Dominican representative announced his government's willingness to admit fully 100,000 Jews, thereby placing Dominica on record as the only nation in the world prepared to open its doors wide to the victims of Nazism. Hereupon, the Dominican regime drew up an agreement with the Joint Distribution Committee in January 1940. Under its terms, Jewish farmers would be settled on land to be donated by "El Benefactor" himself, the nation's dictator, Rafael Trujillo. The expenses would be underwritten by the Joint and other Jewish organizations. Accordingly, the Joint proceeded to bring over some one hundred young German and Austrian Jews, settled them in the Dominican province of Sasua, and provided them with land, housing, tools, and credit.

The project failed. The homesteaders soon drifted away to the cities, where they subsisted as clients of the Joint. President Trujillo did not take the fiasco as a personal affront. In ensuing years, he continued to make friendly gestures toward the Jews. His government issued a postage stamp honoring the Sasua project, and Trujillo donated $60,000 of his own money toward the construction of a synagogue in the capital. By the 1950s, however, the goodwill campaign was undertaken almost exclusively to evoke Jewish support in the United States, on the assumption that the "Jewish-controlled" press would help sanitize "El Benefactor's" regime. In the end, not more than 800 refugees passed through Sasua. Another 3,000 Jews obtained Dominican visas, but never actually settled there. As of 1984, less than 200 Jews remain, a majority of them small merchants of Syrian background. They are mirror images of the approximately 150 Jews who remained in Nicaragua until the late 1970s, tradesmen who flourished under the patronage of the Somoza dictatorship until the Sandinista revolution sent all but a handful of them into flight.

During the 1960s and early 1970s, meanwhile, spokesmen for Jews in six of the Caribbean nations—Panama, Guatemala, El Salvador, Costa Rica, Nicaragua, and Honduras—made a rather poignant effort to sustain a Federación de Comunidades Judías de Centro América y Panamá (FEDCO). Representing a combined Jewish population of less than 7,000, the joint body held a few conventions, even organized a "youth council" that functioned essentially as a marriage bureau. But with the political turmoil in El Salvador and Nicaragua in recent years, and the near-total departure of Jews from those nations, the federation operated only intermittently. As early as 1959, as it happened, Caribbean Jewry suffered a shattering blow. This was the collapse of its principal demographic hinterland, the once-impressive Jewish enclave in Cuba.

The most densely inhabited island in the Spanish Antilles, Cuba had attracted individual Jewish families as early as the turn of the century. These were *turcos*, the characteristic early vanguard of Sephardim from Turkey and the Balkans. Even a generation later, at the height of the diverted East European migration to Latin America, the Sephardim numbered fully a third of Cuban Jewry. Although most of the *polacos* became small or middle-sized businessmen in Cuba, they also included a significant number of manual workers, principally semi-skilled "finishers" who labored in the garment industry. It was this Jewish proletariat, tending to political leftism, that established a link with the radicalism that was to surface in the Castro revolution of 1959. An elder of the East European workers, Pablo Gribart, served as a member of the Communist central committee and remained a confidant of Castro's. Nevertheless, within two years of the establishment of the Castro regime, the majority of Cuba's 12,000 Jews joined the exodus to the United States—where most of them later resumed their careers in Florida. In ensuing years, attrition depleted the remaining Jewish population to less than 1,000 and, in some estimates, to less than 500.

Castro has been more than willing to accommodate this remnant. Six synagogues functioned in the 1960s, and five survive today, all of them in Havana, all without rabbis. A kosher restaurant and a ritual slaughterer are still available. The government sees to the maintenance of the nation's two Jewish cemeteries, provides the school bus that transports some twenty children to the afternoon Hebrew classes at the Alberto Einstein School, and supplies additional food for the Jewish community's Passover meals. Cuba's position toward Israel has been as hostile as that of other Communist-bloc nations, and in 1973 it severed diplomatic relations with Jerusalem. Yet this anti-Zionist stance has had no effect on the treatment of Cuba's Jewish minority. Like Trujillo and Somoza at the other end of the political spectrum, Castro was persuaded early on of Jewish "influence" in the Western media. He is uninterested in gratuitous blemishes on his image as revolutionary liberator.

Revival at the Source: Portugal and Spain in the Twentieth Century

If the Jewish presence in Central America was initially revived by a fin-de-siècle wave of pioneering Sephardim, a renewal of Jewish life took place later in another historic Jewish setting, but in this case the unlikeliest. It was the Iberian peninsula, in the very nations that had cast out Sephardic Jewry in the great convulsions of the late-fifteenth century. For many years, the revival was barely perceptible. In the mid-eighteenth century, a group of Sephardic Jews living as British citizens in Gibraltar established the nucleus of a community in Lisbon. In 1820, another congregation was organized in Faro, Portugal. The tiny enclave was joined in the last years before World War I by forty or fifty East European Jews. In 1917, while exploring a group of mining properties in Portugal's Sierra da Estrella region, a Polish Jewish engineer, Samuel Schwartz, stumbled upon a pocket of marrano communities in the northern provinces of Trás-os-Montes, Beira Alta, and Entre-Doure-Minho. Investigations by Schwartz, and by Jewish scholars whom he alerted, later turned up entire villages whose inhabitants for generations had been maintaining a kind of crypto-Judaism. After the war, a group of American rabbis arrived to distribute Hebrew prayerbooks and ritual objects to their newly discovered kin. A Portuguese army captain, Arturo Carlos de Barros, whose parents had secretly practiced Jewish rites, established a center in Oporto for the full return of the marranos to their ancestral religion.

Accounts of the discovered marranos continued to circulate throughout the Jewish world, and were lavishly embellished by rumors that as many as twenty thousand of them were waiting breathlessly to return to Judaism. A "Pro-Marrano Committee" was established in London, with associate committees in the United States. Elie Kedoory, the renowned

Jewish merchant prince of India, built a synagogue for the marranos in Oporto—the Mekor Chaim Kedoory. Additional congregations soon were established in other towns, the largest of them in Bragança. Meanwhile, responding to church pressures, the government intimated that employment opportunities for those returning to Judaism would be distinctly limited. The movement died. Afterward, only the Kedoory synagogue in Oporto survived, attended desultorily by less than one hundred professing Jews, most of these Moroccan or Gibraltar immigrants. During World War II, they were joined by refugees from Nazi-occupied France, but few of the latter remained on after 1945. The current identified Jewish population of Portugal has stabilized at about eight hundred, and consists largely of Moroccan immigrant families in Lisbon.

At the same time, an unobtrusive Jewish resettlement was taking place across the frontier, in Spain. During the sixteenth and early seventeenth centuries, descendants of *cristianos nuevos,* Jewish converts to Christianity, may have comprised fully a third of the population of the larger Spanish cities. Francisco Franco's ancestors were said to have belonged to this group. It was unlikely that significant numbers of marranos existed among them any longer, for the Inquisition continued to operate until 1834. By the latter nineteenth century, however, even Spain was beginning to enter the Western world. A new constitution, promulgated in 1876, went so far as to assure "freedom from molestation" to non-Catholics. Under the dictatorship of Prime Minister Primo de Rivera, a 1924 decree recognized descendants of the exiled Sephardim as Spanish citizens.

Although Rivera's gesture had little practical effect—at most, several hundred European Jews were doing business in Spain by the eve of World War I—a more significant inducement was the birth of the Spanish republic in 1931. Assured of full religious toleration under the new constitutional regime, groups of Italian, North African, and Balkan Jews, all Sephardim, began settling in Barcelona. Quite poor, subsisting at first as peddlers, they managed nevertheless to purchase a house on Calle Provenza for worship and communal purposes. Their congregation was augmented by a later influx of German Jewish refugees in the mid-1930s. Other, smaller Jewish enclaves appeared in Madrid and Seville. Numbering six thousand, this minority population represented the first identifiable Jewish community in Spain in four centuries.

The outbreak of the Spanish Civil War in 1936 fatally undermined their security. The Nationalists soon invested the largest part of the country, and the Jewish settlers paid the price for their known Loyalist sympathies—indeed, for the worldwide Jewish support of the republican government (four thousand Jewish volunteers served in the International Brigade). Isolated from any contact with their kin in other lands, the immigrants either returned to Morocco or crossed the frontier to Portugal. Following the Nationalist triumph in 1939, all earlier republican legislation establishing religious liberty was abrogated, together with the 1931 constitution itself. The synagogues in Madrid and Barcelona were closed and Jewish religious worship was forced underground. Except for isolated cases of police brutality, however, the Fascist government refrained from overt or systematic persecution of Jews. Rather, during World War II, Franco allowed Jewish and other refugees to pass through his country; and, as a result, fully thirty thousand Jews crossed Spain to Portugal, where many journeyed on to freedom in Allied countries.

Yet the Franco government categorically forbade Jewish refugees to settle permanently in Spain. If Jews made their way across the Pyrenees, but did not possess visas for Portugal or other nations, they were interned in concentration camps and reduced to near-starvation. In this respect, Spain was less than the haven the Franco government claimed (after the war) to have provided. The notion that the Falangist regime extended its diplomatic protection indiscriminately to Sephardic Jews throughout Europe was another myth that was sedulously fostered by the postwar Spanish government. With a single exception, the Jews of Hungary in 1944, Spain offered its diplomatic protection exclusively to Spanish nationals in other European nations, and even this gesture was halfhearted during the first part of the war, when it appeared that Hitler was winning.

Tierra Bonita, Tierra Redescubierta

Spain's post-1945 approach to the Jews was curiously ambivalent. Throughout the war, and for at least a decade and a half afterward, the nation's press and pulpit continued to disseminate anti-Jewish propaganda. Newsstands and bookstores, some of them owned by ex-Nazis or by expatriate French Algerians, were allowed to distribute antisemitic literature, including *The Protocols of the Elders of Zion*. Additionally, Franco's postwar ambition to succeed Mussolini as "protector of Islam" led him to flirt with the Arab League, and to applaud Arab efforts to destroy Israel. On the other hand, during the 1950s and 1960s, the Spanish government displayed a willingness to assist Jews in distress. Denied entrance to the United Nations, Franco's regime eventually recognized the need to cultivate goodwill in traditionally liberal circles. To that end, Madrid cooperated with the Jewish Agency and the Joint, which were directing the mass emigration of Moroccan Jews to Israel and France, by offering transit facilities in Spain. Later, during the 1956 and 1967 Middle East wars, the Falangist government extended its diplomatic protection to numerous Sephardic Jews in Egypt, enabling them to leave the country. For its part, Israel was prepared to reciprocate. In 1975, it ceased to oppose Spain's application for membership in the United Nations.

By then, Jewish resettlement within Spain itself had picked up noticeably. At the end of the war, the 1,000 (or fewer) Jews remaining in the country were almost all Ashkenazic refugees from the Nazis. Their legal status was tenuous, and as a result their numbers increased to only 2,500 in 1950. Later, however, with the Spanish economic boom of the ensuing decade, Jewish immigration gained momentum. A majority of the newcomers arrived from Spanish Morocco, and most of these took up residence in the southern part of the country, principally in Barcelona. Several hundred others were European Jews, former victims of Hitler. By 1976, there were not less than 10,000 Jews in Spain altogether, most of them holding permanent resident status. Despite their lack of citizenship, they were not hesitant in pressing their demands. This was particularly true of the Moroccans, devout and ethnocentric, who were intent upon living in Spain as identified Jews.

The government was prepared to accommodate them. As early as July 1945, bowing to Allied pressures, the Franco regime enacted a series of laws defining the "basic rights of Spaniards." While Catholicism was proclaimed as Spain's official religion, the new measures guaranteed non-Catholics the right to practice their religion, although not in public buildings. The legislation at least ended the juridical limbo that the approximately 1,000 Jews (and some 35,000 Protestants) had endured in Fascist Spain since the abrogation of the republican constitution. That same year, the Jewish inhabitants of Barcelona were allowed to conduct religious services in a rented apartment, a private place of worship acceptable under Spanish law. "Cultural" gestures of goodwill were also forthcoming. In 1959, the government arranged an imposing exhibition of documents on the Golden Age of Jewry in Spain. Courses in Semitic studies were expanded at the universities of Madrid and Barcelona. In June 1961, an international congress of Spanish-language organizations was convened in Madrid, and was attended by delegations of Sephardic communities from throughout the world. In June 1964, a ten-day official symposium on the status of Sephardic culture in other lands was organized in Madrid by the Institute of Sephardic Studies. That same year the cornerstone was dedicated for a new Sephardic synagogue in Toledo. To commemorate the occasion, the government issued a postage stamp inscribed with the picture of Toledo's renowned fourteenth-century El Tránsito synagogue.

Then, in 1966, the climate for Jews changed even more decisively. Widening prosperity, the growth of a reform-minded middle class, the annual incursion of millions of Western tourists who moved and talked freely—all contributed to the demand for peaceful change. Moreover, the government was determined to win American endorsement of Spain's application for full membership in NATO and in the United Nations. In this period, too, the ecumenical position of the late Pope John XXIII was beginning to register, together with the decision of the Vatican Council to pass the *Schema* on the Jews. In December 1966, then, after nearly two years of study and extensive revisions, the draft of a law on religious freedom was completed and sent on to the Cortes. There it was passed officially in June 1967. Under its terms, the government accepted "religious liberty as a fundamental right of the dignity of the human person," and granted non-Catholics the right to worship in public, to place identifying signs on synagogues or churches, to form religious associations, to publish their religious literature, even to hold any office except that of chief of state (still restricted to Roman Catholics). The law was a cataclysm for Fascist Spain. In the case of the Jews, the government provided an additional, poignant gesture of reconciliation. On December 16, 1968, it formally revoked the 1492 expulsion edict of the Catholic monarchs Ferdinand and Isabella.

Francisco Franco died in November 1975. Thereupon, after thirty-seven years of Fascist rule, Spain gingerly reverted to a constitutional monarchy under Juan Carlos de Borbón. In June 1977, the citizens of Spain participated in free secret elections. The following year, a democratic referendum approved a new constitution. One of its provisions guaranteed all Spaniards "freedom of ideology, religion and worship for individuals," and for the first time confirmed that "there shall be no state religion." By then, the Jews were far more comfortably aware of where they stood. Two years earlier, in February 1976, King Juan Carlos had tendered a warm reception to delegations arriving for a congress of the World Sephardic Federation, and Queen Sophia had attended a Friday evening service in the Madrid Synagogue the following May. Although these gestures were not accompanied by official recognition of Israel, trade between Israel and Spain nevertheless grew steadily, and Spain maintained a consulate-general in Jerusalem.

In the latter 1970s, responding to the new mood of goodwill, additional numbers of Jews immigrated. This time most of them came from Argentina and Chile, where political conditions were worsening. Currently, some 13,000 Jews reside in Spain, a number larger than the Jewish populations of Austria and Denmark. Approximately 4,000 of them live in Barcelona, 3,000 in Madrid, 400 to 700 along the southern coast from Málaga to Gibraltar, where several scores of families are also to be found in Seville, Valencia, and the Canary Islands. Nearly 2,000 other Jews remain in the Spanish enclaves of North Africa—1,200 in Melilla and 600 to 700 in Ceuta. Most are businessmen. Few are naturalized citizens. Indeed, the Moroccans (still the majority) have not yet applied for citizenship. Even so, as permanent residents, they are in no sense limited in their religious or communal activities.

Those activities have been vigorous and extensive. As early as 1954, the Jews of Barcelona established a community center in a comfortable middle-class neighborhood on Calle Porvenir. It has since been enlarged with the help of Joint and Claims Conference funds. In the entrance lobby of the rather muted, five-story structure, just beyond the iron gates, a tablet inscribed in Hebrew and Spanish dedicates the building to Maimonides. Except for its two synagogues (one Sephardic, one Ashkenazic), the center is given over to classrooms and space for other cultural and recreational functions. Its day school, attended by nearly half of Barcelona's Jewish children, has grown impressively enough to require the services of imported teachers from Israel. In Madrid there has been a parallel expansion of Jewish activity. By 1977 two community center–synagogues were functioning in the capital, and 90 percent of all Jewish children were attending the Jewish community day school. Madrid also supports a kosher restaurant. Palma in Majorca boasts a kosher hotel, although principally for Western tourists.

Jewish communal life in Spain owes much to an enterprising Ashkenazic immigrant, Max Mazin. Polish-born, Mazin survived the mass

Jewish migration beyond the Urals in World War II, and after 1945 made his way to Belgium, to Israel, and ultimately, in 1950, to Spain. Since then, he has lived in Madrid with his Jerusalem-born wife and their four children. From the outset, Mazin proved to be a dynamic and imaginative businessman. Within less than a decade, he put together a consortium dealing in real estate, coal, oil, and steel, and later was appointed chairman of the nation's World Trade Center. Like many émigrés from Israel, too, Mazin became an overcompensator in his Jewish identifications. His success in interfaith activities has been particularly striking. Forceful and ingratiating, Mazin persuaded several friendly Catholic clergymen to join him in establishing an Amistad Judeo-Cristiana in 1961, then in fostering branches of this friendship society in Barcelona and Seville. Due largely to Mazin's persistence, and that of his cochairman, Father Vicente Serrano, Spanish school textbooks were cleansed of antisemitic materials. In 1969, Father Serrano and his colleagues in Madrid established the Centro de Estudios Sobre Judaísmo; and three years later, by decree of the Bishop of Madrid and Alcalá, the center became an official institution of the bishopric. Its seminars on Jewish subjects for Catholic clergy have since been organized both in Israel and Spain, in close cooperation with the Israel Interfaith Committee of Jerusalem.

By the late 1970s, the militant antisemitism of the early Franco years had largely disappeared. Jews currently appear to be as secure in Spain as in any Western European nation. To be sure, as recently as 1973 the Amistad was obliged to protest a number of vestigial neo-Nazi groups. Several of these apparently were funded by Arab sources. Yet there is little evidence that they represent the wave of the foreseeable future in prosperous, industrializing Spain. Much plainly will depend on the monarchy's success with the revived experiment in constitutional democracy. Thus far, Spanish Jews have remained detached from the nation's political issues; they tend to express their sympathies with Israel more discreetly than do Jews in other Western countries.

Conceivably the most poignant episode in the resuscitation of the Spanish-Jewish relationship occurred in 1965 when the government— the Franco government—approved the first Jewish public religious service on the island of Majorca since the Inquisition. Among the worshipers were several descendants of the *chuetas,* Majorcan Jews who had been converted to Catholicism in the fifteenth century. Although in no sense marranos, and functionally integrated into the larger Catholic community, the chuetas until recently had lived in their own ghetto quarters. The choice had been a voluntary one. Despite the sincerity of their Catholicism, somehow they had nurtured the memory of their Jewish ancestry, their sense of separateness. With the help now of emissaries from the Madrid Jewish community, they expressed an interest in reviving an all-but-forgotten creed. Their numbers did not exceed forty. Yet, old and young alike, they entered the makeshift synagogue that had been established for them in an aged apartment building, and prayed—initially in Spanish, then later in an uncertain Hebrew—with growing and obvious emotion. Their collective memory was of a far older deracination than Hitler's. Their return now to their ancestral faith, on soil that once had nurtured the Diaspora's most creative and venerated community, was perhaps as noteworthy in its way as the far more extensive return of Jews to the Land of Israel itself.

X

Brazil and the Multiracial World of the South

The Sephardic Foothold Renewed

With his sallow complexion and comfortable belly, Isaac Athias could have passed for a river planter whose best years of dissipation were behind him. Dignified in his late seventies, monolingual in Portuguese, he bore little resemblance to the stereotypical European Jew, living on his nerves and his languages. Athias was as indigenous to this vast Amazonian behemoth of a nation as any *seringueiro* plantation owner. He was born in the interior of Pará at the opening of the century, sixteen miles from the town of Belém, at the juncture of the Atlantic Ocean and the Amazon's southern estuary. With its population of nearly 300,000, Belém was a substantial, if rather somnolent, community. Once it had served as a major rubber center, the inducement that had brought Athias's father from Morocco as a young man and provided him with his livelihood as a broker of raw gum extract from the jungle's interior.

Other Sephardic Jews had long since found their way to Brazil. The connection was resumed as early as 1822, when the country achieved its independence from Portugal. Two years later, Brazil's first constitution proclaimed toleration for all non-Catholics, and a marrano group in northern Pará thereupon declared its Judaism openly and established a synagogue in the town of Manaus, the nation's rubber capital. In time, new Sephardic immigrants arrived, many of them settling in the northeastern provinces, and particularly in Belém. A synagogue was erected in Belém, and here the Athiases worshiped, amid a local population of Portuguese, blacks, and mestizos. When his family moved later to a smaller community, Isaac Athias, his brothers, and his sisters were sent upriver for their schooling in the town of Breves. There the proprietor of a Jewish boardinghouse gave the youngsters afternoon lessons in Hebrew.

Some 500 Jewish families lived in the vicinity in those early years, almost all of them Moroccan Sephardim, almost all as forthrightly Jewish as the Athiases. Yet they mixed freely with non-Jews, for Brazil by the twentieth century was an easygoing blend of meridional and African languor. So it was—and is—in Belém and Manaus; in Recife, the capital of Pernambuco, where 200 Jewish families currently live in a flourishing city of nearly a million; and in Salvador, the capital of Bahia, supporting 170 Jewish families in a population of 740,000. Predominantly Sephardic even now, the Jews of Belém and Manaus sustain their traditions of Iberian piety and dignity.

Isaac Athias would have found it unthinkable to abandon those traditions. As an adult, working first as a bookkeeper, then as a traveling salesman for a paint company, he followed the dietary laws even in the isolated towns and villages of the interior. Settling later in São Paulo, with its much larger Jewish population, Athias thereafter regarded observance as a matter of convenience no less than of principle. Here he opened a furniture store in partnership with one Moisés Hakim, an Egyptian Jew married to Athias's distant cousin. "We were proud of our Sephardic heritage," Athias recalled, "but we were never snobs. We intermarried." "Intermarriage" then signified a wedding of Sephardim and Ashkenazim. Athias himself married Amelia Dimanstein, an ophthalmologist of Polish extraction—upon satisfying himself first that she was prepared to maintain a strict Jewish home. In this racially open society, ethnicity was less important than observance. Indeed, Athias and his friends conceded that they had more in common with the early Ashkenazic settlers than with many of the second wave of Moroccans.

These latter arrived in the post–World War II era. Numbering perhaps two thousand, the Moroccans tended to bypass São Paulo in favor of Rio de Janeiro, their Brazilian Casablanca. Awaiting them on the Copacabana's Rua Barata Ribeiro was a magnificent Sephardic synagogue, founded decades earlier by immigrants from Turkey, Greece, and Rhodes. Their children had gone to university, and not a few later prospered. Rio was a lure that frightened Athias. Childless, he watched in dismay as six of his nephews flourished there—and eventually married non-Jews. Was it the wave of the future? Not if he could help it. For nearly fifty years he had devoted a major portion of his leisure time to his Moroccan-Sephardic kehilla, with its own social welfare fund, its own four synagogues. "But we aren't snobs," he emphasized again. Balkan and Italian Sephardim were welcome in the Moroccan congregations. In recent decades, they intermingled freely. If Syrian and Egyptian Jews did not join, that was by their own choice.

"Our tradition is a very old one, you see," explained Marco Farhi, in his pellucid French. Sixtyish, with finely chiseled features, he was as lean as Athias was portly. "We think it's even older than the Moroccan tradition." Farhi was born in Damascus, moved to Beirut as a youth, then emigrated to Brazil in 1961. Like many of his compatriots, he was drawn initially to the easygoing ambience of Rio. Nearly two hundred Lebanese Jewish families had settled there as early as the turn of the century, discerning in Brazil a country with a need for a commercial class. Five decades later, that need remained. Sentient to the usefulness of enterprising foreigners, the government reopened its doors to immigration and cordially received a second, larger wave of Lebanese-Syrian Jews.

This time, most of the newcomers were Aleppines. While Aleppo remained the poorest Jewish community in the Near East, its émigrés later became Westernized as they passed through the alembic of Beirut before traveling on to the New World. "We were jewelry merchants in the old country," remarked Albert Jamus, a clone of Farhi in age and appearance. "We arrived after 1956, when Israel's campaign in the Sinai shook up our part of the world." Ultimately, some three thousand Syrian-Lebanese Jews made their homes in Rio and São Paulo, where they prospered as merchants and small manufacturers. Farhi owned a chain of clothing stores. Jamus owned a large textile factory. One of their number, Edmond Safra, now owned the twelfth-largest bank in Brazil. Here as elsewhere, they maintained separate communities, synagogues, and philanthropies. Perhaps they no longer drew narrow distinctions between Aleppines and Damascenes in this multiracial society, between Turkish, Balkan, Egyptian, or Moroccan Jews. They would intermingle, even "intermarry." But they would never compromise their Jewish loyalties. Fully 30 percent of their children attended the Jewish day schools, a much higher ratio than among the "European" Jews. Observance of Jewish traditions, of the dietary laws, attendance at synagogues, all remained a central feature of their existence.

"I corroborate that," declared Ibram Salama, vice-president of Brazil's Egyptian Jewish community council. A dark, heavyset man, he wore a pin-striped cashmere suit. In his native Alexandria, one did not dissemble about wealth, and his family had it. They owned a large cotton gin and a flour mill. A spacious home, servants, private schooling, and European vacations were their way of life. Then, in 1957, Nasser liquidated the majority of Jewish holdings. It was the Salamas' good fortune, as that of other Jews in Egypt, to claim a variety of nationalities—Italian, Spanish, Turkish. Israel's doors were open, to be sure, but the prospect of life in another poor country was not enticing. Salama's brothers and two of his sisters ended up in France. He was attracted to Brazil, by its vast resources, and by President Juscelino Kubitschek's proclaimed desire for immigrants with entrepreneurial experience. Tens of thousands of Syrians and Lebanese of all religions were pouring into Brazil. Some nine thousand Egyptian Jews now joined them. "We were not beggars," Salama insisted. "We had a little money laid by in Europe. We purchased our own tickets to Brazil."

Arriving with his wife and two children in São Paulo, where his in-laws had settled four years earlier, Salama quickly got the lay of the land. With a bank loan, he opened a small workshop to manufacture clothing labels. Within ten years, the workshop grew into a small factory employing one hundred workers. Five years after that, it employed three hundred and was the largest producer of labels in Brazil. A millionaire again, Salama reappraised his opportunities. Since the mid-1960s, the government had imposed import quotas on foreign automobiles and automobile parts. Accordingly, Salama sold his label company, bought control of an automobile parts factory—and soon became a millionaire twice over.

"Mine is hardly a unique success story," he admitted. "After all, we Egyptian Jews bring special advantages with us. We spoke French or Ladino at home, and so we had no difficulty with Portuguese afterward. With our linguistic skills and business experience, we could always count on salaried jobs. Many of our people have become managers of banks, insurance companies, import-export houses. My son, Eric, has a fine executive position at the Bank Safra. My daughter, Maureen, had an excellent position in an import house before she married."

"Whom did she marry?"

Salama nodded. "Ezekiel Shalom is his name. From Aleppo." He anticipated the question. "I'm not complaining. We're not snobs. Their culture may be lower than ours, but they're hard workers and even richer than we are. Ezekiel is a factory representative." Salama allowed himself a complacent smile. "He's done well enough to own four apartments. One of them is next to ours in Garujá—at the seaside."

Like their Syrian, Moroccan, and Turkish predecessors, the Egyptians founded their own congregation, Mekor Chaim. Established in 1948, it eventually became the second-largest congregation in Brazil. In later years, many Syrian and Rhodian Jews availed themselves of its ample facilities and well-trained Egyptian and Lebanese rabbis. "We're probably not quite as devout as the Syrians," Salama confessed. "Our people received a much wider cultural training, after all. But we stick to the straight and narrow. Our children attend the day schools here. We're active in our Jewish community. Our social life is exclusively among our own."

It is an opulent social life. Parties, weddings, Bar Mitzvah receptions, are lavish. Handsome apartments and seaside villas are the norm. But the Sephardim also remain generous to Jewish charities. One of these, São Paulo's Jewish old age home, is a facility worth seeing. A complex of eight buildings, some of them ten floors high, it is all but a four-star hotel in comfort and decor. In proportion to their numbers, the Sephardic communities have matched the Ashkenazic Jews cruzeiro for cruzeiro in support of this institution. It is a matter of caring for family.

"Family integrity," asserted Salama. "That's where we can still teach the Ashkenazim a thing or two. We'll intermarry with them now, but we'll not intermarry with the Gentiles." He paused. "I don't say that we may not lose a few of our people to intermarriage"—here plainly he was speaking of marriage between faiths—"but hardly to the extent that the Ashkenazim do. We flatly will accept no converts." His face became hard. "In our synagogue, no man who marries a Gentile will ever be called to the Torah. Loyalty, pride of peoplehood—we don't compromise there." It is a fact. Numbering thirty thousand now, over a fifth of Brazilian Jewry, these Sephardic communities from the Balkan and Moslem worlds serve as the conscience of their fellow Jews.

An Equivocal Welcome to Europeans

One gains some insight into the expansion of this giant southern domain, as large as the continental United States, with room for another Texas, by appreciating that its population has quintupled since World War I, and that, until very recently, its rate of economic growth has consistently surpassed that of the United States. European Jews were slower than the Sephardim in grasping its potential. Only a few hundred of them arrived in the nineteenth century, essentially technicians, mining engineers, businessmen from Germany. Then, in the early 1900s, attracted at last by the nation's evidently limitless supplies of rubber, diamonds, and timber, immigrants from throughout Europe suddenly began pouring into Brazil at the rate of about 100,000 a year. Among these were some 2,000 Russian Jews.

Most of them were brought over by the renowned Bavarian Jewish philanthropist, Baron Moritz de Hirsch, an enormously wealthy financier, builder of the Trans-Balkan Railroad, who settled them on his farm colonies in the southern Brazilian state of Rio Grande do Sul. Known as Philipson and Quadro Irmãos, the two colonies were an extension of a much larger project de Hirsch was underwriting for Jews in neighboring Argentina—and they proved even less enduring than their Argentine counterparts. The Jewish farmers soon began wandering from the soil to the cities. By the eve of World War I, the Jewish population of Brazil reached 7,000, almost equally divided between Europeans and non-Ashkenazim. The influx gained momentum after 1921, once the United States restricted immigration. For East European Jews, fleeing the crypto-Fascist regimes of postwar Romania and Poland, the Caribbean basin and South America emerged as major sanctuaries. By 1933, Brazil's Jewish population had climbed to 42,000.

Leon Feffer remembers. A slim, quietly dressed little man of eighty, he sat in his modest office in downtown São Paulo and reminisced about the early years. His father had arrived from the Ukraine in 1912 in search of a foothold for his wife and children. As a retailer of paper goods in São Paulo, he did well enough to send funds home regularly. Then, with the outbreak of the World War, his family was left on its own and nearly perished in the upheavals of transplantation, revolution, and civil war. The ordeal ended only in 1920, when a letter arrived from the father, containing funds for boat tickets to Brazil. The voyage consumed a full month; the ship dropped anchor in Rio de Janeiro in late January 1921. The father was waiting. That night the Feffers left for São Paulo by train.

As drab as Rio was glamorous, São Paulo even then was the locomotive pulling Brazil. By 1921, it accounted for half the nation's industrial output and was on the threshold of even more impressive growth. The Feffers could sense it. Like most of their fellow Jewish immigrants, they rented a flat in the lower-middle-class Bom Retiro quarter. The father was earning a tolerable livelihood in his paper products trade; but Leon, who mastered Portuguese within a year, was chafing to be on his own. With two other young immigrants, he opened a small distributorship, buying paper from factories, selling it to wholesalers and retailers. He did not work on commission, as his father had, preferring instead to rely on the market for his profits. The enterprise went spectacularly well. By 1930, he was able to buy out his partners. By 1939, with its two hundred employees, Leon Feffer & Cia. had become the largest wholesale paper company in São Paulo, and one of the three largest in Brazil.

Years later, Feffer asked himself how he could have missed. He had arrived in this abundant, easygoing land with a fanatical determination to succeed, and with a family legacy of mercantile experience. Others of the Jewish immigrants brought skills as spinners and weavers, as tailors and seamstresses, as shoemakers and furniture-makers. Working from dawn to dusk in their tiny stores or workshops, they almost invariably saved enough to open larger retail establishments or small factories. From then on, growth was exponential. By 1939, Jews owned several of the nation's largest textile mills, many of the largest wholesale distributorships, retail shops, and department stores. Even smaller businessmen were earning livelihoods that permitted a certain leeway for relaxation. In Leon Feffer's case, his free hours were spent at the Círculo Israelita do São Paulo, a social club that had sprung up among the immigrant children of Bom Retiro. There he met his wife. Like him, Antoinette Tepperman was reared in an observant home. After their marriage in 1925, they resolved to maintain that tradition. It was still the widely held expectation of their generation.

The world depression struck Brazil hard. The international market for coffee diminished sharply. Exploiting the crisis, Getúlio Vargas, a wealthy landowner and president of the state of Rio Grande do Sul, seized control of the nation's presidency in 1930. In the following years, Vargas silenced opposition through censorship, arbitrary arrest, torture, and assassination. While not overtly antisemitic himself, the president tolerated Jew-baiting to placate his right-wing landowner and lumpenproletariat supporters. Many of the latter gave their support to the Integralista Party, a collection of green-shirted ruffians who drew their inspiration from Italian and Portuguese fascism. With the tacit support of important church leaders, the Integralistas devoted an entire branch of their secret service organization to the surveillance of Brazilian Jewry. Not since the Inquisition had Jews faced such organized hostility in this land. The danger proved to be short-lived, however. Vargas began to have second thoughts about flagrant pro-Axis propaganda on Brazilian territory, and in 1935 he suppressed the Integralistas. Three years later, in an effort to combat Nazi influence among the large German enclave in the Rio Grande do Sul province, the Brazilian dictator curtailed foreign-language schools and cultural activities, and eventually banned foreign-language periodicals—German, Italian, Japanese, among them.

The Jews drew an uncertain reassurance from these measures. Much of their press was still Yiddish, and was disallowed with the other foreign-language publications. Their libraries and schools were also tightly circumscribed. More ominously, in 1937 the Vargas regime introduced severe restrictions on immigration—at the very moment that Jewish refugees from Hitler were turning to Brazil for sanctuary. Approximately fourteen thousand Central European Jews entered before the outbreak of war, and afterward perhaps four thousand others made their way from neighboring countries. It was by no means a negligible total, and in time German-speaking immigrants comprised a fourth of São Paulo's Jewish population. But their early years were hard. Most of the newcomers gained admission only by bribing Brazilian immigration officials. Frequently they were obliged to continue paying blackmail to corrupt go-betweens. Nor could they be employed without a permanent residence permit, and this was difficult to obtain. The multiple harassments drove a number of the refugees to suicide, among them the eminent writer Stefan Zweig.

Meanwhile, Brazil's small community of naturalized German Jews worked assiduously to help the refugees through the red tape, to find them employment and housing. A legendary figure in this effort was Dr. Ludwig Lorch, a surgeon who had arrived from Germany several years earlier and had established a thriving practice. Well respected and connected, Lorch played a leading role in settling German Jews during the 1930s and 1940s. If the newcomers had business experience, Lorch somehow negotiated credit lines for them at banks. If they were harassed by the police, Lorch had an instinct for the appropriate officials to accommodate. The newcomers did the rest on their own. Often their business experience was prized highly enough for Brazilian firms to take them in as managers or even as partners.

By and large, the Germans avoided São Paulo's East European ghetto in Bom Retiro and took up residence in the comfortable, middle-class Jardim America quarter. The Jewish day schools were not for them. Their children attended either Brazilian or English-language institutions. But they involved themselves in other Jewish activities, particularly those that fostered their acculturation. Again under Dr. Lorch's leadership, the Central Europeans organized their own welfare and employment services, their own cultural and musical societies, their own synagogue, Congregação Israelita Paulista—the CIP. Nominally Liberal, the CIP was somewhat akin to American Conservative, and its first rabbi, Dr. Fritz Pinkuss, had been a distinguished spokesman for Liberal Judaism in Germany. More a community center than a synagogue, the CIP was a place to find good books and journals in the German language, a source of information on legal and administrative matters, a kind of unofficial employment exchange. Today, with a membership that is Ashkenazic but no longer exclusively German, the CIP is the largest synagogue in Brazil and the second-largest in Latin America.

Prosperity and Anchorage

In 1945, President Vargas was deposed and constitutional government was restored in Brazil. Immigration restrictions were eased soon afterward. Between 1945 and 1965, approximately 20 million newcomers of various backgrounds were admitted into the country. These included Jews from Hungary, Syria, Lebanon, Egypt, and Turkey. By 1965, the Jewish population had reached 110,000. Twenty years later, estimates of Jewish growth ranged between 120,000 and 150,000. If the figure is calculated at 130,000, it would represent less than one-fifth of one percent of the total Brazilian population of approximately 130 million by 1984. Currently, about 60,000 Jews are living in São Paulo, another 45,000 in Rio de Janeiro, 13,000 in Pôrto Alegre, 3,000 in Recife, with perhaps 1,000 each in Bahia, Belo Horizonte, and Curitiba, and a few thousand others scattered elsewhere.

With rare exceptions, they had achieved economic security by the end of World War II, and they continued to prosper afterward. By 1964, the last year of Brazil's democratic government, less than a third of São Paulo's Jews still lived in the Bom Retiro district. Highly literate and well-versed in business affairs, they were in the forefront of Brazil's remarkable economic takeoff. A military coup in 1964 accelerated this progress. The new regime was technocratic and pro-capitalist. It encouraged Brazil's transformation from an agrarian economy, based essentially on coffee, to an industrial one. The annual growth rate in the 1960s and 1970s was spectacular. Profits were high, jobs plentiful, as the government orchestrated the massive construction of roads, dams, and power plants. The Jews shared in that action. They, too, had shifted the scale of their operations from the immigrant vocations of merchandising to large-scale manufacturing, the range of products extending beyond clothing and furniture to plastics, electronics, metals, chemicals, pharmaceuticals. And paper.

Imports into the country all but ceased with the outbreak of World War II. If he wished to continue selling paper, Leon Feffer decided, he would have to produce it himself. To that end, he built his own plant and set about distributing the finished paper products through his already impressive network of wholesalers and retailers. By 1945, he was employing five hundred workers. During the next few years, he imported new paper-making equipment from Sweden and the United States, and by 1950 his company was the largest manufacturer of quality paper in Brazil. At this point, he might have followed the example of the Klabins, East European Jews whose firm was the largest manufacturer of paper products in Latin America. Venturing into pulp production, the Klabins had chosen to build their factories at the source of supply, the pine forests of the state of Paraná. To service this plant, however, it had been necessary for them to open new roads, to build housing and other facilities for the workers' families. At one point, the Klabins had almost gone bankrupt. It was not a risk that appealed to Feffer.

As early as 1942, Feffer's son Max, a trained engineer, had become intrigued by another source of pulp. This was the eucalyptus tree, which grew in vast quantities near São Paulo. The eucalyptus was not a long-fibered wood, the kind that normally was used to manufacture quality pulp. But Max Feffer wondered if a chemical process might not be devised for bleaching the tree's shorter fibers. He and his research staff set about conducting experiments, and at last, in 1954, they came up with a promising method. The next step was to build new facilities. In 1957 the family completed its first pulp mill in Suzano, thirty miles from São Paulo. Both the pulp and the paper manufactured from it proved to be of excellent quality. Within the next four years, 100 percent of the company's output was being produced from local eucalyptus supplies.

Today, it requires a helicopter journey to gauge the extent of the Feffer company's holdings. Not less than 70 million trees are growing in Feffer-owned forests, and 10,000 men are working there. Another 3,000 employees labor in the Feffers' huge integrated pulp-and-paper factory, and 1,300 in three smaller factories. The results of this prodigious investment have been dramatic. In the largest integrated pulp, paper, and board operation in Latin America, the Feffer company is currently producing a daily output of 1,000 tons of paper, 500 tons of pure pulp, 400 tons of board. In addition to its domination of the Brazilian market, the company exports some $40 million worth of its products, and projects a goal of $100 million by the end of the 1980s. This is the empire created by a Ukrainian Jewish immigrant family.

If the Jews encountered no significant political or legal obstacles to their economic advance after World War II, a certain public esteem for Israel may have been a factor. Relations between the two countries remained cordial, scientific and cultural exchanges between them extensive. A more decisive influence, however, was the Brazilian economic miracle. Well into the 1970s, the nation's indicators seemed headed uninterruptedly upward. Even the military coup of 1964, which established a technocratic autocracy, did nothing to arouse antisemitism or to exploit group frictions. "Obviously, there is antisemitism here and there," observes Rolf Herzberg, director of the Jewish Federation of São Paulo. "This is a Catholic country, after all, and the church's influence is quite strong in the interior. The simple people there may still regard Jews as Christ-killers. But the emotion has never become malevolent or even open. Brazilians are too soft, too 'African,' for that kind of imported European phobia."

The barriers to political activity have been as minimal as those in the economic sphere. Between 1949 and 1959, a Jew, Horacio Laufer, served consecutively as minister of finance and of foreign affairs. In later years, Jews sat in state and municipal cabinets. Max Feffer, the son of Leon, and the technological genius of the Feffer paper and pulp empire, was appointed secretary of culture, science, and technology for the state of São Paulo (and by common consensus was the ablest man ever to hold that post). His predecessor, José Mindlin, was also a Jew. Jews have been mayors of Curitiba and Rio de Janeiro, where squares and streets are named for Theodor Herzl, David Ben-Gurion, Anne

Frank, and other Jews. There have been Jewish generals in the armed forces—six of them in 1966. The nation's cultural life has been as widely influenced by the Jewish leaven as in any Western land, from the conductor of the national symphony orchestra to directors of state academies and institutes to deans of universities. Public officials attend the dedications of Jewish institutions. Interfaith activities are common, with church leaders benignly participating. Descriptions of Jewish holidays, interviews with Jewish leaders, appear in the general press. The tone is invariably friendly.

Adaptation to an Open Society

I sat with Leon Feffer in the sunroom of his luxurious duplex. With a vivacity that belied his years, he recalled the crises of World War II, the Vargas era of homegrown facism, the postwar influx of nearly ten thousand displaced persons, the attempt to legitimize Zionism in Brazil. The organizational pattern of Brazilian Jewry was still determined by origin and language, with separate communities of Sephardic, German, Polish, and Hungarian Jews maintaining individual synagogues, networks of social services, and burial societies. In those days, there was even a separate Jewish burial society for the dozen or so madams of São Paulo's most popular brothels. While the fund-raising campaigns of the various communities were invariably productive, there was growing recognition in later years that a centralized body was required to deal with the government and the outside world, to foster understanding for the Jewish National Home in Palestine.

Accordingly, the Jewish Federation of São Paulo was established in 1946, then similar federations in Rio and in other cities soon afterward, and finally a national Confederation of Brazilian Jewish Communities. Feffer was a pioneer in these unifying ventures, and he and his associates did not have an easy time at first. Dr. Ludwig Lorch, doyen of the German Jewish community, was opposed to the notion of an umbrella body in which German efficiency would be subordinated to *ostjüdisches Politik* (and, he feared, to East European Zionism). Eventually, he was outvoted. To no one's surprise, Feffer was elected chairman of the federation, and in later years he remained one of its permanent vice-chairmen. Since then, elections have taken place biennially. Once they were vigorously contested, with candidates running on Zionist-style party lists that were replications of the Knesset electoral system in Israel—and evidence of the enormous impact of Zionism on the Diaspora (precisely as Lorch had anticipated). But since the 1970s, elections have become somewhat perfunctory, with fewer than five thousand local Jews voting. The number is even smaller in Rio. There is no mystery to the dropoff. Brazilian Jews have long since developed political and social interests beyond their own community.

For decades, the bedrock of Jewish ethnicity lay in education. "The *Deitcher* [German Jews] didn't always agree," Feffer recalled, with some amusement. "Their children were sent to the state schools or the English-language private schools. But that was not our way, or the way of the Sephardim." Between the 1920s and 1950s, nearly half the Jewish children in São Paulo and Rio received their primary education in a cluster of privately funded Jewish day schools, where the level of study was reasonably high. Yet, in ensuing years, there has been a decline in both the quality of teaching personnel and the quantity of students. With the exception of the more recent Sephardic immigrant groups, Jewish parents discern little need any longer to "ghettoize" their children. Currently, less than 20 percent of the Jewish students in São Paulo attend the community's seven day schools; although in Rio, the proportion remains closer to 50 percent.

Within the University of São Paulo, meanwhile, efforts to establish an "Interdisciplinary Center for Jewish Studies" have been less than successful. Few Jewish students have been induced to attend. Dr. Walter Rehfeld, an early faculty member, put the issue succinctly: "We have thousands of Jewish students at the universities, hundreds of Jewish faculty, even a few deans. They're quite unselfconscious as Jews. But as intellectuals, they tend to gravitate to 'progressive' social causes. There's no middle ground here in Brazil. I don't suggest that they move to the radical Left," he added quickly. "That period in our history ended in the 1930s. But they simply can't be indifferent to the horrifying economic inequities in our society. In the university context, unfortunately, those issues claim most of their extracurricular time. Jewish cultural activities come in a poor second." Among students in any Diaspora community, they usually do. Rehfeld's discouragement notwithstanding, Jewish culture is far from moribund in this land. The various federations, congregations, and Zionist organizations sponsor lectures, art festivals, occasional theatrical performances. In Rio and São Paulo, several publishing houses have intermittently brought out translations of well-known Jewish volumes. Israeli ensembles perform quite often, before large audiences, and local Jewish youth groups enthusiastically participate in festivals with Israeli themes, particularly in Chanukkah and Purim celebrations.

There are alternate routes to identification, beyond schools and institutes. Interestingly enough, synagogue attendance is one of them, and it has as little to do with religiosity in Brazil as in other Western communities. The Sephardic synagogue, Mekor Chaim, is a spacious building, constructed in the traditional Near Eastern manner, with the dais in the center of the sanctuary. The Sabbath morning I walked in, nearly every seat was filled. Crowned with an imposing silk biretta, the rabbi was intoning the week's scriptural portion. Congregants circulated, shaking hands with friends, chatting in a low undercurrent of mild cordiality. Wives and other womenfolk in the balcony murmured cozily to each other. The atmosphere was warm, homey, yet without the chaotic lack of decorum often encountered in Orthodox Ashkenazic synagogues.

Less than three blocks away, on Rua Antonio Carlos, services were being conducted at the Congregação Israelita Paulista. I strolled over. The building was modernistic and vast, seven stories high. It was a community center, after all. Here, too, the sanctuary was all but filled; at least a thousand congregants were present. The CIP remained the prestige address for Brazil's Ashkenazic Jews. Unlike the Sephardic congregation, formality was the rule here. The ambience was cordial, but restrained. There was no chitchat. On the dais—this time at the front of the sanctuary—Chief Rabbi Emeritus Pinkuss was enthroned, flanked by three younger associate rabbis. One of the latter was an American, with blond, modishly long hair. Plainly quite taken with himself, he was delivering the sermon in a Portuguese insipid enough even for me to grasp, and as readily to forget. It was all very comfortable. The turnouts I had seen that morning were not unusual, friends assured me later. Brazilian Jewry is gregarious. Sabbath services are friendly social occasions.

One cannot predict how long even this free and easy, typically Brazilian, version of social Judaism will survive. The reservoir of Portuguese-speaking rabbis is limited for São Paulo's thirty synagogues, Rio's twelve synagogues. Few Americans can be induced to serve here. Nor would they deal any longer with a captive constituency. Between them, the CIP and Rio's ARI temple alone perform over one hundred conversions a year, even convert children of mixed marriages to enable them to be Bar Mitzvahed. However enlightened the practice, the sheer number of conversions is evidence of a rising wave of intermarriages (most of them, no doubt, unaccompanied by conversions) that would have been unimaginable a generation earlier. Hard statistics on mixed marriages are nonexistent, but estimates range between 25 and 30 percent. As elsewhere in the West, exogamy is the price Jews and other ethnic minorities pay for an open society.

As in other countries, too, the more isolated Jewish communities— Belém, Belo Horizonte, Pôrto Alegre—are dying on the vine for lack of spiritual or cultural leadership, even for lack of Jewish contacts. Their association with the major Jewish organizations in São Paulo or Rio is limited to periodic confederation or B'nai B'rith meetings. Emissaries from the larger cities tend to be fund-raisers, hardly ever teachers or rabbis. "Why don't our Jews follow the example of the Catholic Church, which sends missionaries here?" lamented Raúl Doctorchik, a B'nai B'rith officer from Recife, in a letter to the *International Jewish Monthly*. "What will happen to our children in this Jewish cultural wilderness?" No doubt they would undergo the fate of small-town Jews in any other Western country. Some unquestionably would be lost. Some would not. And, generations later, some would revert. All is comparative. Brazil's Jewry is still of more recent vintage than Argentina's. With few exceptions, even the most acculturated Brazilian Jew remains closer to his Jewish roots than his second-generation Argentine Jewish counterpart.

The Accommodation of Congeniality

Devotion to Israel meanwhile remains as powerful a gravitational field for Brazilian Jewry as for any community in the Diaspora. Between 1948 and 1983, three thousand Brazilian Jews settled in Israel. Still others maintain apartments in Israel and live there part of the year. Israeli themes remain central to Jewish communal and cultural life in Brazil—as evidenced (we recall) in the Knesset-style party lists for the federation elections. "This is a Zionist community," insisted Fiszel Czeresnia, chairman of Brazil's Zionist Organization. "Zionism animates every Jewish institution we have in this country. It's the link with Israel that has kept Brazilian Jewry from expiring as a community."

Czeresnia's view was too draconian. Ethnic gregariousness alone probably would have done the job. In São Paulo, as in Mexico City or

Buenos Aires, a major focus of Jewish identity is a luxurious sports facility-country club-community center. Located in the affluent Jardim America quarter, the center encompasses a two-thousand-seat auditorium, a theater, ample classroom and office space, an indoor swimming pool, two outdoor swimming pools, a score of tennis courts, as well as picnic and playground areas. Like its model in Buenos Aires, it is called Hebraica, and its Hebraic dimension typically may be identified less in its occasional Hebrew or Yiddish lectures, or performances of Jewish or Israeli music, than in the scope of its Jewish membership. On a summer Sunday, as many as ten thousand Jewish Paulistas can be seen decked out here in swimming or tennis garb. In the later hours, entire families, or the younger Jewish smart set, will have their dinners served in one or another of the Hebraica's dining rooms, then dance to fashionable society orchestras. Not to be outdone, the Jews of Rio have constructed their own modern Hebraica building on the prestigious Rua des Laranjeiras. A seven-story building, it is equipped with comparable facilities.

Undoubtedly, these luxurious monuments to Jewish success, love of comfort, and gregariousness serve their purpose in allowing young Jews and old to meet under convivial surroundings. They are hardly a Jewish innovation in hedonism. Germans, Japanese, Italians, and other ethnic communities similarly maintain their own community center-country clubs. A respectable number of cultural activities do in fact take place within the Hebraica's premises. Yet it is questionable if the club's charter members (Feffer, of course, preeminent among them) anticipated that this *palácio* ultimately would transcend synagogue, federation, school, or university classroom as the single most tangible manifestation of Jewish identity in Brazil, other than Zionism. In earlier years, during the crest of the Brazilian economic boom, the effulgence of Jewish communal life tended to blend with a more widely diffused prosperity. Yet even during the affluence of the 1960s and early 1970s, the nation's income was far from adequately distributed, and the lower 40 percent of the population actually lost ground. Uncontrollable inflation was steadily outstripping the modest rate of wage improvement. Malnutrition was becoming widespread even before soaring energy costs in the 1970s drove Brazil to the threshold of insolvency. At the time of writing, as many as 90 percent of the Brazilian people are believed to be afflicted with a near-medieval array of diseases, from tuberculosis to parasitic infestations. Almost surrealistically in debt, threatening to default on some $90 billion in foreign bank loans, the government no longer can give even passing attention to measures for social improvement. The political implications for Brazil are not encouraging.

With a few exceptions—mainly university students and a handful of progressives in the state and national legislatures—Jews have not taken a stand on the nation's horrifying economic inequities. Living in comparative prosperity, accepted by the elite strata of Brazilian society, they appear content with the political status quo. Most of them do not seem fazed by a military regime that is benign by Latin American standards. As in Chile and Argentina, the largest numbers of Brazilian Jews remain suspicious of populist democracy. They take no position against social change or for it. Discreetly, most of them prefer to avoid the risk of ending up in the wrong camp.

Benno Milnitzky knows his people. The son of Ukrainian Jews who had settled originally in the Baron de Hirsch colony of Quadro Irmãos, he moved later with his parents to the ghetto of Bom Retiro. Working his way through night law school, Milnitzky soon afterward developed a respectable general practice. Almost from the beginning of his career, too, he identified himself with Jewish affairs. President of São Paulo's Zionist youth movement, vice-president of the Círculo Israelita, he rose in later years to the presidency of the Zionist Organization, then of the São Paulo Jewish Federation, and finally of the national Confederation of Brazilian Jewish Communities. No man, not even Leon Feffer, has won greater attention or respect from his fellow Jews.

They do not listen to his exhortations comfortably, for Milnitzky is a Cassandra. Sixty-two years old when we met in 1982, with a vast proboscis jutting aggressively beneath a flamboyant pompadour, he ventilated his misgivings amid clouds of cigarette smoke. "I don't mind that Brazilian society is open," he insisted. "Heaven forbid. I *do* mind that the openness of society here has undermined our Jewish integrity. Isn't it true that since the beginning of the Diaspora we Jews haven't learned to live in an open society, haven't found the proper balance?" He looked at me, awaiting confirmation. As I contemplated an answer, his son—one of three who shared his practice with him—apologetically interrupted us. A special delivery letter had arrived. Milnitzky read it carefully, brow furrowed. "It's from the Confederation," he explained to me. "Another appeal for an 'emergency' meeting tomorrow." Sighing, he handed the letter back to his son. "We'll cancel our appointments, then. It's the only thing to do." The son shook his head and departed.

"There's no strong leadership here," Milnitzky continued, mercifully sparing me the need for reply, "certainly no rabbis worthy of anyone's attention. If only someone could instill in our people a feeling for the old Jewish ethical values, not the fake materialistic values of the Brazilian elite. Our people simply are too attracted by Brazilian materialism. It's the kind of behavior that we Jews of all people can't afford to emulate." He shrugged resignedly. "I suppose I antagonized a lot of my friends several weeks ago at a community banquet. Of course, it was at the Hebraica. Of course, they were dressed to the hilt. I watched the waiters staring at the food the guests left on their plates. The scraps would have fed those poor wretches' families for a week. And when I spoke, I spoke in plain language. 'Don't commit yourselves politically, if you're afraid to,' I said. 'But you also don't have to make every communal function, every synagogue gathering, the occasion to air your fashionable worries about the dangers of intermarriage, of the "assimilation" of your children. It's your own behavior you have to worry about. Clear out of this place. Organize your community activities at the synagogue. Be modest in your personal demeanor. You live among a desperately poor people. In your social and communal lives, at least, try to set a standard of ethical values, of our historic prophetic values. The most important contribution you can make to Jewish survival here will be the example you set in your behavior as human beings.'"

As I left his office, it occurred to me that the Benno Milnitzkys I had met in my travels—in my own country, for that matter—I could count on the fingers of one hand.

A *Mestizo Diaspora: Prosperity and Isolation*

Of the multiracial nations sharing Brazil's frontiers, Venezuela is by far the best endowed. Yet, as in Brazil, its immense natural wealth has not ensured a broadly diffused prosperity. Out of Venezuela's current population of approximately fourteen million, four-fifths are mestizos, Indians, Negroes. Their cultural level is as marginal as their economic level. The best soil has remained concentrated in the hands of a minority of *latifundistas*. The oil deposits that transformed Venezuela into the fifth-largest petroleum exporter in the world diverted attention and investment from agriculture altogether. In recent decades, serious efforts have been made to introduce economic and political reforms. In 1975 and 1976, the government nationalized the steel and oil industries, and applied their profits to a vigorous program of social welfare. Thus far, however, the nation's problems remain, its widespread poverty, unemployment, and illiteracy seemingly ineradicable. The exquisite villas and gleaming skyscrapers of Caracas overlook a nightmare of slums. The gap between rich and poor continues to widen.

In the worst and best of times, nevertheless, Venezuela has provided a cherished sanctuary for Jews. The first marrano refugees from the Portuguese Inquisition arrived here from Brazil early in the seventeenth century. As elsewhere in Latin America, their descendants intermarried and were numbered eventually among Venezuela's most aristocratic families. Early in the nineteenth century, the nation's recently won freedom from Spain began to attract professing Jews, including a contingent of some four hundred Sephardim who arrived from Curaçao. By the opening years of the twentieth century, a functioning Sephardic community was in place, with its own synagogue, mutual aid society, and newspaper. In ensuing decades, the enclave was broadened by newcomers from Morocco and the Near East. Essentially small retailers, the Sephardim today number about three thousand.

Jewish life in Venezuela achieved its most impressive growth after World War I, when East Europeans began arriving in substantial family groups. In the characteristic immigration profile, they were followed by German Jewish refugees in the 1930s, then by smaller quantities of displaced persons after 1945. The current Jewish population of Venezuela is estimated at 17,000, of whom the largest majority lives in Caracas. They are middle class. While important numbers of them are importers, Jews also own some 350 factories producing clothing, textiles, and furniture. By now, their children occupy important positions in the professions, and notably as faculty members of the National University in Caracas. They have encountered no significant problems of antisemitism, except for immigration restrictions during the late 1920s and 1930s. Relations with the Catholic clergy and the government are quite equable.

Two large synagogues function in Caracas, one Ashkenazic, one Sephardic, along with a dozen smaller congregations. Although each group maintains its own communal center, the Ashkenazic and Sephardic kehillas work together amicably in the usual confederative roof organization and in a joint fund-raising drive for Israel. Here, too, Zionism is primus inter pares among Jewish communal endeavors. Nearly a thousand Venezuelan Jews have settled in Israel. Zionism is also the principal motif of Venezuelan Jewish education. Shunning the state schools, with their Catholic instructional programs, the Jewish communities maintain several excellent day schools that are attended by virtually all their children. The Herzl-Bialik School is regarded as the best private institution of its kind in Venezuela and has been attended by the children of high-ranking (non-Jewish) officials, including those of the minister of education. Enjoying a certain degree of critical mass, then, Venezuelan Jewry is affected less by an erosion of identity than by the nation's uncertain economic future.

Directly to the west, Colombia, the fourth-largest state in Latin America, possesses an agricultural economy and a racially blended population of marginal literacy. After a decade of civil war, from 1948 to 1958, the nation entered an era of relative quiescence under a kind of presidential democracy. Since the early 1970s, however, Colombia has endured the regional afflictions of runaway inflation, chronic unemployment, and a staggering population growth of 600,000 a year. The largest numbers of its 25 million inhabitants function at the subsistence level, and its middle class remains narrowly based. The Jews traditionally belonged to this latter stratum, of course. In the sixteenth century, as many as four thousand marranos settled here, many of them arriving direct from Spain, others from neighboring lands. Medellín, capital of the province of Antioquia, was founded by marranos, and descendants of the Antioquians over the years evolved into a distinct ethnic group known as the Palas, a mixture of Jews and Basques. Among them was Jorge Isaacs, Colombia's national poet and a renowned nineteenth-century Latin American writer (whose great-granddaughter in the 1950s sought to convert back to Judaism).

It was only when Simón Bolívar threw off the Spanish yoke, however, and abolished the Inquisition, that small numbers of professing Jews began to settle in Colombia. Their vanguard, too, was Sephardic, and their foothold was strengthened in the twentieth century by three or four hundred kinsmen from Morocco and the Balkans. One of these, Bernardo Elbert, was the first navigator of the Magdalena River. Another, Ernesto Corescos, founded the Colombian airline (now Avianca). Yet the Jewish population of the 1980s consists largely of East European Jews who arrived in the interwar period, with the usual smaller influx of German Jewish refugees afterward. Theirs was the familiar vocational odyssey, from small shops to larger-scale merchandising and manufacturing. Settled in Bogotá, their principal components—Sephardic, East European, Hungarian, German—jointly support a community center and a day school that today is attended by more than half the nation's Jewish children. It is a staunchly Zionist Jewry, basking in the congenial relations between Colombia and Israel, proud of the special agricultural programs Israel established for the Colombian government in the 1960s.

If there is lingering uncertainty among Colombia's Jews today, it relates to the precariousness of the nation's democracy—the consequence in turn of an increasingly shaky economy. Elections are greeted with apathy by the public, leftist guerrilla groups are resorting to terror tactics, and the government is reacting with stern military measures. As a result, there has been a significant Jewish exodus in recent years. As late as 1980, twelve thousand Jews lived in Colombia. Today, there are perhaps six thousand. The émigrés have departed mainly for the United States, and in smaller numbers for Israel. Those who remain are a significantly more isolated Jewish community than Venezuela's. They are off the Caribbean tourist route. Participation in international Jewish organizations does not yet compensate for the desperate shortage of rabbis, teachers, and communal leaders, or for Colombian Jewry's remoteness from the major power centers of Jewish life.

The problem of isolation is compounded for the five thousand Jews of Peru. Abutting the Pacific Ocean, a country of imposing size and geographic diversity, Peru is also one of the poorest nations in the Southern Hemisphere. Its mineral resources in copper, silver, zinc, and lead are substantial; but here also, the nation's eighteen million—predominantly Indian—inhabitants share only marginally in the economic return. The wealth remains solidly in the hands of the white criollo elite. Not a few of these are of Jewish origin; for, next to Brazil's, Peru's Jewish past is the richest in Latin America. A powerful marrano community lived here throughout most of the sixteenth century. Eventually, most of these underground Jews were discovered by the Inquisition and tortured, burned, or driven into flight. Yet the few remaining families produced several notable figures. In 1864, the abandoned mercury and silver mines of Peru were revived by the Salcedo family. A great-grandson, Augusto Leguia Salcedo, was twice president of Peru, from 1906 to 1912, and from 1919 to 1930.

Today, not less than 90 percent of the Jewish population comes from Eastern Europe, particularly from Bessarabia. Virtually all of them now conduct their businesses in Lima, although a few pioneering Jewish storekeepers are still to be found along the primitive Andean stretches of the Pan American Highway. Many of their children and grand-children occupy positions of respect in the nation's economic and cultural life. It is a tightly knit, quite ethnocentric community, with a markedly lower record of intermarriage than in many other Latin American nations. Supporting an effective central committee, a reasonably active B'nai B'rith lodge, traveling frequently to Jewish conferences in other Latin American countries and in the United States and Israel, Peruvian Jews appear determined to sustain their identity. The alternatives, immersion in an Indian-mestizo culture, or adaptation to the Catholicism of the criollo aristocracy, still remain unimaginable to them.

There are Jewish communities even more isolated in the vast southern hinterland. Paraguay is one of the unlikeliest locales in the Diaspora. Landlocked and economically underdeveloped, this middle-sized nation has oscillated for 150 years between anarchy and autocracy. During the past generation it has been ruled by the iron hand of the president-dictator Alfredo Stroessner. Decimated by repeated wars with its more powerful neighbors, and particularly by the savage Chaco conflict with Bolivia in the 1930s, Paraguay suffered so many casualties in battle that even today women do the heaviest work and age cruelly.

Nevertheless, a tiny Jewish population of six or seven hundred (out of three million Paraguayans) conducts a reasonably active mercantile life in the capital city of Asunción. Half are veteran Sephardim, descendants of Near Eastern immigrants who arrived at the turn of the century. The rest are East Europeans, some of them postwar displaced persons, others refugees from Argentina. Although far from wealthy in a nation of limited resources, they are moderately well off. Antisemitism remains endemic to the country's sizable German and White Russian minorities, but has not evoked much interest among the Indian majority. Few Jews have been affected by it. Characteristically, they have organized efficient communal aid societies, a small Orthodox synagogue (without a rabbi), and a quite vigorous youth club. Paraguayan Jewry's struggle to remain a viable community is as courageous as it is poignant.

An even more improbable setting for Jews is to be found on the roof of the southern continent, twelve thousand feet high, in the chill, rain-lashed Bolivian capital of La Paz. More than half the Bolivian population of 5.6 million are Indians, another quarter are mestizos. Poor beyond any North American understanding of the term, Bolivia has been described as a "beggar sitting on a pile of gold"—in this case, zinc.

For years, the country was ruled by a privileged group of criollo magnates, who exploited their workers in the mines at starvation wages. As
a consequence, the nation was torn by periodic revolutions, over one
hundred since it became an independent state in 1825. Wars with its
neighbors, Chile, Argentina, and Peru, also took their toll. With death
by violence a commonplace in this ravaged land, it was not a destination
that appealed to Jews. But with the rise of Hitler, they took their
asylum where they could find it, and by 1939 some ten thousand German and Austrian Jews found it in Bolivia.

Then, at the first opportunity after World War II, most of them
departed for Argentina or Chile. It was not loneliness and poverty alone
that sent them on their way. Influential German and White Russian
minorities poisoned the government against them. In recent decades,
nevertheless, the approximately six hundred Jews who remained have
encountered a more congenial atmosphere. The success of Israel has
enhanced the Jewish image, and in the 1960s, several Israeli technical
aid programs embellished it further. Remarkably, Bolivian Jews have
managed to sustain three synagogues, separate communal centers, and
a handful of other Jewish organizations. Their B'nai B'rith, Zionist, and
World Jewish Congress delegates have occasionally visited other Latin
American nations and the United States as participants in international
Jewish conventions. They are rarely visited in return.

A comparable Jewish settlement will be found in the northeastern
corner of the hemisphere. Like Paraguay and Bolivia, the scenic mountain nation of Ecuador is a poverty-stricken third world backwater, its
seven million Indians kept in a state of near-permanent revolution. Devoutly Catholic, its government offered no hospitality to nonbelievers
throughout the nineteenth century. It was only when the ban was lifted
in 1903 that several hundred East European Jews began drifting in. Yet
the major Jewish immigration consisted of some four thousand refugees
from Germany. Arriving in the 1930s and early 1940s, they made their
living essentially as retailers. A few became managers of Quito's larger
hotels, and others resumed the practice of medicine. They founded a
synagogue, as did the smaller East European group, and even a day
school for their children. In later years, however, the Jews of Ecuador
began departing for the United States or for other, larger countries in
South America. Currently, less than a thousand remain. They survive
in an atmosphere of intense anomie. Their loneliness is soul-destroying.
"Are we Jews, heirs to one of the world's most sophisticated civiliza-

tions, to end our days here," they lament to visitors, "among illiterate Indians?"

Essentially the same question is being asked by Jews in scores of towns and villages throughout the breadth of Indian, mestizo, or black Latin America. Their endurance is not undeserving of praise. Yet, encountering these people, one instinctively recalls the prologue of Hemingway's tale "The Snows of Kilimanjaro." The cadaver of a leopard was discovered far up the slope of a great African mountain. There was admiration for the creature's tenacity in reaching this height. Even so, "No one has explained what the leopard was seeking at that altitude."

XI

A Transplanted Europe Under the Southern Cross: Argentina, Chile, Uruguay

Chile and Uruguay: Latin Sisters

Manuel Tenenbaum, a native Uruguayan, is the regional director of the World Jewish Congress for the Southern Hemisphere. "My map of Latin America is a Jewish map," he explained. "In that map there is one large community, Argentina, and one half as large, Brazil. They're the only parts of the map you hear about in the States, I imagine."

"Mexico and Venezuela aren't altogether off the Jewish tourist route," I reminded him. "Not during the winter months."

He nodded. "But you see, Uruguay's Jewish population is larger than Mexico's. Chile's is larger than Venezuela's. More important, Uruguay and Chile share Argentina's cultural profile. They're both far more 'European' than other Latin American nations."

Perhaps. But we both knew that Uruguay rated little more than an afterthought to Americans who traveled as far south as Buenos Aires. Their loss. Were they to make the twenty-minute flight to Montevideo, they would encounter the "Switzerland of Latin America." Like Argentina, Uruguay is indeed an oasis of Europe in an Indian or mestizo continent. Almost all of its three million citizens are descendants of Spaniards, Italians, or French. They inhabit a beautiful little country, with a temperate climate, scenic grasslands, and snow-capped mountains. Deriving their income from cattle, wood, and light industry, the Uruguayans are unique in Latin America for the breadth of their middle class. A full decade before Franklin Roosevelt's New Deal in the United States, President José Batille y Ordóñez introduced social reforms under the slogan "Bread and Work," including an eight-hour working day and early retirement with full wages. For years afterward, the nation's political ambience was as mild as its climate. Almost unbelievably for

Latin America, Uruguay remained a functioning democracy for a century and a half.

It was an attractive sanctuary for Jews. With little significant marrano prehistory, their settlement here was almost entirely a twentieth-century phenomenon. Initially, in 1907–1908, it was a limited immigration of a few hundred Sephardic Jews from Smyrna, and fifty or sixty East Europeans who crossed over from Argentina. The first sizable influx, 18,000 Polish Jews, occurred in the 1920s. It was followed a decade later by a wave of German Jewish refugees, and after World War II by a smaller group of displaced persons. Currently, Uruguayan Jewry numbers 44,000. Of these, about 30,000 are East Europeans, 7,000 are Sephardim, and perhaps 7,000 are Central Europeans. Settled in Montevideo, they comprise the third-largest Jewish community in Latin America and the fifth-largest in the Western Hemisphere.

Theirs was the usual odyssey for this part of the world. The East Europeans started out as credit peddlers in the countryside ("my father's beginnings," Tenenbaum remarked), and worked their way up to retail and wholesale proprietorship. The Sephardim tended to gravitate into manual trades and modest shopkeeping. German Jews provided the first industrialists. In varying degrees, they all prospered during the war. Moving from their former lower-middle-class quarter in Villa Múñoz to the more fashionable Pósitos and Carrasco neighborhoods, they sent their children to universities, and increasingly into the professions. No obstacles barred their way. In recent decades, there have been Jewish senators, ministers and deputy ministers, directors of the central bank and the central tax-collection office, a rector of the university. Uruguay was the first Latin American government to recognize Israel. Since then, the two states have found much in common as small, democratic, quasi-Socialist nations.

From the beginning, each wave of Jewish immigrants followed the traditional ethnic pattern, organizing its own communal institutions. Thus, the East Europeans currently support twenty small, and three large, synagogues. The Sephardim maintain only one, although it is by far the largest and most beautiful in Montevideo. The Germans similarly maintain a large, handsome synagogue. Each community has underwritten its own social services. The East Europeans have also established three day schools that today are attended by students from all the Jewish communities—although not more than 20 percent of Montevideo's Jewish youngsters are registered in these institutions. A

Jewish program in Spanish, *Kol Zion en Uruguay*, broadcasts on the state radio station two hours each day at the choice afternoon siesta listening time, a privilege unmatched in any other Diaspora community. As in São Paulo, Rio de Janeiro, Mexico City, and Buenos Aires, a lavish sports-communal center, Maccabi, is the focus of social life.

In 1940, a unified organization, the Comité Central Israelita, was founded as Uruguayan Jewry's spokesman to the government. Its role was perfunctory for many years. The nation basked in a climate of democracy and toleration. After 1968, however, serious inflation began to undermine Uruguay's formerly stable economy. To the horror of the country's substantial middle class, outbursts of violence were launched by the Tupamaros, perhaps the most tightly organized leftist guerrilla group on the Latin American continent. For a while, the danger of a Communist takeover was quite real. It required four years of aggressive counterterrorist warfare before the military succeeded in quashing the Tupamaros. After that, the generals turned their attention to the "economic crimes" within the administration, and in 1975 overthrew the government altogether. Dissolving the legislature, the military regime systematically expelled "leftists" from the executive branches and from other public positions. The purge was bloodless. If there was a redeeming feature to the army junta, it was the officers' Brazil-like emphasis on technocracy, their rejection of totalitarian populism. The regime presented no threat whatever to the Jewish minority. Although some four thousand Jews had fled initially to Israel, most returned within the next two or three years and thereafter managed to achieve a modus vivendi with the rightist administration as easily in Uruguay as in Brazil. Afterward, Jewish life resumed as placidly, and as prosperously, as before.

The single lingering consequence of these political changes has been an intensification of Uruguayan Jewry's Zionist commitment. As in Brazil and Argentina, election contests for the Ashkenazic kehilla are waged between party "lists" identical to those in the Israeli Knesset. Leaders of Jewish institutions dutifully consult the Israeli ambassador—their status symbol—on matters relating not only to Israel but to domestic Jewish affairs. During the Middle East crises of 1967 and 1973, Uruguayan Jews rallied to Israel's aid, contributing over $1 million on each occasion, while nearly a hundred Jewish volunteers departed for Israel. Jewish education, both in the day schools and in some eleven afternoon and Sunday schools, has remained Israel-centered. So have Jewish dance fiestas, music, and art exhibitions.

"Sounds familiar by now," I remarked to Tenenbaum.

"I never suggested that Jewish life in Uruguay was uncomfortable," he replied. "It's simply . . ." He searched for a word.

"Parochial?"

"Dull."

Chile, the other middle-sized "European" component on Tenenbaum's Jewish map, is a somewhat different proposition. Its population of eleven million is stratified quite sharply between a criollo elite, 30 percent of the nation, and an impoverished mestizo majority. Its Jewish history is also to be differentiated from Uruguay's. Marranos figured prominently here among the early conquistadores and Jewish converts of the sixteenth century. Günther Böhm's volume, *Chilean Jews in the Colonial Period*, published by the National Academy, lists 150 names of marrano origin currently borne by aristocratic Chilean families. Religious toleration came late to this country—again in contrast to Uruguay. Freedom of religion was not explicitly recognized until the new constitution of 1925.

The first significant influx of professing Jews accordingly was quite recent. The newcomers arrived from Poland and Romania in the years immediately before and after World War I. This time they were welcome as white immigrants. The criollo aristocracy regarded immigration as essential to the nation's economy and racial composition. Later, in the depression years, the quotas for immigrants would be tightened. Yet even in the 1930s, fully 18,000 German Jews managed to find their way into the country, becoming Chile's single largest Jewish community. After World War II, 8,000 displaced persons and some 2,000 fugitives from North Africa and the Middle East augmented the earlier settlement. By 1970, approximately 30,000 Jews were living in Chile, two-thirds of them Central Europeans. Settling for the most part in Santiago, they rapidly achieved their characteristic eminence in commerce and played the major role in the establishment of Chilean light industry. With true Germanic discipline, they were swift and thorough in their linguistic acculturation. Their children and grandchildren comprised 4 percent of the student body of the University of Santiago, and most of these gravitated almost reflexively to law, medicine, music, or academia.

Although each group—German, East European, Sephardic—followed the traditional pattern of maintaining its own community, its own spectrum of synagogues and social welfare services, this was a more

Central European, a more "integrated" Jewry than Uruguay's, even as Chilean culture altogether was more sophisticated and attractive to Jews than its Uruguayan counterpart. By 1970, virtually all communal activities were conducted in Spanish, including a weekly Jewish radio hour. As in Uruguay and Brazil, the Jewish school system attracted only a minority of Jewish children; the German Jewish approach was to avoid "ghettoization." Meanwhile, interfaith relations in Chile were exemplary. So, too, were relations between the Chilean and Israeli governments. Here, as elsewhere in the West, Zionism served as the binding integument in Chilean Jewish life. If there was the faintest lingering reserve toward Israel among the German Jewish community, this was dissipated in the crisis and euphoria of the Six-Day War, and the warm Chilean national support for the Israeli defense effort.

Only three years after the June 1967 war, commitment to Israel suddenly was revealed as a farsighted personal investment. In 1970, an avowed Marxist, Salvador Allende, was elected president of Chile; and upon his inauguration, he embarked upon the nationalization of Chile's banks and largest industries. Although a small number of Jewish professionals had become active in Chile's leftist movement, and assumed office under Allende as middle-level technocrats, the new regime's policies were as terrifying to Jews as to other middle-class elements of the population. Not less than six thousand Jews fled to Israel or to the United States as the nationalization program developed.

The leftist era was a brief one, however. In 1973, the Allende government was overthrown by a military coup. Under the ensuing right-wing regime of General Augusto Pinochet, the nationalization of property was entirely reversed. Factories were quietly returned to their owners, to Jews and non-Jews alike. At that point, many of the émigrés returned, although the number of Jews in Chile did not reach 30,000 again, and possibly not 25,000. Their security appeared ensured as fully under the Pinochet autocracy as under the pre-Allende government. Indeed, the commander of the Chilean air force was a Jew, as was Chile's ambassador to Israel. Two or three hundred other Jews held administrative positions, served as deans and department chairmen in the nation's universities. To businessmen, the new economic atmosphere was especially appealing, for in 1975 the Pinochet government embarked upon a free-market, virtually laissez-faire, economy.

At first, the results of the new capitalism were impressive. Between 1977 and 1981, the GNP rose at the unprecedented rate of 7 percent a year. The Jews shared in the surging prosperity. Then suddenly, at the end of 1981, the boom collapsed. Chile suffered a catastrophic drop in exports and production, and the unemployment rate climbed to fully a quarter of the nation's work force. Until this setback, most Chileans had been prepared to overlook Pinochet's quasi-dictatorship, his repressive campaigns against leftists, in which as many as fifteen thousand persons were jailed. In 1982, however, the deterioration of the Chilean economy provoked a series of large-scale demonstrations against the military regime, and by 1983 the violence led to scores of deaths and thousands of additional arrests.

It is too soon to predict the future of the nation's Jews in the likely event of still another upheaval. Thus far, however, antisemitism does not appear to figure in the ideology or strategy of either Chile's Right or its Left. Perhaps this very silence testifies to the thoroughness of Jewish integration. It is a striking achievement for an otherwise insecure minority living in the midst of a proudly Europeanized society, winning acceptance from a criollo establishment that shares fully in the Latin *grandeza* of Argentina, directly to the east. And yet no contrast between Jewish communities in neighboring sister republics could possibly be more vivid.

Argentina: Chimerical Utopia on the Pampas

In July 1889, a German Jewish sanitary engineer, Dr. Wilhelm Löwenthal, was journeying by train through the Argentine province of Entre Rios. As the train stopped at a village depot, Löwenthal climbed down to stretch his limbs. His attention was drawn to a gathering of perhaps two hundred wretched-looking individuals clustered near the tracks. Literally in rags, their faces drawn and ashen, several of the emaciated men and women held out cups and hats to awaiting passengers. A number of their children appeared near death, their eyes glazed. Something in the beggars' accent, in their cast of face, evoked recognition. In German, Löwenthal asked: "Who are you?" Immediately, an older man stepped forward. "Is Your Honor perhaps a Jew?" he whispered, in Yiddish. The engineer nodded. "Help us, then," pleaded the elderly man. "When we came here several months ago, we were nine hundred. Now we are less than seven hundred. Our children and old people are perishing before our eyes." The tale the man subsequently related was a shock to Löwenthal. District officials later filled in the missing facts.

Only two years before, Julio Roca, president of Argentina, had dispatched agents to Europe to seek out cheap agricultural labor for his country. The vast plains of the interior were underpopulated, except for the backward, half-Indian gauchos. Europeans were needed. Learning of the suffering of the Jews in tsarist Russia, Roca's agents visited the Pale of Settlement. There they met with Jewish leaders and assured them that ample homesteads and excellent credit terms awaited any Jews who were prepared to settle in the Entre Rios province. The offer was widely circulated. Among the first to respond to it some months later were 130 Jewish families of Kamenets-Podolsk. The Alliance Israélite Universelle then took over the negotiations, and provided the largest share of the passage money. But when the Kamenets-Podolsk families at last reached Argentina after a two-month journey—from Odessa to Genoa to Buenos Aires—and arrived in Entre Rios province, they discovered that neither the owner of the promised tract (Moisésville, they had already named it) nor the government was prepared to offer financial support. The ensuing year turned out to be a nightmare for the immigrants. Adrift in a strange country, without seed or farm equipment, they soon were reduced to beggary in a country railroad station.

Hearing this story, Löwenthal emptied his wallet, then arranged for his employers to provide the forlorn Jews with temporary shelter. Later, upon returning to Europe, he immediately brought their tragedy to the attention of the Alliance. The Alliance in turn notified Baron Moritz de Hirsch, the railroad tycoon, and a man renowned for his generosity to Jewish philanthropies. De Hirsch promptly sent money to the Moisésville Jews. Several weeks later, the great financier had a brainstorm. Consulting the Argentine government with a number of agronomists, he set about organizing a charitable foundation to buy extensive tracts of land for permanent Jewish settlement in Argentina. Funded with $40 million of de Hirsch's private fortune, and titled the Israelite Colonization Association (ICA), the foundation would supply transportation, homes, farm equipment, and training for the new settlers.

Ultimately, the ICA purchased over 1.4 million acres—eleven vast tracts in Argentina as well as two in Brazil. Located along the perimeter of the humid pampa, the Argentine tracts were light in their soil texture and somewhat alkaline. Even so, de Hirsch was confident of their potential, if farmed intelligently. He was equally confident of his ability to bring to Argentina no less than 3 million impoverished Russian Jews during the next twenty-five years, and to transform them into a self-reliant agricultural race. Indeed, the fame of the ICA colonies became so widespread that some Russian Jews embarked for Argentina on their own to seek out their new homesteads. Yet they came in relatively small numbers. In 1891, the first year of the ICA experiment, only 1,348 Jews settled on its tracts. Nor did the immigration increase significantly in any future year. By 1927, the Jewish farm population in Argentina reached its highest figure of 33,084 persons, barely 1 percent of the massive transplantation de Hirsch had envisaged. The vocational patterns of the Diaspora evidently could not be transformed within the space of a single generation.

Nevertheless, the experiment was by no means an unqualified failure. As late as 1922, nearly a quarter of Argentina's Jews were working in agricultural communities, a higher proportion even than in Palestine, and they proved to be capable farmers. "[They] have nothing of the ghetto bend about them," marveled a visiting observer, Elkan Adler, in 1903. "Fearless and high-spirited, the boys and girls ride the horses bareback, and they at least are really attached to the land." The cooperatives the Jews organized for bulk purchase and sale and for crop loans were pioneering institutions in the Argentine countryside, and served as models for the Jewish banks that later would be established in the cities. As in Palestine, these settlers and their descendants eventually became an aristocracy of sorts among Argentine Jewry. Well into the 1960s, the community's leaders still tended to be drawn from the sons and grandsons of the original colonists.

Metropolis and the Challenge to Tradition

Of the numerous cities I visited in the course of my research and earlier travels, Buenos Aires may well have been the most fascinating. It was darkened and rationed in its meat supplies during my first trip, in 1974, and on the threshold of total economic collapse when I returned in 1982. During my second tour, its sidewalks and avenues frequently were in disrepair, its public buildings shabby, its citizens visibly threadbare. Yet, however faded, the elegance somehow remained, a unique architectural blend of Paris and Madrid, an intriguing amalgam of Italian intonation and provincial Mediterranean cuisine. Nothing in Europe itself, not even Vienna, struck me as so quintessentially fin-de-siècle as this flawed but still luminous outpost of Western humanism in a mestizo-Indian-black continent.

This was the tradition that Argentina in its entirety had embodied only seventy-five years earlier. It was still a land with seemingly inexhaustible supplies of grain and cattle, endowed with a superb ocean port and inland waterways, and with a relatively homogeneous, temperate, and literate white population that produced the largest middle class and one of the longest records of political stability in Latin America. Little wonder that in Spain and Italy, in the Balkans and southern Russia, Europeans responded to the inducements of Argentine immigration agents. Between 1890 and 1914, 4 million people migrated there. The largest numbers were Italians, followed closely by Spaniards. Of these, hundreds of thousands resumed their former livelihoods as agricultural laborers. Others built the railroads, erected the first factories and refineries in the industrial towns of the interior. By 1914, however, one in four of them was living in Buenos Aires, and almost half of Buenos Aires's 1.5 million inhabitants were foreign-born or the children of foreign-born.

Jews were the third-largest immigrant group. Indeed, of the 150,000 Jews in all of South and Central America by the First World War, 113,000 were in Argentina and 90,000 of these were already in Buenos Aires. Even after 1920, when immigration restrictions were gradually introduced, a significant number of East European Jews who were turned away from the United States managed to enter Argentina. Between 1890 and 1950, Argentina absorbed 5 percent of the total European Jewish migration overseas, and by far the lion's share within Latin America itself. This figure included some 45,000 Central European Jews who came during the Hitler era, and an additional 10,000 displaced persons who arrived after World War II. Yet even as early as 1935, not less than 175,000 Jews were already living in Buenos Aires— 80 percent of the nation's Jewish population.

During these same fifteen years after World War I, the Jewish farm settlement on Baron de Hirsch's ICA tracts crested, then steadily declined. The war and its immediate aftermath had opened out great prosperity for Argentine agriculture, and the value of the ICA farms had quadrupled. Many of the colonists began to press the ICA administration for title to the homesteads, often well before their eight-year apprenticeship had expired (a condition Baron de Hirsch had imposed to prevent land speculation). When the management decided to acquiesce, several thousand farmers sold out immediately and used the funds to open businesses in Buenos Aires. Others followed in ensuing years, animated not only by economic considerations but by the isolation and other hardships of the countryside. On the eve of World War II, less than seven thousand Jews remained on the ICA tracts. Twenty years later, the number was half that.

The movement from the countryside to the city was hardly limited to Jews. Discouraged by the land monopoly of the great *estancieros*, immigrants and natives alike flocked to Buenos Aires after World War I. Much to the discomfiture of the criollo elite, the hardworking immigrants soon took over much of the capital's retail and wholesale urban commerce. Even more unsettling to the aristocracy was the influx of an urban proletariat, whose members often brought Syndicalist or Socialist ideas with them from Europe. These elements were already at work in the prewar period, organizing unions, fomenting strikes. Jews were prominent among them. Many had shared in the revolutionary ferment of tsarist Russia. The majority were single men, and sexual frustration undoubtedly played a role in their political extremism. So did sheer distance from the Old World's religious influences. Most of the East European rabbis had gone to the United States. In Argentina, the void in Jewish spiritual leadership was filled increasingly by social activists. More than any other Diaspora community in the West, Argentine Jewry would foster a highly secularized and politicized culture.

The growth of this large, militant proletariat ended any lingering criollo illusions that European immigrants were indispensable as "whiteners" and "enlighteners" of the mestizo races. On May Day 1909, during a workers' demonstration in Buenos Aires, a Jewish anarchist murdered a local police chief. Retaliation was savage. Rioters attacked the Once quarter—the Jewish ghetto of Buenos Aires—raped several Jewish women, sacked Jewish shops. Even this violence was overshadowed by the outburst that followed a decade later, in January 1919. Alarmed by labor unrest, conservative elements published newspaper warnings against the "Jewish Bolshevik conspiracy." Whereupon police and right-wing agitators descended on the Once ghetto again, vandalizing shops and eventually killing sixty Jews and injuring hundreds more. In Argentine folklore, this episode is recalled as "La Semana Trágica," the tragic week. The wave of reaction that swept Argentina in the 1920s reached its climax in 1930, when a military coup under General José Uriburu overthrew the middle-class Irigoyen government. During the next thirteen years, the rural aristocracy tightened its grip on the nation. For the Jews and other Southeastern European peoples, the aftermath of the "Semana Trágica" brought tightening immigration restrictions until, by 1939, Argentina was all but closed to refugees from abroad.

Even for veteran Jewish settlers, the postwar repression discouraged political activity for the ensuing quarter-century. From 1919 on, rather, they tended to channel their Socialist convictions into Jewish communal life. Their leftist approach to social and religious issues was also vividly reflected in their literature. With the United States, Argentina emerged during this period as one of the two great centers of Yiddish language and culture outside Europe. Both in the capital and in the towns of the interior, the immigrant community supported an abundance of Yiddish-language libraries, of drama and lecture groups. As late as 1938, thirty-four Yiddish newspapers and periodicals were being published, many of them by unions and cooperative societies, and most of Argentine Jewry's literary writing first appeared in them. The Yiddish theater also played a major role in Jewish life. By the 1930s, four repertory companies were giving performances throughout the nation. Whatever the medium, themes of social protest became even more characteristic a feature of Yiddish literature in Argentina than in Western Europe. Jacobo Streicher's poems, Noé Vital's stories, Jacobo Aisenstein's novels, all lamented the workers' hard fate of poverty and oppression in Buenos Aires.

The Socialist ethic was equally apparent in Ashkenazic Jewry's highly organized welfare program, its cooperative loan banks, its powerful support for Labor Zionism. As far back as 1894, the East European immigrants established a cemetery and burial society, the Ashkenazi Chevra Kadisha, which soon afterward expanded into a complex of welfare institutions. In effect, this network became the kehilla, the communal organization for the East European majority in Argentina, which sponsored a wide variety of philanthropic, mutual insurance, and educational programs under the name Asociación Mutual Israelita Argentina. The AMIA's services included old age and orphan homes; facilities for the indigent and ill; a hospital, Ezra, which developed into one of the country's most advanced medical institutions. From the earliest decades of settlement, then, the emphasis upon social welfare influenced almost all Jewish communal activities, even the first B'nai B'rith lodges. Religious worship was distinctly secondary in the Ashkenazic community's sense of priorities. To be sure, Jewish social activism tended to become more domesticated and respectable than the fiery radicalism of the Jewish Communists. For some years between the world wars, the Communists battled aggressively for control of the kehilla, and with their characteristic tactics of stridency, obstructionism, and intimidation. It required almost superhuman forbearance for the kehilla's moderate majority to purge the radicals from organized Jewish life; but eventually they succeeded, in the mid-1930s.

During the same period, the Ashkenazic community was obliged to fight off a threat from another quarter. This was a small, but ruthless, Polish Jewish syndicate of white slavers. Until their arrival, prostitution had largely been monopolized by French entrepreneurs. The Jews proved to be even better businessmen. Pooling their financial resources in a kind of guild, the newcomers by 1909 controlled slightly more than half the nearly two hundred licensed brothels in Buenos Aires. Jewish women served as their madams, and Jewish immigrant girls often were recruited or lured into their hands as prostitutes. Outraged in turn by the cancer in their midst, Jewish vigilantes soon began raiding the white slavers' premises. Throughout the 1920s, physical battles were carried on in the bordellos, even in a small Yiddish theater used by the procurers as the showcase for their "actresses." Finally, in the early 1930s, Argentina's tightened immigration laws effectively undermined the white slavery rings by closing off their principal source of raw material. By 1934, the Jewish "guild" was out of business.

The German Jews meanwhile succeeded during the early 1930s in forming their own *Gemeinschaft* for the maintenance of synagogues and cemeteries, of loan funds, of old age and medical facilities. Their role in pioneering Buenos Aires's first B'nai B'rith lodge also produced important consequences for Jewish defense. It happened that, within a short period of its accession, General Uriburu's cabal began displaying a warm and vocal admiration for the Fascist regimes in Italy and Portugal. The implications of that friendship soon became apparent to the Jewish minority. "We had to respond quickly," explained Alberto Klein, "and with discipline and dignity."

A straight-backed little man of eighty-four, Klein was the son of German Jewish immigrants who had settled in Rosario in the latter nineteenth century. He had secured a degree in engineering at the

University of Buenos Aires, and later his success as a civil engineer won
him a professorship at the National Technical University. Klein's Jewishness was never an issue in his career, as evidenced by his membership on numerous government panels and commissions. Yet he was
also active in his Jewish affiliations, president of his synagogue, then of
Buenos Aires's first B'nai B'rith lodge. In the mid-1930s, when the
Uriburu government turned toward fascism, Klein realized that Argentina's Jews no longer could afford the luxury of fragmentation. Under
the aegis of B'nai B'rith, he and his fellow lodge members founded a
kind of Argentine anti-defamation league; then, in 1934, a more widely
based central organization to represent the various communities—Polish, Hungarian, German, North African, Aleppine, Damascene, Turkish, Rhodian, Balkan. Entitled Delegación de Asociaciones Israelitas
Argentinas—DAIA—the new body quickly won recognition as the authoritative spokesman of Argentine Jewry. Klein was elected its first
president. "From that point on, the government had to take us into
account as a united entity," Klein recalled. "We were already five percent of Buenos Aires, after all. Now we had an address."

The Two Faces of Juan Perón

The new united front was opportune, for the ensuing years of depression and World War II turned out to be hazardous ones for
Argentine Jewry. General Uriburu's military regime was buttressed in
its Fascist sympathies by the army command's long tradition of friendship with the German Wehrmacht. In 1943, a number of these officers
handpicked General Pedro Ramírez, a flagrant pro-Nazi, as the country's new president. Whereupon Ramírez immediately dissolved the
congress, restricted the press, and outlawed the nation's Allied support
organizations. As if these developments were not threatening enough to
the nation's precarious liberal heritage, there existed within the army a
number of younger officers, led by Colonel Juan Perón, who became
impatient with the narrow base of the Ramírez government, particularly
its unwillingness to attract the working classes by offering more extensive wage and unemployment benefits. This appeal to populism was a
dangerous political tactic in an increasingly volatile Latin country, but
Perón managed to bring it off. With widespread trade unionist support,
he maneuvered himself into the position of vice-president and minister
of war in 1944, and eventually into the presidency itself.

A handsome, charismatic man of Italian origins, Perón conceivably was influenced in his populist approach by his wife, Eva Duarte, a former radio actress of easy morals, whose insight into the Argentine masses was even more incisive than her husband's. Assured of large-scale national support, Perón at this point might have continued as a democratic president in the postwar era. Instead, he developed an increasingly authoritarian regime. In 1949 he summoned a constitutional assembly to legislate a vast increase in his powers and in those of the vice-president (soon to be his wife, Eva). Freedom of the press was now entirely abolished, and scores of newspapers were closed. Opposition political parties were subjected to close surveillance and their leaders frequently were jailed or exiled.

The worst of Jewish fears apparently were to be fulfilled in this regime of demagoguery and dictatorship. Issuing thinly veiled statements of friendship for the Axis during the war—and thereby provoking a United States embargo of Argentina—Perón accepted substantial quantities of Nazi assets after 1945 both to relieve the economic pressure of the American trade quarantine and to line his own pockets. In return, he quietly allowed some 7,500 fugitive Nazis to enter Argentina or to pass through the country before settling elsewhere in Latin America (Adolf Eichmann and Dr. Joseph Mengele were among these secret immigrants), and even appointed several ex-Nazis to important posts in the Argentine police and armed services. More ominously yet, Jew-baiting emerged as a popular tactic in Peronist mass rallies. A number of Jewish newspapers and printing houses were closed down. Although United States pressure after the war secured the abrogation of these measures, rallies against Jews and periodic defacements of Jewish institutions continued with little police interference.

In the meanwhile, Perón devoted his major efforts to the achievement of national economic self-sufficiency. Taxing the vast sums accumulated by Argentina's wartime cattle and wheat exports, the colonel-president invested heavily in industrial development. A high protective tariff was imposed on foreign manufactured goods. While programs of rapid economic expansion and diversification were hardly unprecedented among developing nations, this one was fatally undermined by indiscriminate wage handouts to the workers and lavish social welfare benefits channeled through Eva Perón's personal "foundation." As the Argentine balance of payments was wiped out, a disastrous inflation soon liquidated the real wage gains achieved by Argentine labor during Perón's first half-decade in power.

It was these reverses, combined with the defeat of Germany and a growing need for United States goodwill—and spare parts—that induced Perón to shift his approach to the Jews. Purging the Fascists from his government, he now began expressing his friendship for Jews and (after 1948) for Israel. Important public positions suddenly were opened to Jews. Angel Borlenenghi was appointed minister of the interior, Abraham Kirslavin became his subsecretary, and Liberto Rabovitch was named a federal judge. Several Jews were allowed to hold responsible positions in Perón's Justicialista Party. Notwithstanding their instinctive distaste for populist demagoguery, most Jews also appreciated that Perón at least was a strong man, and probably their best hope of restraining the "authentic" Fascists. Moreover, Jews had shared in the Argentine war boom. Their proletariat had largely disappeared and they were a middle-class community now. Although they suffered in common with other businessmen from Perón's bloated social welfare program, they could hardly disapprove the president's enforced industrialization and tariff protection. Many Jews had begun to thrive in the closed Argentine market, and a few even became millionaires.

The Banco Mercantil Argentino is a multistory steel-and-glass building in the heart of Buenos Aires's financial district. Julio Werthein received me in the top story's luxurious executive office. A plump, immaculately tailored man in his early sixties, he owned this bank. Werthein was the son of Bessarabian Jewish immigrants, the youngest of eight children who had been reared in Riveia, a small town eighty miles from Buenos Aires. From Riveia, his childhood was a succession of other small towns—Salbiquelo, Lago Epecuén, Charhué—where the family bought and operated modest hotels. In 1933, the year their father died, the Wertheins owned four.

Settled by then in Buenos Aires, the brothers had more ambitious plans for their future. Over the years, the pioneer Jewish cooperative credit associates had grown into full-scale banks, their loans playing a vital role in the Jewish business community. The two older brothers, Gregorio and Nino, already were operating their own small bank in the province of La Pampa, and had acquired several small ranches there. The venture succeeded handsomely. By 1933, then, the family envisaged banking and ranching, not hotels, as the basis of their future expansion. While a student at the University of Buenos Aires, Julio worked part-time at Banco Popular Israelita, learning the mechanics of higher finance in this largest of Jewish savings and loan institutions. His brothers moved ahead during the war period with a vigorous banking and land-development program. Eventually selling off their last two hotels in 1953, the Wertheins used the proceeds to organize an import-export company, El Pampero. One of their most profitable lines was television sets. When the Perón government imposed import restrictions, the brothers secured a license from the Dumont Company, opened their own television factory, and within two years became Argentina's biggest television manufacturer. Soon afterward, they obtained a franchise from the Allen Bradley Company, the world's largest manufacturer of electric resistors and circuit breakers. By 1960, the Wertheins were millionaires.

Even that late, some ten thousand Jews still operated market stalls in the Once ghetto quarter. But most had achieved their foothold as self-employed tradesmen, and many of their children were attending university. As elsewhere in Latin America, the German Jewish refugees of the 1930s were swiftly recouping their fortunes. Aided by the Peronist emphasis upon economic self-sufficiency, they emerged among the most successful light industrialists in Argentina. By the early 1950s, their mills and clothing factories were the nation's largest. Some Jews, both German and East European, were pioneers in food products, in lumber and steel, in printing and publishing houses. Others were achieving eminence as builders and developers. In growing numbers, Jews made their homes now in Buenos Aires's affluent Belgrano and Palermo quarters.

In 1959, meanwhile, the Wertheins purchased the controlling interest in a modest Buenos Aires bank, Banco El Hogar Argentino. Four years later, they sold it to a Spanish consortium, then used the proceeds to buy full ownership of Banco Mercantil Argentino, an institution with four small branches. The venture was a risky one. The new acquisition had lost 360 million pesos the year before and was nearly insolvent. Julio and his brothers would have to raise millions more to revive it. They did. By 1982, Banco Mercantil Argentino, twenty branches strong, had become the nation's twelfth-largest bank doing foreign business, and functioned as the only private bank in the country. Yet, from the outset, the Wertheins had regarded Banco Mercantil Argentino as the instrument with which to finance additional ventures.

In later years, their enterprises came to include ISA Fábrica, the largest woolen mill in Latin America; Valley Evaporating Company, a huge manufacturer of apple extract products and other dehydrated fruits for export; a major fashion house, and numerous subsidiaries in the clothing industry. By 1982, the brothers had structured the most diversified farming-business conglomerate in Argentina. "And even that isn't our principal activity," chuckled Julio Werthein. "Ranching and cattle is what we're mainly into these days. We've come full circle." They were estancieros, then, in the oldest Argentinian aristocratic, criollo tradition, with ten large ranches comprising 250,000 acres and 60,000 head of pedigree Angus cattle.

"How do you manage it all?" I inquired. "That's a lot of territory for one family to cover."

"Why, with our charter air taxi company for executives, of course," blandly replied this son of Yiddish-speaking Bessarabian immigrants.

From Perón to Perón: The Vulnerability of Chaos

The Peronist regime, the source of much of this new Jewish wealth, was nearing its end by the mid-1950s. Years of mismanaged government investment, featherbedding, wage increases, and social welfare programs had created fiscal chaos. Inflation was soaring out of control. The administration was becoming notorious for its corruption, as well, even as the church and the armed forces had growing misgivings about Perón's unsavory personal extravagances. Following the death of their beloved "Evita" in 1952, moreover, large elements of the working classes became disgruntled. Finally, in June 1955, a military coup drove Perón into exile.

During the following eleven years, the army, although nominally giving way to elected politicians, monitored the latter's actions for evidence of "Peronist" (that is, populist) backsliding. Intimidated by this threatening military presence, the civilian officials in turn failed to revive the nation's pillaged economy or to placate its restive industrial proletariat. Taking office in 1958 under Arturo Frondizi, a respected lawyer and veteran liberal, a cabinet of moderate centrists struggled for four years to reconcile fiscal stability with economic development and social reform. But when the president impulsively allowed the Peronists to reorganize their own party, the armed forces interceded, deposing him. Late in 1963, the military once again permitted a new

civilian government to take office, this one under the presidency of
Arturo Illia, a colorless hack politician. Illia's timidity, however, in coping with Argentina's strident union leadership threatened to open the
door to Peronism. Thoroughly exasperated at this point, the armed
forces deposed Illia and organized a military administration of their own
under General Juan Ongania. So ended all pretense to democratic government in Argentina. For the next eight years, the government functioned under military rule. The 23 million inhabitants of Latin
America's most sophisticated "European" nation once more found themselves living under the kind of regime associated with the lowliest Caribbean banana republic.

The two decades of alternating turmoil and autocracy in the post-
Perón era were the grimmest in Argentine Jewish history. Thousands of
Jewish small businesses were bankrupted. So were many Jewish banks
and credit cooperatives—and their failure in turn crippled a large
number of Jewish communal and educational institutions. More ominously yet, the post-Perón years were those of the Jews' most acute
political vulnerability. They learned then that even an elected civilian
government did not necessarily produce a democratic society. Rather,
their mortal enemy turned out to be chronic economic and governmental instability. Intent upon diverting worker unrest, the nation's right
wing tacitly countenanced underground hate groups that swelled in
numbers and boldness after the fall of Perón. Between 1955 and 1958,
pro-Nazi and other Fascist elements occasionally bombed synagogues
and defaced Jewish property. Even when Jews were momentarily encouraged by the election of the Frondizi government in 1958, their
optimism was cut short by the events following Israel's abduction of
Adolf Eichmann from Buenos Aires in 1960. Indignant at this violation
of national sovereignty, the Argentine government withdrew its ambassador from Israel. Eventually, the crisis between the two countries was
resolved through the good offices of the United States, and diplomatic
relations were restored. But the episode triggered an unprecedented
increase of antisemitic activity within Argentina itself. Firebombings of
synagogues and Jewish homes, beatings of Jewish adults and schoolchildren, increased sharply in 1961 and 1962.

The most notorious of the fringe elements was the Tacuara, an ultra-
nationalist group founded and led by a Jesuit priest, Julio Meinville.
Meinville's followers often were youths from the upper strata of Argentine society. Their political position was classically Falangist, in the

Spanish style, and was by no means aimed exclusively at the Jews, but rather at democratic ideology and institutions altogether. Yet, as always, the Jews served as the most convenient target, and particularly after the Eichmann episode, when the Tacuara launched into systematic attacks on Jewish property and individuals. More alarming even than these assaults was the government's indifference to them. Gang beatings of Jewish youths during the High Holidays in 1961 went unpunished. So did bomb and gun attacks against the Argentine press association and the University of Buenos Aires department of philosophy, both of these substantially Jewish in their membership. Hundreds of less widely publicized outrages against Jews occurred during the early 1960s.

Frondizi was too weak to move against this violence. And upon his overthrow in March 1962, the army-controlled Guido regime allowed the Tacuara and other gangs of right-wingers virtual carte blanche. Nazi-style rallies were mounted throughout the country. In June 1962, a group of Tacuara hoodlums abducted a nineteen-year-old Jewish university student, Graciela Sirota, as she was waiting for her morning bus. Knocked unconscious, she was stripped, burned with cigarettes, and her breast was incised with a swastika—"in revenge for Eichmann," an accompanying note declared. Although the girl's abductors were known, the police refused to file charges against them. They suggested rather that "left-wing" Jews had staged the episode. Outraged, the Jewish community of Buenos Aires responded to an AMIA—kehilla—appeal by engaging in a half-day strike. All Jewish businesses were closed. The gesture was effective. Embarrassed by it, President José Guido promised stern measures against future offenders. Yet the respite was a brief one. The attacks gained momentum again in 1963, and included the bombing of a synagogue and the machine-gunning of two girls inside.

The accession of the "liberal" Arturo Illia to the presidency in July 1963 brought no relief to Argentine Jewry. During Illia's tenure, antisemitic episodes occurred at the rate of nearly one a day. These included physical assaults, sniper shootings, fire and tar bombs thrown at synagogues, schools, and private homes, the desecration of cemeteries, threats by mail and telephone. In February 1964, a Jewish student was shot dead in his home by Tacuara members. Two years after the execution of Adolf Eichmann in Israel, Eichmann's son (also Adolf), twenty-four, organized the "National Socialist Party in Argentina," replete with a swastika and a promise to destroy "the oppressive rule of international Zionist Jewry." By then, a major element in the constellation of anti-semitic groups was the Arab League of Latin America. Organized in Buenos Aires by Hussein Triki, a Tunisian who had collaborated with the Nazis in World War II, the Arab League worked closely with the Tacuara, even helped subsidize the latter's anti-Jewish rallies. The DAIA—Jewish community council—and other Jewish spokesmen were in despair. All the more so, in 1966, when the military staged yet another coup under General Ongania, to snuff out civilian democratic government altogether. No institution in the country, not even the church, was as unremittingly reactionary as the army. Drawn essentially from the criollo elite, its officer class was prepared to exploit any technique necessary to suppress Peronist—that is, worker—unrest. Antisemitism was a time-tested one.

In his first months as president, then, Ongania canceled two decades of Jewish integration by the simple device of removing all Jews from civil service positions. Even as the Tacuara and other ultra-nationalist groups continued to run riot, the government itself in July 1966 launched a series of raids in the heavily Jewish business areas of Once and Calle Libertad, arresting eighteen officials of Jewish credit cooperatives for alleged peculation. Eventually the prisoners were freed for lack of evidence, but Police Chief Enrique Green, Ongania's brother-in-law, proceeded afterward to launch a "morality campaign" against "liberal atheism." To the shouts of antisemitic epithets, police attacked Jewish students and professors at the University of Buenos Aires. A spasm of fear passed through the Jewish community. Reflecting that anguish, the DAIA leadership transmitted a full account of Argentine Jewry's ordeal to Jewish leaders in the United States. It was at this point that Senators Robert Kennedy and Jacob Javits of New York urged President Lyndon Johnson to withhold recognition of the Ongania government. Johnson agreed. Given pause in turn by Washington's stern reaction, Ongania finally began taking firmer, if belated, measures against terrorism. A certain physical security at least returned to Jewish neighborhoods.

The respite continued for three years. Then, in 1970, responding to a new upsurge of student and labor unrest, the army deposed Ongania for another general, Roberto Livingston; and nine months after that, for still another, Alejandro Lanusse. Once more, in the midst of economic paralysis, of labor hostility and political chaos, Jews remained the favored right-wing scapegoat for the nation's ills. Antisemitic violence mounted throughout 1971 and 1972. It was accompanied this time by an exotic twist of propaganda. The Jews were accused of plotting the transformation of Patagonia, the southern third of Argentina, into a Zionist state. The charge was as gratuitous as it was inane. By then, the single Zionist address of any compelling interest to Argentine Jewry was the State of Israel itself. Between 1948 and 1972, not less than twenty thousand Argentine Jews departed for Israel, eight thousand of them during the post-Perón era.

An Uncertain Cultural and Religious Identity

The malaise of Argentine Jewry was intensified by a crisis of self-appraisal. In the earliest years of their settlement in Argentina, their social profile was almost exclusively one of ethnocentrism, following the old East European *shtetl* pattern. In those days, few homogenizing influences of any kind were at work in Argentine society, neither tax-supported public schools, universal military service, nor widespread industrialization with its attendant mobility of labor. The immigrant communities—Jews, Italians, Germans, Syrians—were left on their own, and tended in each case to perpetuate the Old Country's way of life. Thus, the various Jewish kehillas, with their elaborate skeins of educational, cultural, and welfare institutions, functioned as replicas of their East European Jewish predecessors.

The Ashkenazic kehilla, the AMIA, ultimately became the largest organized Jewish community in the Southern Hemisphere, and the fourth-largest in the Diaspora. Its headquarters currently are located in the heart of the Once district. An imposing, twelve-story structure, the AMIA building encompasses offices, lecture halls, classrooms, meeting rooms, a theater auditorium, and dining facilities for every variety of communal function. As late as the 1950s, the triennial AMIA elections were contested vigorously. But afterward, interest began to erode. The young, the native-born, the better-educated, tended to focus their interests increasingly on the attractive secular world of the university, the press, the theater. The decline of communal Jewish participation in Buenos Aires was largely paralleled in Córdoba, Corrientes, Paraná, Mendoza, Santa Fé, La Plata, and other provincial cities.

During the earlier years of the twentieth century, Jewish day schools had played a crucial role in sustaining Jewish identity. By 1967, however, only 17 percent of the Jewish school-age population of Buenos Aires was enrolled in these institutions. To some degree, the gap was filled by afternoon synagogue classes. But in that year the government increased the hours of instruction in state schools through the midafternoon; and, as a result, Jewish afternoon education immediately became unviable. Argentine Jewry responded to this crisis in the next half-decade with a prodigious "crash" program of fund-raising, school-construction, and teacher-training. For a brief period, the number of Jewish youngsters attending day schools climbed again, to nearly 60 percent on the elementary level. But the exertion could not be sustained. In common with the rest of the nation's middle classes, Argentine Jews were severely affected by the deteriorating economy. Only a minority of the day schools survived. Today, not more than 12 percent of Jewish youth receive any form of Jewish education whatever after the age of fourteen.

Under the circumstances, the influence of the synagogue normally would have been minimal. Yet there is less certainty about this prognosis than about any other feature of Argentine Jewish life. Much of the debate has focused on the role of an American rabbi, Marshall Meyer, whose presence in Buenos Aires since 1959 has exerted a curious impact upon the most thoroughly secularized Jewish community in the Western Diaspora. Many of the communal leaders whom I met regarded Meyer as arrogant and flamboyant, and my initial encounter with him tended to verify their reservations. We met at the rabbinical seminary he had established in Belgrano, the elegant upper-middle-class quarter where a majority of Buenos Aires Jewry lives. The seminary building was a sleek basalt-and-glass structure, its interior tastefully functional in decor and immaculately clean. Greeting me in his office, Meyer was in his early fifties, a chunky, clean-shaven man wearing a black turtleneck sweater and tan loafers. As we chatted, he put me off at first by his disconcerting fondness for Freudian and mod-sociological terminology. Yet his evaluation of recent Argentine Jewish history rang true.

The religious life Meyer had encountered upon his arrival twenty-two years earlier was a wasteland. With few exceptions, Argentina's two-hundred-odd synagogues were Orthodox, the thirty or so rabbis essentially recycled Hebrew teachers, most of them without formal seminary training. Preaching in the various languages of the Old World—Yiddish, German, Hungarian, Arabic, Ladino—they had little to offer the younger generation. Even as late as 1970, less than 10 percent of Argentina's Jews belonged to religious institutions of any kind; not more than 14 percent set foot in synagogues even for Yom Kippur services. Meyer was an unlikely candidate to reverse this trend. The product of a well-to-do family in Norwich, Connecticut, he had attended Dartmouth, then studied at the (Conservative) Jewish Theological Seminary. Following his ordination and a brief postgraduate stint, he sought a "challenging" pulpit overseas. Eventually, he was placed as assistant rabbi in Buenos Aires's Congregación Israelita, the largest Conservative synagogue in Latin America, and—with the CIP of São Paulo—the most prestigious. Centrally located on Calle Libertad in the heart of the city, it is a massive old stone building, its sanctuary as vast and intimidating as the Temple Victoire's in Paris. "The rabbi was a dignified old gentleman, Guillermo Schlesinger," recalled Meyer. "His congregants were the cream of Jewish society, but they were all aging, even then. There was no life there. Friday nights were moribund. There was no youth attendance whatever."

Meyer regarded the establishment of a youth group as his first priority. On his own, he raised money to open a summer camp (Ramah) outside Buenos Aires. He himself did much of the hammering and sawing, the cooking, teaching, and athletic instruction in the camp's first years. When a larger site became available outside Córdoba, he hurled himself into the effort once again. The project took off like a rocket. Today, the camp has a staff of forty, and the children of Argentina's most prominent Jewish families vie to attend it. In the meanwhile, chafing at the restrictions of the Congregación Israelita, Meyer launched into the formation of his own congregation. It began in 1962 with a nucleus of thirty families. Meyer's willingness to innovate, to introduce changes in the ritual, to involve lay people—particularly young people—in the services, proved to be effective. Within twenty years of its founding, the congregation, Beth El, had grown to over a thousand families, and was housed in an attractive modern building in Belgrano. I attended a Friday night service there. The sanctuary had seats for twelve hundred congregants. Twelve hundred seats were filled, at least a third of them by young people.

From the onset of his career in Argentina, moreover, Meyer was acutely aware of the dearth of younger, locally trained, Spanish-speaking rabbis to meet the shortage in Buenos Aires and the provinces, as well as in Latin America at large. In 1962, the year he organized his own congregation, he embarked upon the establishment of a Conservative rabbinical seminary in Buenos Aires. There were no premises, no trained faculty besides himself and a handful of local rabbis. Neither was there so much as a Spanish-Hebrew prayerbook in the Conservative tradition, certainly no textbooks in Spanish. Within the space of twenty years, Meyer solved these problems. A competent faculty was engaged, with the help of visiting professors from the Jewish Theological Seminary in New York. A respectable curriculum was devised. The text and prayerbook translations were completed. It was an achievement that removed the single most formidable barrier to modern rabbinical training in the Spanish-speaking world. Finally, Meyer raised the funds to transfer his seminary from its makeshift headquarters in an old house to its current premises in Belgrano. By 1984, twenty-six full-time rabbinical students from throughout Latin America were studying there. After graduation, they would staff new congregations opening in the provinces, as well as a number already functioning in the capital.

Well before then, Meyer had also projected a new image of the rabbi in Latin America by his vigorous spokesmanship for civil rights. Alone of the nation's senior rabbis, he publicly and repeatedly condemned the excesses of the military regime. By his persistence, he became the only rabbi permitted to visit Jewish political prisoners. The mandate was not an easy one. Meyer was stripped naked by the guards and searched in a particularly brutal and humiliating fashion. "It was worth it," he insisted. "Once I established contact with a prisoner, that person could no longer simply 'disappear.'" Unfazed by threatening letters and telephone calls, he continued to publish articles and to speak out on radio and television in behalf of human rights. Even his harshest critics acknowledged his courage. Watching him in action over the next few days, I was prepared to grant him his charisma. His version of Judaism breathed. It does not seem capable by itself of reversing the determined secularism of the Jewish majority, not even the erosion of their ethnic creativity. But history is not made by majorities.

In other spheres, auguries of that diluted creativity are less encouraging. The Yiddish theater, once embracing four repertory companies, has long since been reduced to intermittent performances at the AMIA auditorium. Its actors are foreigners now, essentially from Israel and the United States. Only a handful of Yiddish weekly newspapers survive. In recent decades, writings on Jewish themes have been pub-

lished almost exclusively in Spanish. Well and good, but these are
narrow in scope and theme. The best of the Spanish-language writers
belonged to an earlier generation. Thus, Alberto Gerchunoff's autobiographical novel, *Los gauchos judíos*, a highly romanticized version of
Jewish agricultural life on the pampas, became a classic that still is read
in Argentine schools. In the 1930s, the playwright and poet César
Tiempo (born Israel Zeitlin) dramatized a Jewish community in Buenos
Aires that had been integrated into Argentine society. Despite its bur-
lesque style, his best-known work, *Para la pausa del sábado* (For the
Sabbath Rest), was as optimistic in its own way as Alberto Gerchunoff's
novel, suffused with confidence in the future of Jewish life in Argentina.
It won the first Municipal Prize of Buenos Aires for poetry. A cofounder
of the Argentine writers' association, Enrique Espinoza (born Samuel
Glusberg), warmly affirmed his Jewish heritage in a series of elegant
short stories and essays. Espinoza's most important works dealt with the
pre-World War II period. So did those of Lazar Lischo, who was well
regarded for his tales of Jewish immigrant life on the farm colonies, and
for his poems limning the relations between Jews and Christians in Argentina.

In more recent years, the quality of Argentine Jewish writing declined as its mood darkened. By the time Marcus Soboleosky's novel
Enfermo la vid (The Vine Sickened) was published in 1948, the precariousness of the Jewish condition in Argentina was reflected in its
melancholy themes of intermarriage, cultural and psychological limbo,
and eventually suicide. It was this characteristic pessimism that suffused Bernardo Verbitsky's *Etiquetas a los hombres* (Labels for Men),
published in 1972. Again the protagonist was an intermarried Jew grop-
ing painfully, if sometimes fatiguingly, for his identity in Argentina.
From the 1960s on, the ablest Jewish writers preferred to devote themselves almost exclusively to Argentine topics or to narratives of torrid,
star-crossed love affairs. "We don't even have a Philip Roth to mock
us," muttered Simcha Sneh, a grizzled old Yiddish writer who scratched
out his weekly column in a tiny office of the AMIA building. "There's
hardly a writer left here who is prepared to write even negatively on
Jewish themes. It's a desert."

The Jewish community itself publishes journals and newspapers.
Since 1931, a Spanish-language weekly, *Mundo Israelita,* has been
widely read by the Sephardic community. For some twenty-five years,
the American Jewish Committee published an Argentine version,

Comentario, of its well-known American monthly. But together with a few lingering Yiddish weeklies, the combined sum of these newspapers and magazines represents a fifth of those published by South African Jewry, a far smaller community than Argentina's. Unlike the United States, where the condition of Jewishness has long been a favored literary theme, Jewish culture in Argentina is regarded as parochial. Jewish intellectuals are by no means lacking. Indeed, they remain extremely influential in the arts and journalism. Jews comprise 20 percent of the university student body, attend medical and law schools freely, and are widely represented on university faculties. But if few of these younger people are consciously intent upon "assimilating" into Argentine culture, fewer yet—Marshall Meyer notwithstanding—appear to be interested in identifying affirmatively with Jewish culture.

A certain ethnic cohesiveness is offered by the Hebraica Sports and Community Center. The inspiration for its later counterparts in São Paulo, Rio, Santiago, and Mexico City, the Hebraica was founded in 1926, and during the war boom opened its own building in the heart of Buenos Aires's Once district. It is a massive, fourteen-story edifice containing lecture halls, a well-stocked library, an auditorium, a film theater, as well as extensive sports facilities. The evening I visited, bulletin boards in the lobby announced an impressive schedule of lectures and musical performances. I looked in on several of these. They were sparsely attended, mainly by older people. The gymnasium, the ballet rooms, the swimming pool, were a different story. These had been taken over wall to wall by the younger generation. Several years earlier, a country club had been added to the Hebraica's portfolio of offerings. "Jewish 'culture' at the Hebraica?" I could still hear old Simcha Sneh guffawing. "It's a sport and social center, pure and simple." Pure or simple, its social function is not altogether to be scoffed at. It provides a central meeting place for young Jews.

Doubtless there are others. Marshall Meyer's synagogue and camp are among them. Several B'nai B'rith lodges throughout Argentina are active, and even socially quite prestigious. Nonetheless, in their eagerness to join the mainstream of Argentine life, Jews unquestionably have been leaving their Jewishness behind. Cultural pluralism is in any case difficult to maintain in this essentially monoracial society. No official statistics are kept on intermarriage, but the most commonly cited figure is 30 percent for Buenos Aires, and nearly twice that for many of the smaller cities. In the towns of the interior, the rate evidently approaches 100 percent.

Here as elsewhere in the Diaspora, however, Zionism has managed to infuse some of the vacuum of Jewish identity. The movement quickly took root among Argentine Jewry, its first societies dating back to 1897. An early competitor was the ICA colonization project on the pampas; but with the latter's demise, the principal ideological competition took place between the Zionists and the Socialists—and in time Labor Zionism emerged as an acceptable compromise. Once Israel was born, too, Jewish pride and security were fortified by the amiable relations that developed between Argentina and Israel (with the exception of the Eichmann episode). From Perón to the military regimes of the 1960s and 1970s, diplomatic and cultural exchanges were frequent, and reasonably well reported in the local press. Even the most thoroughly acculturated Argentine Jews identified fullheartedly with Israel. Julio Werthein, his walls festooned with letters from political leaders and financiers on two continents, reacted to Israeli appeals very much as did Leon Feffer in São Paulo. The year of Israel's birth, Werthein established a fruit concentrate company, Pricuz, outside Tel Aviv; later, he sank a small fortune into Clal, an Israeli investment company. Gregorio Werthein served for nearly a decade as president of Israel Bonds in Argentina. Noel Werthein was the latest of the three brothers to serve as president of ORT, the worldwide vocational training program that gave its heaviest emphasis to Israel. Gregorio and Nino Werthein endowed a wing of the biology building at Tel Aviv University and Nino Werthein built Casa Argentina, a guesthouse, on the campus of the Hebrew University of Jerusalem.

Even among the middle class, few Jewish families hesitate to contribute generously of their funds and energy on behalf of Israel. The rallies and volunteering during the 1967 and 1973 Middle East wars were exceeded by few other Jewish communities. The Israeli ambassador has been an esteemed patron at every major Jewish function. Since 1956, the Israeli party list system has been incorporated directly into elections for AMIA, the Ashkenazic kehilla. However bizarre the transplantation of Israeli-style politics to an aging and shrunken Diaspora electorate, the phenomenon is evidence again of the gravitational field projected by the revived homeland. It is less a cultural projection, conceivably, than a pragmatic one. For since the 1960s, Argentine Jewry, like South African Jewry, has regarded Israel as its ultimate guarantee of sanctuary.

Civil War and a Search for Refuge

In July 1981, the Association of Latin American Immigrants in Israel made the initial contact for me. It was not a simple matter. Mauricio Helfman* was skittish and reluctant to be interviewed. But after a little persuasion, he agreed finally to talk to me the next afternoon. We met at a coffee shop near the Habimah Theater. In his early thirties, Mauricio was tall, round-faced, and wore a thick handlebar mustache. A burly older man accompanied him. Together, they gave me the once-over, then scrutinized the coffee shop and the approaches to it from both ends of the street. Afterward, the companion took up a position near the corner, scanned the neighborhood again for several minutes, and finally departed. "My control," explained Mauricio, in heavily accented Hebrew. "If I don't report back to him in three hours, he and others will want to visit you."

Mauricio's maternal grandparents were pioneer Jewish settlers in Córdoba, arriving shortly after World War I. They were veteran Bundists, and Mauricio's mother, a schoolteacher who settled in Buenos Aires, and his father, a stitcher in a Buenos Aires handbag factory, shared this Socialist tradition. Mauricio and his younger sister, Laura, did not set foot in a synagogue throughout their youth. In 1964, Mauricio enrolled at the University of Buenos Aires, one of 16,000 Jews who were registered there, fully 20 percent of the university's huge student body (Jews comprised 1 percent of the Argentine population of 23 million). Those of Mauricio's friends who were Jewish fully shared his radical political interests. During the Six-Day War crisis in 1967, he experienced a tremolo of Jewish awareness and joined an ultraleftist Zionist youth group. The flirtation with Zionism was brief, although through it he met Felicia Cohen, whom he married in 1970.

Within the year, Mauricio found himself involved in "straightforward" radical activities again, pasting Communist slogans on walls, distributing handbills secretly to his fellow students. In 1971, he joined his comrades in locking a right-wing professor in his classroom. They were all arrested and sentenced to a week's detention. Four of the eleven jailed students were Jews. "A high proportion," Mauricio admitted, "but that was our tradition. We had been raised to protest social injustice, and there was plenty of it in Argentina. We saw entire families sleeping in metro stations. The military oligarchy hounded them from

---

*At the request of the subject, the family name has been changed to protect relatives in Argentina.

pillar to post. Who could sit still for that sort of thing?" If few Jewish students were leaders of radical organizations, they comprised an important minority within them.

Mauricio and his comrades were products of the chaos that developed in the 1970s. By 1973, the nation had reached a political crossroads. For eighteen years civilian government and intermittent military regimes had proved either inept or lawless. Perón's party had been outlawed during that time, but Peronism itself manifestly remained a vital force among the workers. No other figure could match the ex-president's near-mystical appeal. In the election of 1973, with the country already in turmoil, the army no longer dared risk a revolution by denying Peronists the right to campaign. The latter triumphed decisively. Soon afterward, Perón returned from exile in Madrid to become president once more. By then he was seventy-eight years old, his dyed hair and fixed smile barely disguising his physical exhaustion. Elected with him as vice-president was his new wife, Maria Estela (Isabelita) Martínez, a former cabaret dancer. The most dedicated of his followers were young leftists in the Montonero guerrilla organization, who were convinced that he would set the government on a revolutionary Fidelist course. But others among the president's supporters were right-wingers—businessmen, ranchers, even a few army officers—who expected him to restore some degree of order and stability to the nation. Before Perón could manage to reconcile these conflicting forces, he died, in July 1974.

He was succeeded by his widow, a pitiable, hysterical figure who almost immediately became the puppet of her minister for social welfare, José López Rega. A committed reactionary, López Rega set about violently purging leftists from the government and the party. The latter fought back no less violently. The reign of murder, kidnapping, and other forms of terror continued between the right and left wings of the Peronist movement, until the army eventually lost patience with the facade of "Isabelita" and with López Rega. In 1975, it deposed the president and her advisers and established yet another military junta, this one under the presidency of General Jorge Videla. Henceforth, there was no further pretense to constitutional or representative government of any sort. Under a proclamation of martial law, crimes involving "national security"—a term that was very broadly defined—would be tried by military courts, with the accused persons subject to indefinite imprisonment without the right of habeas corpus. Not even the Ongania regime of 1966 had been quite this implacable.

At the time of Perón's death, the Montoneros and other leftist fringe groups may have numbered 400,000. Operating as guerrillas, they were responsible in 1974 for at least 1,100 political murders, and in 1975 for twice that many. Entire families often were wiped out in these lethal forays. Accordingly, with the tacit support of "respectable" society, the Videla military regime embarked on a drastic and no less ruthless countercampaign against the guerrillas. In some provinces, thousands of troops fought thousands of Montoneros. It was civil war. Mauricio Helfman was fully involved in it by then, although with growing misgivings about the brutality of his own FAL—Trotskyite—group. In December 1975, this unit made preparations for a large-scale attack against the army camp of Monte Chingolo, north of Buenos Aires. On Christmas night, covered by tarpaulins, Mauricio and 150 of his companions set out for the camp in a procession of fuel trucks. Once they reached Monte Chingolo, however, the army was waiting. The guerrillas were ambushed and at least one hundred of them were killed. Only nine, including Mauricio, succeeded in escaping.

Mauricio reached his own apartment in the small hours of the morning. His two-year-old daughter was sleeping. His wife Felicia regarded him in cold terror, but said nothing. Later in the day, Mauricio reported to the cell's secret headquarters across Plaza Irlanda. Two other survivors were there, reporting to the unit leader, a hardened guerrilla known simply as Lucio. They informed him that his own girlfriend, Piojo, a brave and dedicated comrade, had been killed. She had been three months pregnant. Lucio said nothing for a moment. Then, filling his glass with whiskey, he remarked coldly: "Long live the revolution!" At that moment, Mauricio realized that he had had enough. He could not live with this callousness. The terror was becoming mindless on both sides.

His decision coincided with the government's climactic offensive against the Montoneros. The campaign included massive arbitrary arrests, torture, abductions, and murders. Often the prisoners had had little or nothing to do with left-wing activities. Among those held were honest liberals, intellectuals, priests, exiles from other Latin American countries. Nevertheless, in common with captured guerrillas, they were murdered or simply disappeared. Prisoners who were Jewish often were subjected to an extra refinement of brutality. This knowledge, too, was sobering to Mauricio. Then, in September 1976, he learned that the entire leadership of his cell had fallen into the hands of the police. Fearing that they might divulge his name under torture, he decided to leave the country immediately.

The problem was to find a safe haven. As Mauricio saw it, there were three possibilities: Cuba, Angola, or Poland. Any one of these Marxist regimes would accept a political fugitive from Argentina. He discussed the matter with Felicia. She would have none of it. Pregnant again, she was not about to expose her children to another dictatorship, whether of the Right or the Left. It was at this point that Israel came to mind. In fact, the idea had already occurred to several thousand other Jews, but hardly for reasons of Zionism—or radicalism. Most of them were small businessmen. Like their Gentile counterparts, they were facing ruin. It was not the government they were fleeing, but the leftist groups, the "living curse" that had destroyed their livelihoods and security. Of the 6,000 Jews who departed in 1975 alone, radicals like Mauricio were in the minority. But whatever their motives, not less than 35,000 Argentine Jews were living in Israel by 1981.

Mauricio established his contacts in early October of 1976. At the local Jewish Agency office, the Israeli representative warned him that, as one whose passport had been confiscated at the time of his arrest as a student, Mauricio faced a serious risk in trying to leave the country. For that matter, Israel might jeopardize its relations with Argentina by issuing him a visa. In some anguish, Mauricio replied that Israel was his one alternative to certain death. "Israel cannot abandon me," he pleaded. The Jewish Agency official was less than moved by this appeal. He had had his fill of these leftist fugitives who had cared little or nothing about Israel all these years. Now, suddenly, they were becoming instant Zionists. But in the end, he promised to look into the matter.

Three days later, the Israeli sent a messenger to Mauricio's flat. The Helfmans were to make ready quickly. They would depart that very evening on the night ferry up the La Plata River to Montevideo. A passport was not required for travel to Uruguay, and in Uruguay many things could happen. Packing swiftly, then, Mauricio and his wife bade hurried goodbyes to their families. The leavetaking from Mauricio's sister Laura was painful. Following her brother's earlier example, Laura had recently joined the FAL and was fully committed to its goals. Mauricio's heart ached for her, but there was no time for appeals or warnings. The ferry was waiting. The young couple and their daughter embarked. It was an overnight journey. The next morning, they arrived safely in Montevideo. Registering at a prearranged hotel, they were driven that night to the city's Jewish Agency office. There they were supplied with Israeli laissez-passers and airline tickets. Flying out of Uruguay the next day, they landed in Israel thirty-six hours later.

The Jewish Agency arranged housing for the family. The Association of Latin American Immigrants found Mauricio employment as an assistant manager of an appliance store outside Tel Aviv. He saw it as a way of marking time. Once the revolution toppled the Argentine junta, he would return home to Buenos Aires. A year passed. The military government remained unshaken—and evidently all but unchallengeable. It was Laura who provided Mauricio with the facts of life. Her letters arrived weekly, always from a different address and over a different signature. She remained active in the movement, she explained, but took no part in its military actions. Fewer of these were taking place, in any case. The government was tightening the vise, capturing and disposing of the best comrades, gradually breaking the back of the radical movement. Some twenty thousand "subversives" or "ideologically tainted" people had been killed or had disappeared. Most of them were no more than honest liberals. It was a grim period for the nation.

A year and a half went by. On March 25, 1978, Mauricio received a letter from a family friend in Buenos Aires. Two weeks earlier, the man wrote, an automobile had pulled up to Laura as she waited at her accustomed bus stop. Two men in black masks had seized her and carried her off. The abduction was typical of the secret service. Possibly it had been intended as an act of government revenge for Mauricio's departure. So far, there had been no word from Laura. Nor was there ever to be. The mother, half mad with grief, was still knitting sweaters for her missing daughter. The father, broken, said nothing. "Laura, my baby sister, twenty-four years old," murmured Mauricio, his voice barely above a whisper. "The day I came here, I signed her death warrant."

The Case of Jacobo Timerman

The darkest period of military rule followed the overthrow of the "Isabelita" Perón government, in 1976. In fact, the junta's relentless countercampaign against Montoneros and other leftist Peronists was only partially responsible for the brutality of suppression. Chaos within the government itself was also a factor. Under General Videla, the senior officers organized their personal domains, each commander functioning as an independent warlord in the fiefdom under his control, each responsible for his own prisoners. The rightist terrorism of the generals and admirals was not directed specifically against Jews, although fully nine hundred Jews were among the lists of "disappeared" prisoners, and those who survived continued to be singled out for particularly harsh interrogation and other privations. After 1973, moreover, antisemitism appeared to shift from random violence against Jewish property and individuals to a more widespread, if more subtle, press and propaganda offensive against the Jews as a community.

The campaign became evident in the Videla government's reaction to a series of "Jewish scandals." One episode involved the Madanes family, principal owners of the great Aluar aluminum corporation, whose name was placed under a cloud for reputed questionable transactions. Then came the Gelbar scandal, involving the first Jew to serve in a Perón cabinet. The cases were interrelated. In May 1974, José Ber Gelbar, a major stockholder in Aluar, was accused of graft in accumulating the fortune required for purchasing his vast investment. He fled to the United States, allegedly with millions of embezzled dollars. In May 1977, the Argentine government sought his extradition. Two years later, as the case was being litigated in American courts, Gelbar died. By then, he had become a central figure in Argentine press accounts of a "Jewish conspiracy" to sap the nation's economy. Gelbar was described as the mentor of David Graiver, who was involved in still another "scandal."

The Graiver affair in fact was the linchpin of these interrelated charges. David Graiver had originally married the daughter of a Buenos Aires construction tycoon, then used her dowry to purchase his first bank in La Plata. In 1971, at the age of thirty, he bought his way into the post of deputy minister of social welfare. His connections and influence grew. With several other Jewish investors, most of them Mexican, Graiver used his family bank to purchase controlling shares of the American Bank and Trust, a major New York financial institution. He then skimmed $50 million out of ABT, precipitating its collapse and the liquidation of $180 million of its deposits. Most of the American depositors were insured, but the Mexican Jewish investors were not. And several other losers, as it happened, were generals in the Argentine government cabal. The scandal rocked the Argentine financial community. Graiver was in Mexico then. A warrant for his extradition accordingly was issued. But in August 1975, a private airplane in which he was flying crashed into a mountain near Acapulco. When his second wife immediately ordered the recovered body to be cremated, the suspicion mounted that Graiver was alive.

In the meanwhile, the Argentine government took Graiver's parents, wife, brother, and other members of his family into custody, where they remained without being formally arraigned for personal involvement in the swindle. It is likely that they were hostages in the event that Graiver was still alive, for the charge against him was much more far-reaching than simple embezzlement. He was accused of having served as the banker for the Montonero terrorists, of paying them interest of $14 million on capital the family had invested for them. So far, there was no hard evidence of this complicity. Under financial pressure, however, the family attempted to sell its 45 percent share of the news magazine *La Opinión,* edited by Jacobo Timerman, and it emerged that the Graivers were the principal minority shareholders in Timerman's influential journal. Timerman himself was taken into custody the very week members of the Graiver family were arrested. As matters turned out, he, together with Graiver, Madanes, Gelbar, and other prominent Jews, was not only a convenient target for distracting public attention from government brutality and ineptitude, but also the object of government revenge.

The oldest of eight children, Timerman was born in Poland and brought to Argentina at the age of five. His father died as a comparatively young man. His mother went to work as a street vendor. For a while, young Timerman served as janitor of the building in which the family received its lodgings. An intelligent, ambitious youth, he secured a position in 1950 as reporter for *La Razón,* a major evening newspaper, and within four years achieved his own signed column. By 1958, widely respected as a journalist, he won financial backing to launch *Primera Plana,* a kind of Argentine version of *Time.* Succeeding in that venture, Timerman then sold out, buying a series of other newspapers, nurturing each of them to a respectable circulation, then selling them for a handsome profit. In May 1971, he launched into the publication of *La Opinión.* Modeled after the Paris daily *Le Monde,* the paper became the organ of intellectuals, liberals, and moderates. It accurately reflected the ferment in Argentine political life, as well. In 1973, *La Opinión* initially supported the regime of General Alejandro Lanusse, but then suddenly shifted its support to the Peronists. It was a shrewd gamble. The Peronists won.

Assured of the benevolence of the government, of substantial quantities of government advertising, *La Opinión* prospered. In 1974, with cash borrowed from David Graiver, Timerman built a large, modern printing plant. Then Perón died and the corrupt Isabelita–López Rega regime took over. Once it became clear that the government could not survive the spreading anarchy, Timerman began editorializing in favor of a military coup to restore order. And when the Videla junta assumed power, Timerman promptly supported it, conveniently looking away from the horrors of extortion, mass abduction, torture, and murder. Several months later, to his credit, Timerman did in fact begin to report the atrocities of the military cabal. It was under these circumstances, with the Graiver scandal and the evidence of the earlier Graiver-to-Timerman loan, that the government in 1977 acted decisively to remove Timerman from the public scene.

In April of that year he was arrested. Unlike an earlier period of brief custody and questioning upon the detention of the Graiver family, the publisher this time was locked in prison. Without being informed of the specific charge against him, he was subjected to intermittent periods of torture. Few beyond his family raised questions about his imprisonment. His professional colleagues chose to remember his political contortions, his wheeling and dealing. Eventually, Timerman was brought before a military tribunal, where he was accused of complicity in the Graiver affair, and then cleared for lack of evidence. Still he was kept in prison, interrogated, and tortured—but this time to reveal his involvement in "the Zionist conspiracy against Argentina." In November 1977, he was stripped of his civil rights and control over his assets, and *La Opinión* was taken over by the military.

Finally, in April 1979, Timerman was released from prison, but kept under house arrest in Buenos Aires. The internment was imposed notwithstanding a supreme court decision in July 1979 that his original arrest and continued detention were illegal. It was only then that protests finally were heard from overseas, from Amnesty International and the International League for Human Rights, from President Ephraim Katzir of Israel and President Jimmy Carter of the United States. The accumulation of these pressures registered. In late September 1979, following a second supreme court decision against the government, the military regime came up with a solution. It annulled Timerman's citizenship and exiled him from the country. Whereupon the publisher boarded an airplane and flew off to Israel to join his family, which had preceded him there.

In Israel, Timerman immediately set about chronicling his ordeal. The account, *Prisoner Without a Name, Cell Without a Number*, was a skillful job, hardly less than a prose poem about the force of life against the Nazi force of death. Laying his major emphasis upon the antisemitism of his captors, Timerman insisted that it was his Jewishness and his undisguised Zionism that his interrogators most resented and feared. Whether or not this was true, his description of the gauntlet of bigotry he endured was both harrowing and convincing. Yet the evidence was also compelling that Timerman's Jewishness had less to do with his initial imprisonment than with his ultimate release, when State Department and White House officials had interceded on his behalf essentially as a victim of antisemitism. Timerman may have been closer to the mark in charging that the Argentine Jewish leadership had displayed timidity, even cowardice, in failing to protest his imprisonment. Before his arrest, he wrote, Dr. Nehemia Reznitzky, president of the DAIA (the central Jewish council), had urged him not to protest every alleged injustice of the military regime. Better to protest "some" injustices, he was cautioned, and to remain silent about others. This was a *Judenrat* mentality, Timerman argued.

Despite the man's flamboyance, his well-developed ego, the glaring silence in his book about his close financial relationship with David Graiver (the most far-reaching scandal in the history of Argentine Jewry, after all), his trivialization of the Holocaust by a disingenuous equation of Argentine Jews with European Jews under the Nazis—despite all these lapses and excesses, Timerman could not be dismissed in his exposure of Argentine Jewish leadership. Many Argentine Jewish intellectuals similarly criticized the establishment newspaper, *El Mundo Israelita*, for its near-total silence on the question of human rights. Nor was Timerman exaggerating the reaction of Bernardo Fain, legal adviser to the DAIA, who had equably observed that Timerman's continued imprisonment, following the initial supreme court order for his release, was "not necessarily illegal."

I discussed the behavior of the Jewish leadership with Fain. A slim, youthful-looking man in his early fifties, a native of Buenos Aires, Fain had acquired considerable experience as an administrative lawyer, including a stint as a state attorney-general in Neuquén, then as president of an audit court in Buenos Aires. He knew his way around the bureaucracy. "I'm the first to admit that the DAIA has only the most limited influence with the military junta," he explained forthrightly. "The best we can do is simply maintain as friendly a relationship as possible with various individuals in the government." For Fain and his colleagues, there were priorities to be maintained. One of them definitely was not the fate of an "operator" like Jacobo Timerman. The welfare of other prisoners had to come first. "For years, we've been interceding quietly with the government on behalf of about one hundred fifty missing Jewish prisoners. We no longer have any illusions about those who have disappeared. But if there are surviving prisoners we know about, we can be reasonably sure at least that they don't disappear." It was Marshall Meyer's argument, and no doubt valid.

It was equally certain that the DAIA's posture, if often gratuitously restrained, was by no means that of a *Judenrat*. When the military regime made noises about reinstating Catholic instruction in the public schools, the DAIA vigorously and successfully protested (much to the gratification of Argentina's Protestants). From the beginning, the DAIA identified itself unreservedly with Israel, and organized protest meetings on behalf of Soviet Jews and Jews in Arab lands. In 1981, embarrassed by the hue and cry raised in the United States by the Timerman book, the government asked the DAIA if it would issue a statement repudiating Timerman. The DAIA board members flatly and unanimously refused. There was no retaliation. "It's difficult to prophesy," reflected Fain, slowly and carefully, "but my instinct tells me that we're on the other side of the crisis now. We're all breathing a little easier."

Fain's "instinct" was based on signs that presumably he was expert in reading. The manifest loyalty of Argentine Jewry during the Malvinas (Falkland) Islands crisis evidently had registered on the public. There had been extensive press and television coverage of six young rabbis, in army fatigues, at the front line with Jewish troops. Julio Werthein joined a blue-chip commission of leading Argentinians that flew to Washington to explain Argentina's position. At that moment, too, Israel was forthcoming in the sale of airplanes and weapons systems to the Argentine air force. Gratitude to Israel spilled over in some degree to the local Jewish community.

Under the circumstances, Argentine Jewry now finds itself less at bay than in the 1960s and 1970s. Numbering some 250,000 in 1984, it remains the sixth-largest Jewish community in the world and plays an important role in Argentine economic and cultural life. Sociologists are inclined to regard the gravest threat to Argentine Jewish viability as demographic rather than political. It is the old story: of a low birth rate, an aging population, rising intermarriage, and substantial emigration. But for those who remain, settled comfortably in Buenos Aires's Belgrano or Palermo quarters, maintaining servants and vacation houses in Punta del Este, Uruguay, there is no sense of urgent danger. Their future status probably will depend less upon political liberalization than upon the recovery of the Argentine economy. Here the prognosis remains unfavorable. Inflation currently is running at 350 percent a year, and there is little compensating economic development at any level. No minority, least of all the Jews, can function with self-assurance in a nation where hunger is a tangible presence. "I feel myself a second-class citizen," admitted Elias Zviklich, a lawyer and president of the B'nai B'rith Council of Argentina. "Anyone who tells you otherwise is living in a dream."

Was Zviklich exaggerating? He had encountered no difficulty in being accepted in law school and practicing law, nor had any of his Jewish friends in studying and practicing law, medicine, or engineering. "It may be changing," warned Leonardo Senkman, a young professor at the University of Belgrano, and chairman of that institution's modest Judaic studies program. "Laicism still functions in the municipalities. The public schools are safe. But the universities are national, and that depends on the government of the moment. Presently, the regime is sending up trial balloons about the need for 'good Catholics' in the academic administration. Some antisemitic deans are beginning to come in. The situation isn't serious yet—nothing like the López Rega period—but it bears watching."

"And yet you accept the government," I reminded him. "It doesn't seem to frighten you."

"Because internally, at least, it's getting more efficient," Senkman explained. "We can live with an efficient autocracy, one that at least keeps antisemitic hooliganism off limits. Democracy, on the other hand, very rapidly becomes anarchy in this country. That's our danger."

"But Timerman . . . ?" I left the question uncompleted.

Leo smiled wryly. "We fear a Sirota affair [the girl whose breast was incised with a Tacuara swastika] more than a Timerman affair. Where there is order, at least we know where we stand. With the civilians, the Peronists . . ." The mob? He shook his head.

It was a curiously nineteenth-century Jewish answer. But this was a nineteenth-century land. The wisest old Jew I met in Argentina confirmed Senkman's evaluation. Mark Turkow, the retired former director of the World Jewish Congress in Latin America, was a man in his eighties. Profoundly cultured in many languages, spare as a white-headed bird, he sat before his extensive private library and reviewed his half-century of public service in this land. "Leo is right," he nodded, tapping Senkman's knee. "Political chaos is our enemy, not autocracy." In so many words, Turkow intimated his distinct lack of enthusiasm for the free national elections promised by the military for the autumn of 1983. He had seen many, far too many, of those charades in his life-time.

"Is there a future for Jews in this land?" I asked bluntly.

Understanding well that he would appear in my book, that he was obliged to continue living in Buenos Aires, he shrugged. "It depends," he murmured.

I asked the identical question of Maximo Yagupsky, director emer-itus of the American Jewish Committee office in Argentina. Also a man in his eighties, Yagupsky turned his head discreetly, gazing down at the flood of traffic on Calle Libertad. Half the shops on this elegant down-town street were Jewish. "Argentina is not an antisemitic country," he remarked at last. "There are simply antisemites living here."

These shrewd old diplomats of imprecision. Still, I pressed on. "Would you advise your grandchildren to remain here?"

"But, my esteemed friend"—he was ready for that one, too—"a man surely cannot tell his grandchildren what to do."

XII

False Dawn in the Communist Satellites

Bulgaria: Vanishing Sephardic Enclave

Sofia's Great Synagogue resembles many in the eastern Balkans, with its curious mélange of traditionally Jewish and Byzantine styles, its onion-shaped cupola and bell-like turrets, its immense chandelier hanging from the main sanctuary's one-hundred-foot-high ceiling. Cobblestones in its courtyard sprout grass. Its wrought-iron gate, crowned by a Star of David, is petrified in rust. Its snapped lock is a poignant superfluity. Rabbiless since 1962, the Great Synagogue is designated a national monument. It memorializes a community that even before the war was renowned not for its size or its wealth—as late as 1940 the Jews of Bulgaria numbered 48,000, less than 1 percent of the nation's population of 5.2 million—but for its Sephardic "integrity."

Most of these Sephardim were modest tradesmen and craftsmen. In an underdeveloped agricultural nation, they were less than prosperous even in the best of times. Yet, in the 1920s and 1930s, there were among them doctors, lawyers, members of the civil service. A handful of Jews sat in the Bulgarian parliament. Veterans in the land, tracing their lineage to sixteenth-century Spanish Jewish refugees, they lived comfortably with their Bulgarian neighbors. Their reaction to antisemitism elsewhere was essentially that of Elias Canetti's mother: Jewhatred "was meant for Kornfeld [i.e., the Ashkenazim], not for you." Native chauvinism appeared late, and was almost exclusively a German importation. Like Germany, Bulgaria was a victim of World War I, and therefore a revisionist state. When Adolf Hitler offered inducements for an alliance, there were nationalist elements eager to accommodate him. Throughout the 1930s, nevertheless, Nazi racial ideology evoked little response among the Bulgarian people.

The change occurred in February 1940, with the appointment of
Bogdan Filov as premier. Virtually a Nazi puppet, Filov introduced a
numerus clausus for Jews in the professions. Other measures quickly
followed. Jews were prohibited from bearing Bulgarian surnames, deprived of employment in the civil service, then of the right to vote, to
rent or own real estate in the countryside, to marry Bulgarians. In
1941, following Bulgaria's entry into the war at the side of Germany,
discriminatory taxes were imposed on Jewish property, curfews imposed on Jewish movement, telephones and radios removed from Jewish homes. By 1942, Jews were stripped of their civil rights altogether
and expelled from the larger cities, their able-bodied men were dispatched to labor camps, their homes and businesses were sequestered
by a Commissariat for Jewish Affairs, then resold to non-Jews. Finally,
some eleven thousand Jews living in the Bulgarian-occupied territories
of Yugoslav and Greek Macedonia were handed over to the German SS,
and murdered.

Yet even in the darkest period of German intimidation, not a single
Jew within the borders of Bulgaria itself was surrendered to the Nazis.
After 1943, with the Axis in retreat, protests against Jewish deportations
were raised by members of parliament, by government ministers, by
Bulgarian intellectuals and professionals, and not least of all by King
Boris I, who repeatedly and vigorously affirmed his sympathy for the
Jews. In September 1943, a new cabinet began gradually reversing the
former anti-Jewish policy. Jews were allowed to return to their homes.
The following August, all remaining anti-Jewish decrees were abol-
ished. And in September, the government signed an armistice, taking
the nation out of the war against the Western Allies. Then the Red
Army moved in.

Some 44,000 Jews remained alive in Bulgaria. It was the largest
proportion of Jews to survive in any Axis nation. Their problems were
not over. Many found their homes destroyed or damaged by air raids,
or occupied by squatters. At Soviet orders, priority in housing was
given to Communists and former partisans. Few Jews belonged to these
categories, and months passed before their lodgings were returned,
usually in wretched condition. Restored business premises often had
been gutted. Bulgaria's postwar economic circumstances clearly were
grave for everyone, but the Jews were reduced to utter destitution. If
they entertained hopes of reviving their former mercantile careers,
these were destroyed by the Communist nationalization decrees of

1947. The Joint moved quickly, setting up cooperatives, a central Jewish bank. The ORT vocational training organization hurriedly began retraining white-collar Jews for manual livelihoods. Yet these efforts were less than successful. As late as 1948, Bulgarian Jews remained desperately impoverished, subsisting largely on philanthropy, envisaging no prospects for themselves except emigration. They had long been Zionists. Now they required no further incentive to leave for Palestine.

Following the Communist line, the new regime initially had outlawed Zionism. In 1947, several Zionist party leaders were arrested on trumped-up charges of black marketeering. But a few months later, reflexively adapting to the twists of Moscow's diplomacy, the Sofia government reversed itself, supported the partition of Palestine, and agreed to a certain limited Jewish emigration. The first wave of departing Jews consisted of seven thousand younger men who were permitted to leave as "fighters against British imperialism." Then, in 1948, the Jewish Agency negotiated a secret and wider-ranging deal with the Bulgarian regime. Jews of all categories who chose to leave for Israel would be allowed to do so—provided they renounced their holdings, their chattels, their real estate. Under this formula, the departures picked up momentum and continued well into the summer of 1950. By the end of the year, less than five thousand Jews remained, essentially older or more assimilated people, including a tiny minority of Communists.

Slightly over half of them continued to live in Sofia, with the rest scattered between Plevna, Plovdiv, Varna, Yambol, and other, smaller towns. Many worked in state industrial enterprises or in workers' cooperatives. No more than three hundred Jews were professionals, but these were impressively represented in the nation's cultural life, in theater, journalism, and the university. With the passage of time, the Jews developed a workable relationship with the Communist government. They were permitted a religious and communal life of sorts. A Central Religious Council of Israelites, government financed, paid the salaries of the few remaining rabbis and kosher butchers. In 1957, a Jewish confederation was established as the umbrella organization for Jewish activities. The body was in Communist hands, of course, and in 1961 it turned over to the state all remaining Jewish community buildings, including schools and clinics, and retained only a small cultural house in Sofia and a few properties in other cities. If fewer Jews made use of these resources, it was essentially because fewer of them remained. Over the years, several hundred additional Jews had emigrated to Israel. Others had intermarried or died. Currently, some 3,000 Jews are left in Bulgaria, a feeble remnant both acculturated and aging.

Yugoslavia: Survivors of Third World Communism

During the Six-Day War in 1967, urgent radio communication frequently was necessary between Israel's deputy chief of military staff, General Chaim Bar-Lev, and the commander of Israel's northern (Syrian) front, General David Elazar. To save time, the two officers spoke on open, uncoded radio frequencies. There was little chance of interception by Arab intelligence, for the language they used was Serbo-Croatian. Both Elazar and Bar-Lev were Yugoslav-born, progeny of yet another of the wide-flung Balkan Jewish dispersion. On the eve of World War II, 76,000 Jews were living in Yugoslavia, slightly more than 0.5 percent of the nation's population of 14 million, and its smallest minority group. Approximately 25,000 of them were Sephardic, the community from which David Elazar sprang. The rest—the majority—were Ashkenazic, Bar-Lev's community.

Although they intermingled in Israel, this had not been their custom in prewar Yugoslavia, where each community followed the well-worn Diaspora tradition of maintaining its own religious and cultural institutions. They tended also to live apart, the Ashkenazim in the more urbanized northern parts of the country, the Sephardim (many of whom still preserved their Ladino dialect) in the poorer areas of the south. The Ashkenazim generally were upper middle class; the Sephardim, lower middle class. As in Bulgaria, there was little history of anti-semitism in a country that had been governed for many centuries by the Ottoman Empire. Communal Jewish schools received partial state funding. Jewish traditions were respected. Jews were exempt from appearing in court on the Sabbath and on Jewish holidays. In Sarajevo, where Jews comprised 10 percent of the population, Jewish holidays were legal for the entire city.

This tranquil existence ended, of course, with the German occupation of May 1941. Under direct Nazi occupation, Yugoslavia ceased to exist as a state; the machinery of Jewish deportation and extermination worked freely here. By 1944, approximately 55,000 Yugoslav Jews had been wiped out, while 18,000 others saved their lives by taking refuge in the Italian-controlled zone in Dalmatia. After the war, many of these survivors chose to depart for Austria and Germany, and from there to

Palestine. The Tito regime did not stop them. Nor did it stop others who joined them, once Israel was born. Between 1948 and 1952, approximately 7,600 Jews embarked, 7,000 remained. Their "ethnic" ratio, interestingly enough, was essentially that of the prewar: two-thirds Ashkenazim, one-third Sephardim. Their economic condition slowly improved, together with the rest of the population's. Following Tito's break with the Kremlin in 1948, the Communist economy was decentralized. Small traders, retailers, and commercial managers were permitted to function again, and Jews were well represented in these vocations. Almost as many other Jews earned their livelihoods as middle-level civil servants, or as private professionals.

There were several Jews, too, who played leading roles in the government. The most eminent of these was Moshe Pijade. A Sephardi, Pijade had spent fourteen years in prison before the war for Communist activities, much of that time as Tito's cellmate. The two men became inseparable friends. During the Nazi occupation, Pijade emerged as one of the most daring of the Partisan leaders, serving by Tito's side until the liberation. Subsequently, he represented Yugoslavia at the peace conference, then served as president of the Yugoslav National Assembly. Upon his death, Pijade was buried in the Crypt of National Heroes, one of five men granted this honor, and he is further memorialized by a huge stone likeness in Belgrade's Moshe Pijade Square. His eminence, like that of lesser Jewish government or professional figures, occasioned no special comment among the citizenry. Antisemitism altogether remained as thinly rooted among the people of Yugoslavia after 1944 as it had been in the prewar years. The government, meanwhile, fiercely maintaining its independence of Moscow, scorned the very notion of parroting the Soviet antisemitic line. Although Tito adopted an essentially pro-Arab diplomatic position, even severed relations with Israel after 1967, his Middle East policy did not affect his friendship for Yugoslav Jewry. Neither did that of his successors. For that matter, the government always understood and accepted the Jewish community's emotional identification with Israel (however discreetly expressed), and contact between Israelis and Yugoslav Jews was never broken. To this day, travel between Yugoslavia and Israel remains free and open.

Religious services currently take place in a handful of synagogues throughout the country. Laymen preside. The community's last rabbi died in 1969 at the age of eighty-seven. A single old age home is maintained in Zagreb, with its own synagogue. Several rather decrepit Jewish libraries and reading rooms are still to be found in the larger cities. Two Jewish kindergartens survive in Belgrade and Zagreb. An officially recognized Jewish Federation is supported by voluntary contributions and subventions from the Joint and the Memorial Foundation. Representing both the Ashkenazic and the Sephardic communities, the Federation maintains a Jewish historical museum and archive in Belgrade, operates a summer camp, publishes a monthly bulletin, sponsors women's and youth groups, lectures and musical events. But participation in these events does not appear to be extensive. There is not enough critical mass. The demography of Yugoslav Jewry is an all too familiar one, particularly in Eastern Europe. The birth rate is low, the death rate high. In the last two decades, the Jewish population has numbered barely five thousand, with intermarriage the norm. There is no reservoir of available spouses.

On a Sabbath eve a number of years ago, watching the two or three dozen aged worshipers seated in Belgrade's venerable Sephardic Synagogue on Cara Urosa, I recalled Alihodja, the old Turk in Ivo Andric's haunting novel *The Bridge on the Drina*. To my eyes, this synagogue was as doomed as the bridge of Andric's volume. The congregants here must have known that their world was disappearing, as Alihodja sensed it in July 1914: "Only in dreams could one see and experience such things any longer. Only in dreams."

Postwar Czechoslovakia: The Demise of Decency

In the autumn of 1952, Rudolf Slansky, former secretary-general of the Czech Communist Party, and thirteen other eminent former officials of the party and government, went on trial in Prague for high treason. The charge against them was espionage on behalf of Tito, Israel, and the United States. By then, purge trials were old stories in Communist nations. What distinguished this one was its openly antisemitic character. Of the fourteen defendants, eleven were Jews, and were plainly identified as Jews. Countless other Jews were mentioned as co-conspirators, including the dead and the living. Six weeks later, when the Doctors' Plot was announced in Moscow, it became evident that the Slansky trial represented but a prelude to Stalin's climactic purge of Jews behind the Iron Curtain.

This bizarre episode unfolded in the one Communist-dominated nation that had achieved a consistent prewar record of democracy and toleration. When the Czechoslovak republic first won its independence in 1918, some 285,000 Jews were living there, and conducting their affairs in a freedom they had taken for granted during the previous three-quarters of a century, under Habsburg rule. Between the two world wars, they remained by far the most prosperous Jewish community in Eastern Europe, with a distinguished professional and cultural tradition. Then, following the Nazi occupation in March 1939, with their numbers swollen to 325,000 by earlier refugees from Germany and Austria, they also became the largest hostage Jewry in the Greater Reich. Indeed, as the war unfolded, their tragedy was as far-reaching as that of any Jewish population west of the Vistula. In Theresienstadt, in Auschwitz, and in other camps, the great majority of that historic community perished—270,000 souls.

At the end of the war, barely 51,000 Jews survived, and of these, 11,000 were refugees from Carpatho-Russia. Yet prospects for the remnant population were not unpromising at first. Although well within the Soviet sphere, Czechoslovakia's initial postwar election was free. The nation's president, Edvard Benes, and its foreign minister, Jan Masaryk, exerted themselves fullheartedly to alleviate the Jewish plight. Between 1945 and 1947, Czechoslovakia served as the principal transit route of Polish Jews to the American zones of Germany and Austria, and the Czech government offered every facility to the refugees. Following Moscow's lead, Czechoslovakia became a major source of weapons for Israel in its military struggle for independence.

Nevertheless, even in the first postwar years, Jewish survivors began encountering difficulties. Their restitution claims often were denied on the pretext that Jews belonged to the despised "German" or "Hungarian" minorities. In backward Slovakia, with its more deeply rooted folk antisemitism, objections to the return of Jewish property erupted into occasional violence. Government officials warned Jews not to press their claims. The minister of information, Vaclav Kopecky, a Communist, sought to mobilize public support for his party by describing the Jews as "bearded Solomons," "Jewish scum." An official organ of the ministry of education insisted that the capitalists in Czechoslovakia had always been of foreign—that is, Jewish—origin, and that "native" rights ought now to be respected. Once the Communists launched their coup in February 1948, moreover, and officially transformed Czechoslovakia into a Socialist People's Republic, there was no question of returning businesses or factories to anyone, Jew or non-Jew. These enterprises were nationalized altogether. The Council of Jewish Communities (together with non-Jewish religious organizations) was soon taken over by Communist apparatchiks. Contact with Jewish organizations abroad was stopped. Within the ensuing two years, Jewish welfare institutions were nationalized, Jewish schools were closed, and the Joint was ordered to terminate its activities in Czechoslovakia. These developments, coinciding with the birth of Israel, resulted in a mass wave of Jewish emigration. By 1952, approximately 34,000 Jews had left the country.

The government's acquiescence in their departure was unrelated to its harsh anti-Zionist policy at home. Rather, it was influenced in part by the desire to end Czechoslovakia's chronic minorities problem (Germans and Hungarians, too, had been encouraged to leave the country), and in part by a quiet agreement to grant exit permits in return for a substantial Jewish Agency payoff in dollars. Following the post-Israel exodus, therefore, not more than 17,000 Jews remained in the country, some two-thirds of them in Bohemia and Moravia. Except for occasional pockets of traditionalists in Slovakia, it was an assimilated group, consisting largely of intellectuals, professionals, and administrators. Many of them were dedicated Communists.

The Purge Trials: Czechoslovakia as Weather Vane

The Communist takeover in February 1948 occurred immediately following the Kremlin's break with Yugoslavia's Marshal Tito, a development that provoked Moscow in turn to fasten its grip decisively on the satellite nations. The possibility of a Titoist "infection" elsewhere in the Communist world henceforth became Joseph Stalin's devouring obsession. To the Soviet ruler, the leadership cadres within the various satellite nations were instantly suspect as former associates or friends of Tito. Thus, at Stalin's instigation, a chain reaction of purges was launched throughout the satellite nations in 1949 and 1950, and culminated in the trial, execution, or imprisonment of high party and government officials. Among all the "Socialist People's Republics," however, the most brutal and extensive purge occurred in Czechoslovakia. Here the residual tradition of idealistic democratic socialism was known to be strongest; and here, as a result, not less than 25,000 people were arrested between 1940 and 1951. Among them were numerous members of the party, the government, the armed forces, the professions.

In 1951, the regime began changing the ideological basis of the alleged plot against the nation from "bourgeois nationalism" to "Zionism." When the first great trial began in November 1952, the defendants included: Rudolf Slansky, secretary-general of the party and a vice-premier; Bedrich Gemeinder, director of the party's foreign affairs department; Ludvik Frejka, author of the nation's five-year plan; Josef Frank, deputy secretary-general of the party; Vladimir Clementis, minister of foreign affairs; Bedrich Reicin, deputy minister of national defense; Karel Svab, deputy minister of state security; Artur London and Vavro Hajdu, deputy ministers of foreign affairs; Evzen Loebl and Rudolf Margolius, deputy ministers of foreign trade; Otto Fischl, deputy minister of finance; Otto Sling, district secretary of the party in Brno, the capital of Moravia; and André Simone (né Otto Katz), foreign editor of the party newspaper. Of these fourteen persons, only Clementis, Frank, and Svab were not Jews, and after the name of each Jewish defendant the indictment added the words "of Jewish origin."

The defendants' alleged crime, "Zionist conspiracy," was depicted as a widely based plot, led by Jewish leaders in the United States and Israel, to undermine the Socialist order and to give away billions of Czechoslovak kroner to foreign capitalists. The Joint Distribution Committee was identified as the conduit of this Zionist penetration, its techniques purportedly ranging from espionage and sabotage to black market operations and smuggling. Even the charge of medical assassination was raised in the Prague Trial (two months before the Doctors' Plot in Moscow), with the Joint accused of helping Slansky arrange the attempted poisoning of President Klement Gottwald.

There were several explanations for this furiously anti-Jewish and anti-Israel campaign. One clearly related to the fear of heterodoxy that had plagued Stalin since his break with Tito in February 1948. As a minority group with extensive connections abroad, particularly in the West, the Jews, like the Titoists, appeared to represent a "deviationist" threat to the Soviet ruler. They were known, too, as a repository of the old, idealistic Trotskyite socialism that Stalin had feared, execrated, and purged since the 1920s—although Slansky himself was a veteran hardline Stalinist. Antisemitism as a well-perfected distraction from internal economic failures was undoubtedly a factor, and this classic device was applied with a special virulence during Stalin's paranoia-ridden last year. Of particular importance, finally, between 1950 and 1953 was the growing suspicion of Israel as a potential ally of the Western powers in the Middle East.

In Prague, meanwhile, the defendants, who had been held incommunicado for many months, now vied with each other in confessing to their ostensible crimes, and the trial proceedings were widely published and broadcast. Among those testifying were two Israeli citizens (and former Czechs), Mordechai Oren and Shimon Ohrenstein, leftists who had been visiting their former homeland at the time of their arrest in late 1951. They, too, confessed to their participation in the "Zionist" plot. On November 27, 1952, the court handed down the sentence of death by hanging for Slansky and ten of the other defendants, with three receiving life terms. The executions were carried out on December 3. In May 1953, a second trial was begun in Prague. This time the defendants were Richard Slansky, brother of Rudolf and a former diplomat; Edvard Goldstücker, a former Czech minister to Israel; and Pavel Kevan, former secretary of the Czech embassy in London—all Jews. The first two were sentenced to life imprisonment, and Kevan to twenty-five years imprisonment.

From the outset of the first trial, an intensive press and radio barrage was mounted against the "Zionist" conspiracy. Jews in every echelon of national life were expelled from their positions in government, party, industry. Numbers of Jewish communal leaders were jailed, then tried secretly on charges of "economic crimes" or of illegally restoring Jewish properties during the early postwar period. Even Stalin's death in March 1953, and the ensuing "thaw" within the Soviet Union itself, did not initially ease the Jewish ordeal. Another year would elapse before the anti-Jewish campaign guttered out in Czechoslovakia. And a decade would pass before the imprisoned survivors of the original trials were legally rehabilitated and politically exonerated. The trauma was not one from which Czechoslovak Jewry would soon recover.

The Prague Spring—and Its Aftermath

By 1963, the nation's Jewish population was listed as 14,000, of whom 9,000 lived in Slovakia. Clearly, there had been much attrition over the previous decade through intermarriage, nonregistration as Jews, or death. Only 1,500 of the estimated 5,000 Jews living in Prague were registered with the Jewish community; the purges had had a shattering moral and psychological impact on them. Some liberalization took place in the latter 1950s and early 1960s, to be sure, following the accession of Nikita Khrushchev in Moscow. Plans even were laid to commemorate the millennium of Prague Jewry. Yet, in the aftermath of the Six-Day War in 1967, the Novotny regime followed Moscow's lead in severing diplomatic relations with Israel, and then in launching an anti-Israel propaganda campaign more far-reaching and violent than any outside the Soviet Union. There was reason for this spleen and vitriol, and it was a classic diversionary one: the attack on Israel was obliquely directed against mounting liberal sentiment within Czechoslovakia itself. As the surrogate of that liberalism, and also as the symbol of resistance to Soviet client nations in the Arab Near East, Israel became the target now for "spontaneous" mass demonstrations and for a savage press campaign against "Zionism"—a pejorative that subliminally could be read as liberalism, or Titoist deviationism. The remnant Czechoslovak Jewish minority was not spared this vindictiveness. The millennium celebration was abruptly canceled.

It was in the wake of these developments, several weeks later, that there occurred the mysterious death of Charles Jordan, executive director of the Joint Distribution Committee, who was visiting Prague. On the evening of August 19, 1967, his body was found floating in the Vltava River. The Czech police attributed his death to drowning, but there was a compelling suspicion of foul play. At the insistence of the Joint Executive in New York, the Czech government agreed to allow a famous Swiss pathologist, Dr. Ernst Hardmeier, to conduct an autopsy. Hardmeier found traces of a powerful drug in Jordan's pancreas. Subsequently, American investigators accumulated information that Jordan was to have been assassinated in Romania before his visit to Prague. Either the plot was foiled by the Romanian security apparatus or the killers simply were unable to carry out the deed. Apparently, Jordan's murderers then followed him from Bucharest to Prague, where they finally managed to abduct and kill him. The evidence was overwhelming that the assassins were Czech.

The concatenation of these events was not lost on the reformers within Czechoslovakia. The government's slavish obedience to Soviet pro-Arab policies deeply angered them, as did the vicious "anti-Zionist" campaign. Indeed, millions of Czechs discerned a parallel between Israel's unyielding stand against the Arabs and the current situation of Czechoslovakia in the midst of a Communist sea. Criticism was directed as well against the Novotny regime's ossified Stalinism, its deadening intellectual repression, its ineffectual economic policies. The spokesman for this discontent was Alexander Dubcek, the party chairman in Slovakia. Dubcek's open broadside against Novotny, loosed in October 1967, coincided with growing student riots in Prague. The party leadership was intimidated by the unrest. After a series of intra-presidium crises, Dubcek was finally offered the first secretaryship of the central committee.

A committed Marxist in his own way, Dubcek was intent now upon revamping the system into "socialism with a human face." To that end, he embarked on a series of innovations, emphasizing freedom of expression, justice, and legality—in short, an end to terror. So began the "Prague Spring," an effort to wed socialism's concepts of economic justice with the Western traditions of political and cultural freedom. By early 1968, the nation's radical change of direction had developed into hardly less than a quiet but thoroughgoing revolution. For the Jews, the most important of its changes was a decisive repudiation of anti-semitism. In radio broadcasts and newspaper columns, vigorous warnings were issued against "anti-Zionism" as a weapon of reaction. On February 15, 1968, the writers' union demanded the rehabilitation of all citizens wronged under the previous regime, and particularly during the Slansky trials. Responding to this appeal, the government in May did in fact grant amnesty to some twenty thousand prisoners, and to all those who had fled during the purge era of the 1950s. President Svoboda now posthumously restored their former decorations to Slansky and Otto Sling, and awarded the Order of the Republic to four other executed Jewish victims and also to three Jewish survivors of the trial. That same month, it was also announced that the celebration of the millennium of Prague Jewry would take place after all between June 5 and 6, 1969, and Jewish participants from throughout the world would be invited. It was a fresh new wind, and altogether a thrilling one for the nation's thirteen thousand Jews.

The Prague Spring did not survive the summer. On the night of August 20, divisions of Polish, East German, Hungarian, and Bulgarian troops crossed Czechoslovakia's borders from four directions. They met no resistance. Dubcek and several other members of the Czech presidium were swiftly taken into custody, then forced to accede to the "reconstruction" of their government. The invasion coincided with a full-scale "anti-Zionist" offensive that was launched simultaneously in the various East European capitals. Within Czechoslovakia itself, the occupying forces seized the newspapers and radio stations, then embarked on a farrago of accusations specifically against Dr. Edvard Goldstücker, chairman of the writers' union, charging him with the identical crimes for which he had been imprisoned by the Slansky court fifteen years earlier. Czechoslovak Jews altogether were identified as "part of the spiderweb of Israeli aggression." The intensity of the hate campaign did not abate even after the last of the Czech rump presidium resigned, and Dubcek himself stepped down in April 1969. Gustav Husak, Dubcek's successor as first secretary, made clear afterward that Jewish members would not be welcome again on the presidium. The outpouring of official antisemitism continued, this time under the direction of Soviet agents well entrenched in Czechoslovakia. The old conspiratorial relationship between the CIA, the Joint, and international Zionism was played overtime.

The invasion and its aftermath similarly ended all plans for celebrating the millennium of Prague Jewry. There were few enough identified Jews in any case to observe the event. Between August 1968 and February 1969, approximately 35,000 Czechs left the country, and Jews accounted for at least 10 percent of these. Heavily assimilated and intermarried, they bypassed Israel for Western Europe. Approximately 8,500 Jews remained in Czechoslovakia. Only one aged rabbi continued to serve the tiny minority of traditionalists among them. In the 1970s, the anti-Jewish atmosphere gradually was dissipated, in common with a relaxation of oppression in Czechoslovakia altogether. By then, only one Jewish school, in Bratislava, was still functioning. All but three of the nation's synagogues were abandoned. The most impressive surviving testimonies of a Jewish population that once had been among the most dynamic and accomplished in Europe were the tourist showpieces in the capital—the Old-New Gothic Synagogue, the Jewish "town hall" of the old medieval ghetto area with its Hebrew dial, and the remarkably well preserved Jewish museum (which in later years of brief East-West détente lent its superb collection of artifacts to Jewish communities abroad). If the anniversary had been celebrated in 1968, it would more appropriately have commemorated the demise of ten centuries of Jewish vitality in this land.

Jewish "Revival" in Poland

Jerzy Panski was seventy-three years old when we met. His heavy-set body gave evidence of a once powerful musculature. His face was strong and deeply lined, under thick gray hair. His manner was

"Slavic," hearty and open. Born in Lodz, he was the son of a businessman who moved to Warsaw after World War I to operate a small paper factory. The family's comfortable apartment was located on Warsaw's Churentokshuska Street, in a mixed Jewish-Gentile neighborhood. Determined that his two sons become "authentically" Polish, the father sent them to a state gymnasium. "He was insistent that we have a decent chance among our Polish fellow citizens," Panski recalled, his smile cynical. A "decent chance" manifestly was not to be achieved in postwar Poland. Fully a third of the reborn nation's population of thirty million were members of non-Polish minorities—Ukrainians, Hungarians, Romanians, Lithuanians, Germans, Jews. Fearing and distrusting these "alien elements," the government ignored its treaty promises to accord them civil equality, and engaged instead in a policy of thinly disguised repression.

With no "brother" state to intercede on their behalf, Poland's three million Jews were the most vulnerable of all the minorities. In the immediate postwar period, Jews living in border communities were exposed to physical assaults, even killings. From the 1920s on, as a lower-middle-class element, they endured a "cold" pogrom of economic discrimination. "If the aboriginal nation reaches economic maturity," explained one Polish senator bluntly, "the immigrant nation must step aside." It was a widely held conviction that a Polish middle class could grow and flourish only through the displacement of non-Poles. Accordingly, the government assumed control of specifically those industries—tobacco, liquor, salt, matches, transportation—in which Jews had long been heavily represented. The latter were "displaced," hundreds of thousands of them reduced to the barest subsistence level. Throughout the 1920s and 1930s, the Joint was obliged to labor overtime in Poland to maintain an extensive program of food and medical dispensaries, of credit cooperatives and employment agencies.

The Panski family, however, managed to preserve its standard of living. Upon completing gymnasium in 1929, Jerzy Panski registered in the state maritime college, in Gdynia. He was one of four Jews admitted in a class of one hundred, and from the outset he ran a daily gauntlet of antisemitic abuse. Upon completing of the program in 1933, the Jewish students were singled out for more "sea experience," and Panski and the three others were obliged to spend two additional years as common sailors before they were allowed to take their examinations and receive their lieutenants' commissions. Even then, they were fortunate by comparison with the Polish Jewish majority. In 1937, the National Unity Coalition announced openly that "business and culture henceforth should remain exclusively in Polish hands." From then on, the Sejm—the Polish parliament—steadily debated the Jewish problem, which had become that of a "surplus population," or of "aliens." With government encouragement, the nation's trade, professional, and artistic associations imposed a quota that all but excluded Jews. Accepted only in token numbers, Jewish university students were intimidated by their classmates into accepting "ghetto benches."

Although Panski himself was aboard ship as a maritime officer during the most virulent period of Polish antisemitism, he was well aware of the unfolding campaign of chauvinist repression. Traditional political remedies would not suffice to alleviate the Jewish plight, he believed, or that of the Polish "common people." With his secularist background, Panski regarded communism as the logical solution—"the only way then of declaring war on the Fascist establishment," he insisted. There were other Jews of his background who agreed. Only five thousand of them were party members, in a total Jewish population of over three million; but they comprised fully 26 percent of the party's Polish membership in 1938. During his travels through the Baltic and North seas that year, Panski was put in touch with Communist groups in other nations, and smuggled their propaganda home. He was at sea when the German invasion began, and spent the early war years aboard various Allied merchant vessels.

The stroke of timing almost certainly saved Panski's life. Approximately 2,700,000 Polish Jews were liquidated by the Nazis. Another 350,000 escaped from eastern Poland into the Soviet interior, principally into the Central Asian republics, where a third of them perished of exposure or starvation. Panski's family remained in Warsaw. Seeking to disguise their identity, they were informed on by a neighbor. Panski's father was shot. His brother, Alexander, joined the Polish Communist underground; but, captured later by the Gestapo, he was tortured to death, his body then publicly hanged. The news was relayed to Panski in 1944 in Sweden, where he was working in Stockholm with other émigré Poles. "I don't believe I wept," he recollected, "but my Communist commitment became even more unshakable." Following the directives of the Lublin—Communist—government in liberated Poland, he set about vigorously organizing his fellow expatriates into a Communist front organization. In February 1945, he was appointed his country's chargé d'affaires in Stockholm, then in April was summoned to Warsaw for more extensive responsibilities.

He returned to a Jewish graveyard. In the spring of 1945, only 85,000 Jews remained alive on Polish soil. Their numbers did not yet include any of the 230,000 Jews who had survived in the Soviet Union, most of whom would be repatriated only the following year. The treatment meted out to the survivors by the Poles, who had long since taken over Jewish homes, shops, and businesses, was more brutal than anywhere else in liberated Europe. In 1945, some 350 Jews were killed. On July 4, 1946, 41 Jews were slain in the town of Kielce, and shortly afterward, 33 other Jews were pulled from trains en route to Germany and beaten to death. "The fact that this condition is deteriorating," blandly explained Cardinal August Hlond, primate of Poland, "is to a great degree due to the Jews who today occupy leading positions in Poland's [Communist-dominated] government, and who endeavor to introduce a governmental structure which the majority of the people do not desire." Thus, even as Polish Jews were returning from the Soviet Union in the following two years, a simultaneous flight of Jews from Poland itself was taking place to the American zones of Germany and Austria. Directed by Jewish Agency representatives, the emigration of Jews reached 150,000 in the spring of 1946, and increased even more rapidly following the Kielce pogrom. The tide did not ebb until the summer of 1949, when the exit routes finally were sealed. By then, not more than 90,000 Jews remained in Poland, and in the next four years another 9,000 would succeed in making their way out.

Panski did not join the exodus. A dedicated Communist, he understood that the party needed his skills, and those of his Jewish colleagues. Large numbers of these people had lived abroad during the war, and particularly in the Soviet Union. Among them were three leading members of the politburo, Jakub Berman, Hilary Minc, and Roman Zambrowski, and two of the three deputy members of the politburo. Many of the key directors-general in the government ministries were Jews. So were numerous police chiefs and army officers. In eastern Poland, Jews seemed to be the only reliable Communists available. Their visibility without doubt was an intolerable provocation to the local inhabitants, and all the more so after the Holocaust and the recent flight of tens of thousands of other Jews to the West. In effect, the Jewish Communists represented a large head on a virtually nonexistent body, a tiny minority of despised "aliens" administering a hated system on behalf of a traditional enemy power.

If the Jewish Communists were sentient to the hatred around them, it was not Marxist idealism alone that persuaded them to remain. Postwar Poland had shifted westward, acquiring the highly industrialized former German territory of Silesia and eastern Prussia. Once the German inhabitants of this area were forcibly repatriated to Germany, a need existed for skilled, educated personnel to take their place. More than the Poles, the Jewish survivors possessed the necessary background. Accordingly, they were offered comfortable (formerly German) apartments and good salaries to remain on. Many accepted. Physically and emotionally drained by their wartime ordeal, they welcomed an oasis in their wanderings.

Yet for Panski, the compelling inducement was the "opportunity to serve." He was appointed deputy minister of commerce and shipping. Invested with wide-ranging authority and provided with an extensive budget, he managed within two years to rehabilitate several of the nation's most important harbors, to increase their capacity by constructing new wharves, rail sidings, sheds, cattle pens. In 1947, as a reward for completing his projects ahead of schedule, he was appointed Polish consul in New York, and the following year, Polish maritime attaché in London. In 1950 he was back in Warsaw to reorganize the ministry of shipping. As special assistant to the minister, Panski now made the key decisions on expenditures, material imports, personnel. Frequently he traveled abroad on purchasing missions, and in Western countries he was able to buy clothes and household appliances. In 1952 he married an attractive Polish woman of aristocratic background. It appeared to him by then that he had achieved all a Pole legitimately could expect out of life. His sense of accomplishment and relief was shared by perhaps the largest number of Jews who remained. A fifth of them were employed directly by the government, usually in responsible, well-paying positions. Others were heavily represented as executives in public corporations and in nationalized industry. More than a third of them were professionals—accountants, economists, statisticians, scientists, physicians. By the early 1950s, incidents of antisemitism had been contained under threat of harsh prosecution.

The revival of Jewish communal life was less assured. At first, the postwar Polish government authorized the establishment of a Central Jewish Committee, even helped subsidize it with grants of over 100 million zlotys. Jewish schools were opened with funds provided by the Joint, which also underwrote Jewish newspapers, journals, libraries, theatrical and cultural activities. After 1948, however, the transformation of a "people's democracy" into an outright Communist dictatorship all but aborted this revival. Jewish schools were the first to be nationalized, followed by Jewish credit cooperatives, then welfare institutions, including old age homes, children's homes, the Jewish theater. The Jewish writers' association and Jewish youth organizations were dissolved. The Central Jewish Committee itself was taken over entirely by Communist leadership, and the parallel Union of Jewish Religious Congregations was restricted afterward exclusively to internal religious matters. The Joint, the ORT, and other international Jewish philanthropies were ordered to close their offices. It was in this period of cultural strangulation, during the 1950s, that rivulets of illegal emigration further depleted the Jewish population, to about sixty thousand by 1956.

Nonreligious himself, Panski was unconcerned about the fate of Jewish communal life. He shared with his Jewish friends a certain quiet pride in the birth of Israel, a sense of gratification that the old stereotype of the Jews as perennial martyrs had been shattered. But otherwise his interests were exclusively Polish. It was the Moscow Doctors' Plot early in 1953, and the impact of the Soviet "anti-Zionist" campaign, that gave him pause. In April of that year, Panski and numerous other Jewish officials suddenly were called up before an administrative court on charges of inefficiency. They were demoted and sentenced to three months of surveillance. Yet this abrupt fall from favor was a brief one. After Stalin's death, the "crimes of the secret police" were exposed. Jewish officials were promptly reinstated at their former ranks. If the system was not yet perfected, Panski decided, at least in its fundamentals it appeared to be just and self-correcting.

The Price of "Liberalization"

The death of Stalin loosed far-reaching changes throughout the Soviet empire, and particularly after Nikita Khrushchev's famous speech at the Twentieth Communist Party Congress in February 1956, denouncing the late dictator's crimes. In Poland, as elsewhere in Eastern Europe, the relaxation of Soviet rule opened a major schism within the party leadership. Since the last months before liberation, control of the party had been firmly in the hands of the "Muscovites," those Polish émigrés who had lived in the Soviet Union during the war and who had returned to assume power in Warsaw, directly under Soviet sponsorship. By contrast, the "Partisans"—Communists who survived as members of the underground in Poland itself during the war—had largely been dismissed from positions of leadership. Much of the Polish people's growing resentment of Communist domination was focused on the Muscovites, and, as has been seen, specifically on the prominent Jews among them.

The opposition became almost uncontrollable following the death in March 1956 of Boleslaw Bierut, the party chairman in Poland, and a veteran Stalinist. A series of popular demonstrations culminated in a workers' riot in Poznan late in June 1956. Army units were required to suppress it. Hereupon, the Muscovites in the politburo deemed it expedient to invite a number of Partisans to share responsibility with them. One of these was Wladyslaw Gomulka, a wartime Communist leader who had been kept under house arrest in recent years. He was brought back into the central committee now as a gesture of placation. Another gesture was the dismissal of Hilary Minc from the central committee, the last remaining Jew. Yet it was too late to appease the Partisans. In mid-July they seized control of the central committee, and in the ensuing half-year fended off all efforts by the Muscovites to retrieve their position. Finally, deeply alarmed, a Soviet delegation led by Khrushchev himself flew into Warsaw on October 20 to "confer" with the Polish leadership. It was a tough bargaining session, but eventually Khrushchev and his colleagues agreed to enlarged Polish autonomy in domestic matters, provided the Polish government maintained its commitment to the Warsaw Pact—to Communist bloc military solidarity.

The next day, October 21, Gomulka was elected first secretary of his party's central committee. Then and later, he kept his part of the bargain, remaining loyal to Soviet policy on the international scene; his "national communism" was applied exclusively to Polish affairs. Gomulka's domestic innovations were more than perfunctory, however. He decentralized the economy, turning away from agricultural collectivization and simultaneously permitting a wider latitude in public discussion and press reportage. Catholic religious instruction was reintroduced into the public schools, and Catholic newspapers and magazines reappeared. It was these latter measures, above all, that gave the new regime a certain measure of popularity and staying power.

So did a shift in the government's approach to the Jews. On the one hand, Jewish communal institutions were allowed a limited revival and rehabilitation. Several Jewish schools were reopened and even permitted to offer religious instruction. A Yiddish newspaper, *Folksztyme,* was authorized to publish news about Israel and about Jews in other lands. World Jewish Congress leaders were permitted to visit Warsaw, to re-establish contacts with Polish Jewry. The Joint was invited to open its offices again, to provide food and medical help to needy Jews. But at the same time, the new "liberalization" unleashed an upsurge of popular antisemitism. Poison-pen letters appeared in the newspapers, urging Jews to leave the country. Jewish children were taunted, even assaulted, in the schools and streets. Gomulka himself was not an antisemite. Indeed, he was married to a Jewish woman. At his orders, a systematic campaign against prejudice was undertaken by press and radio. Yet the first secretary knew his own people. If restraints on their traditional chauvinism were loosened now, the Jews inevitably would feel the consequences. Gomulka made it clear, then, that those who wished to leave for Israel could do so. In response to this shift in emigration policy, thousands of Jews rushed to the nearest passport offices to secure exit visas. Between 1956 and 1958, fully 33,000 of them streamed out of Poland and journeyed directly to Israel.

By 1959, the 27,000 or so Jews who remained in Poland included not only the aged, who were fearful of abandoning their pension benefits, but others, unwilling to give up well-paying positions, who were convinced that the revived antisemitism soon would burn itself out. It had received no government benediction, after all. Thus, at the outset, Panski was an ardent admirer of the Gomulka revolution. "I favored any change that would introduce liberalization into the country," he admitted. But four months after the new regime began, he was called to the public prosecutor's office. "Did you purchase a Swedish ship, *Helga*, for half a million American dollars?" he was asked.

"I did."

"The same ship that could have been purchased for three hundred thousand dollars?"

"Certainly not," responded Panski. "You're confusing the *Helga* with another ship, a coal-burning ship. The *Helga* is a motor ship."

"What was the difference?" persisted the official.

"Bunkering stations," explained Panski. "We purchased the *Helga* for our new line to China. En route to China, there aren't enough bunkering stations for a coal-burning ship. A motor ship is more expensive, but we had no choice."

The prosecutor dropped the issue. Several months later, however, the audit of Panski's office accounts was resumed. Again, the inquiries were inconclusive. Despite this harassment, Panski held on. Finally, in 1964, his job status was reduced to that of a "ministerial consultant." His salary remained high—he had a famous reputation—but his authority gradually was stripped from him. It was suggested that he might enjoy serving as a maritime officer again. He did not protest. His route afterward took him to the Mediterranean, to the African coast, and he was permitted at least to bring his wife and daughter with him. Yet the comedown was humiliating. Brooding on it, he was aware that many of his Jewish friends, including decorated war heroes and others who were linguistically and culturally as Polish as any Roman Catholic, were also quietly being reassigned. Even for a committed Marxist like Panski, the atmosphere was unsettling.

Antisemitism Without Jews: A Polish Joke

As late as 1964, few of the Jewish Communists would have predicted another venomous campaign of antisemitism within the near future, and particularly under the aegis of the government. Yet this time the onslaught was the consequence of a three-way rivalry for leadership within the party itself. Throughout the 1960s, the Gomulka regime had shown itself incapable of resolving the nation's economic problems. Agricultural and industrial production lagged, and the temper of the country was becoming increasingly restive. It was in this darkening mood that General Miczlyslaw Moczar, the interior minister, saw his opportunity. Of peasant ancestry, a coarse, bull-necked straw boss, Moczar exhibited little ideological bias toward either the Muscovites or the Partisans. His sole obsession was power, and his route to it was through the unscrupulous manipulation of his nation's patriotism. To that end, Moczar's first step in 1966 was to establish a special "Jewish department" in his ministry, its main purpose to delve into the "questionable" pasts of well-known Jews and other "suspicious" Poles.

Moczar was not the only competitor for Gomulka's seat. Edward Gierek, party chief for upper Silesia, also developed into a serious rival. A technocrat, Gierek preferred to concentrate his attack less on the Jews than on the government's inept economic policy. For the while, then, Gomulka was able to play his rivals against each other, and he was reelected first secretary at the party congress in November 1967. But in the spring of 1968, discontent among the intellectual community suddenly boiled over. Outraged by the government's decision to cancel performances of Adam Mickiewicz's *Dziady* (The Forefathers), a classic nineteenth-century play with anti-Russian overtones, the nation's writers, artists, and students petitioned the government to rescind its decision. Then, late in March, several thousand students at Warsaw University held a rally to demand the reinstatement of two students (both Jews) who had been expelled for protesting the ban of *Dziady*. When the meeting was brutally suppressed by the police, riots followed, and with them further police repression. Under General Moczar's direction, the arrest and expulsion of students soon far outstripped the actual provocations. Here, Moczar believed, was an ideal opportunity to expose Gomulka's policies as lacking in Polish nationalism. Surely it was no accident, he suggested, that the country's institutions were riddled with "non-Poles."

Discerning which way the wind was blowing, Gomulka himself now belatedly adopted the hard-line approach. In a televised speech of March 19, the first secretary joined in condemning "antipatriotic elements." Although he insisted that he was attacking Zionists, not Jews, neither he nor his listeners appeared interested in drawing lines of distinction. A series of party-organized meetings took place throughout Poland, demanding that Jews identify themselves, and beating the drum against "Zionist" influences. These were followed almost immediately by a far-reaching purge of Jews in all echelons of Polish life.

At first, the authorities concentrated upon dismissing Jewish government officials whose children were implicated in the student demonstrations (although the majority of protesters were non-Jews). But afterward, Roman Zambrowski, the most eminent of the former Jewish members of the politburo, was expelled from the party. A wave of other party expulsions followed, including among its victims three former members of the central committee; the former ambassador to the United Nations; the director of the state scientific publishing house; the director of light industry; and numerous other Jewish deputy ministers, department directors, and editors. Between March and June 1968, some eight thousand Jews at all levels of government, party, and cultural life were dismissed from their positions. Professors, factory administrators, doctors, scientists, all were expelled from their party and professional associations, and thus were automatically deprived of their jobs. Politically motivated as the cold pogrom was, it served the additional practical purpose of upward mobility for Poland's new middle class. A vacancy in one hitherto "Jewish" post in the government, in a state enterprise, a newspaper, a university, or a hospital, often meant that a dozen officials could move up a rung on the ladder. It also meant the availability of Jewish apartments in overcrowded urban centers, enabling the same dozen moves up the ladder to improved housing. The ulterior purpose at times became quite explicit, and reminiscent of the Polish senator in the 1930s who had alluded to the "aboriginal" nation that had reached "maturity."

As a result of firm Kremlin support against his rivals, Gomulka felt secure enough by the autumn to curb the Jew-baiting hysteria. The "anti-Zionist" campaign in the mass media began to subside. Yet the purge quietly continued. Jewish communal life, too, which had been tentatively restored after 1956, this time was decisively liquidated. Jewish schools and youth clubs were closed, together with the Yiddish newspaper, *Folksztyme*, and Jewish publishing houses. The Jewish state theater ceased its operation, and its renowned directress, Ida Kaminska, was among those deprived of a livelihood. By late 1969, the Jewish minority was ruined financially and psychologically. Jerzy Panski shared in the ordeal. Well before the student riots and the "anti-Zionist" campaign, his daughter, Eva, had been suffering acutely in school. Classmates mocked her almost daily as a "Zhidovka" (although she was half-Jewish). Now, during the 1968 purges, her teachers began to share in the harassment, reviling the fourteen-year-old child as a "Jewish whore."

By July 1969, Panski finally accepted the harsh truth that there was no future for him and his family in Poland. He resigned from the party that month. In response, he was expelled from his job. At the main visa office at the Palace Mostovski, he informed the authorities that he, his wife, and his daughter had decided to leave for Israel—the one official destination permitted Jews. Whereupon the Panskis were given three months to depart. Had it been up to their fellow citizens, the time would have been less. Knots of them in the streets were waving placards: "Jews, clear out" . . . "Pack your bags" . . . "Your time is coming." More painful yet was the abusive behavior of Panski's former colleagues. They insulted him coarsely, brutally, not sparing him expletives. But within three weeks the bureaucratic procedures were completed. As the family closed the door of their apartment for the last time in September 1969, only the janitor and his wife bade them goodbye. The rest of their neighbors either were silent or ostentatiously turned their backs.

Between 1969 and 1970, approximately seventeen thousand Jews forfeited their apartments and pensions and departed Poland. Veteran Communists, extensively intermarried, most of them were uninterested in resuming their lives in Israel. Upon reaching their initial way station in Vienna, they opted for other, Western lands. Many preferred the Scandinavian countries, which traditionally had maintained an open-door policy for Eastern bloc refugees. "The simplest way would have been to go to Israel," Panski admitted, with some discomfiture. "But I had never done anything useful for Zionism and probably would have met a hostile reception there." Fear of the Israeli rabbinate too, of the complications that awaited his daughter—the product of a mixed marriage—could not have been absent from his mind. "Anyway, I was quite familiar with Sweden," he explained. "I had lived there briefly during the war, after all, and could get by in the language. I felt the chance was good of finding employment."

By the time the Panskis arrived in Stockholm, they were without resources. The expense of purchasing "exit visas" and tickets had cleaned them out. Fortunately, a representative of HIAS, the international Jewish immigration organization, met them at the station and arranged their temporary lodgings at a small hotel. The local Jewish community provided them with food and pocket money for their first weeks in the country. Earlier Polish Jewish émigrés had organized their own Union of Polish Jews, and it was this group that assisted the Panskis and other immigrants with housing. Finally, the Swedish government made available a special language and orientation course, then employment services. Almost every Polish Jew eventually found a job in Sweden. Panski himself was placed in the Institute of Economics at the University of Gothenburg, where he earned an adequate livelihood—and later a doctorate—as a research specialist on East European economics. His wife was given employment as a librarian. Eva, their daughter, was admitted tuition-free to the University of Stockholm. They were safe.

So, it appeared, meanwhile, was Wladyslaw Gomulka in his position as party secretary in Warsaw. The Soviet invasion of Czechoslovakia had served as a tacit warning to his nationalist enemies. Both Moczar and Gierek muted their criticism for the time being. A year and a half later, however, authorizing the dismissal of "redundant" workers, Gomulka triggered a chain reaction of demonstrations and strikes. These were suppressed by army units, causing the death of several hundred workers and the wounding of thousands of others. Public opinion was outraged; no comparable violence had occurred in twenty-six years of Communist rule in Poland. Terrified of an even wider-spread revolt, a majority of the politburo in December 1970 voted to dismiss Gomulka in favor of Edward Gierek.

Yet the Gierek era was hardly an improvement. Throughout its ensuing ten years, this regime, too, failed to cope with the ongoing shortage of food and the escalating cost of living. By August 1980, the economic situation had deteriorated so alarmingly that some half-million Polish workers went out on strike for eighteen days. Their demand now was government recognition of their own newly established labor organization, Solidarity. Completely unnerved by this upheaval, Gierek entered into negotiations with Solidarity's leader, Lech Walesa, and capitulated entirely. For the first time in an Eastern bloc nation, a workers' organization unaffiliated with the Communist Party was recognized. Additionally, the government permitted the church to broadcast Sunday mass over the national radio. These were concessions potentially as extensive as those of Czechoslovakia's Prague Spring in 1968. Even so, they were not sufficient to rescue Gierek's personal authority. Faced with the threat of additional demands and strikes, the first secretary bowed to the pressure of his colleagues and resigned his post in favor of a moderate, Stanislaw Kaniz. For a brief moment, it appeared that meaningful liberalization, so often promised and so often betrayed, was taking place in Poland at last.

The turmoil also provided an unanticipated benefit for the nation's remaining ten thousand Jews (and half-Jews). For the Polish establishment, the 1968 hate campaign had been a skeleton in the closet. That closet had been kept tightly shut under Gierek. But in the upheaval that was shaking the country, it was now being reopened. The national debate allowed liberals and other victims of the 1968 campaign to speak out for the first time about this "black page" in Polish history. At meetings of intellectuals and students, in letters to newspapers, in radio discussion programs, the "shame" of 1968 was openly condemned and warnings were issued against its recurrence. On the thirteenth anniversary of the March 1968 students' uprising, the academic branch of Solidarity organized a commemorative meeting at the University of Warsaw. A collection of documents, photographs, and other items relating to the tragic events of 1968 was put on exhibition, and attention was called to the historic contributions of Jews to Polish national culture.

These allusions to the Jewish question represented a direct challenge to General Moczar. For several months, recriminations against
the government had kept the interior minister and his followers on the
defensive. In late March of 1981, however, responding to the commemorative event at the university, Moczar instructed his partisans in the
national veterans organization to conduct their own rally to honor
"Polish patriots murdered and jailed in 1948–56 by torturers under the
banner of Berman, Zambrowski, Fegin, Fozansky, Michnik, etc."
Placards warned the "Zionist clique" to "keep their hands off Poland."
Taking the offensive against the liberals, then, Moczar encouraged the
circulation of antisemitic books and pamphlets. One of the most notable
was a volume published by a journalist, Zdzislaw Ciesiolkiencz, entitled
Invasion of the Phantoms, 1944–70. Purporting to divulge the role of
Jews in Polish history, its subtitle was: "Who Are They? Where Are
They From? How Have They Harmed Poland?" Throughout 1981 and
1982, while it outlawed Solidarity, arrested Walesa, then momentarily
stepped back from harsher action, the government issued antisemitic
posters bearing Nazi-like caricatures of Jews as agents of "international
Zionism." Although the placards were torn down at night by Solidarity
members, they were replaced each morning. Facing economic chaos,
acute food shortages, and chronic unrest, the regime felt itself on safer
ground by invoking Poland's endemic xenophobia. In this nation, it
knew, Jew-hatred was the one virus that could never be eradicated.

"They can only eradicate Jews," muttered Panski dourly. Iron-gray
hair rumpled over his vast temples, he sat in his modest flat on the
northern fringe of Stockholm, in a sprawling workers' housing complex
inhabited by Spaniards, Turks, Algerians, and other enclaves of
Gastarbeiter. Children played outside in a babel of languages. "Myself,
I don't get around much anymore," he continued. "The heart went bad
three years ago." He retired then. His wife, still trim and handsome,
kept her job in the municipal library. Between his pension and her
salary, they lived adequately. Eva, twenty-six, a graduate of the University of Stockholm, now worked in Paris as an economist in a bank.
"I'm not entirely out of action, though," Panski added. "I'm secretary of
the Union of Polish Jews here." There was a note of muted embarrassment in his voice. "The first time in my life I've been active in anything
Jewish." Did he maintain any of his former Polish or Communist associations? He smiled coldly then. "Not one. I try not to think of the years
I wasted in that pitiful love affair. It was all one way." He recalled again

that it was specifically Jews like him, thoroughly assimilated and un-affiliated with Jewish life, who had been rooted out and destroyed by the successive Communist regimes. Even so, he was reminded, the government was planning a fortieth anniversary commemoration next year of the Warsaw ghetto uprising. Rumor had it that delegations of foreign Jews were to be invited.

"Foreign Jews, indeed," he scoffed. "The entire ceremony will be a public relations gesture for foreign consumption. Ask, rather, how many Polish Jews will be invited to return." He shook his head. "With this people, nothing has changed. Nothing will change."

He was fond of Sweden. He would fight for it. "But I would fight even more willingly for Israel," he added. During the Yom Kippur War of 1973, he joined the Stockholm Jewish Community in its mass meet-ings on behalf of Israel. Three weeks later, he visited Israel for the first time. Would he move there? "No, I have only two or three years left. Too late for any more moving around." Then he added quickly: "But at least I'm identified as a Jew. After the 1973 war, I began attending a synagogue for the first time since my Bar Mitzvah. Just to show that I'm part of the Jewish people." On the mantel stood a portrait of his daugh-ter, a slim, quite striking young woman. He gazed at it reflectively. "She's strong and hard, like her parents," he observed then. "She won't even go back to Poland for a visit. She doesn't want to hear about it." His wife, silent until that point, whispered something to him, and he nodded. "Yes. When we first arrived in Sweden, I registered our daughter with the Jewish community in Gothenburg, in order to help her find her own identity. Two years later, at her own express wish, she attended classes with the rabbi and accepted the Jewish faith officially." He smiled again, this time with a certain shy pride. "I'm satisfied that she's learned a good lesson from her old father's mistakes. There has to be at least one identity no one can ever take from you."

XIII

The Wages of Collaboration:
Hungary and Romania

The Glory That Was Budapest

A taxi ride from Budapest's central railroad station to the Hotel Royal challenged all my expectations of the grim austerity awaiting in a Socialist "people's republic." A week of touring the Hungarian capital all but obliterated them. Magisterial public buildings dating from the Habsburg era matched anything I had seen in Vienna. So did the half-dozen bridges arabesquing over the Danube; the brilliantly chandeliered theaters and opera; the scores of churches, mullioned and frescoed in an amalgam of Romanesque, Italian Renaissance, and Gothic styles; the sweeping boulevards, public squares and parks; the cascading fountains and floodlit statuary; the pedestrian malls, subway stations, shopping arcades; the modern hotels (a Hilton among them); the crowded restaurants and coffee shops.

There was nothing tentative or jerry-built about shops stocked with consumer goods, market stalls laden with fruits and vegetables, streets humming with private automobiles (most, to be sure, of East European manufacture). Was Big Brother watching? His eye surely was not on the hotel bookshops, with their Western newspapers and magazines, from *Stern* and *Paris Match* to the *International Herald Tribune, Time,* and *Newsweek;* or on the cabarets with their rock bands and spoofs of inept bureaucrats. "Socialism with a Human Face," Party Chairman Janos Kadar had promised his nation (Dubcek in Czechoslovakia later preempted the slogan). He may well have kept that promise. "Long life to him!" my hosts murmured fervently, when his name came up in our discussions. I believe they meant it.

They were Jews, and they understood this country, this city, with a proprietary insight. In the years following Jewish emancipation in 1867, every right, every career opportunity was theirs. No ethnic strain in all Hungary became as thoroughly magyarized as they. It was no accident that the Great Synagogue, on Dohany utca 2, a century and a quarter old, with its seating capacity of 3,000, its two balconies, its giant organ a respiratorium of 5,000 pipes (Liszt and Saint-Saëns had played their compositions on it), was the largest synagogue in Europe. As late as 1914, Jews numbered over 900,000 in Greater Hungary, and comprised a fifth of Budapest's population of a million ("Judapest," cynics dubbed it). They were Hungary's middle class par excellence. By 1914, fully 60 percent of the nation's merchants were Jews. In Budapest, Jews constituted 42 percent of the journalists, 45 percent of the lawyers, 49 percent of the doctors. Many held important positions in government, and hundreds bore the patent of nobility. In no other country was the share of Jewish authors in the national literature as extensive. Ferenc Molnar was the nation's most popular playwright. Jewish producers and directors were preeminent in the theater, Jewish conductors and instrumentalists in the concert halls. If this influence provoked antisemitism, it was far less virulent than the Austrian variety. In 1913, Jeno Heltai, a cousin of Theodor Herzl, was elected chairman of the Hungarian Writers' Association.

Jewish eminence in the pre-1914 era was achieved in a prosperous and transcendant imperial setting. The Hungary that emerged from World War I was dismembered more cruelly than any of the other Central Powers. Two-thirds of its territory was severed by the Treaty of Trianon, and half its population with it, leaving only 9 million people. The 445,000 Jews who remained in postwar Hungary were still a middle-class community, but their status now was an exposed target for an impoverished and chauvinist petite bourgeoisie. Their vulnerability became particularly acute in the immediate aftermath of the war. For 133 days, Hungary was ruled by a Communist dictatorship. Its party boss, Bela Kun, was a Jew. So were 31 of the 49 commissars in Kun's regime. When the Red cabal finally was overthrown by the Hungarian military, the full force of the counterrevolution was turned against Communist and non-Communist Jews alike. By early 1920, some 3,000 Jews had been murdered, 5,000 wounded, and an antisemitism that had been essentially fitful and ineffectual in the prewar years was now all but institutionalized among the nation's lower middle classes.

To be sure, the regency of Admiral Miklos Horthy spared Hungarian Jewry's economic position. Horthy was uninterested in fanning the flames of populist antisemitism. He counted a number of prominent Jews among his closest financial advisers and even among his personal friends. Until the mid-1930s, the circumstances of the Jewish middle class remained tolerable, particularly by comparison with those of Jews in Poland and Romania. It was the onset of the world depression, then the rise of Nazism in Germany, that shattered the illusion of restored normalcy. Following Hitler's Anschluss with neighboring Austria in 1938, the Hungarian government began slowly to ingratiate itself with the Nazi Führer. Parliament enacted a law restricting the quota of Jewish employees in private business to 20 percent of the work force (a figure later reduced to 12 percent) and 6 percent of those employed in the higher professions, and barred Jews altogether from "responsible positions" in the media. Nor could Jews acquire Hungarian citizenship any longer by naturalization. After Germany's occupation of Czechoslovakia in March 1939, the Führer's "Vienna Awards" returned to Hungary extensive tracts of its pre-1919 territories from Czechoslovakia and (under intimidation) from Romania and Yugoslavia. In these regions lived some 224,000 Jews, who now also became subject to Budapest's anti-Jewish legislation.

What did the discrimination mean in practical terms? Agnes Gergely remembers. Born in an eastern Hungarian village near Endrod, she was the daughter of a journalist, originally Gyorgy Gutmann (the name was later magyarized to Gergely). Although he was a devout patriot, in 1939, under the quotas of the antisemitic legislation, he was dismissed from his position as deputy editor of the local newspaper published by the Smallholders Party. Moving to Budapest, he was obliged to work as a chauffeur, then as a garage mechanic. He lodged his family in a roach-ridden basement flat. Agnes, an only child, was dressed in secondhand clothes provided by relatives. Like many Jewish children, she attended a Jewish day school. Many of her schoolmates came from the upper-middle-class Jewish quarter of Lipotvaros. Their snobbery was more painful to her than the bigotry of her Hungarian neighbors. "It was a two-pronged assault from antisemites and wealthy Jews," she recalled. "I suspect that's what made a lot of us susceptible to communism in later years."

World War II completed the destruction of Jewish self-esteem. Only a generation before, many of these people had regarded themselves as the aristocracy of Hungary. Now, shamed and broken by the antisemitic legislation of the 1930s and 1940s, they possessed less moral defense in depth than did their kinsmen in Poland and Romania. The latter's burden of persecution at least did not include the weight of hubris. The physical ordeal of Hungarian Jewry began only later in the war. Once the Horthy regime entered the conflict at the side of Germany in 1941, its role in the anti-Jewish "actions" was not directed at first against the Jews of pre-1938 Hungary, but rather against Yugoslav Jews, then against Jews in the formerly Slovakian regions of Carpatho-Ukraine. These were slaughtered. Additional thousands of Jews in the Vienna Awards territories were shipped to the zone of direct German occupation, for murder at the hands of the SS. Ultimately, the largest number of Jews in these areas perished.

Yet within "integral" Hungary, no serious restrictions were imposed on Jewish freedom of movement during the early war years. Hungarian citizens, Jews and Gentiles alike, were entitled to the same food rations. In 1940, Agnes Gergely's father was taken into the army, together with all Hungarian men of military age. Under intense German pressure, too, Jewish soldiers were separated from non-Jews, obliged to wear yellow stripes, then assigned to special penal work battalions. But even then, Hungarian Jewish patriotism was not entirely dissipated. With others of their Jewish friends, Agnes's family still shared the sense of outrage at the 1920 Treaty of Trianon, even a certain convoluted gratitude to Hitler for the Vienna Awards. In common with other Hungarians, they were horrified by the Don Catastrophe in 1943, when eighty thousand Hungarian troops froze to death at Voronezh during the Soviet campaign. All the while, Admiral Horthy and Prime Minister Miklos Kallay refused to turn their Jewish citizens over to the Germans. Their stubbornness was fortified in 1943, as they sensed that the Axis had shot its bolt. Indeed, by then the government was determined to extricate Hungary from the war altogether. It was to abort this move, in turn, that on March 19, 1944, Hitler ordered the occupation of Hungary by the German Wehrmacht.

The evening of the Nazi occupation, Agnes's father was on leave from his battalion and attending an operetta with his family. In the parterre during intermission, he overheard an urgent conversation between a group of Hungarian army officers. Horrified, he rushed back to the auditorium to inform his wife and daughter. "The Germans are in Budapest," he whispered. "Let's commit suicide." Instead, they returned to their basement flat and waited. Within days, thousands of SS and German regular army troops began fanning through the city, rounding up Jews from prepared lists, then herding them into special ghetto areas. With scores of other Jewish families, the Gergelys were crowded into a six-story building on St. Stephen's Boulevard, in the Erzsebetvaros—Jewish—quarter. The numbers were reduced in ensuing days as Jewish men were marched off to forced labor camps. Returned to his battalion, Gyorgy Gergely wrote his wife and daughter, begging them to convert. His wife would not hear of it. Rather, months later, she visited the Swedish embassy to request documents of protection. Word had already circulated through the ghetto of Raoul Wallenberg's heroic rescue efforts. The papers were forthcoming the same day. Mother and daughter then were transferred to a special "protected" house, with the Swedish crest on it.

The Hungarian regime would countenance only a limited number of "diplomatic" exemptions, however. The great majority of Budapest Jews was exposed to the Final Solution. By the tens of thousands, they were dispatched to Auschwitz. On November 22, Gyorgy Gergely managed to secure a week's furlough to visit his family. It was a harassed, poignant reunion, bereft of privacy, racked by hunger. On the thirtieth, Gergely was shipped back to his unit. He never returned. A month later, all "protected" Jews in Budapest were gathered at St. Stephen's Park and transferred with the others to the principal ghetto, the Dohany Synagogue complex. In the Great Synagogue itself and its connected buildings, and through the rest of the street, were packed fully 130,000 people. Each day, the ghetto was "thinned out" by death camp deportations. It was at this point, as the Soviet army approached the gates of Budapest, that Adolf Eichmann, who had taken personal charge of the Final Solution in Hungary, ordered the shrinking pocket of Budapest Jewry out of the city and force-marched westward on the highway to Vienna. In the course of this trek, an additional 50,000 Jews perished. For the small remaining minority in the capital, waiting its turn for expulsion, death came from starvation, disease, and random Arrow-Cross shootings.

Agnes was nearly one of the victims. Scavenging for food in the ghetto's refuse bins, she came down with dysentery. Convulsed by spasms, she prayed for the attacking Soviet bombers to end her misery. Others were equally certain that the end had come. Ilona Seifert, later to become executive director of the Central Board of Hungarian Jews, was hiding with her mother and sister in a pension near the Gergelys. As the Russians drew close, she watched the Arrow-Cross guards mining the ghetto, preparing to demolish it together with its Jewish occupants. Rabbi Sandor Scheiber, standing with outstretched arms in the doorway of the Swiss legation, watched his approaching mother shot dead in the street by an Arrow-Cross hooligan. His father died of malnutrition that same December. With his wife, his brother, and his sister, Scheiber also now silently awaited the end.

The Red Army arrived first. On January 18, 1945, a young Soviet Jewish lieutenant walked into the building where the Gergelys and other Jews were hiding and informed them that they were free. Nearly two years would pass before the final account would be drawn up on the Holocaust in Hungary. By then, it was the consensus of historians that 450,000 Jews had died—70 percent of the Jewish population of post-1938 Hungary. Within the boundaries of integral—prewar—Hungary, half the Jews were annihilated. Approximately 155,000 survived in Budapest, and about 55,000 to 65,000 in the provinces. It was an all but mortal blow to a community that, like Germany's, had regarded itself as native to the bone and marrow.

The Litany of Postwar Hopes

When the war ended, Hungary lay in ruins, its economy shattered, its population on the verge of ruin. The ordeal of the Jews was particularly acute. Debilitated by hunger and illness, they died off at the rate of seven hundred a week throughout the winter and spring of 1945. Agnes and her mother were among the survivors. Within ten or twelve days, the worst of Agnes's dysentery passed. Afterward, mother and daughter began the trek to their native town of Endrod, nearly one hundred miles from the capital. They walked through snow, in ragged shoes and clothing, begging their food from peasants en route, occasionally receiving lifts in Soviet army vehicles. By the time they reached Endrod, Agnes was suffering from frostbite. A local physician examined her feet and recommended immediate amputation. Hereupon a neighboring peasant woman, an old acquaintance of the Gergely family, took the youngster in hand and massaged her ankles twice a day with cattle dung. Agnes recovered. During the next three months, the Gergelys spun wool for the peasants and received food in return. In the late spring, with their strength reviving, they moved on to a larger town, Szeged. There a family friend took them in. Agnes returned to school. Mrs. Gergely found work in an orphan hostel operated by the Joint. By the autumn of 1945, Joint funds were arriving in substantial quantities. Joint canteens were opening in Budapest and in other communities. The Jewish death rate declined.

The prospects for Hungary seemed hopeful at first. A free election took place in November 1945, and the Communists won only 8 percent of the vote. Soviet forbearance was destined to be short. With the intimidating presence of the Red Army behind them, the Communists turned their efforts in the next year to infiltration. As elsewhere in Eastern Europe, their strategy was to participate in "coalition governments," while systematically building their cadres. Their Soviet-trained leadership included a large majority of Jews. Although many of the commissars from the Bela Kun era in 1919 had been killed, a number of them had survived in Soviet exile. These were the men who returned now in the wake of the Red Army. Their spokesman was Matyas Rakosi.

The illegitimate son of a Jewish miller's daughter and a Gentile coachman, Rakosi was a brilliant student who had attended the Habsburg monarchy's elite school for diplomats in Vienna before joining the Communist movement. A thoroughly unscrupulous apparatchik, physically unprepossessing with his fleshy bald head and squat body, Rakosi had spent a decade and a half in Hungarian prisons after an international campaign had saved him from a death sentence for his role in the commune of 1919. In 1940, he was released and went to Moscow. Now, four years later, he returned at the head of a quintet of fellow Jews that included Erno Gero, who would become the Communist government's economic overlord; Mihaly Farkas, its military and defense chieftain; Jozsef Revai, its cultural "pope"; and most important, Gabor Peter, who would be named chief of the dreaded security police. Of the twenty-five members of the first Communist central committee in postwar Hungary, no fewer than nine were Jews; while at the lower echelons, Jews were widely, even preponderantly, distributed in key positions. It was precisely this Jewish leadership that tolerated a renewed wave of antisemitism. Time was needed, they believed, to recruit a larger party membership. Thus, in 1946, when Jewish efforts to secure the return of homes and businesses touched off pogroms in communities such as Miskolc and Kunmadaras, the Communists refrained from intervening. Gabor Peter, the Jewish chief of the security police, declined to act. When Jews appealed for protection or pressed their claims for restitution, they were advised by the authorities to "be patient," to display "understanding."

Within three years after the end of the war, the Communists had sufficiently infiltrated the political system to assume decisive control. The change at first brought little improvement for the Jews. Although the regime no longer found it necessary to tolerate pogroms, the wholesale Communist nationalization of property, of large and small businesses alike, all but liquidated the Jews as a middle class. Throughout 1948, the number of Jews dependent on Joint relief funds rose to 94,000 out of a total Jewish population (by then) of 143,000. In 1951, the Rakosi government began to deport expropriated "capitalists" and similar "unproductive" elements from Budapest and other cities to distant villages, where they were confined under inhuman conditions. It was a curious twist, then, that Rakosi and his detested regime, identified by the Hungarians as Jewish, should have dealt with the Jews more brutally than with any other group in Hungary.

In 1948, Agnes's mother lost her job in Szeged when the Joint's network of orphan hostels was closed. Returning to Budapest, she finally secured employment as a clerk in a state clothing shop. Agnes left school to work as a steam-presser in a clothing factory, then as a lathe operator in a locomotive factory. Her ambition was to study at the Drama Academy. In fact, she was accepted by the academy in 1950, but was dropped several weeks later as a political "unreliable" when it was learned that her father had worked for the Smallholders Party. Applying later to the University of Budapest, she was denied admission. Remarkably, both her Socialist idealism and her Hungarian patriotism remained intact.

Seventeen years old in 1952, Agnes was only faintly aware of the purges ravaging the party in Hungary and elsewhere in the Communist world. The struggle thrust the Jewish issue directly into public consciousness. Faced with Stalin's antisemitic frenzy in 1952, which led to the fall of Rudolf Slansky in Prague and Anna Pauker in Bucharest, and which culminated in the Doctors' Plot in Moscow, Rakosi hastened to save his own skin by jettisoning his Jewish colleagues. He ordered the arrest not only of his closest allies, including Gabor Peter and other Jewish officials of the security police, but also of other Communists who happened to be Jews. The roll call extended from the chairman of the Jewish Community and the president of the Hungarian state radio to scores of Jewish physicians, journalists, and executives at all levels of society.

But, in the end, Rakosi himself could not escape the antisemitic terror. Fully aware of the depth of Jew-hatred in Hungary, Stalin decided that Jews in key positions weakened the party's position. In February 1953, the order came down from Moscow that Rakosi should leave his post as premier (he was allowed to continue as party leader), although this decision was not put into effect until several months later—ironically, after Stalin's death. Two other members of the "Rakosi quintet," Farkas and Revai, also lost their posts. Later, at Moscow's instructions, the Hungarian Communist politburo appointed a compromise figure, Imre Nagy, as the new premier, and warned him to protect the party's image by cleansing it of Jewish influence. Although a number of Jews had long been among Nagy's closest friends and associates, the premier dutifully complied.

How had the Hungarian Jewish population fared by remaining in the country? Some had anticipated a meaningful revival of Jewish communal life. Three decades later, Sandor Scheiber, now in his late sixties, bespectacled and brush-mustached, reminisced in the ancient rabbinical seminary building on the Jozsef Korut. A Neologue (Conservative) rabbi, Scheiber held a doctorate from the University of Vienna, and had achieved a reputation as a promising scholar before the war. Following the liberation, he resumed his career as a professor in the seminary. The circumstances were grim. Students and faculty alike spent much of their time scavenging for food. "That wasn't important," Scheiber insisted. "At least we were able to conduct our studies without political interference. The first postwar government meant to do the right thing for our community." It was a fact. Jewish religious, cultural, and educational institutions were reactivated. Under a cabinet decree of 1945, the property of the decimated religious communities was taken over by the Central Board of Hungarian Jews. A Jewish museum was reestablished, even a Jewish Free University and music school. Two dozen of the former 147 Jewish elementary schools and five Jewish high schools were reopened. "That was our postwar golden age," Scheiber remarked.

It lasted barely two and a half years. As the Communists tightened their grip on the nation after 1948, they similarly assumed full control of the Central Board of Hungarian Jews. Although Jews shared with other denominations a constitutional guarantee of religious freedom, the "atmosphere" changed (here Scheiber became somewhat vague in recollection). Jewish newspapers and periodicals were discontinued. The curriculum of the Jewish day schools was thoroughly reoriented to communism, and the schools themselves later were nationalized. One of the most important casualties was the Joint's network of institutions. Between 1945 and 1952, American Jewish philanthropy had poured $52 million into Hungary for relief and welfare. Except for the DP camps of Germany, this was the Joint's single largest program in any European country. In 1953, it was all closed down and many of its Hungarian employees were arrested.

Zionist activity also experienced the vicissitudes of Communist rule. Before 1940, Zionism had not been one of the stronger political or cultural movements among the extensively acculturated Hungarian Jewish population. This changed substantially after 1945, of course. Zionism after the war became virtually the raison d'être of the Jewish school network, even of the Central Board of Hungarian Jews. If emigration to Palestine was smaller from Hungary than from Poland or Romania, age may have been a factor. The survival rate of middle-aged Jews here was somewhat higher than in other European countries, and presumably this older group was less inclined to face the hardships of starting over in DP camps or in Israeli relocation camps. Of the approximately 70,000 Hungarian Jews who made their way to the American zone of Germany, anticipating a swift emigration from there to Palestine, most were younger people. (Agnes Gergely's mother was one of those who stayed behind, and her daughter would not leave her; afterward, there would be no opportunity for reappraisal.) By the late 1940s, the party was committed to the harsh Soviet line against Zionism. It disbanded the Zionist organization altogether in March 1949 and began arresting its leadership. The arrests continued throughout 1949 and 1950. Unlike the other Communist satellites, which in 1949 regarded Jewish emigration to Israel as an anti-British measure, the Budapest regime maintained its ban precisely because the key members of the ruling elite were Jewish. The 135,000 Jews who remained evidently were trapped.

Thaw and Revolution, Hungarian Style

The purge of Rakosi and his last Jewish associates, following the death of Stalin in March 1953, lifted the worst of the terrorist repression in Hungary. The new premier, Imre Nagy, was a man of unexpected moderation. In June 1953, he abandoned forced collectivization, endorsed a shift to the production of consumer goods, then opened the doors of prisons and labor camps and authorized the return of the "parasites" who had been exiled from Budapest. The reversal evoked heartfelt relief among the Jews. Thousands of them were among the "capitalists" who had been shipped off to the provinces under penal conditions, together with hundreds of others convicted by the Rakosi regime for "Zionist activities." "I was admitted to the university at last," recalled Agnes Gergely. "My bourgeois background no longer was held against me. My mother and I even were allowed to move into a larger room." Jewish communal institutions revived, several newspapers reappeared, a few schools were reopened.

The loosening of restraints was curtailed again within a few years. The power struggle within the Soviet Union, especially the fall of Gyorgy Malenkov in February 1955, enabled Rakosi to unseat Imre Nagy in Budapest, to dismiss him as premier, then to have him expelled from the party. But the Hungarian people no longer were as easily intimidated. Learning of the revolutionary events in Poland in October 1956, intellectuals and workers alike demanded the return of Nagy, the withdrawal of Soviet troops based in Hungary, the introduction of free elections. Taken aback by the mounting unrest, the Hungarian politburo moved quickly to reinstall Nagy as premier. Yet the gesture failed to abort the incipient revolt. The rebels pressed their demands even more forcefully. For his part, Nagy seemed prepared to accommodate them. He promised free elections, a Western-style government, and closer relations with the West altogether. This time, however, the provocation was too much for Moscow. On November 4, 1956, Soviet army units stationed in the Hungarian provinces unleashed a massive attack on Budapest. The revolutionaries were swiftly crushed. Even as Nagy and his colleagues took refuge in the Yugoslav embassy, the Russians installed Janos Kadar, a more reliable pro-Soviet party drone, as the new premier of Hungary.

Jewish students and intellectuals participated in the demonstrations. Agnes Gergely was among them. She remembered the marches and protests as "beautiful, heroic." Most of her fellow students favored a progressive Socialist administration. There was never a question of a return to the older prewar tradition of reactionary government. Nevertheless, once the uprising was suppressed, the Kadar regime argued in its "White Book" that if the "counterrevolution had not been put down within a comparatively short time, it might have spelled death for Hungarian Jewry." The statement has been contested. Historians such as

Paul Lendvai insist that the absence of serious antisemitic outbursts was actually one of the "miracles" of the October uprising. Agnes is less certain. In October 1956, as she stood in the midst of crowds besieging the Hungarian state radio, she sensed the underlying malevolence of many of the demonstrators, especially of the workers. Epithets were shouted about "that damned Jew Rakosi," and "Judeo-Bolshevism." The Star of David was scrawled on the doors of numerous Jewish homes. "These episodes simply devastated me," Agnes confessed. "I left the demonstrations and went home. From then on, I took no further part in the protest movement."

Other Jews shared her misgivings at the events of late October. Of the 170,000 refugees who fled to Vienna during the uprising and its aftermath, at least 20,000 were Jews who feared that the hatred accumulated over the Rakosi years soon would be aimed at them. Their fears may have been groundless. On June 17, 1958, Moscow completed its retaliation with the announcement that Imre Nagy and three other leaders of the October insurrection had been executed in Budapest. One of them, Miklos Gimes, was a Jew, as well as a brave liberal. But after the revolution, the Jewish origin of a politician or an intellectual did not significantly affect Soviet or Hungarian policy.

By mid-1959, the Kadar regime was well enough established to permit an extensive relaxation of the police state. In return for "stability," Kadar was prepared to offer his people major concessions, particularly an improved standard of living. Some years later, in 1968, a New Economic Model was introduced, opening up profit opportunities equally for farmers, professionals, and managers of industrial and commercial enterprises. A much wider freedom of expression was introduced into Hungarian cultural life. Western influences everywhere were apparent throughout the 1960s and 1970s, in music, drama, literature, in coffee shops and discussion groups. Kadar had long since adopted a famous slogan: "Who is not against us is with us." And he got away with it, for in matters of foreign policy he remained loyal to Moscow. The Hungarian people understood, and were not dissatisfied.

No element of the population expressed the prevailing sentiment, "Long life to Kadar," with more enthusiasm than did the Jews. Economically, they shared in the blessings of the new liberalization. From the 1960s on, they were to be found prominently among owners of textile workshops, of small furniture and appliance shops. Large numbers of them resurfaced in the professions. Jews served as editors and deputy editors of many newspapers. Theater and cinema in Hungary were overwhelmingly Jewish again. Possibly more than half of Budapest's physicians and lawyers were Jews, and surely more than half the nation's university professors—a proportion exceeding that of the pre–World War I era, when Jews comprised a far larger percentage of the Hungarian population. Nor did the Jews' middle-class origins pose further obstacles to their advancement in the government. Within a single decade after the revolution, the list of Jews serving in the administration included the deputy prime minister, the ministers of foreign trade, of transport and posts, of the treasury; the deputy ministers of defense, foreign affairs, the treasury, internal commerce, transport and posts; the president of the national bank, several score government department and bureau directors. As late as 1974, of thirteen members of the politburo, at least three were Jews—Gyorgy Aczel, Antal Apro, and Dezso Nemes. In 1979, eight Jews sat in the presidium, and thirty-seven in the parliament. If the Jews then comprised only a tiny fraction of the population, by the 1980s they remained far more visible in Hungarian public and intellectual life than in any other Communist nation.

Their opportunities were not unlimited. Although travel to the West was more open under Kadar, constraints were still imposed on emigration. These applied to Jews and non-Jews alike, for the government would not accept the loss of skilled personnel at a time when it was reviving its economy. If Jews occasionally defected to other countries (although rarely to Israel), the reasons had little to do with anti-semitism, but rather with their dislike of the regime. Indeed, Jews were disproportionately represented in the nation's tiny dissident movement. By 1984, it was intermarriage and the attrition of an aging community that had reduced Hungarian Jewry to some 75,000 in a population of 10 million. Of these, approximately 50,000 live in Budapest.

Upon her graduation from the university in 1957, Agnes Gergely looked forward to becoming a teacher of Hungarian and English in an elementary school. Although she had participated in the 1956 student demonstrations, within a year she was given employment in the school system and allowed to teach the subjects of her choice. From then on, Agnes encountered no further obstruction to her career. Diligently studying and perfecting her English, she moved to the state radio in 1963 as a producer of programs dealing with the English-speaking world. She and her mother were able to purchase a modest private apartment. In 1971, she left the radio to become a staff member of the

Hungarian literary weekly *Elet es Irodalom* (Life and Letters). Three years later, she was appointed a senior editor in the state publishing house; and in 1977, senior editor of *Nagyvilag* (Entire World), a respected monthly devoted to translations of foreign literature. Meanwhile, she had been publishing her own poetry, fiction, and criticism. Like the majority of Hungarian Jewish intellectuals, Agnes was secure—and comfortable. "Long life to him [Kadar]," she murmured repeatedly in our discussions.

Neither Agnes nor any other Jew doubted that antisemitism survived in Hungary. But it received no government sanction, not even under the euphemism of "anti-Zionism." Kadar's personal goodwill was above reproach. As an impoverished youth of the lowest class, he had literally been taught to read and write by a kindly Jewish family, and afterward had received his Marxist education from Jewish friends. He never abandoned those relationships. Indeed, Kadar repeatedly alluded to the wartime suffering of the Jews and to the right of Israel to exist as a Jewish homeland. "Thus, we are against the imperialist policy [of Israel] and not against the Jewish people," he emphasized, somewhat embarrassedly, in 1967, when he was obliged to follow Moscow's lead in breaking relations with Israel. "Nor are we against the State of Israel." By East European standards, subsequent criticism of Israel has remained comparatively moderate in Hungary. As for popular antisemitism, the government ensures that even an anti-Jewish remark is punishable by jail. Possibly no other measure would be effective.

An Island of Normalization?

The Central Board of Hungarian Jews is located in an aged building at Sip utca 12, off Rakoczi Boulevard. The site of the Jewish kehilla before the war, it occupies three stories, each shabbier than the next. The day of my first visit, Mrs. Ilona Seifert, the secretary-general, received me in her spacious office. Silver-haired, plumpish, with violet eyes of arresting beauty, she wore a stylish dress. Mrs. Seifert was a product of a middle-class Lipotvaros family. Her late husband, Geza Seifert, a lawyer, served as the Central Board's president for ten years, until his death in 1976. His leadership would have been unthinkable before the 1956 revolution, for he had never been a party member. But afterward, the changed psychological climate had permitted a certain revival of autonomous Jewish life.

Currently, Mrs. Seifert explained, some thirty synagogues function in Budapest and the provinces, as well as eleven Jewish old age homes, a two-hundred-bed hospital, a religiously oriented high school, a secular Jewish gymnasium, and of course the rabbinical seminary. Cultural and artistic programs are organized by the Central Board in Budapest and by branches in the larger provincial communities. *Uj Elet*, the Jewish communal newspaper, publishes fortnightly editions. After years of isolation, Hungarian Jewry has been permitted to resume extensive contacts with international Jewish organizations, and in 1981 the Central Board itself was authorized to become a member of the World Jewish Congress. It is all a pale shadow of prewar Hungarian Jewish life, perhaps, but still a dramatic contrast to the circumstances of many other East European Jewries.

Zionist activities remain banned. Nevertheless, Hungarian-born Jews living in Israel are allowed to pay return visits. During the Six-Day War, Geza Seifert publicly insisted that the hearts of Hungarian Jews were with Israel. The courageous remark was quoted widely in the press and evoked respect among the Hungarian people. When Seifert died, important government officials attended his funeral. His widow was asked to assume the position of secretary-general of the Board, and thereafter replaced her husband as the moving force in Jewish affairs. Chatting with me in German, Mrs. Seifert acknowledged as much. "It's a lot of work," she observed, smiling charmingly, her violet eyes doing a job on me that could not have been less effective with her government contacts, "but I love every minute of it. The government is so very cooperative now. We even get financial help from them." Most of the funding, she admitted, still came from membership dues. "But no one is obliged to be a member in this country," she assured me. "Thousands of Jews have defected, have intermarried. Dues would never begin to cover our expenses." What of the Joint? "Yes, of course," she agreed. "Their funding is invaluable. All those old age homes, our hospitals . . . But still, the government is our indispensable partner. Without its goodwill, we couldn't function." The Kadar government, of course. "God bless him," she whispered fervently.

The following day, I resumed my conversation with Rabbi Scheiber. He described the hardships of religious life immediately after the war, when barely 25 rabbis survived of the 115 who had held pulpits. As late as March 1944, on the eve of the Final Solution in Hungary, over 100 students had been preparing for their ordination at the seminary. In

1946, the total was 14 half-starved young men; and in 1948, half this tiny group joined the exodus to Israel. When the dean, Dr. Samuel Löwinger, similarly departed for Israel in 1950, Scheiber himself assumed the directorship. The next years were exceptionally difficult. Here again in our conversation, he became guarded. He did not deny that government officials monitored the classes in the early 1950s. "But there was never any question of closing the seminary," he assured me. "Anyway, all that nonsense stopped a year or two after the 1956 revolution. From then on, we conducted our courses as we liked."

Through all these vicissitudes, Scheiber managed to produce a succession of erudite books dealing with Jewish inscriptions in Hungary, codices in German libraries, Genizah studies, and his monumental two-volume *Jewish Folklore and History of Motifs*. In addition to numerous academic honors awarded him in the West, invitations came his way to teach—at Marshall Meyer's rabbinical seminary in Buenos Aires, at Jews College in London. "I was never tempted," he stated flatly. "This is the only rabbinical seminary in Communist Europe. My mission is to keep my community alive."

After our talk, Scheiber invited me to join his pupils for Friday night dinner at the seminary, and to attend services afterward. I wandered through the building again. Could this actually have been the renowned Ignac Goldziher Theological Seminary, the "beacon" of East European Jewry? It was decrepit, neglected, moldering. Overlooking a common courtyard, some of its offices intermingled with private apartments. On the upper levels, women were beating carpets strung out on balcony rails. The seminary's lone bathroom was filthy, its empty scroll socket and towel bar crusted with disuse. Joining the seminarians later for dinner, I sat with five young men. They were an unimpressive crew, sour-looking and gruff-mannered. Two were Hungarians, one was Czech, and one was Bulgarian. And one of them—no mistaking that mouthful of steel dentistry—recently had arrived from the Soviet Union. I recognized a youth seated to my left. The day before, in Ilona Seifert's office, he had dropped by to have some papers signed. Mrs. Seifert had explained to me that he had been ordained a few months earlier and the government was allowing him to depart to assume a pulpit in Norse Bay, Ontario. I had questioned the young man briefly, speaking to him in Hebrew. His own Hebrew responses were stumbling. Well—Norse Bay. Discreetly testing the Hebrew of the other seminarians around me, however, I encountered an identical level of competence.

Services were conducted in the small adjoining synagogue. It was filled with some two hundred worshipers. In common with 95 percent of the professing Jews of Hungary, the congregants belonged to the Neologue trend. Virtually all the nation's Orthodox Jews—Chasidim, almost every one—had departed. The services now were on the brief side. The prayers were the conventional ones. To my delight, the young cantor intoned the Hungarian *nigun* in a truly beautiful tenor. His Hebrew pronunciation was pure Sephardic. After the services, I glanced at his text. It was transliterated Hungarian. Never mind. The most important feature of the services was the remarkable number of young people attending. Friday nights at the "Scheiber synagogue" were social events. "I'm the best *shadchan* [matchmaker] in Hungary," he had joked earlier. It was not the least of his importance to a community half of whose young Jews already were intermarried. I thought of Agnes Gergely, once betrothed to a Gentile, once briefly married to a Jew, and now entirely eclectic in her circle of friends.

Following the services, the congregants ascended the stairway to a third-floor auditorium. Tables had been arranged in a great horseshoe. At the head table, Scheiber ceremoniously intoned the blessing over an immense challah, personally distributed morsels of the bread to each of the two hundred people in the room, then delivered a brief speech. It was a review of a newly published book on Hungarian folk legends, some of which he traced back to Hebrew sources. The audience listened raptly. During the social hour that followed, the mood was one of mild conviviality. Several of the congregants turned out to be Israelis on a return visit to family and friends. I could only wonder again at the political light-years that had passed from the murderous insecurity of the early 1950s to the current ambience of relaxed unselfconsciousness.

Had I gauged the atmosphere correctly? I posed the question to Agnes Gergely two days later, as we sat with her mother on the porch of their vacation villa at Lake Balaton. "I would say so," she replied finally. "Of course, it didn't hurt that Scheiber had picked a comparatively innocuous theme for his little speech. If you had understood Hungarian, you would have noted that he carefully abstained from any reference to Israel, even to the Jews of the United States. But commentary on a scholarly theme is entirely the Jewish cup of tea in this country." She looked at me to ensure that I understood. "It has nothing to do with assimilation. This is a sophisticated Jewry in Budapest. It always has been. It bears no comparison with the Jews of Romania or with those in most of the other East European communities. A quiet and unaggressive Jewishness, its roots intermingled with Hungarian folklore—how did Scheiber put it?—is the best we can hope for today. And believe me, we've come far these last thirty years to be able to express even that much."

Agnes had come far. In her passage from membership in the Young Communist League, her revulsion at the Lipotvaros Jews, her obsessed love affair with the Hungarian language and literature, she apparently had found a balance of her own. One of her nation's most respected writers, she had published ten volumes of her literary work. In 1963, her first book of poetry bore the title *You Are a Sign on My Doorjamb*. It was dedicated to the memory of her father, and the poems alluded frankly to the Holocaust. Her second novel, *The Interpreter*, described a love affair between a Hungarian Jewish woman and an Armenian sculptor, and the impact of the Holocaust as it lingered in the woman's life. The critics ignored the book for several years. "As I look back, I'm surprised it was published at all," she remarked. "It was public policy then not to draw attention to the Holocaust. The critics' silence broke my heart, though." She smiled. "Gave me ulcers, anyway." Later, the volume was translated and sold widely in Sweden. Only then did the Hungarian literary establishment turn their attention to it, deciding that they might safely praise it. "That broke the logjam," she explained. "Within the next few years, some ten or twelve Jewish authors began writing about the Jewish problem." Since then, more books on the Holocaust have been published in Hungary than anywhere else in the Communist world. "Like me, my fellow Jewish writers have had to come to grips with the issue, to work it through. I think I've worked it through." In later books, she was able to deal with more general themes. "But my current manuscript has returned to the subject of what it means to be a Jewish woman in Hungary. It's a novel and goes up to the revolution of 1956." She reflected for a moment. "I'm reasonably sure it will be accepted."

Agnes spoke in flawless English, and her words were a writer's, carefully chosen. ". . . Will be accepted."—the phrase remained with me during the train trip back to Budapest. Two days before, I had accompanied Scheiber from the synagogue for a brief pre-Sabbath stroll. During our earlier conversations, I had refrained from pressing him on the current attitude of the Hungarian people toward their Jewish neighbors. Nor was it really necessary to do so now. Inadvertently, I had left a skullcap on my head as we walked along a main thoroughfare. Wearing a conventional hat himself, Scheiber caught my lapse after several minutes. His voice was level, and very quiet. "It might be advisable for you to take off the yarmulke," he remarked gently.

Romania: Outpost of Asia

The undersized Czech locomotive hauled us into Bucharest shortly before midmorning. The terminal was the usual Near Eastern maelstrom—not quite as bad as Cairo, not much better than Istanbul—thronged with city dwellers, farmers, soldiers, most of them weighted down with tacky pressboard or vinyl suitcases, sacks of fruit, boxes of chickens, bags of laundry. Outside, the spectacle was of decrepit shops, kiosks, and "luxury" hotels—even these visibly in need of refurbishing—of streets overrunning with litter, of ill-shaven, patch-trousered men and heavy-legged women in shapeless print dresses. The taxi ride to my hotel carried me past foodshops besieged by lines of customers awaiting their week's quota of meat, eggs, milk, sugar. The Grand (or was it the Lux?) was three stars in my travel guide and intermittent hot water and a malfunctioning television set in my room. Not to worry. France and Italy had been worse in the early postwar years, and Arab hostelries were no picnic even now.

Downtown later that afternoon, I was approached by a dark man, his hair jet black and thickly oiled. His language was pidgin French. "Dollars? Travelers' checks? Je vous donne quatre mille pour cent dollars." Suddenly he was joined by his clone, equally dark, hair pomaded and gleaming.

"I give forty-five hundred," the newcomer shouted, in English.

Romania was a police state and I was a Western tourist. The newcomer sensed my consternation. Seizing my elbow, he attempted to guide me into a nearby shop. It may have been a clothing store. Four or five other dark men were waiting, and all but pulled my arms off with their supplications—"quarante-six mille," "forty-six fifty," "laissez-moi voir votre montre . . . je vous donnerai deux bijoux pour votre montre." It took me a good minute or two to shake them off, to refasten the snap on my watchband, to make my way back into pedestrian traffic. Even then, my original assailant harangued me down the street for the better part of a block.

"I see a lot of dark little people pestering tourists in town," I remarked to the hotel concierge later that day. "Their speech doesn't sound like Romanian to me."

"Should think not," the concierge replied. "They're Zigeuner."

Zigeuner—Gypsies! I had seen them before, perhaps twenty years earlier, their orchestras fiddling away in the restaurants of Belgrade and Zagreb. I should have remembered. "What do they do now?" I inquired. "Still musicians?"

"Still thieves," scoffed the concierge. "Only that. It's their only way of life."

A hotel functionary should not have been the last word on social history, of course. But others, the Romanian Jewish intellectuals I met later, confirmed the man's remarks. The Gypsies remained a historical anomaly, surviving generation to generation by theft and ruse. Efforts to lure them into productive livelihoods had never been successful. Before the war, a quarter-million of them had lived in Greater Romania, and smaller numbers throughout other Balkan nations. Hitler had made their liquidation a priority second only to the Jewish Final Solution. Contemplating my encounter with them, I suspected that their diminished members would have reduced them from a major social problem to a public annoyance.

My introduction to this land had been suggestive. For more than a century, Romania (its Gypsies and non-Gypsies alike) had been widely regarded as the last outpost of Asian vice on European soil. After World War I, the nation's legacy of Ottoman corruption was extended to a vast expansion of population and territory. The peace treaty converted Romania from a provincial backwater, with a population of barely 7 million, into the largest of the Balkan states, with 18 million inhabitants. The additions, from the ruins of the Habsburg and Romanov empires, and from Bulgaria, were hardly unmixed blessings. With the inherited territories came the ensnarled problems of minority groups—of some 2,500,000 Hungarians, 1,100,000 Ukrainians, 340,000 Germans, 300,000 Bulgars, together with several hundred thousand Turks, Poles, Serbs, and Gypsies.

Not less than 760,000 Jews were scattered through all the provinces. Before 1920, approximately 300,000 of them had lived within the frontiers of integral Romania—the Old Kingdom. Descendants of fugitives from tsarist Galicia, they maintained a vibrant Jewish culture. In addition to hundreds of synagogues and scores of venerated rabbis, Romanian Jews nurtured the first Yiddish theater and one of the earliest and most powerful Zionist movements in Europe. The quality of their intellectual life possibly was less austere than that of Hungarian Jewry; but Romania altogether was a less sophisticated realm than Hungary. On the other hand, representing a sizable component of the nation's middle class, the Jews contributed far beyond their numbers to Romania's cultural and artistic life. The author of the first Romanian grammar and the first Romanian dictionary, several of the country's outstanding writers and composers, were Jews.

Their contributions were less than appreciated. Nowhere did nineteenth-century parochialism and twentieth-century xenophobia blend more savagely after World War I than in Romania's paranoid suspicion of its large Jewish minority. For decades even earlier, Romania had bred an antisemitism as implacable as that of tsarist Russia's. Jews who had petitioned for citizenship found innumerable bureaucratic obstacles in their way. Others were subjected to physical pogroms. And then, after 1920, this engorged successor state was obliged to deal with a Jewish presence two and a half times larger than the substantial prewar enclave. Comprising 4 percent of the nation's population and 30 percent of its urban population, Romanian Jewry had become the third-largest Jewish community in Europe, after those of Poland and the Soviet Union.

The government confronted this vast "alien" settlement with little less than horror. From the 1920s on, Bucharest consciously exploited every legalism, every diplomatic wile, to evade its peace treaty obligations to its minority subjects—and specifically to its Jews. The half-million Jews of the annexed territories were deprived of full Romanian citizenship, and thereby not only of political rights but also of social insurance and other welfare benefits. Even the 300,000 indigenous Romanian Jews were relentlessly scourged through a shrewd government policy of étatism. Selected enterprises in which Jews had long been heavily represented were transformed into state monopolies, and their Jewish employees were dismissed. In smaller outlying towns with large Jewish minorities, physical beatings and lootings rarely were prosecuted, still less punished.

There appeared at first to be no political "logic" to this judeophobia. Unlike the nation's other minorities, who were regarded as irredentist outposts for neighboring "brother" states, the Jews represented no threat to Romanian sovereignty. But in fact their very helplessness was their undoing. They were an ideal target for a chauvinism that was skillfully manipulated by the boyar oligarchy. Dominating the government throughout the 1920s and 1930s, intent upon diverting and aborting peasant and lower-middle-class resentment under a quasi-feudal economy, the territorial magnates stigmatized the Jews as the authentic source of the nation's inequities and shortcomings. A cold pogrom tightly limited the number of Jews in the universities, in the civil service, in the professional and trade associations. In June 1938, the Jews of "integral" Romania were called upon to "prove their claims to citizenship." Whereupon the length of settlement of tens of thousands of native-born Romanian Jewish families was now exposed to examination. Nowhere outside Nazi Europe, not even in Poland, was a Jewish community subjected to so relentless a deprivation of political and economic status.

Then, in 1940, Greater Romania crumbled under the pressures of foreign imperialism. Only months after signing the Molotov-Ribbentrop Pact, the Soviet Union preempted Bessarabia and northern Bukovina. With German support, Hungary and Bulgaria annexed northern Transylvania and southern Dobruja. The Romanian Fascists, in turn, blaming King Carol for supinely accepting the nation's dismemberment, compelled the monarch to abdicate and then assumed power themselves. Under the dictatorship of General Ion Antonescu, the rightwing cabal launched into a policy of "national unification" in league with Germany. Its purpose was both to recover the territories lost to the Soviet Union and to wage a "national Christian crusade" against communism. These were code words that the Jews, of all peoples, had learned to dread. In October 1940, the Antonescu regime fulfilled their premonitions by decreeing the "romanianization"—that is, the confiscation—of Jewish industrial and agricultural property. Jews were subjected to forced labor instead of military service.

In the little Bukovinan town of Suceava, a young lawyer and parttime rabbi, Moses Rosen, acquired his own foretaste of the Jewish future on June 12, 1940. Infuriated by the Soviet occupation of nearby Bessarabia, the local population launched into a three-day orgy of beating Jews and sacking Jewish shops. The police did not intervene. Rather, when Rosen protested the outrage, he himself was arrested for "provocation," and during the next two months was held in a concentration camp. Upon his release, Rosen moved immediately to Bucharest, where he assumed Jews would be safer. He was naive. In January 1941, the Iron Guardists, largest of the country's Fascist paramilitary groups,

embarked on a systematic pogrom in the capital itself. Running wild in
Jewish neighborhoods, the black-shirted thugs spent two days shooting
and beating, then marched 170 Jewish men to a forest, shot them, and
hung their bodies on meat hooks in a Jewish abattoir. Rosen barely
escaped their fate by hiding in a synagogue.

Soon afterward, Antonescu purged the Iron Guard, and ensured
that "military order" was returned to the nation. The respite for the
Jews would be brief. In June 1941, Germany launched its invasion of
the Soviet Union. Collaborating in the assault, the Romanians similarly
coordinated their Jewish policy with the Nazis. In the first week of the
war, following a Soviet air raid on Jassy, the Romanian army organized
a "retaliatory action" against the city's Jewish "traitors." It was systematic killing this time. Some 8,000 Jews were shipped off in cattle
cars from Jassy to deadleg sidings, and all but a few hundred of them
perished of suffocation. Three thousand other Jews were shot or hacked
to pieces in the streets. As the war progressed, another 12,000 Jews
were shot in Czernowitz. In Bessarabia, the Romanian army slaughtered 50,000 Jews—shocking even the Germans with their indifference
to the disposal of corpses. Then, in August, the government found it
simpler to herd Bessarabian Jews across the Dniester, to concentration
camps operated by Romanians in territory—Transdniestria—under direct German occupation. By November 1942, approximately 200,000 of
the deportees were liquidated.

Except for the inhabitants of Jassy, the Jews of integral Romania
fared somewhat better than those in the reoccupied "treaty" territories.
It was a close thing. Early in the summer of 1942, Adolf Eichmann's
personal representative, SS Hauptsturmführer Gustav Richter, negotiated an understanding with the Antonescu government for the deportation of Romanian Jews into German-occupied territory. But Antonescu
changed his mind a few months later, as the war began to turn against
the Germans, and particularly after the disaster of Stalingrad. With the
threat of Allied retribution no longer remote, a decision was immediately reached to "protect" Romanian Jews. Their condition remained
marginal, to be sure. By then, tens of thousands of them had been
driven from their positions in industry and trade, in the professions and
handicrafts, and reduced to subsistence within their own closed economy. Nearly 40 percent of the Jewish male population was serving in
the penal labor force. Their ordeal was compounded by the widespread
looting of Jewish property, and intense pressure on Jews to "contribute"

money and clothing for social welfare. Once the Bucharest government surrendered in August 1944, the wider consequences of Romanian collaboration with the Germans could be assessed. Fully 90,000 Jews were killed in northern Bukovina, 100,000 in Transylvania (most of them at the hands of Hungarians), 200,000 in Transdniestria (essentially "dumped" Bessarabian and Bukovinian Jews). In short, out of the 1938 Jewish population of approximately 800,000 in Greater Romania, not less than 440,000 had perished.

Unlike the Jews of Hungary, then, who evidently still nurtured illusions about their Gentile neighbors, the Jews of Romania experienced no psychological ambivalence after the war in confronting the full dimension of native brutality. Their museum, superbly organized and maintained in the premises of a former synagogue, provides extensive coverage of the Holocaust. Record books, mementos, scores of photographs, are exhibited with elaborate accompanying documentation. On the lectern of the synagogue platform, a "book," bound in leather, is prominently displayed. During my visit, the curator invited me to open it. Within its hollowed interior lay nine bars of soap, their stamped indentations reading: "Rein Jüdisches Fat." The soap had been manufactured from the melted fat content of Jewish bodies, and was part of a large consignment allocated for the Wehrmacht. The samples on display in the museum had been sold to a barber in Bucharest by a group of departing German soldiers. Reverently now, the curator closed the book. "Half of us liquidated," he murmured. "Those who survived represented a more 'manageable' number for our Romanian friends, you see."

I did not rest well that night. It was not the chamber of horrors in the Jewish museum that preyed on my memory. Over the years, I had visited the death camps themselves, seen crematoria, examined vivisection chambers. Rather, it was the curator's remark that gnawed at me: "a more 'manageable' number." If the Nazis used the term in carrying out the Final Solution, they had little difficulty in securing the collaboration of the Romanians—or, for that matter, of the Hungarians, the Poles, the Ukrainians, or even substantial numbers of Vichy French. For the collaborationist nations, as for the Germans, the Final Solution was not a question of slaughter but of demographic management. One need hardly have been a monster, after all, to regard these issues "administratively." Hannah Arendt's thesis in chapter and verse.

I knew then what was robbing me of my sleep. God help me, I had accepted the formula myself. Consciously or otherwise, a civilized American and a Jew had fallen into that trap. *Their diminished numbers would have reduced them from a major social problem to a public annoyance.* My reflection on the Gypsies after my encounter with them. Was it the perspective of a historian, conditioned to the long view? Too easy a rationalization. More probably it was the flawed conscience of the Western humanist, insulated from the Final Solution by distance and the surrealism of compounded statistics. In that shocked moment of personal recognition, I understood in the most intimate and visceral way that Arendt was describing the "banality" latent not alone in the Eichmanns of the world.

The Joy of Instant Communism

During the initial postwar period, a coalition government was established in Bucharest. Despite the presence of the Red Army, King Michael (son of the abdicated Carol) was allowed for the while to remain on the throne. Private property, in land and businesses, went untouched. These were tactical gestures, of course. As elsewhere in Eastern Europe, the Soviets were buying time for the local Communist Party to consolidate its power. Following the signing of the Romanian peace treaty in February 1947, tougher Soviet measures were increasingly imposed. Within the ensuing eighteen months, Romania was systematically transformed into a Socialist People's Republic, a dependable satellite of the USSR. The party's enemies were arrested, convicted, executed. The principal sectors of the economy were nationalized.

By then, some 360,000 Jews remained within the treaty frontiers of postwar Romania, the largest surviving Jewish community in Europe, except for the Soviet Union. Facing imminent starvation at war's end, they were kept alive during 1945–46 almost exclusively by the Joint's massive program of emergency relief. The most urgent of their requirements were not only food and medical services, but restored housing and business property. Yet in Romania, as in Czechoslovakia and Hungary, the Communists were unwilling to press the issue of restitution. Here, too, Jews were prominent within the tiny Communist nucleus, and had been since the inception of the party in Romania in 1921. Throughout the 1920s and early 1930s, nearly half the party's central committee were Jews.

At the end of the war, moreover, the architects of the Communist takeover as usual were the "Muscovites," those who had returned from the Soviet Union in 1944 in the wake of the Red Army. Their leader was Anna Pauker, daughter of a *shochet*, a Jewish ritual slaughterer of animals. A formidably plain woman of harsh dynamism, it was she, not the party's chairman, Gheorghe Gheorghiu-Dej, who made the key policy decisions in her triple capacity as deputy premier, foreign minister, and deputy secretary of the central committee. Pauker and her colleagues were faced with the immediate need of staffing thousands of vital posts, in the police, the army, the foreign service, the local administrative bodies. To that end, they launched a massive recruiting drive, accepting into the party large numbers of ex-Fascists and other collaborators. Few of these people were sympathetic to the plight of the ravaged Jewish minority. Not only were Jewish claims for restitution ignored, but the enforced nationalization of medium- and larger-scale economic enterprises after 1947 simply completed the Jews' economic ruin. Forty percent of Romania's Jews were in commerce. New laws against "elements in speculation" were aimed precisely at their class. By 1950, fully 140,000 Jews were deprived of any source of regular income. Together with other, non-Jewish "capitalist elements," some 20,000 Jews were mobilized as forced labor for the construction of roads, railroads, the Danube–Black Sea Canal.

The one consolation for the Jewish survivors was their confirmed status as "equal citizens" in an authoritarian state. Citizenship was guaranteed to all national minorities, and for several years after the war, Jews and other non-Romanian ethnic groups were allowed to revive their communal organizations, even to "tax" their constituents. Thus, a Federation of Romanian Jewish Communities was established to administer Jewish religious and social welfare institutions. By unifying Jewish communal life, of course, the Communists were in a position to dominate it, and eventually to emasculate it. As a result, from 1949 on, at the height of the Stalinist purges, the number of Jewish public institutions was substantially reduced. At a time when Jewish economic circumstances bordered on mendicancy, all Joint activities were terminated and the Joint's offices and equipment were "co-opted" by the Romanian government. Jewish publishing houses and the Jewish press were drastically curtailed. The schools were nationalized and their teaching curriculum was largely purged of Jewish content. The famed Yiddish theater in Bucharest was still allowed to give performances, but not its counterpart in Jassy. Repertory was limited to revolutionary themes. The synagogues were enlisted to fight "reaction" in all its forms, including Jewish nationalism. Rabbis were ordered to recite special prayers against Zionism and Israel and to participate in Communist "peace" drives.

As much as any Jew, Moses Rosen was caught in the vortex of these pressures. By war's end, he had abandoned the practice of law in favor of the rabbinate, and was serving as associate rabbi of Bucharest's Great Choral Synagogue. Soon afterward, he was elected to the senior position. The choice seemed logical. Rosen already had won a reputation as a learned Hebraist and a dynamic speaker. Photographs of him in this period reveal blue eyes gazing soulfully from deep sockets, wide lips delicately pursed above an elegant goatee. His popular following was extensive. More important, he had become an active member of the Social Democratic Party, which played a significant role in the government coalition during the early postwar years. In 1947, at the age of thirty-five, he was appointed chief rabbi of Romania. In that position, Rosen may still have entertained hopes of functioning as his own man. He felt no compunction about joining the Romanian "Peace Committee," to be sure, and afterward—following the Communist takeover—about dutifully echoing the party line in its attacks on Western "imperialism." Yet, for the time being, he somehow resisted the pressure to condemn Israel. It was a painful tightwire act.

By then, mass emigration plainly was becoming the only solution to Romania's Jewish question. Long before the war, the political ideology of Romanian Jewry was already overwhelmingly Zionist. In 1946, the Romanian Zionist Organization listed over 100,000 members and maintained ninety-five branches and twelve pioneering youth training farms. The emigrationist purpose of this elaborate network was never disguised. By June 1947, some 150,000 Jews were registered for departure—over a third of the Jewish population. They encountered little initial opposition. The Bucharest regime discerned only advantage in reducing its impoverished and economically redundant Jewish minority to "manageable" size. Thus, in the first two years after the war, thousands of Jews were quietly, if unofficially, allowed to depart, either via the port of Constanta, or overland to the American occupation zones of Austria or Germany.

Following the Soviet break with Tito, however, Zionism suddenly came under renewed suspicion as a "deviationist" movement. In June

1948, the government attached Zionist funds, liquidated Zionist training farms, and finally outlawed the Zionist Organization altogether. Yet even then, Jewish emigration was not foreclosed. In private negotiations early in 1949, Anna Pauker reached an agreement with the Israeli ambassador for the departure of four thousand Jews a month. Although the decision unquestionably was influenced by a handsome Jewish Agency subvention to Romania in dollar currency, it may also have betrayed Mrs. Pauker's lingering *Judenschmerz*. Far from being a "self-hating Jew" (Ben-Gurion's contemptuous description of her), she had once been a Hebrew teacher. Her brother lived in Israel. Those who knew Mrs. Pauker insisted that she continued to feel deeply the plight of her people. Whatever her motives, the permission she granted was selective. Departure was limited essentially to ruined businessmen and other *luftmenschen*, people without economically useful skills. Between the end of the war and December 1951, fully 160,000 Romanian Jews emigrated to Israel.

It was at this point that "anti-Zionist" purges began sweeping through the Communist world. The Romanian Jewish exodus was stopped in its tracks. Anna Pauker was removed from office in May 1952 and Gheorghe Gheorghiu-Dej assumed decisive control of the party and state apparatus. By contrast to Czechoslovakia and Hungary, interestingly enough, the purge in Romania was not overtly antisemitic. Another Moscow-trained Jewish functionary, Iosif Chisinevschi, was promoted to full membership in the politburo. Simeon Bughichi, Mrs. Pauker's successor as foreign minister, was also Jewish. Nevertheless, the anti-Zionist campaign was fierce. Even after Stalin's death, scores of Zionist leaders were sentenced to long prison terms and those who survived were released only during the "thaw" after 1956.

These were Moses Rosen's most difficult years. In November 1948, the Jewish federation was obliged to take an anti-Zionist stand, and he was asked to endorse it. By his own account, he refused. "Following the party line against the West was one thing," he insisted later. "Traducing one's ancestral homeland was another." At first, he was not molested. Then, early in 1949, at a time when identified Zionists were being arrested wholesale throughout the country, Rosen ceremoniously received Israel's newly appointed minister to Romania at his synagogue, and the choir sang the Israeli national anthem, *HaTikvah*. The following morning, a government agent visited Rosen at the rabbi's home and threatened to have his "beard pulled out." Rosen's diplomatic response

was to pray the following Sabbath for both Romania and Israel. Thereupon, he began receiving threatening telephone calls and was the subject of abusive newspaper commentary. On one occasion he informed
the minister of cults that he would resign if the intimidation did not
stop. "No one resigns here," the minister replied coldly. "You'll simply
disappear." Rosen's prayers on behalf of Israel went on. Had they been
discontinued, he knew, he would have lost his credibility with the Jewish population.

The pressure intensified. During the period of the Slansky trial in
Czechoslovakia, Rosen developed an acute case of eczema. At one
point, a government official approached him with a "suggested" draft of
a sermon attacking Zionism. Rosen shook his head, saying nothing.
"Comrade rabbi," the man warned, "it would be a pity if you yourself
suffered the fate of Slansky."

"In God's hands," was Rosen's only comment.

On Friday evening, the chief rabbi delivered his prepared sermon,
ignoring the lurid trial sessions in Czechoslovakia. Early the next day,
he learned that the press had turned his address into an attack on Israel. But he was not "visited." Apparently, he remained untouchable. "I
took no particular joy in that victory,'" Rosen observed later. "I knew
the government's patience with me was running out."

The crisis came to a head at the time of the Moscow Doctors' Plot.
In January 1953, the party representative on the board of the Jewish
federation appeared at Rosen's office and ordered him straightout to
condemn the Moscow doctors publicly. Rosen would not commit himself. The apparatchik warned him of "serious personal consequences."
The rabbi felt himself paling, but said nothing. Returning home later in
the day, he caught sight of police agents surrounding his apartment
building. At that moment he experienced the fear he had known during
the wartime "relocations." Still, he played for time. In the following
weeks, as the threats mounted, he remained closely in touch with the
board of the federation, pleading with its leadership to remain firm.
The effort failed; the federation board eventually condemned the Moscow doctors in the "name of Romanian Jewry." The gesture at least
bought several additional weeks of leeway for Rosen. Then the warnings
resumed, the cordon of secret agents around his building returned, a
telltale echo was audible during his telephone conversations. "I'm not
sure what I would have done if the ordeal had gone on much longer,"
he confessed.

Stalin died then, and within days the Kremlin itself repudiated the Doctors' Plot as a fabrication. The cordons and telephone taps ended. Two years later, Rosen flew to Moscow to attend a conference of Socialist bloc clergymen. During a free afternoon, he waited in line over an hour outside Stalin's tomb. "I simply wanted to reassure myself that the monster was dead," he explained, smiling.

Romania Takes a New Line

The Soviet "thaw" gave Gheorghiu-Dej and his associates in Bucharest an opening for a more flexible stance in foreign affairs. So, too, did the emergent Sino-Soviet confrontation, and the temporary immunity from Soviet retaliation that schism afforded the Romanians. In July 1958, Bucharest negotiated the departure of Soviet troops from Romanian soil. Four years later, seizing upon Khrushchev's humiliation during the Cuban missile crisis, the Bucharest regime announced that henceforth it would adopt an "independent Socialist policy." Gheorghiu-Dej's death in March 1965 did not reverse this new approach. Nicolae Ceausescu, the newly appointed first secretary (and later his country's president), was determined to maintain his government's independence from Moscow.

Bucharest's daring move toward independence was not accompanied, as in Poland, by an upsurge of antisemitism. To be sure, chauvinism was hardly lacking in the new mood of self-assertiveness, and several Jews were dropped from key positions in the central committee and the government. Yet Jewish Communists were less flagrantly identified with the "Muscovites" in Romania than in other Eastern bloc nations, the examples of Pauker and Chisinevschi notwithstanding. In its divergence from Moscow, the Bucharest regime was also urgently in search of new links with the West. Thus, swallowing the myth of behind-the scenes Jewish influence in the United States, Gheorghiu-Dej and his colleagues began to examine the possible usefulness of the Jews as intermediaries. Here it was that Moses Rosen played a key role. In 1961, the chief rabbi was allowed to travel to the United States to deliver a guest lecture at Yeshiva University. It was a gamble by the regime, for Rosen had insisted on taking his wife with him, and they had no children; had he chosen to defect, no hostages would have remained. But Rosen had other ideas in mind. Indeed, they had been put in his mind by the Romanian government.

Speaking in New York, then traveling to other American cities, Rosen revealed to Jewish audiences the unsuspected vitality of Jewish life in Romania. At press conferences, then in private meetings with government officials in Washington, he made a point of emphasizing the "fairness" with which Bucharest was treating its Jews, the "alleviation" of all the old constraints upon Jewish religious and cultural expression. The chief rabbi was embellishing the facts, of course, describing a freedom he would have preferred to achieve. Nevertheless, his statements were given wide coverage. They unquestionably mitigated several of the graver American reservations toward the Gheorghiu-Dej government. Soon afterward (although plainly not as a consequence of Rosen's visit alone), relations between Washington and Bucharest eased, and the Romanian minister joined his Yugoslav counterpart as a recipient of special confidences from the State Department. By the time Rosen flew back to Bucharest, he was received as a hero. Gheorghiu-Dej personally expressed his gratification at the rabbi's "marvelous diplomatic accomplishment."

The new atmosphere of trust also made it possible for the government to accept with a certain equanimity the growing role of Jews in public life. Gheorghe Gaston-Marin and Leonte Rautu continued on as deputy prime ministers. At different periods, Simeon Bughichi served as foreign minister or deputy foreign minister. As in Hungary, several of the nation's leading intellectual positions were held by Jews, who emerged as professors, writers, editors, doctors, critics, theater directors. Rosen, meanwhile, exploiting his leverage, was able gradually to extract several tangible concessions for his people. With quiet government approval, a network of talmud torahs was revived through the late 1960s and early 1970s. In that same period, approximately 120 synagogues were repaired or refurbished. The government itself contributed 3 million lei to the project. Additional funding was provided for the maintenance of Jewish cemeteries. Memorials were erected for Jewish martyrs, again with financial contributions from the government, and the ceremonies of dedication invariably were attended by public officials. A Jewish museum was established. The Yiddish theater was enlarged, modernized, and authorized to present a wider choice of plays dealing with more traditional Jewish themes. Since 1956, Rosen had edited a bimonthly journal, *Revista Cultului Mozaic*. Now, in the 1960s, he was allowed to increase the number of its issues, and to include news of Jewish communities throughout the world.

Whether at Rosen's or at the government's initiative, moreover, the idea was accepted by Gheorghiu-Dej in 1965 that heads of "cults" should also sit in parliament. The chief rabbi thereupon became a legislator of the nation. In 1967, Ceausescu personally approved Rosen's "election" as chairman of the Jewish federation. A year later, on the twentieth anniversary of Rosen's election as chief rabbi, elaborate festivities in his honor were prepared within the Jewish community (Rosen himself was not laggard in orchestrating this event). Jewish representatives arrived from throughout the world to pay tribute to the "father" of Romanian Jewry. Government officials attended the climactic ceremony in the Choral Synagogue, together with the Orthodox patriarch, the Catholic archbishop, and the Moslem mufti. "I did not need all this for myself, you understand," Rosen insisted later. "The ceremony was important for the security and status of Romanian Jewry." No doubt he had a point. In 1969, the government authorized the resumption of contacts between the Romanian Jewish federation and international Jewish bodies, including the World Jewish Congress, B'nai B'rith, and various rabbinical organizations.

By far the most important of these international agencies was the Joint. In 1969, for the first time in twenty years, the great American philanthropy was permitted to resume its activities in Romania, where it immediately began underwriting a wide spectrum of social welfare institutions, among them clinics, hospitals, old age homes, kosher kitchens, and clothing warehouses. Bucharest's permission clearly was influenced by the Joint's disbursement of millions of dollars in hard American currency. Yet President Ceausescu wanted access to an even more meaningful dispensation from the United States. This was nothing less than Washington's approval of most-favored-nation trading privileges for Romania. Here again, Rosen was among those selected to play an intermediary role. The wily chief rabbi was more than prepared to cooperate. In exchange for American goodwill, he knew, the Romanian government was willing to pay in coin of almost unimaginable significance to the Jews. The compensation this time would be a relaxation on the ban against emigration to Israel.

As far back as the early 1960s, as it explored a new leeway for itself in international affairs, the Bucharest regime was developing a more flexible Middle East policy. The government began to abstain in the United Nations on various Soviet-sponsored resolutions against Israel, and agreed to a substantial increase in trade and scientific cooperation with the Jewish state. But its most significant departure from the Kremlin line was its refusal to sever diplomatic relations with Israel following the June 1967 war. Identifying with a small nation that had withstood the might of Soviet weaponry, the Ceausescu government dispatched its trade minister to Israel in December 1967, the first East European official of that rank ever to make the journey. Arrangements were reached for joint industrial enterprises, and direct air routes, between the two countries. El Al and Tarom thereafter flew regularly between Tel Aviv and Bucharest, and thousands of Israelis began spending their vacations in Romanian mountain resorts. On the diplomatic level, too, Ceausescu came to envisage himself as something of an "honest broker" between Israel and its Arab enemies. In 1972, he tendered an elaborate state reception to Prime Minister Golda Meir. Five years later, in the autumn of 1977, he conducted extensive private discussions in Bucharest with Menachem Begin and (afterward) with Anwar al-Sadat. Those meetings helped pave the way for Sadat's historic visit to Jerusalem.

Once the specter of Israel was exorcised from Romanian foreign policy, it was an easier matter to contemplate Jewish emigration there. As late as 1958, some 200,000 Jews lived in Romania, still the largest enclave of Jews in Eastern Europe except for the Soviet Union. In that year, Gheorghiu-Dej first studied the possible advantage of "thinning out" this minority population. Jewish departure would provide jobs and apartments for the belatedly emerging Romanian middle class. If the emigration of Jews would produce additional dividends in American goodwill, so much the better. In September 1958, then, the government authorized a limited number of Jewish exit visas to Israel. The response was a tidal wave of applications. More than 100,000 Jews hurried to register for departure. But, in fact, only 33,000 managed to leave before the Gheorghiu-Dej regime abruptly shut the door again. As Rosen discovered later, the Jewish Agency had publicized the emigration for its fund-raising purposes. Once the Arabs got wind of it, they protested vigorously, and Moscow in turn applied intense pressure on Bucharest. "I learned an important lesson then," Rosen admitted. "Noisy publicity was not the way to deal with such matters."

When the Bucharest government finally agreed to resume the emigration in 1961, the departures were handled quietly. Between 1961 and 1975, fully 160,000 additional Jews left the country. Most of them settled in Israel, where they soon comprised that nation's second-largest bloc of immigrants. Some 45,000 of their kin remained behind, a number that would continue to diminish, to less than 30,000 in 1984. For its part, the Ceausescu regime by then had achieved its cherished ambition of most-favored-nation trading privileges with the United States. In late 1974, when the Jackson-Vanik amendment in the American Congress (see page 445) linked this privileged status with free Jewish emigration, Rosen became the guarantor of Romanian compliance. At the request of the State Department and of the Romanian government itself, he took on the responsibility of maintaining an accurate count of Jewish applications and departures, and of transmitting the information to Washington.

A Residual Gerontocracy

Calea Vacaresti-Dudesti is a section often described as the "Brooklyn of Bucharest," for it is the major concentration of Jewish settlement in the capital. On an adjoining street, Calea Sfanta Vineri, the Federation of Jewish Communities makes its headquarters in a two-story building attached as a kind of annex to the Great Choral Synagogue. The executive director of the Bucharest kehilla at the time of my visit, Teodor Blumenfeld, was a pleasant-spoken man in his early seventies. A retired engineer, he had been "elected" to his current position upon the nomination of "His Eminence, Chief Rabbi Dr. Moses Rosen." Blumenfeld's associates and assistants similarly were pensioners. "There aren't that many young people left here," he explained. "Most of them depart for Israel as soon as they complete their education. Occasionally, they send for their parents. Usually not." Here he offered a resigned shrug. "They know they can depend on the federation to take care of the old folks."

It was a fair assumption. Every institution I visited in the ensuing five days was administered by pensioners for pensioners. Even the Yiddish theater was obliged to "co-opt" the services of non-Jewish actors to perform the younger roles. In the kosher canteens of Bucharest and the provinces, it was essentially older people who availed themselves of the thousands of free lunches that were served daily. As I was ushered through the vast clothing storehouse in the federation's social welfare building, it occurred to me only afterward that amid the hundreds, perhaps thousands, of neatly arranged suits, dresses, sweaters, skirts, and shoes, I did not encounter a single item of children's clothing. In the rather dingy polyclinics, it was the same story—of doctors and dentists who had retired from government service, of aging patients.

The care at least seemed quite adequate. The meals were ample, the clothing good, the equipment in the clinics of West European quality. Bucharest's largest Jewish old age home was as impressive as any facility of its kind I had seen in Europe. On the lobby wall, a plaque offered the by then familiar tribute to "His Eminence, Chief Rabbi Dr. Moses Rosen." The home's medical director, Dr. Marcel Saragea, a white-haired gentleman bearing a striking resemblance to Marc Chagall, was a retired professor of "pathphilstology" at the University of Bucharest Medical School. Several of his colleagues were also former staff members of the medical school or of the nation's leading hospitals. Altogether the building employed 123 people. "The operations budget is 89 million lei [the equivalent of $2 million]," Dr. Saragea informed me. It showed. I made the rounds of the patients' rooms, the physiotherapy facilities, the recreation pavilion. My guide was Saragea's deputy, a woman who had completed her medical training in France. "Many of the patients are suffering more from psychic than from physical illnesses," she pointed out. "They've never really recovered from the war. But they receive the identical round-the-clock attention we give the organically afflicted." I did not doubt it. Most of these people were just hanging on, but they were getting a decent sendoff, among their own.

Some things at least were working well in this heavy-handed regime. I took a certain pride in knowing that Jews were responsible for the best of them. Several days later, waiting for my flight to be announced at the airport, I noted a line of tourists filing in from an arriving Tarom jetliner. They were chattering away to each other in Hebrew and Romanian. "Returning to the old homestead?" I inquired of one middle-aged couple. Surprised and pleased, they wasted no time filling me in excitedly on all the particulars. They had left Romania fifteen years earlier and this was their second visit back. "I suppose you're looking up relatives, then," I went on. They shook their heads. No relatives left, but an Israeli travel agency had been able to make the arrangements "dirt cheap . . . a bargain. How could we turn it down?" Easily, I should have thought, contemplating Romania's historic record on the Jews.

Rosen doubtless would have been more philosophic. A few tourists notwithstanding, the Jewish connection with this land would end soon enough. "Our little community is so aged," he explained, "that I, seventy years old, am among the youngest of its servants. Once we boasted six hundred rabbis. Today, we have three. Not more than three thousand young people among us, and within a couple of years even they will be gone." His eyes brightened. "But at least they've remained proud Jews. You don't hear of them veering off from Vienna to the United States." It was a barbed allusion to the Soviet Jewish émigrés. "They go to Israel and stay there." Possibly they had no choice. Unlike Soviet Jews, they were flown directly to Israel; and once in Israel, a free country, they no longer qualified as political refugees under United States immigration law. "No, no, they're proud Jews," Rosen insisted. "They never were interested in 'passing,' as the Hungarians were." That was a point. "There are two kinds of candles," the chief rabbi went on. "One burns for a while, then twists and crumbles before it gutters out. The other burns straight down, remaining erect to the last. Romanian Jewry is the second candle. We've remained straight to the end, proudly identified to the end."

It was a touching simile, and perhaps not an inaccurate one. Yet the image that remained fixed in my mind was of a white-haired, profoundly emaciated woman in the old age home. Helpless on her bed, tethered to a cluster of bottles and tubes, she was being tenderly spoon-fed by a nurse. "In a government institution, they would have let her slip away months ago," confided Dr. Saragea. "Here—you can see— she may be on borrowed time, but at least we let her have that time. As long as she can use it."

XIV

Frankenstein Utopia: The Soviet Union

From the Revolution to Stalinism

"My maternal grandfather was a remarkable person," Mikhail Zand reminisced. "When I was born, he circumcised me personally. That was in 1927, mind you. What he did was strictly against Soviet law—a 're- ligious barbarism.' Well, the old man was religious, he made no pre- tense about it. But he had fought in the Red Army, too, and that got him off." As for Zand's father: "His name was Yitzchak, and he came from a small town in Poland. I remember him as a short, wiry man, with glasses. He was also a dedicated Communist." In 1919, Yitzchak Zand escaped a Polish firing squad by crossing the frontier into the Soviet Ukraine. There, in Kamenets-Podolsk, he met his wife, T'chila. She was Yiddish-speaking, he was Polish-speaking. From then on, they spoke only Russian to each other. "Both sides of my family were tough," remarked Mikhail Zand, his tone matter-of-fact. "Nothing could break them."

The early years of the Revolution both tested and rewarded that endurance. Although their incipient middle class was wiped out, the Jews of the former Russian Pale received the blessings of full equality and mobility in the new society. Highly literate and heirs to a powerful reformist tradition, Jews like Trotsky, Joffe, Zinoviev, Litvinov, Kamenev, and Kaganovich were prominent in the leadership of the So- viet regime. Others swelled the ranks of the state and party bureau- cracy. As late as 1938, Jews occupied 10 percent of the civil service posts in Russia, 20 percent in the Ukraine, 30 percent in Byelorussia.

In 1930, Zand's father brought the family to Moscow. A scholarly man and a prolific writer, he was appointed instructor of Marxist- Leninist philosophy at the Research Institute for Colonial Problems, an agency of the Comintern. Later, he became chairman of the department, and in that capacity was awarded "special" housing. It was a single room on the sixth and top floor of the institute building, on Tversly Boulevard. Nineteen other instructors' families similarly occupied rooms on the upper floors. For young Mikhail Zand, life at the institute was fascinating in its opportunities to meet his father's colleagues and students. Most of the latter came from the eastern reaches of the Soviet empire, and their Turkic or Persian languages evoked romantic associations for the youngster. Several of the instructors were Jewish, and six of them had lived for a while in Palestine. Mikhail Zand picked up a smattering of Hebrew from their children. This was the "ancient Jewish language," explained his father. In his commitment to a classless society, Yitzchak Zand was opposed to "particularism."

Yet there were many other Jews who were not willing to be "departicularized" that quickly. The numbers of their people, approaching three million by 1939, were equal to the populations of four of the (then) fourteen Soviet republics. They remained heavily concentrated in the western areas, especially in Russia, Byelorussia, and the Ukraine. In the first decade of Soviet rule, moreover, the government was prepared to help them safeguard their identity and culture. The Kremlin leadership understood the anomalous status of the Jewish nationality, which possessed no territory or peasant class of its own. In the hope of providing the Jews with a meaningful alternative to Zionism, and of ensuring their very physical survival, the government resettled many thousands who had been peddlers or small merchants in agricultural villages of their own in the southern Ukraine and Crimea. By the early 1930s, these Jewish collective farms numbered around 500, and supported fully 225,000 individuals—a population larger than that of the Zionist farm colonies in Palestine during the same period.

A "Jewish Autonomous Region" was also established in the remote Asian fastness of Birobidzhan, near the Chinese border. Comprising 14,000 square miles, the region was all but uninhabited and subject to Chinese infiltration. It was essentially to preempt that danger that the Soviet government in 1926 created an autonomous Jewish entity in the area. The experiment was less than successful. The colonists' life was harsh in this frigid and marsh-ridden wilderness, and as late as 1938 not more than 15,000 Jews had settled there. Skeletal as this outpost was, however, it allowed the Jews to maintain their own administration and to conduct their public affairs in Yiddish. Streets and entire neighborhoods in Birobidzhan's tiny ramshackle "capital" bore the Yiddish names of celebrated personalities. Elsewhere in the Soviet Union, Jews similarly were allowed to preserve their ethnic identity. Fifteen years after the Revolution, three-quarters of them continued to speak Yiddish as their first language. In areas of their heaviest concentration—the Ukraine, Byelorussia, even Russia itself—hundreds of Yiddish-language schools were functioning, together with a score of Yiddish theatrical companies, newspapers, and publishing houses.

Yet this efflorescence proved to be brief. In the same decade of the 1930s, much of the Jewish population gradually shifted inland. Intermingling with Russians at all levels, they wasted little time in adopting Russian as the indispensable language of employment and education. There was an additional factor that proved inimical to Jewish cultural identity. It was the Stalinist purge campaign of the mid- and latter 1930s. Even in the prewar period, the nightmare of arrests and murders carried certain overtones of Great Russian chauvinism. The Zand family was not spared this ordeal. Until 1937, their circumstances had been improving, their lodgings enlarged to two rooms. But in that year, sixteen of the institute's twenty faculty members were arrested and carried off. Then the wives began disappearing, and the children were sent to orphan homes. Finally, on the afternoon of September 14, 1937, Mikhail Zand and his younger sister Rosa returned from school to learn that the police had taken their father.

Four months later, T'chila, their mother, received an official notice that her husband had been sentenced to ten years hard labor, without right of correspondence. At this point, friends pleaded with her to flee Moscow before she, too, was arrested. After several days of hesitation, T'chila departed for a "safe" town 120 miles inland, where she found employment as a teacher in a steelworkers' school. The two children were left behind. Mikhail was ten, his sister was five. Each night, their grandmother, T'chila's mother, returned from work to prepare their dinner. Strangers, too, occasionally came to give them food. Otherwise, the youngsters cared for themselves, continuing to attend school, enduring the taunts of their classmates. "Once I survived that period, there was no danger I could not face later in life," Mikhail Zand recalled.

Hundreds of thousands of Soviet families were broken by this first convulsion of Stalinist terror, and most of them were not Jews. Yet if the Jews had benefited in disproportionate numbers from the Revolution's earliest phase, they were now among its most prominent victims. Stalin's suspicion had been aroused by their sheer visibility in the party apparatus and government during the 1930s. His obsession was with Trotskyism, with the international socialism that historically had been closest to the Jewish tradition. As will be seen, the fixation would loom even larger in Stalin's mind after the war; but even now its consequences were disastrous. The entire intellectual elite of Birobidzhan was branded as "bourgeois nationalists" and carried away. So was the leadership in the Crimean Jewish farm colonies, not to mention thousands of other eminent Jewish intellectuals.

In 1938, the worst of the purge ended with the completion of the infamous Moscow trials. Early that year, T'chila Zand journeyed home to rejoin her children. A kind of dazed normalcy set in as the three clung to each other, still nurturing the illusion that Yitzchak Zand would be released before completing his sentence. The hope of better times was particularly intense among the Jews. With Nazism triumphant in Germany, and Jew-hatred rampant in Poland, Hungary, and Romania, the Soviet Union still appeared to be their most dependable bastion. They continued to enjoy full access to higher education, to employment at every level of the economy. If their faith in the Revolution had been shaken, it was by no means shattered.

The Great Patriotic War

The Soviet Jewish population of three million was suddenly and substantially augmented following the outbreak of World War II. Within three weeks of the Nazi invasion of Poland, Soviet troops moved into areas of Eastern Europe that had been allocated to them by the Molotov-Ribbentrop Pact. These included the three Baltic states of Latvia, Lithuania, and Estonia, together with eastern Poland and Bessarabia. Thus, in the Baltic republics alone, the Soviets assumed control of 232,000 Jews; in Bessarabia, of 210,000; in eastern Poland, of fully 1,100,000, and soon an additional 300,000 who arrived as fugitives from Nazi-dominated western Poland. The Soviet occupation was accompanied by a brutal campaign against all forms of political and religious "competition," including Jewish Bundist (Socialist) and Zionist organizations. In early 1940, approximately 70,000 "suspect" Jews were deported to the east, where large numbers of them perished of cold, hunger, or punitive labor conditions.

Then, in June 1941, the Germans launched their invasion of the Soviet Union. Mikhail Zand recalled the savage Luftwaffe bombings of Moscow, the nights spent in crowded shelters. In late summer, as the German armies pushed nearer the capital, he, his mother, sister, and grandmother were swept up in the vast civilian migration toward the Urals. Loaded into a cattle train with nearly a thousand other families, the Zands were moved to Yaroslavl, a town on the Volga. From there they were transferred to a river barge. Packed into the vessel's hold, the émigrés were transported hundreds of miles farther south. It was a twenty-five-day voyage. After two more train journeys, they finally reached Kazakhstan, a Turkic-speaking Soviet republic.

Here the Zands were settled in a kolkhoz, a collective farm, and housed with a Kazakh family. T'chila Zand found employment in a nearby factory. Mikhail and his sister Rosa were set to work on the farm. With his ear for languages, the boy picked up numerous words and phrases in the local Kazakh dialect (working barefoot in the field, he picked up leeches and lice, as well). He was one of the more fortunate refugees. Among the 350,000 Jews who had been moved eastward beyond the Urals, to Central Asia and Siberia, 100,000 perished of hunger, cold, and disease. In the early spring of 1942, the Zand family was carried farther east again, this time by boxcar to Dombarovski, a settlement of Kazakh coal miners. Working in the fields and mines, or spending a few hours a day in school with them, Mikhail continued to study their language and customs.

In time, his family was joined by additional Jewish refugees, including a number who had escaped from Poland and the Baltic countries. It was then that the Zands first learned of the organized Nazi slaughter of Jews. They were also exposed to the unquenchable folk Jewishness of these Polish and Baltic survivors. Determined then to master the Yiddish language, Mikhail made use of the old Soviet Encyclopedia in the town library. Its article on Yiddish contained an accompanying diagram of Hebrew characters. In a local bookstore, he found a volume of Yiddish poems and slowly began teaching himself the rudiments of word- and sentence-construction. Other Jews occasionally helped him. Then, in December 1943, he, his family, and other refugees were loaded again into cattle cars for the return trip west. The Nazi armies were in retreat. Several years would pass before the full magnitude of their *Schrecklichkeit* would be calculated, the massacre of 20 million Soviet citizens. Among these casualties would be reckoned 1.1 million Jews trapped in the western Soviet territories, including those of recently incorporated eastern Poland, Bessarabia, and the Baltic republics, and 100,000 others who perished from submarginal conditions as fugitives in Central Asia or Siberia.

The Zands returned to the institute building on Tversly Boulevard, to their identical room on the sixth floor. They shared it now with a worker's family. Mikhail and his sister returned to school. They anticipated a civilized reception. During the war, the government had displayed a new solicitude for Jews. It had even authorized the establishment of a Jewish Anti-Fascist Committee under the chairmanship of Solomon Mikhoels, director of the Jewish state theater, in the hope of mobilizing goodwill for the Soviet war effort among Jews in the West. Including among its membership some of the nation's most respected Jewish authors and intellectuals, the committee appealed to "our Jewish brethren the world over," repeatedly invoked the unity of the Jewish people, its common history and traditions, and emphasized the specifically Jewish genocide then unfolding under the Nazi invasion. Mikhoels and other eminent Jews were sent to the United States to lecture before Jewish audiences. At the same time, the organization began to function as a kind of center for Jewish cultural activities in the USSR itself, and its Yiddish-language newspaper, *Eynigkeit*, became the forum for all genres of Yiddish writing in the Soviet Union. Throughout the country, Jews discerned in this awakening a hopeful augury of their future under Stalin.

But if the Soviet dictator tolerated a limited Jewish cultural revival during the "Great Patriotic War," he simultaneously appealed to Great Russian nationalism, and the seeds of antisemitism were never lacking in this emotion. It was to avail the Jews little that a half-million of their men had fought in the Red Army, including 100 Jewish generals and thousands of colonels and lieutenant colonels; that the commander of the Red Air Force, Yakov Smushkevich, was a Jew; that 340,000 Jews had been awarded medals and orders. Once demobilized, or coming home as civilian refugees from the eastern republics, Jews confronted widespread charges of shirking and draft-dodging. In the western Soviet regions, fully 60 million citizens had been exposed to Nazi racist propaganda. As these areas were liberated, the returning Jews were met with a blast of antisemitism even more intense than in the prewar period. The atmosphere of Kiev was very nearly that of an imminent pogrom. Soviet officials were not likely to antagonize these local populations by supporting Jewish restitution claims.

The Zand children experienced the full force of that local animus upon their return. The taunts of cowardice and desertion they endured were uttered by schoolmates and teachers, by neighbors, government clerks, and shopkeepers. They cut Mikhail to the heart. His response was to volunteer for the army. Upon reaching the age of seventeen, he was cleared for service. Then it was learned that his father had been an "enemy of the people." The war was approaching its end. The colonel at the recruiting headquarters saw no need to go into detail. "We don't need you," he remarked tersely to Mikhail Zand. "Go home." The words were seared into the youth's consciousness.

The Face of Stalinism: The Israeli Connection

The Jewish Holocaust registered on Mikhail Zand with particular intimacy in 1946 during a family visit to Kamenets-Podolsk, his mother's birthplace. It was a Jewish charnel house. The Nazis had machine-gunned tens of thousands of Jews there within the space of two days. A few bones actually were protruding from the ground. Encountering a skull, obviously a child's, Mikhail imagined it as that of his cousin Ina, who had been nine at the time of the Nazi invasion (years later, he would give his daughter the same name). Statistics eventually revealed the extent of the genocide. In 1959, a decade and a half after the liberation of Soviet territory, the official census recorded the Jewish population as 2,268,000, including 2,047,000 in the pre-1939 Soviet area and 221,000 in annexed eastern Poland, Moldavia (formerly Bessarabia), and the three Baltic republics. The figure signified a reduction by almost one-third of the prewar Jewish population, losses that were proportionately four times as severe as those of the Soviet population as a whole.

In 1945, Mikhail Zand finished high school. By then, he had determined to become a specialist in Oriental languages. Yet when he applied to the Oriental Institute, he was turned down as the son of an "enemy of the people." Submitting a new application to Moscow State University, he disguised the circumstances of his father's imprisonment, and was accepted. He found his vocation then in the department of philology. Hurling himself into the study of the Turkic and Persian language groups, he mastered their essentials with phenomenal speed.

Normally, it would have been an idyllic period for a young man on the threshold of his keenest intellectual awakening. But in his opening university year he met a man named Davidowicz, one of the instructors who had lived in the institute building during the 1930s. He had been in prison camp with Yitzchak Zand, and he informed Mikhail now that his father had perished of exposure and brutality soon after arriving at the camp in 1937.

Other shocks lay ahead. For Soviet Jews, the postwar years represented a darker epoch even than the great purges of the 1930s. Once loosed, the nationalist passions of wartime could not easily be contained. The Soviet leadership had been enraged during the Nazi invasion by evidence of disloyalty among the non-Russian minorities. The most notorious of the Nazi collaborators had been the Baltic Germans and the Crimean Tatars, but scarcely a non-Slavic nationality escaped the accusation of treason. Innumerable non-Russians—Kalmuks, Karachais, Chechens, Balkars—were imprisoned or executed in the postwar period. The Jews obviously would have been the last element to collaborate, but as a perennially suspect "alien" minority, they were uniquely vulnerable to the explosion of embittered chauvinism. It had not escaped Stalin that Jewish soldiers had encountered foreign Jews in the liberated death camps, and had mingled with the Jewish troops of other armies. Conceivably, they had been "infected" by Western ideas.

More ominous yet, from the Soviet ruler's viewpoint, was the possibly infectious role of Jewish survivors in the annexed Baltic states of Latvia, Lithuania, and Estonia, as well as in eastern Poland and Moldavia. The remnant Jewish communities in these formerly independent or autonomous lands were ethnocentric, "authentic" Jews, with recent memories of a vigorous independent Jewish communal life. As fellow citizens now of the more acculturated Jews of Great Russia, Byelorussia, and the Ukraine, these newcomers were a potential conduit for Western Jewish influences. Of all the races and nations in the Soviet empire, Stalin knew, the Jews alone possessed their largest numbers among the Western democracies. All the old fears of the Jews as carriers of this Western "virus" flared up again in 1948, with the defection of Yugoslavia's Marshal Tito. As a potentially "deviationist" element, the Jews were identified thenceforth with the heresy of Titoism; and Titoism, in the eyes of the Soviet dictator, was the cutting edge of the ultimate danger of Trotskyism. This time, too, Stalin's paranoia was further exacerbated by the emergence of Israel in the same year. The Jews surely could not be immune to the gravitational pull of the Zionist republic.

Indeed, many of them were not. Mikhail Zand greeted the news of Israel's birth by attending services in the Great Choral Synagogue. The building was packed with old and young, many intoning prayers of gratitude. Zand's fellow Jewish students at the university discussed the historic event openly, daringly, enthusiastically. Yet if Israeli independence was a momentous development, it was also a remote one. Most of Zand's Jewish friends were citizens of the Russian Federated Republic. Enjoying full access to the mighty cultural resources of the Soviet Union, they found it difficult to sustain a vision of life in an exclusively Jewish nation. Given the public mood of xenophobia, moreover, the faintest hint of identification with Israel was dangerous. Zand, whose Jewish consciousness by then was more intense than that of most of his classmates, was moved once to write Stalin, urging Soviet help to newborn Israel and permission for Soviet Jews to enlist in the Israeli army to fight the "British." Fortunately, he did not sign the letter. Several who did, including one of Zand's closest friends, were arrested, tried, and imprisoned.

By 1948, then, the campaign of Russian chauvinism, launched under the aegis of Stalin's deputy Andrei Zhdanov, was focusing on the Jews. The most frequently used pejoratives were "homeless," "rootless," "strangers to the people and the national culture," or "tribeless vagabonds." Although individuals who were singled out as bearers of these anti-Soviet qualities were not specifically mentioned as Jews, their original Jewish names usually were printed in the newspaper accounts. "They are persons devoid of any sense of duty toward the people, the state, or the party," thundered *Pravda*. "It is our pressing task, therefore, to smoke them out of their lairs." The campaign was also waged against Jewish institutions. A number of Yiddish-language journals were closed, among them *Eynigkeit*, organ of the Jewish Anti-Fascist Committee. In December 1948, finally, the committee itself was disbanded.

The government in fact had been taking aim at the committee for many months. Well before the end of the war, this organization had moved beyond the narrow goal originally set for it—that is, of assuring Western Jewish goodwill for the Soviet war effort. By 1944, its leadership was concentrating increasingly on the task of "safeguarding the future of the Jews as a people." Implicit in this objective was the need to revive Jewish cultural and communal life after the war. In the postwar years, the committee's chairman, Solomon Mikhoels, was engaging in "questionable activities," encouraging Jews to use his organization to help the needy and to intervene on behalf of Jewish victims of discrimination. Then, in February 1948—the month of the Soviet break with Tito in Yugoslavia—the director was killed, according to the official version, in an automobile accident. The circumstances of the "accident" were mysterious. So was the subsequent disappearance of a number of other eminent committee members. Soon afterward, the Jewish state theater in Moscow was closed, as were Jewish theaters in Kiev, Minsk, Kharkov, Odessa, even distant Birobidzhan.

These events turned out to be the prelude to a massive campaign of antisemitic terror. Twenty-five other prominent figures of the Jewish Anti-Fascist Committee were arrested without charge, held incommunicado under brutal circumstances for four years until, in July 1952, they were put on trial. The accusation that eventually was leveled against them offered a fascinating insight into the Stalinist mentality. The defendants were alleged to have plotted the "amputation" of the Crimea from the USSR and its establishment as a "Zionist bourgeois republic"—which in turn would serve as a base for American imperialism against the Soviet people. The instrument of this ostensible conspiracy was the American Joint Distribution Committee (a familiar villain by then), whose agents had "manipulated" the 1943 wartime visit to the United States of Solomon Mikhoels and several of Mikhoels's colleagues. However surrealistic the accusations, they were routinely accepted by the court. The hapless Jewish prisoners were found guilty, and on August 12, 1952, twenty-four of them were executed for treason. Lina Shtern, the one woman in the group, was sentenced to life imprisonment. So were hundreds of Jewish writers, almost all of whom eventually died in prison. These included the remaining original members of the Jewish Anti-Fascist Committee. By then, virtually the entire cultural leadership of Soviet Jewry had been eradicated.

Allusion to Jewish themes in the Soviet Union now became altogether taboo. No mention was made of Jews or of Jewish history in Soviet literature or schoolbooks. Hardly any reference to the most distinguished Jews, as Jews, appeared in the *Great Soviet Encyclopedia*. Moreover, the names of Jewish war heroes were removed from monuments, streets, war histories. No published work referred to the Holocaust in its Jewish implications. In the same period, from 1948 to 1953, all state and party agencies, all propaganda organs, were employed in a campaign of unremitting antisemitic incitement. Articles were filled with innuendos about "rootless cosmopolitans," "parasites on the healthy body of Russian culture"—code phrases for Jews. At the universities, snide remarks appeared on official bulletin boards, implying that certain faculty members (always with Jewish names) were denigrating true Russian culture.

Mikhail Zand meanwhile carried on his studies, making himself indispensable to his professors as a research assistant. In 1950, he received his M.A. summa cum laude. His intention by then was to continue on for his Ph.D. It meant reapplication. This time, in a mixture of anger and pride, he did not conceal the circumstances of his father's death. He was rejected. The year before, he had married. His wife, Nellie Shainin, a fellow Jewish student, was now pregnant. Desperate for employment, Zand applied to a friend in Kirghizistan, a member of the Kirghiz branch of the Soviet Academy of Sciences. Again he was turned down.

Zand's fate was shared by thousands of other Jews between 1948 and 1953. It was a painful comedown for a people that had represented the single most trusted nationality in the early Communist regime, and an undiminished source of talent for public service. Until the mid-1930s, the foreign ministry had largely been dominated by Jews such as Joffe, Radek, Litvinov, Suritz, Maisky. Although reduced in numbers by the purge trials of the 1930s, Jews remained prominent in the ministry's research departments, or as professors in the diplomatic training colleges. All this changed now, and Jews were barred totally from the foreign service and its institutions, from the foreign trade institutes, from the senior military command and the military academies. They were barred as well from the party's central committee, except for the wily veteran Moshe Kaganovich, from executive posts in the state bureaucracy and the Komsomol youth organization. Moscow State University, the flagship of the Soviet educational system, was purged not only of scores of its Jewish faculty members but of hundreds of Jewish students. So were other institutions of higher education, and even the institutes of science.

Zand was a casualty of this purge. For nearly a year, until March 1951, he remained unemployed. He earned his bread by hackwork, first ghostwriting a doctorate for a Tadzhik student at the interpreters' institute, then ghost-editing an updated version of a *History of Tadzhikistan* for Bobojan Gafurov (who later was appointed first secretary of the party in Tadzhikistan). He finished the history in two months, essentially writing it anew. On the basis of the revision, Zand's sponsor was elevated to the Tadzhik Academy of Sciences, and it was he, later in the year, who found a slot for Zand as a technical assistant in the academy's department of folklore.

The Tadzhik capital, Dushanbe (a.k.a. Stalinabad in those days), was a town of some 45,000 people, and most of its inhabitants were Russians, or Russian Jews, who had fled the well-organized machinery of repression in the "heartland" Slavic republics. Indeed, as a refuge for Jewish intellectuals, Dushanbe was known as the "Elephantine Center," after the ancient Egyptian Jewish Diaspora. There at last, for a marginal salary, Zand managed to support his family for the next seven years, working in the research institute, investigating classic Persian— the parent of the Tadzhik language—writing articles, then books, in Tadzhik. His magnum opus, an analytical catalogue of Tadzhik manuscripts, published in four volumes, became a primary source in the field. Widely translated into Russian and into other, oriental, languages, many of his writings eventually became classics.

As in many of the Communist satellite nations, meanwhile, the Jewish minority in the western Soviet empire faced its acutest danger between 1952 and 1953. The Slansky trial in Prague ended in late November 1952. Two days later, the "Kiev affair" was publicized throughout the USSR, with reports of individuals tried before the military court in the Ukrainian capital for profiteering and embezzling state property. All the defendants were Jews. Three were sentenced to death and were executed, the others received long prison terms. The Kiev trial in turn inaugurated a flood of Soviet press accounts dealing with alleged Jewish embezzlement of clothing, building materials, food products, private vehicles, appliances. The accusations manifestly served to conceal the regime's economic failure in these vital consumer areas.

The antisemitic onslaught reached its climax in January 1953. Lydia Slovin, a Latvian Jew, gave birth to her second daughter on the thirteenth of that month. In the maternity ward later, she was routinely examined by the attending physician, also a Jewish woman, who continued afterward to the other patients. But as the doctor began examining a Russian woman, the latter suddenly screamed, "Don't touch me." Others took up the refrain, pleading to be spared from the "Zhidovka." The doctor fled in tears. Astonished, Lydia Slovin asked the patients what was the matter. One of them handed her the day's edition of

Pravda. Its front-page account described a conspiracy of "physician-saboteurs," most of them with obviously Jewish names, who in recent years were guilty of causing the death of high Soviet officials. These "monsters in human form" were identified as "hirelings" of the "international bourgeois-nationalist organization," the Joint Distribution Committee, which had been established by United States intelligence to "destroy the leading cadres of the Soviet Union."

Many of the Soviet officials had been "murdered" years before, among them Viktor Shcherbakov in 1945 and Andrei Zhdanov in 1948, but the world evidently had to wait until 1953 for the "true facts" of their deaths to emerge. Long regarded as Stalin's heir apparent, Zhdanov had been the very symbol of Soviet anti-Westernism and leader of the earlier campaign against "cosmopolitanism." The "murder" perpetrated by the doctors clearly was an act of reprisal by a vengeful people. "The black hatred of our great country," declared the Soviet journal *Krokodil*, "has united in one camp American and British bankers, colonialists, kings of arms, Hitler's defeated generals dreaming of vengeance, representatives of the Vatican, and loyal adherents of the Zionist kahal [government]." Waves of accusations quickly followed against other Jewish doctors throughout the USSR for alleged negligence and abuse. The cases were widely publicized and widely believed. The government hardly needed to orchestrate the panic. It drew from native wellsprings of antisemitism that extended back to the Mendel Beilis case, a notorious ritual-murder fabrication of tsarist times, and even earlier. Patients now refused medicines from Jewish physicians. Hundreds of Jewish doctors were dismissed from their hospital positions.

By no coincidence, the Soviet press diatribes against Israel and Zionism became almost psychotically virulent during the period of the Slansky trial in Czechoslovakia and the Doctors' Plot in Moscow. On February 9, 1953, a bomb went off (harmlessly) in the garden of the Soviet legation outside Tel Aviv, an event that led to a brief rupture of diplomatic relations between the USSR and Israel. The Soviet press then noted that the victims of the murder doctors, the actions of the Zionists on trial in Czechoslovakia, and the terrorist act against the Soviet legation in Israel were links in the same chain. It was manifestly Stalin's intention to use the anti-Zionist campaign to tighten his grip on Eastern Europe. Calls were issued for "revolutionary vigilance" against "Zionist nests" throughout the Socialist world. In the Soviet Union, thousands of Jews were dropped from state enterprises. Jewish children were harassed in school. The former foreign minister, Vyacheslav Molotov, was obliged to remain silent as his wife, a Jew, was exiled from Moscow. On the eve of his death, Stalin was rumored to have formulated a plan for the mass evacuation of Jews from the western regions of the Soviet Union to the remote eastern and northern parts of the country.

For Jewish community life, as well, these last years of Stalinism represented a period of strangulation. Nowhere was there to be found a single Yiddish-language school. The teaching of Hebrew was banned entirely. Not one book on Jewish history was published even for Jewish use, or one monograph dealing with the Holocaust. No museum, not even a section of a museum, was devoted to Jewish history, culture, or ethnology. A few score synagogues remained open throughout the Soviet empire—the majority of these in Soviet Asia—but most were in terminal disrepair. Although the nation's dozen aging rabbis were tolerated, they no longer appeared at official receptions together with Christian and Moslem clergy. Religious education and religious publications were banned. The acquisition of religious articles proved far more difficult for Jews than for other religious communities. Except as objects of revilement, the Jews became a nonpeople in Soviet public consciousness.

The psychic trauma this represented is difficult to gauge. Plainly, the Jews had never been a monolithic entity. In many ways, they were more heterogeneous than other ethnic and national groups within the Soviet realm. Until 1941, many had been inhabitants of *shtetls*—small villages—and had preserved their Jewish culture intact. This was particularly true of Jews living in the Baltic republics and eastern Poland. Others were marginal Jews, citizens of the "heartland" Slavic republics, who functioned between the Jewish and Gentile spheres; and by World War II, most were well along the road to assimilation. By then, possibly a seventh of Soviet Jewry, and fully a third of Russian Jewry, were intermarried. During the Holocaust, the principal victims were the shtetl Jews, who bore the brunt of the initial Nazi invasion. The others, better integrated and more acculturated, managed to escape to the trans-Ural area, or to remain alive in the interior regions around Moscow and Leningrad. Normally, this would have been the group least concerned with the survival of Jewish culture.

Yet even among these, a sense of Jewish identity was tentatively stirring. The stimulus was provided less by the birth of Israel than by the Holocaust. The thoroughly assimilated Russian Jewish writer Ilya Ehrenburg was sufficiently shocked by the war period to admit that "[the] Nazis reminded me that my mother's name was Hannah." (After the war, he would toe the party line again.) Mikhail Zand was even more profoundly shaken afterward by the lack of a single memorial, even a designated cemetery, for the Jews murdered in Kamanets-Podolsk. Both reactions were shared by tens of thousands of cultured, often assimilated, Soviet Jews. For them, no horror was more symbolic of the Nazi inferno than the liquidation of 33,000 Jewish men, women, and children outside Kiev, their bodies dumped into the abandoned lime-and-sand pit known as Babi Yar (Grandmother's Ravine). A memorial was not erected to this atrocity, no more than at Kamenets-Podolsk. And then came the orgy of Stalinist antisemitism of 1948–53. Not even the birth of Israel could relieve the impact of this sequence of blows to Jewish pride and security.

Nevertheless, it was the Israelis who were the first to transform the embittered awakening of Soviet Jews into a tentatively organized movement. In September 1948, Golda Meir (then Meyerson) arrived in Moscow as Israel's first minister to the USSR. She and her colleagues were intent upon determining the extent of surviving Jewish identity in the Soviet Union. Mrs. Meir had little reason to be sanguine, and would have been even less so had she depended upon the observations of the few eminent Soviet Jews who were allowed to publish. Two days before Rosh HaShanah, the Jewish New Year, as Mrs. Meir was preparing to attend services at Moscow's Choral Synagogue, a long article by Ilya Ehrenburg appeared in *Pravda*. "Let there be no mistake about it," wrote Ehrenburg, "the State of Israel has nothing to do with the Jews of the Soviet Union, where there is no Jewish problem and therefore no need for Israel. That is for the Jews of the capitalist countries, in which, inevitably, antisemitism flourishes. And in any case there is no such entity as the Jewish people." The article plainly was a warning for the Jews of Moscow to stay clear of the Israeli emissaries. In her autobiography, Mrs. Meir herself later described the "effect" of Ehrenburg's warning.

The street in front of the synagogue . . . was filled with people, packed together like sardines, hundreds and hundreds of them, of all ages, including Red Army officers, soldiers, teenagers and babies carried in their parents' arms. Instead of the 2,000-odd Jews who usually came to synagogue on the High Holidays, a crowd of close to 50,000 people was waiting for us. For a minute, I couldn't grasp what had happened—or even who they were. And then it dawned on me. They had come—these good, brave Jews—in order to be with us, to demonstrate their sense of kinship and to celebrate the establishment of the State of Israel. Within seconds, they had surrounded me, almost lifting me bodily, almost crushing me, saying my name over and over again. Eventually, they parted ranks and let me enter the synagogue; but there, too, the demonstration went on. Every now and then, in the women's gallery, someone would come to me, touch my hand, stroke or even kiss my dress. . . . The service ended, and I got up to leave, but I could hardly walk. I felt as though I had been caught up in a torrent of love so strong that it had literally taken my breath away and slowed down my heart. I was on the verge of fainting, I think. But the crowd still surged around me, stretching out its hands and saying "Nasha Golda" (our Golda) and "Shalom, shalom," and crying.

It was apparent, then, that Soviet Jewry was rather more than a non-"entity." The task of linking it with Israel was subsequently assigned to Nechemia Levanon. A stocky man, then in his early thirties, a demon for work, Levanon had immigrated to Palestine from Estonia in 1938 and had become one of the founders of Kibbutz Kfar Blum. Several years later, he had served as a Zionist youth official in England. In January 1953, he was called back to Jerusalem by Shaul Avigur, the former Haganah director of clandestine immigration and one of the founders of the Mosad, Israel's "CIA." Currently, Avigur was serving as intelligence adviser to Prime Minister Ben-Gurion. Impressed by Levanon's East European background and his credentials as an organizer, Avigur proposed that he put his experience to work in Moscow, operating through the Israeli embassy. The idea did not spring from the brow of Avigur alone. Ben-Gurion himself had emphasized his unwillingness to write off Soviet Jewry as "lost" to Israel, and in fact was intent upon forging a network of contacts between the Soviet Jewish hinterland and the new Jewish state.

Levanon responded to the challenge with enthusiasm. Taking up his duties in Moscow as Israel's agricultural attaché, he was permitted routinely to tour and inspect the outlying Soviet agricultural areas. During these visits, he managed to revive a number of Latvian Jewish contacts from his youth, and with the help of the survivors to arrange for the quiet circulation of Russian-language publications that had been prepared in Israel. The KGB knew what Levanon was up to, and kept him under continual surveillance. Yet its agents rarely intervened directly;

they wanted no reprisals against their own diplomatic personnel in Israel. Moreover, the KGB soon learned that Levanon and his staff were uninterested in intelligence, that the Israelis in fact rejected intelligence data, and restricted themselves exclusively to the transmittal of Jewish and Zionist information. For a time, then, Levanon and his colleagues moved relatively freely.

Thaw and Schizophrenia

On March 4, 1953, Joseph Stalin died. Within weeks, a process of liberalization was inaugurated at almost every level of Soviet life. Emerging afterward as the leader of his party and nation, Nikita Khrushchev called a halt to the worst excesses of Stalinist terrorism. Hundreds of thousands of prisoners of all nationalities were released from concentration and labor camps, even as the reputations of thousands of Stalin's former victims, living or dead, were rehabilitated and their families were emancipated from pariah status. For the first time, a certain openness of expression was permitted in Soviet arts and literature.

The Jews initially were among the beneficiaries of the new "freedom." Less than a week after Stalin's death, the Doctors' Plot was officially denounced as a criminal fraud, and the surviving physicians (one had died in captivity) were promptly released. The alleged instigator of the ghoulish affair, Mikhail Ryumin, then deputy minister of security, was himself denounced, tried secretly, and shot in July 1954. Among other prisoners to be released now was the small number of Jewish poets and writers who had survived the nightmare of arrests and convictions following the liquidation of the Jewish Anti-Fascist Committee. Throughout 1955–56, these people were slowly returned from the Gulag Archipelago, broken in health, shaken, incapable of further productive work. In the latter 1950s, the Sovetski Pisatel publishing house in Moscow was authorized to bring out selected works of the Jewish poets who had been exterminated. In this fashion, a limited financial and moral compensation was provided to the writers' families, and the world was informed obliquely that Jews in the USSR were respectable again.

It was evidently to court Western goodwill, too, that the Soviets in 1959 tolerated a modest publication of works in Yiddish, mainly by such classic nonpolitical writers as Sholom Aleichem, Y. L. Peretz, and other pre-Soviet figures. A Yiddish-language journal, *Sovetish Heymland,* was inaugurated, the first publication of its kind to appear since the demise of *Eynigkeit* in 1948 (its topics were predictably noncontroversial). The Kremlin even displayed a new moderation toward Judaism. Jewish leaders from abroad were welcomed to the USSR and encouraged to attend the nation's synagogues. The visits were at once poignant and ineffectual as propaganda, for they revealed worshipers as essentially small numbers of aged people. In 1957, the government responded to Western pressures by authorizing the publication of ten thousand prayerbooks, the baking of matzot for Passover, even by establishing a small rabbinical seminary—which soon expired for lack of students. Moscow's chief rabbi, David Levin, served mainly as an apologist for the Soviet state.

This cautiously permissive approach to the Jewish question during the first post-Stalin decade reflected the government's ambivalence toward the welter of Soviet nations and races. Under Stalin, priority had been given to the support of Russian culture, and the Russian language was promoted as the lingua franca of the non-Russian republics. Then, after Stalin's death, the policy was briefly relaxed. The non-Russian peoples were allowed to resume their cultural traditions, to teach their own histories, to rehabilitate their national heroes. In this sense, Khrushchev reverted to Lenin's approach of sensitivity and concessions to a multinational empire. As in the satellite states, however, the new approach carried with it the danger that the non-Russian peoples might venture too far in the direction of autonomy. Thus, at the Twenty-first Party Congress in 1959, Khrushchev pointedly warned against "local chauvinism." The prime minister's volte-face in fact was evoked by a startling demographic shift among the Soviet peoples. The census that year revealed that the highest population growth rate in the USSR was to be found in Central Asia and in the Moslem Caucasus. Nothing in the Slavic "heartland" republics could match this rate. Soviet demographers now calculated that the Russian percentage of the total Soviet population might drop below the 50 percent mark by the end of the century.

In recognition of this danger, the Kremlin preserved the theory of federalism, but in practice revived and intensified the earlier program of integration. The nationalities continued to be represented fairly in the Supreme Soviet. But in the institutions where state power meaningfully resided—in the presidium (formerly the politburo), in the council of ministers, and in the state committees—the proportion of Slavs was kept at over 90 percent. While hundreds of national languages survived, Russian continued as the official language of military command, even in the remotest non-Russian areas. Military recruits throughout the USSR increasingly were stationed outside their geographic areas to ensure that they mastered Russian. This ambivalent policy, of encouraging a certain cultural and administrative self-expression among the non-Russian peoples, on the one hand, and of asserting the political and linguistic primacy of the Russians, on the other, in the end produced a whipsawing effect upon the Jews.

To begin with, the Jews remained an exceptionally visible group. Numbering 2,150,000 in 1970 (a drop of 5 percent since the 1959 census), they were dispersed through all fifteen of the union's republics. In Russia that year, they numbered 808,000; in the Ukraine, 777,000; in Byelorussia, 148,000; in Uzbekistan, 103,000; in Moldavia, 98,000; in Georgia, 70,000; in Latvia, 37,000; in Lithuania, 24,000. By 1970, at least 95 percent of the Jews lived in urban areas. The census listed the Jewish population as 252,000 in Moscow (but it may have been far higher), 163,000 in Leningrad, 143,000 in Kiev, 47,000 in Minsk, 50,000 in Kishinev, 31,000 in Riga, 20,000 in Tbilisi (Tiflis), and 16,000 in Vilnius (Vilna).

It was precisely this urbanization, accompanied by the russification of Soviet Jewry, that accelerated the characteristic Jewish trend toward elitism. Even the "black years" of Stalinism did not quite succeed in reversing the process. As late as 1959, fully 295,000 Jews were party members, a number equivalent to nearly 13 percent of Soviet Jewry. No other national group matched this percentage. Some 180 Jews were among the deputies to the Supreme Soviet. Despite the expulsion of all Jews from the central committee (including finally even Kaganovich, dropped in 1957), other Jews remained active within the party at lower levels, and Venyamin Dymshits continued as a kind of showcase Jew in the position of deputy chairman of the council of ministers.

Moreover, if Jews were substantially purged from the foreign ministry and the armed forces in the late 1940s, they continued to be widely represented on the secondary and tertiary levels of government in administrative posts, and as executives of state enterprises. Their representation in education was still extraordinary. Notwithstanding the restrictions on their access to the better universities, Jews continued to produce three times the normal ratio of university graduates to a given nationality. And among those graduates, the ratio of professionals was nothing less than remarkable. As late as 1963, Jews comprised 15 percent of all Soviet doctors, 10 percent of all lawyers—possibly half the lawyers in Leningrad and Kharkov, and 40 percent of those in Moscow—8 percent of all writers and journalists, 7 percent of all actors, sculptors, musicians, and artists. Jewish membership in the prestigious Academy of Sciences was an astonishing 10 percent.

Nevertheless, this inordinate prominence in many of the higher echelons of Soviet life was precisely the measure of Jewish vulnerability to Khrushchev's "federalism." The process of local administrative and cultural decentralization, adopted as a placatory gesture to the various nations of the USSR (at a time when meaningful—that is, centralized—political power was steadily russified), was inimical to Jewish advancement. To be sure, the brutal and physically threatening antisemitism of the Stalin years was ended. Yet something nearly as ominous was afoot. The hale and hearty Khrushchev, with his Jewish grandson, was the first to begin speaking openly about a need for an adjustment in the "ethnic balance." The party chairman's personal dislike of Jews no doubt was also a factor. He was a Ukrainian, a member of the most antisemitic of the Soviet Union's nationalities. In the presence of journalists, he had occasionally alluded to Jews as "incorrigible individualists" and "ambitious careerists." But personal animus was less important to Khrushchev than policy considerations, and decisive among these was the need he perceived for "adjustments" to sustain the political loyalties of the USSR's ethnic nationalities. Khrushchev's "adjustments," then, however cosmetic in their unwillingness to affect meaningful, central political control, allowed the local nationalities preferential treatment in staffing their local bureaucracies. Ukrainians tended to favor their own, as did Byelorussians, Uzbeks, Kazakhs, and—not least of all, the Russians themselves. Under these circumstances, the Jews were expendable, or at least reducible, to less important jobs in the party, the government, the economy.

Nowhere, surely, did this revived numerus clausus exert a profounder impact upon Soviet Jewry than in higher education. As the press now began stressing the importance of bringing the "national composition of the intelligentsia in line with the national composition of the population of the USSR," the Jews, formerly the nation's educational elite, were shunted even more flagrantly than in the early and mid-1950s into second-rate institutions. The implications of this shift were deeply unsettling to a people who had regarded educational discrimination as the single most painful feature of their life under the tsars. The end of these restrictions after 1917 had aroused such gratitude among Soviet Jews that they were prepared later to accept all the inequities and constraints of Communist rule. The sons and daughters of shoemakers, peddlers, and talmudists had become the intellectual aristocracy of a mighty nation. Now, however, Khrushchev and his successors were threatening severely, even harshly, to attenuate that coveted access to higher education and its opportunities. The shock to the Jewish intelligentsia was profound. In the early 1960s, then, some among them began to turn inward, to examine their Soviet status and the Jewish identity they had sacrificed earlier.

This was Mikhail Zand's intellectual odyssey. In Dushanbe he had been respected and liked by his Tadzhik colleagues and students. It was only in the latter 1950s, deprived of their former role in the central government, but encouraged by way of compensation to develop their own ethnic identity and administrative presence, that the Tadzhiks began to reject their Jewish colleagues. Their chauvinism eventually became truculent enough to cause Zand serious discomfort. He was neither a Russian among Russians, nor a Tadzhik among Tadzhiks. In 1956, as it happened, he learned that his father had been posthumously "rehabilitated." The opportunity was open for him now to return to Moscow. At first, with his painful memories of life in the Soviet capital, he was reluctant to take the step. But finally, in 1960, Zand, his wife, and their two children went "home." In Moscow he found work as a deputy editor of the *Journal of Soviet Orientalia*. It was a decent enough job for a gifted scholar who had been effectively closed out of an academic affiliation.

Yet the anomaly of the Jews' status in this widely heralded pluralist society haunted him. In April 1957, while still living in Dushanbe, Zand had accompanied the Tadzhik cultural delegation to Moscow to participate in the annual celebration of Soviet Peoples' Week. That particular April, in fact, was the year of the Tadzhiks. Zand understood well the public relations purposes these events served, the fact that real power emanated from Moscow, wielded by the Russian "big brothers." Even so, it was surely an emotional solace that a Tadzhik, a Ukrainian, or a Georgian youth could progress from kindergarten through university using only Tadzhik, Ukrainian, or Georgian as his first language; that each nationality was allowed to teach its own history in its own schools and in its own national idiom; that monuments and squares honored the national heroes.

Were the Jews, then, not a nationality? So they were defined under Soviet law. Indeed, they were eleventh in numbers among the Soviet Union's score of nationalities. Yet what had they been given for that status except a certain collective oblivion at best, and educational and cultural discrimination at worst? The few dozen Yiddish-language books that had been published since the death of Stalin, the occasional local dance troupe, the rare performance of a Yiddish theatrical group, the intermittent reception given visiting Jewish delegations from abroad— all were bogus gestures, less meaningful than any made to other Soviet nationalities. Threatened with the collapse of their god of education, where were Jewish intellectuals to find self-awareness? As they turned to the immediate Jewish past, they beheld a wasteland. Jewish culture, history, the Yiddish and Hebrew languages, lay in ruins. In Moscow, Kiev, Odessa, Kharkov, and other major Jewish population centers in the western USSR, the practice of religion had been reduced to haphazard meetings in a handful of dilapidated synagogues, virtually all of them without rabbis. The wasteland was not entirely of Khrushchev's making, or even of Stalin's. The parents and grandparents of the Jewish intellectuals—Zand's father among them—had been collaborators in the process.

If the Jews were losing ground in the 1950s and 1960s, however, it was not only as a consequence of decentralization among the ethnic nationalities, whose "aboriginal" elite was coming of age. The political manipulation of antisemitism was also a factor. Having failed to improve the nation's standard of living, the regime once again sought to dissemble—and divert. It embarked on a new series of trials against "parasitism" and "economic crimes." During 1962–63, some 250 persons were reported to have been executed for these crimes, with the total number of victims possibly much higher. Nearly two-thirds of the executed defendants were Jews. Surely not all of them were innocent. Neither could all of them have been guilty. It was significant that the publicity given the defendants in lurid newspaper accounts emphasized Jewish names and featured antisemitic caricatures.

The assault was not directed against the Jews' financial "corruption" alone, but also against their intellectual "domination" and their "web" of international connections. In this flailing offensive, even their religion became a target, although the antireligious campaign was not aimed exclusively against Jews: Catholicism and Islam were similarly impugned. But in the case of the Jews, the denunciations were launched against a people few of whose members were still observant and whose religious institutions were all but invisible. As such, the "antireligious" campaign plainly was another technique of defaming the Jews as a people. Propaganda against Judaism depicted elderly pious Jews as profiteers, and compared rabbis to "loathsome and filthy ticks" that were "blood-sucking and feeding on all kinds of rubbish." In 1961 and 1962, a series of articles was published on "The Reactionary Essence of Judaism." In 1963, the Ukrainian Academy of Science published Trofim Kichko's *Judaism Without Embellishment*. In this account, Judaism was equated with "money-worship," "thievery," "bribery," and "exploitation of non-Jews." The book's jacket displayed a "rabbinical" figure, with hooked nose and thick lips, leaning from a pulpit with a sack of overflowing gold coins in his clawlike hands. Indeed, the work was altogether so reminiscent of the Nazi journal *Der Stürmer* that it provoked outrage among Communist parties in the West, and their protests eventually induced the Soviets to withdraw it.

If these strictures were intended as diversion from the Kremlin's failures, why were the victims still the Jews? And why so long after Stalin's death? For one thing, they still remained an exposed target for accumulated generations, centuries, of folk suspicions. They were still a territorial anomaly, an appendage of an international people—most of whose kin lived in the West. They were also still the demographic hinterland of the State of Israel, an ostensible "outpost of Western imperialism" in the Near East, the partner of the NATO air forces and navies whose planes and missiles were directed against the USSR's exposed southern belly. Not long before, in 1956, the Israelis had collaborated with those Western nations in an offensive against Moscow's client, Egypt. Manifestly, then, the Jews were not like the rest of the Soviet peoples, however diverse. None other was as vulnerable to a far-reaching campaign of diabolization.

Israel's Silent Counteroffensive

In 1958, Nechemia Levanon's successor in Moscow as liaison to Soviet Jewry was Arieh (Lova) Eliav. A respected figure among Israel's Labor leadership, Eliav was thirty-seven years old. Warm, even endearing in personality, he brought to his new assignment an extensive background of military and civilian responsibilities. Born in Moscow, he had emigrated with his parents to Palestine as a child in 1924. Later, as a young man, he interrupted his studies at the Hebrew University to serve in the Haganah, then in the Palestinian unit of the British army in World War II. Following the surrender of Germany, Eliav participated in the underground Jewish emigration to Palestine. A lieutenant colonel in the Israeli army, he fought in his nation's war of independence and in the 1956 Sinai campaign, where he engaged in the daring commando action that rescued Port Said's Jewish community. During his civilian years, Eliav served as assistant director of the Jewish Agency settlement department, organizing the Lachish group of cooperative settlements in the northern Negev. Like his predecessor, Levanon, Eliav was a doer, and in 1958 he was selected by the Mosad to be its man in the Soviet Union. He would operate in Moscow under the title of first secretary of the Israeli embassy.

There appeared little doubt by then that Soviet Jewry was sentient to its collective identity. Golda Meir had verified the fact. So had Levanon. So too, in 1957, had Israel's delegation to an international youth festival in Moscow. The 150 youngsters had come simply to perform as dancing and choral groups. But their presence in the USSR was a revelation for the Soviet Jews who saw them in action. Mikhail Zand was one of these. Still living in Dushanbe that year, he had returned to Moscow as a member of the Tadzhjik entourage. From a street curb, he watched as the various national delegations marched by under their respective flags. The crowd was silent as the Israeli troops passed. Overcome with emotion, Zand suddenly called out to them: "Shalom." Spectators backed away. Unfazed, he hurried after the Israelis. So did a hundred or more other Jews. Soon the gathering became a crowd, weeping, shouting, cheering. Wherever the Israelis went afterward, even larger crowds of Jews awaited them, following Zand's example, uninhibitedly crying out, "Shalom, Shalom," mingling with the visitors to shake their hands, even embrace them. Despite Soviet efforts to alter the Israelis' schedule, to cancel their occasional appearances, the encounter was repeated in the various cities and towns they visited. By the time the group returned to Israel, its members were in shock. Shaul Avigur, still in charge of the Mosad's "Soviet project," debriefed them personally, together with Lova Eliav. The soil was fertile, they agreed.

Arriving in Moscow then with a staff of eight, Eliav understood that his mission was specifically to seek out Jews, to distribute material on Israel, to intensify Jewish nationalism. The challenge was a formidable one. The Soviet Union remained a closed society. Within its frontiers, the Israeli emissaries would be under continual KGB supervision. Their telephones would be tapped. Eliav's initial tactic was to use the Choral Synagogue as his "headquarters"; at least one Israeli diplomat was present each day to pray. Word of the Israelis' presence traveled fast among Moscow Jewry. Soon hundreds of Jews were turning up to see them, occasionally venturing to speak to them. Eliav and his staff began to distribute religious material—prayerbooks, prayer shawls, mezuzahs, Star of David insignia. Most of the gifts were miniatures that could be passed on unobtrusively, with a handshake. During the festival of Chanukkah, the Israelis were able to distribute thousands of miniature menorahs. On the spring festival of Purim, miniature festive noise-makers were passed out; on Passover, miniature matzot, or tiny bottles of Israeli wine. The distribution went on in synagogues in other major cities with substantial Jewish populations. A rhythm gradually developed for these events, with embassy staffers certain to appear in the larger synagogues, even as far distant as the Caucasus republics.

Other channels of communication were the rare Jewish concerts or theatrical performances authorized by the government (essentially between 1958 and 1962) as public relations gestures to the West. Thus, when a classic Sholom Aleichem play was scheduled, thousands of Jews attended in the certainty that Israeli diplomats would be in the audience. Eliav and his staff, their wives and children, transformed themselves into "walking signals" (Eliav's phrase). Every stroll, every trip in the metro underground, was carefully arranged to draw attention to themselves. Carrying El Al bags, wearing Stars of David on their briefcases, on their collars, the diplomats could sense Jews watching them. Eventually, individuals began to approach them. There were quick, furtive conversations and the Israelis swiftly distributed coins, stamps, postcards, miniature plastic records of Israeli songs, miniature Hebrew-Russian dictionaries, Jewish histories, even miniature translations of Leon Uris's novel *Exodus*. When traveling outside the capital, the diplomats carried suitcases filled with these mementos. The work was prosaic, but vitally important. "We were reaching out to a Jewish archipelago," Eliav recalled.

The Soviet regime did its utmost to deter the Israelis from traveling outside Moscow. As a rule, Eliav and his colleagues were permitted to do so within the framework of reciprocity that operated between nations with diplomatic relations. But the Israelis often were kept waiting, or required to change itineraries, or deprived of train or air schedules. It was a complicated business. "We were the most persistent diplomats in the the USSR," Eliav boasted, with some amusement. "No other embassy staff traveled even a tenth as much as we did." They traveled where they knew substantial numbers of Jews were likely to be, particularly during holiday periods. Yalta was virtually a Jewish resort in summer, with as many as 100,000 Jews on the beaches. To a lesser extent, this was true of the beaches in Riga. Together with his colleagues and their families, Eliav, his wife, son, and daughter journeyed the length and breadth of the USSR, distributing their Israeli artifacts.

By the 1960s, too, the Israelis were making use of Jewish tourists as an important means of communication. Western Jews frequently arrived in delegations attending various international congresses or other special events. They were willing, often eager, to cooperate in the Israeli program of gift distribution, to "contribute" prayerbooks or prayer shawls at synagogues. Over the years, the practice gained momentum as Western Jewish tourists regularly made their first order of business a visit to the Israeli embassy to pick up their material and instructions. The scope and persistence of Eliav's operation became intensely frustrating to the Soviet authorities. They watched. The Israelis evaded. They tapped telephones. The Israelis transmitted their messages outside the embassy premises. On one occasion, a Soviet foreign ministry official invited Eliav to a restaurant and plied him with vodka. But five years in the British and Israeli armies had taught Eliav to drink. He gave out no information, while the Russian soon was in his cups, admitting to Eliav that there were only three great espionage organizations in the world: the Soviet MVD, the Vatican, and the Israeli Mosad. "It made my day," Eliav recalled.

During his first months in the Soviet Union, Eliav was contacted by Jewish activist groups. They alerted him, as they had Levanon, that they were available to disseminate information about Israel. Initially, the center of this activity was in Riga. The Latvian Jewish community had been fearfully depleted by the Nazi liquidation, but 31,000 Jews survived there. As in the prewar years of Latvian independence, the Jewish population fiercely maintained its identity, even an uncompromising version of right-wing Zionism. Throughout the 1950s, its members conducted Zionist underground meetings. Late in 1961, several hundred young Riga Jews began holding memorial gatherings at the Rambuli Forest, one of the major Nazi killing grounds, to sing

Zionist songs and celebrate Jewish holidays. In *samizdat,* underground literature, they spread the word of Israel's growth, of its military prowess.

From the outset, Lydia Slovin was deeply involved in these activities. A blond, blue-eyed woman of deceptively gentle features, Lydia worked as a lawyer in the Latvian ministry of justice. Passionately committed to Jewish nationalism, she was the first Jew in Riga to develop the samizdat operation. From an official of the Israeli embassy, she acquired an English-language copy of the novel *Exodus,* and with friends began translating it into Russian. Over the course of a year, the little group distributed some three hundred individually typed copies to friends in other Jewish communities throughout the Soviet Union. Copies even made their way into the labor camps. Ultimately, *Exodus* became the all-time samizdat best-seller among Soviet Jewry. Eliav and his staff meanwhile kept the underground groups informed of each other's activities, carried messages between them, and offered advice for transcribing samizdat literature. Their efforts were fortified by Kol Yisrael, the Israeli state radio. In the late 1950s, Jerusalem transmitted its first broadcasts to the USSR, in both Russian and Yiddish. The programs refrained from criticizing the Soviet Union, or taking a position on the cold war. While the broadcasts may have sounded unduly timid to militants like Lydia Slovin, at least they were not jammed, and eventually they reached thousands of Soviet Jewish listeners every year.

Mikhail Zand was one of these. Kol Yisrael's Hebrew lessons were indispensable to him. By the late 1950s, he was devouring the few Hebrew books he could find at the Oriental Institute library in Dushanbe, then later in Moscow. In Moscow also he learned of an elderly scholar, Felix Shapira, who was at work on a new Hebrew-Russian dictionary commissioned by the Oriental Institute. At considerable personal risk, the old man allowed Zand to consult a draft manuscript of his dictionary. Afterward, Shapira even agreed to organize a clandestine Hebrew study group in his own apartment. Zand participated in the weekly sessions. Soon he was devoting himself to a wider study of Semitic languages, and eventually he became known as an authority on the subject. In 1964, much to his delight, he was invited to lecture on the "Connections Between Yiddish and Modern Hebrew" at the Soviet Congress on Semitic Studies. The address was well received. Later, it was published and widely disseminated in the Soviet Union and other lands, including Israel, where it enhanced Zand's already formidable reputation among Israeli philologists and

Orientalists. Several of them began to correspond with him.

There was yet another important consequence of his lecture. One afternoon in May 1965, an aged man approached Zand outside the Oriental Institute, greeted him briefly in Israeli Hebrew, then hurried on. Zand soon discovered that the man was Zvi Plotkin, one of the nation's most renowned Hebrew scholars during the pre-Soviet era. Several days afterward, he located Plotkin's flat and visited him. Zand learned then that several other Hebrew writers were living in Moscow, among them such legendary figures as Grigory Preigerzon and Meir Ba'azov, the last survivors of the famous pre-Soviet Hebraic literary circle. Informed that they still were meeting cautiously from time to time, Zand joined their little group. He was not yet aware of the samizdat cells being organized by Lydia Slovin and other Jews in the Baltic republics and elsewhere in the Soviet Union. But he was committed now to a clandestine Hebrew renaissance in Moscow, in the very nerve center of the Soviet empire.

Israel Lays the Groundwork for Protest

As early as 1955, Nechemia Levanon had discussed with Shaul Avigur the possibility of focusing world attention on the plight of Soviet Jewry. Although reserved at first, Avigur finally agreed to open a "liaison office" in Israel's foreign ministry under Levanon's direction. Its mandate was nothing less than to awaken the West to the cultural strangulation of Soviet Jewry—and then gradually to seek methods of fostering Jewish emigration. To avoid compromising Israel's delicate relations with Moscow, however, the project was organized under the auspices of local Jewish institutions within Western capitals. Thus, in London, it functioned under the guise of the "Contemporary Jewish Library." Similar "libraries" were established in Paris and Rome, in Buenos Aires and São Paulo. Their initial task was to enlist the support of overseas Jewish communities, which would then recruit non-Jewish diplomats and public figures. To that end, in 1961, Levanon also organized an International Conference of Intellectuals devoted to the cause of Soviet Jewry. Most of the delegates who attended the Paris gathering were Jews, and included such eminent figures as Martin Buber, Nahum Goldmann, and André Meyer; but a few leading non-Jewish figures also attended, including Lord Bertrand Russell. The participants denounced Soviet oppression and appealed for an end to the cultural persecution of Soviet

Jewry. Press coverage was extensive. Similar protest meetings were organized throughout Latin America.

The task of recruiting the Jewish establishment in the United States took longer. American Jews had only slowly recovered from the shock of the Nazi Holocaust. Since the war, they had devoted themselves almost exclusively to the establishment and sustenance of Israel, and several years of patient education were required by Levanon and his staff to direct their attention to the plight of Soviet Jewry. In 1960, Lova Eliav was recalled from his Moscow post to help in the campaign of public enlightenment. Slowly he began to make headway with American Jewish leaders. By the mid-1960s, Levanon and Eliav had put together a worldwide organization of Jewish leadership, as well as an impressive roster of non-Jewish public figures willing to speak out for Soviet Jews. The United States government was entirely prepared to exert its influence with Moscow. Operating for several years out of the Israeli embassy in Washington, Levanon developed excellent contacts with State Department and National Security Council personnel by sharing his expertise on Soviet affairs with them. President Lyndon Johnson, in his 1964 summit meeting with Soviet Prime Minister Kosygin, in Glassboro, New Jersey, raised the issue of Soviet Jews. Kosygin was less than cooperative, of course. In recent months, he had been outraged by the succession of public meetings on Soviet Jewry that Levanon had organized in the West, by the "vigils" of American and European Jews outside Soviet embassies, and by the protest demonstrations outside theaters and concert halls whenever visiting Soviet artists performed.

It had taken seven years of hard work for the liaison office to effect this coordination, but its structural fulfillment at last had taken "official" form. In the same year as the Glassboro conference, an urgent convocation of Jewish leaders in Washington established the National Jewish Conference on Soviet Jewry. The new body included twenty-five American Jewish organizations, and was coordinated by an office in New York. Under the aegis of the Conference, a mammoth protest rally on behalf of Soviet Jewry was held in Madison Square Garden. It was the Conference that also obtained a resolution from both houses of Congress calling on Moscow to grant Soviet Jews the "rights to which they are entitled by law." Groups of jurists, scholars, clergymen, and labor leaders were enlisted to endorse the resolution. It is worth noting that these appeals, in the United States and in other nations, were concerned only with Jewish legal "rights" within the Soviet Union. They said nothing yet about the "right" of emigration.

To most, but not all, Soviet Jews, such a "right" was still all but unthinkable. Mikhail Zand experienced this fact of life personally. In 1966 he was permitted to take his first trip abroad, as a delegate to the International Congress of Iranian Scholars in Tehran. There he met a number of Jewish Orientalists from the United States and England, including the eminent historian of the Middle East, Bernard Lewis. During a break in the congress proceedings, which took place in the palace of the shah, Lewis and the other scholars discussed Jewish matters with Zand. It was an entirely new world to him, and a thrilling one. At the end of the congress, joining his delegation at Tehran's airport for the return home, Zand passed the El Al counter, then caught sight of an El Al passenger jet on the tarmac. The compulsion to defect and to seek asylum in Israel was overwhelming. But his wife and children were in Moscow, and he resigned himself to the likelihood that he would never leave the vast Communist house of correction.

This was not a fate that all Soviet Jews were prepared to accept by then. The Riga activists were continually pressing Israeli diplomats to speak out in behalf of Jewish emigration. Here they encountered resistance. Yosef Tekoah, Israel's ambassador to Moscow between 1962 and 1965, understood well that a campaign for Jewish rights as an equal nationality within the Soviet Union conceivably was viable. The Soviet leaders had a certain respect for legality, provided their government's self-interest was not threatened. Emigration was a very different matter, however, for no Soviet nationality possessed this right—not in a closed society that was susceptible to infection by Western ideas. In any case, the USSR had lost over twenty million of its citizens in World War II. Laboring to achieve a certain parity with the Western industrialized nations, it could ill afford to lose its Jewish scientists, engineers, and other contributors to its technology. Moreover, the grant of exit permits to one people would set a dangerous precedent for other nationalities, and particularly for the USSR's southern Moslem peoples, whose kin lived directly over the frontier, in Turkey, Iran, Afghanistan, and elsewhere.

Israel's embassy officials accordingly were obliged to move far more circumspectly on this issue. Time was needed, both for a general softening of Soviet policy vis-à-vis all its nationalities, perhaps in response to better relations with the West; and for Israel's campaign of fortifying

Jewish consciousness in the Soviet Union to take wider effect. The "authentic" Jews of the Baltic communities were far more willing to contemplate emigration than were the more integrated and intellectually sophisticated Jewish populations of Russia, the Ukraine, or Byelorussia. For the moment, the wiser policy was to ensure that Soviet Jews not be encouraged to take a premature stance on emigration. That kind of impulsiveness might well expose them to the persecution they had endured in the Stalin era, and place them beyond the reach of Israel altogether.

On the other hand, the Israelis assuredly were not prepared to forgo the issue of emigration indefinitely. All their efforts since the 1950s had been directed to that goal, after all. In recent years, Levanon and his colleagues at the liaison office had been interviewing the small numbers of Soviet Jews who had made their way to Israel via the Polish and Romanian repatriations of 1946–48 and 1958–60. Names of their remaining relatives were catalogued. Levanon then explained the procedures that were available for extricating their kin. The invitations would have to be sent very cautiously, and under no circumstances to the wrong "addresses." Once a direct link was established between a Soviet Jew and a blood relative in Israel, then, in very limited and specific instances—illness or old age—the Soviet authorities might permit the reunification of a family in Israel. In the mid-1960s, Ambassador Tekoah occasionally presented lists of applicants on this narrowly technical basis, and always in a matter that did not threaten Soviet policy or pride. As a result, some 4,500 special cases eventually were permitted to leave between 1966 and 1967. Although these were aged pensioners, for the most part, of no further use to the Soviet economy, they comprised a larger number than had been allowed to depart in the entire previous decade. Even so, there appeared little possibility of a more substantial emigration in the near future.

In 1963, Lydia Slovin left her employment in the ministry of justice in Riga to accept a position as legal adviser to a film company based in Minsk. Traveling extensively throughout the Soviet Union to negotiate contracts with suppliers and actors, she found the assignment an excellent cover to organize Zionist groups and to arrange for the exchange of samizdat materials between communities. Whenever she visited Moscow or other large cities, Lydia sought to develop her own contacts with visiting American Jews, particularly those attending international congresses, and to raise the issue of emigration with them. The Israeli embassy staff learned of these meetings only after the fact. In some consternation, it warned Lydia to stop. Matters of emigration should be handled entirely by embassy personnel, it insisted; the KGB was only waiting for the chance to arrest any Soviet Jews found to be engaged in emigration activity, and to prosecute them for "treasonable complicity."

The warning was appropriate, Lydia admitted. She sensed that she was already under KGB scrutiny. Nevertheless, Israel's caution was a source of growing irritation to her. By then, she and her friends were convinced that the regime was vulnerable to a mass appeal for a Jewish exodus. In 1966, during a secret meeting with an Israeli embassy official, she gave vent to her exasperation. "What would happen," she demanded, "if my friends and I were to face the issue head-on and repudiate our Soviet citizenship? If we were simply to declare ourselves to be Israeli citizens? Sooner or later we'll have to take that step, you know. Do you think those bureaucrats are anxious for a public exposé of the repression in this land? I doubt it."

Lydia recalled that the man went pale. Bluntly, then, he told her what that kind of declaration would cost her. She was not impressed. "How long have you been here?" she asked. "Two years? Three years?"

"Two years," he replied. "And?"

"And my friends and I have been here all our lives," she continued. "I can assure you that we're not the shtetl Jews you and other Israelis remember from your childhood under the tsar. There are *some* advantages at least we've gotten from the Soviet system. We're educated people now and we've traveled to every corner of this land. We know whom we're dealing with here. Better than you do."

The conversation became acrimonious. Finally, losing patience, the official gave Lydia an ultimatum. It was to await further instructions. Either that, or the embassy would terminate its contacts with her, along with its funds for translations, and its communications between Riga and Jewish communities elsewhere in the Soviet Union. "I'm quite serious," the man insisted. "I hope I'm registering with you."

"We'll wait," Lydia replied then, aware that her cheeks were burning. "But don't imagine that we'll wait forever. When your tour of duty is over, you'll be going home. You won't just leave us behind, though. One way or another, we'll be joining you. Even if our route takes us through prison."

XV

The Jews of Protest: The Soviet Union

Prefigurations of Unrest

By 1964, Nikita Khrushchev's failures had come home to roost. He had blundered in the Cuban missile crisis, exacerbated the rift with China, seriously aggravated the shortfall of agricultural production. An embarrassment to the central committee, he was replaced. His successors as premier and party first secretary, Alexei Kosygin and Leonid Brezhnev, were "safe" party bureaucrats with none of Khrushchev's populist impulses. They were expected to keep liberalization within narrow bounds and they did. The outpouring of anti-Stalinist revisionism abated. Ideological and intellectual controls were discreetly but unmistakably tightened.

Yet the post-Khrushchev regime was unable to turn the clock back altogether. The developing nationalism of non-Russian peoples refused to be stilled, particularly in the Ukraine, in the recently annexed Baltic republics, and in the Moslem East. The local populations bitterly resented the implacable policy of russification, the officially sponsored transplantation of Russians to minority areas, the obligatory use of the Russian language for administrative and military purposes. In Lithuania, dissent approached the threshold of a mass movement, with large-scale demonstrations and occasional riots. In the Ukraine, unrest became sufficiently vehement in 1965 to provoke the arrest and imprisonment of twenty prominent intellectuals. Other arrests and heavy sentences would follow in later years. The Baltic Germans, a diffused group of nearly two million who had been driven far into the interior republic during the war, launched impassioned protest marches—and suffered the attendant punitive arrests and convictions.

So, too, did a half-million Crimean Tatars. Deported to Uzbekistan and to other Soviet Asian republics in 1944 for having collaborated with the invading Germans, they embarked on vigorous demonstrations throughout the 1960s, demanding the right of return to their ancient homeland. In July 1968, nearly seven thousand Mtshtekhians, representatives of another Turkic people who similarly had been deported from their homeland in southern Georgia to Central Asia during World War II, converged on Government House in Tbilisi, where they were beaten back by police and army detachments. Dissidence also flared up in the Caucasus republics of Armenia and Georgia, with protests and demonstrations eliciting the usual harsh countermeasures. Evidence of the mounting resentment among these nationalities gravely concerned the Soviet leadership, and turned its suspicions even more vindictively against the Jews. By the same token, the groundswell of protests created both setting and precedent for Jewish self-assertion.

So, to an even greater degree, did the emergence of a vibrant human rights movement among Soviet intellectuals. The phenomenon was partly a response to the tightened literary censorship under Brezhnev and Kosygin. Its initial catalyst was the arrest in February 1966 of Andrei Sinyavsky and Yuli Daniel, whose novels and essays, published abroad, had trespassed an unspoken boundary in their criticism of the system and its literature. Alarmed, many Soviet intellectuals detected in the government's retaliation against the two writers a harbinger of revived Stalinism. Their determination to challenge this threat was stiffened by other arrests and trials of prominent critics. By 1968, the human rights ferment had developed into a formidable movement. Its underground journal, *Khronika*, began appearing every two months as an information clearinghouse in the struggle against "Stalinist lawlessness." For the first time in years, people dared to organize in groups on behalf of persecuted individuals, to stage demonstrations, to transform samizdat into a large-scale cottage industry, to convey news of government abuses to *Khronika* in Moscow and to foreign journalists, tourists, and diplomats. The human rights movement was hardly a threat to the regime; but it did become an embarrassment and a provocation. In January 1972, as preparations were being made for Richard Nixon's first presidential visit to Moscow, the KGB struck hard, arresting scores of dissidents, jailing or intimidating others, and driving several into exile. *Khronika* was silenced. Yet by then the movement had drawn world attention to the repressiveness of Soviet rule.

From the outset, fully a third, possibly half, of the leadership of the

human rights movement was Jewish. Yuli Daniel, whose arrest triggered the dissident protest, was a son of the Yiddish writer
Meyerovich. Tried and convicted for "anti-Soviet slander," Daniel was
sentenced to forced labor together with Andrei Sinyavsky, who, although non-Jewish, wrote under the name of Abram Tertz, an anonymous Jewish underworld figure. Daniel's wife, Larissa, also the child of
a Jewish writer, became a principal force in the movement and ultimately was exiled to Siberia. The movement's star, the physicist and
Nobel laureate Andrei Sakharov, was not Jewish; but his wife, Yelena
Bonner, was half-Jewish. Dozens of other Jews were active in the dissidents' leadership, among them Pavel Litvinov (the son of Maxim),
Yevgenya and Aleksandr Ginzburg, Venyamin Kovesin (né Zilberg),
Yosif Brodsky, Piotr Yakir.

"I had my period with them," Mikhail Zand recalled. "By the mid-
sixties, I had formulated something of an inner philosophy. Its central
feature was a categorical rejection of the Soviet system. I wanted no
part of the regime's fake elections, its fake dialectic." In 1966, chivied
by an apparatchik in the Oriental Institute to join the party, Zand exploded in scatological language. Almost immediately afterward, he
joined the human rights movement, contributing a few articles to its
samizdat literature, sharing its discussions in private homes. "Those
were among the most emotionally fulfilling months of my life," he recollected. "It was a great thing to know Solzhenitsyn, Mrs. Mandelstam,
Nadia Krupskaya [Lenin's widow], Aleksandr Ginzburg, and many
other famous writers. Their courage gave me the strength and purpose
I needed later for my 'Jewish protests.'" Many of the Zionists tended in
later years to denigrate the human rights advocates as utopian dream-
ers. But those like Zand who had briefly participated in the movement
knew what they owed it. From the dissidents, they learned the technique of invoking the Soviet constitution itself as legal justification for
their demands, of reaching the West by exploiting the presence of
Western diplomats and newsmen. It was the dissidents who first broke
the hermetic seal of Soviet society. At a symposium in Jerusalem years
later, Zand paid tribute to these former colleagues:

> Our national [Jewish] movement could not and would not have existed
> without the democratic movement. They were our mentors. They created
> the climate that made dissent possible. . . . Without their bravery and as-
> sistance, it would have been difficult to give vent to our views, because we
> had little experience in such things. . . . To turn our backs on them would
> be impossible to us as Jews.

And yet, eventually, the Jews did turn away from the dissidents. They had little choice after June 1967. It was the Six-Day War that marked them again as targets of Soviet frustration and vindictiveness. The Arab debacle was at once an economic, diplomatic, and political defeat for the Soviet Union itself. Not less than $2 billion worth of Soviet military equipment was destroyed by the Israeli armed forces. Nor was Moscow capable even of mobilizing support for a United Nations resolution demanding Israeli withdrawal from captured Arab territories. More painful yet was the Soviet government's loss of prestige among its own satellites. Although most of these Communist regimes followed the Kremlin's lead in severing diplomatic relations with Israel, it was evident that popular sentiment among the East European peoples markedly favored the victors. In their eyes, Israel was a symbol of effective resistance to Soviet might, and they drew the appropriate parallels. Within the Soviet Union itself, Lithuanians, Latvians, and other contentious nationalities exulted at Moscow's discomfiture. "Many of my non-Jewish acquaintances approached me to shake hands and congratulate me," Lydia Slovin recalled.

Rarely in its history did the Soviet leadership react to a foreign policy setback with a more explosive outburst of vilification. In late July 1967, a massive propaganda campaign was launched against Zionism as a "world threat." Defeat was attributed not to tiny Israel alone, but rather to an "all-powerful international force." As in the Stalin era, that "international force" was equated now with Jewish communities everywhere, and not least of all with expressions of national feeling among Soviet Jews themselves. The term "Zionist" henceforth became interchangeable with "Zionist Jew," or with the "rich Jewish bourgeoisie." In its vulgarity and intensity, this new propaganda assault soon rivaled that of Adolf Hitler.

The Soviet public was saturated with racist canards. Extracts from Trofim Kichko's notorious 1963 volume, *Judaism Without Embellishment,* were extensively published again in hundreds of Soviet newspapers, pamphlets, and broadcasts. Yuri Ivanov's *Beware Zionism,* a book that was essentially a rephrasing of *The Protocols of the Elders of Zion,* was given nationwide coverage. Two antisemitic novels, *In the Name of the Father and the Son* and *Love and Hatred,* by Ivan Shevtsov, were published under the imprimatur of the ministry of defense. Never before in Soviet literature had such a rogues' gallery of Jews been portrayed, most of them sinister power brokers who were funded surreptitiously by the unlimited wealth of world Jewry. The Israelis,

too, were depicted as hook-nosed Jewish stereotypes in the typical caricatures of this period. Western observers, even members of Communist parties in Western lands, were stunned by the Nazi-like onslaught.
It had its effect on Soviet Jewry, as well.

The June Trauma: Reaction and Action

The Six-Day War electrified this beleaguered minority people. For
years, even before the fighting began, Soviet Middle Eastern policy had
kept the Israel issue alive in the press, and thus in the consciousness of
Soviet Jews everywhere. Avid readers, they were made aware that Israel and the Jewish Diaspora evidently were a powerful force on the
international scene. In the aftermath of the war, the Kremlin inadvertently reinforced this dynamic image by exaggerating even further the
"power of world Jewry." In Moscow, Zand was stirred to his depths by
Israel's spectacular victory. Overcome by relief and pride, he hurried to
a jeweler and purchased rings for himself and his wife with the Hebrew
initial *heh* inscribed on them. *HaYom*—The Day—was its secret meaning, the day when he and Nellie would emigrate with their children to
Israel. A vague, inchoate dream now was transformed into a burning
determination.

It was in the non-Russian territories, particularly the Baltic republics in the west and the Caucasus republics in the east, with their
"authentic" Jewish populations, that the impact of the Six-Day War was
most far-reaching. "For us in Riga it had never been a question of
whether we would depart for Israel," Lydia Slovin recalled. "But after
June 1967, there was simply no further time for waiting." The effort
that had begun more than a decade earlier as a small nucleus of cultural
Zionists swelled now into a militant, widely organized Jewish emigration movement. Ironically, the closure of the Israeli embassy offered a
certain advantage to the Jewish activists. From then on, Lydia and her
friends were able to mount their campaign without fear of injuring
Soviet-Israeli relations. They could even take the decisive step at last of
petitioning for the "right" to leave the USSR.

On February 15, 1968, a group of twenty-six Jewish lawyers, doctors, and scientists in Vilnius addressed a letter to Lithuania's party
central committee. Alluding to widespread government discrimination
against Jews, to the suppression of Jewish culture, the letter appealed
in straightforward language for the opportunity to emigrate to Israel.

Through Western tourists, a copy of this document made its way to the United States, where it was published in the *Washington Post*. Other equally forthright appeals followed. One of the most dramatic was that of Mendel Gordin, a young Riga physician, who in February 1968 applied for an exit permit to settle in Israel. When he was rejected, he sent an open and signed letter to President Nikolai Podgorny, renouncing his Soviet citizenship and declaring that Israel henceforth was his only motherland. Gordin was promptly fined and demoted from his position in Riga's bacteriological research institute. But again, his appeal was smuggled out to the West and given extensive publicity. Other letters followed, all addressed to Communist officials, all demanding the "right" of repatriation to the "ancestral Jewish homeland." With few exceptions, the letters were reproduced in Western and Israeli newspapers.

The emphasis upon the "right" to emigrate was not merely rhetorical. In Jewish samizdat literature, much attention was being paid to Dr. Boris Zuckerman, a forty-one-year-old Moscow physicist. Following the example of the dissidents, Zuckerman and his Russian wife had been studying the Soviet constitution, as well as the legislation passed in recent years by the Soviet presidium. Stung by an editorial in *Literaturnaya Gazeta* that had branded as a traitor anyone wishing to forsake Mother Russia, Zuckerman wrote the editor arguing that neither the constitution nor Soviet legislation denied a citizen the right to leave his country. When he received no answer, Zuckerman prepared a second letter, this time invoking a law requiring an answer within eight weeks to any letter written to a newspaper on a constitutional issue. Finally, he received his reply, and although it was vague, he had forced the authorities at least to hedge. Satisfied then that the law could be a weapon in the struggle to emigrate, Zuckerman alerted the extensive samizdat readership.

Lydia and her friends in turn broadened their travels throughout the country, raising funds to publish samizdat material and to provide emergency relief for other Jews who had renounced their Soviet citizenship, applied for exit visas, and been deprived of their livelihoods. The first breakthrough came entirely unexpectedly. On September 23, 1968, a friend telephoned Lydia. "My application's been approved," the woman cried out, almost beside herself with excitement. "The people at the visa office told me that other applications will also be regarded favorably." Incredulous at first, Lydia decided to test the waters. She contacted her network throughout the country, urging its members to apply immediately, en masse. The response was overwhelming. On October 11, she received another telephone call at her home in Riga. It was an official of OVIR, the passport office, suggesting that if she and her family applied for exit visas, they would be approved. "It was true, then," Lydia recalled. "I was stupefied."

Her reaction was shared by hundreds of other Baltic Jews who earlier had made applications. The unimaginable had come to pass: Jews were being allowed to depart. In Lydia's case, approval came for herself, her husband, her parents, and—so she was informed—her three children. She and her husband, Boris, promptly set about completing the formalities, arranging for papers to be signed, tax vouchers to be stamped. Then, several weeks later, the Slovins were informed that their oldest daughter, Naomi, eighteen, had been "reevaluated" and would not be granted an exit visa. As the OVIR official explained it, Naomi had been an operator at the central telephone exchange and thus had been privy to security information. "In the end, Naomi herself insisted that we go without her," Lydia said. "Once we left the country, she was sure we could make the necessary diplomatic contacts to get her out. The OVIR people looked at matters differently, of course. They regarded Naomi as a hostage for my 'good behavior' after we reached Israel." Lydia smiled coldly at the recollection. "My 'good behavior.'"

Even as the Slovins departed, without Naomi, thousands of Jews were lining up each day at the OVIR offices in Riga and other cities— still largely in the Baltic republics. They lined up outside post offices, too, to cable relatives in Israel for the required *vyzovs*, invitations authenticated by the Finnish embassy in Tel Aviv (which handled Soviet affairs after the severance of diplomatic relations in June 1967). After obtaining a vyzov, the applicant was obliged to secure a *kharakteristika*, a character reference from his employer or school; then to obtain documents certifying that his lodgings were returned in proper condition, that he had resigned his job or his position in school, returned his trade union and military service books. If the exit visa was approved, the applicant was then charged 900 rubles ($1,000) for each family member. The sum represented about six months wages for the average Soviet professional. The number of Jews receiving the coveted pink-and-white triplicate exit permits jumped from 213 in 1968 to 3,033 in 1969.

Why had the Soviet government permitted this increase? It was still interested in a détente with the West, for one thing. The current, rather modest, loosening of its emigration restrictions evidently served as proof of its good intentions. The gesture was hardly a risky one for the Soviet leadership. The Jewish activists were not demanding political reform (the objective of the dissidents), but simply the opportunity to be "repatriated," a concession that could be granted without fundamentally affecting power relationships. There were even precedents in recent Soviet history for this type of repatriation. In 1956, approximately 200,000 Poles, living in the Soviet interior since 1939, had been repatriated to Poland. Four years later, Moscow had quietly allowed about a thousand Soviet citizens of varying nationalities to rejoin their families in Western countries. Additional thousands of Volga Germans, Mongolians, and Koreans had similarly been "reunited" with their families. And so, it is recalled, had nearly 4,000 Jews in the mid-1960s— although most of them were older pensioners.

If, then, some Jews—especially in the recently annexed Baltic provinces—were agitating to leave for Israel, perhaps (the Soviet leaders apparently reasoned) it would be better to allow them to depart, and thereby remove the danger of "infection" spreading to the Jews of the "heartland" republics, including those of integral Russia. If these were the Kremlin's assumptions, they soon proved to be radically in error.

An Uncertain Israeli Response

News of the relaxed emigration policy caught Soviet Jewry by surprise. Only 7,000 of them applied for exit visas in 1968. Once the government's policy was verified, however, the figure soared to 27,000 in 1969, and by then not all the applicants were from the border areas. Accordingly, as the evidence accumulated of a widening Jewish passion for departure, the Soviet hard-liners asserted themselves decisively. In 1969, the issuance of visas abruptly dropped by two-thirds, to less than a thousand, and then was all but terminated. Whereupon, having burned their bridges by applying, thousands of Jews now found themselves suspect in the eyes of the party and of their employers. Many of them were dismissed from their jobs or demoted, and their children were harassed in school. With little to lose, then, they decided to fight openly for their right to emigrate. From 1969 on, they dispatched thousands of letters and petitions to the Soviet government, and to influential figures and institutions in the West.

During the same period, Jewish samizdat writing developed a new momentum. In 1970, its first journal, *Iton Alef* (Primer A), was "published" in Riga. It was followed by successive editions, *Iton Bet* and *Iton Gimel*. Crudely mimeographed in batches of one or two thousand copies, the issues included a rapturous account of life in Israel, a report on the Six-Day War, and the first open letters to Soviet and international organizations demanding free Jewish emigration from the Soviet Union. In April 1970, a more professional-looking magazine appeared, this time in Moscow, entitled *Iskhod* (Exodus). Its model was the dissident journal *Khronika*, but its emphasis was exclusively on Jewish and Zionist themes. Mikhail Zand participated in these ventures, writing a number of articles for *Iton* in 1970, stressing the legal basis of Jewish emigration. Zand's was a classic example of the overlapping contributions to *Khronika* and to specifically Jewish samizdat. Otherwise, Jewish underground literature scrupulously avoided *Khronika*'s criticism of Soviet society. When, in an article for *Iton*, Zand once attacked the Soviet regime, the committee refused to publish it.

The growing network of activists also concentrated increasingly upon mobilizing public opinion abroad. Once more they employed techniques they learned from the dissident movement. These were letters, cables, and, frequently, telephone calls to the West and Israel. When applications for exit visas were rejected, or premises were searched by the KGB, or Jews were detained or arrested, full accounts were promptly transmitted by samizdat material and by registered letters sent abroad. The Soviet authorities meanwhile were unsettled, then outraged, by this spreading "infection." Yet they were hesitant to resort to the repressive methods of the Stalin era at a time when they were seeking détente with the West. Instead, the regime engaged in indirect harassing measures, dismissing or demoting applicants for emigration, waging a propaganda campaign against "parasitism" (the code word for Jewish emigration).

The government's counteroffensive reached a climax of sorts on March 2, 1970, a nationwide Day of Protest Against Israeli Aggression. Its highlight was the presentation of an anti-Israel petition signed by thirty-seven eminent Soviet Jewish intellectuals, among them two Nobel Prize laureates in physics. Several days later, forty additional Jews were co-opted for a televised press conference, including Vice-Premier

Venyamin Dymshits, Generals Dragunsky, Milshtein, and Beinchik, Aron Vergelis (editor of *Sovetish Heymland*), Aleksandr Chakovsky (editor of *Literaturnaya Gazeta*), and other famous academicians, actors, writers, doctors, and scientists, together with the violinist Leonid Kogin and the comedian Arkady Raikin. It was a blue-chip group, most of them appearing publicly as Jews for the first time. They read a statement condemning Israel and "international Zionism," and denying the existence of antisemitism in the Soviet Union. It was a pitiable spectacle.

No more so, however, in the eyes of the Jewish activists, than Israel's public silence on the issue of Jewish emigration. The lapse was even more inexplicable after all Israel had done to foster Jewish identity in the USSR, to organize foreign support and diplomatic pressure on behalf of the Jews' right to emigrate—not to mention the thousands of vyzovs dispatched from family members in Israel. In view of this record, why should the Israeli government have been unwilling to fight back in Moscow's campaign against Soviet Jews, particularly for those trapped in the emigration process Israel itself originally had encouraged? An official Israeli campaign to marshal world opinion was desperately needed at a moment when Soviet Jews in the tens of thousands were risking their very livelihoods to break free of Communist rule and make their way to Israel.

As late as 1969 Shaul Avigur, the founder of the liaison office, still determined Israeli policy on East European Jewry. Conditioned by his years of cloak-and-dagger intelligence work, Avigur maintained his passion for secrecy. He remained convinced, too, that Soviet Jews were more likely to be extricated through clandestine negotiations, the method he had used successfully for rescuing Jews in the pre-state period of 1945–47, and for achieving the Jewish exodus from Romania, Bulgaria, and Poland during the 1950s. Avigur retired in 1969, but his handpicked successor, Nechemia Levanon, continued his predecessor's approach and Prime Minister Golda Meir continued to rely heavily on Avigur's advice. Avigur and Levanon still believed that Israel's role behind the emigration movement must not be publicly acknowledged—even though Moscow was entirely aware of it. Otherwise, the Soviet leadership would be provoked into exploiting the relationship to extract concessions from Israel in the Middle East. It was vital for Israel to keep the two issues entirely separate. In any case, nothing was likely to be gained, and conceivably much lost, by putting the Soviet ruling elite (with its chronic paranoia) on the defensive.

By 1969, Soviet Jews had learned the techniques of reaching Western news media on their own. The human rights movement had taught them. Their plight was out in the open, after all. Indeed, the leadership of the Jewish activist movement insisted that it was specifically the glare of public attention that had driven the Kremlin into a relaxation of its emigration policy. With its economy faltering and Red China looming on the horizon, the Soviet government was willing to pay almost any price now to gain access to Western technology and to ease tensions with the West. This was the argument of the Baltic Jews who had recently arrived in Israel and who met with a group of Israeli newspaper editors. The editors were impressed. Early in August 1969, a number of their various party spokesmen raised the issue in the Knesset security affairs committee (in executive session), asking if the time had not come to adopt an alternative approach to Soviet Jewry. That same month, Lydia Slovin and twenty-eight of her fellow Soviet émigrés secured an interview with Prime Minister Meir. Lydia recalled the meeting vividly. "We've risked everything to launch the emigration movement," they argued. "Tens of thousands of our brethren in the Soviet Union continue to face the risk of arrest and imprisonment—and mainly because of the inspiration provided by our courageous Israeli kinsmen. Now we come here, to discover that Israel's government is constrained by the identical ghetto mentality that once was ascribed to us."

Although moved, the prime minister still believed that the cause of Soviet Jewish emigration would be harmed by public clamor. She reminded her visitors that premature publicity had interrupted the emigration of Romanian Jews in 1958. But Lydia and her friends also held fast. It was their own "noisy" activism, they insisted, not Israel's quiet diplomacy, that had achieved the breakthrough of recent years. The discussion became heated. "Put padlocks on your mouths," warned Mrs. Meir, ending the interview. "If you continue, I'll be obliged to impose censorship on anything you leak to the press. We already have such a law, and I'm quite prepared to enforce it."

Lydia Slovin was cast in the same iron mold as Golda Meir. She would not be deterred in her course. With the help of several prominent American Jews who had taken up the cause of Soviet Jewry, she flew to the United States the next month and met with Senators Abraham Ribicoff and Jacob Javits, asking them to intercede with both the

American and the Israeli governments. Lydia's sponsors then brought her to Los Angeles. There she was interviewed on television and described the personal tragedy of her own daughter held hostage in the Soviet Union. Petite, blond, attractive, and impassioned in the Slavic manner, she made an extraordinary impact. For hours after the interview, telephone calls of support poured into the television station. By the time Lydia returned to New York, the *Times* had picked up her story and given it extensive coverage. So had newspapers in Britain and France. Following these accounts, the Israeli press began questioning the government more sharply about the wisdom of its policy of silence. And finally one Israeli newspaper, *Yediot Acharonot,* defied the censor altogether by printing a lengthy account of the burgeoning emigration movement among Soviet Jewry. At this point, Prime Minister Meir faced a crucial decision: whether to prosecute *Yediot Acharonot* or to give open Israeli support to the emigration cause.

In fact, Mrs. Meir had already undergone a reappraisal. It was influenced by a heartrending letter she had received from eighteen Jewish families of Tbilisi, Georgia, forwarded by the Netherlands embassy in Moscow. Avoiding any criticism of the Soviet regime, the Georgian Jews described the love their people historically had nurtured for the "beloved motherland of Israel," and their willingness now to risk everything in applying for emigration visas. Yet their departure could only be achieved, they went on, if their Israeli kin spoke out vigorously on their behalf. "In all our centuries in this faraway land, we have never abandoned you," they concluded. "We beg you now not to abandon us." Those close to Mrs. Meir recalled that the appeal brought tears to her eyes. For the moment, she held firm. But the mounting pressure of other letters, of the Israeli press, of several close political advisers, finally altered her course. On November 19, 1969, the prime minister's office announced that, whatever the risks, the government of Israel henceforth would take the lead in openly championing the cause of Soviet Jewish emigration. A Knesset resolution all but unanimously endorsed this policy. "We felt that Israel had definitely heard our call," one of the Soviet Jewish activists, Alla Rusinek, was later to write, "and was trying to help. . . . Now we could feel that the second front was open."

An Airport in Leningrad

The front proved to be an active one. By the spring of 1970, Soviet Jewish immigrants to Israel were holding collective prayer sessions at Jerusalem's Western Wall and outside the United Nations in New York.

On March 15 of that year, a mass protest rally against the Soviet emigration ban was conducted in Buenos Aires. Ten days later, a similar rally took place in Melbourne. A day after that, several thousand Jewish students demonstrated outside the Soviet consulate in New York. On April 3, a crowd of Jews and non-Jews maintained a torchlight vigil at the Soviet embassy in Copenhagen. The next day, Jewish students conducted a hunger "sit-in" at newspaper offices in Johannesburg and Cape Town. Three days later, a Jewish demonstration was mounted on the Piazza Navona in Rome. On April 26, tens of thousands of Jews shared in a Passover "Exodus March" from the Soviet mission at the United Nations to UN headquarters.

Although orchestrated in large measure by Levanon's office in Israel and by the National Conference on Soviet Jewry in the United States, these demonstrations unquestionably were heartfelt and passionate. They coincided with an escalating and frustrating Soviet involvement in the Egyptian-Israeli "war of attrition," and with a Soviet propaganda campaign against Israel that had reached unprecedented fury. With Jewish applications for exit visas altogether out of control, especially in the Baltic republics and in the Caucasus, Moscow now had decided to crush the emigration campaign once and for all.

It happened that a few months earlier, in December 1969, several Jewish activists in Leningrad had begun developing a plan for abducting a Soviet passenger airplane. Their objective was to publicize the emigration campaign dramatically and decisively. Several weeks afterward, the discussion was extended to Riga, and apparently knowledge of it reached a number of Jews in Kishinev, Moscow, and other communities. The originators of the scheme were Mark Dymshits and Edward Kuznetsov. Dymshits was forty-three years old, an engineer and a former aviator with a first-rate wartime air force record, who had endured a galling period of unemployment in the postwar wave of Stalinist antisemitism. He had applied for permission to emigrate to Israel in 1968, but had been ignored. Kuznetsov, thirty-eight, was the son of a Jewish father and a Russian mother. In the 1960s, he had become involved in the dissident movement, and had edited and published numerous samizdat articles. Eventually he had been arrested and imprisoned. Upon completing his seven-year sentence in 1968, he asked that his passport registry be changed back to "Jew" (after his father's death, he had been re-registered as "Russian"). In common with tens of thousands of Soviet Jews, he had been inspired by the Six-Day

War. His request was denied. Soon afterward, in January 1970, Kuznetsov married Sylva Zalmanson, an engineer from Riga and a committed Zionist. Settling with her in the Latvian capital, he hurled himself full-heartedly into the Jewish emigration movement.

One of the couple's close associates in the movement was Gillel Butman, a young lawyer in Leningrad, who was fluent in Hebrew and well read in Jewish history. In February 1970, Butman telephoned Sylva Zalmanson in Riga to arrange an urgent meeting. Several days later, in the Kuznetsovs' Riga flat, Butman outlined a scheme for commandeering a Soviet airliner. Under the plan, Sylva's friends in Riga would join the group Butman had recruited earlier in Leningrad. Posing as a wedding party, they would purchase tickets and occupy a large number of seats in a regularly scheduled Aeroflot flight from Leningrad to Murmansk. Once the plane was en route, they would take it over and fly it to Sweden. The Kuznetsovs reacted to the plan with enthusiasm. Yet, in subsequent weeks, Butman and the others decided that too many people were involved (both the early planners and the later participants) and that secrecy was likely to be breached. The final version was to abduct a smaller craft, a twelve-seat Antonov-2 biplane scheduled to depart from Smolny Airport, an auxiliary field near Leningrad. Through a contact, Sylva Zalmanson then sent word of the plot to the liaison office in Israel. Nechemia Levanon, still directing the office, discussed the matter immediately with Prime Minister Meir. Both agreed that the plan was "insane." The very notion of an air hijacking was appalling to a government that had been the target of many PLO attempts against its own El Al planes. Levanon communicated with Riga, strongly condemning the idea. Whereupon Sylva Zalmanson assured her contact in Israel that the plan would be canceled.

It was not. Rather, a new scheme was devised, calling for the "wedding party" to divide into two parts. Kuznetsov and Dymshits would lead the main group to Leningrad's Smolny Airport, where they would board the AN-2 and fly from Leningrad to Priozersk, a middle-sized town thirty-nine miles from the Finnish border. At Priozersk, in turn, Sylva Zalmanson and several others would board the craft. While the AN-2 was still on the ground, the passengers would seize the crew members and bind them. Then Dymshits would fly the group to Sweden, where they would release the crew, request sanctuary, and eventually travel to Israel. The target date was set for June 15.

On June 14, Sylva Zalmanson and three other participants set out from Leningrad by train for Priozersk. Reaching their destination the same evening, they entered a forest abutting the small Priozersk airport. That night, while sleeping in the forest, they were arrested by KGB agents. Five hours later, in the early morning, Kuznetsov, Dymshits, and their friends in the second group unsuspectingly walked out of the terminal building at Leningrad's Smolny Airport and headed for the waiting AN-2 that was scheduled to depart for Priozersk. Crossing the tarmac, they too were arrested by KGB men.

Clearly, the plot had somehow leaked—and well in advance. The ensuing arrests were efficient and far-reaching. The same afternoon of June 15, KGB agents searched over sixty Jewish apartments in various parts of the country, arresting 232 other persons in Leningrad, Riga, Moscow, Kishinev, and Kharkov. It was a devastating roundup. That evening, the Soviet press carried a brief report: "On June 15 a group of criminals trying to seize a scheduled airplane was arrested at Smolny Airport. Investigations are in progress." Indeed, those investigations would continue for months, as additional apartments were searched, and additional members of the Jewish emigration movement were detained and questioned. But in the interval, the sheer scope, rapidity, and thoroughness of the KGB crackdown left Jewish activists throughout the USSR in a state of shock.

The formal investigation of the abortive hijacking ended on October 27, 1970. The trial date was scheduled for November 20, then postponed until December 15. That delay may have been the Kremlin's mistake. Recovering their composure meanwhile, the activists began deluging their Israeli and Western contacts with letters of protest. In Israel, Prime Minister Meir denounced the impending trial as a "farce." Gideon Hausner, who had prosecuted Adolf Eichmann, labeled it a "fraud." A number of Western attorneys and law professors sought permission to assist the accused in their defense—and of course were refused. The protests and intercessions were given extensive coverage by the Western press; and when the first group of defendants, consisting of the original plotters, finally went on trial in Leningrad, scores of reporters from numerous Western countries thronged the steps of the courthouse.

At that time, no Soviet criminal statute applied specifically to hijacking. The charges leveled by the prosecution were "betrayal of the Fatherland" (treason), efforts to commit "large-scale theft of state property," and "anti-Soviet" agitation and propaganda. All these charges carried the death penalty. The right of defendants under Soviet law to counsel of their own choice now was declared inapplicable in "political" cases. Consultations between the defendants and their court-appointed lawyers were severely restricted, and the lawyers were forbidden to make written notes. Many of the defendants' requests for witnesses were denied, while the prosecution's witnesses were spared cross-examination.

It is likely, nevertheless, that the prosecution struck bargains with a few of the accused. Shortly before the trial, Mark Dymshits's wife and two daughters were unexpectedly released from arrest as "an act of clemency." In the opening statement presented by his lawyer, Dymshits admitted that he had been the ringleader. Sylva Zalmanson and two other prisoners also pleaded guilty to some charges, innocent to others. All the accused denied any intention of harming anyone. Without exception, they courageously affirmed their Jewish identity and defended their action as their only way of emigrating to their "ancestral homeland." These statements were wasted on the prosecutor. Concluding his summation with a vigorous peroration against the "intrigues of international Zionism," he requested the death penalty for Dymshits and Kuznetsov, and heavy sentences for the others. On December 24, the judge concurred. Dymshits and Kuznetsov were condemned to death. The others received prison sentences ranging from life to fifteen years. After the sentencing, each of the prisoners was permitted to address the court. Again, Dymshits and Kuznetsov spoke movingly on behalf of their Jewish rights. A wife of one of the condemned men jumped on a bench and cried out: "We will wait for you! All Jews are with you. All the world is with you. We will all meet in Israel one day." The families of the condemned men then began singing the *Sh'ma Yisrael*, the ancient credo of the Jewish people. The prisoners in turn called out: "We'll all be in Israel. You will be free. *Am Yisrael Chai* [the People of Israel lives]." These reactions stunned the Soviet authorities.

Determined to convey the news to the West, friends of the prisoners outside the court rushed to the nearest telephones. In Moscow, Zand received the full account by long-distance telephone. Jotting down notes in lengthy detail, he then transferred the information to a visiting American Jewish businessman, Jean-Jacques Newman. Newman in turn carried the notes with him by airplane from Moscow to Vienna (under acute tension, he suffered a heart attack upon reaching the Austrian capital). Other reports were transmitted by Jewish students at the University of Moscow, acting as "red line" couriers to foreign journalists. And, as anticipated, Jewish organizations throughout the Western nations denounced the sentences.

In New York, the American Jewish Congress announced that its Soviet Jewry "hot line," a recorded telephone message giving callers news of the most recent developments on Soviet Jewry, would be expanded to additional cities and would be updated daily, even hourly. Within days, too, hundreds of public meetings were organized in major cities across the United States, climaxed by a National Emergency Conference on Soviet Jewry on December 30 in Washington. Meanwhile, governments of twenty-four nations intervened diplomatically on behalf of the Leningrad defendants. Even the Communist parties of several countries, including those of France and Italy, cabled protests to Moscow. The Kremlin was deluged with appeals for mercy from the Vatican, from Protestant religious leaders, Nobel laureates, and other public personages. Within the Soviet Union itself, Jewish activists spoke out vehemently. Here they were joined by spokesmen of the human rights movement, led by Andrei Sakharov. It was altogether an avalanche of protest unlike any the Soviet regime had encountered in its earlier criminal trials and verdicts.

Taken aback by this international reaction, the Kremlin moved to stem the tide. The supreme court of the Russian Federal Republic convened only six days after the original verdict of the Leningrad district court. Crowds of dissidents, many of them non-Jews, picketed the courthouse (Zand was among them). In an unprecedented gesture, then, the tribunal substantially reduced all the sentences, commuting the death sentences to life imprisonment. Determined to present a more humane face to the West, the Soviet leadership plainly recognized that the initial convictions had been a blunder of the first magnitude. Instead of treating the planned hijacking as the foolish and widely execrated crime that it was, they had chosen to transform the trial into a full-scale ideological attack, and a savage frontal campaign, against the entire emigration movement. By overplaying their hand, they had stiffened Jewish defiance rather than chilled it. Worse yet, from their viewpoint, they had focused world attention on the plight of Soviet Jewry, and had done so far more effectively than had even the liaison office in Tel Aviv.

The revised sentences of course were hardly mild. The convicted defendants now were dispatched to Soviet prison camps. Moreover, trials of twenty-two other conspirators followed in Leningrad, in Riga, in Kishinev—all linked by the prosecution to the hijacking attempt. Again, all the defendants were found guilty, all sentenced to prison terms ranging from one year to ten years (in the case of Gillel Butman), all at "strict regime" labor. As at the first Leningrad trial, full accounts of the proceedings were smuggled to Western newsmen from notes jotted down by relatives. Published in Israel and in the West, the rough transcripts once more elicited intense compassion and outrage. The penalties imposed on the defendants were unquestionably severe. But for the Soviet government itself, the consequences in world obloquy had become prohibitive. Indeed, beginning in December 1970, as the reaction to the original Leningrad death sentences began flooding in, the price already was being paid.

A Crescendo of Soviet Jewish Applications

As it turned out, the Leningrad trial and its successors evoked the harshest and most extensive condemnation of the USSR since the invasion of Czechoslovakia. From his office in Tel Aviv, Nechemia Levanon set about exploiting it. If world support had been formidable enough to reverse the original Leningrad death sentences, its pressure would have to be maintained on Moscow. To that end, the liaison office encouraged demonstrations and vigils outside Soviet embassies in almost every Western capital. Petitions and letter-writing campaigns were organized on behalf of Soviet Jewry. At the initiative of the National Conference on Soviet Jewry in New York, posters appeared at synagogues and at the offices of Jewish organizations throughout the United States, with appeals to "Save Soviet Jewry" and "Let My People Go." Rallies, symposia, lectures, "remembrance days," television interviews, editorials, were effectively orchestrated to publicize the circumstances of Soviet Jewish life. In the United States and Europe, political and religious leaders of all backgrounds lent their names and often their presence to these campaigns.

One of the most effective projects undertaken by the Tel Aviv and New York offices was the organization of a World Conference of Jewish Communities on Soviet Jewry, which took place in Brussels in February 1971. Soviet concern for the adverse effect of the conference was evident in its threat to break off relations with Belgium if the event were held. Yet the Belgians defied the threat without any reprisals. A total of 760 delegates arrived from thirty-eight countries, including some of the leading Jewish figures in communal and public life, from the arts, sciences, and professions, men of the prestige of former United States Supreme Court Justice Arthur Goldberg, Nobel Laureate Albert Sabin, the renowned Jewish scholar Gershom Scholem, as well as media personalities such as Otto Preminger and Paddy Chayevsky. The aged David Ben-Gurion came out of retirement to lend dignity to the conference. In its panoply of flags and floodlights, its television and press coverage, its sheer drama, the Brussels conclave was a triumph of Jewish imagination and resourcefulness. No episode in recent Jewish history better demonstrated the depth of the Jewish people's defense as a world movement and world force. Five years later, in February 1976, a second Brussels Conference would be convened, this one attended by 1,200 delegates, including Golda Meir.

Moscow's efforts at intimidation were visibly failing. Thanks to "Brussels I" and the ongoing campaign abroad, Soviet Jews now realized that widespread communication and publicity protected them far more than endangered them. If they were punished, news of their fate almost immediately would be known in the West. Accordingly, various code techniques and subterfuges were developed by the activists to transmit their information. These involved telephone and mail, the use of foreign newsmen, tourists, occasionally even foreign diplomats—all devices that had been perfected earlier by the dissident movement. Meanwhile, throughout 1971 and 1972, Jews applied for their exit visas by the tens of thousands. The largest numbers of applications still came from the border communities, but within the Slavic republics of Byelorussia, the Ukraine, and of Russia itself, the emigration movement was gaining momentum.

In the Ukrainian Black Sea port of Odessa, Raiza Palatnik, a young librarian who had been sentenced to two years imprisonment for requesting an emigration visa and renouncing her Soviet citizenship, went on a hunger strike in protest. Demonstrations on her behalf were carried out by hundreds of Odessa Jews. In Czernovitz, another Ukrainian community, a young woman, Lilia Ontman, was arrested for having renounced her Soviet citizenship upon being rejected for emigration. During the court proceedings, not a single Jew would cooperate with the prosecution, and militants demonstrated at the courthouse. In Minsk, the capital of Byelorussia, Colonel Lev Ovsischer, a wounded hero of Stalingrad, the possessor of fifteen medals and orders, was reduced to private and denied his pension for having applied to go to Israel. Immediately, several other distinguished Jewish officers protested, then stocially faced demotion for "slander."

Fulfilling the worst of Soviet anxieties, moreover, the "infection" of Jewish emigrationism had spread by then to Moscow itself. Here lived possibly as many as 340,000 Jews by the early 1970s, a population that tended to be far more acculturated than the Jews of the hinterland. At least a third of them were intermarried. If the upsurge of emigration sentiment among them did not reflect piety or even Zionist conviction, it was influenced far more by their threatened status as an intellectual elite. The omens had been evident for several years. In the aftermath of the 1967 war, the number of Jews admitted to universities began to decline absolutely as well as proportionately for the first time in Soviet history—from 112,000 in 1968 to 88,000 in 1972. Between 1970 and 1974, the number of Jews admitted to graduate work fell by 30 percent. The number of Jews entering the ranks of the "scientific community" during 1972–73 was a bare 1,000, in contrast to an annual average of 2,000 to 3,000 between 1955 and 1971. The numerical decline of Jews was evident in the field of medicine, as well, and in the faculties of universities. And one area of Soviet employment had become altogether *Judenrein*—the "secret scientific agencies" that dealt with research in military technology.

In the non-Russian areas, it will be recalled, the rationale for this discrimination was cosmeticized as the "rectification" of ethnic "imbalances" in education and career opportunities. Within Russia itself, the narrowing quotas were motivated by plain and simple Great Russian chauvinism. But for the victims of a discrimination more flagrant and massive than any encountered since the days of the tsars, motives were less important than consequences, and the consequences of reduced educational opportunities proved to be the compelling inducement for Russian Jewish emigration.

The ordeal of those who sought to leave was harrowing. In the non-Slavic hinterland, it occasionally entailed imprisonment for "hooliganism." More commonly, retribution took the form of economic punishment. Scientists and engineers, denied visas for having been privy to "secret, classified material," were demoted or deprived of their jobs altogether. Even those who managed to secure exit visas found the process infinitely difficult and onerous. Together with the complicated and intimidating bureaucratic requirements, prospective immigrants and their children were subjected to mortifying social abuse. The process was expensive, as well. The government continued to require the visa recipient to pay 900 rubles (about $1,000) for himself and for each adult member of his family. This impost, together with a loss of livelihood the emigrants suffered before their departure, frequently reduced them to penury. If they borrowed from relatives to see them through, their families might be left in economic straits. In the end, the Jewish Agency in Israel—the body traditionally responsible for transporting and settling immigrants in the Jewish state—was obliged to devise methods for using "tourists" to convey the necessary fees and to provide food and clothing parcels for Jews waiting out their applications. But until these techniques were refined, in 1971, the experience of departure was an obstacle course that approached a Kafkaesque nightmare.

The Dynamics of Jewish Confrontation, of Soviet Retreat

Whatever the acculturation of the Moscow Jews, their influence on the emigration movement was destined to be particularly far-reaching by virtue of their sheer presence in the capital. Here they were in intimate contact with the dissident movement, often with foreign ambassadors, journalists, and tourists. These advantages, together with the greater numbers of threatened intelligentsia among them, accounted for the shift of strategic direction of Jewish activism to Moscow after the heroic beginnings of the Riga and Leningrad groups. It was in the capital, therefore, during 1971, that the wave of applications for departure was accompanied by newer and even more audacious protest tactics.

Zand played a major role in this development. At the beginning of 1970, he had received his vyzov from a distant cousin in Israel. Initially he refrained from making use of the document, preferring to wait until his older child finished high school. But in February 1971, he was hospitalized with stomach ulcers. During his month's confinement, uncertain of the time he had left and increasingly involved in the emigration movement, he decided not to postpone his application. As soon as he was released, he carried his vyzov to the director of the Oriental Institute, asking for the kharakteristika that would enable him to proceed to the OVIR, the passport division of the ministry of the interior. Shocked, the institute director asked time to consider the matter. Zand was not about to keep a low profile in the interval. Even then, on February 24, an unprecedented confrontation was taking place at the Supreme Soviet in Moscow. It had been planned with the knowledge and advice of Zand himself during his hospitalization.

The episode involved twenty-four Jews, most of them from Riga, who presented themselves collectively at the presidium's reception room and demanded the right to quit the Soviet Union for Israel; they wanted their exit visas then and there. Throughout the day, the visitors continued to hold their positions in the reception room, awaiting an answer. Finally, at nightfall, representatives of the presidium sent word that they would take the applicants' request under advisement and give their answer not later than March 1. The group then dispersed. No one was arrested. Subsequently, on March 1, the original petitioners (joined by eight others) turned up once more at the presidium. Awaiting them this time was a group of officials, including the chief of the OVIR. As a larger crowd of other Jews waited outside, the government representatives assured their visitors that the emigration question would be properly considered; that the OVIR would assist applicants in obtaining kharakteristikas from their places of employment; and that the authorities meanwhile would investigate all complaints of postal delinquency in transmitting vyzovs that had been mailed to applicants from Israel.

Exhilarated and emboldened by the government's apparent cooperativeness, a much larger group, 156 Jewish activists from eight cities—again, a majority from the Baltic republics—marched once more to the presidium ten days later, this time to demand an immediate audience with officials of the secretariat. They were rebuffed. At a signal, then, the petitioners squatted on the floor, refusing to move, and declared a hunger strike. Twenty-four hours went by. At that point, a large force of riot police suddenly descended upon the visitors and evicted them by force. But no one was arrested. The following day, the group marched through the street to the ministry of the interior, insisting that their entire delegation be received forthwith by the minister himself. Impervious to all warnings, they threatened a sit-down strike again if their demands were not met. Finally, several hours later, the paunchy, bemedaled figure of the minister appeared, Colonel General Nikolai Shchelokov. In a conciliatory posture, Shchelokov answered all questions, promised the group that the government would adhere strictly to "Socialist legality," although he refused to make a blanket promise on emigration. As the hours passed, other high officials from OVIR and even from the KGB addressed the delegation, repeating the minister's assurances. At last the group disbanded early on the morning of the eleventh. Once more, incredibly, none was arrested. Within the day, news of this unprecedented "triumph" was relayed to activist groups throughout the USSR, and to Israel and the West.

Zand was now determined to mount a confrontation of his own. It happened that on March 23, the Kremlin, which had been incensed by the Brussels Conference of the month before, organized a conclave of rabbis, cantors, and Jewish lay leaders. Gathered from Leningrad, Kiev, Odessa, Baku, and many other cities, as well as from the capital itself, these handpicked representatives were assembled in Moscow's Great Choral Synagogue. It was the government's intention that the Jewish dignitaries issue a formal denunciation of Israel, Zionism, and the Jewish emigration movement altogether. This was Zand's opportunity. Hurrying to the Choral Synagogue, he found its doors closed to the general public. Large numbers of foreign newsmen were similarly denied entrance. On an impulse, Zand then presented his "press card" as a consulting editor of the *Journal of Soviet Orientalia*. The ruse worked. He was admitted, and took his seat in the gallery with Soviet journalists and authorized observers. There he watched in growing revulsion as the official delegates, reading from prepared texts, vied with each other in echoing the government's line. Eventually, a draft resolution was prepared, repudiating the "claim of the rulers of Israel . . . to defend us . . . against nonexistent wrongs or restrictions."

Outside the synagogue, meanwhile, several hundred outraged Jewish activists were denouncing the assembly as a sham, assuring foreign newsmen that these poor "housebroken" rabbis did not speak for Soviet Jewry. Inside, Zand went further. Leaping to his feet, he cried out: "I am a religious Jew who wishes to emigrate to Israel, and I am not the only one." As the chairman banged his gavel in dismay, Zand refused to be silenced. Shouting above the hubbub, he condemned the assembly as a "disgrace and a scandal." The meeting was thrown into confusion. Guards hurried toward Zand. Only then did he leave the synagogue. But outside, surrounded by the foreign journalists—some of them extending the microphones of their tape recorders—he declared in careful, measured English that there was no future for Jews in the USSR, that their one opportunity for a meaningful Jewish life was in Israel. He would have continued, but at this point he was hustled away by the police.

At police headquarters, Zand was formally booked on charges of hooliganism and trespassing, then put in a cell. He waited, without food or water, his stomach throbbing. Four hours later, much to his astonishment, he was informed by a senior police official that he was being released. The man actually apologized "for the inconvenience." Returning home, Zand promptly telephoned his colleagues. Within hours, news of his detention and release was transmitted to Israel and the West. The activists were satisfied by then that in Moscow, at least, they had won a certain immunity. The government understood that its every move against Jewish protesters was monitored by foreign journalists and "couriers," who instantly dispatched abroad all the latest developments.

Yet the government's tolerance of provocation was soon breached. The Twenty-fourth Soviet Communist Party Congress was scheduled for March 29, 1971. During the nine days of congress sessions, world press attention would be focused on Moscow. This was the occasion Zand and his colleagues had awaited to dramatize their cause. For Zand himself, there was a new, personal grievance that spurred him on. The directorate of the Oriental Institute had just refused him his kharakteristika. On the morning of March 24, even as foreign newsmen and Communist delegations began gathering in Moscow, Zand joined a hundred other Jews in marching again to the presidium building. There they submitted a petition demanding that all Jewish defendants who had been tried or who were still to be tried on the air hijacking charge be released on bond, or that "open" trials be held at once.

This time the police were waiting. Descending on the Jewish protesters, they loaded them into vans and ambulances. Several Jews were carried off to the notorious psychiatric hospitals, others were placed in the central jail, where they were held overnight and denied food and telephone facilities. The next day, the women were fined and released. The men were still held. Eventually, ten of them were given a fifteen-day jail sentence for "hooliganism." Zand was among these. Despite his painful stomach condition, he embarked then on a hunger strike, defiantly wearing a skullcap as his new symbol of Jewish identity. Prisoners who were released before him met with foreign journalists to describe his resistance. The news was instantly sent on to the West. In Israel, and on the Jewish "hot line" in the United States, Zand's fate became a matter of international concern, and he himself was transformed into something of a public figure. News of his eventual release, and of the blood transfusions that were needed to restore his health, was given extensive coverage in the Israeli and Western press.

After March 1971, hardly a month went by in which Soviet Jews did not undertake some form of overt public protest, either demonstrations, sit-down strikes, or hunger strikes at government and party offices. The activists seemed infused now with a fever of determination, a near-mystic fanaticism (which some observers insisted was typically Russian) to force a showdown with the authorities. No other group, neither the Baltic Germans, the Mtshtekhians, the Crimean Tatars, the Ukrainians, nor the Russian Pentecostalists, had displayed a comparable skill in manipulating Western opinion and support against Soviet oppression. To be sure, of all the Soviet dissident movements, only the Jews had access to a centrally directed, heavily financed, politically well-connected network of lobbies in the West. Effectively mobilizing the sympathy of governments and distinguished public figures, this network both exacerbated and "confirmed" the Soviet government's paranoia that world Jewry was indeed engaged in a far-reaching and sinister anti-Soviet conspiracy.

The Kremlin responded to the threat with characteristic Russian ambivalence. On the one hand, the avalanche of "anti-Zionist" abuse continued, in books, press editorials, broadcasts. Yuri Ivanov's notorious *Beware Zionism* was reprinted and distributed in tens of thousands of copies. The malevolence of the campaign resembled in every respect that of the last days of Stalin—or of the tsars. The occasional arrests and trials of activists similarly continued. At the same time, new measures were devised to negate the torrent of visa requests. One of these was a crippling "diploma tax," imposed on would-be emigrants who had received their higher education in the Soviet Union. The rule manifestly penalized a wider proportion of Jews than of any other Soviet nationality. Those who had completed their studies in a technical institute were required now to pay the equivalent of $7,700 before receiving an exit visa. For those who had completed undergraduate university programs, the tax was raised to $12,200. For those who held a medical degree, it was $18,400. And for those who had received doctorates in the sciences, it was $20,000. To these sums were added the price of the visa and a tax for the renunciation of Soviet citizenship, about $1,000. Passed by the Soviet council of ministers in August 1972, the decree was retroactive and affected Jews whose applications had been approved earlier but who had not yet received their visas.

In response to the shocked reaction in the West, which drew analogies with the Nazi ransom for Jews in the 1930s, the Soviet government explained that those who had profited from the nation's provision of free education had the obligation of reimbursing the state for its expenditures, if not by service, then by rubles. The argument was a fake. An educated specialist in the USSR, woefully underpaid by Western standards, repaid the state in service for all the costs of his training within five or six years, and most of the Jewish applicants had possessed their degrees much longer. Freed of all pension obligations, the government actually saved money by their departure. But the decree probably was based on an assumption more cynical than its official rationale, namely, that international Jewry had the means to pay. In fact, the staggering ransoms were far more than the Jewish Agency could provide, even with its access to Western Jewish funds. Nor would the Agency have acquiesced in the payment of this blackmail, had money been available.

Yet if harsh retribution and intimidation represented one Soviet approach to the Jewish emigration movement, it could not be the only one. In the late 1960s and early 1970s, Chairman Brezhnev had made plain his desire for access to Western technology. To achieve this objective, Brezhnev and his colleagues were prepared to make significant concessions, including efforts to defuse the misgivings of the United States Congress. It was common knowledge that the Senate had been effectively cultivated in recent years by the National Conference on Soviet Jewry, and had agreed in principle to lay down a firm quid pro quo for expanded trade relations with Moscow. A key feature of that bargain would have to be a liberalization of Soviet emigration policy. As shall be seen, discussions on this issue would be long and painful, but on one point the Soviets were willing to back down surprisingly quickly. In April of 1973, they deactivated the diploma taxes.

As far back as March 1971, moreover, in tandem with its campaign of repression, the Soviet government had quietly begun increasing its number of exit visas altogether. It was a curiously devious policy, all in all, and in that respect typically Russian. By the end of 1971, nearly 15,000 Jews had been allowed to depart for Israel. The number more than doubled throughout 1972, notwithstanding the diploma taxes, and reached 31,652 by the end of the year. During the course of the United States presidential campaign of 1972, over 4,500 Jews a month were leaving the Soviet Union. The records kept by Levanon's office were scrupulously accurate. They indicated that from January 1968 to June

1973, fully 62,600 Soviet Jews had arrived in Israel; and in the peak years of Jewish emigration—1972 and 1973—not less than 53 percent of those who had been sent vyzovs from Israel succeeded in emigrating. By Soviet standards, it was an unprecedented exodus.

It was also an uneven one. Nearly half the Jews permitted to depart still came from annexed territories, essentially from the Baltic republics; while another 30 percent were Jews from the Caucasus republics of Georgia and Azerbaijan. In these essentially peripheral areas, some 30 percent of the local Jewish populations were emptied during the upsurge of emigration. By contrast, the 12,000 Jews who were allowed exit from the "heartland" republics of Russia, the Ukraine, and Byelorussia represented not only a bare 10 percent of the total Soviet emigration in the peak years of 1971 and 1972 but also less than 0.5 percent of the Jewish populations in these republics. The pattern was significant. It revealed that the Kremlin still intended to solve its Jewish question through forced acculturation, that it was opening the doors principally to those Jews who were least educated and least assimilable, the intensely religious Jews of Soviet Asia and the "authentic" Jews of Lithuania and Latvia. Yet whatever its demographic profile, in scope and political impact this Jewish exodus unquestionably dwarfed the emigration permitted any other Soviet minority. More Jews left the USSR in 1972–73 than all other Soviet citizens of all ethnic groups during the entire previous forty-five years of Communist rule.

Following his two-week jail detention in March 1971, meanwhile, Zand persisted in his efforts to secure his kharakteristika from the Oriental Institute. To his dismay, colleagues who had been his good friends, even those whom he had helped professionally, now succumbed to party pressures and denounced him. Within the month, he was dismissed from his position and deprived even of translating opportunities as a free-lancer. As a nonperson, he was left without an income. Twenty years had passed since Zand had first vainly applied for admission to graduate school, had been rejected and reduced to hackwork for survival. Now he had come nearly full circle. Periodically, he was called in by the KGB for interrogation on his "activism." He was not about to recant or compromise. Instead, seized by a fervor, he insisted upon wearing the beard and skullcap of an Orthodox Jew, upon responding to his interrogators exclusively in Hebrew, "my ancestral Jewish language." Zand's intransigence left the KGB officials frustrated and baffled. Yet they feared imprisoning him, for he was well-connected.

During the spring of 1971, it was known that he was transmitting daily accounts of his circumstances overseas. Each night, an American Jewish colleague, Professor Avram Udovich, called him from Princeton, New Jersey. The renowned Orientalist, Professor Bernard Lewis, telephoned daily from London. From Levanon's office in Tel Aviv, calls arrived on a near-daily basis from a former Soviet Jewish activist, a Mrs. Margolin.

Their solicitude transcended the fate of one man alone. It was understood by then that Zand was a leading spokesman of the emigration movement in Moscow. It was to him now that Western correspondents turned for their progress reports on the activist campaign. Visiting his apartment, they transcribed the latest information for dispatch to their newspapers and television networks abroad. It was this sustained individual contact, in turn, that protected Zand and his family from more dire action by the authorities. The contact sustained them physically, as well. Jewish tourists, several of them Israelis carrying American passports, visited the Zands repeatedly, bringing money transfers, cartons of food and clothing.

Early in May 1971, Zand was called to OVIR headquarters. As a crowd of Jews gathered excitedly in the hall, he entered the passport office. A panel of officials awaited him. The chairman informed him then that he and his family would shortly be granted their exit visas. Zand said nothing. But the moment he left the room, he raised his arms in victory. The crowd cheered. Afterward, he rushed back to his flat to telephone the news to Mrs. Margolin in Israel. Then he and Nellie began selling off their furniture to purchase air tickets to Vienna, to pay their exit fees. Three days later, Zand was summoned back to the OVIR office. "Your visas are being postponed," the official announced. "We've been getting too many complaints about you from honest proletarians. They tell us you advise Jews how to go to Israel, that you receive telephone calls from overseas and transmit information abroad. You can be imprisoned for this, you know." Again Zand said nothing. "We have to examine these complaints," the official went on. "We advise you to keep quiet about this, to say nothing to your contacts." Zand nodded. Leaving the office, he entered the nearest public telephone booth and put in a local call to one of his best contacts, Theodore Shabad, Moscow correspondent for the *New York Times*. He followed with calls to other Western correspondents. Sharing his outrage, the journalists assured him that the news would be on the wires immediately. Within hours,

Zand began receiving calls from Israel and the United States, promising that the campaign for his release would be intensified.

The Zands were without employment, without funds, even without furniture. Additionally, they had been stripped of their citizenship upon applying for exit visas and were liable to arrest as "illegal residents." The ensuing weeks were the most precarious of their existence since the Stalin era. Knowing that silence would have been fatal, Zand wrote a letter to United Nations Secretary-General U Thant, protesting his treatment under the UN Declaration of Human Rights (of which the Soviet Union was a signatory). The letter of course was published in New York by the National Conference on Soviet Jewry. Zand's wife and daughter wrote letters of complaint to the district court of Moscow. Remaining in the spotlight, Zand led demonstrations outside government offices, participated in two additional sit-ins in the corridor of the Soviet presidium.

The technique was shrewd. Western protest rallies and vigils outside Soviet embassies by then were conducted on his behalf almost on a daily basis. Letters and appeals were pouring in to the Soviet government. Money transfers were delivered periodically by tourists, by Soviet Jews, and occasionally by non-Jewish leaders in the dissident movement—who shook his hand silently and then departed. The KGB knew everything, of course, but refrained from taking direct action. Then, one morning, as Zand descended the steps of his apartment building, a huge truck roared down the street. Swerving off the roadway, the vehicle climbed the lower steps and came within inches of striking him before returning to the street and disappearing around the corner. Was it a deliberate effort to put him out of the way? To this day, Zand is not certain. Yet it was plain that he was living in Moscow on borrowed time.

In mid-June, Zand was summoned back to the OVIR office. The official handed over a packet of four exit visas. "These are conditional, you understand," the man warned. "No 'extracurricular' activities from now until you get on the plane." Zand merely smiled at that one. In spite of himself, the official smiled back. As Zand departed the ministry of the interior, the policeman outside, a Tatar, winked at him. "On your way out, are you?" he asked. Zand nodded. "It seems all my Jewish clients have left for Israel," continued the policeman, with a mock sigh, "and I haven't even received a postcard from a single one of them." Zand triumphantly waved the exit visas in the air. A group of sixty or seventy friends cheered.

They cheered again eight days later, on June 24, as they waved goodbye to the 'Zands' departing Aeroflot transport at Moscow's Chodovno Airport. The following afternoon, Mikhail and Nellie Zand and their two children boarded an El Al jetliner in Vienna. Five hours after that, they disembarked at Israel's Lod Airport. Hundreds of former Soviet Jews awaited them, together with scores of newsmen and television cameramen. The moment was sweet for the son of Yitzchak Zand, murdered in a Stalinist penal camp. He and his family had come home.

XVI

Hostages of Détente: The Soviet Union

A World Passed By—and Reclaimed

Among the tens of thousands of Soviet Jews who poured into Israel during the great wave of migration in the 1970s, nearly a third were inhabitants of the Asian reaches of the USSR. Their arrival in these disproportionate numbers was a source of confusion and some dismay to Israel's leaders. Government and Jewish Agency officials still were coping with the task of acculturating earlier transplanted Jewish communities from North Africa and the Middle East. They had not anticipated yet another influx of "orientals." In their remote native habitats, after all, these exotic Asians had numbered barely 120,000 or 130,000 out of the 2,150,000 Jews listed in the Soviet census of 1970, and had represented not more than 6 percent of the totality of the Soviet Jewish population. Could they be regarded as "authentic" specimens of Soviet Jewry? In fact, these dusky newcomers comprised by far the most "authentic" and venerable Jewish communities living within the frontiers of the USSR. Their origins predated those of their European kinsmen by at least a millennium.

So far as is known, most were descendants of Palestinian Jewish exiles who migrated east into the Assyrian, Babylonian, and Persian empires some 1,500 years ago. Penetrating the outlying regions of the future tsarist empire, they managed over the centuries to establish enclaves in the remote lands of Armenia and Georgia in the Caucasus, on the eastern and northern shores of the Black Sea, on the banks of the Caspian, and in territories lying along the "Silk Road" extending from Persia and Turkey through Central Asia to the Far East. Grouped loosely into three major categories—Bukharan, Dagestani (Mountain), and Georgian Jews—they tended to adopt the dress and often the languages and folk mores of their host societies. Like their neighbors, they placed much emphasis upon the integrity of the *chamoula*, the extended family. It was this intense filial solidarity, in turn, that preserved the ancestral Jewish faith. Even if a father was a member of the Communist Party, the male child was circumcised, and later Bar Mitzvahed. Unlike Russian Jews, moreover, those of Soviet Asia invariably married among their own, and according to Jewish tradition. They owned their own Jewish cemeteries, and baked their matzot openly during the Passover season.

None of these communities was older or more tenacious in its religio-ethnic loyalties than were the Bukharan Jews of Central Asia. Numbering approximately sixty thousand by 1970, they derived their name from the medieval emirate of Bukhara, a Moslem realm whose inhabitants were of mixed Iranian and Turkic extraction. Under the Soviets, not less than two-thirds of the Bukharan Jews lived in the republic of Uzbekistan, particularly in the larger cities of Tashkent, Samarkand, Kokand, Khiva, and Bukhara itself. The rest were settled in the neighboring Tadzhik Republic, essentially in its capital, Dushanbe. Perhaps ten thousand others were to be found in the Turkmen, Kazakh, and Kirghiz republics. Well into the Soviet era, Bukharan Jews maintained their traditional mercantile vocations, dealing in silk, cotton, wool, cloth, and carpets. The officials and salesmen of the large government bazaars and of smaller market booths were still likely to be Bukharan Jews.

Their cultural traditions included not only a warm Jewish piety, but also a distinctive language, similar to the Tadzhik dialect spoken by the neighboring Moslems, except for the Hebrew characters that were used in its written form. As traveling silk merchants in the years before the Revolution, Bukharan Jews also managed to develop important contacts with Jews in Middle Eastern lands, even Palestine. From these associations a rejuvenated Hebrew educational system and an important early Zionist movement developed in Bukhara, and by World War I some 2,500 Bukharan Jews had migrated to Palestine. This Hebraic revival was seriously shaken by the later sovietization of the Bukharan Jewish school system; then by the imprisonment of Bukharan Jewish writers in the 1930s; and finally, in 1938, by the replacement of the Hebrew alphabet with Cyrillic characters for rendering Bukharan Jewry's Tadzhik dialect. Yet even Stalinist oppression failed to shake the community's intense ancestral loyalty. Thereafter it was essentially the family that preserved those cultural and religious traditions.

The family—the *chamoula*—invariably was the key, and no less among the forty thousand "Mountain" Jews who were scattered among the Dagestan Autonomous Republic (technically, part of the Russian Federated Republic), and in smaller numbers in the Azerbaijan Republic, along the Caucasus shore of the Caspian. Most of the Jews of Dagestan proper lived in the town of Derbent and in the Dagestani capital of Makhachkala. In Azerbaijan, they were to be found in the capital of Baku and in the city of Kuba. The origins of these Jews, like those of Bukhara, were lost in the mists of folklore. Possibly they were descendants of the famed Khazarian Jewish converts of the Middle Ages. In later centuries, they were easily identified by the biblical root of their names, followed by a typically Russian suffix—for example, Davidov, Yechezkelov, Danielov. Their language, in common with that of the surrounding tribes, was Tati, an old Persian dialect, which they wrote in Hebrew characters until this practice was banned in 1938.

Like their Moslem neighbors, the "Tats"—Mountain Jews—were a hardy group, living not only as tradesmen but as artisans and even as farmers, especially of tobacco. Close to the earth, they were trusted as loyal Soviet citizens. During World War II, they fought gallantly in the ranks of the Red Army, and two of them were among the first Soviet troops to battle their way to the Reichstag in Berlin. Their literature, in Tati, similarly emphasized the legends of ancestral heroes and fighters, rare subjects among Diaspora Jews. Their national epic, *Shirago* (from the Hebrew word *shir*—song), extolled the mighty deeds of Samson I, Samson II, and Samson III.

> Like kernels
> under millstones
> our tribe has lived.
> Heavy and cruel
> were the millstones,
> but we, the Tats,
> the small kernels,
> have strengthened and stiffened
> our hearts,
> and have transformed into rock
> the shells of the kernels.

Even during the post-Revolution years, as the Mountain Jews began moving from their villages to the larger cities, to Derbent and Baku along the shores of the Caspian, they managed to preserve their Tati dialect, their religious and ethnic cohesiveness. No pressures exerted by the Soviet regime would shake those mores.

Their dream of Zion survived, as well:

> the old homeland,
> ancient, gray,
> is close
> and before our very eyes.
> Just stretch out your hand
> and you will reach her.
> But the mirror of waters
> has separated
> and not united us.

The first emissaries from Palestine arrived in Dagestan and Azerbaijan in 1890, and their political Zionism received a warm reception. A delegation of Mountain Jews, booted and bandoliered in their traditional garb, attended the Second Zionist Congress in 1898. Early in the twentieth century, hundreds of them began settling in the Holy Land, a migration that was not choked off until the mid-1920s. During World War II, Zionism revived and intensified among the Mountain Jews as a dynamic contemporary force. Large numbers of Polish and Lithuanian Jewish fugitives were beginning to arrive in the area then, bringing with them a powerful tradition of Zionist activism. Thousands of these Europeans remained after the war, and the passion of their Zionist commitment was infectious. So, after 1948, was sheer pride in the reborn Jewish state.

The decisive initiative for emigration among these Asian Jewish communities was provided by the third and largest component among them, the Jews of Georgia. Mikhail Kaecheli in many ways was typical of that community. Short, thickset, swarthy, mustachioed, he looked as "Georgian" as any of his neighbors. A native of the capital city of Tbilisi, he fully shared his neighbors' pride in their beautiful land, unfolding luxuriantly from the shores of the Black Sea to the snow-crowned peaks of the Greater and Lesser Caucasus Mountains. While considerably less venerable than the Jewish presence in Bukhara or in Dagestan, the settlement of Jews in Georgia extended back at least to the tenth century. Numbering approximately seventy thousand by 1970, and overlapping into the neighboring republics of Azerbaijan and Armenia, they shared with their Georgian neighbors a common language, even a common nomenclature. Their last names carried the identical -shivili, -adze, and -eli suffixes.

For Mikhail Kaecheli's family, as for other Georgian Jews, ancestral traditions were maintained at home, and they were strong. Synagogue attendance on Sabbaths and holidays was the established routine. Almost half the remaining synagogues in the USSR during the 1940s were still to be found in Georgia. The local authorities could not have cared less. They were typically proud Georgians, a people with a long history of enmity toward Greater Russia. Disliking Moscow's "colonial" rule, they made a point of respecting and protecting local religious and cultural traditions. During the Stalinist "black years," when an ethnographic museum of Georgian Jewry was closed and much of its material destroyed, when a wave of searches and arrests swept over Georgia, and prayerbooks and Jewish history books were confiscated—even then, periodic Soviet efforts to close the synagogues failed.

Meanwhile, the largest numbers of Georgian Jews continued in their traditional livelihoods as businessmen, particularly in textiles, or as middle-level bureaucrats. They persisted in these vocations even under Soviet rule. Mikhail Kaecheli's background was characteristic. His father, who died in 1934, when the youngster was four, had been a clerk in a government office. Afterward, his mother worked as a supervisor in a textile factory, raising her three young children on her own. As government employees, the Jews distinguished themselves as managers and distributors. They were also permitted to operate their own "artisan cooperatives" under loose government supervision, and a few accumulated tidy nest eggs for themselves. They were particularly adept at wending their way through the rules and regulations of state "ownership." With a shrewd understanding of the corruptibility of Georgian officials, they found it possible to distribute a portion of their factories' output on the "open market." Thus, Mikhail Kaecheli's uncles, who were managers of a dress factory, found ways to dispose of their surplus output at more "realistic" prices than those set by the government. The local bureaucrats and police, all collecting their share, rationalized this entrepreneurship as the fulfillment of an "economic need." In practical fact, the black market in Georgia was the real economy, and no one mastered its intricacies better than did the nation's Jewish businessmen.

Until World War II, Georgian Jews tended to proceed directly into business upon completing their schooling. The tradition changed after 1945, as higher education became increasingly available. Thus, when Mikhail Kaecheli finished secondary school, he was accepted by the polytechnical institute in Tbilisi. After five years, he received his degree in mechanical engineering. His first employment, as a plant engineer, was in Kutaisi, Georgia's second-largest city. Many Jews worked there at the higher professional levels. There were no tensions. Prejudices were directed mainly against the Russians, or against the Azerbaijanis and Armenians. Kaecheli enjoyed his job, his excellent salary, his equable relations with his fellow workers, his membership on the factory soccer team. While the Stalinist terror was ravaging Jewish communities in European Russia, Kaecheli and his kin experienced little of its impact in Georgia. Those who disappeared invariably were Russian Jews. In 1957, Kaecheli married Tina Sepiashvili, the daughter of a neighboring Tbilisi Jewish family. Soon afterward, he obtained a job in Tbilisi, working there in an engineering institute. The ensuing thirteen years were good ones. Rising to the position of deputy director of design, he was appropriately rewarded, was settled in a three-room apartment, lived comfortably with his wife and two daughters.

The nature of his work enabled Kaecheli to travel extensively, supervising the construction of semiautomated factories for the nation's defense industry. In common with other Jewish professionals and businessmen who traveled, he frequently visited his fellow Jews in the cities and small towns of the Caucasus and Central Asia. "We were one large chamoula," Kaecheli recalled. "Everybody knew everybody else." In truth, contacts between the Georgian and Mountain Jews were more intimate than those between the Ashkenazic communities of the western Soviet Union. It was this mutual intermingling that had informed Georgian Jews early on of the Zionist effort in Palestine. Six or seven hundred had departed to settle there as early as the turn of the century; and for a number of years after the Revolution, handfuls of others managed to join their families in the Holy Land. The birth of Israel decisively revived this interest in Zionism. In Kaecheli's home, Israel was a perennial subject of conversation. During his visits to other communities, he enjoyed sharing with his fellow Jews the latest broadcast news from Kol Yisrael. His friends boasted of the matzot, amulets, and prayer shawls they had acquired from Israel. The most exhilarating moments of the Kaechelis' lives as Jews were their encounters with visitors from the Israeli embassy, including Nechemia Levanon and Lova Eliav.

The experience was reciprocal. Years later, the Israelis still recalled the warmth and enthusiasm of their reception. Heedless of onlooking KGB agents, Georgian Jews literally shouted with joy in the streets when the Israelis appeared. The visitors were honored with calls to the Torah in the synagogue, intensely questioned during private—and lavish—dinners afterward. One of the visiting diplomats, Zvi Netzer, was in Tbilisi on June 5, 1967, when the Six-Day War broke out. Attending the main synagogue on Leslidze Street, he found the building filled with some two thousand men, women, and children, praying their hearts out for Israel. After the services, the congregants besieged Netzer to clutch his hand, to express their blessings and good wishes. A veteran of many poignant experiences during his years as an emissary in Eastern Europe, Netzer still shook his head disbelievingly years later as he described the episode. "It was a shock to us, too," Kaecheli admitted afterward. "The Six-Day War was the great moment of awakening for Georgian Jewry." As almost everywhere else.

It was also the point at which Kaecheli and his friends decided to prepare for departure to Israel. Early in the winter of 1967–68, the first several hundred Jews applied for exit visas. They were indifferent to possible government reprisals. Indeed, Georgian Jews had been indifferent to the government for decades, and were not about to quail in anticipation now. But if they were not punished, neither did they receive their visas. They reapplied then, together with hundreds of friends and neighbors who had received invitations from distant relatives in Israel. And at last, in the winter of 1968–69, forty-nine families were notified that their visas had been approved. Within days, the news reached every Jewish family in the Georgian republic. Thousands now clamored for permission to depart. This time the government struck back. Many adults were dismissed from their positions, students from school. They would not be intimidated. Kaecheli's experience was typical. Determined to preempt any OVIR excuse for rejecting him, Kaecheli gave up his job, with its quasi-military connections, and accepted a lesser assignment in a textile factory. "It was no sacrifice," he insisted later. "Many of my friends did more." To be sure, the change meant a lower standard of living, and several years would have to pass, Kaecheli knew, before he would be considered a safe candidate for departure.

In the meanwhile, the famous appeal to Prime Minister Golda Meir from the "Georgian Eighteen" in 1969 had finally induced the Israeli government to go public in behalf of Soviet Jewish emigration. For their part, the Soviet authorities wanted an end to this embarrassment. They would grant the Georgian, the Bukharan, and the Mountain Jews the same preferential status that had been extended the Jews of the Baltic republics. No serious obstacles would be put in their way. Thus, from 1971 to 1974, a larger percentage of Jews emigrated to Israel from Soviet Asia than from any other region of the USSR. In 1972, Jews from Georgia comprised a third of Soviet Jewish emigration, with the Bukharans representing a twelfth, the Mountain Jews about a thirteenth. It was an exodus of eighty thousand human beings within less than a decade—again, nearly a third of the totality of Soviet Jewish emigration. As the Israeli government struggled with this inundation of Central Asians, it well understood the coldblooded rationale of Soviet emigration policy. Minor merchants, still comparatively undereducated, the orientals represented no important technological or economic loss to the Soviet empire—or gain to Israel. All they brought with them was a fervent, messianic love of Zion that seemingly was untinctured by even the remotest interest in alternative, Western lands.

Kaecheli's father-in-law departed for Israel in 1972. Within days of his arrival, he dispatched the requisite vyzovs to his daughter, son-in-law, and grandchildren. Kaecheli's time had come. In April 1972, he completed the application questionnaire, then presented it to OVIR. Months went by. Finally, in August, he was informed that he would have to pay a 7,700-ruble education tax, his due as an engineer. His wife, a graduate of a linguistic high school, would have to pay 6,600 rubles. Kaecheli was unperturbed. Payment to officials was an old story, one he and his people understood well. Within days, he obtained the necessary funds from relatives and friends. Less than a fortnight later, the emigration visas were handed over. In November 1972, the Kaechelis flew off to Moscow, then to Vienna, then to Israel. Several months afterward, all their possessions arrived at their new apartment in the Tel Aviv suburb of Cholon, all their furniture, even their grand piano.

Mikhail Kaecheli secured a good job in a furniture factory and became an important recruiter for Israel's Labor Party among his fellow Georgian immigrants. Why Labor? "It was the party in power when I came here," he explained. But was not his family's background, his people's background, entrepreneurial? "Just the point," he continued smoothly. "I was never a fanatic about matters of 'Communist oppres-

sion.' Communism never oppressed me. It's the Russian and Baltic
Jews who feel themselves oppressed. They're the fanatics about right-
wing revisionism. We Georgians are not fanatics about anything. We
adjust." How, then, was it with Mikhail Kaecheli now that a right-wing
government was sitting in Jerusalem? Would not a right-wing regime
limit his opportunities as a Laborite in Israel? "Adoni," he remarked
patiently, "all our lives we've learned to adjust to any government in
power in Georgia." His hand came off his breastbone and he nodded
meaningfully. "We'll adjust here, too."

Congress Enacts an Amendment

It is recalled that the Soviets' decision to allow this emigration was
animated by the need to achieve détente with the United States. The
evolving rapprochement between Washington and Peking merely un-
derscored the urgency of a new understanding. So did Moscow's fixation with access to Western technology. The Kremlin was intent, too,
upon securing that access on terms not less advantageous than those
Washington offered its best Western trading partners—in short, on a
most-favored-nation credit basis. It was known that the Nixon administration regarded this dispensation as a vital emollient for improved
Soviet-American relations. In 1971, the United States had approved a
new trade treaty with the USSR, setting higher quotas for purchases
and sales between the two nations. As the president saw it, the inducement of most-favored-nation privileges now would lock the Soviets into
more normalized dealings with the West.

Yet in one respect this Soviet-American diplomatic courtship was
embarrassing and potentially dangerous for Moscow. It raised the issue
of Jewish emigration. It was now that the Jewish lobby's years of
cultivation among American congressional leaders paid off. The road to
legislative approval of most-favored-nation privileges ran through the
office of Henry Jackson, a vastly influential Democratic senator with
ardent presidential ambitions. In 1971, two of Jackson's staff members,
Richard Perle and Dorothy Fosdick, visited Israel. There they met with
Nechemia Levanon, who provided them with a full account of the Jewish plight in the Soviet Union. The Americans then returned to devise a
strategy with Jackson, which jelled once the Kremlin began imposing
"diploma taxes" on Jewish exit visas. It took the form of a proposed
amendment to the draft of the most-favored-nation agreement. Under

the terms of the amendment, which was co-sponsored by Congressmen Wilbur Mills and Charles Vanik in the lower house, any nation within the "non-market economy" bloc would be denied participation in the United States credit and investment guarantee (most-favored-nation) program "unless that country permits its citizens the opportunity to emigrate to the country of their choice."

This "trade for freedom" draft amendment set in motion two years of diplomatic maneuvering between Washington and Moscow. It is worth noting that at least one "non-market" nation, Romania, had already met the standards of the Jackson-Vanik proposal by quietly allowing its Jews to depart. In the United States, on the other hand, Nixon and his security adviser, Henry Kissinger, were dismayed by the amendment, regarding it as a serious and gratuitous obstacle to normalized relations with the Soviet Union. Even American Jewry was divided on the issue. Levanon and the National Conference on Soviet Jewry found it necessary to mount a strenuous campaign for the amendment—first among the American Jewish leadership, then among the members of Congress. To abort that developing campaign, Moscow itself tacitly dropped the "diploma taxes" in April 1973. Additionally, several Jewish activists who until then had been denied their exit visas were permitted to depart for Israel. These included Sylva Zalmanson, who had languished in prison for three and a half years for her part in the Leningrad hijacking episode. The remaining six years of her sentence now were commuted. Lydia Slovin's daughter, Naomi, similarly was allowed to leave.

Yet these gestures were insufficient to head off mounting congressional support for the Jackson-Vanik amendment. Negotiations on the subject between Washington and Moscow, and between Congress and the White House, continued for months, and agreement was reached only on October 18, 1974, in an exchange of letters between Kissinger and Jackson. The accord clearly reflected a parallel understanding that first had been reached between the two governments. Under its terms, as outlined in Kissinger's letter to the senator, the Soviets in effect agreed to cease harassment of applicants and to end all impediments to their emigration. In his reply to Kissinger, Jackson indicated that "we understand that the actual number of emigrants will rise promptly from the 1973 level [of 34,300] to about 60,000," a figure that the Senate henceforth would use as a benchmark.

It was an extraordinary feat, the ultimate fruition of the Israeli effort that had begun ten years before, and the vindication of its strategy of working through foreign channels—in this case, the National Conference in New York. In the entire history of the Soviet regime, no such wide-ranging agreement on emigration had ever been extracted on behalf of any Soviet ethnic or political group, not even the Baltic or Volga Germans. Presumably the Kremlin understood that the concession, painful as it was to Soviet pride, would be less costly than some other quid pro quo the Americans might have demanded: for example, a pledge to reduce the Soviet flow of arms to the Arabs or to North Vietnam. There remained a certain calculated advantage, too, in letting Jewish troublemakers out.

As the final vote on the amendment approached in December 1974, Levanon returned to Washington to work closely with the National Conference in a last-minute campaign of Jewish telegrams to senators and congressmen. The bill easily passed the Senate on December 13. Yet all was not over. The Jewish lobby had assumed that United States credits to Moscow would be sufficiently generous to provide an ongoing inducement for the Soviets to fulfill their part of the bargain of Jewish emigration. To the shock and dismay of Levanon and his colleagues, however, at almost the last moment before the Senate vote, Senator Adlai Stevenson of Illinois added a new qualification, in effect an amendment to the amendment. Its most important feature placed a ceiling of a relatively meager $300 million in credits to the Soviets over a four-year period. Additional terms constrained the president to extend the credit ceiling only on the specific conditions that the Soviets: (a) eased emigration procedures; (b) exercised moderation on Middle Eastern questions; and (c) negotiated in good faith on arms control and military force reduction. Despite the protests of the Jewish lobby, the Senate approved the Stevenson amendment on December 19. The House added its own endorsement almost immediately. The damage was irretrievable. Deeply affronted, the Kremlin on January 10, 1975, announced that it would not avail itself of the Trade Reform Act—nor, by implication, would it honor its prior understanding on Jewish emigration. Two and a half years of strenuous Israeli and Jewish diplomacy had gone down the drain.

For Soviet Jewry, the consequences of the failed negotiations were felt both individually and collectively. The most tragic victims were the imprisoned defendants of the 1970–71 Leningrad hijacking trials. Their families had regarded Sylva Zalmanson's release in the spring of 1973 as a positive omen that others would follow. Now these hopes apparently were doomed. The ordeal of Gillel Butman was typical of the group's experience in Soviet prisons. After receiving his ten-year sentence, in May 1971, Butman was returned to the KGB internal security prison— the Leteiny Street Prison—in Leningrad, where he spent the next sixteen months. Afterward, he was shipped to a work camp in Shcharansk, two thousand miles to the east. His rail carriage on the train was a "Stolypin wagon," a conveyance first devised in the days of the tsars. Twenty-five men were penned together, three to a cage, on three levels of the rail car.

At the work camp, Butman and his fellow Jewish prisoners were locked in a concentration complex surrounded by barbed wire and guarded by heavily armed soldiers. Some one hundred prisoners were confined to each prison block, among them many former Nazi collaborators—Latvians, Ukrainians, Lithuanians. The Jews were harassed with a vengeance. "There were thirteen of us," Butman recalled, "all imprisoned for our Zionist activities. We either had to show our Jewish pride and defiance, or allow ourselves to be brutalized indefinitely. We fought back." There were vicious fistfights. Although the Jews were punished afterward by solitary confinement, the other prisoners eventually left them alone. "A small victory," Butman admitted, "but it saved our morale." In July 1972, the Jewish prisoners were transported another thirteen hundred miles southward, to Camp Number 34 in the Urals. Also known as Vladimir, it was the camp in which Lenin himself once had been imprisoned. Living conditions in Vladimir were no worse than those in Shcharansk, but the work regimen was much harsher. The Jewish prisoners did not make life easier for themselves by their determination to assert their "rights." Protesting the wretched food and the brainwashings, they went on hunger strikes. Their punishment was solitary confinement and deprivation of all mail contact with their families. Upon release, they were permitted a weekly shower, but the water was deliberately heated to the boiling point. Once Butman risked it, and fainted. One slop bucket in each cell served all five men, and wastes from the prisoners in the cell above dripped down. Medical care was virtually nonexistent.

In October 1978, Butman was transported another three hundred miles to the south, to the town of Chistopol, in the former Tatar Republic. Unlike the vast work camps of Vladimir and Shcharansk, the prison here was a small two-story building with room enough for only thirty-five men. "I considered it an improvement," Butman remarked.

"There were fewer common criminals there." The warden and guards were local Tatars, however, quite primitive and brutal. They also intercepted Butman's letters, leaving him entirely cut off from the world and from knowledge of his family. Two prisoners shared his cell. One was a Russian youth, a devout Orthodox Christian who had been sentenced for membership in the dissident movement. The other was a fellow "plotter," Yosif Mendelevich. The adjacent cell was inhabited by another Jew, Anatoly Shcharansky, who had been active in both the human rights and the Jewish emigration movements. "I remember him as a little man with a large balding head," said Butman. "He was very brave and endlessly in good humor." Communication between them was forbidden. Once, sending messages through the wall, Butman was caught and given ten days solitary confinement. Neither man would be broken. The messages continued.

Although they were not religious, Butman and Mendelevich insisted upon observing the Sabbath on Friday evenings. Fashioning skullcaps from rags, they lit threads as their Sabbath candles. "It gave us a sense of commitment," Butman recalled, "and it was also the only way we could keep track of time. How long had I been in prison by then? It was getting foggy. I tried to remain strong, to retain my sanity. But the effort was increasingly difficult. None of us could see the light at the end of the tunnel any longer. Our lives were running out. . . ."

The Crisis of the Intellectuals

With the breakdown of the most-favored-nation trade agreement between Washington and Moscow, the circumstances of Soviet Jewry deteriorated rapidly. Nowhere was this more apparent than in the realm of education. Between 1970 and 1977, the number of Jews admitted to universities dropped from 111,900 to 66,900, a decline of 40 percent in seven years, and a catastrophe for a people that had lived or died by education. By the mid-1970s, not more than three or four Jews were admitted to Moscow State University each year, and from 1977 to 1979, not a single Jew was registered. The figures were identical at the University of Novosibirsk. On the graduate level, discriminatory quotas were even harsher. Science students were particularly hard hit. Prestige institutions such as the Moscow Institute of Physical Engineering and the Moscow Physical-Technical Institute were accepting only a token number of Jews by mid-decade—in fields that had all but been dominated by Jews until then. In the latter 1940s, 30 percent of the students in the mathematics department at Moscow State University were Jews. By 1972, the figure was 1 percent.

Boris Ulyanovsky, a student of mathematics at this institution, remembered the ordeal facing even those Jews who were currently registered. Shortly before his scheduled graduation in 1973, he and the single other Jew in his class, Anatoly Shcharansky, were informed that their comprehensive examination marks were unsatisfactory and that they would not be allowed to graduate. The statement was preposterous on the face of it. Both men were known as outstanding students. Yet their experience was characteristic. By then, Jews who received superior grades, who were awarded prizes, almost invariably were subjected to "special" examinations. Thus, the oral examination, normally lasting an hour and a half, often was extended up to five hours for Jewish applicants, and was made fiendishly complex. In the cases of Ulyanovsky and Shcharansky, as it happened, the decision of the administration was reversed under intense student pressure; but even those Jews who passed their examinations and received their graduate degrees were denied appointments to universities or to scientific institutes.

It was inevitable, then, that the intellectuals, deeply resentful of the cold pogrom in higher education, increasingly took over the leadership of the emigration movement. There was a certain irony here, for by tradition the Jews of the Slavic republics, and particularly of Moscow, were the most thoroughly assimilated in the Soviet Union. For that reason, until the mid-1970s, the number of applicants for emigration was smaller in the "heartland" areas than in other regions of the country. As late as 1980, only one-third of the Jews in the Ukraine applied for vyzovs from Israel. In Byelorussia, the figure was one-fourth. In Russia itself, the figure never exceeded one-sixth. Not a few of the new emigrationist leaders had been raised in such ignorance of the Jewish tradition that they had sought to fulfill the spiritual void of Communist life by flirting with other religions, and several of them had converted to the Russian Orthodox Church—following the example of two of the greatest Jewish literary figures of the postwar period, Boris Pasternak and Nadezhda Mandelstam. Anatoly Krasnov-Levitin, perhaps the Soviet Union's foremost Christian writer, was similarly of Jewish origin, as were the Russian Orthodox essayists and poets Aleksandr Galich and Mikhail Meerson-Aksenov.

As has been seen, it was not uncommon for Jewish intellectuals, whether marginal or committed in their Jewish identification, to gravitate first into the human rights movement. Yet by 1973, the dissident effort appeared all but moribund. Accordingly, with all their cosmopolitan background and prestige, the Moscow Jewish academicians and scientists turned to the cause of Jewish emigration as their final alternative. Their ranks included such eminent figures as Professor Venyamin Levich, physical chemist and corresponding member of the Soviet Academy of Sciences; Mark Azbel, senior fellow in the Moscow Institute of Theoretical Physics; Aleksandr Voronel, nuclear physicist and laboratory director of the Moscow Research Institute of Physics; Vladimir Slepak, a leading electronics engineer; Aleksandr Luntz, director of the mathematics department of the Computer Institute; his coworker, Viktor Brailovsky; Vitaly Rubin, senior fellow of the Asian Institute of the Soviet Academy of Sciences; Mikhail Agursky, director of postgraduate studies at the Institute of Cybernetics and a member of the Academy of Sciences. It was a formidable group. Others of similar reputation gave weight to their appeals abroad, and helped them mobilize their professional colleagues in the United States and elsewhere.

By 1973, their role became decisive. The first wave of mass emigration had fairly well cleared out pioneer activists like Mikhail Zand from the Russian and Ukrainian republics. A second wave did not appear likely to follow. In that year, Agursky was turned down flat in his request for an exit visa. Resigning under pressure from the Cybernetics Institute, he subsisted as a free-lance industrial consultant. Aleksandr Luntz, applying for his exit visa in 1972, was summarily forced to resign from the institute. Azbel, Rubin, and Levich experienced the same fate. As scientists who had had access to classified security information, they and their colleagues were also kept under tight KGB supervision. If their reputations offered them a certain immunity from arrest, by the same token they all but ensured the refusal of their applications as well as their dismissal from their posts. The government was prepared to suffer the disadvantage but not the humiliation of losing prominent figures in the sciences.

The Moscow activists sustained their effort and morale with considerable imagination. Voronel and Azbel launched a weekly series of science seminars. Each Sunday morning, in the apartment of one or another of the "refuseniks"—as the rejected visa applicants came to be known—a scientist would deliver a paper on his specialty to a gathering of other refusenik scientists. In his presentation, the speaker would make use of the latest research papers and published material from overseas. These had been transmitted by colleagues in the United States and elsewhere in the West, who were determined that the refuseniks should suffer no intellectual deprivation as a consequence of their professional disbarment. Early in 1974, too, the idea was conceived for staging an international seminar, a gathering of scientists from both within and outside the USSR. Scheduled for July 1–5 of that year, the seminar would at once provide the latest findings of different sciences and dramatize the cause of the refuseniks to the world. Preparations were made throughout the emigrationist underground, and the seminar in fact took place, in Aleksandr Voronel's apartment, crowded with some two hundred scientists from the USSR and the West. The event was given front-page coverage in Western newspapers.

At the same time, Hebrew lessons became a passion among the intellectual elite of Soviet Jewry. Private, "unlicensed" teaching of the language was still forbidden in the USSR. In 1970, however, Erned Trachman, the son of Communists expelled from Palestine in the 1920s, began secretly organizing the first large-scale Hebrew classes. The pupils included six or seven particularly brilliant members of the mathematics faculty of Moscow State University. Several of Trachman's graduates in turn began conducting their own classes for other mathematicians and scientists. Despite the anxiety and inconvenience of secrecy, by 1975 some forty Hebrew teachers were giving courses for approximately five hundred adult students, using textbooks transcribed from smuggled Israeli copies.

The government's response to these scientific seminars and Hebrew classes during the mid-1970s was more restrained than might have been expected in a period of waning détente. But in Moscow, after all, the refuseniks had developed their contacts with foreign journalists, American diplomatic personnel, visiting Western political figures and scientists. Indeed, the Jewish activists had refined the technique, pioneered originally by men like Mikhail Zand—and the Russian dissidents before them—of holding press conferences and special information sessions for Western newsmen and tourists. The ablest of their spokesmen, as it happened, were Anatoly Shcharansky and his former classmate Boris Ulyanovsky.

A promising young computer scientist, Shcharansky had started out in the human rights movement, then in 1973 had thrown himself heart and soul into the cause of emigration. The most active of activists, he led public demonstrations, organized letter-writing campaigns, held frequent press conferences with foreign journalists. Dismissed from his position in 1974, Shcharansky depended entirely on American Jewish money transfers. Nothing would stop him. His meetings with American and European political figures, with Western Jewish officials and traveling celebrities, were masterpieces of public relations. His charm and enthusiasm, his fluency in English, made him a favorite of these contacts; and, by the same token, no one in the emigration movement was more feared by the Soviet authorities. His closest ally and fellow computer scientist, Boris Ulyanovsky, was an early graduate of Trachman's Hebrew classes, and himself a dedicated Hebrew teacher. In May 1974, the two young men led a procession of fifty Jews along a central Moscow boulevard to the passport office in the interior ministry. The marchers all wore yellow Stars of David on their sleeves. The group was broken up by the police, but no one was arrested; too many Western correspondents had recorded the event. Shcharansky and Ulyanovsky were harassed, their apartments searched, and they themselves were detained and questioned, even threatened with arrest for "parasitism." Throughout 1974, however, the harshest punishment meted out to the refuseniks was loss of employment. The dissidents, imprisoned or confined to mental hospitals, usually fared much worse.

The retribution that pained most was the tightening limit on exit visas. In 1972, a total of 31,681 Jews had been allowed to depart. In 1973, the number rose to 34,733. Then, in 1974, the figure sank back to 20,628; and in 1975, to 13,221. The decline was alarming enough for Levanon's office and the National Conference to organize a second Brussels Conference, in February 1976. Yet, even in the mid- and latter 1970s, Soviet policy appeared to oscillate. Unprepared to write off American goodwill, the Kremlin refrained from a total ban on Jewish emigration. Occasionally, it even experimented with brief relaxations in its visa policy. Perhaps the most telling evidence of this equivocation was the unexpected release of the Leningrad hijacking prisoners. With the failure of the Jackson-Vanik amendment, all hope for the other prisoners had seemed lost. As time went on, however, their sentences were quietly reduced and they were granted exit visas for Israel. In April 1979, even Mark Dymshits and Edward Kuznetzov, whose sentences had been reduced from life to fifteen years, were released for a number of Soviet spies caught in the United States—an exchange that was discreetly arranged between Chairman Brezhnev and President Jimmy Carter.

For Gillel Butman and Yosif Mendelevich, the spring of 1979 differed little from their previous eight years of captivity. In Chistopol Prison, on April 11, the eve of Passover, they managed a little holiday celebration in Butman's cell, sharing the "festivities" with their Russian Orthodox cellmate. Their symbolic matzot were dried pieces of bread. Their candles were rags. Their prayers were only vaguely remembered. None of the prisoners could perceive even the faintest glimmer of light at the end of the tunnel. Then, on the evening of April 20, a duty officer appeared and ordered Butman to pack his things. With more than a year remaining on his sentence, Butman assumed that he was about to be transferred to another prison. It was the gaunt Russian boy who was certain that a more important change was pending. "You're being released, Gilya," he assured Butman. "Mark my words." Butman laughed cynically, but then the two embraced. The following morning, after a restless night in another cell, Butman was awakened and informed that he was being "moved." As he was ushered out of the courtyard, he shouted a Hebrew farewell to the other Jewish prisoners. Their "Shalom"s brought tears to his eyes.

Transported in a six-hour drive to the Tatar community of Bogolma, Butman was confined in a local jail. After four days there he was driven to the local airstrip, still handcuffed and in his prisoner's uniform, and hustled into a small transport craft. The flight was a short one, to the great Tatar city of Kazan. In Kazan, he was transferred to a larger airplane. The flight was a long one this time, seven hours across much of the width of the Soviet Union. As the plane began its descent, Butman recognized the city beneath him. It was his native Leningrad. "By then, I began to get the picture," he recalled. He was being given his release. It was conditional upon his willingness to sign for his exit visa at the local OVIR office, then to depart within the next ten days. "The terms were distinctly acceptable," Butman recalled, smiling. On April 27, he left by airplane from Leningrad for East Berlin, then connected on to Vienna, where he was received by Jewish Agency officials. On April 29, his El Al flight brought him to his wife and children. It was two years before Yosif Mendelevich followed—and finis was written at last to the Leningrad hijacking episode.

The Soviet Vise Tightens

The release of these prisoners was accompanied by another unanticipated Soviet gesture to the Jews in the late 1970s. The rate of emigration had dropped to 13,221 in 1975. It rose minutely to 14,261 in

1976, then to 16,736 in 1977. The modest rate of departures in the early months of 1978 suggested that Jewish emigration had reached a plateau. But then, suddenly, in June of that year, the number of authorized exits began to climb sharply. The government's purpose was entirely functional. Rapprochement between the United States and China appeared to be gaining momentum again, an ominous development in Soviet eyes. Conversely, Washington's ratification of the SALT II agreements seemed to be an augury of better relations, one that was worth encouraging. Not less important, the Kremlin detected a hint of flexibility in Washington's position on the Jackson-Vanik amendment. In recent months, Senator Adlai Stevenson had intimated his willingness to raise the ceiling for Soviet credits to $2 billion, provided there were a quiet understanding on emigration. Additionally, the Moscow Olympics were scheduled for the summer of 1980, and the Soviets were intent upon cultivating as much goodwill as possible. For these reasons, the Kremlin permitted an increase in Jewish emigration, to 28,865—and then, even more dramatically, to 51,333 in 1979. It was an unprecedented figure in the history of the emigration movement.

But the gesture also proved to be typically Russian in its unwillingness to offer the carrot without showing the stick. Even as the number of exit visas was increasing, the stick was being applied against the emigrationist leaders, particularly the Moscow scientists, who were hounded far more relentlessly now than in the mid-1970s. Their seminars were banned. Detentions and arrests suddenly mounted. In March 1977, Anatoly Shcharansky was taken into custody for "anti-Soviet activities," then held incommunicado for a year without an attorney or a trial of any sort. Earlier, as an act of tantalizing cruelty, the OVIR had granted his young wife, Natalia (later Avital), an exit visa for Israel within hours after she and Shcharansky were wed. She was obliged to depart almost immediately, for the visa's grace period was ten days. That perverse gesture turned out to be a miscalculation. When her husband subsequently was arrested and jailed, Avital Shcharansky became a poignant advocate for his cause, touching the hearts of Jews and non-Jews, including those at the highest echelons of power. President Jimmy Carter was moved to denounce Shcharansky's arrest and detention. Within the year, the Jewish prisoner became something of an international cause célèbre, his face appearing on the covers of several American news magazines. Yet, in this case, world pressure was unavailing. In July 1978, Shcharansky finally was tried and convicted, then sentenced to thirteen years imprisonment. He was carried off beyond the Urals to Chistopol Prison in the former Tatar Republic (where he shared a common cell block with Gillel Butman and Yosif Mendelevich). There he remains to this day.

By the latter 1970s, none of the leaders of the emigration movement was spared the tightening Soviet vise. Between 1978 and 1981, Dr. Aleksandr Paritsky, organizer of an unofficial "Jewish University" in Kharkov, was arrested and his makeshift institution was closed. Other eminent refuseniks, the scientists Viktor Brailovsky, Ida Nudel, and Vladimir Slepak, were arrested, tried, and convicted on charges of defamation. During the same period, half a dozen other scientists were arrested and put on trial. Even those refuseniks who were spared arrest were exposed to an especial refinement of harassment and public degradation. Unemployable, execrated for disloyalty, they were driven into isolation and impotence. In 1981, fifteen additional Jewish activists were seized and placed in detention. Not since the roundup of the hijack plotters and their friends in June 1970 had the authorities conducted so unremitting a campaign of intimidation against Soviet Jews.

In the early 1980s, the brief, promising emigration upsurge of previous years was decisively reversed. In 1980, the number of exit permits was reduced to 21,471; in 1981, to 9,443; in 1982, to 2,688; in 1983, to 1,314. During this period, moreover, the OVIR had perfected methods to deter Jews even from applying. One was simply to enact tough new guidelines on "family reunifications." In the past, any family member in Israel, whether an aunt, an uncle, or a cousin, was eligible to dispatch a vyzov for a relative in the Soviet Union as the first step in the emigration process. But in 1980, the new definition of family member applied only to children and parents, spouses and siblings—a far narrower category. And increasingly now, a vyzov from Israel was intercepted by the Soviet postal authorities. At the same time, the diminishing number of applicants underwent increased harassment. Their children were humiliated in school. Older children frequently were expelled from university and, having lost their educational exemptions, were conscripted immediately into the armed forces. For their parents, the trauma included endless social obloquy and ostracism, carried out over a much longer period than before.

By the end of the decade, the leadership of the emigration movement had been decapitated, either by imprisonment, emigration, or intimidation. Voronel, Azbel, Agursky, Ulyanovsky had gone on by

then to Israel—to join Zand, Lydia Slovin, Dymshits, Kuznetsov, Butman, and other, earlier activists. It was the government's last gesture of
selectively "excising" troublemakers by allowing them to depart. The
newer applicants were not cast in the same mold. The sheer physical
hardships that faced them now were overwhelming. If they were dismissed from their jobs, the dollar transfers their predecessors had received from abroad no longer possessed their former buying power.
The government halved the exchange value. Families that had survived
on fifty-dollar monthly transfers now were reduced to penury and confronted with a genuine threat of starvation. It was a demoralizing prospect. By 1982, the Jewish emigration movement was all but paralyzed.

What had happened? Why had the government now conclusively
resolved its former stop-and-go ambivalence toward Jewish emigration?
The danger of setting an example for other nationalist movements—
Tatar, Ukrainian, Volga German—plainly was a factor. So was the possibility of a "brain drain." Intent upon achieving a quantum improvement in the nation's standard of living, the regime had not anticipated
so far-reaching an exodus of doctors, physicists, engineers, and other
Jewish professionals. It felt keenly both the disadvantage and the embarrassment of losing prominent figures in the sciences and arts. But
even more significant in the decision to foreclose Jewish emigration was
the renewed strain in Soviet-American relations. Whatever hope the
Kremlin may have entertained as late as 1979 of meaningful détente
with the United States had been dissipated by 1980. The Soviet occupation of Afghanistan, President Carter's response in boycotting the Moscow Olympics, the tough anti-Soviet pronouncements of President-elect
Ronald Reagan, all indicated a harsh chill in Great Power relations. At
the Madrid Conference on Security and Cooperation in Europe, which
opened late in 1980, a Soviet spokesman, Sergei Kondrashev, explicitly
linked any future progress in the "reunification of families" to the circumstances of Soviet-American détente.

There was yet an additional factor that influenced Soviet policy.
"Reunification of families" had been the government's face-saving rationale for acquiescing in Jewish emigration (and theoretically, under
the Helsinki Agreement, in the emigration of other citizens), so long as
the Jewish visa recipients departed for Israel. Israel was the self-pro-
claimed homeland of the Jews, after all, and thereby fitted into a pattern of other recognized homelands for the USSR's plurality of races
and peoples: the Ukraine for Ukrainians; the Baltic republics for Letts,

Estonians, and Lithuanians; Azerbaijan and the Turkmen Republic for the Turkic peoples; Uzbekistan and Tadzhikistan for peoples of Iranian descent. While Israel was a palpable embarrassment in Moscow's dealings with the Arabs, and the object of limitless denunciation in the Soviet media, Jewish departure to the Jewish homeland of Israel at least presented no serious threat to the Leninist concept of national homelands and identity.

On the other hand, emigration that aberrated from the officially countenanced pattern did present a threat. This was departure to another country—to the United States, for example. Such a development would represent an altogether intolerable precedent, one that might swiftly be adopted by millions of Soviet citizens of all backgrounds, with their own dreams of an easier life in the West. Emigration of this nature, with its implicit challenge to the integrity of the Soviet empire, would under no circumstances be tolerated. By the mid- and latter 1970s, however, it was becoming clear that thousands of Soviet Jewish applicants for exit visas had in mind precisely this alternative new course.

A New Promised Land

Until 1973, not more than 2 percent of all Jews who left the USSR chose destinations other than Israel. Their departure accordingly supported the thesis that Jewish emigrationism was indeed a "repatriation movement." Yet in April 1973, Israeli sources acknowledged that 4 percent of the Soviet Jews who had managed to reach Israel were re-emigrating subsequently to other countries. Of even graver concern, far more of those who received their OVIR documents were not coming to Israel at all, but were turning to other lands once they reached the initial way-station of Vienna. It was the first hint that the emigration of Soviet Jewry, the consummation of years of Israeli efforts, was not working out entirely as planned. The statistics in ensuing years confirmed this premonition. The number of Soviet Jewish "dropouts," either from Israel or en route to Israel, climbed to 19 percent in 1974, to 37 percent in 1975, to 49 percent in 1976. For the Israeli government, the shift in the migration pattern was no longer merely unsettling. It was shattering.

It is recalled that fully two-thirds of those reaching Israel between 1968 and 1974 had come from the Baltic republics and from Soviet Asia, regions that encompassed less than 10 percent of Soviet Jewry. Conversely, the far larger Jewish population in the urban "heartland" republics—Russia, the Ukraine, Byelorussia—had produced less than 14 percent of the Jewish immigrants during the same period. These latter often were third- or fourth-generation Soviet citizens, heavy consumers of Russian culture, and people deeply impressed by Western technological values. By the mid-1970s, then, as the reservoir of "authentic," committed Jews was gradually drained in the Baltic and Asian regions, the relative percentage of acculturated Jews from the Slavic areas climbed significantly. Their reasons for leaving Moscow, Leningrad, Odessa, Kiev, Kharkov, or Minsk had little to do with Zionist idealism, but rather with far more practical grievances of reduced educational and professional opportunity—itself the consequence of a revived tactical antisemitism.

Soviet Jews of all backgrounds were received with enthusiasm in Israel. They were provided with housing often superior to that enjoyed by Israeli citizens. Employment opportunities were literally manufactured for them at public expense, and included well-paying jobs in universities and industry. No other immigration wave in Israeli history had been extended comparable benefits, and at such prodigious cost both to Israel and to Western Jewish philanthropy. The effort manifestly was worthwhile. Many of the newcomers were well educated, particularly those from the Baltic and Slavic republics. They appeared to be superb human material for Israel's still thinly stretched population. The Israeli government and public were gratified, and for a while even quietly euphoric, at this unprecedented transfusion of manpower and talent.

Their exhilaration was premature. The Zionist commitment of the more recent acculturated newcomers was often less than resilient upon confronting the shortcomings and inequities of Israeli life. Few Soviet Jews had ever imagined that Israel suffered from class conflict, from the problems of deprived minorities, from cultural discrimination, or from serious pockets of poverty. Fanatically anti-Socialist themselves, they were repelled by the prevalence of Socialist ideology in the Jewish state, by the penetration of Israel's labor federation into almost every level of the nation's economy (even under the Begin government). Often married to Gentile spouses, too, the Soviet immigrants were horrified by the power of Israel's Orthodox parties, and the difficulties the chief rabbinate created for children of mixed marriages. In any case, many of the newcomers regarded the help extended to them as their just due as heroes and martyrs. Israel's obligation was to them, and to the extent that this debt was not paid immediately and generously, the later wave of Soviet Jewish immigrants responded with growing criticism and resentment.

In letters to their relatives at home, the new settlers frequently expressed their disappointment, even their bitterness. Their correspondence in turn was given extensive coverage by the Soviet media. If this disaffection was a body blow to the Israelis, it was hardly less so to tens of thousands of Jewish vyzov-recipients in the Soviet Union itself. Awaiting their exit visas for months, these people had ample opportunity to brood upon the unhappy fate that evidently awaited them in Israel. Perhaps other alternatives were worth exploring.

Those alternatives were not lacking. Under legislation initially passed during the Kennedy administration, the United States attorney general announced in September 1971 that he would exercise his parole authority under the Immigration and Naturalization Act to admit refugees from communism on a priority basis. "The United States wants these people," explained the Jewish Agency representative in Vienna. "If it didn't take them, it would have to fill its quotas with blacks from Cuba. At least Soviet Jews are white—those who apply to the United States. They're educated and hard-working. And the Jewish lobby in the States has reminded Washington that these immigrants never, ever, become welfare cases. It's a compelling argument, and the State Department has swallowed it whole. Their visa office admits newcomers under the category of 'political refugees.' Obviously, if these Soviet Jews go first to Israel, a free country, they're no longer regarded as political refugees, and they enjoy no further priority for admittance. And so, increasingly, they've learned to apply to the United States from the moment they reach Vienna." The Jewish Agency official, a woman, smiled resignedly at this point. "After all, they realize they can always go to Israel later if they choose. So why not pick the bountiful United States first? They know the American government wants them, that anyone with a Soviet passport is pure gold in the eyes of the State Department. Washington even helps defray the cost of their transportation and settlement. It matches every dollar provided by the various Jewish charities with a federal dollar. Who could resist such temptation?"

The woman spoke with understandable bitterness. A former Soviet Jewish émigrée herself, she had long since paid her dues in dramatizing her kinsmen's passionate wish to return to their "ancestral homeland, Israel." She was Lydia Slovin, the heroine of the Riga emigration movement. Qualifying for the practice of law after settling in Israel, Lydia had continued to devote almost every moment of her free time to the cause of her people in the Soviet Union. Forty-nine years old in 1979, with her energy and eloquence at full maturity, she was the Agency's logical choice that year as its emissary to Vienna, the first transit-point of Soviet Jewish debarkation. It was she who met the emigrants at the airport or railroad station, who took them in hand, arranged their hostel facilities and their subsequent transportation to Israel.

Over the months and years, however, fewer emigrants were willing to be taken in charge by her. A majority preferred to head directly for a bus placed at their disposal by the Joint and HIAS (the Hebrew Immigrant Aid Society), which in turn carried them off to temporary lodgings in Vienna, and to the ministrations of American Jewish personnel who were skilled in finding alternative sanctuaries for Jews. Lydia was permitted to make a final appeal on behalf of Israel to these "defectors," as they gathered at the HIAS-Joint office on the Brahmsplatz. But if the appeal failed (as it usually did), the defectors then were carried on to Rome. There, in the Italian capital, procedures were begun to arrange transportation for them, either to the United States or—occasionally— to other Western countries. "It's been a heartbreaking experience," Lydia admitted.

More than heartbreaking, the arrangement was intolerable for the Israelis. They were outraged at the notion of being forced into competition with the United States, and with American Jewish philanthropies. It was shocking to them that their years of patient worldwide diplomacy, their mass appeals on behalf of "family reunions" in Israel, should be dissipated now by the blandishments of a free and easier life in wealthy America. In 1981, the chairman of the Jewish Agency Executive, Arieh Dulzin, issued a warning. If the competition did not cease, he and his associates would simply decline any longer to turn over the names of arriving Soviet Jews to HIAS and Joint representatives in Vienna; the Americans would have to find any prospective "dropouts" on their own. Here the American Jewish establishment— which also provided the bulk of the Jewish Agency's funds—cautioned Dulzin that he was going too far. A compromise would have to be found. Eventually, in December 1981, a series of urgent meetings in Jerusalem between the leadership of the Jewish Agency, the Joint, and HIAS produced a new formula. It was the so-called Naples Agreement.

Under this new format, HIAS and the Joint would extend their services only to would-be defectors who possessed "first degree" relatives in the United States—that is, parents or children, spouses or siblings. These people would be conveyed from Vienna directly to Naples, together with other Soviet Jews who did not possess "first degree" relatives. There, for a two-week period, the entire group would be exposed to the exhortations of Jewish Agency representatives on behalf of Israel. Afterward, "qualified" defectors who remained adamant against Israel would receive the full spectrum of HIAS and Joint help in transportation to the United States and settlement there. The rest, without access to "first degree" relatives, would be left on their own, and presumably in the end would have no choice but to depart for Israel. Dulzin was convinced that the agreement ultimately would reverse the alarming rate of defections, and by the same token counter one of the principal Soviet objections to the issuance of exit visas. Whether or not the Jewish Agency chairman's instincts were sound would remain a matter for speculation. The Naples Agreement hardly was allowed to get off the ground. On April 26, 1982, the HIAS board of trustees decided to end its cooperation in the experiment. After a three-month trial period, it argued, the results, in defectors who changed their minds in favor of Israel, simply did not justify the heartache inflicted on those who were left in limbo.

"That wasn't the whole story," insisted Lydia Slovin. "By then, the dropouts had discovered another convenient source of help in getting them to the States. It was the Satmar Chasidim [an ultra-Orthodox sect that traditionally opposed the existence of the State of Israel as a "heresy"]. The Satmar people have offices throughout Europe, and they maintain their own extensive connections in the United States and Canada. Their official rationale in taking over Soviet Jews is that they're performing a *mitzvah* [holy deed] by keeping Jews away from Israel." Lydia inadvertently lowered her voice. "Anyway, not only are the Satmar people performing a 'mitzvah,' but they bear no real expenses, certainly none comparable to ours. The Agency maintains a big transit camp here in Vienna, a clinic, a large group of skilled professional personnel. The Satmar have nothing like it, and so their operations hardly represent a financial burden to them." Lydia spoke calmly, even with a certain grudging admiration for her adversary's resourcefulness. "The dropouts couldn't care less, of course. By the time they clear out of the Soviet Union and reach Vienna, they've already memorized the address of the 'good rabbi'—the Satmar organization—on Afrikanergasse. They head there like a shot."

In Tel Aviv, Nechemia Levanon offered his own explanation for the failure of the Naples Agreement. HIAS and other American Jewish social service organizations maintained an "army" of personnel. Each Soviet Jewish family arriving in the United States received care that gave responsibility and employment to successive echelons of social welfare professionals. It was specifically these staffs who induced the lay boards of HIAS and the Joint to veto continuation of the three-month experiment. Ultimately, the dispute was carried to the top levels of American Jewish philanthrophy. Dr. Baruch Gur, a young Israeli academician-diplomat who served as Levanon's deputy in the liaison office, evaluated the episode succinctly. "It represented the decisive triumph of Jewish Federation [domestically oriented] leadership over United Jewish Appeal [Israel-oriented] leadership," he insisted.

Possibly yet another explanation related to the guilt feelings of American Jews, who were themselves principally of East European descent. No one had inhibited the migration to America of *their* parents and grandparents, after all. How could they deny the same right to their own kin now? This was not an argument that had been used in the 1940s and 1950s, as it happened. In those days, the American Jewish leadership gave unquestioned priority to Israel's urgent population needs. Even the local and national Jewish federations had not lifted a finger to seek wider immigration quotas for Jewish refugees who preferred the United States to Israel. But of course, most of the refugees then were dark-skinned Jews from North Africa and the Middle East.

During the late 1970s and early 1980s, therefore, Soviet Jews who rejected Israel were sent by HIAS and Joint representatives directly from Vienna to Rome, usually within seventy-two hours of their arrival in the Austrian capital. In Rome, the Joint provided funds for the immigrants' room and board. HIAS, with its staff of nearly seventy people and its generous United States government subsidies, handled the procedures for securing American visas. Meanwhile, the Satmar organization devised parallel arrangements that were not substantially less efficient. The entire process usually took between two to six months, and afterward the dropouts proceeded on to the United States or (less frequently) to other Western nations. The statistics of defection continued to mount alarmingly against Israel. It will be recalled that by 1976, half the emigrants were refusing Israel. By 1977, the figures were

8,483 out of 16,737; in 1978, 16,967 out of 28,865; in 1979, 34,056 out of 41,333; in 1980, 14,078 out of 21,472; in 1981, 7,932 out of 9,443; in 1982, 2,321 out of 2,688; in 1983, 727 out of 1,314. Even if the Naples Agreement had been in effect from 1981 on, the rate of defection would not have been appreciably less. For by then a majority of Soviet Jewish emigrants already possessed "first degree" relatives in the United States or elsewhere in the West—essentially defectors who had preceded them.

Those, by contrast, who fulfilled the long odyssey of application and emigration, who settled and remained in Israel, had their own evaluation of the dropout phenomenon. It was summarized by Mark Azbel:

> The very possibility of anyone leaving the Soviet Union was due to the heroic efforts of Jews who dreamed of Israel, who sacrificed their liberty, and in some cases their lives, to build the road to freedom. In our opinion, those who rejected Israel cast shame and mockery upon the memory of these people. We couldn't forget that it was Israel—and Israel alone—that had aroused the world's sympathy on behalf of Soviet Jews. . . . We knew Israel was not perfect. . . . [Israel] has innumerable very serious problems, but . . . for this very reason it devolved upon us to try to alleviate those troubles. To abandon our country [Israel] in favor of another that offered more goods, more choices—I couldn't stop feeling ashamed of the people who made this choice. These same people would run to Israel if the need arose, and if Israel should ever be annihilated again, the rest of the world would despise the Jews who let it happen. And they would be right.

A Leave-taking in Vienna

The flame of Jewish creativity has by no means guttered out in the Soviet Union. Appeals for Jewish educational material and Hebrew teaching tools continue to reach Israel from refuseniks in integral Russia and from the depleted Jewish hinterland in the Baltic republics and Soviet Asia. The most recent international book fairs in Moscow, in September 1981 and September 1983, attracted many thousands of Jews from throughout the Soviet Union, who flocked to the exhibits presented by the (American) Association of Jewish Book Publishers and by a number of Israeli publishers (none of these books would ever be placed on sale, of course). But occasional sunbursts of activity and curiosity are deceptive. In 1984, the assimilationists in Soviet Jewry appear far to outnumber the hard core of identified emigrationists. By the most knowledgeable Israeli and Soviet calculations, the former still represent the "silent majority."

Thus, in 1970, the intermarriage rate of Soviet Jews was estimated at 40 percent. The figure doubtless has climbed in ensuing years, and unquestionably is higher within the Russian Federal Republic. The trend of intermarriage is as evident among Soviet Jewish emigrants, particularly those from the "heartland" areas, most of whom in any case appear to be interested less in going to Israel than in leaving the Soviet Union. Although not all Soviet Jewish "defectors" to the United States are indifferent to their heritage, there surely are more of them than of identified, committed Jews. Nevertheless, like émigré Israelis, they remain the objects of admiration and solicitude by American Jews and Jewish communal organizations.

The number of Jews who left the Soviet Union between 1968 and 1984—259,634, or more than one in every ten—can only be described as extraordinary, certainly unprecedented in the postwar history of Soviet emigration. At least that many others have received vyzovs from relatives in Israel. If not all of them have yet applied for emigration visas, it is likely that at least half a million Jews are still anxious to depart. Even so, these figures are by no means proof of a resurging Jewish identity. Of the 260,000 emigrating Jews, after all, some 90,000 have chosen not to settle in Israel. At least two-thirds of Soviet Jewry have not requested vyzovs at all, and apparently intend to remain where they are. They may not be enamored of life under Soviet rule, but neither are tens of millions of other Soviet citizens. Except for the educational numerus clausus that "rectifies" the historic disproportion of Jews among the intelligentsia, most Soviet Jews are not suffering active persecution. Although the atmospherics of antisemitism in the media and in the schools have unquestionably been demoralizing, and Jewish religious and cultural opportunities are all but foreclosed, Soviet Jews have experienced less danger of antisemitic violence than have the Jews of Argentina, or even of France. Settled in the larger cities, they may no longer enjoy their former status as the USSR's intellectual elite, but they continue to enjoy livelihoods at least as remunerative as those of the majority of their non-Jewish neighbors. They have access to a limited but intense cultural life. Indeed, many Soviet Jews regard Israeli culture as rather feeble by comparison. Those who have emigrated to Israel and the West still confess to a fondness for the Russian people, for their warmth and kindness, their lack of "natural" antisemitism.

Some demographers in Israel and elsewhere have even speculated that within thirty or forty years, Soviet Jewry may disappear altogether. It is a dire prophecy which can be made of Jews elsewhere, of course—in Scandinavia, in the Lowlands, in Italy, assuredly in other Communist lands. The prognosis is a time-honored one. Usually it is wrong.

The train from Moscow was due to arrive at Vienna's Westbahnhof at 12:10 P.M. From their border station near Bratislava, the Austrian police had already telephoned Lydia Slovin that a number of Soviet Jews appeared to be on board. It was a routine call, and it set in motion a routine response. A member of the Jewish Agency staff, Ze'ev, a tall man in his late thirties and a former Soviet émigré, brought me with him to the station. There he exchanged perfunctory greetings with four or five Austrian policemen, Uzi submachine guns in hand. Alert for Arab terrorists, they too awaited the arrival of the train. It pulled in on schedule, eight decrepit carriages linked to a rickety Czech locomotive. Ze'ev entered one of the carriages and shortly afterward emerged with six people. Two of them were a couple in their late sixties, of less than middle height, and plainly of European origin. Within seconds, they were taken in hand by a rather substantial middle-aged woman, blond and bejeweled. I was informed that she worked for the "good rabbi," that is, the Satmar organization. Arrangements for the elderly couple evidently had been made in advance. The newcomers allowed the blonde to shepherd them off without so much as a backward glance at Ze'ev. Rather, they consciously avoided his gaze.

Ze'ev was preoccupied with a younger group of immigrants. There were four of them—two parents, a small boy, and a girl. Slight of stature and shabbily dressed, they were as dark as Cochin or Yemenite Jews. The husband's mouth glittered with Soviet dentistry. The wife was very pregnant. Their Russian was heavily accented enough even for me to notice. Ze'ev explained that Tati was the family's vernacular, that they came from Baku, Azerbaijan. The husband was a sheet-metal worker, and apparently he was prepared to go to Israel. His wife was not. Emphatically not. She argued shrilly with Ze'ev, warning that she would fill out no questionnaires, wanted no part of any Jewish Agency arrangements. All her "first degree" relatives were in the United States, she insisted. Ze'ev shook his head at that one, then patiently assured the couple that they might go wherever they wished, but that the procedure for everyone was a twenty-four-hour stopover at the Jewish Agency hostel.

Loading the family's meager baggage, the six of us climbed into Ze'ev's automobile and we drove off. Austrian police vehicles flanked us fore and aft. During the half-hour trip to the hostel, the Azerbaijani woman continued her strident protest. At times, her determination to travel on to the States approached hysteria. Ze'ev's replies were calm, reassuring. But occasionally he made the point that there was no future for dark-skinned Caucasus Jews in the West. He promised her that she could speak by telephone to her family members in Israel (she no longer denied their presence there) before making a final decision. "If this woman weren't pregnant," Ze'ev whispered to me then, "I'd tell them to go to hell and turn them over to HIAS here and now." The hostel was located in a remote suburb, enveloped by farmland. It had been leased from the Red Cross since 1974, following the closure of the Jewish Agency's original transit facility at Schönau Castle. Once a monastery, then an orphanage, it was an aged, dormitory-style edifice capable of accommodating up to five hundred people. In recent years, the building rarely housed more than two dozen people at a time. A police contingent guarded the entrance. My credentials were checked thoroughly before I was admitted.

It was 1:00 P.M., and some thirteen or fourteen Soviet Jewish transients were seated in a cavernous dining hall, eating a hot lunch. I joined them. A motherly-looking woman of about sixty sat beside the newly arrived Azerbaijani family, studying the children intently as they ate. She informed me that she was a nurse on the Agency staff, that she herself had been born in Russia and had arrived in Israel in 1948. Her Russian was still quite adequate, and she chatted gently with the newcomers. The Azerbaijani wife responded in a staccato, defiant tone. The husband said nothing. "It looks hopeless," the nurse whispered to me. "They're determined to try for the States. We'll put in a call now to their 'cousins' in Jerusalem." She rose and entered an adjoining office. Five or six minutes later, the connection was made, and the nurse beckoned urgently to the Baku couple. They rushed into the office. The wife seized the telephone and began shrieking in her exotic Tati dialect. After two or three minutes of this, the nurse cut in on an extension telephone, speaking in Russian. She listened to the reply, nodded cynically, allowed the woman to continue. Afterward, she gave me the gist of the conversation. "Her 'cousins'!" she scoffed. "It was the woman's father. He ordered her not to come. 'We're sitting on our suitcases ourselves,' he told her." Behind me, Ze'ev shook his head glumly. "An old story for the Europeans," he muttered. "We still would have expected better from these Caucasus types."

After lunch, I strolled into the courtyard. Seven or eight transients were standing about. I was informed that this was an "authentic, committed" group. They were preparing to depart for Israel that afternoon on the daily El Al flight. Among the bystanders were a middle-aged European woman, her daughter-in-law, and a grandson of about eight or nine. The daughter-in-law was Russian but not Jewish, I was told, and was divorced from her husband—the middle-aged woman's son— who himself had departed earlier to Canada. Even so, grandmother, daughter-in-law, and grandson were leaving together now for Israel. Intrigued, I watched the child. He was playing on a makeshift swing with the Azerbaijani boy and girl. Enjoying themselves hugely, the latter two squealed and laughed. Their father stood a few paces away, watching, saying nothing, reflectively levering a toothpick around his mouth. Sensing an opening here, Ze'ev murmured to him, "You see, these parents are educated people. They can go anywhere they want, but they're heading for Israel. They don't want their children traipsing around the world trying to find a place where they belong." The Azerbaijani woman hissed something in reply. The husband remained silent.

I was invited into the office to meet a Mr. Yuli Ber, director of the hostel. In his early forties, Ber had gone this route himself ten years earlier as an immigrant from Lithuania. He knew these people backward and forward, and all their tricks. "The younger couples will often bring their aged, ill parents with them," he explained. "On the train, they'll seat the old folks in a separate carriage and warn them to pretend that they're traveling alone, not to betray the family relationship. The idea is to get us to send the parents on to Israel, where free welfare care will be provided for them. The young ones—usually with small children of their own—will then demand to be turned over immediately to the HIAS people, so they can be sent directly to the States or Canada." He grinned in spite of himself. "If we don't comply on the spot, they threaten to head straightaway for the 'good rabbi.' We'll agree to turn them over to HIAS, all right. But we won't be fooled about the old parents. We won't separate families. If they want us to care for the parents in Israel, they'll have to accompany them. That gives them pause. About a third of them usually will go on to Israel then. The rest will drag the old folks to the HIAS office and take their chances there."

"What about this latest family?" I asked.

Ber shrugged. "We'll wait a few hours and then turn them over to the Austrian authorities. The Austrians will turn them over to HIAS, and that will be that."

Ze'ev had joined us. "At least we give them an honest choice," he explained. "But once they get into the hands of the 'others'"—he mentioned no names—"they're drilled in lying. They're taught to inform the United States immigration officials that they're religious or political persecutees. That way they can qualify for admission under the United States Refugee Act. The charade puzzles the immigrants. 'What persecutees?' they'll ask. 'We were never persecuted. On the contrary, we're members of the party. We just want to live in America.' 'Oh, no,' they're warned, 'you don't dare do that. Do as we tell you.'" Ze'ev grimaced. "That's their 'freedom of choice'!" Ber nodded in agreement. I could only contemplate the irony here. During the Nazi epoch, Jewish organizations had pleaded with the United States government to lift the immigration ban on Jewish refugees. Could they now ask Washington to reimpose the ban?

At that moment, the nurse rushed in, her face flushed. "Prepare their papers quickly. They're coming." I was informed later that, watching his children, the Azerbaijani man had suddenly stiffened and barked to his wife, "You do what you want, but I'm going to Israel." The woman had hesitated, then wilted. Ber and Ze'ev were momentarily dumbstruck now. "Let's move!" the nurse cried. "There are only a few minutes left to get them to the airport." At that point, the three staff members jumped into action, sorting out and stamping papers. The Azerbaijani husband entered the office, carrying the family's two frayed vinyl suitcases and a plastic sack of dried Caspian fish. The Agency officials dropped the entire load into a single carton and sealed it.

"What about the plane tickets?" I asked.

"No time for that," snapped Ze'ev. "We'll work out the formalities with El Al later. They're used to these last-minute operations. The important thing now is to get these people on board before they change their minds again."

The family was hustled into a waiting Agency van. The "authentic" emigrants were already seated. The instant the Azerbaijanis climbed in and their carton was loaded, the vehicle roared off. From the office window, Ber and his staff watched, almost beside themselves with delight. They had retrieved another Soviet Jewish family. It might not have been ideal human material for Israel, but it was a family, and perhaps something yet could be made of the children. By the summer of 1982, these four warm bodies could be regarded as a small triumph.

Three days after this episode, the Jewish Agency reached the decision to close the hostel. With only handfuls of immigrants selecting Israel as their destination, accommodations could be provided more economically in local pensions. The gates of the hostel then were padlocked by the police.

XVII

The Diaspora Condition

A Waning of Dissonance

In his volume *The Exiled and the Redeemed*, Yitzchak Ben-Zvi, second president of Israel and distinguished scholar of crypto-Jewish communities (among them, the Karaites of Russia and the Dönmehs of Turkey), suggested that it was preeminently the factor of common religion, not of race or language, that linked the "judaized masses" into a single entity known as the Jewish people. Except for the earliest centuries of their history, "racial" Jews or "ethnic" Jews did not comprise the Jewish majority. In recent decades, Ben-Zvi's generalization has been confirmed by the evolving demography of the State of Israel. A palimpsest of the Diaspora, the Jewish citizenry of the Zionist republic comprises a vast melding of races, ethnic types, even colors, as well as of linguistic groupings and subgroupings. The people of Israel in fact are the peoples of Israel. In their variety and diversity, they are living testament to the integrative power of an extraordinarily tenacious creed.

But over the millennia, even as a religious ethos projected its unifying influence on a constellation of peoples, so a network of regional, tribal, and ethnic characteristics shaped the profiles of individual Jewish communities. Whenever those distinguishing traits were physical, they could be ascribed almost exclusively to commingling between Jews and their neighbors, or even—as in the case of the Moroccan or Yemenite Jews—to a common ethnic origin. Intellectual resemblances, however, are more subtle than physical ones. They tend to reflect both hereditary and environmental factors. The role of environment is writ largest in cultural interaction. Raphael Patai, venerated doyen of Jewish social anthropologists, has made clear that a renaissance within the host society invariably produced a cultural flowering among the Jewish minority. The obverse was also true. In recent centuries, Jews from Moslem lands appear to have shared in the intellectual backwardness of the surrounding non-Jewish population, to have displayed the identical characteristics of reduced literacy, high fertility, strong family solidarity, and religious traditionalism. The disjunction of this pattern from that of Ashkenazic Jews has been verified in Israel by research carried out under near-ideal social laboratory conditions.

Patai has also traced the behavioral patterns of individual Jewish communities to specific historic conditions. For centuries, it is recalled, Sephardic Jews generated a certain compensatory esteem for the alleged "purity" of their family line. In fact, this aristocratic posture was characteristic in Spain of Moslems and Christians, and it was from them that the Jews acquired their own preoccupation with *limpieza de sangre*. The impact of the host culture was equally apparent on other Jewish societies. It affected German Jews, who internalized the traits of their German neighbors, the latter's good manners, punctuality, seriousness, affinity for higher culture; Scandinavian Jews, who shared the secularism and fluid ethnic identity of their Danish and Swedish fellow citizens; Russian Jews, who since the 1880s identified with the native intelligentsia's long struggle for political and social justice.

Yet the Diaspora experience was not only one of adoption and adaptation. For the Jewish minority, it was also a long and painful litany of culture shock and discrimination. Nor was the clash limited to that between Jews and Gentiles. In the seventeenth and eighteenth centuries, the contempt of Sephardic Jews for the "backward" Ashkenazim was a classic example of this encounter. So was the self-esteem of modern Germany's acculturated Jews, who applied austere Teutonic standards to the evaluation of their East European kinsmen. Moses Mendelssohn, "father" of the German Jewish Enlightenment, and later Jost, Zunz, Graetz, and several other scholars of the nineteenth century *Jüdischewissenschaft* school, despised the characteristics they imputed to the *Ostjuden* (even as the Germans imputed them to the Slavs)—slovenliness, boorishness, parochialism, medievalism. As late as the post–World War I era, the German Jewish statesman Walter Rathenau could refer disparagingly to the Polish Jews who were beginning to make their way in Berlin as "the oriental horde camped on the Brandenburg sands." East European Jews in turn developed an ethnic snobbery of their own. For them, German Jews were *Kaiserjuden*, that is, self-seeking assimilationists. Veteran Zionists, they reacted with bemusement to the immigration of German Jewish refugees to Palestine in the 1930s, and some among them could not resist the opportunity to welcome the newcomers with derisive placards: "Nur Sie, Herr Doktor, haben wir erwartet"—We've been waiting only for you, Herr Doktor.

Both eastern and western Ashkenazic Jews, moreover, shared a distaste for the exotic oriental mores and manners of Jews from Islamic countries. Throughout the 1950s and 1960s, as North African and Middle Eastern Jews flooded into Israel by the hundreds of thousands, the Europeans were aghast at the newcomers' seemingly retarded educational and cultural level. Even the nation's leading figures revealed this Ashkenazic bias. As minister of education, Abba Eban could state in a public address that "one half of our population comes from countries which, since the decline of Islamic culture, have had no educational history or environment." "Shall we be able to elevate these immigrants to a suitable level of civilization?" Golda Meir once publicly asked. In a newspaper interview, Chaim Haziz, one of Israel's leading writers, stated this concern forcefully: "We must try to bring European culture to the oriental communities. We cannot afford to become an oriental people. I feel great resentment at such a development. We had to travel a road of two thousand years to become a European Jewish cultural division, and now it is impossible to turn the wheel backward. . . ." Until the mid-1960s, the Israeli school syllabus emphasized the Ashkenazic heritage almost exclusively, with detailed courses in European Jewish history and literature. The response of the orientals, particularly of the North Africans, vacillated between resentment and shame—a mirror image of the early-nineteenth-century West European Jewish reaction to Gentile prejudice. When queried on their origins, Moroccans often dissembled, suggesting that they were "French."

These tensions between Jews, as well as the residue of Diaspora insecurity toward Gentiles, would have asserted themselves much more flagrantly had it not been for the trauma of the Holocaust, then the resurgence of pride fostered by the birth and growth of Israel. The transformation of French Jewry is a case in point. Members of a community that once had been the epitome of impassioned acculturation, they had identified themselves for decades as "français de confession Israélite." After 1944, that designation was consigned to the dustbin of history. Even the mandarins of the Consistoire referred to themselves

now as "French Jews," or, at the least, as "Jews of French nationality."
From the 1950s on, French Jewish natives no less than North African
Jewish newcomers regarded the concept of "Jewish Frenchmen" with
suspicion. What had it availed them? It was not the Nazis, after all, who
had revoked their citizenship during the war, but rather the Vichy government of their compatriots. Their renewed status afterward emerged
less from their own protestations of loyalty than from the birth of the
State of Israel and from their willingness to adopt an aggressive group
identity.

Whatever the cultural and social gulf between West European and
East European Jews, then, between occidental and oriental Jews, the
schism was largely bridged in the Diaspora by Zionist, philanthropic,
and mutual defense activities. The centralized structures of French and
other Western Jewish communities, their joint demonstrations on behalf of Israel, offered testimony to the new awareness of a common
destiny. For better or worse, all Jews everywhere now were prepared
to accept Theodor Herzl's maxim: "We are a people—*one* people."

An Uncertain Vulnerability

Although this solid front was adopted far too late to be of use against
Hitler, it has since been well defined against anticipated future dangers. Western Jews were political sleepwalkers before the Holocaust.
They have been political insomniacs ever since, endlessly alert and
united against the threat of revived antisemitism. In many ways, the
statistical evidence of their security is encouraging. By the 1980s, not a
single major party of any significance in a Western country dares openly
to espouse antisemitic policies. In not a single West European country
are the rights of Jews circumscribed in any fashion, not even in Spain.
In the Western Hemisphere, the security only of Argentine Jewry has
remained less than total; and even in Argentina (before the recent free
elections), governmental oppression rarely was directed specifically
against Jews. In the 1930s, the struggle against antisemitism was conducted essentially against hostile or indifferent governments. During
the 1970s and 1980s, one could fight antisemitism in Western Europe
assured of warm official support. It is significant that the largest of the
right-wing parties vigorously deny the charge that they are antisemitic,
for it has well registered on them that society disapproves of politicized
Jew-hatred.

Moreover, these rightist movements currently appear to be in a state of disarray. Not one of them can be equated with a serious neo-Fascist revival. In the West German elections of 1980, the National Democrats, the country's most chauvinist party, won a pitiable 68,000 votes in a total vote of 38 million—0.2 percent. In the 1980 Austrian presidential election, a bare 3.2 percent of the electorate cast their votes for Dr. Norbert Burger, the leader of the right-wing National Democratic Party. In Spain, a nation emerging from thirty-seven years of Franco dictatorship, fewer than 2 percent of the 18 million voters in the 1979 election were cast for the neo-Fascist National Union. In Britain, the National Front, a right-extremist party that appealed largely to the unemployed and to elements frightened by the nation's large colored immigrant population, attracted 0.6 percent of the vote in the 1979 elections. The single radical-right party to achieve a certain parliamentary leverage was the Movimiento Sociale Italiano; but its vote also declined in each of two consecutive elections—to 8 percent in 1972 and 4.3 percent in 1979.

Accordingly, it is not the political strength of the far Right that has fostered the vigilance, even the anxiety, of Jewish leaders, but rather the ominous shift from propaganda and recruitment to violence and terrorism. From 1978 on, as a reaction in some degree to the terrorism of the Left, neo-Nazi groups began to launch their own acts of violence, particularly in Germany and France, and these have since included assaults, kidnappings, bombings, arson, assassinations. Most of the attacks have not been directed against Jews. In general, the targets have been the coloreds in Britain, the foreign workers in Germany, and left-wingers in France. But there have been increasing numbers of Jewish victims, as well.

On June 15, 1982, a bomb destroyed an Israeli restaurant in West Berlin, killing an infant and injuring fourteen adults. In Rome, on October 9, 1982, two masked men threw grenades and machine-gunned a festive Sabbath gathering outside the Great Synagogue, killing a child and wounding thirty-seven others. The day after the attack, ten thousand Jews marched silently from the synagogue to the Italian parliament, bearing candles and wearing skullcaps. Police patrols were subsequently assigned to all Jewish communal buildings. In France, the objects of attack have included synagogues, Jewish schools, student centers, cemeteries, the Tomb of the Unknown Jewish Martyr. During the summer of 1982, nearly a dozen Jewish or Israeli targets were hit.

On the morning of August 9, terrorists entered Goldenberg's, a popular Jewish restaurant in Paris, and opened fire with machine guns. Six people died and twenty-two were wounded in the single most shocking anti-Jewish episode since the rue Copernic synagogue bombing. Immediately afterward, police guards were assigned to all Parisian Jewish institutions, to community centers, schools, and synagogues.

There is still uncertainty whether those responsible for the upsurge of violence are local Fascists or one or another of the various PLO factions; whether the assaults are motivated by classic antisemitism or by anti-Zionism. The evidence appears weighted toward the latter. It is hardly coincidental that the atrocities reached a climax of sorts during the Israeli invasion of Lebanon in the summer of 1982. In France, many Jews were dumbfounded by the palpable hostility of the nation's press and television reporting during the Middle Eastern war. The attitude of Communist and pro-Palestinian groups throughout Paris could have been taken for granted. These elements organized demonstrations against Israel almost on a daily basis. But French media coverage was another matter. It was intensely emotional and unanalytical. The number of Lebanese victims was consistently exaggerated. Beirut was compared to the Warsaw ghetto. Israel was accused editorially of exterminating the Palestinians, of committing "genocide."

Much of the hyperbole and misinformation reflected the characteristically emotional and tendentious nature of French journalism. Even so, newspaper and television commentary in other Western lands was not significantly less polemical. Throughout Europe and Latin America, the media accounts invariably emphasized the tragic fate of Lebanese and Palestinian civilians under Israeli air and artillery attack. The preoccupation with civilian casualties surely was not unwarranted. It was shared by the Israeli press and by a large section of the Israeli population. Nevertheless, in Europe and Latin America virtually no attention was given to the prolonged nightmare of infiltration and murder endured by Israeli civilians at the hands of irregulars based in southern Lebanon and directed by PLO headquarters in Beirut; and still less to the proclaimed intention of all PLO organizations to eradicate the Israeli republic altogether. Rather, in cynical Paris, in flamboyant Rome, in gentle Copenhagen, in phlegmatic Stockholm, in lackadaisical São Paulo, the analogies were drawn continually between the fate of Beirut and the fate of Warsaw. "What better way for the Europeans to exorcise their own guilt toward the Jews," suggested Bernard Henri-Lévy, a

French Jewish philosopher, "than to say that the former victims have become the executioners? What better way to deny the unprecedented and unparalleled character of the Holocaust than to say that it is not unparalleled because it is happening again—and the Jews themselves are the perpetrators?"

In its most extreme form, the repudiation of Western guilt for the Holocaust has taken the guise of a deliberate falsification of history, a denial that the Nazi genocide actually took place. Although the center of the revisionist effort most recently has been in the United States, it began, we recall, with Paul Rassinier in France as far back as 1949, and its leading European exponents included Richard Harswood in Britain, the author of *Did Six Million Really Die?*, and Robert Faurisson, a one-time professor of French literature at Lyons University, whose articles expanded on this theme. The skewed equation of Lebanon with the Holocaust appeared to validate the observation once made by Hannah Arendt on Moses Mendelssohn admirers and other philosemites of the German Enlightenment: that they expected their favored Jews to be not only exceptional specimens of the Jewish people, but exceptional specimens of humanity altogether. There is nothing just about this double standard. It is simply a cruel, but apparently irremediable, certitude of Western behavior.

Israel's Prime Minister Begin evidently chose to ignore it, a fact of life that rendered the Diaspora vulnerable not only to Gentile but to Israeli *Realpolitik*. Neither did he appear sentient to the complexity of the nexus linking Diaspora Jewish liberals to Israel. Between 1980 and 1983, in meetings with Jewish communal leaders, with Jewish intellectuals in almost every corner of the world, I was made aware of the curious delicacy of that relationship. Perturbed by Israel's annexationist policy, many of these contacts appeared to have become beleaguered in their efforts to justify the behavior of a nation whose existence still remained central to their lives. A particularly traumatic consequence of the Begin years was evident in France. Shortly after Christian Phalangists massacred several hundred Palestinian refugees in Lebanon, an Israeli embassy car was bombed in Paris, and a Brussels synagogue was attacked. Immediately, then, the Renouveau Juif in Paris called for a demonstration "in memory of all the victims of terrorism—Christian, Jewish, or Palestinian."

Many of the 1,500 Jews who gathered for the event in a pouring rain waved Israeli flags and carried signs proclaiming: "Long Live Israel,"

"Six Million Is Enough," "Thursday: Arafat in the Vatican; Friday, car bombing; Saturday, attack in Brussels." When Henri Hajdenberg, leader of the Renouveau Juif, took the microphone, the atmosphere was already volatile. "After the carnage in the Palestinian camps of Sabra and Shatila," he began, "whether the authors were the Phalangists or Major Sa'ad Hadad's militia, it appears that the Israeli army did not intervene, did not fulfill its mission of maintaining order. . . ." Stunned by this reaction from the most militant of French Jewry's pro-Israel leaders, the crowd instantly began hooting. Hajdenberg was unable to continue, as hecklers (the majority of them North African Jews) shouted him down and denounced him as a "traitor." Fistfights broke out. Crestfallen, Hajdenberg was ushered away by the Renouveau Juif's security units.

A parallel disarray and confusion was gradually overtaking not only Zionist organizations in France and elsewhere, but the central organs of Jewish life. I encountered this phenomenon in tense gatherings of Jewish leaders from Stockholm to São Paulo, and even within the Board of Deputies of British Jews during an argument on Israel's recent annexation of the Golan Heights. For Jews who typically had adopted the restrained manner of their British neighbors, the debate in Woburn House was conducted with uncharacteristic acrimony. At no time was there any doubt that Israel remained the very wellspring of Anglo-Jewish loyalty and pride, or that the wounds of confusion and disagreement ultimately would heal. Yet one could not help speculating on the residual scar tissue, both in fund-raising for Israeli causes and in such purely domestic programs as Jewish education, with its markedly Zionist orientation.

Israel and the Diaspora Future

If Diaspora Jews have been the victims of anti-Israel terrorism, if Jerusalem's policies lately have distressed and disoriented them, it may be pertinent to inquire whether, in the 1980s, the existence of Israel has not exacerbated, rather than mitigated, the Diaspora's historic vulnerability. Perhaps the answer is implicit in the very structure of Jewish communal life. The political scientist Daniel Elazar has incisively defined five major categories of postwar Jewish communal organizations: the "subjugated" communities in the Communist nations and in several Moslem countries—Egypt, Syria, Iraq; the "state-recognized" communities of continental Western Europe (except France); the state-recognized "religious structures" of France's and Belgium's Consistoire Israélite; the "tacitly recognized" communal organizations of Latin America; and the "voluntary" communal structures of the British Commonwealth and South Africa. (The pluralism of American Jewry is sui generis.)

In whichever category these kehillas belong, all except those in the Moslem and Communist blocs have undergone an unofficial but profound "constitutional" metamorphosis after 1948. Whether in Argentina or Britain, Italy or France, their decision-making processes have been routed increasingly through Jerusalem. The trend became particularly noticeable after the Six-Day War, when the Israeli government embarked upon a conscious program to shape, strengthen—that is, to zionize—the institutions of world Jewry by identifying them more closely with the Jewish state. With few exceptions, the attempt was successful. In some instances, notably in Argentina and Brazil, the very party structures of the local federations came to emulate those of the Israeli Knesset. There developed a tacit assumption in nearly every free Diaspora community beyond North America that Israel's greater ability to deal with political matters, and its vital stake in strengthening the Jewish confederacy throughout the world, would allow it to assume the role of protector and spokesman for all Jews everywhere.

Over the years, that assumption has been proved valid. Few communal leaders remain oblivious of the unique prestige enjoyed by a sovereign Jewish state in dealing with sovereign governments. Thus, in the 1950s, when the Greek-Turkish conflict over Cyprus touched off a series of anti-Greek riots in Istanbul, several Jewish shops were inadvertently ransacked. Instantly, the Turkish government, fearing diplomatic repercussions, extended its profuse apologies to the Israeli ambassador. In South Africa, the Afrikaners' subliminal tendency to identify with Israel has offered a certain mantle of protection to an otherwise suspect local Jewish minority. In Argentina, during the outburst of anti-Jewish violence in the 1960s and 1970s, the military junta was deterred from lending antisemitism its "official" approbation. The Israeli ambassador had issued a plainspoken warning of diplomatic consequences—which, inferentially, would have extended on from Jerusalem to Washington. In 1982, Israel's Foreign Minister Yitzhak Shamir made a highly visible visit to Buenos Aires on behalf of abducted Jews, and specifically at a time of critical Israeli arms sales to

Argentina (the Argentine-British confrontation on the Falkland Islands was developing). Once in the Argentine capital, Shamir handed over to the government a list of twenty-eight detainees known to be alive in specific prisons. All twenty-eight were released in the next few months. Elsewhere in Latin America—in Brazil, Chile, Uruguay—the elaborate annual festivities organized for Israel Independence Day served as deliberate reminders to the host governments of the sovereign force that stood behind local Jewish communities.

Western Jewry's enhanced legal and physical security, then, the fortified political status conferred on it by Israel, have more than compensated for its vulnerability to occasional PLO or right-wing violence. It is questionable, too, that local Jewish minorities have been placed in substantially greater peril even in nations overtly hostile to Israel. Was it the rise of Israel alone that doomed the largest number of Jewish communities in the Moslem world—or more generally Islamic xenophobia and the departure of the European powers, a departure that in North Africa and in Egypt similarly doomed other non-Moslem minorities? Was "anti-Zionism" the pathology that terminated the last remnants of organized Jewish life in Eastern Europe—or plain and simple anti-semitism thinly disguised and manipulated as "anti-Zionism" for domestic political purposes? Even if it was the latter, were the Jews of these totalitarian nations ultimately less secure as a consequence of Israel's existence? One must speculate whether, without Israeli affidavits and the Israeli-organized network of pressures on the USSR, some half-million Soviet, Polish, and Romanian Jews would have managed to secure emigration visas from these Communist regimes.

In Western nations, too, Gentile admiration for Israel ultimately affected the Jews' own sense of identity and self-esteem. The impact of Zionism and the establishment of Jewish statehood dissipated the bankrupt "cultist" approach to Jewish identity that had characterized the prewar leadership of France, Italy, the Netherlands, in some degree even of Britain. By the same token, the birth of Israel energized Jewish life even in the most thoroughly acculturated Western communities. It hebraized Jewish school systems, and was largely responsible for the growth of the Jewish day school movement in Britain, South Africa, Australia, even in Denmark and Sweden. Jewish music and drama, Jewish arts and crafts, Jewish camps and youth movements, all have since profited decisively from the stimulus of the Zionist renaissance. No student of Jewish history would gainsay that the existence of Israel,

and surely the policies of Israel's recent governments, have not complicated, occasionally endangered, individual Jewish lives in the vast hinterland beyond the Jewish state. But it would require a myopic view of
the world scene to ignore the profoundly infused quality of Jewish identity for which Israeli statehood, more than any other single factor, has
been responsible. That infusion has been evident not only in Western
nations, but in such East European countries as Hungary, Romania,
and other Balkan states—and not least of all, the Soviet Union.

Yet if the Diaspora communities know what they owe Israel, the
Israelis have been curiously slow to reciprocate. For many decades, it
was a principle of Zionist ideology to write off the Diaspora, to regard
Jews overseas not only as half-Jews but virtually as half-men. At times,
criticism of Diaspora Jewry approached a kind of involuted antisemitism. A. D. Gordon, a Tolstoyan prophet of manual labor in the
Holy Land, leveled the accusation of parasitism at Diaspora Jews.
Other Zionist ideologues echoed this charge. Thus, the Palestine Jewish
writers David Frischmann and Yosef Chaim Brenner labeled Diaspora
Jews as "Gypsies, filthy dogs, inhuman." For Avraham Schwadron, they
were "slaves, helots," a people of the "basest uncleanliness, worms,
filth, rootless parasites." Again and again, the Zionists described Jewish
life in *Galut*—itself a pejorative term for the Diaspora, connoting a
state of permanent alienation—as one of poverty, powerlessness, and
degradation. Jewish labor parades in Palestine in 1933 carried a banner
reading: "A parasitic people has become a people of workers." Well
after the birth of Israel, native-born Israelis, and notably Israeli writers,
persisted in characterizing Diaspora Jews as a servile and timorous people, exhibiting neither shame nor honor. Until the Eichmann trial in
1961, and its revelation of Nazi power and brutality, even the Holocaust
was regarded by many Israelis in these terms.

Interestingly enough, Zionist contempt for the Diaspora was in
some degree prefigured in the modern era by devoutly religious Jews.
When Napoleon Bonaparte first opened the ghettos of Western Europe, there were Jewish communal leaders who were fearful of accepting the challenge of emancipation, of mingling cheek by jowl with the
Gentile world. Would not acquaintance with the majority culture erode
the cohesion that traditionally had ensured Jewish survival? From the
insularity of their recent quarantined existence, and without access yet
to the tools of contemporary scholarship, few of these spokesmen enjoyed the luxury of historical perspective, or could have thought deeply

about the kind of survival that was worth having. Only later was the evidence disinterred of the fate of peoples sealed off hermetically from advanced surrounding cultures. In the case of the Jews, that fate was one of spiritual and intellectual malaise. The examples abounded: of the cabalistic sterility left in the wake of the Crusades; the hysteria of the Chasidic epoch following the partitions of Poland; the cultural atrophy of Maghreb Jewry, locked off from Europe in the post-Renaissance, thrust exclusively into dealings with primitive Berber tribes.

It was only in later years that the uniqueness of Jewish history became clearer, the odyssey of a people whose authentic genius was to be found in its ability to absorb, transmit, and often to inform with its own individuality the talents and progressive ideas of advanced surrounding cultures. In this fashion, the Jews acquired their vaunted intellectual tradition, by exposure to Hellenistic logic and inquiry. The "Golden Age" of Spanish Jewry was ignited by Islamic scholasticism. Jewish music and dance, much of it later to resurface in Israel, drew its principal inspiration from Russian and Balkan folklore. Was the Mendelssohnian Enlightenment in Germany to be deplored for having produced a generation of retrograde salon Jews? If that were the case, then all its ensuing blessings would similarly have to be written off, among them mastery of the Western languages, of the humanism that produced the German Jewish intellectual efflorescence of the nineteenth and twentieth centuries. It was access to Russian and Western literatures under Tsar Alexander II that nurtured the *Haskalah*, a Russian Jewish cultural awakening that, in tandem with exposure to Pan-Slavist nationalism, played a decisive role in the birth of modern Zionism. For that matter, the Israelis of all peoples should have been aware of the debt they owed the British mandate for thirty years of juridical and administrative training in statecraft; of the extent to which their survival as an independent nation depended not only on financial infusions from the Diaspora but on the skills of Jews who returned, after centuries in Europe, as a modern, sophisticated, technologically advanced people.

Even those Israelis who acknowledge the indispensable heritage and support of the Diaspora occasionally have been reluctant to anticipate its future. For all its two-millennia longevity—so the argument runs—was this epoch not terminated by the Holocaust? The revival of the postwar years may be a valiant experiment, yet is not its failure augured by the trauma of Soviet and East European Jewry, by the mercurial antisemitic juntas of Argentina, the suppurating racism of South Africa?

The argument is worth consideration. But so is the likely future of Is-rael itself in the event catastrophe should befall the free and democratic societies of the United States and other Western communities. The term "epoch" may in any case be a misnomer for the history of the Diaspora, as if organized Jewish life beyond the frontiers of the Holy Land were delimited tightly between two statehoods, one ancient, one contemporary. Long before the fall of the Jewish Commonwealth of antiquity, other communities—Babylon, Alexandria, Rome itself—sus-tained densely inhabited and productive Jewish enclaves. Indeed, they ensured the very survival of the Jews as a civilization following the de-struction of their statehood. In ensuing centuries, these and later émi-gré settlements became dynamic centers of Jewish economic and cultural life, their names synonymous with vibrant periods of Jewish creativity: Sura and Pumpedita in the third and fourth centuries; An-dalucía and Córdoba in the tenth and eleventh centuries; the Ottoman Empire in the sixteenth and seventeenth centuries; Germany and the Habsburg Empire in the late nineteenth and early twentieth centuries; the English-speaking world—and increasingly the French-speaking world—of our own era.

If there is a present threat to that Diaspora, it is conceivably less political or economic than demographic. In 1939, the world Jewish pop-ulation was estimated at approximately 16.5 million. More than a third that number was destroyed in the Holocaust, reducing world Jewry to less than 11 million. The Jews have shared in the postwar population growth, to be sure, but at a slower rate than any other people. In 1984, the number of Jews worldwide barely exceeds 13 million. Of these, approximately 6 million live in the United States and Canada; 495,000 in Central and South America; 1,260,000 in Western Europe; 1,880,000 in Eastern Europe and the Balkans; 3,380,000 in Israel; 45,000 in other Asian countries; 21,000 in Northern Africa; and 105,000 in Southern Africa. The Israeli demographers O. Schmelz and P. Glickson have ac-cumulated compelling evidence that world Jewry is facing a steady ero-sion of population. The reasons are the familiar ones of low or negative natural increase and, in lesser degree, of assimilation. In those Diaspora communities for which data are available, the fertility of the Jews be-tween 1945 and 1983 has been calculated at well below the general population's. In recent decades, Jews have tended to marry later than their neighbors, to produce fewer children. Intermarriage is becoming widespread among them, particularly among the decimated Jewish populations of Europe, where the number of Jewish partners remains limited.

The Diaspora's future growth thus appears to be dependent almost entirely upon new infusions of immigration. But what would be their sources? The Soviet Union and Romania? North Africa? South Africa? That kind of migration would effect a shift of population, but hardly a replenishment of population. Its one useful result could be envisaged as the movement of Jews from less free to more free communities. There is another source, which for three and a half decades has been modestly stabilizing the relative population loss of the Jewish hinterland. It is the State of Israel itself, which has fed back into the Diaspora on a permanent or provisional basis conceivably as many as 600,000 Jews. For reasons both of ideology and security, it is a subject on which Israeli authorities are taciturn. And whatever its demographic impact on the Diaspora, this exodus-in-reverse manifestly has done nothing to enlarge the world Jewish population.

The reader will hardly be faulted, then, for discerning in these statistics the possibility of a diminution, if not an ultimate demise, of the Jewish leaven in contemporary society. Yet he could as easily, and as logically, have anticipated an identical Jewish fate in earlier times. The late Uri Zvi Engelman, a distinguished scholar of Jewish economic history, calculated that if hundreds of thousands of Jews "passed" into Christianity during the medieval period to escape the torments of persecution and forced conversion, the process worked both ways. The Gentile peoples who "passed" into the Jewish ambit included tens of thousands of Berbers whose descendants today represent almost all of Israel's and France's Moroccan Jewish populations. The origins of Yemenite Jewry, of Ethiopian Falashas, of important strains among the Jews of the Crimea, of the Caucasus, of Bukhara, even of India, at the least are clouded in obscurity.

As late as the Middle Ages, there existed no religious or legal bias against Jewish proselytization, and assuredly not against the acceptance of converts, individual or collective. Rather, in the last millennium, it was Jewish custom, not law, that hardened against the acceptance of "outsiders." One cannot predict the degree to which that tradition of inhospitality may change; whether the Viking women proudly wearing Stars of David in Stockholm and Copenhagen may not yet be joined in future years by other Europeans and Latin Americans. In any event, the historian's task is to deal not in speculation but in facts. It is the

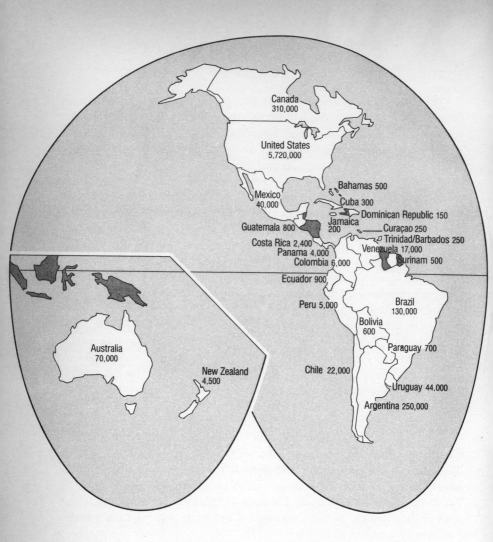

World Jewish Population, 1984
(A Synthesis of Current Estimates)

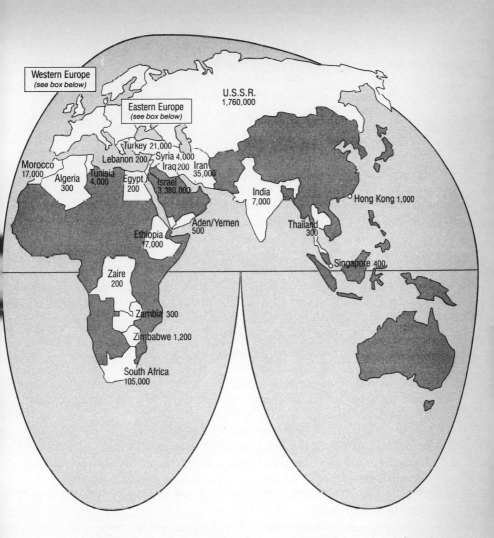

Western Europe
(see box below)

Eastern Europe
(see box below)

U.S.S.R.
1,760,000

Turkey 21,000

Lebanon 200   Syria 4,000

Iraq 200   Iran
35,000

Morocco
17,000

Algeria
300

Tunisia
4,000

Egypt

Israel
3,380,000

India
7,000

Hong Kong 1,000

Aden/Yemen
500

Ethiopia
17,000

Thailand
300

Zaire
200

Singapore 400

Zambia 300

Zimbabwe 1,200

South Africa
105,000

Western Europe				Eastern Europe	
Austria	12,000	Ireland	3,500	Bulgaria	3,400
Belgium	41,000	Italy	35,000	Czechoslovakia	8,500
Denmark	7,500	Luxembourg	700	East Germany	1,500
Finland	1,500	Netherlands	28,000	Hungary	75,000
France	670,000	Norway	1,100	Poland	5,000
West Germany		Portugal	800	Romania	30,000
(incl. W. Berlin)	42,000	Spain	13,000	Yugoslavia	5,000
Gibraltar	600	Sweden	15,000		
Great Britain	360,000	Switzerland	21,000		
Greece	5,000				

magister of contemporary Jewish historians, Salo Baron, who has given profoundest thought to the most ominous and most challenging of those facts: that among all the peoples ravaged in the Second World War, only the Jews—and the Gypsies—have failed to regain their former demographic strength.

It was twilight of a frigid January afternoon when I prepared to take my leave of Gerhart Riegner. The tour d'horizon had left us both quite exhausted. Riegner's career as the watchman of world Jewry for nearly half a century could only be touched on in thirty hours of intensive conversation. The things he had seen, the things he had done, the vicissitudes of a people etched in his face, no doubt in his very soul! What was there left for him to say about his people's regenerative strength? I reminded him of the ominous statistics, and he nodded soberly. The telephone rang then. The call was from the World Jewish Congress's New York office. In excellent English, Riegner chatted patiently for several minutes. After hanging up, he returned to my question. "A timely break," he smiled. "It's allowed me a chance to reflect. Now let me answer with a little story."

Early in 1951, Riegner was visited in Geneva by Dr. Albert Vajs, president of the Federation of Jewish Communities of Yugoslavia, and a professor of law at the University of Belgrade. "My wife has a strange idea," Vajs confessed, "even a *meshuggene* one." Mrs. Vajs, who had lost her children and first husband to the Nazis, was one of the few Yugoslav Jewish women to have survived the war. Vajs had married her shortly after his own liberation from a POW camp. "My wife proposes that we create a Jewish kindergarten for Belgrade, and I would like to ask your opinion of the plan. Do you think we might get a little funding from the Congress?"

Riegner said nothing at first. Both he and Vajs were aware that the small minority of Jewish men who survived the years of death camps and partisan fighting in the mountains had lost their parents, wives, and children. When they married again, they married the only women available, non-Jews. The couples remaining in Yugoslavia after the emigration to Israel were largely those who had intermarried.

"How many children do you have in Belgrade?" Riegner asked finally.

"Twenty to twenty-five of kindergarten age in the city," replied Vajs. "Perhaps thirty if we include the suburbs."

"Hmm."

"There's a risk, of course," added the professor. An understatement. All the children were the products of these mixed marriages, of Gentile mothers. Under Orthodox law, they were not regarded as Jews.

"We might be able to locate a few thousand dollars," Riegner answered then. "Let me worry about the risk." The arrangements were made soon afterward.

Sixteen years later, Riegner visited Yugoslavia. The country's Jewish federation had dreamed up another of the "events" that enabled remote Jewish communities to invite Jews from the West and Israel, and thus for several days to become the focus of the international Jewish community. Riegner encouraged these celebrations; they helped keep the Jewish spirit alive. The pretext this time was the 350th anniversary of Jewish settlement in the provinces of Bosnia and Herzegovina. The day of his arrival in Sarajevo, Riegner was seated in his hotel lobby, waiting for Vajs to pick him up. A tall, handsome man in his early twenties approached him. "Dr. Riegner, may I have an interview with you?" he asked. "I'm the editor of *Kadimah*. It's our Jewish youth journal here in Yugoslavia."

That was a revelation. Riegner had not been aware such a newspaper existed. The fact that it did, and in a Communist nation, delighted him. Willingly, then, he granted the interview, offering the young man a number of observations on the Jewish condition in other lands. As the discussion neared its end, Riegner saw Vajs approaching from the far side of the lobby. "Riegner," cried the professor, "do you remember our conversation in your apartment years ago about the Jewish kindergarten?" Riegner did. "So, this is the result of that kindergarten." Vajs beamed, gesturing to the young editor.

Riegner needed several moments to digest this intelligence. "How many of these young people do you have?" he asked.

"About fifty boys and between twenty and thirty girls—all 'graduates' of those early classes. And you can believe me, Riegner, they're all like this." The professor clenched his fist proudly. "They're a wonderful lot. When the Six-Day War began and Yugoslavia severed its diplomatic relations with Israel, it took all our efforts to dissuade them from demonstrating in the streets against the government. That would have been a bit much, even for a 'tolerant' Communist regime. They're passionate, loyal Jews, our young people."

Coming back to me, Riegner shook his head in wonder. "You see, if you had asked me in 1947 or 1948 how long Yugoslav Jewish life could have existed after the Holocaust and the departure of survivors, I would have said twenty years, certainly not longer. Have you been to Yugoslavia? Yes? Have you seen what's there?" I nodded. Old people like Alihodja, were they, the Turk in Ivo Andric's *The Bridge on the Drina*? Living exclusively in a ruined dream world of their own? I remembered the facile analogy I had drawn in a Belgrade synagogue. "And what's happened in Yugoslavia is happening even in the most moribund of Jewish communities elsewhere," Riegner continued. "Consider what's been going on in the Soviet Union for the past dozen years. Who could have predicted such a development? There's simply no logic in Jewish history. If there were, we would have disappeared a hundred times over by now. We surely would never have had a state of our own. I think our prophets of doom have never left quite enough leeway for the unexpected. Don't you agree?"

Wise man, Riegner. With the children of Israel, this sleepless little coruscation of a people, it was never otherwise.

Bibliography

This compendium is presented topically. Some works are listed, as appropriate, under more than one heading. Titles are limited to the major Western languages and to Hebrew. The *Encyclopedia Judaica* (16 vols., Jerusalem, 1971) and the *American Jewish Year Book* (Philadelphia, published annually) will also provide useful brief reference information. Barnet Litvinoff's *A Peculiar People* (London, 1969) similarly offers a concise, penetrating insight into contemporary Jewish life.

Prologue

Agar, Herbert. *The Saving Remnant*. New York, 1960.

Bauer, Yehuda. *A History of the Holocaust*. New York, 1982.

————. *American Jewry and the Holocaust: The American Joint Distribution Committee*. Detroit, 1981.

Breitman, Richard, and Alan M. Kraut. "Who Was the 'Mysterious Messenger'?" *Commentary*, October 1983.

Davidowicz, Lucy. *The War Against the Jews*. New York, 1973.

Farrer, David. *The Warburgs: The Story of a Family*. New York, 1975.

Feingold, Henry. *The Politics of Rescue: The Roosevelt Administration and the Holocaust, 1938–1945*. New Brunswick, N.J., 1970.

Friedlander, Albert H., ed. *Out of the Whirlwind*. Garden City, N.Y., 1963.

Gilbert, Martin. *Auschwitz and the Allies*. New York, 1981.

————. *Exile and Return*. New York, 1981.

Glatstein, Jacob, Israel Knox, and Samuel Margoshes, eds. *An Anthology of Holocaust Literature*. Philadelphia, 1969.

Gun, Nerin E. *The Day of the Americans*. New York, 1956.

Gutman, Yisrael. *The Jews of Warsaw, 1939–43*. Bloomington, Ind., 1982.

Handlin, Oscar A. *A Continuing Task*. New York, 1964.

Hilberg, Raoul. *The Destruction of the European Jews*. Chicago, 1961.

Joint Distribution Committee. *The Story of the Joint Distribution Committee*. New York, 1958.

Lambert, Gilles. *Operation Hazalah*. New York, 1974.

Laqueur, Walter. *The Terrible Secret*. New York, 1980.

Leavitt, Moses. *The JDC Story*. New York, 1953.

Morse, Arthur. *While Six Million Died*. New York, 1968.

Reitlinger, Gerald. *The Final Solution*. New York, 1961.

Sachar, A. L. *The Redemption of the Unwanted*. New York, 1983.

Schwarz, Leo W. *The Redeemers*. New York, 1953.

Vida, George. *From Doom to Dawn: A Jewish Chaplain's Story of Displaced Persons*. New York, 1967.

1. The Vortex of Guilt: Germany and Austria

"Alles—Nur Kein Deutscher Mann." *Stern*, June 30, 1970.

Amerongen, Martin van. *Deutschland und seine Juden*. Hamburg, 1979.

Anti-Defamation League. *Germany: Nine Years Later*. New York, 1955.

Balabkins, Nicholas. *West German Reparations to Israel*. New Brunswick, N.J., 1971.

Baum, Phil, and Carol Weisbrod. "Austria—Lingering Shadows." *Congress Bi-Weekly*, September 12, 1962.

Bentwich, Norman. "The Jewish Remnant in Germany." *Contemporary Review*, February 1953.

"Bewältigung oder Verdrangung? Juden in des BRD." *Links*, January 8, 1982.

Blumenfeld, Kurt. *Erlebte Judenfrage*. Stuttgart, 1962.

Broder, Henryk M., and Michel R. Lang. *Fremd in Eigenem Land—Juden in der Bundesrepublik*. Frankfurt a/M, 1979.

Cahnman, Werner. *Völker und Rassen in Urteil der Judend*. Munich, 1965.

Conference on Jewish Material Claims Against Germany. *Twenty Years Later*. New York, 1974.

Dam, Hendryk van. "Jews in Germany." *World Jewry*, September 1966.

Deutschkron, Inge. *Bonn and Jerusalem: The Strange Coalition*. Philadelphia, 1970.

Edelsberg, Herman. "The New Germany—A Home for Jews?" *National Jewish Monthly*, August 1972.

Elon, Amos. *Journey Through a Haunted Land*. New York, 1967.

Engelman, Bernt. *Deutschland ohne Juden*. Munich, 1970.

Fischer, E. "Seven Jewish Families from the Ghetto to the Holocaust and Beyond." *Jewish Social Studies*, Summer–Fall 1980.

Fleischmann, Lea. *Dies ist nicht mein Land*. Hamburg, 1980.

Fraenkel, Josef. "Jewish Books in Germany." *World Jewry*, March 1961.

———. *The Jews of Austria*. London, 1970.

Fried, Leonard. *Deutsche Juden Heute*. Munich, 1965.

Germany. Ministry of the Interior. *Jüdische Religiongesellschaften*. Bonn, 1969.

Gershon, Karen. *Postscript*. London, 1969.

Gimbel, John. *The American Occupation of Germany*. Stanford, Cal., 1968.

Giordano, Ralph, ed. *15 Jahre Allgemeine Wochenzeitung der Juden in Deutschland*. Düsseldorf, 1961.

Goldmann, Nahum. *Sixty Years of Jewish Life*. New York, 1969.

Gruber, Ruth. "Austrian Justice—After a Fashion." *Congress Bi-Weekly*, December 19, 1966.

Halpern, Irving. *Here I Am: A Jew in Today's Germany*. Philadelphia, 1971.

Heller, James E. *Our Share of Morning*. Garden City, N.Y., 1961.

Horne, Alistair. *Return to Power*. New York, 1956.

Joseph, Nadine. "We Feel Like Strangers." *Present Tense*, Summer 1983.

Jouhy, Ernest. "German Youth and German History." *Commentary*, April 1960.

"Juden in Deutschland." *Spiegel*, July 31, 1963.

Katcher, Leo. *Post-Mortem: The Jews in Germany Today*. New York, 1968.

Klause, Jacob H. "East Germany's Jews." *Reform Judaism*, November 1973.

Kuschner, Doris. *Die Jüdische Minderbeit in der Bundesrepublik Deutschland: eine Analyse*. Cologne, 1977.

Lang, Daniel. "A Reporter in Germany." *The New Yorker*, October 3, 1977.

Lerhman, Hal. "The New Germany: Her Remaining Jews." *Commentary*, December 1953.

Levine, Herbert S. "Munich Thirty Years Later." *Present Tense*, Spring 1975.

———. "The Two Berlins." *Present Tense*, Spring 1975.

Levkov, Ilya. "Russian Jews in West Berlin." *Midstream*, June–July 1980.

Maor, Harry. *Über den Wiederaufbau der jüdischen Gemeinden in Deutschland seit 1945*. Mainz, 1961.

Moser, Jonny. *Die Judenverfolgung in Österreich, 1938–1945*. Vienna, 1966.

Muhlen, Norbert. *The Survivors: A Report on the Jews in Germany Today*. New York, 1962.

Martin, P. "Planting New Jewish Roots." *Newsweek*, April 7, 1980.

"Operation Reconciliation: Atonement by German Youth." *Jewish Digest*, October 1967.

Oppenheimer, Jacob. *Jüdische Jugend in Deutschland*. Munich, 1967.

Postal, Bernard, and Sam Abramson. *The Traveler's Guide to Jewish Landmarks of Europe*. New York, 1971.

Rosenkranz, Herbert. *Verfolgung und Selbstbehauptung: die Juden in Österreich, 1938–1945*. Vienna, 1978.

Ross, Martin H. *Marrano*. Boston, 1976.

Rothschild, Sylvia. "Wien bleibt Wien." *Present Tense*, Spring 1974.

Rückerl, A. *The Investigation of Nazi War Crimes, 1945–1978*. Heidelberg, 1979.

Samuels, Gertrude. "The Jews in Germany Today." *Harper's*, May 1964.

Schoenbaum, David. "West Germany and Israel: The Odd Couple." *Present Tense*, Autumn 1974.

Schulz, Günter, ed. *Kritische Solidarität*. Bremen, 1971.

Strauss, Herbert A., and Kurt P. Grossman. *Gegenwart im Rückblick: Festgabe für die Jüdische Gemeinde zu Berlin*. Heidelberg, 1970.

Vogel, Rolf, ed. *Deutschlands Weg nach Israel*. Stuttgart, 1967.

Walch, Dietmar. *Die jüdischen Bemühungen um die materielle Wiedergutmachung durch die Republik Österreich*. Vienna, 1967.

Weizierl, Erika. *Zu wenig Gerechte: Österreicher und Judenverfolgung, 1938–1945*. Graz, 1969.

Werner, Alfred. "Germany's New Flagellants." *American Scholar*, Spring 1958.

Wiesenthal, Simon. *The Murderers Among Us*. New York, 1967.

Wilder-Okladek, F. *The Return Movement of Jews to Austria After the Second World War*. The Hague, 1969.

Wistrech, Robert. "Bruno Kreisky and Simon Wiesenthal." *Midstream*, June–July 1979.

II. A Prolonged Convalescence in Western Europe

Ashkenazi, Tovia. *Saloniki HaYehudit* [Jewish Salonica]. Jerusalem, 1960.

Bassani, Giorgio. *The Garden of the Finzi-Continis*. London, 1965.

Bedarida, Guido. *Ebrei d'Italia*. Livorno, 1952.

Benvenisti, David. *Kehilot HaYehudim b'Yavan* [Jewish Communities in Greece]. Jerusalem, 1979.

———. *Yehudei Saloniki b'Dorot HaAcharonim* [The Jews of Salonica in the Last Generations]. Jerusalem, 1973.

Bermant, Chaim. "Rome Report." *Present Tense*, Winter 1978.

Boas, Henrietta. "Jewish Figures in Post-War Dutch Literature." *Jewish Social Studies*, June 1963.

Bondy, Ruth. *The Emissary: Enzo Sereni*. Boston, 1972.

Carpi, Daniel, Attilio Milano, and Umberto Nahon, eds. *Scritti im memoria di Enzo Sereni*. Milan, 1970.

Cohen, Naomi. *Not Free to Desist*. Philadelphia, 1972.

Della Pergola, Sergio. *Anatomia dell'ebraismo italiano*. Rome, 1976.

———. "A Note on Marriage Trends Among Jews in Italy." *Jewish Social Studies*, December 1972.

———. *Jewish and Mixed Marriages in Milan, 1901–1968*. Jerusalem, 1968.

Dunne, Leslie C., and Stephen P. Dunne. "The Jewish Community of Rome." *Scientific American*, March 1957.

Ehrlich, Israel. *Italiyah: P'rakim b'Toldot HaKehilot HaYehudiot* [Italy: Chapters in the History of the Jewish Communities]. Tel Aviv, 1974.

Ellen, Max. "Belgian Jewry Today." *World Jewry*, March 1966.

Falconi, Carlo. *The Silence of Pius XIII*. Boston, 1970.

Felice, Renzo de. *Ebrei in un paese arabo*. Bologna, 1978.

———. *Storia degli ebrei italiani sotto il fascismo*. Turin, 1963.

Fortus, Umberto. *Jews and Synagogues: Venice, Florence, Rome, Leghorn. A Practical Guide*. Venice, 1973.

Furbank, P. N. *Italo Svevo: The Man and the Writer*. London, 1966.

Galanté, Abraham. *Histoire des Juifs de Rhodes, Chio, etc*. Istanbul, 1935.

Garfinkels, Betty. *Les Belges face à la persécution raciale, 1940–1944*. Brussels, 1965.

Gutwirth, Jacques. "Antwerp Jewry Today." *Jewish Journal of Sociology*, June 1968.

Hellman, Peter. *Avenue of the Righteous*. New York, 1980.

Hirschhorn, Paul. "Very Much Greek." *Present Tense*, Winter 1982.

Hughes, H. Stuart. *Prisoners of Hope: The Silver Age of the Italian Jews*. Cambridge, Mass., 1983.

Leboucher, Fernando. *Incredible Mission: Rescue Efforts in France, Italy.* New York, 1969.

Levi, Primo. *Survival in Auschwitz.* New York, 1961.

Lottman, Herbert R. "Diamonds in the *Shtetl.*" *Present Tense*, Winter 1976.

———. "Venetian Ghetto." *Present Tense*, Winter 1974.

Martin, Malachi. *Three Popes and the Cardinal.* New York, 1972.

Michaelis, Meir. *Mussolini and the Jews.* Oxford, 1978.

Milano, Attilio. *Storia degli Ebrei in Italia.* Turin, 1963.

———. *Storia degli Ebrei italiani nei Levante.* Florence, 1949.

Molho, Michael. *In memoriam: hommages aux victimes juives des Nazis en Grèce.* Salonica, 1978.

Morley, John F. *Vatican Diplomacy and the Jews during the Holocaust, 1939–1942.* New York, 1980.

Nola, Alfonso Maria di. *Antisemitismo in Italia, 1962–1972.* Florence, 1973.

Patai, Raphael. *The Vanished Worlds of Jewry.* New York, 1980.

Poliakov, Léon. *Jews Under the Italian Occupation.* Paris, 1955.

Postal, Bernard, and Sam Abramson. *The Traveler's Guide to Jewish Landmarks of Europe.* New York, 1971.

Presser, Jacob. *The Destruction of the Dutch Jews.* New York, 1967.

Reichman, Jerome, and Mariangela Reichman. "How the 6-Day War Hit an Italian Community." *National Jewish Monthly*, December 1967.

Reiss, Johanna. *The Journey Back.* New York, 1976.

Rossi, Mario. "Italy: Viva la Palestina Ebraica!" *Commentary*, July 1947.

Roth, Cecil. *The History of the Jews of Italy.* Philadelphia, 1945.

Rovner, Ruth. "Come to Beautiful Switzerland." *Present Tense*, Autumn 1978.

Sabatello, Franco, and Sergio Della Pergola. "Background and Ideological Trends of the Leadership of the Jewish Youth in Italy." *Dispersion and Unity*, 11, 1971.

Sluyser, Meyer. *Before I Forget.* New York, 1963.

Valabrega, Guido. *Ebrei, fascismo, sionismo.* Urbino, 1974.

Wachsstock, David. "Jewish Antwerp—A Shtetl in Transition." *Dispersion and Unity*, Spring 1966.

Zweiggbaum, A. "Swiss Jewry." *Dispersion and Unity*, 13–14, 1971–72.

III. Oases of Uncertain Tranquillity: Switzerland and Scandinavia

Brandes, Georg. *Reminiscences of My Childhood and Youth.* New York, 1975.

Garfinkel, Jacob. "Copenhagen: New City of Refuge." *Conservative Judaism*, Winter 1973.

Guggenheim-Grünberg, Florence. *Die Juden in der Schweiz.* Zurich, 1961.

Herz, Liva. "A Note on Identificational Assimilation Among Forty Jews in Malmö." *Jewish Social Studies*, December 1969.

Israelitische Gemeinde Basel. *Zum Zentenarium der Basler Synagogue, 1868–1968.* Basel, 1968.

Külling, Friedrich. *Bei uns wie überall? Antisemitismus.* Zurich, 1977.

Melchior, Marcus. *A Rabbi Remembers.* New York, 1963.

Postal, Bernard, and Sam Abramson. *The Traveler's Guide to Jewish Landmarks of Europe*. New York, 1971.

Rothschild, Lothar. *Gesinnung und Tat*. Frauenfeld, 1969.

Rovner, Ruth. "Finnish Jews." *Present Tense*, Winter 1978.

———. "Living in Sweden." *Present Tense*, Autumn 1974.

Schmid, Max, ed. *Schalom! Wir wirden euch töten! Texte und Dokumente zum Antisemitismus in der Schweiz, 1930–1980*. Zurich, 1980.

Valentin, Hugo M. *Judarna i. Sverige*. Stockholm, 1964.

Yahil, Leni. *The Rescue of Danish Jewry*. Philadelphia, 1969.

IV, V. France and North Africa

Albert, Phyllis Cohen. *The Modernization of French Jewry: Consistory and Community in the Nineteenth Century*. Hanover, N.H., 1972.

Anschel, Robert. *Les Juifs de France*. Paris, 1946.

Ansky, Michael. *Les Juifs d'Algérie du décret Crémieux à la liberation*. Paris, 1950.

———. *Yehudei Algeria* [The Jews of Algeria]. Jerusalem, 1968.

Aron, Raymond. *De Gaulle, Israël, et les Juifs*. Paris, 1968.

Aubery, Pierre. "Jewish Attitudes in French Politics." *South Atlantic Quarterly*, Winter 1958.

———. *Milieux juifs de la France contemporaine à travers leurs écrivains*. Paris, 1962.

Ben-Ami, Issachar. *Yehudei Maroc* [The Jews of Morocco]. Jerusalem, 1975.

Benguigui, Georges, Josiane Bijaoui-Rosenfeld, and Georges Lévitte. *Aspects of French Jewry*. London, 1969.

Bensimon-Donath, Doris. *Immigrants de l'Afrique du Nord en Israël*. Paris, 1970.

———. *L'intégration des Juifs nord-africains en France*. Paris, 1973.

———. "North African Jews in France: Their Attitudes to Israel." *Dispersion and Unity*, 10, 1970.

———. *Un mariage: deux traditions: chrétiens et juifs*. Brussels, 1977.

Berg, Roger, Chalom Chemouny, and Franklin Didi. *Guide Juif de France*. Paris, 1971.

Bloch-Michel, J. "Anti-Semitism and the French New Right." *Dissent*, Summer 1980.

Blumenkranz, Bernhard. *Histoire des Juifs en France*. Toulouse, 1972.

Bourdrel, Philippe. *Histoire des Juifs de France*. Paris, 1974.

Braun, Henry W. "The Jewish Communities of France and Germany." *Conservative Judaism*, Summer 1971.

Centre de documentation juive contemporaine. *Activité des organisations juives en France sous l'occupation*. Paris, 1946.

Chouraqui, André. *Cent ans d'histoire. L'Alliance israélite universelle et la renaissance juive contemporaine (1870–1970)*. Paris, 1970.

———. *La saga des Juifs en Afrique du Nord*. Paris, 1972.

———. *Les Juifs d'Afrique du Nord*. Paris, 1953.

Cohen, David. *Le parler arabe des Juifs de Tunis*. Paris, 1964.

Coryell, Schofield. "Anti-Semitism in France." *Jewish Currents*, December 1980.

Crosbie, Sylvia K. *A Tacit Alliance: France and Israel from Suez to the Six-Day War*. Princeton, 1974.

Davis, Moshe. "Mixed Marriage in Western Jewry." *Jewish Journal of Sociology*, December 1968.

Derogy, Jacques, and Edouard Saab. *Les deux exodes*. Paris, 1968.

Deutsch, Naftali. "The Strasbourg Community: Stronghold of French Jewry." *Dispersion and Unity*, Winter 1964–65.

Diamant, David. *Héros juifs de la résistance française*. Paris, 1962.

Eder, R. "The Jewish Question in France." *New York Times Magazine*, November 30, 1980.

Elgraby, Jordan. "The Sephardic Community of Paris." *Present Tense*, Summer 1983.

Fleg, Edmond. "Revival in France." *Menorah Journal*, Autumn 1945.

Friedmann, Georges. *Fin du peuple juif?* Paris, 1963.

Goldberg, Michel. *Namesake*. New Haven, 1982.

Greilshammer, Ilan. "The Democratization of a Community: French Jewry and the Fonds Social Juif Unifié." *Jewish Social Studies*, December 1979.

"Guilty Conscience Forty Years Old." *Economist*, October 25, 1980.

Harari, Yosef. *Toldot Yehudei al-Magreb* [History of the Jews of the Maghreb]. Tel Aviv, 1973.

Harris, André, and Alain de Sédoury. *Juifs et Français*. Paris, 1979.

Hirschberg, Chaim. *M'Eretz m'voh HaShemesh: Im Yehudei Afrika HaTzfonit b'Artzoteihem* [From the Land of the Setting Sun: With North African Jews in Their Own Lands]. Jerusalem, 1957.

Hyman, Paula. "Challenge to Assimilation: French Jewish Youth Movements Between the Wars." *Jewish Social Studies*, December 1976.

——. *From Dreyfus to Vichy: The Remaking of French Jewry, 1906–1939*. New York, 1979.

Ikor, Roger. *Les eaux mêlées*. Paris, 1967.

Inbar, Michael. *Ethnic Integration in Israel: A Comparative Case Study of Moroccan Brothers Who Settled in France and in Israel*. New Brunswick, N.J., 1977.

Korkaz, Sylvie. *Les Juifs de France et l'Etat d'Israël*. Paris, 1969.

Kraus, J. Russell. "Report from Belleville." *Present Tense*, Summer 1980.

Latour, Anny. *The Jewish Resistance in France, 1940–1944*. New York, 1981.

Leboucher, Fernande. *Incredible Mission: Rescue Efforts in France, Italy*. New York, 1969.

Malka, Elie. *Essai de folklore des israélites du Maroc*. Paris, 1976.

Mandel, Arnold. "French Jewry in a Time of Decision." *Commentary*, December 1954.

Mangan, Sherry. "The Outlook for France's Jews." *Commentary*, November 1947.

Marrus, Michael. *The Politics of Assimilation: French Jewry at the Time of the Dreyfus Affair*. Oxford, 1971.

——, and Robert O. Paxton. *Vichy France and the Jews*. New York, 1981.

Martin, Claude. *Les Israélites algériens de 1830 à 1902*. Paris, 1936.

Memmi, Albert. *La terre intérieure*. Paris, 1976.

Nataf, Félix. *Juif maghrébin*. Paris, 1978.

"New Life in France's Jewish Community." *Christian Century*, December 7, 1966.

Raphael, Freddy, and Robert Weyl. *Juifs en Alsace*. Toulouse, 1977.

Ravine, J. *La résistance organisée des Juifs en France, 1940–44*. Paris, 1973.

Roditi, Edouard. "Anti-Semitism in France." *Midstream*, November 1980.

Roussel, Odile. *Un Itinéraire spirituel: Edmond Fleg*. Paris, 1978.

Sabille, Jacques. *Les Juifs de Tunisie sous Vichy et l'occupation*. Paris, 1954.

Schnapper, Dominique. "A Remarkable Revival." *Present Tense*, Summer 1983.

————. *Juifs et Israélites*. Paris, 1980.

Segal, Aaron. "The Jews of Algeria." *Spectator*, February 23, 1962.

Schoenbrun, David. *Soldiers of the Night: The French Resistance*. New York, 1980.

Sitbon, Claude. "The Jews of Sarcelles—Integration and Identity." *Dispersion and Unity*, 13, 1971.

Soustelle, Jacques. *La longue marche d'Israël*. Paris, 1968.

Stahl, Avraham. *Toldot Yehudei Maroc* [The History of Moroccan Jewry]. Jerusalem, 1966.

Szajkowski, Zosa. *Jews and the French Foreign Legion*. New York, 1975.

Tapia, Claude. "North African Jews in Belleville." *Jewish Social Studies*, June 1974.

Tessler, M. A., and L. L. Hawkins. "The Political Culture of Jews in Tunisia and Morocco." *International Journal of Middle Eastern Studies*, February 1980.

Tsur, Ya'akov. *Prélude à Suez: Journal d'une ambassade, 1953–1956*. Paris, 1968.

Walker, Gila. "Divided They Stand." *International Jewish Monthly*, March 1983.

Weinberg, David H. *A Community on Trial: The Jews of Paris in the 1930s*. Chicago, 1973.

Winegarten, Renée. "French Culture and the Jews." *Commentary*, January 1968.

Woodward, K. L., and E. Behr. "France's Proud New Jews." *Newsweek*, June 30, 1980.

World Council for Progressive Judaism. *French Jewry*. London, 1981.

Yetiv, Itzhak. "Marseilles Jewry at the Crossroads." *Dispersion and Unity*, 2, 1963.

Zafrani, Haïm. *Pédagogie juive en terre d'Islam*. Paris, 1969.

VI. The Jews of Complacence: Great Britain

Aris, Stephen. *But There Are No Jews in England*. New York, 1970.

Association of Jewish Refugees in Great Britain. *Britain's New Citizens: The Story of the Refugees from Germany and Austria, 1941–1951*. London, 1951.

Benski, T. "Identification, Group Survival and Inter-Group Relations: The Case of a Middle Class Jewish Community in Scotland." *Ethnic and Racial Studies*, July 1981.

Bermant, Chaim. "Anglo-Jewish Culture." *Present Tense*, Autumn 1976.

————. *Coming Home*. London, 1976.

————. *The Cousinhood*. London, 1971.

————. *Troubled Eden: An Anatomy of British Jewry*. London, 1969.

Bunt, Sidney. *Jewish Youth Work in Britain*. London, 1975.

Charles, Gerda. "Anglo-Jewish Writing Today." *Dispersion and Unity*, 13–14, 1971–72.

Edgar, David. "Britain's National Front." *Present Tense,* Spring 1978.
Fraenkel, Josef. *The History of the British Section of the World Jewish Congress.* London, 1976.
Friedman, Maurice. *A Minority in Britain.* London, 1955.
Gartner, Lloyd. *The Jewish Immigrant in England, 1870–1914.* London, 1973.
Goodman, Mervyn. "Liverpool Jewry." *Dispersion and Unity,* Spring 1966.
Gould, Julius, and Shaul Esh, eds. *Jewish Life in Modern Britain.* London, 1967.
Goulston, Michael. "The Anglo-Jewish Rabbinate, 1840–1914." *Jewish Journal of Sociology,* June 1968.
Hanman, Charles. *Almost an Englishman.* London, 1979.
Holmes, John. *Anti-Semitism in British Society, 1876–1939.* New York, 1979.
Institute of Jewish Affairs. *Jewish Voters in the United Kingdom.* London, 1980.
Jones, Catherine. *Immigration and Social Policy in Britain.* London, 1977.
Katz, Herschel, and Ofra Seliklar. *Jewish Political Behavior: Two Studies.* Glasgow, 1974.
Kimmel, Hans. *The Structure and Regime of the Board of Deputies of British Jews.* London, 1969.
Krausz, Ernest. "British Jewry Today." *Dispersion and Unity,* Winter 1963.
———. "Jewish Students in Britain." *Dispersion and Unity,* Winter 1964–65.
———. *Leeds Jewry: Its History and Social Structure.* Cambridge, 1964.
Levine, Harry. *The Jews of Coventry.* Coventry, 1970.
Lipman, V. D. *Social History of the Jews in England, 1850–1950.* London, 1954.
Marcus, Solli. "British Jewry." *Israel Horizons,* November 1973.
Moonman, Jane. "The Gilded Ghettos, London Style." *Present Tense,* Spring 1976.
Prais, J. J., and Marlena Schmool. "Size and Structure of the Anglo-Jewish Population, 1960–65." *Jewish Journal of Sociology,* June 1968.
———. "The Social-Class Structure of Anglo-Jewry, 1961." *Jewish Social Studies,* June 1975.
Rees, Goronwy. *A History of Marks and Spencer.* London, 1973.
Roth, Cecil. *A History of the Jews in England.* Oxford, 1964.
Rubinstein, William D. "Jews Among Top British Wealth Holders, 1857–1969: Decline of the Golden Age." *Jewish Social Studies,* January 1972.
Shaw, Henry. "Jewish Social Classes." *Twentieth Century,* Spring 1973.
Sherman, A. V. "Epitaph for the East End." *Commentary,* November 1960.
———. "The Jacobs Affair." *Commentary,* October 1964.
Shimoni, Gideon. "Selig Brodetsky and the Ascendancy of Zionism in Anglo-Jewry, 1939–45." *Jewish Social Studies,* December 1980.
Steinberg, Bernard. "Jewish Schooling in Great Britain." *Jewish Social Studies,* December 1980.
Stevens, Austen. *The Dispossessed.* London, 1975.
Wasserstein, Bernard. *Britain and the Jews of Europe, 1939–1945.* London, 1979.

vii. The Progeny of Empire: Australia and South Africa

Arkin, Marcus. *Aspects of Jewish Economic History.* Philadelphia, 1975.
Barwin, Victor. *Millionaires and Tatterdemalions: Stories of Jewish Life in South Africa.* London, 1952.

Berger, Nathan. *Jewish Trails Through Southern Africa*. Johannesburg, 1976.

Bermant, Chaim. "Report from Johannesburg." *Present Tense*, September 1979.

Bernstein, Edgar. *My Judaism, My Jews*. Johannesburg, 1962.

Brasch, Rudolf. *Australian Jews of Today*. Stanmore, Australia, 1972.

Buckley, Berenice, and Sol Encel. "The Demographic History of the New South Wales Jewish Community, 1933–1966." *Jewish Social Studies*, April 1972.

Bullivant, Brian M. *The Way of Tradition: Life in an Orthodox Jewish School*. Hawthorn, Australia, 1978.

Crown, Alan D. "The Initiatives and Influences in the Development of Australian Zionism, 1850–1948." *Jewish Social Studies*, Fall 1977.

Dubb, Allie A. *Jewish South Africans*. Grahamstown, 1977.

Encel, Solomon. *Equality and Authority*. London, 1970.

Engelman, Matyida. *The End of the Journey*. Melbourne, 1978.

Feldberg, Leon, ed. *South African Jewry*. Johannesburg, 1965.

Getzler, Israel. *Neither Toleration nor Favour: The Australian Chapter of Jewish Emancipation*. Melbourne, 1971.

Goldman, Lazarus M. "The Demography of Australian Jewry." *Jewish Social Studies*, December 1966.

———. *The History of the Jews in New Zealand*. Wellington, 1958.

Goss, Isaac. *Adventures in Jewish Education*. Johannesburg, 1961.

Katzew, Henry. *Apartheid and Survival*. Cape Town, 1955.

Kemelman, Y. *Can Sydney Jewry Survive? A Survey of New South Wales Jewry*. Sydney, 1969.

Levi, John S. *Australian Genesis: Jewish Convicts and Settlers, 1788–1850*. London, 1974.

———. "The Lucky Country?" *Present Tense*, Autumn 1975.

Lippman, Thomas. "Harry Oppenheimer." *Washington Post*, April 11, 1982.

Lippmann, Walter M. *Australian Jewry Five Years Later*. South Yaira, Australia, 1970.

———. "The Demography of Australian Jewry." *Jewish Social Studies*, December 1966.

Mass, Rose. "Return to South Africa." *Present Tense*, Winter 1977.

Medding, Peter Y. "Jewish Voting Behavior in Australia." *Jewish Social Studies*, June 1971.

———, ed. *Jews in Australian Society*. Melbourne, 1973.

Porush, Israel. *The House of Israel*. Melbourne, 1977.

Price, Charles. "Chain Migration and Immigrant Groups, with Special Reference to Australian Jewry." *Jewish Social Studies*, December 1964.

———. *Jewish Settlers in Australia*. Canberra, 1964.

"Progressive Jews in South Africa Speak Up." *Jewish Currents*, October 1960.

Rabinowitz, I. L. "South African Jewry Today." *Dispersion and Unity*, 2, 1963.

Rachleff, Owen. "Antisemitism Down Under." *ADL Bulletin*, April 1973.

Rubenstein, W. D. "The Australian Left and the Jews." *Midstream*, December 1980.

Saron, Gustav, and Louis Hotz, eds. *The Jews in South Africa*. Cape Town, 1955.

———. "The Organization of South African Jewry and Its Problems." *Jewish Social Studies*, June 1963.

Shimoni, Gideon. *Jews and Zionism: The South African Experience, 1910–1949*. London, 1980.

Steinberg, Isaac N. *Australia, the Unpromised Land*. London, 1948.

Stevens, Richard P., and Abdelwahab M. Elmissiri. *Israel and South Africa: The Progression of a Relationship*. New York, 1976.

Strelitz, Ziona. "Jewish Identity in Cape Town." *Jewish Social Studies*, June 1971.

Ungar, André. "South African Jews and Apartheid." *Worldview*, August 1973.

Uys, Stanley. "Helen Suzman, MP." *Present Tense*, Autumn 1974.

Weisbrod, Robert G. "The Dilemma of South African Jewry." *Journal of Modern African Studies*, 5, 1967.

VIII. Stepchildren of the East: The Moslem World and India

Abduh, Ali Ibrahim, and Khairieh Kasmieh. *Jews of the Arab Countries*. Beirut, 1971.

American Jewish Congress. *The Black Record: Nasser's Persecution of Egyptian Jewry*. New York, 1957.

Avidov, Yani. *Alilot Iraq* [Iraqi Adventures]. Tel Aviv, 1959.

Barer, Shlomo. *The Magic Carpet*. London, 1952.

Bar-Yosef, Yitzchak. *Y'tziat Iraq, 1945–50* [Exodus from Iraq]. Jerusalem, 1977.

Ben-Ya'akov, Avraham. *Kehilot Yehudei Kurdistan* [Kurdish Jewish Communities]. Jerusalem, 1961.

Ben-Zvi, Yitzchak. *The Exiled and the Redeemed*. Jerusalem, 1957.

Berkson, Carmel. "India." *Present Tense*, Spring 1976.

Brauer, Erich. *Yehudei Kurdistan* [The Jews of Kurdistan]. Jerusalem, 1947.

Cohen, Hayyim J. *The Jews of the Middle East, 1860–1972*. New York, 1973.

Cohen, Naomi. *Not Free to Desist*. Philadelphia, 1972.

Elias, Flower. *The Jews of Calcutta: The Autobiography of a Community, 1798–1972*. Calcutta, 1974.

Emanuel, Yitzchak M. *Tzahak Yehudei Mitzrayim—Hatzilu!* [Egyptian Jewry's Cry for Help]. Tel Aviv, 1967.

Galanté, Abraham. *Histoire des Juifs d'Anatolie*. 2 vols. Istanbul, 1937–39.

Gilbert, Martin. *The Jews of Arab Lands: Their History in Maps*. London, 1976.

Goitein, S. D. *Jews and Arabs: Their Contacts Through the Ages*. New York, 1974.

Grunzweig, Bedrich. "Istanbul." *Present Tense*, Summer 1977.

HaCohen, D'vora, and Menachem HaCohen. *One People: The Story of the Eastern Jews*. New York, 1969.

Hameiri, Yehezkal. *Prisoners of Hate: The Story of Israelis in Syrian Hands*. Jerusalem, 1969.

Harris, Alan C. "The Jews of Turkey." *Jewish Digest*, November 1967.

Hodes, Lionel. "Jews in Arab Lands." *World Jewry*, April 1968.

International Conference for the Deliverance of Jews in the Middle East. *The Plight of Syrian Jewry*. New York, 1975.

Israel, Benjamin J. *Religious Evolution Among the Bene Israel Since 1950*. Bombay, 1969.

Jonas, André. *Jews in Arab Countries*. London, 1971.

Kashani, Reuven. *Yehudei Afganistan* [The Jews of Afghanistan]. Jerusalem, 1975.

Landau, Jacob. "Bittersweet Memories: Memoirs of Jewish Emigrants from Arab Countries." *Middle East Journal,* Spring 1981.
————. *Jews in Nineteenth Century Egypt.* New York, 1969.
Landshut, Siegfried. *Jewish Communities in the Moslem Countries: A Survey.* Westport, Conn., 1976.
Lewis, Bernard. *The Jews of Islam.* Princeton, 1984.
Loeb, Lawrence D. "Dhimmi Status and Jewish Roles in Iranian Society." *Ethnic Groups,* December 1976.
————. *Outcasts: Jewish Life in Southern Iran.* New York, 1977.
Lottman, Herbert R. "The Last Indian Jews." *Present Tense,* Summer 1976.
Mandelbaum, David G. "Social Stratification Among the Jews of Cochin in India and in Israel." *Jewish Journal of Sociology,* December 1975.
Meir, Yosef, *Me'ever laMidbar* [From Across the Desert]. Tel Aviv, 1973.
Mizrachi, Hanna. *Yehudei Paras* [The Jews of Iran]. Tel Aviv, 1959.
Murad, Emil. *MiBavel baMachteret* [From Iraq by Underground]. Tel Aviv, 1972.
Musleah, Ezekiel N. *On the Banks of the Ganga: The Sojourn of Jews in Calcutta.* North Quincy, Mass., 1975.
Nathan, Naphtali. "Notes on the Jews of Turkey." *Jewish Social Studies,* December 1964.
Patai, Raphael. *The Vanished Worlds of Jewry.* New York, 1980.
Rhode, Harold. *The Iranian Revolution.* New York, 1981.
Roland, J. G. "Jews of India: Communal Survival or the End of a Sojourn?" *Jewish Social Studies,* Winter 1980.
Roumani, Maurice M. *The Case of the Jews from Arab Countries.* Tel Aviv, 1978.
Sachar, Howard M. *Egypt and Israel.* New York, 1981.
————. *From the Ends of the Earth.* New York, 1964.
Schechtman, Joseph B. *On Wings of Eagles: The Plight, Exodus, and Homecoming of Oriental Jews.* New York, 1961.
Shtainhorn-Halu'ani, Ester. *Damasek Iri* [Damascus Is My City]. Jerusalem, 1978.
Spicehandler, Ezra. *Yahadut Iran* [Iranian Judaism]. Jerusalem, 1970.
Sutton, Joseph A. *Magic Carpet: Aleppo in Flatbush.* New York, 1979.
"Take Me, Take My Rug." *Economist,* February 17, 1979.

ix. The Legacy of Iberia: Spain and Central America

Adler, Elkan. *Auto da fé and Jew.* London, 1908.
Alan, Ray. "Spanish Anti-Semitism Today." *Commentary,* August 1964.
Arkin, Marcus. *Aspects of Jewish Economic History.* Philadelphia, 1975.
Austri, Dan. "The Jewish Community of Mexico." *Dispersion and Unity,* 1, 1963.
Avni, Haim. *Spain, the Jews, and Franco.* Philadelphia, 1982.
Barnett, R. D., ed. *The Sephardi Heritage: Essays on the History and Cultural Contribution of Spain and Portugal.* New York, 1971.
Becker, Lavy. "Jews in the Caribbean." *World Jewry,* October 1971.
Beer, Yitzhak. *A History of the Jews in Christian Spain.* Philadelphia, 1961.
Beller, Jacob. *Jews in Latin America.* New York, 1969.
Bloom, Herbert I. *The Economic Activities of the Jews of Amsterdam in the Seventeenth and Eighteenth Centuries.* Williamsport, Pa., 1937.

Bocanegra, Matias de. *Jews and the Inquisition of Mexico*. Lawrence, Kan., 1974.

Brainstein, Baruch. "Shenanigans in Spain." *Menorah Journal*, Winter 1947.

Cheuse, Alan. "Not Quite at Home: Enigma in Mexico." *Present Tense*, Summer 1976.

Cohen, Martin A. *The Martyr: The Story of a Secret Jew and the Mexican Inquisition in the Sixteenth Century*. Philadelphia, 1973.

Davis, Nicholas N. *Notes on the History of the Jews in Barbados*. New York, 1909.

Diaz, Adolfo S. "Spain's Wandering Jews." *Américas*, July 1953.

Elkin, Judith L. "A Demographic Profile of Latin American Jewry." *American Jewish Archives*, November 1982.

———. *Jews of the Latin American Republics*. Chapel Hill, N.C., 1980.

Emanuel, Isaac S., and Suzanne A. Emanuel. *A History of the Jews of the Netherlands Antilles*. 2 vols. Cincinnati, 1970.

Karner, Frances P. *The Sephardics of Curaçao*. Assen, Netherlands, 1969.

Katsch, Siegfried. *Sasua, verheissenes Land*. Dortmund, 1974.

Katzin, Donna. "The Jews of Cuba." *Nation*, May 25, 1974.

Lerner, Ira T. *Mexican Jewry in the Land of the Aztecs*. Mexico City, 1973.

Lewin, Boleslao. *Mártires y conquistadores judíos en la América Hispana*. Buenos Aires, 1954.

Liebman, Seymour B. *The Jews in New Spain*. Coral Gables, Fla., 1970.

Lindo, Elias H. *The History of the Jews of Spain and Portugal*. New York, 1970.

Lottman, Herbert. "Aliens in an Alien Land: Spain's New Jews." *Present Tense*, Summer 1974.

Neuman, Abraham. *The Jews in Spain: Their Social, Political and Cultural Life during the Middle Ages*. Philadelphia, 1942.

Patai, Raphael. *The Vanished Worlds of Jewry*. New York, 1980.

Postal, Bernard, and Malcolm Stern. *A Tourist's Guide to Jewish History in the Caribbean*. New York, 1975.

———, and Sam Abramson. *The Traveler's Guide to Jewish Landmarks of Europe*. New York, 1971.

Roth, Cecil. "On Sephardic Jewry." *Dispersion and Unity*, 5, Spring 1966.

———. *The Spanish Inquisition*. New York, 1964.

Sapir, Boris. *The Jewish Community of Cuba: Settlement and Growth*. New York, 1948.

Schers, David, and Hadassah Singer. "The Jewish Communities of Latin America." *Jewish Social Studies*, Summer 1977.

Schifter, Jacobo. *El judío en Costa Rica*. San José, 1979.

"Spain Opens the Door to Jews—Slightly." *Christian Century*, February 1949.

Srebrnik, Henry. "The Cuban Outpost." *Present Tense*, Winter 1978.

Wisnitzer, Arnold. *Jews in Colonial Brazil*. New York, 1960.

Zucker, Norman, and Naomi Zucker. "Survivors on a Desert Island: Curaçao." *Present Tense*, Summer 1977.

x. Brazil and the Multiracial World of the South

Beller, Jacob. *Jews in Latin America*. New York, 1969.

Elkin, Judith L. "A Demographic Profile of Latin American Jewry." *American Jewish Archives,* November 1982.

———. *Jews of the Latin American Republics.* Chapel Hill, N.C., 1980.

Graziani, Robert. "Latin American Jewry: At the Crossroads?" *Conservative Judaism,* Spring 1972.

Kaufman, Edy, Yorem Shapira, and Joel Barromi. *Israel–Latin American Relations.* New Brunswick, N.J., 1979.

Lerner, Natan. *Jewish Organizations in Latin America.* Tel Aviv, 1974.

Levine, Robert M. "Brazil's Jews During the Vargas Era and After." *Luso Brazilian Review,* June 1968.

O'Mara, Richard. "Brazil: The Booming Despotism." *Nation,* April 1974.

Plaut, Juan. "South of the Border." *National Jewish Monthly,* April 1968.

Sable, Martin H. *Latin American Jewry: A Research Guide.* New York, 1978.

Twinam, A. "From Jew to Basque: Ethnic Myths and Antiqueño Entrepreneurship." *Journal of Inter-American Studies,* February 1980.

Varig Airlines. *A Jewish Traveler's Guide to Brazil.* São Paulo, 1979.

xi. A Transplanted Europe Under the Southern Cross: Argentina, Chile, Uruguay

Adin, Julio. "Nationalism and Neo-Nazism in Argentina." *Dispersion and Unity,* Spring 1966.

———. "Neo-Nazism in Argentina." *Jewish Frontier,* December 1966, February 1967.

Adler, Elkan. *Jews in Many Lands.* Philadelphia, 1905.

American Jewish Committee. *Jewish Community in Argentina.* New York, 1967.

Avni, Haim. *Argentina: HaAretz HaYe'udah* [Argentina: The Promised Land]. Tel Aviv, 1973.

———. "Argentine Jewry: Its Socio-Political Status and Organizational Patterns." *Dispersion and Unity,* 1971, 1972.

Beller, Jacob. "Jews in Argentina." *Jewish Frontier,* April 1966.

———. *Jews in Latin America.* New York, 1969.

Böhm, Günter. *Los judíos en Chile durante la colonia.* Santiago, 1948.

Cohen, Stu. "The Case of Jacobo Timerman." *Present Tense,* Autumn 1978.

Delegación de asociaciones israelitas argentinas. *Cinquenta años de colonización judía en la Argentina.* Buenos Aires, 1939.

Dulfano, Mauricio J. "Antisemitism in Argentina: Patterns of Jewish Adaptation." *Jewish Social Studies,* April 1969.

Elkin, Carlos Esteban. *Abraham León y el pueblo judío latinamericano.* Buenos Aires, 1954.

Elkin, Judith L. *Jews of the Latin American Republics.* Chapel Hill, N.C., 1980.

Friedländer, Günter. *Los héroes olvidados.* Santiago, 1966.

Kalechofsky, Roberta, ed. *Echad: Latin American Jewish Writings.* Marblehead, Mass., 1980.

Lerner, Natan. "A Note on Argentine Jewry Today." *Jewish Social Studies,* July 1964.

————. *Jewish Organizations in Latin America*. Tel Aviv, 1974.

Lewin, Boleslao. *Cómo fué la inmigración judía a la Argentina*. Buenos Aires, 1971.

————. *La colectividad judía en la Argentina*. Buenos Aires, 1974.

Liebermann, José. *Los judíos en la Argentina*. Buenos Aires, 1966.

Penalosa, Fernando. "Pre-Migration Background and Assimilation of Latin American Immigrants in Israel." *Jewish Social Studies*, April 1972.

Perera, Victor. "Argentina After Perón." *Present Tense*, Autumn 1975.

Rapaport, Nicolás. *Desde lejos hasta ayer*. Buenos Aires, 1957.

Rozitchner, León. *Ser judío*. *Buenos Aires, 1967*.

Sadow, Stephen A. "Judíos y gauchos: The Search for Identity in Argentine Jewish Literature." *Jewish Social Studies*, November 1982.

Sapolinsky, Asher. "Jewish Education in Uruguay." *Dispersion and Unity*, Winter 1963–64.

————. "The Jewry of Uruguay." *Dispersion and Unity*, Summer 1963.

Schers, David, and Hadassah Singer. "The Jewish Communities of Latin America." *Jewish Social Studies*, Summer 1977.

Segal, Bernard E. "Acá se habla Idish." *Present Tense*, Autumn 1973.

Sofer, Eugene F. *From Pale to Pampa: A Social History of the Jews of Buenos Aires*. New York, 1982.

————. "Terror in Argentina." *Present Tense*, Autumn 1977.

Solberg, Carl. *Immigration and Nationalism: Argentina and Chile, 1890–1914*. Austin, Tex., 1970.

Timerman, Jacobo. *Prisoner Without a Name. Cell Without a Number*. New York, 1981.

————. "The Silence of the Jews." *Harper's*, November 1971.

Weisbrot, Robert. "Antisemitism in Argentina." *Midstream*, May 1978.

Wieseltier, L. "The Many Trials of Jacobo Timerman." *Dissent*, Fall 1981.

Winsberg, Morton D. "Jewish Agricultural Colonization in Argentina." *Geographical Review*, October 1964.

————. "Jewish Agricultural Colonization in Entre Rios, Argentina." *American Journal of Economics and Sociology*, July 1968.

Zeliger, Gerald L. "Argentina and Its Jews: Hints of Crucial Change." *National Jewish Monthly*, October 1969.

xii. False Dawn in the Communist Satellites

Andreski, S. "Communism and Jewish Eastern Europe." *International Journal of Comparative Sociology*, March, June 1979.

Anti-Defamation League Report. *Polish Antisemitism and the Solidarity Crisis, 1981*. New York, 1982.

Arditti, Benjamin J. *Yehudei Bulgaria baShanot HaMishtar HaNazi* [Bulgarian Jewry Under the Nazi Occupation]. Cholon, Israel, 1962.

Bartoszewski, Wladyslaw. *The Blood That Unites Us: Pages from the History of Help to the Jews in Occupied Poland*. Warsaw, 1970.

Brzezinski, Zbigniew. *The Soviet Bloc*. Cambridge, Mass., 1967.

Canetti, Elias. *The Tongue Set Free.* New York, 1982.

Chary, Frederick B. *The Bulgarian Jews and the Final Solution.* Pittsburgh, 1970.

Checinski, Michael. *Poland: Communism, Nationalism, Anti-Semitism.* New York, 1982.

Dagan, Avigdor, ed. *The Jews of Czechoslovakia,* vol. 3. Philadelphia, 1983.

Eitzen, Stanley. "The Jews of Poland." *Jewish Journal of Sociology,* December 1969.

Freidenreich, Harriet P. *The Jews of Yugoslavia.* Philadelphia, 1979.

Goldberg, Itche, and Yuri Suhl. *The End of a Thousand Years: The Recent Exodus of the Jews from Poland.* New York, 1971.

Heller, Celia S. *On the Edge of Destruction: Jews of Poland Between the Two World Wars.* New York, 1977.

Institute of Jewish Affairs. *Jewish Aspects of the Changes in Czechoslovakia.* London, June 1968.

————. *Jewish Themes in the Polish Crisis.* London, August 1981.

————. *The Current Polish Crisis and the 1968 Antisemitic Campaign.* London, December 1980.

————. *The Use of Antisemitism Against Czechoslovakia.* London, 1968.

Jelen, Christian. *La purge: chasseau juif en Pologne populaire.* Paris, 1972.

Jewish Publication Society. *The Jews of Czechoslovakia: Historical Studies and Surveys.* Philadelphia, 1968.

Koen, Albert. *Le sauvetage des Juifs en Bulgarie, 1941–1944.* Sofia, 1977.

Kulka, Erich. "1,000 Years in Czechoslovakia." *National Jewish Monthly,* July–August 1968.

Lendvai, Paul. *Antisemitism Without Jews.* Garden City, N.Y., 1971.

Lippman, Harley. "Poland's New Anti-Semitism." *National Jewish Monthly,* June–July 1981.

Lourie, R. "The Last Jew in Poland." *Dissent,* Fall 1982.

Meyer, Peter, B. D. Weinryb, E. Duschinsky, and N. Sylvain. *The Jews in the Soviet Satellites.* Westport, Conn., 1953, 1971.

Moszcz, G. "Persecuting Stalin's Jews." *New Statesman and Nation,* March 20, 1981.

Ringelblum, Emanuel. *Polish-Jewish Relations During the Second World War.* New York, 1976.

Sachar, A. L. *Sufferance Is the Badge.* New York, 1940.

Sachar, Howard M. *From the Ends of the Earth.* New York, 1964.

"Someone Denounced Us." *Newsweek,* January 12, 1970.

Szulc, Tad. *Czechoslovakia Since World War II.* New York, 1971.

Tamir, Vicki. *Bulgaria and Her Jews.* New York, 1979.

Vergelis, Aron. *On the Jewish Street: Travel Notes.* Moscow, 1976.

Weydenthal, Jan de. *The Communists of Poland.* Stanford, Cal., 1978.

XIII. The Wages of Collaboration: Hungary and Romania

Andelman, David. "Rumania." *Present Tense,* Summer 1980.

Biss, Andreas. *A Million Jews to Save.* South Brunswick, N.J., 1973.

Braham, Rudolph L. "Hungarian Jewry: An Historical Retrospect." *Journal of Central European Affairs,* April 1960.

———. *The Politics of Genocide: The Holocaust in Hungary.* 2 vols. New York, 1981.

———, and Mordecai M. Hauer, eds. *Jews in the Communist World: A Bibliography, 1945–1962.* New York, 1963.

Brzezinski, Zbigniew. *The Soviet Bloc.* Cambridge, Mass., 1967.

Du Broff, Sidney. "The Jews of Romania." *The Jewish Spectator,* August 1968.

———. "Two Views of Jews in Hungary." *National Jewish Monthly,* November 1967.

"Ecumenism in Bucharest." *World Jewry,* June 1968.

Fischer-Galati, Stephen. *Romania.* New York, 1957.

———. *The Socialist Republic of Romania.* Baltimore, 1969.

Fisher, Julius S. *Transnistria: The Forgotten Cemetery.* South Brunswick, N.J., 1969.

Handler, Andrew, ed. *Ararat: A Collection of Hungarian-Jewish Short Stories.* Rutherford, N.J., 1977.

Institute of Jewish Affairs. *The Jews of Hungary.* New York, 1952.

Kovrig, Bennett. *The Hungarian People's Republic.* Baltimore, 1970.

Lambert, Gilles. *Operation Hazalah.* Indianapolis, 1974.

Lavi, Theodore. "Jewish Journals in the Romanian People's Republic." *Dispersion and Unity,* 1963.

———. *Yehudei Romania b'Ma'avak al Hatzlatam* [The Jews of Romania in Their Struggle for Survival]. Jerusalem, 1965.

Lendvai, Paul. *Antisemitism Without Jews.* Garden City, N.Y., 1971.

———. "Jews Under Communism." *Commentary,* December 1971.

Leval, Jeng. *Hungarian Jewry and the Papacy: Pope Pius XII Did Not Remain Silent.* London, 1967.

Meyer, Peter, B. D. Weinryb, E. Duschinsky, and N. Sylvain. *The Jews in the Soviet Satellites.* Westport, Conn., 1953, 1971.

Romanian Ministry of Cults. *Jewish Life in Romania in 1978.* Bucharest, 1978.

———. *The Mosaic Denomination in the Socialist Republic of Romania.* Bucharest, 1982.

Rosenfeld, Harvey. *Raoul Wallenberg: Angel of Rescue.* Buffalo, 1982.

Szulc, Tad. "Nationalism Is Rampant Again." *Present Tense,* Winter 1977.

Werbell, F. E., and T. Clarke. *The Lost Hero: The Mystery of Raoul Wallenberg.* New York, 1982.

xiv, xv, xvi. The Soviet Union

Alexander, Zvi (Netzer). "Immigration to Israel from the USSR." *Israel Yearbook on Human Rights.* Jerusalem, 1977.

Altshuler, Mordechai. *Ancient Mountain Jews.* Jerusalem, 1974.

Axelbank, Albert. *Soviet Dissent: Intellectuals, Jews, and Détente.* New York, 1975.

Azbel, Mark Ya. *Refusenik: Trapped in the Soviet Union.* Boston, 1981.

Ben-Ami (Arieh Eliav). *Between Hammer and Sickle.* Philadelphia, 1967.

Ben-Horin. *MaKoreh Sham: Sipuro shel Yehudei MeBrit HaMoatzot* [What Is Happening There: The Story of Soviet Jewry]. Tel Aviv, 1970.

Bergelson, David. *The Jewish Autonomous Region*. Moscow, 1939.

Bland-Spitz, Daniela. *Die Lage der Juden und die jüdische Opposition in der Sowjetunion, 1967–1977*. Diesenhoffen, 1980.

Brown, Archie, and Michael Kaser, eds. *The Soviet Union Since the Fall of Khrushchev*. New York, 1975.

Carrere d'Encausse, Hélène. *Decline of an Empire*. New York, 1979.

Chesler, Evan R., ed. *The Russian Jewry Reader*. New York, 1974.

Cohen, Richard, ed. *Let My People Go*. New York, 1971.

Eliyashvili, Natan. *HaYehudim HaGruzim baGruziyah u'veEretz Yisrael* [Georgian Jews in Georgia and in Israel]. Tel Aviv, 1975.

Fluk, Louise R. *Jews in the Soviet Union: An Annotated Bibliography*. New York, 1975.

Friedberg, Maurice. "From Moscow to Jerusalem—and Points West." *Commentary*, May 1978.

———. "Jewish Ethnicity in the Soviet Union." *Midstream*, August–September 1972.

———. "Soviet Jewry Today." *Commentary*, August 1969.

———. *Why They Left: A Survey of Soviet Jewish Emigrants*. New York, 1972.

Friedman, Michel. *Ils ont fui la liberté: la tragique odyssée des juifs qui veulent retourner en U.R.S.S.* Paris, 1979.

Gilboa, Yehoshua A. *The Black Years of Soviet Jewry*. Boston, 1971.

Gitelman, Zvi. "Baltic and Non-Baltic Immigrants in Israel: Political and Social Attitudes and Behavior." *Studies in Comparative Communism*, Spring 1979.

———. "Moscow and the Soviet Jews: A Parting of the Ways." *Problems of Communism*, January 1980.

Goldhagen, Erich, ed. *Ethnic Minorities in the Soviet Union*. New York, 1968.

Goodman, Jerry. *The Jews in the Soviet Union*. New York, 1981.

Grienbaum, Alfred A. *Jewish Scholarship in Soviet Russia, 1918–1941*. Boston, 1954.

Halevy, Jacob. *Genocide of a Culture: The Execution of the 24*. London, 1972.

Howe, Irving, and Eliezer Greenberg, eds. *Ashes Out of Hope: Fiction by Soviet Yiddish Writers*. New York, 1980.

Institute of Jewish Affairs. *Soviet Jewry: A Selected Bibliography*. London, 1971.

———. *Statistical Data on the (Soviet) Jewish Minority*. April, September 1980.

Jacobs, Paul. "Let My People Go—But Where?" *Present Tense*, Winter 1979.

Kantor, Levi. *Meah Shanot Ma'avak, 1865–1965: Poalim Yehudiyim baRusia HaSovyetit* [One Hundred Years of Struggle, 1865–1965: Jewish Workers in Soviet Russia]. Tel Aviv, 1968.

Kochan, Lionel, ed. *The Jews in Soviet Russia Since 1917*. London, 1978.

Korey, William. *The Soviet Cage*. New York, 1973.

———. "With Andropov in Power, Will the Hammer Fall?" *International Jewish Monthly*, February 1983.

Krammer, Arnold. *The Forgotten Friendship: Israel and the Soviet Bloc, 1947–53*. Urbana, Ill., 1974.

Lazaris, Vladimir. "The Saga of Jewish Samizdat." *Soviet Jewish Affairs*, Jerusalem, 1979.

Lendvai, Paul. "Jews Under Communism." *Commentary*, December 1971.

Markish, Esther. *The Long Return*. New York, 1978.

Markish, Simon. "Passers-By: The Soviet Jew as Intellectual." *Commentary*, December 1978.

Meerson-Aksenov, Michael. "The Jewish Exodus and Soviet Society." *Midstream*, April 1979.

———, ed. *The Political, Social and Religious Thought of Russian "Samizdat": An Anthology*. Belmont, Mass., 1977.

Meir, Golda. *My Life*. New York, 1973.

Naishtal, Mordechai. *Yehudei Gruziyah* [The Jews of Georgia]. Tel Aviv, 1970.

Namir, Mordechai. *Sh'lichut b'Moskvah* [Mission in Moscow]. Tel Aviv, 1971.

National Council for Soviet Jewry. *Hostages for Trade: Soviet Jews*. Miami, 1979.

Novosti Press Agency. *Soviet Jews: Fact and Myth*. Moscow, 1970.

Orbach, William W. *The American Movement to Aid Soviet Jews*. Amherst, Mass., 1979.

Pinkus, B., and A. A. Greenbaum, eds. *Russian Publications on Jews and Judaism in the Soviet Union, 1917–1967*. Jerusalem, 1970.

Rabinovich, Solomon. *Jews in the Soviet Union*. Moscow, 1969.

Rass, Rebecca. *From Moscow to Jerusalem*. New York, 1976.

Redlich, Shimon. "Khrushchev and the Jews." *Jewish Social Studies*, October 1972.

———. "The Jewish Anti-Fascist Committee in the Soviet Union." *Jewish Social Studies*, January 1969.

Rosenberg, Louise R. *Jews in the Soviet Union: An Annotated Bibliography, 1967–1971*. New York, 1971.

Ross, J. A. "The Relationship Between the Perception of Historical Symbols and the Alienation of Jewish Emigrants from the Soviet Union." *World Political Quarterly*, June 1979.

Rothenberg, Joshua. *An Annotated Bibliography of Writings on Judaism Published in the Soviet Union, 1960–1965*. Waltham, Mass., 1969.

———. "The 'Mountain Jews' of Soviet Russia." *Jewish Frontier*, November 1967.

Rubenstein, Joshua. *Soviet Dissidents: Their Struggle for Human Rights*. Boston, 1981.

Rusenik, Alla. *Like a Song, Like a Dream*. New York, 1969.

Scharansky, Avital. *Next Year in Jerusalem*. New York, 1979.

Schmelz, U. O. "New Evidence on Basic Issues in the Demography of Soviet Jews." *Jewish Journal of Sociology*, December 1974.

Schroeter, Leonard. *The Last Exodus*. Seattle, 1981.

Seeger, Murray. "Episode in Leningrad." *Present Tense*, Autumn 1975.

Sevela, Ephraim. *Farewell, Israel*. South Bend, Ind., 1977.

Shindler, Colin. *Exit Visa*. London, 1976.

"Soviet Anti-Semitism: An Exchange." *Commentary*, January 1965.

"Soviet Jewish Scientists Rebut *Saturday Evening Post* Attack." *Jewish Currents*, December 1960.

Stillman, Gerald. "Soviet Yiddish Fiction." *Jewish Currents*, July–August 1960.

Suller, Chaim. "Soviet Jewish Cultural Revival Today." *Jewish Currents*, September 1960.

Svirsky, Grigory. *Hostage: The Personal Testimony of a Soviet Jew*. New York, 1976.

Taylor, Telford. *Courts of Terror: Soviet Criminal Justice and Jewish Emigration*. New York, 1976.

Teller, Judd L. "USSR: On Its 50th Anniversary, Moscow May Soon Replace Nazi Berlin." *National Jewish Monthly*, October 1967.

Turkow-Kaminska, Ruth. *I Don't Want to Be Brave Anymore*. Washington, D.C., 1978.

United States Congress: House of Representatives. *Anti-Semitism and Reprisals Against Jewish Emigration in the Soviet Union*. Washington, D.C., 1976.

Van Leer Institute. *Jewish Culture in the Soviet Union*. Jerusalem, 1973.

Werth, Alexander. *Russia: Hopes and Fears*. New York, 1969.

Wheen, F. "No Exit for Jews." *New Statesman and Nation*, April 27, 1979.

xvii. The Diaspora Condition

Améry, J. "Anti-Semitism on the Left." *Dissent*, Winter 1982.

Ben-Zvi, Yitzchak. *The Exiled and the Redeemed*. Jerusalem, 1957.

Berger, Graenum. "The Tragedy of Ethiopian Jews." *Present Tense*, Spring 1978.

Dicker, Herman. *Wanderers and Settlers in the Far East: A Century of Jewish Life in China*. New York, 1962.

Elazar, Daniel J. "The Reconstitution of Jewish Communities in the Post-War World." *Jewish Journal of Sociology*, December 1969.

"Fearsome, Fanatic, and Few: Euro-Nazis." *Economist*, October 11, 1980.

Institute of Jewish Affairs. *Antisemitism in the Western World Today*. London, June 1981.

"Jews of the Andes." *Time*, January 18, 1960.

Levy, S. J. "The Falashas of Ethiopia: God's Lost People." *Christian Century*, July 1–8, 1981.

Liebman, Charles. *Pressure Without Sanctions: The Influence of World Jewry on Israeli Policy*. Cranbury, N.J., 1977.

Lowenthal, Rudolf. *The Early Jews of China*. Peking, 1948.

Patai, Raphael. *The Jewish Mind*. New York, 1977.

———. *The Vanished Worlds of Jewry*. New York, 1980.

Pollak, Michael. *Mandarins, Jews, and Missionaries: The Jewish Experience in the Chinese Empire*. Philadelphia, 1980.

Rapaport, Louis. "The Falashas: A Black Holocaust Looms." *New Republic*, February 24, 1979.

———. *The Lost Jews*. New York, 1980.

Salem, A. *Jew Town Synagogue*. Kiryat Motzkin, Israel, 1972.

Schmelz, U. O., and P. Glikson. *Jewish Population Studies*. Jerusalem, 1970.

Velayudhan, P. S., et al., eds. *Commemoration Volume: Cochin Synagogue*. Ernakulam, India, 1968.

Walker, T. "China's Lost Jews." *World Press Review*, July 1982.

Williams, Joseph J. *Hebrewisms of West Africa: From Nile to Niger with the Jews*. New York, 1967.

Index